# GRENADA
# ISLAND OF CONFLICT

*George Brizan*

MACMILLAN

First published by Zed Books Ltd 1984
This edition published by
MACMILLAN EDUCATION LTD 1998
London and Basingstoke
*Companies and representatives throughout the world*

ISBN 0–333–71023–1

10 9 8 7 6 5 4 3 2 1
07 06 05 04 03 02 01 00 99 98

This book is printed on paper suitable for recycling and made from fully managed and sustained forest sources.

Typeset by EXPO Holdings, Malaysia

Printed in India

A catalogue record for this book is available from the British Library.

**Photographic acknowledgements**
The author and publishers wish to acknowledge, with thanks, the following photographic sources.
Naomi Bowen pp 461 top and bottom; 465 top and bottom
The Bridgeman Art Library pp 97 top and bottom; 98
Camera Press p 373 top and bottom
Abbie Enock, Travel Ink p 24
Grenada National Museum Collection pp 54; 138; 142 top and bottom; 179; 226; 229; 232; 266; 355 top; 371; 415 top
Peter Newark's American Pictures pp 90 top and bottom; 91; 108
Popperfoto p 443
Rex Features p 444 top and bottom and cover photograph

All other photographs provided by the author.

# Contents

## Appendices

# List of Tables and Figures

## Figures

# *Acknowledgements*

I would like to thank the following persons for their assistance in the production of this book: the librarian of the Grenada Public Library, Sister Sheila Buckmire and Sister Florence Martin for making archival material available; the attendants at the Government House Archives for facilitating my requirements at some of the most awkward hours; Sisters Sherrie Thomas and Nelli Payne for typing the first two drafts; Sister Marlene Greene of CUSO for financing the first draft; the Ministry of Education for invaluable assistance in securing a publisher for the first edition; Marie at the Centre of Popular Education, who did the final typing; and Evelyn Ross who consented to the use of pictures from his private collection. I am also grateful for the assistance of Michael Jessamy, Susan Hood and Russell Lambert.

The assistance of these, as well as many other people whose names are not mentioned, is appreciated.

George Brizan

*This work is dedicated to Jean, Kwamina,*
*Damani Halim Sheereen and to all the working people*
*of Grenada, Carriacou and Petit Martinique*

# *Chronology*

1498 Columbus sights Grenada on his third voyage
1609 First attempt to settle and colonize Grenada by the English: Caribs resist, the attempt abortive
1626/27 Grenada claimed by both France and England
1638 French under Monsieur De Poincy, Governor of St Kitts, attempt to settle and colonize island: Caribs resist and attempt fails
1650 Arrival of French expedition under Du Parquet
1651/52 French wage war of colonization and conquest on the Caribs; war culminates in the 'Caribs' Leap' at Sauteurs
1654 French wage war of extermination on Caribs
1664 Grenada comes under the administration of the French West India Co.
1674 Grenada comes under administration of French Crown; and becomes officially a French colony
1700 Conducting of the first census: 257 whites, 525 slaves, 53 Free Coloured
1705/10 Fort Royal (now Fort Rupert) constructed
1714 Coffee and cocoa introduced and cultivated
1738 First hospital constructed
1763 Grenada ceded to Britain at Treaty of Paris at the end of seven-year war
1766 First election to the Grenada House of Assembly
1779 Island captured by French
1783 Grenada restored to Britain at the Treaty of Versailles; Grenada *Chronicle* first published
1795 Outbreak of the Fedon Rebellion
1823 Free Coloureds of Grenada demand full civil and political rights
1824 First public primary school established under the auspices of the Church of England
1832 Free Coloureds receive civil and political rights
1838 Slaves freed
1848 Introduction of the metayage system

1854 Outbreak of the cholera epidemic. First East Indian indentures arrive
1857/68 Cocoa replaces sugar as main crop
1872 First secondary school – St Joseph's Convent – established
1877 Grenada becomes a Crown Colony
1884 Government builds first primary school
1885 Grenada Grammar School established (Govt Secondary)
1885 Colonial government closes down William Galway Donovan's newspaper – *The Grenada People*
1885 The Bonfire Riots
1915 *West Indian* newspaper begins
1917 Formation of Grenada Representative Association
1925 First election to Legislative Council since 1876
1951 General strike and popular protest led by E.M. Gairy
1958 Federation of the West Indies
1962 Grenada constitution suspended as a result of the findings of corrupt practices by a Commission of Enquiry into the Control of Public Expenditures of the Gairy government of 1961
1967 Grenada becomes an Associate State of Great Britain
1973 Formation of New Jewel Movement and mass demonstrations against Gairy government
1974 Grenada achieves independence
1976 Formation of a People's Alliance against the Gairy government
1979 Overthrow of Gairy and the advent of the Grenada Revolution
1983 People's Revolutionary Government destroyed

# *Names the Island has Borne*

Grenada has been known by many names throughout history. First, during the period when it was settled by our Carib ancestors it was *Camerhogne*. We know this from the writings of a French Dominican priest, Raymond Breton, who lived for many years with the Caribs on the island of Dominica. His works *Dictionnaire Caraïbe-François* and *François-Caraïbe* were published in 1665 and 1668 respectively.

The second name Concepción was given to the island when it was sighted by Columbus on his third voyage of exploration.

The island's third name was Mayo. Grenada was given this name in 1500 by Alonso de Hojeda, Amerigo Vespucci and the map-maker Juan de la Cosa who sailed up the islands from the Dragon's Mouth to St Kitts, mapping all the islands they saw. As late as 1511 it appears that both names – Concepción and Mayo – were used on *Royal Cedulas* about Grenada, but Concepción was used more frequently.

From 1523 onwards these names were dropped and replaced by 'Granada.' With but one exception, all Spanish maps after 1523 used the name Granada for the island.

In 1650 the French settlers changed the Spanish name 'Granada' into 'La Grenade' and the island bore this name until 1763 when she was given to England by France at the Treaty of Paris. The English then changed the name from La Grenade to Grenada.

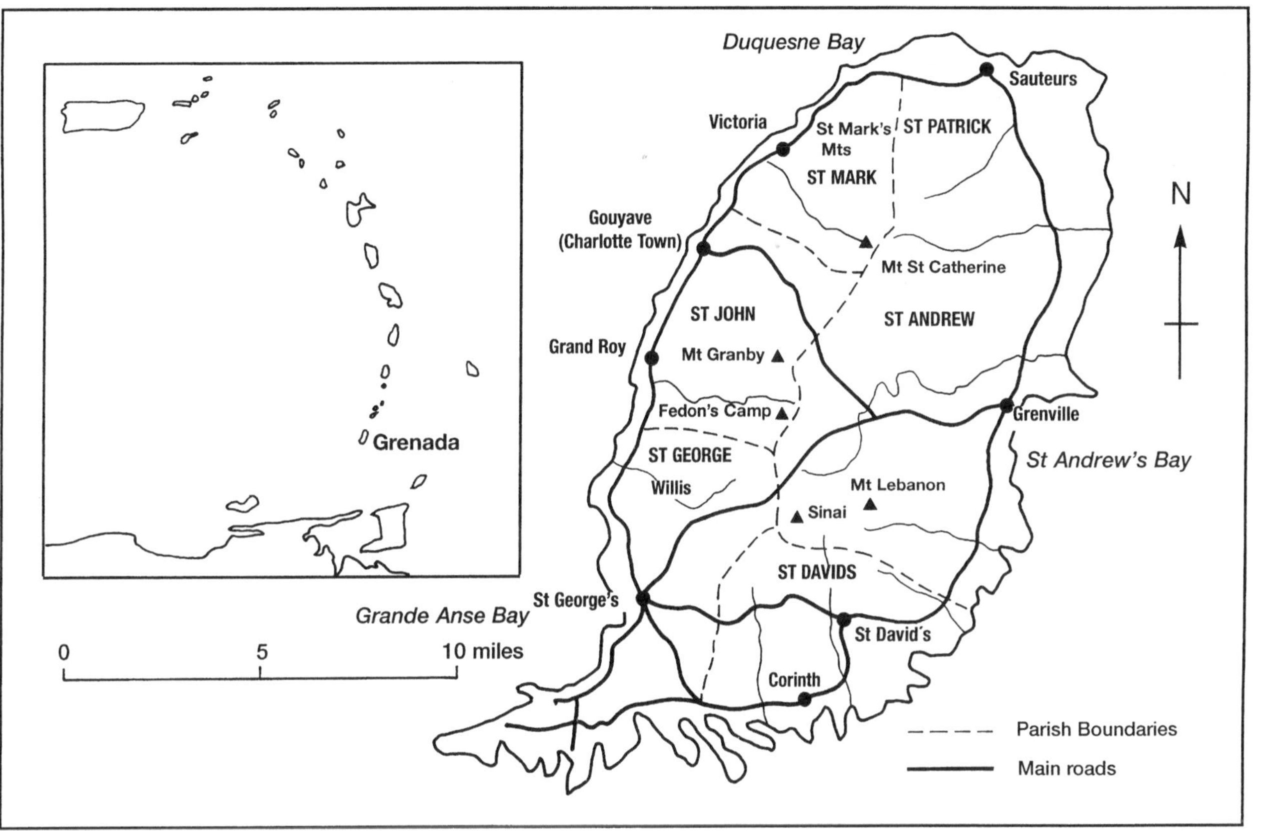


*Map of Grenada*

# *Preface to the Second Edition*

*Grenada, Island of Conflict* is the analysis of six major irreconcilable conflicts in the history of this small Caribbean island, which came to the attention of the world in 1979 when the New Jewel Movement led by a small group of Marxists overthrew the elected government of Eric Gairy. Four years later it again occupied centre stage in world news when the People's Revolutionary Government destroyed itself, and the Prime Minister Maurice Bishop, three of his senior ministers and other followers were executed by members of the People's Revolutionary Army.

The first edition of the book, written in 1981 and published in 1984, studied the first five of these conflicts, up to the demise of Gairy's government in 1979. These were:

1. The Carib/Arawak conflict which ended violently with the destruction of the relatively peaceful Arawaks.
2. The Carib/French conflict which ended in violent confrontation and the mass suicide of the last band of militant Caribs.
3. The French/British conflict – a conflict of two cultures, one Francophone, the other Anglophone – which ended with the Fedon Rebellion of 1795–6.
4. The ex-slave/planter conflict which spanned a period of over a century and ended with the 1951 Social Revolution led by Eric Gairy.
5. The conflict between the forces of Gairyism and the anti-Gairy forces which ended in 1979 with the violent overthrow of the Gairy government.

The second edition includes a new chapter analysing the sixth conflict, which ended yet again in bloodshed, culminating in the execution of Prime Minister Maurice Bishop and others in October 1983. This latest conflict seems to give credence to the saying 'Revolutions tend to be cannibalistic', in that they often devour their own. The author was an eye witness to this latest conflict.

Hon. George Brizan
June 1997

# *Introduction*

Grenada's history from 1650 to 1983 has been one of conflicts, either between local groups and classes or between rival imperial cultures. In each case, when a major conflict arose, the contradictions between the groups were so antagonistic and the differences so irreconcilable, that it was invariably settled violently.

The first conflict arose in the pre-Columbian era (pre-1492) between the relatively peaceful Arawaks and the hostile and warlike Caribs. By the time Columbus arrived, Grenada was firmly under Carib control.

The second conflict was between the native Caribs and the French settlers during the period 1651–54. The French brutally massacred the Caribs in retaliation for sporadic acts of Carib violence; the result was almost total destruction of Grenada's Caribs. The period of French rule followed until 1763 when Grenada was ceded to England at the Treaty of Paris – the Treaty which ended the Seven Years' War.

Subsequently, two rival groups and two rival cultures emerged in Grenada – one Anglo-Saxon, the other Francophone; one Protestant, the other Roman Catholic. This conflict between the established French community and the newly emergent British community prevailed for the next 30 years until it was finally settled in 1795–96, in the Fedon rebellion. Thousands of slaves deserted their masters and rallied behind Fedon's banner, but the rebellion was eventually crushed and the hopes of thousands of the working class were dashed.

After this the English in Grenada continued to be the dominant group – if not socially and culturally, certainly economically and politically. Emancipation came in 1834–38 and the Black section of the population previously kept under the degrading bondage of slavery was freed and fresh energies began to be unleashed.

The next conflict was essentially one of class and was an extension and continuation of the class conflicts of the plantation system in Grenada, which had originated during slavery, between the mass of slaves and the planter class. Now, it was between the Mulattos and White Creoles who owned most of the land, estates and commercial houses, and who monopolized all power – political, social and financial – and the mass of ex-slaves who had recently been freed and were developing an independent life-style after the psychologically dehumanizing experience of slavery; this latter class was powerless, except in terms of numbers.

In 1839 the average wage for labourers of that class ranged from 4d to 1/– per day. By 1939, 100 years later, the daily wage for agricultural labourers was 1/– for women and 1/3d for men. The class conflict that grew and developed during these 100 years exploded violently in 1951 with the rise of Gairy and the coming of the social revolution. It is interesting to note that this conflict too was settled violently.

During the next 28 years, but especially from 1968 to 1979, Gairy ruled Grenada despotically, violating the principles, and exploiting and destroying the very people, for whom he fought in 1951. The voice of dissent was virtually stifled and many basic economic and constitutional rights were disregarded and trampled upon as Gairy and his clique tightened their grip upon Grenadians. Inevitably, this situation generated its own conflicts and contradictions, and opposition grew. In the early 1970s this opposition coalesced and finally became organized into a mass political movement – the New Jewel Movement. The struggle between the Gairy regime and those opposed to it was settled violently when, on 13 March 1979, the Gairy government was overthrown in an armed seizure of power by the New Jewel Movement. This marked the beginning of the Grenadian Revolution.

The Revolution came to a violent end four years later, in October 1983 when a conflict which had developed between two ideologically opposed factions of the People's Revolutionary Government (PRG) resulted in the execution of the then Prime Minister, Maurice Bishop, three of his ministers and many supporters.

G. Brizan
Grenada

# 1

# *First Grenadians: Amerindians of Camerhogne*

## The Antillean Arawaks and Caribs

Grenada was first settled by the Arawaks, an Amerindian tribe which originated around the Amazon basin and then migrated to the coast of Northern South America, from where they proceeded to settle and populate various islands of the Caribbean.

The Arawakan migration was followed by waves of Carib migration many years later. The Caribs themselves, who were less numerous and spoke a language different from that of the Arawaks, originated around Central Brazil and the Guianas. By waging incessant wars, in which they were invariably victorious, they pushed the relatively peaceful Arawaks further and further north.

The main testimony of the Arawaks' presence in Grenada is the pottery and carvings which they left behind. These carvings consist mainly of heads and faces cut into rocks; one of the best examples is to be found on a huge stone in the bed of La Fortune River on Mt Rich Estate.[1]

The Arawaks who inhabited Grenada during the pre-Columban era suffered the same fate at the hands of the insurgent Caribs as did those in the other islands. In fact, being so far south they were among the first to have been affected by Carib incursions and military adventures.

As the number of Caribs in Grenada increased owing to successive waves of migration, conflict soon developed between the two groups of Amerindians. As a result, most of the Arawakan men were killed or forced to flee the island, and the women were kept by the

Caribs as both slaves and wives. We are told that the women continued to speak the Arawakan language up to the time the Europeans arrived in Grenada. They also spoke the language of their Carib captors, but they used their own language among themselves.[2] They were generally segregated from the Carib men and were denied the use of the Carib community hall, a large hut used by the men. On the whole, the Arawak women were a domesticated class whose tasks were cooking, looking after the huts, and satisfying the sexual appetites of the Carib men.

The best way to understand the basis of the Arawak/Carib conflict in Grenada more fully, is to examine and compare the lifestyles of both groups, and their economic and political systems. The deep-seated differences that emerge will thus reveal the inherent causes of conflict.

## The Arawaks

How extensively did the Arawaks populate the Caribbean? What socio-economic system did they develop? What were their cultural and religious values?

### *Cultural groups*

When Columbus arrived, the Arawaks or Taino, as they were sometimes called, inhabited the Greater Antilles. Arawaks were divided into five subgroups: Taino, Sub-Taino, Ciguayo, Lucayo and Igneri. This classification was based on differences in language, technology, and ceramic and artistic styles which had developed as a result of years of isolation.[3]

The Taino inhabited most of Hispaniola except the South-Western and North-Eastern Peninsulas. They comprised the main Arawakan group and, by the time the Spaniards arrived in the West Indies, had achieved the highest level of linguistic and ceramic refinement. It was this group that Columbus and the Spaniards first colonized and virtually exterminated. But the first group that Columbus encountered was the Lucayans of the Bahamas who, isolated for centuries, had developed different ceramic and ceremonial complexes from the Taino.

The Igneri Arawaks inhabited most of the island of Trinidad and seemed to have survived waves of Carib migrations. They spoke a different language from that of the Taino and were found to be far more warlike than any of their other Arawakan counterparts.

The Sub-taino inhabited Central Cuba and Jamaica and were said to have been less culturally developed than the Taino. The Ciguayo, found in the North-Eastern Peninsula of Hispaniola, spoke a different language from that of the Taino. They were said to have been a mixture of Caribs and Arawaks, with Arawakan traits and affiliations being dominant.

According to research by anthropologists Frolich Rainey and Irvin Rouse, the Arawaks' arrival and settlement in the Antilles dated from AD 1089 to 1193; a result arrived at by stratigraphic analysis of refuse deposits, and cross-dating of trade objects. As Grenada is the southernmost island of the Windwards, it is quite possible that the Arawaks could have settled there as early as the first century AD.

## *Political organization*

In contradistinction to the Caribs – whose leader was elected – the office of chieftain among the Arawaks was inherited along matrilineal lines. In both communities, however, the leader was an autocrat and his power was absolute.

The Arawakan territory was divided into provinces and each province had its great *cacique* who governed the province. In the case of Grenada, there was one *cacique* who ruled over the entire island. Hispaniola was divided into five provinces – Caizcimu, Huhabo, Cayaho, Bainoa, Guacayarima – each ruled by a Great *Cacique*. Each Arawakan province was subdivided into around 30 districts, which were ruled by individual sub-chiefs or *caciques* of the second rank. Each district, in turn, was subdivided into about 70 villages, each of which was administered by a headman. The *cacique* of each province had absolute power over his area. The village headman helped to organize the daily routine of work and supervised the storage and distribution of food; the *caciques* presided over dances, feasts, public festivals and law courts.[4]

Arawakan society was rigidly stratified into classes. The upper class consisted of the *cacique* and his close relatives; the middle class of nobles, or *nitaynos* by Spanish interpretation; below them was the lower class of commoners, and finally, at the bottom, there was the unfree or slave class, called *naborias*. Status was determined by birth, especially in the highest and lowest classes.

## *Economic life*

The Arawaks operated a subsistence economy, oriented both to the land and to the sea. Root crops – yams, sweet potatoes, and both bitter and sweet yuca or mandioca[5] – supplied the carbohydrate requirements of the native diet.

The bitter yuca was the great staple of the Arawaks. The untreated roots were poisonous, but grated, drained, and baked into unleavened flat bread, called cassava, they were edible. The sweet or non-poisonous manioc was simply boiled. Manioc grown from stem-cuttings on mounds produced tubers from six inches to one foot after about a year, but the Arawaks left their manioc crop for two to three years, harvesting part of it from time to time. Las Casas said that several cuttings were planted in each mound, and the best results could be had after 18 months.[6]

The second most important crop was the sweet potato. Its yield was lower than that of manioc, but unlike the latter, its leaves were used as a kind of spinach. Two types were planted: the sweet *batata* and the non-sweet, with more extensive plantings of the former, which produced a crop within four months of planting.

The Arawaks also cultivated yantia, canna, arrowroot and peanuts; the Europeans first saw peanuts in the West Indies and prized them for their nutritious value. Beans, squashes and corn were also grown. These originated in Mesoamerica and probably were carried to the West Indian islands by the Indians.

Cultivation included clearing, burning, and digging the land with a pointed and flattened heavy stick – a type of primitive spade; the earth was then heaped into mounds. The tribute in food demanded from the natives by the Europeans was calculated by the number of mounds they were required to plant.[7] The most important agricultural tool among the Arawaks was called the *macana*, a kind of broadsword made of very hard wood with a cutting edge on one or both sides. It was the Arawaks' cutlass and served both as a digging tool and as a bush knife.

The Arawaks also cultivated numerous yard plants, including cotton (*Gossypium Barbadense*), bixa, and tobacco. Bixa, an attractive shrub, produced seeds in capsules which were prized for their colouring matter. They also cultivated the Genepa, a handsome hardwood tree, which produced an edible fruit from which a black dye, used to paint the body, was extracted. Other yard plants were the calabash tree (*Crescentia*) from the fruit of which gourd containers were made; the mameyapple tree, known to have been carried to the island by the Indians, and bearing fruit with a special flavour; papaya; guava; coconut; the manzanilla, whose fruit was prized for its purgative value; and capsicum peppers, used for seasoning.

While fruits and vegetables supplied the sugar and starch, animal protein and fat were obtained from seafood and water fowl. The

Arawaks fished on and off shore, in the estuaries, streams and lakes, harvesting fish, turtles, marine mammals, water fowl, and shellfish, which comprised the predominant flesh eaten in Grenada.

The Spaniards were impressed not only by the abundance of fish but also by the Arawaks' fishing techniques. They fished with nets and hooks but also with the suckerfish; this attached itself to large catches, for example, turtles and manatees, thus enabling them to be easily captured. Marine food was prepared either by boiling in the pepper-pot dish or by roasting. Pigeons, doves and large iguanas were extensively eaten and thus supplemented the fish protein.[8] The Arawak diet was, in fact, admirably balanced.

## *Housing and the village*

Arawak houses were made of wood and palm branches and shaped like an *alfanaque* or Moorish tent; in fact a group of houses in a village resembled a tented encampment. The larger ones, called *bohio*, were inhabited by the *caciques* and political officials, and also served as a venue for ceremonial meetings. The smaller houses, called *caneye*, were shared by several members of the family, including husbands, wives and children – usually about 10 to 15 persons. The houses were cool and rainproof. The interiors were well-swept and clean. Wooden stools and beds resembling cotton nets – *hamacas* – seem to have been their only furniture. The houses were circular in outline and bell-shaped in profile.

Villages usually contained about 100 to 200 households and about 1,000 to 2,000 inhabitants, but the size of the village differed from island to island. Whereas a village in Hispaniola consisted of about 1,000 households, an average village in Grenada consisted of about 20 to 50 households.[9]

In the middle of every village was an open space used for assemblies and festivities. Here, Arawaks held their *areitos* or dances accompanied by drums, rattles and castanets. Their principal sporting activity, a ballgame known locally as *batey*, a game usually followed by dancing, also took place in this space. Other games included athletics and wrestling.

## *Beliefs*

The Arawaks had a well-developed system of rites and ceremonies. They believed in two supernatural beings: 'the god of the sky' and 'the goddess of the earth'; these they called *zemis* and they were supposedly the parents of all other *zemis* or gods. In that they believed that spirits were in all things, animate and inanimate, rocks, trees, and so on, the Arawaks were also animists. They held the view that after death earthly spirits went to an earthly paradise; and that supernatural powers could be obtained by gaining power over the spirits of nature and of their ancestors. They believed too, that certain gods controlled the food supply, brought rain, caused the winds to blow and the sun to shine. Spirits of the living were called *goeiz*, and those of the dead, *opeia*.[10]

From these series of beliefs the cult of *zemiism* developed. The Arawaks made representations or relics of *zemis* from wood, cloth or stone, and each family had its own god. They also kept the bones of dead relatives and used them as relics of gods. They had a well-developed system of shamanism or priesthood. The shaman performed manifold duties of divination, consultation of *zemis* and recourse to them in times of war, curing the sick, and praying for rain during periods of drought.

## *Art and craft*

The Arawaks excelled in the field of art and handicraft. They were artists *par excellence*. Sauer says: ‘woodworking was the craft in which the Islanders (Arawaks) were equal and perhaps superior to natives in any part of the New World.’[11] Of particular interest were their canoes and paddles which were admired for both functional design and elegance. They shaped their dug-out canoes in such a way as to achieve speed, balance and manoeuverability; in this respect their competence was said to be equal to that of the early Polynesian boat-builders.

The making of ceremonial seats, called *duhos*, ranked second in importance to boat-building. These were elaborately carved and highly polished.[12] The tropical cedar and mahogany were the woods most commonly used. Their finely finished bowls of very dark hardwood were traded widely and highly prized.

The Arawaks were skilled in ceramic work, which they practised extensively, and produced some of the finest pottery at the time in the Americas. They also wove cotton into cloth which provided the married women’s short skirts called *naguas*; hammocks, too, were made from woven cloth and from fibre. The fibre of the hibiscus was prized for cordage and for making nets.[13]

The Arawaks in the Lesser Antilles seem to have had no knowledge of metals, not even gold. Therefore, all their tools and weapons were made with stone, shell, bone and wood.

Many Arawakan artefacts have been found in Grenada in recent years; most of them in archaeological sites at Pearls, Westerhall Point,

Calivigny Island and 11 other locations. These include a *zemi*, ceremonial axes, bone needles, shell knives, storage jars, and large bowls. One bowl found on Calivigny Island was decorated with a number of circular designs in black on the red clay background. Another large bowl found at Pearls was decoated with a number of geometric, stylized human faces.

Arawakan pottery in Grenada was divided into two cultures; the Saladoid culture, comprising pottery of an early period – AD 1 to 500; and the Barrancoid culture, which included pottery of a later period – 500 to 1000. Pottery of the early period was thin, hard, fine and smooth. The articles made had flat rather than pedestal bases, 'D'-shaped handles and were painted red. There were few cases of incized decoration, few decorated (*adorno*) handles and no flanged edges. Pottery of the later period was thick, soft and coarse in texture. Articles had pedestal bases, and large, heavily flanged edges. Handles were elaborately adorned, and the articles themselves decoratively incised.[14]

## Technology

The Arawaks' technology was by no means primitive. By the 15th century it was considerably advanced. By then they had developed graters or *metates* for making cassava cake, juice squeezers for extracting poisonous liquid from the cassava and flat ovens of coarse clay for baking it. They also made stone axes, and awls and needles of bone. In the field of agriculture the *macana* or wood machete was their most outstanding achievement. They developed stone mortars and pestles, and grindstones to facilitate food preparation.

The cassava root was first grated on a *metate*, then put into wicker basket and hung from a branch and weighted at the end. This caused the tube to contract and force the poisonous liquid out of the wet cassava. After a day or so the cassava was ground in the mortar, then sifted in a basket sieve to separate the coarse seeds from the fine powder, the former remaining in the sieve while the powder – which was finally baked into cassava cake – was collected below in the wooden bowl or container.

Another technological device worthy of note was the clay 'whorl' or thread spinner used by the Arawaks of Grenada to spin their fibres (cotton thread) into cloth.

The Arawaks' main dish was the pepperpot. This was an ingenious method devised by the early Indians to preserve their meat and fish, all of which they placed in deep earthenware vessels; these were then filled with water and the contents boiled. Pepper (capsicum) and cassareep were also added. The latter is the poisonous juice extracted from cassava after boiling, which is then fermented in the sun, a process whereby all poison is eliminated.[15] Sometimes the cassareep was mixed with salt and pepper and used as a sauce with smoked meat or fish.

### *Health*

Examination of the foods eaten by the Arawaks reveals that they were a well-nourished and generally healthy people. They never threw their garbage in the roads or around their houses; instead, all garbage was thrown in a communal dump outside the village, on the leeward side or down a slope. These communal rubbish dumps were called 'middens' or 'kitchen middens'.

With regard to the health of the Arawaks, Professor Bullbrook says: 'Rickets and dental decay were almost unknown among the West Indian and American aborigines, so that it was obvious that they must have had an ample supply of bone-forming minerals and vitamins.'[16]

## Summary: Characteristics of the Arawak

The following conclusions may be drawn from the foregoing analysis of the Arawaks:

1. They lived a sedentary and settled life.
2. They had passed beyond the predominantly hunting and gathering stage of human development and reached that of subsistence agriculture.
3. They had attained a relatively high level of artistic and technological achievement, and were expert potters.
4. They were a Stone Age people, as the knowledge and use of metals were as yet unknown to them.
5. They had a decentralized political structure with absolute power remaining in the hands of the great *cacique*.
6. They held a complex set of religious beliefs and practices similar in structure to many other aboriginal peoples.
7. They knew the use of the file as can be testified from the shell and bone artefacts found.
8. Most of their tools, weapons and domestic articles seemed to have been made predominantly from wood.
9. They believed in some form of survival after death.
10. They were a relatively advanced and peaceful people.

When the warlike, seafaring, hostile and domineering Caribs came into contact with the Arawaks there emerged in Grenada a clash of two cultures and two incompatible ways of life, even though the two groups were derived initially from a common racial type. This clash of cultures continued until the relatively peaceful and rather sedate Arawaks were finally driven off the Lesser Antilles islands, or were killed.

## The Caribs

The Grenada Caribs, like the Arawaks, were Amerindians who had originated in South America. It is not yet known when exactly they arrived in the islands, but it seems to have been a very long time after the Arawaks, possibly about 1000, for by 1492 the Arawaks had spread as far north as Cuba, greatly improving their culture and refining their skills as they went along. The Grenada Caribs most probably arrived in Grenada about 500 years before Columbus and inhabited the island until 1654 when they were finally exterminated by the French settlers.

The island Caribs had five main cultural, political and economic characteristics:

1. They were warlike in nature and placed much emphasis on military exploits.
2. Their economy was oriented to the sea. They were a seafaring people.
3. Their society was male dominated.
4. They extolled the virtues of the body cult and honoured those among them who displayed great military prowess.
5. They were polygamous.

### *Political organization*

Unlike the Arawaks, there was no Carib aristocracy; neither was their political organization as mature. Each island had one or two belligerent war chiefs elected for life and called *Ubutu*. The basis of selection was bravery and fighting skills, not, as for the Arawaks, along hereditary lines. Men became prominent owing to their military prowess.

A *caracoli* inherited from an ancestor was usually a mark of political status. These were amulets obtained during raids on Arawakan villages or during war with the Arawaks. Rouse described the *caracoli* as 'the most prized possession of the men'. It was crescent-shaped, usually an alloy of gold and copper framed in wood; some were small and served as ear, nose or mouth pendants, others were large enough to be worn on the chest. Petitjean-Roget said: 'They were crescent-shaped ornaments, the Karacouli, probably made of gold, silver or tin.' F. Breton agreed that 'these were their most precious treasure'. Butler identified fragments of stone crescents from the Savanne Suazey site in Grenada, as pieces of stone *caracoli* similar to those identified by Walter Fewkes in St Vincent.[17]

The *Ubutu* had absolute power; he decided on all matters – raids, choosing of commanders, and so on. There were also lesser governors of villages – known as *Tuibutuli Hauthe* – who ruled in times of peace, and supervised fishing and the cultivation, storage and distribution of food. The Caribs kept a slave class of captive women who were given as wives to their bravest warriors; these were the Arawakan women captured either in raids or in war.

The Caribs of Grenada and the Windwards were not isolated and insular groups but a unified race. They used their pirogues (boats 30–40 ft long able to carry about 50 people) for inter-island travel and communication. In times of trouble they would rally to each other's assistance and act in unity.

## *Economic life*

The economy of the island Caribs was oriented to both the land and sea, but predominantly to the sea. All land was held in common by the village but canoes and ornaments were considered to be personal possessions and were excluded from common ownership. The Caribs' main economic activities were fishing and hunting. Their staple food, the crab, was caught by night using a torch; they also ate considerable quantities of other shellfish. Agouti, lizards, birds and iguana were fair game for hunters. Fishing techniques included fish pots, nets, spears, bows and arrows; trained birds – the Pecheur and Grand Gosier – were also used to help locate schools of fish. Canoes some 20 feet long, or about one-half the length of a pirogue, were used for fishing. The process employed in the construction of both types of boat consisted of hollowing out trunks of softwood trees.

Vegetables in the Caribs' diet included bitter and sweet manioc, corn, beans, peppers, yams and sweet potatoes. Their method of preparing cassava was very similar to that of the Arawaks and thus merits special mention for the purposes of comparison. First, the poisonous juice was extracted by allowing the wet powdered manioc to hang in an elongated container, called a cassava press, which had a heavy stone attached to one end. After a day or two, the flour was sifted through a sieve and then baked on a hotplate or clay griddle with the aid of a wooden spatula.

The Caribs' main dish was a stew of crab and cassava seasoned with *tamaulin* sauce. This sauce was made from lemon juice, pepper and the green meat of the crab found near to its shell. With this dish they drank a cassava beer called *ouicou*, which was a combination of manioc and sweet potatoes fermented with syrup and water.[18] Père Labat, who visited Grenada as late as 1700, was given a glass of *ouicou* to drink by a French settler in Grand Pauvre (St Mark's). The Caribs abstained from eating certain foods, including turtle meat, pork and salt, either because they felt these would make them stupid, or because of other, superstitious beliefs.

## *Housing and clothing*

Caribs lived in villages, called *carbets*, comprising about 50 to 60 families each. From the literature it seems they also referred to their houses as *carbets*. The average house was about 60 feet long by 20 feet wide. From the wide distribution of Suazey-scratched pottery in Grenada it is concluded there were numerous Caribs in this island.[19]

Their clothing was sparse and they used *roucou* (vegetable dye of bright orange colour, obtained from fruit pulp of *Bixa Orellana*) paint to decorate and dye their bodies, believing that it toughened the skin and was a protection against insect bites. In times of war they painted their bodies so as to present a terrifying appearance and thus strike fear in the hearts of their enemies. Carib women wore bracelets – *rasada* – on their arms and legs; men wore necklaces made from the teeth of their enemies. They also wore idols around their necks to represent the *Icheriri* or good spirit, and headdresses of feathers. It was the woman's duty to comb and oil the man's hair daily.[20]

## *Social life, beliefs and technology*

The warrior instinct pervaded the entire Carib society. Most boys were trained as warriors, the remaining few were trained as priests. The initiation of a warrior was a major social event in the village and was accompanied by eating, drinking, merry-making and great festivities.

Two other events were celebrated similarly: the birth of a boy and the launching of a canoe. The Caribs also practised *couvade*. This was a system of self-imposed fasting by Carib fathers during the period immediately preceding the birth of a child and while their wife was in labour. This practice was in order to give their womenfolk moral support and courage.

Little can be said about the religious beliefs of the island Caribs. According to Abbé Raynal, 'their religion consisted only in some confused belief of a good and bad principle.'[21] Due Tetre agreed that they recognized two types of gods – one good and the other evil. The good gods were called *Icheriri* and the evil ones *Mabouya*.[22] They believed that everyone had a *Mabouya*, and that all of each person's evil experiences, whether death, sickness or accident, were as a result of a spell put on them by an enemy's *Mabouya*. The task of the Carib priest or *boyez* was to defeat the *Mabouya*'s evil spells and deeds.

The Caribs, in common with other tribes of America, developed specific techniques, as well as tools and equipment, to assist them in their daily lives. One such device was the bow and arrow. They used the *Bois Verde* or *Bois de lettre* (red-streaked brown wood, close grained and very hard) as material for their bows, and the fibre or bark of some trees was used to make the bowstring. The arrow, which was about three and a half feet long, was made from the top shoot of the *roseau* (a reed) and poisoned with the sap of the *manchineel* (*Hippomane Mancinella*, a valuable timber tree, bearing fruit resembling small green apples. The timber is hard to wash because all parts of the tree contain a poisonous white sap). There were three kinds of arrows – those for war, those for hunting and those for fishing. Among other devices that merit mention are graters, cassava presses, sieves and clay platines.

The Caribs in Grenada were not potters; such pottery as they had was made by the Arawak women whom they enslaved. Gradually, the concern of the Arawak women (or their daughters and granddaughters) to make good pottery was lost and they produced only in inartistic, sloppily made work. Ceramic styles introduced by the Caribs included scratched surfaces, large flat-bottomed, fairly straight-sided pail-like cauldrons, and finger-indented rims.[23]

## *Caribs and cannibalism*

Were the Caribs cannibals? They have always been closely associated with the practice of cannibalism; indeed, the two words 'Caribs' and 'cannibalism' have become synonymous in the eyes of many students of West Indian history. Were they pervasive eaters of human flesh as we are made to believe in the general history of the Caribbean? In his *History of the West Indies* Garcia referred to the Caribs as 'a race of cannibals'.[24] Augier et al., in *The Making of the West Indies* described them as 'cannibals who lived by attacking their neighbours'. In neither of these books, however, is there any evidence to substantiate these claims.[25] Sherlock, in *A Short History of the West Indies*, is a little more objective. He asserts that the name Carib was given to them by the Spaniards to whom the word meant cannibal. Although Sherlock eventually admits that cannibalism was one of the traits of these 'canoe-borne marauders', he was uncertain whether it was practised for food or for ritualistic purposes.[26]

Professor Bullbrook who has done considerable work on Trinidad's archaeological history had the following to say:

> That he was a cannibal has to be admitted but he did not eat human flesh because he preferred it. It is even possible that he did not actually like it. He ate no one save a brave enemy, and he ate him entirely for the purpose of gathering to himself that enemy's bravery.[27]

Bullbrook went on to say that Caribs have been greatly maligned on the question of cannibalism. Neither did Eric Williams, in his *History of Trinidad and Tobago*, make any accusations, but merely stated 'that the Caribs were conventionally described as cannibals'.[28] Most writers on Trinidad's archaeological history agree that the Caribs inhabited Trinidad's north-east, yet so far, there has been no evidence of cannibalism in the remnants of animal food found in the middens. This, therefore, throws doubt on the Caribs' alleged cannibalism.

In *From Columbus to Castro* Williams states emphatically that 'Columbus saw in the cannibalism of the Caribs a pretext for their enslavement'.[29] Apparently Columbus was responsible for originating this idea and perpetuating the myth in order to enslave the Indians. While it cannot be denied that the Caribs ate human flesh, the suggestion that it was their staple diet, that they tasted the flesh of all who crossed their path, is a gross exaggeration and distortion, since no credible evidence to that effect exists. Quite clearly, the facts were exaggerated in order to provide a justifiable pretext for enslavement, war and colonization of the islands and their inhabitants in the Antillean chain.

Of all the tribes in the Caribbean and Central America it was the Caribs who resisted European colonization most stubbornly. Europeans who tried to colonize St Lucia in 1605 were all killed; in 1609 over 200 tried to settle in and colonize Grenada, many were killed and the attempt had to be abandoned. When Ponce de Leon was sent to colonize Puerto Rico in 1512 he encountered formidable resistance from the Caribs there, far greater than his counterparts Juan de Esquivel and Diego Velasquez experienced in Jamaica and Cuba respectively.[30] When in 1623 the French and English jointly settled in St Kitts they were so incessantly harassed and attacked by the Caribs there that eventually both groups had to unite in their common defence. Wherever intruders in the Caribbean met Caribs they also met strong resistance.

The *Encyclopaedia Britannica* of 1911 defined 'Carib' as a name first used by Columbus to describe a people of South American origin who inhabited parts of Guiana, the Windwards and other islands at the time of his arrival; the word is derived from *cariba*, which means a valiant man. Columbus, however, tended to confuse such indigenous terms as Cariba and Caribal with Canima, Caniba and Canibal.[31] In his journal he wrote:

> the Caniba are nothing else than the people of the Great Khan who must be very near and possess ships; and they must come to take them captive and as the prisoners do not return they believe that they have been eaten.[32]

Columbus heard this from the Arawaks of Hispaniola, but believing he was in Asia (Cipangu) concluded the Caribs were soldiers of the Chinese Emperor Kublai Khan (in Cathay). His readings of strange descriptions of people in ancient and medieval mythologies would have surely influenced and coloured his perception of the Caribs whom he had never seen. Columbus' biographer, Justin Winsor agrees firmly with this.[33]

Columbus always had ambitions of origanizing a slave trade to Spain; so, upon encountering the Indians he contemplated the possibility of initiating the trade. In 1494, in a letter to the Spanish monarch, which accompanied a shipload of Indians, he wrote: 'These cannibals, a people very sage and suitable for the purpose are well made and of good intelligence. We believe that having abandoned their inhumanity they could be better than any other slaves.'[34] At this time, Columbus had never seen a Carib, but only heard of them. The people he was sending to Spain as slaves were the mild and peaceful Arawaks of Hispaniola. On 30 June 1495, Columbus instructed Antonio Torres, one of his aides, to write to the King and Queen of Spain requesting a permit to sell Indian slaves in exchange for cattle. The instructions went as follows:

> You shall say to their Highnesses that there are now sent with these ships some of the cannibals men and women and boys and girls; it is thought here that in Castille they may be led to abandon that inhuman custom which they have of eating men and much more readily receive baptism.[35]

Columbus' request to Ferdinand and Isabella for 'a license and permit' to supply cattle, etc. for the colonies, for which payments would be made in slaves from among 'these cannibals', was fortunately rejected.

Even Du Tetre, who visited the Winwards in the 17th century and recounted how Caribs found French and Spanish flesh delicious, expressly stated that: 'I have heard it said many times.' Thus, what he wrote about the Caribs was based on hearsay and was probably a distortion or exaggeration of reality. Du Tetre himself admitted that in Carib ceremonials part of the ritual involved partaking a portion of the flesh of an Arawakan prisoner-of-war. Moreover, he stated emphatically that they ate this 'viand in rage and not from appetite, in order to avenge themselves and not to make a feast for most of them became ill after so partaking.'[36] Thus, any human flesh eaten by the Caribs was for purely ritualistic purposes – a practice by no means unique to them. Finally, Jean Pierre Labat, who visited Grenada and the Windwards around 1700 and actually spent some time among the Caribs stated clearly that: 'It is an error to believe that the savages of our Isles are man-eaters and that they go to war to make prisoners in order to satiate their hunger. I have proof to the contrary.'[37]

NOTES

Full citations only given where work does not appear in the Bibliography.

1. Raymond Devas, *History of the Grenada.*
2. Ibid, p. 25.
3. Julien Steward, *Nature and Peoples.*
4. Carl Otwin Sauer, *The Early Spanish Main* pp. 45–48.
5. Ibid p. 53. Mandioca is a Tupi-Portuguese word, later anglicized to manioc.
6. Bartolome de las Casas. 'Apologetica historia de las Indias' in *Historiadores de Indias* by Marcelino Menendez y Pelayo Ch. 10.
7. Sauer, *Spanish Main*, p. 52.
8. Ibid, p. 58.
9. J.A. Bullbrook, 'Aboriginal remains', p. 18.
10. Las Casas, 'Apologetica', Ch. 46.
11. Sauer, *Spanish Main*, p. 59.
12. Gonzalvo Fernandez de Oviedo y Valdes, *Historia General*, Vol. 1.
13. Sauer, *Spanish Main*, p. 60–61.
14. Many remains of Arawakan art can now be found at the Grenada Museum.
15. Bullbrook, '*Aboriginal Remains*', p. 21.
16. Ibid.
17. Bullen, *Archaeology of Grenada*, p. 58. Irving Rouse, *Handbook*, Vol. 4.
18. E. Brathwaite (ed.), *The People Who Came, Book 1, Trinidad*, Longman Caribbean Ltd, 1972.
19. Bullen, *Archaeology of Grenada*, p. 57.
20. Raynall, *Philosophical and Political History*, Vol. III, Book x, p. 383.
21. Devas, *History ... of Grenada*, p. 26.
22. Garcia, *History of the West Indies*, p. 18.
23. Bullen, *Archaeology of Grenada.*
24. Garcia, *History of the West Indies.*
25. Augier et al, *The Making of the West Indies*, p. 4.
26. Sherlock, *A Short History*, p. 3.
27. Bullbrook, 'Aboriginal Remains', p. 15.
28. Williams, *History of Trinidad and Tobago*, Port of Spain Publishing Co. Ltd, 1962, p. 3.
29. Williams, *From Columbus to Castro*, p. 31.
30. Sherlock, *A Short History*, p. 12.
31. Moore, 'Carib cannibalism', p. 121.

32. Columbus, *Journal of ... Columbus*, p. 62.
33. Winsor, *Christopher Columbus*, p. 166.
34. Williams, *Documents of West Indian History 1492–1655*, p. 54.
35. Ibid, p. 50.
36. Du Tetre, *Histoire General Voyages;* and *Reedition Executée d'Apres L'Edition de 1667–71 aux Frais de la Société d'Histoire de la Martinique* 1959, p. 342; Moore, 'Carib Cannibalism', p. 127.
37. *The Memoirs of Père Labat 1693–1705*. Translated and abridged by John Eaden, London, Frank Cass & Co. Ltd, 1970, p. 103.

# 2

# *The French-Carib Conflict: 1650–54*

## Early Attempts at Colonization

During the first half of the 17th century many attempts were made by Europeans to settle in Grenada and to colonize its inhabitants (Caribs). These attempts were unsuccessful and in some cases, ended in disaster.

The first attempt at settlement was in 1609 when four Englishmen – Godfrey, Hall, Lull and Robinson – together with 199 followers and companions landed in Grenada from the ships *Diana, Penelope* and *Endeavour*.[1] A group of London merchants had undertaken to finance the fitting out of the ships and all other expenses. After the party disembarked in Grenada, the ships proceeded to Trinidad, their original destination.

The Caribs considered the English settlers as intruders and treated them accordingly, besieging their encampment and harassing them unceasingly. Many members of the party fell victim to the Caribs' deadly bow and arrow and to their guerrilla tactics. When the ships returned from Trinidad the little settlement was almost completely destroyed and those who survived were happy to return to England.

Almost three decades later, in 1638, came the second attempt by Europeans to settle Grenada. This was made by Monsieur De Poincy, Governor of St Kitts, and some followers, but the Caribs resisted and eventually drove them off.[2]

It seems that many Caribs were living in Grenada at the time and provided a strong striking force against the intruders. Labat attributed their relatively large numbers to the island's abundant fertility, its prolific fishing grounds and plentiful supply of birds and game.

During this early period, although Grenada was technically a part of the Spanish Empire, both England and France wanted to claim her as their possession. Spain had never either recognized or treated Grenada as being within her Empire; thus, in 1636 the island was included as part of the possessions of a joint-stock company formed in France by Cardinal Richelieu: the French Company of the Islands of America. In 1627, King Charles I of England had included Grenada in the Carlisle Proprietorship, a grant of islands in the Eastern Caribbean to the Earl of Carlisle, cousin to the King. Nevertheless, until the abortive attempt by the French under De Poincy, neither Spain, France nor England had made any attempt to colonize Grenada. That Grenada was claimed by one imperial power and given as a gift by another, when it was inhabited solely by the Caribs, indicates the pervasive colonizing ambitions of early European powers, and their contempt and disrespect for the rights of native peoples.

In 1644, a Spanish ship bound for Venezuela on the mainland (Tierra Firme) called at Grenada for firewood and food; the Caribs treated the captain and crew very hospitably. Don Tiburcio Radin, a member of the crew, was so impressed that he never forgot these inhabitants and later, in 1649, when he became a priest and joined the Capuchin Franciscans as Father Francis of Pamphona, he decided to return and evangelize the Caribs. On his arrival, however, he found the French in control of Grenada and saw a Dominican priest among them. He left immediately and returned to Cumana in Venezuela.

## *Colonization by Du Parquet: 1650*

The first successful attempt by Europeans to settle Grenada was in the year 1650, under the leadership of Monsieur Du Parquet, the then Governor of Martinique. Both Du Tetre and Labat claimed that Du Parquet was invited to Grenada by Caribs who visited Martinique.[3] If this was so, and Du Parquet came to Grenada as an invited guest, why did he come heavily armed with all the necessary materials for settlement and colonization? Clearly Du Parquet planned to colonize Grenada, establish plantations and use the natives to provide the work force. He came not as visitor and guest but as conqueror and colonizer. In fact the *Grenada Handbook* records that in 1650, MM. Houel and Du Parquet, shareholders of the Company of the Islands of America, bought Martinique, St Lucia and Grenada from the Company for 1,660 livres.

Before leaving Martinique for Grenada in 1650, Du Parquet made careful and elaborate preparations. He advertised for men willing to join the expedition and emigrate to Grenada, offering tax exemptions as an incentive to all prospective settlers. From those who came forward he chose 203 strong men[4] who were to form the backbone of the projected new settlement. Du Parquet then ordered that the ships which were to transport them be packed with cassava bread, turtle, salted sea-cow, peas, beans and corn, three barrels of brandy, two casks of Madeira wine, a quantity of linen cloth, iron tools, glass beads, textile fabrics, cannon and barrels of gunpowder. Each man was given a rifle, two belt pistols, a sword, a bayonet and adequate ammunition. Also accompanying Du Parquet on this expedition were his personal priest, Monsieur Le Compte, his cousin, and a Monsieur Le Fort.

The expedition left Martinique on 16 June 1650, and arrived in Grenada four days later. On arrival, Du Parquet and his group were welcomed and hospitably treated by the Carib chief (*Ubutu*) Kaierouanne. Du Parquet offered him gifts of cloth, axes, bill-hooks, knives, glass beads, mirrors and two quarts of brandy in an attempt to soften, bribe and temporize with the Caribs for his future colonization plans. Labat suggested that in return for the gifts Kaierouanne cede most of the island to Du Parquet, reserving for his people the *carbets* or villages where they lived. Other writers claim that there was no bargain, but that the Caribs merely accommodated the French and accepted them as visitors. One account relates how the French promised to be peaceful and offered the natives help against the English. The Caribs did not understand and, moreover, could do nothing about the continued French presence as they were terrified by the French cannons.[5]

Immediately after his arrival, Du Parquet erected a prefabricated house, a barricade and a fort with mounted cannons in order to repulse any attack by the Caribs. This encampment was situated on the ballast ground, an area just beneath Islander Hotel (now Butler's House). It was called the settlement of St Louis. Du Parquet was preparing for war and colonization, despite the hospitality extended to his party by the natives, which he found expedient to the achievement of his aims.

After making these security arrangements the colonizers felled the trees around the lake or spout in what is today called the Tanteen area, and started a large tobacco plantation. At that time, tobacco was a major money-making crop, and most European nations with colonies assisted their colonists in developing extensive tobacco plantations. For 250 years after the arrival of the Dutch in Brazil (1531) tobacco was a thriving and vital export crop and a source of much revenue for the metropolis, Holland.[6] Considerable quantities of tobacco had been exported from Spain's American colonies since the

16th century, enriching the coffers of the Spanish sovereigns, and the pockets of the Conquistadores and Hidalgos.

The British colony of Virginia was saved from economic ruin and raised to a position of modest wealth by the cultivation of a single crop of tobacco in the first half of the 17th century.[7] Early English colonists in St Kitts and Barbados exported substantial quantities of tobacco to their metropolis, England. In 1637 and 1638 the Port of London received 1.1 million pounds of tobacco from the Caribbean colonies and 3.4 million from Virginia.[8]

Thus, the French Governor of Martinique, Du Parquet, was well aware of the profits and income to be made from a thriving tobacco trade between Grenada and France: this is why one of his first acts on arrival in Grenada in 1650 was to establish a tobacco plantation in Tanteen. The first crop was reaped early in 1651, about eight months after settlement. By that time Du Parquet had returned to Martinique, leaving his cousin, Monsieur Le Compte, as Governor and man-in-charge.

## Carib Resistance and Death

About seven months after the arrival of the colonizing French, the Caribs began to rebel against them. As the French established themselves and consolidated their position in Grenada during the first year, the Caribs realized they had come not as visitors but as settlers who soon would displace them and drive them off the island. They saw this as a betrayal of their hospitality and friendship. Both John Scot and the Abbé Raynal agree that the Caribs considered themselves to have been duped and as a result became very angry and began to commit isolated acts of violence upon unsuspecting and vagrant French settlers. As Labat explains: Not daring to attack the French openly, they determined quietly to slay all whom they found hunting in the woods far from the fort.[9] These attacks continued for about a year, occurring mostly in 1651, and became so widespread that most of the Frenchmen had to confine themselves to the Fort. The Governor, Monsieur Le Compte, realizing that the situation had become dangerous, especially after the death of Monsieur M. Imbert,[10] decided to retaliate by going on the offensive.

Le Compte planned to attack the largest of the Carib *carbets*, situated on Mount St Catherine, a mountain precipitous from all sides. The attack, however, turned out to be abortive as the Caribs defended the mountain bravely and tenaciously; they repulsed the French, and killed many of them.

In 1652, when Du Parquet received news of this, he sent 300 soldiers and men to reinforce Le Compte's diminished forces; he also sent strict orders to Le Compte to push the Caribs to the extreme north or drive them out of Grenada completely. In the meantime, the Caribs also received reinforcements from their counterparts in St Vincent and Dominica. They planned a general assault on the French fort and settlement, having by then mobilized a fighting force of some 800. But the French learned of the proposed attack and instead of taking the offensive, waited patiently for the Caribs, hoping to surprise them.

On the day of the attack, fully prepared for the counter-offensive, the French remained quiet, until, when the Caribs were within a few yards of the Fort, they opened fire with their cannons and muskets. The Caribs' force was thrown into complete disarray both by the element of surprise and the thunderous sound of the cannons. Many Caribs were killed by the initial outburst of gunfire and the rest ran for cover in the surrounding woods. They fought bravely and unyieldingly, but the French had the superior weapons and continued to track them down and kill them relentlessly.

About 300 Caribs were pursued by the French to a *carbet* at the top of a mountain and about 80 of them were killed. The remainder rushed down the hillsides at dazzling speed, like stones dropping from a 1,000 foot cliff; those able to reach canoes and even logs, escaped to the Cabsterre of the island. A band of about 40 pressed further north until they reached the northernmost point of the island, but realizing the hopelessness of their situation and, with the French soldiers then close at hand, the impossibility of escape, covering their eyes with their hands they plunged into the sea to meet what to them was a glorious end, compared to a base and shameful death at the hands of the Frenchman. The French pursuit of the Carib lasted several days,[11] beginning in St George's (Basseterre) and ending at Le Morne des Sauteurs or Leaper's Hill, the name subsequently given to the spot from which the Caribs plunged (see page 24). In 1664 the Dominican order of the Catholic Church laid the foundation of a church there.

## Carib Resurgence

The Caribs of Grenada, including those who had escaped the first war of extermination, continued to live in the Cabsterre of the island. Sometime around 1653 and 1654 they called a general assembly in which it was decreed that all Frenchmen in Grenada must be killed. In the meantime, the Caribs in the islands to the north, angered by the evil deeds of buccaneers and other ruffians from Europe, began to

*Le Morne des Sauteurs today*

muster their forces to expel the intruders. The word was spread from island to island that every white man found should be put to death – *Kaori homan*, as they called it. Around this time, in St Vincent, two Jesuit priests, Aubergeon and Gueimu, were attacked and killed while celebrating mass, to the dismay of a handful of their Carib neophytes.

In Grenada, the Caribs yearned to revenge the 1652 massacre of their families. In 1654, they formed themselves into guerrilla bands and began to roam the forests killing all Frenchmen they encountered. Realizing that the Caribs were now arousing fear and terror in the French settler community and fearful of an outbreak and spread of general panic, Le Compte mustered a force of 150 men and travelled quickly up the Cabsterre of the island. At daybreak, they made a surprise attack on the most populous *carbet* killing everyone regardless of age or sex; virtually no Carib escaped or survived. To prevent the escape of those who were away from the village at the time of the massacre, the French burned all the canoes and boats, and then formed groups and combed the woods, forests and streams, killing every Carib they met. They then burned the *carbets*. This event, in 1654, marked the almost total extermination of the caribs of Grenada. The few who remained were too isolated and numerically weak to retaliate or pose any threat to the French.

On his return to Port St Louis, Governor Le Compte drowned while trying to save one of his men who had fallen into the sea and was apparently unable to swim. Shortly after, Monsieur Louis de Cacqueray, Sieur de Valminière was appointed Governor of Grenada and successor to Le Compte.

In the meantime, the Caribs of St Vincent, learning the fate of their brothers in Grenada, retaliated by descending upon the island and stealthily damaging as much as possible; an activity both continuous and ubiquitous. Despite this, the few Caribs who inhabited the Cabsterre remained inactive, probably because their numbers were so greatly diminished after the recent French offensive they had no choice but to accept the status quo. The St Vincent Caribs, however, continued to kill and harass many of the French in Grenada, and war on a small scale was renewed, to the extent that from time to time Du Parquet had to send military assistance to the colonists.

## Internal Discontent

But Valminière experienced other troubles, in the form of internal discontent. Several officers among the colonists considered that they should have been appointed governor instead of Valminière. Chief among these was Monsieur Le Fort, First Captain and Major of the French, and an officer of about four years standing in Grenada. He considered that he should have been made Governor, and Monsieur Le Marquis Major of the French forces. As a result discontent spread, and the colonists became divided into rival groups, those loyal to Valminière and those supporting Le Fort. Informed of the crisis Du Parquet sent orders to Le Fort and his followers to accept Valminière as Governor; he also strengthened the latter's hand by sending a company of 100 soldiers – Walloons – who had recently served in Brazil under the Dutch States-General, but who, together with the Dutch, had been expelled by the Portuguese when they regained control of Brazil in 1654.[12]

Upon arrival the Walloons' Captain went to Le Fort's house to hold discussions with him, but Le Fort refused to open his door, whereupon it was broken down. Some shooting ensued and a few members of the opposing parties were killed while others were wounded. Le Fort and Le Marquis were finally overpowered, arrested and imprisoned. While in prison, Le Fort, fearing that he would be sentenced to an ignominious death, took poison and died. Le Marquis was sentenced to death, but Du Parquet later commuted this to banishment.[13] Thus, even in the early years of its colonial history, inhabitants of Grenada had begun to kill each other over the question of political power and leadership.

The Carib wars of 1652–54 had considerably strained Du Parquet's finances. In 1657, realizing that his investment in Grenada had been a financial disaster he sold the island to the Comte de

Cerillac for 1,890 livres, in an attempt to recover some of his losses. It was said that the 'Caribbees proved to be the irreconcilable enemies of the French and that their frequent insurrection at last obliged Du Parquet to sell Grenada.'[14]

The new Governor of Grenada sent by the Comte de Cerillac was a brutal dictator who committed many acts of tyranny against the French colonists; as a result of this oppression many of them emigrated to Martinique. Those who remained eventually rose up in arms against the Governor, arrested and tried him in an *ad hoc* People's Court which condemned him to be hanged. However, the Governor claimed to be a man of noble birth and pleaded for his sentence to be changed from hanging to beheading. His wish was granted, but, as there was no skilful executioner among the ranks the wretched Governor was eventually shot.

When news of this incident arrived in France, the French Court sent out a warship and a commissioner to enquire into the state of affairs in Grenada. But by this time, many of those who participated in the People's Court had emigrated and no one was found who could have been held responsible.

## Grenada Passes To the French Crown

In 1664 the King of France passed an Order in Council transferring the rights of the Company of the Islands of America (founded, as has already been noted, by Cardinal Richelieu in 1635) to the recently established French West India Company. This Company was given full political authority to develop the French Antilles, and had a monopoly of all trade between these colonies and France. Du Parquet, Houel and Cerillac all had shares and vested interest in the Company; at the same time, they were appointed Governors of the established islands by the directors. They acted almost independently of the French Crown and were virtually autonomous in the conduct of the affairs of the French Antilles.

It appeared that in 1664 the Comte de Cerillac was coerced into selling his rights in Grenada to the newly formed French West India Company, for which, in 1665, he was paid the sum of 10,000 crowns. Monsieur de Tracy, a new Commissioner, was sent by the Company in 1664 to rectify the affairs of the island. Arriving in November 1664 he found the colonists in great distress. He redressed most of their grievances, expelled the Comte de Cerillac and appointed Monsieur Vincent as Governor. The Commissioner then left Grenada on 29 November 1664.

When, ten years after its formation, the French West India Company was dissolved in 1674, Grenada came directly under the administration of the French Crown and remained so for the next 88 years, when, as we have noted, it was ceded to England at the Treaty of Paris in 1763.

NOTES

Full citations only given where work does not appear in the Bibliography.

1. Devas, *History of Grenada*. p. 30.
2. *Grenada Handbook*, p. 19.
3. Du Tetre, *Histoire General*; Labat, *Voyages*.
4. Devas, *History of Grenada*, p. 35.
5. *L'Histoire de L'isle de Grenada en Amerique,* anonymous manuscript presented by Jacques Petitjean Rojet, Montreal, Montreal University Press, 1975, pp. 47–66.
6. Rollie Popino, *Brazil* p. 128.
7. J.H. Parry, *The Establishment of European Hegemony*, p. 394.
8. Richard B. Sheridan, *Sugar and Slavery*. p. 394.
9. Devas, *History of Grenada*, pp. 36–37.
10. Monsieur Imbert, supposedly invited to a social gathering in a *carbet* by some Caribs, was on his arrival attacked and slain.
11. *Grenada Handbook*, p. 21, Devas, *History of Grenada*, pp. 39–41.
12. Devas, *History of Grenada*, pp. 39–41.
13. Ibid, p. 52.
14. The amounts given for which Grenada was sold differ. The *Grenada Handbook* (pp. 21–23) gives 1,890 livres; the *Encyclopaedia Britannica*, 1911, 30,000 crowns, Labat gives 90 livers; *L'Histoire de Grenade*, 800,000 francs.

# 3

# *French Colonialism: 1674–1762*

French political structures and administration in Grenada were similar to those in other French colonies in the West Indies. They were based on three essential principles postulated and promulgated by Jean-Baptiste Colbert, Minister of Marine in 1669, with full jurisdiction over the colonies. These principles were as follows:

1. Colonies were necessary to build trade, wealth and economic power for France.
2. The colonies were the exclusive property of the French Crown.
3. Colonial interests must be subordinated to metropolitan or imperial interests.

Thus the French political system was drawn up to foster and build the economic interests and prosperity of France, and to develop her as a nation. Colbert was noted as being the foremost architect of French colonialism and empire-building, and laid the basis for French expansion and hegemony in the 18th Century. He was hostile towards Dutch interests and influence in the West Indies and ordered all Dutch ships to be driven out of French colonial ports or be confiscated. French colonial trade was to be a monopoly of France.

Dutch trade with the French colonies in the West Indies at that time amounted to two million livres of sugar, and one million livres of cotton, tobacco and indigo, and employed 200 or more ships and 6,000 Dutch seamen. It was with a view to seizing this trade that Colbert helped create the French West India Company in 1664.[1]

In assuming direct control of French colonies formerly administered by joint-stock companies, Colbert hoped to maximize the benefits of empire and trade for France. A centralized political administration was seen as essential to the achievment of these objectives; Grenada had to fit into this imperial matrix.

## Administrative Structure

French colonial administration was supervised in France by the Conseil d'Etat, and the supreme command in the French Antilles was entrusted to a Governor-General who resided in Martinique. His duties were to oversee and superintend the administration of French colonies in the Lesser Antilles; he was also Commandant of the army and navy. Grenada like all French colonies had a military governor whose main functions consisted of military duties and the enforcement of commercial restrictions. The Governor-General was assisted by a *conseil souverain* composed of lawyers, planters and army officers, who advised him on matters of policy; its primary function, however, was as a Court of Appeal in the colony, and in this capacity it had the highest judicial authority in Grenada. The authority of the Governor was held in check by the *Intendant* who was primarily responsible for justice, economic regulations and finance. He was an exofficio president of the Council while the other councillors, (usually ten) were the Governor's nominees. The councillors were usually prominent local people who wielded considerable political power. If they either disliked or came into conflict with a particular Governor they could make things difficult for him: it resembled the BWI Assemblies in this regard. It had no power to make laws or vote money. Between 1674 and 1705, of the nine Governors who had served in Grenada, only two were said to have displeased the imperial government in France.

Simultaneous with the establishment of civil government in Grenada was the establishment by the French of the Roman Catholic religion. The first mission, represented by Father Bénin Bresson, was of the Dominican order. The land given to them by Du Parquet to facilitate their missionary work is today called Diamond Estate.

In 1657, the Dominicans were succeeded by the Capuchins, but they later returned and established a settlement in Grand Pauvre. By 1677, however, they had been ordered off the island by the French government and the bearded Capuchins again took their place. The Capuchin settlement in Fort Royal, the capital, consisted of 33 acres extending from Springs Estate to Tempe Estate, and in 1690 they built and blessed a new church there; the site is now occupied by the Anglican church. At that time the Governor, who gave valuable assistance to the Capuchins, was Gabaret, and the priest was Father Victor.[2]

In 1721, more land was given to the Capuchins by Governor Pradine for the establishment of churches in parishes other than Grand Pauvre. Churches were then built: at Megrin (St David's), on Corinth Estate, near the sea overlooking a bay known as L'Ance Pere. Another church was built in Marquis by the main road; and in Sauteurs, the Court House now stands where the church was.[3] There was also a church built at L'Ance Gouyave.

The church was a pillar of the colonial process, and the development of civil-political institutions went hand in hand with that of ecclesiastical institutions. In the Spanish, French, English and Dutch colonies in the West Indies a symbiotic relationship existed between the political administration and the church, especially the established church of the respective metropolitan powers. This is why both Du Parquet and the various governors were disposed to provide resources and facilities to enable the church to function extensively in Grenada.

By 1721 there was disenchantment with the Capuchins and the Dominicans returned to their estate in Grand Pauvre, where they established the parish church dedicated to St Rose.

## Grenada c. 1700

There were in Grenada around this time (1700) some 835 inhabitants (excluding isolated pockets of Caribs); these included 257 whites, 53 Mulattos and 525 Black slaves. Most of these slaves were employed on the island's three sugar estates and 52 indigo plantations. The livestock of these estates comprised 64 horses and 569 head of cattle.[4]

Père Labat, who visited Grenada in 1700, described the existence of a *carbet* of Caribs near Diamond Estate and of many others elsewhere which were tolerated by the French in the Cabesterre of the island. The French colonists were well supplied with fish, venison, fresh cassava, and *quicou* (a wine made from manioc and sweet potatoes and fermented with syrup and water. Pigeons, ramiers, ground doves, grieves, parrots, perriques, tatoos, and agouti provided most of the animal protein.[5]

At that time Grenada was divided into six parishes: Basseterre (St George's), Gouyave (St John's), Grand Pauvre (St Mark's), Sauteurs (St Patrick's), Megrin (St David's), and Marquis (St Andrew's), each separated from each other by rivers and streams. The Paroisse de la Basseterre extended from the Rivière Chemin to the Rivière Douce.

The area between Pointe des Salines and the Rivière du Chemin was dry and barren and sparsely populated; the little water there was came from wells or salt ponds. The salt ponds, when carefully managed, produced a great deal of salt.

The Paroisse de Megrin, on the south-east of Grenada, extended three and a half leagues (one league = three miles) from the Rivière du Chemin to the Rivière du Crochu which separated it at the north from the district of Grand Marquis.

The largest parish was the Quartier du Grand Marquis, situated at the east and extending for four and a half leagues from the Rivière du Crochu to the Rivière Antoine which separated it at the north from the parish of Sauteurs.

The Paroisse des Sauteurs at the north of the island extended for four leagues along the Chemin Royal from the Rivière Antoine to the Rivière de Duquesne.

The Paroisse de Grand Pauvre, the smallest parish, lay to the north-west and extended two leagues (about six miles) from the Rivière de Duquesne to the Ravine Marans, which separated it to the south from the Paroisse de L'Ance Gouyave. The latter parish extended two and a half leagues from the Ravine Marans to the Rivière Douce.

| | | |
|---|---|---|
| Basseterre | 4,345 | quarres |
| Gouyave | 2,657 | " |
| Grand Pauvre | 1,617 | " |
| Sauteurs | 3,078 | " |
| Marquis | 6,212 | " |
| Megrin | 3,000 | " |

Each parish was measured in quarres (one quarre = 3.2 acres in English measurement) of land, and their extent was:

The total area of Grenada was estimated at 20,900 quarres or 60,146 English acres. The principal parish was Basseterre which contained the town, port and fort. The town was first named Fort Louis, (when it was located on the ballast ground). In 1705, under the governorship of Monsieur de Bellair, it was transferred to a new site on the western side of the harbour where it now stands. The French engineer, Monsieur de Caillus, built Fort Royal during 1705 and 1706, and the town itself was renamed Fort Royal in 1705. In 1763 the British changed it to St George's, and the Fort was also renamed Fort George. Today it bears the name Fort Rupert to commemorate Rupert Bishop, the father of the leader of the People's Revolutionary Government (1979) whom police murdered on Monday 21 January 1974, while he was protecting children in Otway House during the demonstrations against the Gairy government.

Around the year 1700 the Fort's military establishment consisted of a garrison of 35–40 soldiers of the Compagine Detachie de la Marine. They were housed in huts, mostly built against the walls of the fort; the officers' quarters were small and poorly constructed buildings.

## Economic Life 1700–50

The cultivation of tobacco and sugar continued to be the principal economic activity until the second decade of the 18th century. Grenada itself continued to be generally neglected by the French government. The colonists were at the mercy of the tax-gatherers who exacted heavy taxes, almost ruining the cultivation of tobacco in the process. At this time the colony was engaged in a considerable smuggling trade with the Dutch in an effort to survive and to overcome the effects of metropolitan neglect. This activity brought increased wealth and prosperity to the island and its inhabitants.

Around the year 1714, Grenada's economic base was diversified, and cocoa, coffee and cotton began to be cultivated. These crops expanded significantly during the next three decades with coffee taking the lead. Tobacco grown in Grenada at the time was said to be of such superior quality that it realized double and triple the price of that grown in the other islands.

During the next 40 years, as the cultivation of these commodities increased, the colony apparently made modest growth; it also became an entrepôt for trade and shipping between Martinique and the Spanish Main. By 1753 the economy had grown considerably and the plantation system had become well established. There were some 83 sugar plantations, 27,525,600 coffee trees, 150,000 cocoa trees, 800 cotton trees, 5,740,450 trenches of cassava and 933,596 banana trees. The island was well supplied with livestock both for meat and draught: 2,456 head of horned cattle, 3,278 sheep, 902 goats, 331 pigs and 2,298 horses and mules. The population had grown significantly to 1,262 whites, 179 free negroes and 11,991 slaves.[6] There were six churches and one hospital, all serviced by three Dominicans, three Capuchins and one Jesuit.

By 1763, there were 81 sugar plantations, 208 coffee plantations and 21 other estates lying fallow.[7] The sugar and coffee estates were distributed as shown in Table 3.1 (page 33). With the consolidation of the plantation system and the consequently increased economic power

**Table 3.1 Distribution of Sugar and Coffee Estates in 1763**

| *Parish* | *Estates* | |
|---|---|---|
| | *Sugar* | *Coffee* |
| Basseterre | 13 | 35 |
| Gouyave | 10 | 38 |
| Grand Pauvre | 6 | 26 |
| Sauteurs | 18 | 29 |
| Marquis | 23 | 53 |
| Megrin | 11 | 27 |

and influence of the planters, the living conditions of the slave labour force simultaneously deteriorated. Ill-fed, over-worked, and considered in law and treated in practice as chattel, the African slave paid the highest price for the plantations' prosperity.

There were 11,911 slaves, and the one hospital in the island was, of course, reserved for the whites and the inhabitants in the town. Estate workers who became sick suffered in pain, died and were buried as beasts of burden. The hospital, on Hospital Hill, (where Presentation College is today) was erected by the French government in 1738 and placed in care of the Brothers of St John of God. It was supported by charity and the profits from a sugar plantation in St George's which had been purchased with the funds of the institution. In 1750, Fr Damien Pillon, who was in charge, seemed to have been more interested in the sugar factory than in the sick and suffering in the hospital. So many complaints were made against him that the hospital had to be placed under the direct management of the French colonial government.

By 1750, numerous small settlements had sprung up in Grenada, including: Sauteurs, Marquis, Grand Bacolet, La Baye, Le Requin, Le Petit Trou, Ville et Fort Royal, Beausejour, Marigot, Le Grand Roy. As early as 1700 Labat likened the settlers in Grenada to peasants and described their manners as crude. Half a century later this peasant-type agriculture was superseded by the plantation system.

## NOTES

Full citations only given where work does not appear in the Bibliography.

1. Williams, *From Columbus to Castro*, p. 160.
2. Devas, *Conception Island* , p. 21.
3. Ibid. pp. 22–25.
4. *Grenada Handbook*, p. 22.
5. *The Memoirs of Père Labat.*
6. Septimus Wells, *Historical Descriptive Sketch.*
7. Ragatz, *Statistics*, p. 5.

# 4

# *The Genesis of British Colonial Rule: 1763–79*

## Grenada Ceded to the British

On 10 February, 1763, the island of Grenada was ceded to England by the ninth article of the Treaty of Paris, and on 10 October, 1763, letters patent were issued creating the government of Grenada. The orders read as follows:

> Comprehending the island of that name, together with the Grenadines, St. Vincent, Dominica and Tobago and providing for councils and assemblies of the representatives of the people therein in such manner and form as is used and directed in those colonies and provinces of America; the legislatures created are empowered to pass laws as may be agreeable to the laws of England and the governor shall create courts of justice with the rights of appeal to the Privy Council.[1]

Thus, from its inception as a British colony the government of Grenada was constituted as part of a federated unit. That unit included Grenada, the Grenadines, St Vincent, Tobago and Dominica, and was called the Government of Grenada.

Immediately after cession all lands were declared Crown property by the Governor; surveys were made, and in March 1764 regulations governing their disposal were issued. These revealed a firm effort to prevent the development of large estates, and large tracts of idle land being held by speculators.

Commissioners were despatched to Grenada with orders to dispose of parcels of land by public sale to British subjects only. No person was allowed to purchase more than 500 acres in Grenada or 300 in Dominica. Of the price, 20% was payable immediately upon purchase; 10% in each of the two years following, and the remaining 60% in three annual instalments of 20% each.[2]

Commissioners were authorized to lease to the French inhabitants, (now called new subjects) for terms of up to 40 years, such lands as had been in their possession under the old regime, provided they swore allegiance to the King of England.[3]

The Treaty of Paris allowed those French subjects who possessed estates in Grenada, but did not wish to live under British rule, to sell them to British subjects. Many such estates and tenements were purchased by British subjects during the next four years, but as the French were allowed to remove all their records to Martinique, countless disputes over titles and claims to these estates and tenements ensued. In order to prevent the new owners from being unjustly deprived of their properties, on 12 January 1767 the Government passed a law securing and confirming the titles of persons possessing lands in Grenada. No defect or informality of law in passing deeds of sale was able to defeat or prejudice the title of purchasers and new owners.

## Melville's Administration

The first British Governor to administer the colony was General Robert Melville, who arrived in Grenada on 13 December 1764, and immediately proceeded to set up a General Council for Grenada, Dominica, Tobago, St Vincent and the Grenadines. He then tried to set up a General Assembly for all the islands but encountered vigorous opposition from planters in Dominica and the other Windwards. This was the first attempt to unite the Windwards politically, and it failed owing to the insularity of the planter class and to their dogged resistance to political unity.

Melville then proceeded to have an Assembly elected for Grenada and the Grenadines; this consisted of 20 members elected from the landed and monied class in the colony, including those French inhabitants who qualified for the franchise. The first election to the Grenada House of Assembly was on 13 April 1766 and the first session of the House began later on in that month. However, its first Bill, 'A Bill for The Better Government Of The Slaves' failed to pass the Council. A conflict ensued over the relative powers of the Assembly and Council and the Assembly claimed the right to adjourn without the Government's permission, whereupon the Assembly was dissolved having existed for a mere 37 days.[4]

On 5 October 1766, a new Assembly was convened, which existed for much longer. In March 1767, the General Council for the

Windwards was abolished and a separate council for Grenada created. On 31 December 1768, the first major change to the constitution was made: the Legislative Assembly was enlarged from 20 to 24 members, and the French section of the population was given the right to stand for election. Provisions were made for the election of three French inhabitants to the Assembly, and for the nomination of two to the island's Council, provided they had sworn alliegiance to the King of England. Moreover, they were exempted from swearing to the 'Test Act' which was a rejection of the belief in the Catholic doctrine of transubstantiation. The more zealous Protestants resented this and bitter inter-group dissensions followed. They strongly contended that it was unjust and against the laws of England to admit Roman Catholics to His Majesty's Council and Assembly. It was popularly believed that the machinations of a French agent in London led the Secretary of State to allow two Roman Catholics to be members of the Council and three others to be eligible for elections to the Assembly; in addition, one Roman Catholic was eligible for appointment as a Puisne Judge of the Court of Common Pleas, and one as a Justice of the Peace for each town, parish or district in Grenada, Carriacou and Petit Martinique.

Governor Melville, the Council, the Speaker and the majority of the Assemblymen had advised the Secretary of State, Lord Hillsborough, against his leniency towards the Roman Catholics. As early as 1766 Ninian Home and 17 other planters sent a petition to Melville protesting over his procurement of the vote for the French subjects. A second petition, however, signed by 23 Englishmen in Grenada, was subsequently addressed to Melville, supporting the idea of a vote for the French subjects; this was reinforced by a third petition, signed by 35 French subjects. Melville eventually gave them the vote but intimated that they would not be admitted to the Assembly. But in 1768, Fitzmaurice, much to the chagrin of Melville, was instructed by Lord Hillsborough to extend to the French subjects the right to be elected to the Assembly and to admit two of them to the Council. During this time both General Melville and Lieutenant-Governor Gore were out of the colony and Lieutenant Ulysses Fitzmaurice had assumed the governorship of Grenada. It was, then, to Fitzmaurice that the Secretary of State sent the following clarification of the political status of the French subjects:

> It is His Majesty's further pleasure that you do acquaint the Assembly to be called ... that the new subjects in the island professing the Roman Catholic religion shall enjoy the free exercise of their right as the Laws of Great Britain permit.[5]

On 12 October 1768, in a subsequent proclamation, the Roman Catholics were officially exempted from the Test Act. On the 16 February 1769, three of the New Subjects (Roman Catholics) took their seats in the Assembly without having subscribed to the Test Act and seven were appointed Justices of the Peace, one in each parish of Grenada and one in Carriacou;[6] on 24 August 1769, a Roman Catholic was appointed Puisne Judge. When, however, Fitzmaurice attempted to introduce into the Council two Assemblymen, Chanteloupe and Devoconnue, he was opposed by Protestants on the grounds that their numbers were complete and that a mandamus from His Majesty was necessary to change the number.[7] Lord Hillsborough wrote that they should be admitted. When, subsequently, Fitzmaurice introduced them into the Council six Councillors walked out, and as a result were suspended by Fitzmaurice on 6 October 1769.

The leading English planters protested against the Governor's action and accused him of acting *ultra vires* and illegally. The Councillors who had walked out convened a meeting of the Council on 25 September 1769, and passed the following resolution condemning Governor Fitzmaurice's attempt forcibly to introduce the two Roman Catholics into the Council, and also offering an explanation of their withdrawal.

> At the last meeting the Council thought it proper to withdraw themselves for that time, not with any design to absent themselves from the public business but merely with the view of preventing His Honour from carrying into execution a measure which appeared to them to be so illegal, it is hoped that upon cooler deliberation the reasons submitted to His Honour may be of sufficient weight to induce him to desist from so dangerous a measure.[8]

Apparently an attempt to settle the dispute was made during the next two days, but Fitzmaurice, realizing he could neither compromise on the issue nor submit to a Council officially bound to support him, issued the notice of suspension referred to above.

The six Councillors immediately convened a meeting and, on the basis of a legal technicality, passed the following resolutions:

1. That according to His Majesty's instructions the Governor cannot suspend any member without a good and sufficient cause and without the consent of the majority of the said Council.
2. That the attempt to suspend the members without having taken the previous steps is a wanton and extraordinary abuse of power.
3. That the said suspension is null and void and that the said Council will continue to sit and exercise the power delegated to it.

The Governor ignored these objections and, on 6 October 1769, proceeded to issue written suspension orders on the six Councillors as follows:

> Whereas I have thought proper, for divers reasons not fit to be communicated to the Council but which shall be laid before His Majesty, to suspend and remove [the six Councillors] I do hereby suspend and remove the said [six Councillors] from sitting, voting and assisting in His Majesty's Council of Grenada and the Grenadines.[9]

Realizing that this suspension was valid, for reasons which the Governor deemed not fit to be communicated to them, the six Councillors submitted and accepted the suspension.

Meantime, there were strenuous efforts to prevent Governor Melville from being sent back to Grenada. During his previous administration he had made himself unpopular with both the French and a large section of the British in Grenada. In October 1769 some English planters resident in England presented complaints against him, in which he was held up to much ridicule. Nevertheless, in 1770, he resumed his governorship of Grenada at the height of Anglo-French conflict over political rights.

On 6 September 1770, the Court of Kings Bench and Grand Sessions of the island was held. Two French subjects whose names were on the Commission of the Peace were again asked to take the Test; one refused and so they were thrown out by a vote of 8:2. The Protestants in Grenada petitioned His Majesty protesting against the principle granted the Roman Catholic New Subjects. They declared that these subjects did not even speak English and were given privileges not enjoyed by their counterparts in England. On 23 April 1771, the imperial government issued letters patent exempting Catholics from the Test Act. Early in 1771, when William Leyborne succeeded Melville (who either resigned or was recalled over this matter) he was instructed that they be sworn in, and so they were. In the same year two French subjects were accepted in the Council and three in the Assembly. On 30 January 1772, the Protestants, unsatisfied at the outcome of the contest over civil rights, petitioned Governor Leyborne, protesting against the inclusion of Catholics in the Assembly; also some Councillors wrote to the Secretary of State at the time intimating that Roman Catholics could not be exempted from the Test Act by the King's order, but only by Act of Parliament. These petitions were followed by the resignations of three Justices from the Court of Common Pleas, and bitter attacks on the new Roman Catholic Councillors and Assemblymen. Relations between the English and Scottish Protestant politicians and the Roman Catholics continued to be very strained, with the ultra-Protestant party remaining uncompromising over this matter of civil liberties. The English Assemblymen continued to show their disapproval by boycotting Assembly meetings until as late as 1779, when Grenada was recaptured by the French during the War of American Independence.

## The Grenada Assembly

Not only was the Grenada Assembly at the time poorly constituted, but it also performed its duties most unsatisfactorily, and members attended meetings very perfunctorily. In 1769, the constituents of the Assembly comprised: one alien, one member under age, five without any qualifications, five or six absent from Grenada, three Army officers, and four Frenchmen who neither spoke nor understood a word of English; a truly motley group!

The English inhabitants complained that the French subjects, who formed the majority of land owners, monopolized elections to the Assembly, and the unsatisfactory constitution of that House was attributed to this. At that time about two-thirds of the property was in the hands of the English inhabitants, most of whom were resident planters. The French-speaking subjects possessed less than one-third, mostly sugar plantations belonging to about 16 Roman Catholics, of whom half were absentees. Many coffee, cocoa, and cotton plots were owned largely by French Roman Catholic subjects, and these medium-sized farmers controlled the balance of power and by and large determined who sat in the Assembly. The quorum for General Assembly sessions was 11 members, and sessions were frequently adjourned owing to the chronic absenteeism of Assemblymen. On 18 March and on 1 April 1772, only nine out of a total of 24 members were present, and these sessions were accordingly cancelled.[10] During the next two years, so much did the situation deteriorate that in January 1774, a law was passed compelling members of the Assembly to attend to their duty, and laying down that a member absent for three successive meetings would forfeit his seat unless within ten days after the last day of the third session he delivered a certificate, sworn before a magistrate and written by a medical practitioner, stating that he was incapacitated by illness during the said three sessions. Any member absent for 12 calendar months was to forfeit his seat; any member absent one hour after meeting began would be fined 7/6d; a member absent for one or more sessions but less than three, and who was resident in the island at the time would be fined 33/-. Also, in the absence of a quorum the Assembly was to adjourn from day to day.[11]

The Assembly was dissolved on 26 June, 1775, and on 30 October there were General Elections in which the 24 representatives were returned for the respective electoral districts. There were four elected representatives for the town of St George and five for the combined parishes of St George and St John; one of the latter was a French Grenadian Etienne Molenier. The combined electoral districts of St David's, St Andrew's, St Mark's and St Patrick's had six representatives each, including another two French-speaking representatives, Francis Laurent and Charles P. Clozier. Carriacou had three representatives.

In 1775, the Assembly consisted of 21 English-speaking and three French-speaking members. As a result of the language problem two French-speaking members (Molenier and Clozier) moved a motion during the first session of the house for the appointment of an interpreter, and one Joseph Malan was appointed.

Being fully aware of the problems of absenteeism and its deleterious effects on the management of the Government of Grenada, the New Assembly imposed 20 restrictions in order to discipline members and help solve the problem. They retained the quorum of 11 members but they ordered that, 'the law that was passed to compell members of the Assembly to attend to their duty in the said Assembly, be strictly enforced.' Additionally, that the Speaker, with the consent of six or more members, should be empowered to send the messenger to any member(s) not attending at the regular hours of the meeting, to demand his/their attendance or, an acceptable excuse.[12] A fine of 16/6d was imposed on each member for non-attendance.

This law was imposed at the commencement of the New House. For the Session of 15 November 1775, one day after the rules were passed, eight members only attended and the Session was cancelled. On 25 November, 1775, nine out of 24 Members were present, and on 4 December 1775, two out of 24 Members were present. Before this, on 20 November, one member, Alexander J. Alexander, was fined £4.19s. for a week's absence; he paid the fine and then resigned.

Clearly, by 1779, the Assembly was in a shambles, essentially owing to two factors; sectarian strife, and elected representatives' subordination of the island's affairs to their own personal affairs and interests.

## Early Political Conflict

Cultural and religious factors provoked the political conflict that raged in Grenada between 1763 and 1779. The cultural factors pertained to traditional Anglo-French differences, while the religious factor was based on the refusal of Roman Catholics to subscribe to the Test Act, which in essence was a forcible rejection of their religion.

The Test Act, which the ultra-Protestant party in Grenada was determined to enfore during and after this period, had five weaknesses:

1. It was a highly speculative doctrine.
2. Its imposition meant a violation of the rights of freedom of conscience and religion.
3. It was never meant to be extended to the Colonies.
4. It originated in an age of frenzy, religious fanaticism and frantic violence.
5. It was promoted by a worthless individual out of animosity to the Duke of York.

The Anglo-Saxon Protestants who supported the Test Act did so more out of traditional Anglo-French religious and cultural rivalry than from a standpoint of doctrinaire conviction.

In 1775, Governor Leyborne had died at St Vincent, and in May 1776, a new Governor, Lord Macartney, took over the administration of Grenada. Shortly after Melville had departed in 1771, the colony had undergone another constitutional change, as Dominica was separated from the joint administration and now had a separate government under Sir William Young. In 1776, St Vincent followed suit and so the Government of Grenada was limited to Grenada, Tobago, and the Grenadines. The year 1776 marked the outbreak of war between the French and the English over the issue of French assistance to the breakaway English colonies in America. One of the main theatres of this war was the Caribbean Sea; since this major external factor affected the defence of Grenada it became the dominant issue in the island and the 14 year old contest over civil liberties was overshadowed by concern for the security of the colony. This was the situation until 1779 when Grenada was captured by French forces under Count d' Estaing.

## Early Colonial Economy 1764–80

Of all the ceded islands, Grenada was the most advanced agriculturally, and at the same time the most exploited, as can be seen clearly from a comparison of the output of the principal staples of these islands for the year 1764 (Table 4.1).

Grenada was the leading coffee, cotton, sugar and cacao producer in the Windward Islands at the time. In 1769–70, 51 ships were involved in trade between Grenada and the Port of London, compared

**Table 4.1 Comparative Production of Ceded Islands 1764**

| *Colony* | *Cacao (lbs)* | *Coffee (lbs)* | *Cotton (lbs)* | *Sugar (lbs)* |
|---|---|---|---|---|
| Dominica | 201,000 | 936,900 | 226,095 | 1,328 |
| St Vincent | 30,600 | 46,700 | 13,000 | 64,458 |
| Grenada | 179,200 | 1,285,700 | 368,032 | 65,669 |

to nine for Dominica, eight for St Vincent and one for Tobago. Grenada's pre-eminence remained generally unchallenged for the rest of the century. By 1775, the year of the War of American Independence, 51 ships were trading to Grenada, 10 to Dominica, 14 to St Vincent and seven to Tobago. By 1795, the year of Fedon's Rebellion, 40 ships were trading to Grenada, compared to 15 for Dominica, 19 for St Vincent and 19 for Tobago.[13] Grenada's exports to Britain surpassed the rest of the Windwards. In 1775 she exported 190,000 cwts of sugar, compared to 40,000 for Dominica, 51,000 for St Vincent and 50,000 for Tobago; 2.4 million pounds of coffee, compared to 1.5 million for Dominica and 1 million for St Vincent: 142,000 pounds of indigo were also exported, compared to negligible quantities for the other colonies.

The plantation system expanded significantly during this period. By 1772, coffee plantations covered 12,796 acres, cocoa 712 and indigo 742 acres. The number of sugar estates increased from 81 in 1763 to 125, occupying 32,011 acres, by 1772. Plantations in Grenada totalled 334 by 1772, 139 of which were operated by the old French residents and 168 by English settlers who had arrived during the last ten years. Ninety-five sugar estates were fitted with water mills, 18 operated cattle mills and another 12 used windmills. By 1776 there were only 106 sugar estates worked by 18,293 slaves who produced an average of one hogshead each. Slaves provided the labour force for the sugar, coffee, cocoa, cotton and indigo plantations, and their labour produced the wealth and profits for planters and their retinue of dependents both resident and foreign.

Grenada's production and export of sugar and rum trebled during the period as Table 4.2 illustrates. In 1764, sugar exports totalled 65,669 cwts, and by 1775 had increased to 189,939 cwts or approximately 200%. From 1775 to 1779 sugar exports declined, owing to the effects of the War of American Independence on Grenada's economy, but from 1769 to 1779 overall sugar production increased to the extent that Grenada became the fourth largest sugar exporter after Jamaica, Antigua and St Kitts.

**Table 4.2 Exports of Sugar and Rum from Grenada to UK 1763–79**

| *Year* | *Sugar (cwts)* | *Rum (gals)* | *Year* | *Sugar (cwts)* | *Rum (gals)* |
|---|---|---|---|---|---|
| 1763 | 71,640 | 366 | 1771 | 157,762 | 161,189 |
| 1764 | 65,669 | 1,629 | 1772 | 194,451 | 90,143 |
| 1765 | 64,458 | 19,490 | 1773 | 198,159 | 63,664 |
| 1766 | 85,543 | 34,916 | 1774 | 179,375 | 72,318 |
| 1767 | 92,766 | 47,827 | 1775 | 189,939 | 143,138 |
| 1768 | 145,532 | 105,215 | 1776 | 147,722 | 292,953 |
| 1769 | 125,227 | 94,030 | 1777 | 115,740 | 98,078 |
| 1770 | 196,130 | 158,066 | 1778 | 122,254 | 148,351 |
| | | | 1779 | 103,291 | 67,223 |

Source: Ragatz, *Statistics*, p. 19

During the second half of the 18th century, Grenada was also the major coffee producer. In 1763 82% of all coffee exported to England from the British West Indies was from Grenada. By 1778, despite the expansion of production in Dominica and Jamaica, she was still producing 60% of all coffee exported from the British West Indies. Table 4.3 provides a year-by-year breakdown of the 28,467,887 pounds of coffee exported from Grenada to England from 1763 to 1780.

**Table 4.3 Coffee Exports from Grenada to Britain 1763–80**

| *Year* | *Coffee exports (lbs)* | | |
|---|---|---|---|
| 1763 | 1,330,998 | 1772 | 2,425,000 |
| 1764 | 1,416,200 | 1773 | 1,739,900 |
| 1765 | 1,285,200 | 1774 | 2,329,900 |
| 1766 | 1,102,498 | 1775 | 2,442,200 |
| 1767 | 1,239,000 | 1776 | 1,640,200 |
| 1768 | 1,899,000 | 1777 | 2,012,300 |
| 1769 | 1,244,300 | 1778 | 1,215,800 |
| 1770 | 1,592,600 | 1779 | 17,500 |
| 1771 | 1,374,900 | | |

Source: Ragatz, *Statistics*, p. 149

Grenada paid a duty of 33/6d into the British Treasury for each hundredweight of coffee exported. Coffee duties were kept exceedingly high in order to protect the tea trade from India and Ceylon. By the 1800s duties were reduced first to 1/5d and then to 7d per cwt. Between 1763 and 1780 coffee import duties paid on the coffee Grenada exported amounted to £414,309; when this is added to the duties paid on sugar, rum, cacao and indigo exports – all of which swelled the British Treasury's coffers – the sum is phenomenal. The only tropical product exempted from duty was cotton until 1798, when a duty of 8/9d per cwt. was imposed.

Grenada was also the largest producer and exporter of cocoa in the 1760s and 1770s, accounting for about 50% of British West Indian exports of cocoa (see Tables 4.4 and 4.5). Grenada's importance as a cocoa producer is indicated by the figures for 1771, when the BWI exported 671,000 pounds, of which Grenada accounted for 505,000 pounds.

**Table 4.4 Exports of Cocoa from BWI to Britain 1763–72 (lbs)**

| *Year* | *Grenada* | *British West Indies* |
|---|---|---|
| 1763 | 196,300 | 242,842 |
| 1764 | 108,100 | 265,500 |
| 1765 | 179,200 | 274,600 |
| 1766 | 242,800 | 486,811 |
| 1767 | 216,000 | 359,614 |
| 1768 | 297,800 | 696,042 |
| 1769 | 234,000 | 622,500 |
| 1770 | 305,400 | 487,800 |
| 1771 | 504,800 | 670,808 |
| 1772 | 343,400 | 642,651 |

Source: Ragatz, *Statistics*

**Table 4.5 Cocoa Exports from Grenada and BWI 1773–79 (lbs)**

| *Year* | *Grenada* | *British West Indies* |
|---|---|---|
| 1773 | 307,400 | 727,400 |
| 1774 | 281,100 | 580,614 |
| 1775 | 266,700 | 533,200 |
| 1776 | 238,600 | 653,300 |
| 1777 | 241,300 | 398,200 |
| 1778 | 239,400 | 338,600 |
| 1779 | 221,700 | 433,700 |

Source: Ragatz, *Statistics* p. 15

Indigo, which had been grown since the late 17th century, continued to be exported in sizeable quantities until the turn of the century, when it ceased to be a major export.

The production of these staples was of much greater benefit to Great Britain than to Grenada. Subject to the mercantile laws of the 17th century, Grenada was prohibited from processing any of her staples. Mercantile theory and practice relegated the role of Grenada, and many other colonies on the outposts of the British Empire, to producers and exporters of staples in a raw or unprocessed form. Processing was done in Britain and, therefore, all the employment, income and technology thus generated accrued to Britain.

Revenues received by the British Treasury from Grenada's exports of sugar and rum alone between 1763 and 1779 amounted to about £1.1 million. This helped to finance British roads, canals, schools, hospitals and industrialization. Together with the above contributions must be added the interests paid by Grenadian planters to the merchants, creditors and financial capitalists in England on loans advanced to Grenadian producers. The establishment of sugar factories, rum distilleries and iron foundries in England was directly linked to the production of the staples in the West Indies, a clear manifestation of the forward linkage effects of sugar production. Eric Williams in *Capitalism and Slavery*, referring to the triangular trade, wrote: 'The profits obtained provided one of the main streams of that accumulation of capital in England which financed the Industrial Revolution.'[14] He then proceeded to show how British commerce, shipping and shipbuilding, the growth of seaport towns, the woollen and cotton industry, sugar refineries, rum distilleries and the metallurgical industries all owed their growth and expansion – sometimes their origin – in the 18th century to the famous triangular trade,[15] in which Grenada was an essential link.

NOTES

Full citations only given where work does not appear in the Bibliography.

1. *Laws of Grenada*.
2. One acre in every 20 was to be cleared annually until half the property was ready for cultivation; failure to do so incurred a fine of £5 per acre. One white man or two white women were to be maintained for each 100 acres cleared, under penalty of a fine of £20 per woman and £40 per man absent. A quit rent of 6d per acre on all was payable to the crown. Eight hundred acres in every parish were reserved for poor white settlers. These were to be given from one to 30 acres each 'in fee simple'; such grants were inalienable for seven years.
3. Ragatz, *Rise and Fall*, p. 113.
4. *Grenada Handbook*, pp. 23–24.
5. Hillsborough to Fitzmaurice, C.O. *Despatches* 7 September, 1768. Devas, *Conception Island*, pp. 43–44.
6. *A Letter to the Earl of Hillsborough*, p. 7.
7. The Council was composed to 12 members – eight of these were present; under the constitution, in no case could the Governor appoint any persons to be members of the Council unless less than seven are present in the island.
8. *A Letter to Earl of Hillsborough*, p. 27.
9. Ibid. p. 42.
10. Grenada, *Notes of the General Assembly* March–April 1772.
11. *Laws of Grenada* No. 18, Jan. 21/774, pp. 24–25.
12. *Notes of the Assembly* May-December, 1775.
13. Ragatz, *Statistics* p. 24.
14. Williams, *Capitalism and Slavery*, p. 52.
15. Ibid. Ch.III, pp. 51–84.

# 5

# *Capture of Grenada and the French Interregnum: 1779–83*

In 1779 Britain and France were at war with each other. Britain was angered by France's assistance to the breakaway North American colonies and anxious to inflict punishment for what she considered undue interference in her imperial affairs. The conflict was European, but as both powers had colonies in the Caribbean, and were concerned to protect them and their interests, part of it was fought out there (see Appendix 8). Both nations had a powerful fleet stationed in the region: the British under the command of Vice-Admiral Sir John Byron based in port in St Lucia, and the French under the Count D'Estaing based in the port of Martinique. In May 1779, however, Byron sailed northwards to St Kitts in order to provide convoy for a fleet of British mechant ships.

By June 1779, D'Estaing, realizing that Byron was well out of the way, set sail from Martinique and on 18 June attacked St Vincent, which capitulated to him. On 27 June, the reinforcements he had requested arrived, under Commodore La Mothe-Picquet, and he decided to attack Barbados. Encountering much difficulty from the prevailing trade winds, however, he instead attacked Grenada.

## French Attack on Grenada

D'Estaing's forces numbered 25 ships of the line, 12 frigates and 6,500 land forces. The French fleet arrived in Grenada's waters on 2 July

1779, and the island was sighted at daybreak; by evening the fleet was anchored at Boismaurice Point in Moliniere Bay. Upon arrival, 1,300 soldiers, commanded by Count Dillon, the senior Colonel, immediately disembarked and occupied the surrounding heights. That night, a portion of these troops led by the Count D'Estaing marched to Hospital Hill where, apparently, the British had stationed their principal forces upon which they based their hopes of defending Grenada. British forces in Grenada at the time consisted of 101 rank and file of the 48th Regiment, 24 artillery recruits, between 300 and 400 militiamen, and in addition, about 200 volunteers, chiefly sailors from ships anchored in the harbour.[1]

At dawn on 3 July, D'Estaing reconnoitered the enemy's position, the steep slope of which was fortified by huge blocks of stone, a palisade at the bottom and three entrenchments, one above the other. Although estimating that the British forces were no match for him, he realized that he had no cannon, all of which were on his ships, anchored too far away. Realizing, too, that Byron's squadrons might arrive unexpectedly, he decided to launch his attack that night and to capture the enemy's position by a general assault. He planned to attack the eastern part of Hospital Hill in three columns; simultaneously, he ordered a false attack on the opposite side of the Hill facing the River St John, or below the hospital. The division of the French forces commanded by Count de Noailles, which occupied Mount St Eloi, on the other side of the River St John a little beyond Queen's Park Savannah, was to join D'Estaing's own forces at the Pradine's Estate.

On the afternoon of 3 July, D'Estaing sent a flag of truce to Macartney summoning him to surrender. D'Estaing felt that the mere sight of his forces would have forced the British to accept defeat as inevitable. The following was D'Estaing's summons:

> Humanity requires it and the personal consideration which the Count D'Estaing has for Lord Macartney induces him in the most solemn and pressing manner to summon his Lordship to surrender – Lord Macartney should know the superiority of force with which he is attacked. If, therefore, he does not surrender he must be personally responsible for all the consequences which his obstinacy may occasion.[2]

Macartney replied that he did not know the strength of D'Estaing's forces but he knew what his was and would do all in his power to defend the island. Thus, as Devas later wrote, was Grenada committed to bloodshed, neither for the first time nor the last time.[3]

Early in the evening of 3 July the French forces mobilized for attack. Three columns, each comprising 300 men, under Arthur

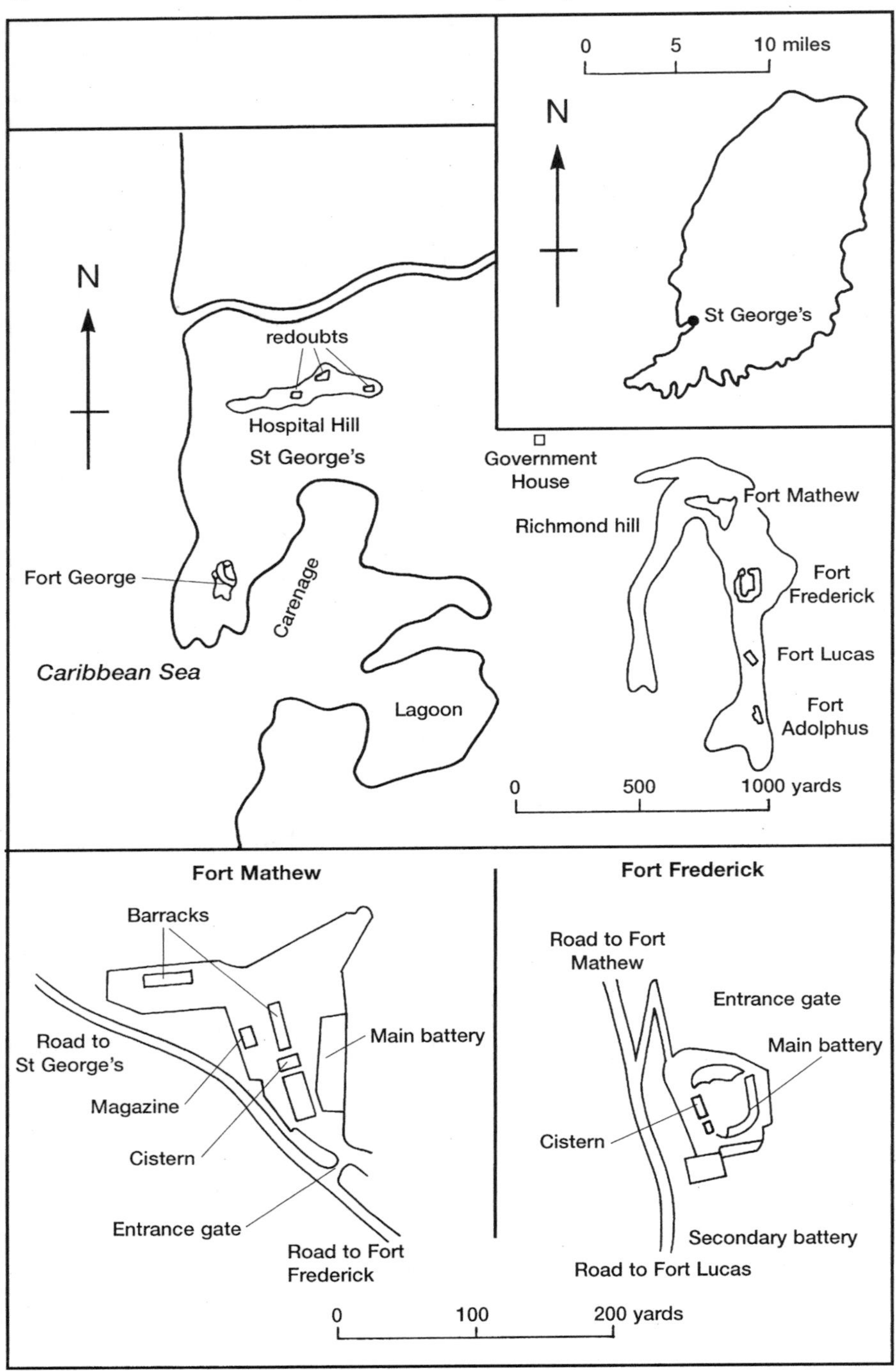


*The fortifications of St George's*

Dillon, Edward Dillon and de Noailles respectively, began their march up the steep incline that led to Hospital Hill. The column on the right was commanded by de Noailles, that on the left by Count Arthur Dillon, and the centre column was under the command of Count Edward Dillon. Arthur Dillon's column was preceded by an advance guard of 180 men commanded by the Count de Durat, the officer who was later to become Grenada's Governor during the period of the French interregnum. The division, comprising 200 men, that was to mount the false attack was commanded by Lieutenant-Colonels Pondevaux and Hussenan and Messieurs de La Bretonnière and de Kerangues. All in all some 1,280 men took part in the assault on Hospital Hill.

The false attack began at approximately 2 a.m. on 4 July, and simultaneously the three columns advanced on Hospital Hill. The British forces finding themselves hopelessly outnumbered rushed down the side of Hospital Hill facing the sea, past the Catholic church (site of the Anglican Church today) and ran for cover in Fort George, the Citadel. Macartney himself admitted that the enemy poured in on Hospital Hill with such impetuosity that it was impossible for the British to mount their cannon. Thus Hospital Hill, the main stronghold of the British in Grenada, was captured on 4 July 1779. All the British cannon, mortars, as well as Macartney's and his officers' jewelry, plate and silver were captured. The British had taken these precious possessions there in the belief that Hospital Hill was impregnable and that they would be secure until reinforcements arrived.

## The British Capitulate

At daybreak on 5 July, the French turned the captured British cannon on the Fort and started to shell it. As shelling began, Macartney, realizing the hopelessness of his position, proposed a surrender. He later wrote that 'without means of resistance or prospect of relief we were obliged to propose a capitulation.[4] D'Estaing gave him three hours to submit his proposals. He then submitted 17 articles of capitulation, including:

1. That the British troops should march round with drums beating and guns firing and be given all the honours of war.
2. That the inhabitants be allowed to enjoy their own civil government, laws, usages, law courts and judiciary.
3. That the inhabitants, both civil and religious, be allowed to keep their property and enjoy their traditional rights and privileges.

4. That free negroes and mulattos should remain free.
5. That slaves should be restored to their respective owners and prisoners be released.
6. That all war material, guns, forts, etc. should be handed over to the French except the personal arms of officers.[5]

These terms of surrender were handed to D'Estaing by Staunton, Macartney's ADC. All 17 were promptly rejected. D'Estaing then submitted 28 articles of capitulation, which, among other things stated that: the British were to come and lay down their arms; prisoners would be shipped on flags of truce; all slaves were to be taken as prize of war, as well as all ships and vessels in the harbour; all free negroes and mulattos with arms were to be considered slaves and would become the property of the French Crown; all military and custom house money was to be handed over; the inhabitants now had to take an oath of loyalty to the French king; the property of absentees was to be appropriated by the Crown; there was to be a period of irrevocable neutrality lasting six months during which no more than four boat-loads of people could leave and during which no ship of war was to come and interfere. Macartney rejected all these terms, but the principal inhabitants with whom he communicated were unanimously of the opinion that it was better to trust to the law and custom of nations and to the justice of one court and the interposition of the other by surrendering at discretion.[6]

On 5 July the French forces took possession of the Fort along with 700 prisoners. They admitted to losses of 107 men – 36 killed and 71 wounded,[7] but the British put the French casualties at around 300.

Thus, from 5 July 1779, Grenada became once more a French colony. The terms of surrender outlined by D'Estaing indicate how Grenada was administered and what prevailed during the next four years. The French King appointed Jean-Francois Comte de Durat Governor-General of Grenada on 7 July 1779, two days after the capitulation. The new Governor-General immediately issued a general decree regarding the administration of the colony's external financial affairs:

> Being informed all all the oppressions exercised by the English government particularly against the French inhabitants of Grenada called the new subjects in contempt of the capitulation of the colony on 4th March, 1762, of the Peace Treaty of Paris of 1763 ... in contempt of natural right and of the right of nations ... and seeing that these vexations have done an injury which has extended to all members of the colony we have from now onwards and forever absolved the inhabitants of Grenada from payment of all mortgages

and pledges of every kind contracted between them in the London market and in other places of commerce without any exception reserving to the court of France to make good all claims just and established resulting from this announcement. Moreover, it is forbidden under penalty, in case of disobedience, of military execution and confiscation of their goods, to all and each of the inhabitants of Grenada to pay anything of what they have or may owe to the subjects of His Britannic Majesty whether directly or indirectly.[8]

This decree was in essentials, very similar to article No.25 of D'Estaing's terms of capitulation. Thus it not only froze all external debts but reserved to the French Court the right to determine which claims were justly established. The *Grenada Handbook* records that for the next four years Grenada was ruled in a most despotic manner by the Comte de Durat, and that the British colonists were heavily oppressed.[9]

One of the first acts of Grenada's new French Government was to commence building a series of forts on Richmond Hill: Forts Adolphus, Lucas, Frederick and Matthew. Mount George Estate, the property of William Lucas, was forcibly appropriated for that purpose. The French realized that had these fortifications existed at the time of their assault on Grenada, their attempt to capture the island could have been abortive.

These forts were completed by the British after the island was returned in 1783 at the Peace Treaty of Versailles. Together they constituted a formidable defence for the remainder of the 18th century and the first half of the 19th century.

NOTES

Full citations only given where work does not appear in the Bibliography.

1. *Relation de La Prise de la Grenada*, 1779, pamphlet anonymously written. Devas, *History of Grenada*, p. 78.
2. Devas, *History of Grenada*, p. 82.
3. Ibid.
4. Ibid. p. 87.
5. Ibid. p. 89.
6. Ibid. p. 91.
7. *La Prise de La Grenada*, 1779.
8. Grenada, *Proclamation of the Comte de Durat*, 7 July, 1779.
9. *Grenada Handbook* p. 26.

# 6

# *Anglo–French Conflict in Grenada: 1783–95*

The eighth article of the Treaty of Versailles, signed on 3 September 1783, restored Grenada to the British. Immediately after his arrival, the new Governor, Edward Matthew, proceeded to establish the Assembly, the Council, and to appoint various officers to fill the civil list. He also restored the same civil and political liberties to the Roman Catholics and French subjects that they had enjoyed before the occupation of Grenada in 1779. Apparently, however, the long-standing differences and grievances of the English inhabitants now came to the fore in all their virulence; more so as they had been the victims of French venom during the occupation of the island. The ultra-Protestant party of the pre-1779 period was now in the vanguard of the attack on the French Roman Catholics. The party was led by Ninian Home, a planter of long standing, a member of the Council, an assistant Justice of the Supreme Court in 1784, and Lieutenant-Governor in the period 1793–95.

## The New British Administration

Despite the internal political and religious conflicts in Grenada during the 12 years after the 'restoration', the Government tried to organize public works, and to create machinery for improving the administration of the colony. Among these were: better regulation of foreign vessels by designating the harbours of Grenville and St George's as the Ports of Discharge (July 1784); fixing the public roads, highways and byways and the declaration to that effect (August 1791); further regulations governing the rebuilding of the town of St George's; raising funds by a public lottery to build a Court House and public Senate in St George's (April 1791), and the establishment of public markets.[1]

Markets were established in St George's, Grenville, Sauteurs, Gouyave, Victoria, Megrin (now St David's town) and Hillsborough. In St George's, the Public Parade was declared to be the marketplace, while in the other towns the sites were fixed by the Justices of the Peace in the area. A comprehensive set of laws was passed governing the operation of these markets. The Governor appointed clerks of the markets, whose duties were to keep scales and weights and determine disputes between buyers and sellers; and to oversee that any meat in the markets judged unfit for sale was sent to the prisoners or given to the poor.[2] Prices in the markets were fixed by a committee of justices, five for St George's and three for each of the other towns. In general, the market was a major social institution for slaves as it was the only central place where they were allowed to meet and gather at the time; other forms of assembly among the slave population were discouraged from fear of insurrection.

For the road construction programme, 40 commissioners were appointed for the island; five for each of the parishes and Carriacou, except St George's, which had six, and Grenville, which had three. The commissioners were to trace out roads from the interior estates to churches, markets and landing places. This same network of roads exists today. Owners and renters of slaves had to provide 10% of their slaves for the road construction programme. In cases of default or negligence, a fine of six shillings per day was imposed on the slave proprietor for each slave not furnished. The programme was to be supervised by the commissioners who were to visit the roads daily during the time the slaves were employed on them.[3]

One noteworthy constitutional change was to extend the life of the Assembly from three years to seven years, accomplished by an act of the Legislature on 4 October 1793. Elections to the Assembly were now to take place once in every seven years. This gave the plantocracy more political leverage and strengthened their hand considerably.

Devas referred to the period 1783–95 in Grenada as the period of persecution of Roman Catholics and pillage of their property. Catholic churches were used by Protestants to conduct services; and in some cases, they were appropriated. In some churches, relics, altars and baptismal fonts were destroyed in what can be termed a display of iconoclasm by the Protestants.

*House used as Roman Catholic Church 1783–84 after Catholic expulsion from their church by the Church of England; it was later used as the first accommodation for Presentation Brothers*

## Internal Rivalry in Grenada

With the accession to power of the British in 1783, many French residents migrated to Trinidad, taking their slaves with them. As early as 1779, Rourne de St Laurent, a resident planter in Grenada, had approached both Governor Martin de Salaverria and the Intendant of Caracas José de Abalos to secure concessions for 383 families, 57 from Grenadian families, 286 from Martinique and 40 from Dominica, to migrate to Trinidad; he even travelled to Europe to put his case before the Spanish crown. The Condé de Aranda, the Spanish ambassador in Paris, gave him official support, as did the French government, and in 1783 his plans were finally approved. Under a *Cedula* for the population of Trinidad, published in 1783, the concessions for French and Irish Catholics to migrate to Trinidad were extended to all Catholics. That *Cedula* marked the beginning of migration of Grenadians from Grenada to Trinidad. Many who left at this time did so in order to escape the wave of persecution now mounted by the Anglo-Saxon Protestants against Catholics.[4]

The dimensions of the Anglo-French conflict in Grenada between 1783 and 1795 differed from those in 1764–79. In the latter period the conflict was essentially one of charges and counter-charges and anti-Catholic propaganda. Neither the Catholics nor their institutions were ever really physically attacked. In one sense the Roman Catholics had won their struggle to participate politically and yet be exempted from the Test. But between 1783 and 1795, the French, all of whom were Roman Catholics, were attacked in four different ways by the British, who usually were members of the Church of England. The conflict was religious, social and political.

The first attack on the French Grenadians by the Anglo-Saxon Protestants involved the forced seizure and use of their Roman Catholic churches. The Revd John Wingate, preaching on the Sunday after he was appointed rector of St George's emphasized: 'No foreign prince, person, prelate, state or potentate hath or ought to have any jurisdiction, power, superiority, pre-eminence or authority ecclesiastical or spiritual within the realm of England or its dominions.'[5] In January 1784, Governor Matthew instructed the Revd Wingate to inform the Catholic churchwardens of St George's that their church was required by the Protestants to hold service. The churchwardens refused to cooperate, intimating that such a matter was beyond their jurisdiction. On the appointed day, the church's door, being found closed, was broken down by the militia at the instruction of the Governor. A few days later the altar, Holy Water stoup and baptismal font were destroyed and the furniture thrown outside. In November 1790 the Roman Catholic church in St George's was still in the possession of the Protestants.

Roman Catholic churches in St David's, St Andrew's and Gouyave were all handed over to the Anglo-Saxon Protestants, but as these were in poor condition they were probably of little use to the new occupants. This state of affairs offended the Roman Catholic, French-speaking mass of the free population, and embittered relations between the French and the Anglo-Saxon plantocracy in Grenada.

The revenue of the Roman Catholic Church was the next object of attack by the Legislature. In 1784 the Government set up a committee to enquire into the state of glebe lands owned by the Church. The leading advocate of anti-Catholic, anti-French sentiments, Ninian Home, was prominent on this committee. The Assembly then recommended to the Council that a joint committee comprising three Councillors and five Assemblymen be formed to investigate a legal and just method of acquiring the revenues of the glebe lands. The Secretary of State found the matter so delicate that he had to postpone a decision until he had had full consultations with his legal advisers. The

Church's revenues from its lands at the time did not exceed £400 and were one-sixth of the £2,400 that the government was spending annually to maintain the establishment of the Church of England. It was, therefore, absurd to argue that these funds were needed to upkeep the established church. More likely the aim was to attack the French Roman Catholics through the main institutions of their community, their religion and their church – an attack with both social and political implications. In 1793, Father Félicien Gachier had to appear before the Court on a civil matter; the judgement handed down was that all images, altar and popish emblems in his church were to be burnt. By then, his church was already appropriated, and he lived and officiated in the adjacent chapel house. In the period 1793–95 Home and Dent made strenuous efforts to take this away from him, but he was saved by the outbreak of the Fedon Insurrection in 1795.

Marriages, baptisms and burials were considered null and void unless celebrated in the Anglican churches, and a law to this effect was passed on 21 October 1785. Also, all baptisms and burials were to be entered on the register of the established church in order to be accepted as evidence in law. Thus, Roman Catholics had to pay two fees: one to their minister for the certificate and another to the rector of the Church of England; this law was revised in 1807, but it remained substantially intact until 1842.

In 1792 the Legislature passed the New Election Act which, effectively, was the fourth blow struck against the French. This Act required all Catholics, *inter alia*, to subscribe to the Test before they could hold political office in Grenada.[6] Only those new French subjects whose parents were resident in Grenada in 1763 and for whom Grenada was their place of domicile were allowed to vote. Moreover, before voting, French subjects were required to swear an oath of allegiance – within 12 months of an election – to the King of England before the Governor, and receive a certificate which they had to produce to the Provost Marshal, or another official, on election day. The effect of the Election Law was to exclude the Roman Catholics from standing for political office and to prevent the Roman Catholic voters, who constituted most of the electorate, from voting. The French in Grenada were, therefore, being gradually reduced to a position of subordination and inferiority by this civil and religious discrimination.

Not only was the Election Act of 23 April 1792 an attack on the French subjects, but it embodied discriminatory and racist legislation against the Free Blacks and Coloureds. In 1771 there were some 451 Free Coloureds; by 1787 there were 1,115.[7] According to the Act, to qualify as a candidate a person had to be a white-skinned male, over 21 years old, and either possess 50 acres of land, of which 25 must be under cultivation, or rent property in town at £100 per annum, and be a natural-born subject and a Protestant.

Similar qualifications applied to a voter, who must be: a white male, over 21, profess the Christian religion, a British subject, possess ten acres of land – five acres cultivated – or rent property in the town at £20 per annum. Thus, the French subjects in Grenada were virtually disenfranchized as, in effect they were debarred from choosing candidates from their own community to represent them.

Even before 1792, successful candidates in elections to the Assembly were blatantly deprived of their rights of membership and violently ejected. Jacques Preudhomme contested the by-elections of 1789 for the combined parishes of St John's and St George's to replace Alexander Sympson who had died. Preudhomme won the seat, took the oath of allegiance, adjuration and supremacy before the Governor, but refused to subscribe to the Test Act. The Assembly was convened on 22 April 1789, and a motion upon whether he could take his seat was put to the House; the House voted 11 to 4 against and Jacques Preudhomme was prevented from taking his seat in the Assembly.[8] This harrassment, violation of rights and persecution of the French continued until 1795.

Conflict between the French and English in Grenada reached its climax in 1795, during the Fedon Rebellion. A main cause of this rebellion lay in the social, cultural and religious differences between the French and the Anglo-Saxons, deliberately perpetuated by an extremist Protestant faction in Grenada led by Ninian Home and other prominent Anglo-Saxon planters. As early as 1776, it was said of Governor Macartney that:

> He found the island distracted by party feuds which impeded all progress. There was the Scotch [sic] Party, the English Party; and of these two the *odium theologicum* of the Scotch was the most violent and the most difficult to conciliate. The Scotch wanted to demolish all the French churches in the island and this violent enthusiasm for the Church of Scotland and rancourous hatred of the Catholic religion would have impelled them to carry out their pious intentions were it not for Sir George Staunton.[9]

In 1776 they were prevented from carrying this out, but after 1784 there was nothing to stop them and the Church of England was behind them all the way.

By 1795 Grenada was divided into two communities each hostile to the other – one Anglo-Saxon and the other Francophone. The quarrels of the 1760s and 1770s had now become open antagonism, which explains why the Fedon Rebellion was so popularly supported by Frenchmen in Grenada.

NOTES

Full citations only given where work does not appear in the Bibliography.

1. 'An Act to Establish Regular Markets'. *Laws of Grenada* No. XXXVII. p. 80.
2. Twenty pounds of guiney (Guinea) grass or 25 pounds of common grass were sold for 9d; slaves demanding more forfeited their grass. One quart of milk was sold for 9d and any milk found to be mixed with water or otherwise adulterated was confiscated. It was illegal for slaves to sell rum in the market. Any person, slave or free, was authorized to kill any pig which was found running loose in any street of any town, and to carry away the carcase for their own use. This was to dissuade market vendors and others from letting their hogs run wild in the streets.
3. 'An Act to ascertain and delcare the Public Roads and Highways in the islands of Grenada and Carriacou' *Laws of Grenada*, St George's, 1840. No. LXVII, 23 August 1791, p. 159.
4. Linda Newson, 'Foreign immigrants in Spanish America: Trinidad's colonisation experiment'. *Caribbean Studies*. Vol. 14, Nos. 2 and 3. April-July 1979, pp. 138–9.
5. *Commissions*, 27 May 1784.
6. Devas, *Conception Island*, p. 62.
7. John Barrow, *The Earl of Macartney*, p. 57.
8. Devas, *Conception Island*, pp. 80–81. 'An Act to establish regular markets'. *Laws of Grenada*, No. XXXVII, p. 80.
9. Bryan Edwards, *History Civil and Commercial*, p. 383.

# 7

# *The Fedon Rebellion*

The decade of the 1790s witnessed a thirst for freedom among the Free Coloured and slave population in the Caribbean. There was the Haitian Revolution of 1791–1804 in the French colony of Saint Domingue; the revolt of the Caribs in St Vincent in 1795; the Maroon uprising in Jamaica in 1795, and lastly, the Fedon Rebellion in Grenada in 1795–96. These demonstrations of popular resistance to the plantocracy and to colonial rule by the slave and Free Coloured population were inextricably bound to events and developments within the French Revolution of 1789–96. They were by no means isolated movements but were considerably influenced by the principles of liberty, equality and fraternity as propounded by the French Revolution.

In the French Colony of Saint Domingue, the Jacobin Government had abolished slavery in 1793; in the British colony of Grenada, Fedon and his compatriots were Republicans and strong supporters of the French Revolution and its political ideals.

Julien Fedon was a Free Coloured Grenadian and owned a large coffee and cocoa estate in Grenada, called Belvedere, in the parish of St John. He was said to have been educated in England. Because of his obvious leadership qualities he was chosen by his Free Coloured associates to lead the rebellion against British rule. His estate at Belvedere was the meeting place and headquarters of the insurgents. The inaccessible nature of the area rendered it the most suitable location for forming a camp.

## Causes of the Rebellion

The Fedon Rebellion was planned and executed by the Free Coloureds in Grenada in collaboration with Victor Hugues and two other French

Commissioners whom the National Convention in France sent to the Windward Islands in 1794 to command French military operations there. Fedon and his men were ably assisted from the start by their own slaves whom they had then freed. Soon after the outbreak of the Rebellion thousands of other slaves joined in and soon it spread into a general slave insurrection led by Fedon, Stanislaus Besson, Charles Nogues and Pierre La Valette, all of whom were Free Coloureds. To understand the underlying causes of this rebellion which lasted for over a year and claimed many lives it is necessary to recall the social situation prior to 1795.

The largest section of Grenada's free population in 1795 as well as a sizeable portion of her entire population was classified as Free Blacks and Coloureds, many of whom owned estates and property and had become quite wealthy. For many decades, however, this class suffered from numerous civil and political disabilities. They were not conceived of as citizens, being denied all civil rights and political freedoms such as were then enjoyed by the Whites. The Election Act of 1792 denied participation in the political process both to them and to white Frenchmen. This discrimination embittered relations between the Free Coloureds and the Whites, especially the Anglo-Saxons who monopolized political power and social prestige in Grenada.

The inhumane and oppressive conditions under which the slave population laboured, and their desire to break the yoke that bound them to the plantation, made them willing to seize any opportunity which presented itself. A further factor was the religious conflict between the predominantly French Roman Catholics and the predominantly British Protestants. As we saw in Chapter 6, this conflict was greatly exacerbated in the period of the restoration of British rule, 1784–95.

Clearly, by 1795 the Roman Catholics, the Free Coloureds and the French-speaking Grenadians had many grievances, having for over ten years been victims of religious persecution and civil and political oppression, while for more than a century the slaves had been victims of the coercive and inhumane plantation system. The outbreak of war between France and England in 1793 intensified these embittered relations.

As early as April 1793 in a letter to a relative in England, William Smith who owned Revolution Hall Estate (now called Brothers) spoke of trouble brewing in Grenada. In 1792 the Grenada legislature passed a law, entitled an Act to Amend an Act, to prevent a further sudden increase in the numbers of Free Negroes and Mulattos. This was intended to verify whether all those Blacks and Mulattos who were not slaves were in fact free. In September 1793 Ninian Home, writing to his fellow planter Alexander Campbell, referred to rascals and vagabonds in Grenada whom the island could not be ridded of. He mentioned too, that Father La Point and other French priests were actively fermenting dissension. On 8 July 1793, Lieutenant-Governor Home, addressing the Board of the Council, referred to the danger that could arise from the number of Free Coloureds who had migrated to Grenada from different French islands.[1] Consequently, the Board passed a resolution stating that 'the numbers of free-coloured people coming into this island were highly dangerous and that the safety of the island required that means be taken for the prevention thereof'. The Governor then issued a proclamation instructing all foreigners without his permission to remain in Grenada to present themselves before him at the Council Chamber on 15, 16 and 17 July 1793; those who refused to do so were to be proceeded against immediately. All arms and offensive weapons were to be delivered, to remain in the possession of the Government during this stay.[2] Many of these Mulattos propagated the French Revolution's doctrines of liberty and equality among their counterparts in Grenada. When ordered to leave Grenada they went into hiding, protected by their new converts and remained underground until the outbreak of the uprising.

Three years earlier, in 1790, a number of French inhabitants in Grenada had sworn loyalty to Great Britain and had requested protection from 'idle and disorderly persons' as well as base and designing Frenchmen who had arrived there from Martinique intending to disturb the peace. Thirty-five Frenchmen, including Julien Fedon, signed the Declaration of Loyalty,[3] but this was nothing but a fictitious show; with one exception they were all to become dedicated revolutionaries by 1795. The exception was Louis LaGrenada, who remained loyal to the British colonial government of Grenada, and actually commanded a detachment of government forces which, on 8 April 1795, attempted to dislodge Fedon from his camp at Belvedere.

The outbreak of the French Revolutionary wars and the subsequent declaration of war between France and England on 1 February 1793 clearly acted as a catalyst to the rebellion of the Free Coloureds and slaves in 1795. As a result of this war the Jacobins sent commissoners to Guadeloupe and Martinique to rally support for the Revolutionary Government from those most discontented with their lot – the *Petit Blancs* and the Free Coloureds. The French planters there were more disposed to support the English, being opposed to the watchwords of the French Revolution. Largely as a result of these planters' assistance the British were able to capture Martinique, Guadeloupe and St Lucia in 1794. These territories were quite valuable to France and the New Republican Government sent Victor

Hugues, a member of the Jacobin Party, with a fleet to help reverse their setbacks in the Caribbean. Guadeloupe and St Lucia were recaptured at once by Hugues after he had declared immediate emancipation of the slaves and encouraged them to rise up against their British overlords and the French planters.[4]

Hugues decided to employ slave or popular uprisings against the British in their territories in order to weaken them. He sent agents to Jamaica and St Vincent, to incite the Maroons and the Caribs to attack the British and resist their rule. In 1795 there were uprisings of both groups.

## Outbreak of Rebellion

The Free Coloureds and Frenchmen in Grenada welcomed the opportunity presented by Hugues to turn against the British. In early 1795 Charles Nogues and Jean-Pierre La Valette went to Guadeloupe where they were briefed by Victor Hugues. They returned with arms and ammunition, caps of liberty, national cockades and a flag of liberation inscribed with the words, 'Liberty, Equality or Death'. They were also furnished with Commissions signed by Hugues, Goyrand and Le Bas. Fedon was appointed Commandant-General of the French Republican Forces in Grenada; Stanislaus Besson, a silver-smith from Grenville, was second-in-command; Charles Nogues, a Mulatto from La Baye, was appointed a Captain, as was La Valette, another Mulatto from the St Patrick's area.[5] The Commissioners promised Fedon and his men speedy and effectual support.

Meanwhile, Governor Home was apparently expecting an invasion from Guadeloupe, as ten days prior to the outbreak of the insurrection he had sent orders to his commanding officers to keep their officers and men on full alert as an invasion was suspected.[6] He neither had information, nor suspicions that an insurrection was planned. When it broke out at midnight on 2 March Home and everyone was taken by surprise.

On 2 March 1795, Julien Fedon, Stanislaus Besson and about 100 ex-slaves and Coloureds from St Andrew's and St Patrick's razed the town of La Baye (Grenville) almost to the ground. Surrounding the town at about 1 a.m. on 3 March, they broke into the homes of the British inhabitants, dragged them into the streets, and shot them; 11 out of the 15 British who lived in the town were executed. Stores were plundered, buildings set on fire, and people living on the outskirts of the town were captured.

By this time slaves of the neighbouring plantations had joined the insurgents and marched along with them towards the mountains. Meanwhile, Captain Jean-Pierre La Valette, commanding a detachment from Sauteurs, had arrived from the north and joined Fedon and as the combined forces made their way to Belvedere, they were joined by more and more slaves as well as some white French inhabitants. Arriving at Balthazar they rested; parties of the insurgents were formed and sent to the neighbouring estates and houses to bring in the British who owned or occupied them.

In this way, the magistrate of St Andrew's, a Mr Ross (the *Narrative* of 1795 gives his name as Rose) who lived about two miles away, was captured and taken to Balthazar, but his relatives were unmolested. At Balthazar, Fedon's party which had by then grown considerably, was given sugar and rum by the estate manager, Charpentier. The Abbé Peissonier, who acted as attorney for de Poulain, the owner of Balthazar, seeing Mr Ross wearing only a shirt in the cold night, brought him a coat and trousers; he was accused of being an aristocrat and promptly shot by Captain La Valette. Shortly after this the insurgents left Balthazar with their prisoners and made their way to Belvedere passing through the coffee estates of Ranaud, Du Parquet and Peschier.

About the same time as La Baye was attacked Gouyave was attacked by another of Fedon's detachment led by Joachim Phillip (a Free Coloured and cotton planter in Petit Martinique) and Etienne Ventour, both of whom formed part of the insurrection's leadership core.[7] The local doctor, John Hay, Revd Francis McMahon, and John Kerr, together with many managers and overseers in Charlotte Town (Gouyave) were seized and dragged off to Fedon's headquarters at Belvedere, but their wives and children were left on the estates, and there were no killings. By the end of the following day (4 March) almost every Frenchman in the northern half of the island had joined Fedon.

## Slaves' Early Involvement

The first slaves to join Fedon, apart from the leaders' own ex-slaves, were the domestics, drivers, tradesmen and other principal slaves on estates; they were the most active in the insurrection.[8] Normally, this class was most unlikely to join any insurrection, and often their members were informers of any planned insurrection. In Grenada they had a close affinity with the Free Coloureds, and were accepted as part of that class.[9] The last to join the insurgents were the field slaves and other, recently arrived, Africans. Many, however, remained loyal and

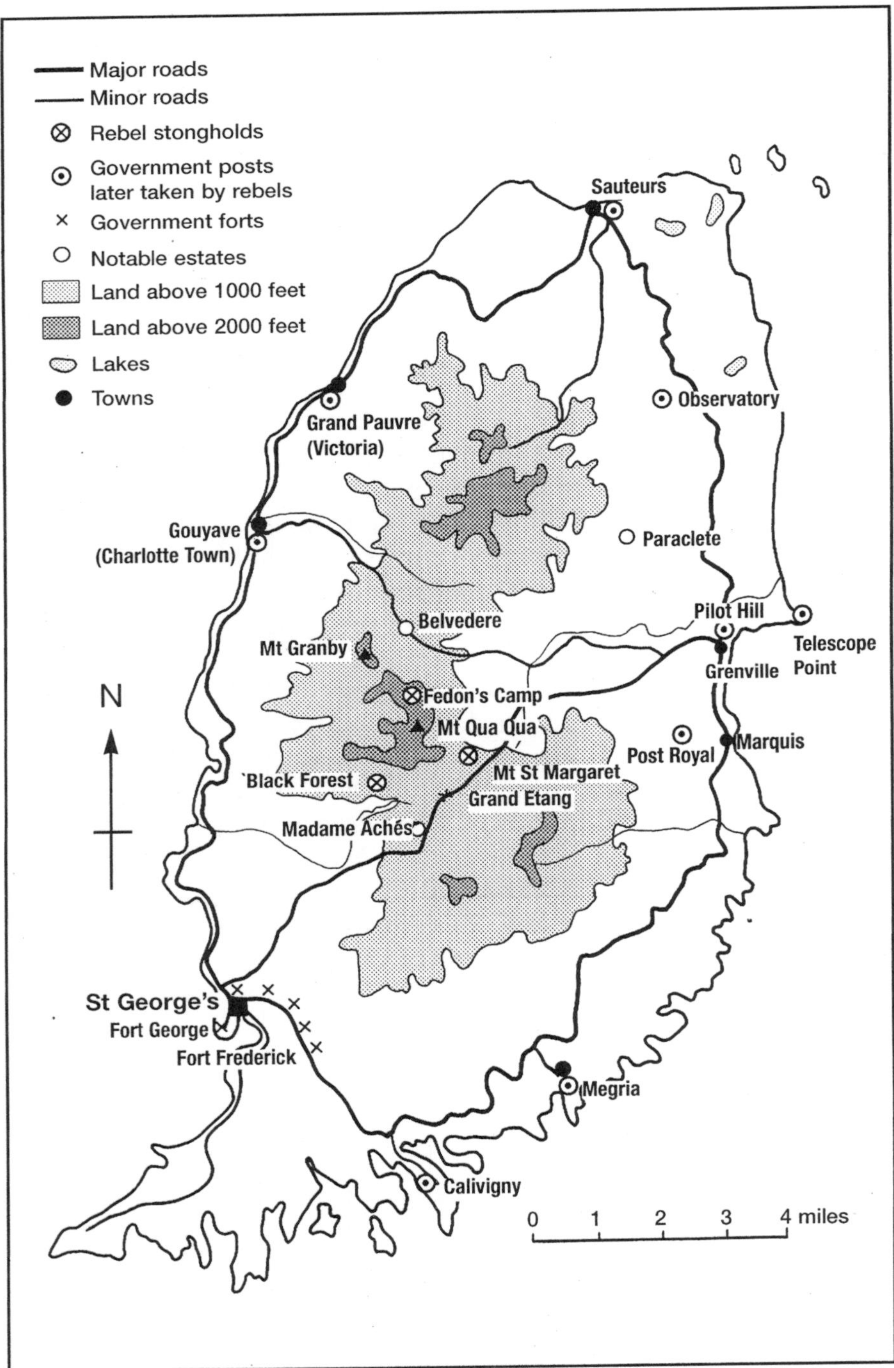


*Fedon's rebellion 1795–96*

when the plantation buildings were burnt down went into hiding. Some later returned to work the fields, on estates close to the military posts established by the middle of 1795. Clearly, however, the outbreak of the insurrection was followed almost simultaneously by a general slave rebellion, as one eyewitness wrote:

> The general *insurrection* of the slaves which soon followed was undoubtedly the work of the same insidious instruments employed in spreading the flame of rebellion, disseminating discord, confusion and anarchy in the minds of all who were susceptible.[10]

The Secretary of the Council Joseph Beete, writing to General Vaughan, admitted that:

> All the coloured people except those who are detained for militia duty in the Fort but on whose fidelity we cannot for a moment depend have joined the insurgents, and we have just learnt that several gangs of negroes have done so and a *mutinous* disposition exists.[11]

Many slaves, heartened by the prospects of real freedom if the insurrection succeeded, accepted Fedon's offer to join his ranks; some not only abandoned the plantations but set fire to them; others became nocturnal incendiaries.

> On the night of the 5th several fires were perceived from the ships in the direction of the upper Pearls and Carriere areas, which proved to be the trash-houses or buildings for preserving the cane-fuel on these estates and some others. The house of Mr. Stuart near De Glapion was also on fire. This was the beginning of a conflagration which was lighted up every night by the negroes in different parts and in the end desolated the whole island.[12]

## Capture of Ninian Home

When news of the insurrection reached St George's, the seat of Government, a Council of State and War was held at the Council chamber on Tuesday 3 March, presided over by Kenneth Mackenzie acting in the absence of Lieutenant-Governor Ninian Home, who was with a hunting party at Paraclete, one of Home's estates. It was resolved that the island be placed immediately under martial law and that the Commander-in-Chief of the British forces in the West Indies and other commanders be alerted and assistance be requested. Assistance was also sought from Don Chacon, Spanish Governor of Trinidad and Governor Seton of St Vincent.

Earlier that day the officers in St George's believed that French forces had landed at La Baye, but this was later corrected by a letter sent by Governor Home to Mather Byles, his secretary:

No French had landed at La Baye, but the Free people have risen against the Whites. Captain Blair and several are killed. I think the Coloured people ought not to have their arms or at least none except Captain La Grenade's company. I shall be in town as soon as possible.[13]

Governor Home was never to see St George's again. On his way there, he and his party embarked at Sauteurs in the New Diamond, with Augustine Cornelia as master, in an attempt to reach St George's by going around the western side of the island. Arriving off Gouyave, they put into the harbour to escape what they mistook to be a French pirate ship. Immediately they arrived in Gouyave Governor Home, together with Alexander Campbell, James Farquhar, Le Pelley and Anthony Kerr, was captured by Fedon's men and carried off to his camp.

Until June 1796 numerous attempts were made to dislodge the insurgents from Belvedere and capture Fedon, but with the exception of the last, all were abortive.

## Fedon's Objective

The aim of Fedon's planned insurrection was to force the British to surrender Grenada to him and his French comrades. On 4 March 1795, he issued a proclamation, in French, from his camp at Belvedere, demanding that every Englishman in Grenada submit to him or die. On the same day he sent both Charles Nogues and Joachim Phillip with a flag of truce, demanding either the surrender of the whole island within two hours, or surrender to the scourges of war.

The following letter was written by Fedon and Besson, and addressed to President Mackenzie and the Council of Grenada:

Without entering into any detail of our rights we summon you and all in this colony to surrender within the space of two hours to the Republican forces under our command. We warrant the safety of your life and property. In case of your not submitting you shall be liable to all the scourges of a disastrous war. All persons whomsoever shall be taken in arms or who shall not have joined the National Flag in such time as we shall judge fit, shall be punished with death, and their estate burnt, and lands confiscated to the use of the republic. The tyrant Home, Alexander Campbell and a great number of the English having been made our prisoners, will answer with their heads for the conduct of those in authority in case of refusal to surrender or submit. If any of our brothers or friends shall become victims or receive any ill treatment on the part of the English such ill treatment shall be retaliated doubly upon each prisoner and death by that of two Englishmen.[14]

By this time some 43 leading British citizens were prisoners at Fedon's camp. Regardless of the safety of the prisoners, the Government rejected Fedon's demands and at the same time offered a general pardon and amnesty to all who had joined the insurrection, except those who had committed murder. Furthermore they wrote:

> If they [Fedon, etc] should be so blinded as to their loyalty and duty and in any degree injure those whom chance has unfortunately thrown into their hands or destroy any property upon the island, they will only have themselves to blame for that severity and rigour which most assuredly will be the consequences of any such proceeding.[15]

Together with his conditions of surrender Fedon had sent to Mackenzie a declaration from Hugues and the other French Commissioners addressed to the British Commanders Vaughan, Caldwell, Thompson, Stewart and Lindsay. It stated that:

> From and after the date of this our official declaration the assassination of each and every individual republican (of whatever colour and in whatever island) shall be expiated by the death of two English officers our prisoners. The guillotine shall at the first notice thereof perform this act of justice. We do further declare that any Frenchman who at the moment of the landing of an army of the French Republic commanded by one of us or any of our substitutes shall not join against our common enemy is outlawed and his property forfeited to the Republic.[16]

President Mackenzie instantly informed General Vaughan and Vice-Admiral Caldwell in Martinique of Fedon's terms of surrender and Hugues's proclamation, and again requested urgent assistance. The Government in St George's meanwhile mobilized a force commanded by Captain Guerdon, in the first of many attempts to subdue the insurgents.

## Attempts to Crush the Rebellion

On 5 March, Captain Guerdon and 40 Regulars of the 58th Regiment, together with 150 volunteers from Colonel Garraway's regiment, under Colonel Park, left for Gouyave in an attempt to dislodge and subdue some of the insurgents.

Landing at Champion Bay they marched through Palmiste and Douglaston to Gouyave, arriving at about 4 p.m. By this time, however, the insurgents had already moved from Charlotte Town and were firmly entrenched in camp at Belvedere.

Guerdon was ordered to march as close as possible to Belvedere guided by Dr Muir, and to attack at daybreak on the 6th with the militia at Sauteurs and St Andrew's co-operating for the St Andrew's end. But Guerdon remained overnight in Gouyave, as some of his men were very tired and others were drunk. He decided to march on the insurgents on the morning of the 6th, and meantime, posted pickets on Gouyave Estate and sentinels around the town.

About 4 a.m. on 6 March, however, 400 of Fedon's men mounted a surprise attack on Guerdon's detachment, killing four of his men, while 12 of Fedon's men were killed and 24 wounded. From the information Guerdon received concerning the insurgents, he decided to postpone further attack until reinforcements arrived from St George's. Some 100 men, under Captain Rogers, arrived on 6 March by the ship *Quebec*.

For the attack on 6 March Mackenzie had written to Colonel Horseford of the St Andrew's militia asking him to arm the trusty negroes of Alexander Campbell's and other estates, to assist. Horsford subsequently stated that he had tried but failed owing to the hostile disposition of almost all gangs of negroes and even the white French planters. The late arrival of the order, and the advice of Smith, a surveyor in the area, that it would have been impossible to arrive on time also contributed to this failure. Mackenzie later rebuked Horsford saying that, 'it is by your united exertions that the island is to be saved and not by hiding your regiments on board ships at La Baye'.[17]

The attack was postponed until 8 March. Fedon, meanwhile, sent another flag of truce (on 6 March) by two white men, DeSuze Cadet and Pierre Alexandre, to the Government in St George's. A meeting of the Council was in progress at the time and the truce bearers were blindfolded and carried in. DeSuze was the son of Chevalier DeSuze and a longstanding French inhabitant of Grenada, while Alexandre was a clerk to M. Baurbousson, a Grenadian planter. The letter they delivered was written by Governor Home and signed by 43 prisoners. It read:

> General Fedon, commander of the French Republican troops now of considerable number, and 43 prisoners, request that I acquaint you with the said General's positive declaration made to me and the rest of the prisoners, that the instant an attack is made on the post where the prisoners now are confined, instantly, everyone of these prisoners shall be put to death. We hope you will take this our representation, into your consideration and not suffer if possible, the lives of so many innocent persons to be sacrificed.[18]

The Council's reply stated:

> We are all willing to spill the last drop of our blood rather than disgrace eternally ourselves and our country by a concession to men capable of such a proposition. We disdain to avail ourselves of our power over the insignificant individuals that have borne this flag but desire that no further communication of the same nature be attempted.[19]

In the meantime, about 80 soldiers from the St Andrew's and St Patrick's regiment left Grenville and proceeded to Gouyave by way of St Patrick's, where they joined Guerdon's men and the detachment which had recently arrived from St George's on the *Quebec*.

This combined force now decided to attack Fedon's camp at Belvedere. They set off on the 8 March but soon found themselves at such a disadvantage they had to abandon the attack. They found that Fedon had occupied an almost impregnable position on a fortified hill with two six-pounders arranged at such strategic points that they were able to smash any incursion. In addition, there were armed posts – one above the other on the highest hill in that area. Discouraged by the general hopelessness of their position, discontent soon spread among Guerdon's men, resulting in many fights; in one instance a private, Mungo McArthur, tried to kill Colonel Park with a bayonet. The men complained that they were volunteers, had left their property undefended in St George's and were unwilling to continue with this futile bush-fighting.[20] A rumour that Fedon's men were within five miles of St George's made the men especially anxious to return. At one point, an officer – Captain Snagg – encouraged the men to leave Gouyave and return to their families in St George's. Beatty, the army's surgeon, had abandoned his post on 6 March and there was no one to care for the sick, wounded and dying men. A Mr Wilson, owner of Gouyave Estate who had been appointed guide to the expedition, left Gouyave on the morning of the attack on the 6th, fearful for his life, as Fedon's men had recently destroyed the estate of a nearby fellow planter who had apparently informed on them.

By this time the insurrection of the slaves was general and widespread. The plundering of estates and burning of houses in Grenada continued almost constantly. The whole island, except St George's and the fortifications and a few estates near the town, were now in possession of the insurgents; the fall of St George's would have ensured total victory. Fedon's main problem, and the main reason for the failure to achieve total victory, appears to have been his inability to mount an all-out assault on St George's.

Between 15 and 22 March 1795 a second attempt was made to dislodge the insurgents. This was organized by General Lindsay, who arrived in Grenada from Martinique on 12 March 1795 on the HMS *Beaulieu*, with 150 men.

Lindsay planned an all-out offensive on the Camp of Liberty, as Belvedere was now commonly referred to. On the 15 March at 4 a.m. he set off at the head of 400 regular soldiers and militia, leaving 200 men to defend St George's. He arrived at Gouyave at 1 p.m. the same day and later was joined by 150 men from the HMS *Beaulieu*. On 17 March, Lindsay set off at the head of this force for Fedon's Camp, leaving the St Andrew's militia and the Corps of Volunteer Associated Cavalry under Lieutenant Gahagen to defend Gouyave. With a detachment of the 9th Regiment under Captain Sandieman he advanced under fire to the insurgents' post at La Croisade and captured it. Then, with a detachment of the 9th Regiment assisted by Captain La Grenade's party, he advanced towards the insurgents' main stronghold. A battle ensued with a party of about 150 insurgents who were forced to retreat into the woods. It was now about 6 p.m. Sandieman and 16 privates were wounded, and two killed. The approach of night made any further movement impossible. This gave Fedon time to carry the prisoners from the lower camp at Belvedere to the highest camp – Camp de La Mort – where he had his quarters. A group of former slaves was left to guard them. Fedon's strategic location consisted of three camps, one at Belvedere estate proper, another beyond and on much higher ground, called Fedon's Camp, and a third beyond Fedon's Camp on Mt Qua Qua. The camps on the highest ground were the most difficult to assail.

When they were in the Coffee House at upper Belvedere Fedon continued to press his prisoner, Lieutenant-Governor Home, to obtain Mackenzie's surrender. 'Ah, tyrant Home; you are now my prisoner. You must cause the forts to be delivered up.'[21] But Home by then had resigned himself to his fate. He replied, 'I am a prisoner and have no longer any power in the colony. I am resigned to my fate whatever you may make it.' On two occasions Fedon had referred to Home as 'Tyrant Home'. Clearly, in the eyes of the Free Coloureds and slaves, Home *was* a tyrannical Governor.

Lindsay determined to attack the camp next morning; he realized his error in resting for an hour. In a letter to Mackenzie, 18 March, he said: 'We hope to be in "their" camp tomorrow'.[22] But that was not to be, as he now had to combat the elemental forces in Belvedere: torrential rains, which fell that morning and continued for the next five days. Fever broke out among the troops; General Lindsay, frustrated and demoralized by the rains, the long wait and the infectious fever which paralysed many of his men, also contracted the fever and in a state of delirium shot himself on the morning of 22 March 1795.[23]

Lindsay's men had deserted him during the rains and he was forced to give leave to the others to go to St George's to revive themselves and return. In a letter to Mackenzie, on 21 March, the day before his suicide, he wrote:

> Upwards of half of the militia having left me contrary to the most positive orders, I have been prevented from carrying my plans into execution and I shall not be able to act offensively until I have at least a number equal to those who have left.[24]

Lieutenant-Colonel Schaw of the 58th Regiment succeeded Lindsay, and both he and Mackenzie were now of the view that the force in Grenada was too small for a general offensive against the insurgents, as, to be effective, such an offensive would have to be from three points simultaneously. On 31 March 1795, Mackenzie accordingly advised the Governor-in-Chief in Barbados that the only effectual way to attack the insurgents was a simultaneous approach to the several avenues to their camp, thus making it difficult for them to take up new positions in the forests. He suggested that forces be deployed in three divisions, one at the Grenville end of the camp, one at the Charlotte Town end and another at the St George's end.

The Government in Grenada was now on the defensive, awaiting the arrival of troops from Martinique. The seas were patrolled constantly to prevent any ship from landing ammunition and stores for the insurgents. Captain Watkins and his men captured one such ship. Another was seized on its way to Guadeloupe along with Pierre Alexandre, who had been sent to Trinidad with one Lussan (a merchant from Gouyave who had been prisoner in the camp, but later released) to procure arms and ammunitions with Lussan's credit there. Lussan, however, escaped from Alexandre and went directly to Governor Chacon, and informed on the insurgents. He was then safely conducted to Grenada on a vessel fitted and equipped by Governor Chacon. From Lussan we learn that there were upwards of 7,000 men in Belvedere as at times they had to kill some 8–10 cattle daily to feed the men. Alexandre, a former member of the British militia, was tried by court martial and condemned to be hanged; he was executed in the market place on 2 April 1795.

The insurgents retaliated to the attack on 17 March by burning Grenville town to ashes on the 18th. They also burnt the pilot's house on the hill and set up a post at Pilot Hill, which they fortified with a nine-pounder, two six- and one four-pounder, thus creating another stronghold, Pilot Hill, in the Telescope Hill area. The Government now realized they had to besiege Pilot Hill to prevent assistance and reinforcements reaching the camp at Belvedere.

On 2 April 1795 the British forces, under the command of Captain Guerdon, landed at La Baye to undertake an assault on the insurgents' post at Grenville Bay which was afforded cover by their forces at Pilot Hill comprising some 200 armed men under the command of Lieutenant Charles Nogues. Nogues was assisted by seven other officers, Jean Peysson, Ignace Dubissett, Jean Francis Camille, Jean Baptiste Edon, Jean Leandre, Michelle Cristoffe and Christome.[25]

Guerdon went into the attack at Pilot Hill on 3 April. The insurgents, with about 100 men, made a stout stand near Paradise Negro-houses, but they were overcome, at the cost of one grenadier. Guerdon then went to Telescope Hill to appraise Nogues' position and strength and was advised that in order to take the camp he would have to lose between one and two-thirds of his men. He wrote: 'They as well as myself thought it were prudent and advisable to return and keep position at Paradise Negro-houses'.[26] Moreover, Guerdon was uncertain whether even if he had captured Pilot Hill, he could have defended it; he, therefore, retreated from Pilot Hill.

At the time Pilot Hill was protected by two companies consisting of almost 200 men, but they were short of ammunition and an attack by Guerdon could have dislodged them. Shortly afterwards they received ammunition from Guadeloupe by a schooner which had escaped the cruisers and got into Marquis on 8 April 1795.[27]

Major Mallory, who was also involved in the Grenville side of the campaign, re-embarked for St George's with his force of some 300 men. On the following day, assisted and escorted by a detachment of light cavalry, his men, under Colonel Este, captured the insurgents' post at Michel – a hill beyond Grand Etang which commanded one of the principal approaches to Fedon's Camp. This was a most strategic position for Fedon to have lost, as it enabled the British forces to cut off his retreat from Camp Belvedere and intercept his heavy supplies from La Baye. Fedon's men stationed at Madame Ache at first stubbornly resisted but were eventually dispersed; British losses were one dead and three wounded. Major Mallory himself, in reconnoitring the situation in the evening, was attacked and wounded by two insurgents. As a result he was replaced by Colonel Este of the Gouyave Division. Mallory died shortly afterwards.

Colonel Este was instructed to proceed to the post at Michel, guided by a detachment of light cavalry under Captain McBurnie.[28] Michel was attacked from two points with two detachments of 50 men each under Lieutenant Walton and Captain Pigot respectively. After much fighting, in the course of which they lost two men, Michel fell.

Colonel Este then sent 250 men under the command of Captain Wright to Grenville Bay to assist the detachment at Observatory. The two detachments, Wright's and Guerdon's, met at Mt Horne Estate on 5 April, but as Wright's men were very tired they went to Observatory for food and artillery. They intercepted a letter from Charles Nogues to Fedon, requesting arms and reinforcements; as we have seen, a ship with arms, ammunition and stores arrived from Guadeloupe on 8 April. The insurgents were still firmly entrenched on Pilot Hill and had just burned down Grand Bras, Mirabeau and Mt Horne estates.

With the arrival of a Colonel Campbell it was decided to launch a full-scale attack on Camp Belvedere, on 8 April 1795. Guerdon and Wright were to guard the rear and if necessary, attack from the Gouyave end. Captain Watkins of HMS *Resource* offered his services and gathered a body of 150 volunteer seamen to assist. They marched to the Gouyave end of Camp Belvedere and joined forces with Colonel Campbell. By midnight on the 7th they were close to Fedon's Camp; at daybreak on the 8th the British forces entered the lower camp of the insurgents.

Fedon's men immediately retreated to the upper and more commanding post. It was strongly defended and made almost inaccessible by the nature of the terrain and the strong battery of trees felled and interlocked with each other. Moreover, the narrow pathway that led up to the upper limits could not have been discovered.

Despite these obstacles, the seamen and troops pressed forward. They tried to capture one of Fedon's guns mounted in the highest position, but after the heavy rains progress up the wet, slippery precipice was difficult. Clustered among trees and scarcely able to keep to their feet, their arms were of little use, and even worse, they were subjected to a heavy volley of bullets from the insurgents. After a gallant effort they were forced to retreat with considerable losses. One quarter of the volunteers under Captain Watkins were killed and wounded; Colonel Campbell's column lost 22 soldiers including Park, Ensign Baillie and Captain Stafford, and more than 48 wounded. Lieutenant Power of the 58th Regiment, six sergeants, two drummers, and 43 rank and file were also wounded.[29]

## Execution of Home and the Other Captives

Shortly after the abortive attempt to dislodge Fedon two more British privates joined the insurgents. On the same day, eight men of Major Wright's detachment, left on the road owing to excessive fatigue, were captured and taken to Camp Belvedere. News of the defeat, the desertion and imprisonment so demoralized President Mackenzie that he admitted his total inability to deal with the situation. The failure of this latter attack was attributable to six factors:

1. Heavy rains.
2. Fallen trees making it difficult for the soldiers to move or use their guns.
3. The rawness and ill-discipline of the new volunteers.
4. The uselessness of the six-pounder 'cannon' of the seamen.
5. The inaccessible nature of the terrain.
6. The enemy's intelligence of the impending attack.

During the assault of 8 April, Fedon lost his brother and a few men. Enraged by this and most probably intent on carrying out the threat he had made to Mackenzie in the second letter of truce, Fedon ordered the summary execution of 48 of his 51 captives on the same day. The *Narrative of the Revolt* reports 50 killed and three – Dr Hay for his professional assistance, William Kerr, son-in-law of Chevalier DeSuze, one of Fedon's top aides and the Revd Francis McMahon – were spared.

After the 48 men, including Governor Home, had been shot, Jean B. Cotton passed from body to body splitting their skulls with a cutlass to make sure they were all dead. The massacre was carried out in the presence of Fedon's wife and his two daughters, who viewed the spectacle with a kind of protean detachment.

In a letter to President Mackenzie on 6 April Fedon wrote:

> It is with indignation that we see the destruction of this flourishing colony by fires by which we are surrounded and which are set by our enemies. It is with the greatest satisfaction that we see the arrival in our camps of a number of English soldiers engaging themselves under the flag of liberty and the French Republic. We faithfully offer all those that will follow their example the same good treatment.[30]

It was this letter, plus the subsequent events of 8 April, that finally demoralized Mackenzie, and in a letter to the Commander-in-Chief in Barbados, General Vaughan, on 9 April, in addition to mentioning Fedon's letter, he wrote:

> The plans I have formed for the restoration of tranquility were the best which I could devise but they have been uniformly defeated by some sinister accident. My profession is not arms and of course, it cannot be expected that the army will act under me with that vigor and confidence which they would feel when commanded by an experienced general.[31]

Mackenzie proposed to General Vaughan that he send a General to Grenada vested with full command to organize a strategy for suppressing the insurrection and rid the country, as he put it, 'of an evil which at present threatens to ruin it'. He then recommended a certain General Arnold, but Vaughan sent General Nicholls.

The French vessel which had arrived on the 8th had brought a Mulatto named LeGrange to assist Fedon, Besson and Hugues. Hugues sent an officer to bring the prisoners from Belvedere to Guadeloupe, but with the exception of Dr Hay, Revd McMahon and William Kerr, whom he took to Guadeloupe, they had already been executed.

## More British Reinforcements Arrive

On 13 April 1795, General Nicholls arrived to take charge of the country's defences, assuming command of the military forces on 16 April. Later that month 300 trusted negro slaves were armed and constituted into a Corps of Loyal Black Rangers, consisting of five companies of about 60 each, with a white Lieutenant in charge of each company, and under the overall command of Major John Farquharson. This corps was soon to provide much valuable assistance to the British; their very existence was a clear manifestation of the old colonial strategy of 'divide and rule'. In 1784, General Nicholls had lived in Grenada during the government of General Edward Matthew; he was then commander of the 45th Regiment.

Nicholls first had a careful surveillance of Fedon's position in Belvedere carried out; he then ordered all troops in the area to withdraw. His plan was first to drive the insurgents from Pilot Hill, set up defensive posts around the island, isolate all Fedon's men at Belvedere and then plan an assault.

On 22 April there was a short skirmish between the insurgents and Major Wright's party at Observatory. Shortly after this a small foraging party returning from Tivoli was nearly surrounded by the insurgents; Robert Turnbull and Langan were killed, but the rest escaped and gave the alarm to Major Wright, who immediately ordered a detachment of regulars, under Captain Guerdon, and the militia, under McCaskill, to march against the post at Pilot Hill. This attack failed. Guerdon was killed early in the action and five regulars and three militia men were wounded.

The Government's posts at Belvedere were evacuated on 22 April and an expedition was mounted against Pilot Hill. Two gunboats each with an 18-pounder, 20 small vessels escorted by HMS *Resource*, and 900 troops left Grenville on 27 April. From St George's troops of the light cavalry and the Corps of Loyal Black Rangers marched through St David's Crochu and Grand Bacolet to Marquis, where the troops that had embarked at Gouyave had landed on 4 May 1795. Immediately on landing Colonel Hope marched with them and easily succeeded in dislodging a party of insurgents on Post-Royal Hill.

Major Wright's party and Lieutenant Gahagan's corps of cavalry were ordered to Grand Bras to cut off the insurgents' retreat from Pilot Hill. But Charles Nogues, realizing that a major assault was planned, abandoned Pilot Hill during the night, spiked the guns, and escaped to Fedon's Camp before the British were able to attack. No doubt Colonel Hope was bitterly disappointed, but nonetheless, a strong detachment under his orders occupied Pilot Hill. General Nicholls then established posts at St Patrick's, Observatory and St David's, while the post at Gouyave was reinforced, and the remaining forces were kept in St George's.

Many days after 22 May 1795 when Pilot Hill had been besieged, about 500 insurgents in the St David's area made a surprise attack at 1 a.m. on around 76 government troops. Caught unawares the sentries on guard were put to death, and those in the church were showered with volley after volley of bullets. The regulars and militia fought back bravely and, nine regulars were killed, 13 were wounded, some very seriously,[32] and 20 insurgents were killed.

After the campaign of 26 May, government strategy was to isolate the insurgents at Belvedere. Forts were set up all around the island to prevent assistance and reinforcements reaching them from outside, but on 10 October 1795 two ships from St Lucia landed reinforcements of 200 armed men for the insurgents. They reached Belvedere without opposition and were seen neither by the British forces nor by scouts on guard at the various lookouts. The government forces also received assistance with 80 members of the Light Dragoons and 200 infantry men arriving from Barbados on 21 October.

On 26 October, apparently, the British forces seized a number of Blacks at Grand Bacolet, who they suspected were in league with the insurgents, carried them off to St George's and hanged them. This infuriated Fedon's men, and on 4 November the Chevalier Sugue sent a letter to General Nicholls under a flag of truce, stating that the war would be carried on with humanity and that the rights of the people of the island should be respected, and finally emphatically stating that the edifice of slavery would be thrown down.[33]

During the next three months the insurrection proceeded with isolated and sporadic attacks from both sides. No large-scale engagements similar to those in the earlier months occurred, except for one on 15 December when the insurgents counter-attacked Pilot Hill, which was stubbornly defended by Captain Wright. The losses, however, were heavy on both sides. The insurgents withdrew and proceeded to Post-Royal in Marquis, which had, by then, been abandoned by government forces in order to set up a new post.

Various acts of sabotage committed by the insurgents weakened the economy and placed the planters' livelihoods in jeopardy. On 8 February 1796 two large canoes of insurgents seized the *Hostess Quickly*, a vessel in government service, captured her Captain, seized her cannons and killed three members of her crew. They then turned the cannons on Pilot Hill, and began to besiege that commanding post. Captain Wright, then the officer in charge at Pilot Hill, was forced to retreat; 10 of his men were killed, 14 were wounded, and the remaining 300 escaped unharmed.[34] The siege ended on 29 February.

## End of the Rebellion

By the beginning of March 1796 the government posts at Observatory in St Patrick's, and Megrin and Calivigny in St David's, were all abandoned under heavy fire from the insurgents. In Gouyave, insurgents captured and held Mt St Margaret; posts at Mabouya and Dalincourt also fell into their hands and were now firmly controlled by Captain Jossey. In addition, Fedon established new posts at Black Forest Estate near Vendomme, and at Beausejour. There was no doubt that at this time five parishes were firmly under Fedon's control. St George's alone eluded his grasp. President Mackenzie, a broken man, resigned and left Grenada on the grounds of ill-health; he was replaced by the Hon. Samuel Mitchell, the most senior member of the Council.

The insurgents and revolting slaves, finding the country areas and estates almost completely deserted and unprotected, as many planters had fled, formed resistance groups, destroyed estates, robbed and burned plantations, dwelling houses and buildings of every kind.[35] By this time, considerable numbers of slaves had rallied to Fedon's banner, as he and the insurgents offered rewards to all slaves who would burn down their masters' plantations, or kill and abandon their masters. Thus by early 1796, a general slave revolt against the plantation system constituted an essential part of the Fedon Rebellion. In one year, Grenada, once a flourishing country, had become a scene of wild desolation and the English plantocracy faced famine and ruin.

This state of affairs had begun to emerge as early as July 1795. By 1796, however, the desolation had become more widespread and the suffering more intense. In August 1795, the Grenada Legislature had sent a petition to the House of Commons explaining these hardships and requesting a loan of £100,000 – of which £40,000 was to be available immediately to buy provisions for the beleaguered population, and those slaves who had remained loyal.[36] Other requests for assistance continued throughout 1795, but they became more urgent in early 1796 when Fedon virtually controlled the entire island and most of the planters were forced to congregate in St George's.

Around March 1796, the British under General Nicholls began to plan a new series of offensives against Fedon, especially as they had just received large reinforcements of both infantry and cavalry. On 19 March 1796, the Legislature passed a law empowering General Nicholls to take from the inhabitants as many male slaves, horses and mules as he needed to complement the new military offensive.

On 22 March, General Nicholls, with 1,000 men, recaptured Post-Royal Hill and thus ensured control over the entire Marquis Bay area. Three hundred insurgents were killed in this fierce battle. Both Post-Royal and Marquis were strategic areas in that they held the key to Pilot Hill. The British lost 40 dead and many wounded.

Fedon, who was supposed to have taken part in the battle at Post-Royal, slipped off to Pilot Hill and gave orders for its immediate evacuation.[37] Accordingly, the insurgents retreated to Camp Belvedere and the surrounding mountains. As the military offensive against the insurgents built up, the fortunes of war slowly turned against them.

The offensive, which had begun on 22 March, was resumed on 9 June with the arrival of General Ralph Abercromby. On 10 June, Captain Jossey, in command of the Dougaldston post, surrendered to General Nicholls. Fedon, who was also then at Dougaldston, escaped to Mt Qua-Qua with 300 men. Abercromby then planned an attack on the Camp of Liberty from three points on Palmiste beach, and offered £500 to any soldier who could bring him Fedon's head. The plan was as follows: General Campbell was to attack from Black Forest and Mount St Margaret after first disposing of the insurgents there. Count D'Hillimer, in command of the Lowensteins Jaggers and the Corps of Loyal Black Rangers together with Colonel Gledstanes in command of the 57th Regiment, were both to assail the headquarters of Fedon's Camp – the Camp of Liberty. Gledstanes was to attack from the head of the Grand Roy valley by Mount Granby, while D'Hillimer was to attack from the Gouyave side of the camp. The Jaggers were specially trained fighters, skilled in this kind of mountain warfare; they silently climbed the mountain during the night, and at dawn launched attack on the insurgents at a post called 'Vigie'. The fleeing insurgents were hotly pursued to their camp at Qua-Qua. By this time all prisoners in Fedon's hands were killed. Vicious fighting ensued; Fedon's side suffered enormous losses while the government forces lost nine dead, with 55 wounded.[38]

When Fedon and some of his lieutenants realized that they would be overpowered and eventually captured and killed, they threw themselves down the precipice. All of Fedon's remaining lieutenants were eventually captured, but Fedon himself eluded the British and was never captured, and there are many speculations regarding what eventually happened to him. The most plausible is that he drowned while trying to make his way in a small boat to his brother in Trinidad. One of Fedon's last lieutenants to be captured was Captain Jacques Chadeau, captured in June 1808 after successfully eluding the British for 12 years. It is said that he was the victim of a love affair with two women. One of them, apparently jealous of the other, informed on him and he was captured by a detachment of the Corps of Loyal Black Rangers, and hanged. His body was left to hang on Mt Eloi (Cherry Hill) as a lesson and a warning of the price to be paid by those who attempted but failed to overthrow governments.

The insurrection, which lasted 15 months from 3 March 1795 to 19 June 1796, resulted in a loss of property estimated at £2.5 million, in addition to the loss of life of insurgents and innocent citizens. Seven thousand slaves died; sugar works, rum distilleries and other buildings were destroyed on some 65 estates; cattle, horses and mules valued at approximately £65,000 were killed. Other buildings, not generally associated directly with sugar production, on 35 estates were burnt to the ground; crops for the years 1794, 1795 and 1796 were lost. All those insurgents who were later captured were executed and their properties, as well as those of all other insurgents, appropriated by the state after all claims against them were settled.[39] A number of persons suspected of harbouring subversive feelings were condemned to transportation; these included 143 slaves, 86 adult Free Coloureds and children, all of whom were taken to Santo Domingo in 1797 in ships owned by James and John McBurnie, who received the contract.

The failure of the Fedon Rebellion marked a failed attempt by the Free Coloureds to free themselves from the civil incapacities which they still suffered and the Blacks to free themselves from the debilitating servitude of slavery. Fedon's failure to mount a full-scale offensive against the British forces in St George's at the outbreak of the insurrection, and again at the end of February 1796, were the main obstacles to victory. Instead of intensifying military pressure Fedon continued demanding that the Government abdicate. The protracted nature of the insurrection afforded the British time to mobilize reinforcements from outside and eventually to isolate Fedon in Belvedere.

The formation of the Corps of Loyal Black Rangers, and the contingent of Black slaves who carried stores and ammunition for the British during the last series of battles, exemplify how the colonizer used Blacks to fight Blacks. It was a clear manifestation of 'divide and conquer', whereby the British enjoyed a double advantage; if the Black Rangers were successful then the British would have achieved their aim; if they were killed, white lives would have been saved.

Fedon was not seeking independence for Grenada, rather he sought to rid Grenada of British colonial rule, abolish slavery and then make her part of the New French Republic created by the French Revolution in 1792. In this aim, Fedon was perhaps deluded, being so distant from the main current of political affairs in France. By 1795 France was in a state of political chaos and the existing leadership had abandoned most of the lofty aims of 1789. That soon afterwards France entered a period of military dictatorship is testimony of such change in political outlook and direction. That Fedon took orders, and received arms, ammunition and other forms of assistance from Victor Hugues, an agent of the Republican Government in Guadeloupe, showed that he was not fully politically autonomous, but was controlled, albeit partially, by external forces.

## NOTES

Full citations only given where work does not appear in the Bibliography.

1. Grenada, *Minutes of the Legislative Body of Grenada, 1792–1797*, 8 July 1793.
2. Ibid.
3. They included: Jean W. Allard, Pierre Julien Valie, Charles Nogues, Julien Fedon, Jean St Bernard, Ignace DuBisset, Louis La Grenada and Stanislaus Besson.
4. *Narrative of the Revolt and Insurrection of the French Inhabitants in Grenada* by an eye-witness (Gordon Turnbull), Edinburgh, 9 November 1795, pp. 3–14.
5. Ibid. pp. 15–16.
6. Ibid. p. 17.
7. Grenada, *Minutes of the Legislative Body*, March 1795.
8. *Narrative of the Revolt*, pp. 3–14.
9. Ibid.
10. Ibid. p. 10.
11. *Minutes of the Legislative Body*, 5 March 1795.
12. *Narrative of the Revolt*, p. 58.
13. *Letter of Home to Mather Byles*, La Fortune, 8.30 a.m., 3 March 1795.
14. *Minutes of the Legislative Body*, 4 March 1795.
15. Ibid.
16. Ibid. Also *Narrative of the Revolt*, pp. 38–40.
17. Mackenzie to Horsford, *Minutes of Legislative Body*, 6 March 1795.
18. Ibid. Friday 6 March 1795.
19. Ibid. Beete to Commander Vaughan, 6 March, 1795; Beete to Fedon, 6 March, 1795.
20. *Minutes of Legislative Body*, 11 March 1795.
21. Ibid.
22. *Narrative of the Revolt;* Lindsay to Mackenzie, 18 March 1795.
23. *Minutes of the Council;* James Park to President Mackenzie, 24 March 1795.

24. *Narrative of the Revolt*, p. 76.
25. *Minutes of the Legislative Body*, 3 April 1795.
26. *Narrative of the Revolt*; Guerdon to Mackenzie, 3 March 1795.
27. Ibid. p. 92.
28. *Minutes of the Council*, 9 April 1795. The *Grenada Handbook* gives figures of 95 dead and wounded. Devas says 40 seamen were killed and wounded and there were 60 casualties among Campbell's men. *Narrative of the Revolt*. pp. 98–99.
29. *Minutes of the Legislative Body*; Fedon to Mackenzie, 9 April 1795.
30. Ibid.
31. Devas, *History of Grenada* p. 143.
32. *Minutes of the Legislative Body*, 1795.
33. Devas. *History of Grenada* p. 150.
34. *Minutes of the Legislative Council*, 'Petitions to the House of Commons', 3 August 1795, 10 March 1796.
35. Ibid.
36. Devas. *History of Grenada*, p. 151.
37. Ibid.
38. Grenada, *Letter Book*, 'Charles Green to the Duke of Portland'. 6 December 1798.
39. Ibid.

# 8

# *Slavery and the Plantation System: 1783–1833*

## Economic and Military Apparatus

The plantation system in Grenada originated during French colonial rule (1674–1762) and continued into British colonial rule. The few changes that did occur in this latter period were purely superficial, involving only those in plantation ownership, names of people, language, and legal and judicial systems. During French colonial rule the colony was oriented towards the French metropole and during British colonial rule towards the British. The local plantation economy was an appendage of first the French economy and in the latter period the British economy. The organizational structure of the plantation, its peculiar psychology, police system, legal system, and degradation of the worker remained essentially unchanged.

The plantation system was built upon the foundations of sugarcane, coffee and cotton production, slave labour and sugar manufacture. It was highly capitalistic with its extensive machinery, equipment, mills, boilers, coolers, stock and land owned by the planter. At the planting and harvesting stages of production the process was extremely labour intensive, but capital intensive at the grinding and boiling stages. Management and capital were provided by the owner, and capital's indispensable complement – labour – was provided by the slaves. From the relationship that developed between the ownership of capital and labour and the production of sugar, four distinct institutions, which were both outgrowths and pillars of the system, were generated

1. A police system was the main device for maintaining the status quo of plantation life. This mechanism of control was intensified

parallel with planters' increasing preoccupation with and paranoia about the slave insurrection.
2. An extensive body of slave laws emerged, aimed at circumscribing the slaves' every movement.
3. A rigid social class structure grew up, and, as a product of that structure, racism.
4. A monopoly of political and judicial institutions was held by the plantocracy or group of estate owners. Such control was considered essential to maintain and defend the economic interests of the planter class.

## Policing System

The heart of Grenada's police system was the island's militia, with the assistance of constables appointed by the Legislature through Justices of the Peace. Its functions were suppression of internal dissent, subversion or revolt, and the protection of the island from external attacks. Thus the economic, political and social status quo was maintained and ensured. In 1779 there were 390 men under arms in Grenada, 90 regular soldiers and 300 militia men. By 1795, the number had grown to a little over 1,2000[1] comprising a garrison of 293 men, together with a militia of 900 (500 British, 80 French and 300 Free Coloureds) and a cavalry detachment of about 40–50. During and after the Fedon Rebellion of 1795–96 the military forces in Grenada were considerably strengthened. The 300 slaves who in August 1795 were hastily constituted into a military corps to assist the island's militia, and to act as a counterweight to Fedon's slave insurgents, continued to operate for many decades after the rebellion, tracking down and recapturing fugitive slaves.

By 1834 there were seven regiments of the militia in Grenada, one in every parish and one in Carriacou,[2] altogether totalling 97 officers and 853 NCOs and privates at an annual cost of between £19,000 and £23,000. This was almost double the amount spent on the civil, judicial and ecclesiastical establishments of the colony.[3]

In the event of slave vagrancy, slave rebellions or any other disturbances the individual estate was unable to handle, the parish militia was called in. In the case of the main threat to Grenada's plantation system during the 1783–1833 period – the Fedon Rebellion – the local militia was unable to restore peace and order and, as we saw in Chapter 7, military forces from outside had to be brought in. There were also the Grenada Maroons, against whom the militia was used from time to time between 1765 and 1795. More will be said about this later.

*A Royal Artillery uniform 1799*

## The Legal Pillar

On of the first Acts passed during the era of British colonial rule was in 1766, entitled 'An Act for the Better Government of Slaves and for the more speedy and effectual suppression of runaway slaves.' In April 1767 another Act followed, making all slaves articles of real estate subject to inheritance, declaring all widows to be dowable of them, in the same way as were lands, houses and animals. Even if slaves were not attached to land, they were to be inherited by the legatees of the owner in the event of death. Deeds and conveyances of slaves had to be proven and recorded in a like manner to that applying to any other article of property.[4] In 1770, an amendment to this law provided for due compensation to the inheritor or administrator in cases where tenants for life might maim, destroy or disable a slave. The compensation was to be three times the value of the slave maimed or destroyed.[5]

In 1770, in order to protect plantations from irresponsible use of fire, and from arson, the Legislature passed 'An act for preventing those who shall willfully fire, burn or destroy canes, dwelling houses or any edifice.[6] Under this law it was expressly forbidden to carry any fire, lamp, lighted torch or candle or to smoke tobacco in any sugar-cane field. Any slave found violating this law was publicly whipped; a free person was fined £5. If a free Negro negligently caused fire to any house the penalty was corporal punishment such as a Justice of the Peace deemed fit and proper; a white person's penalty for the same office was a £20 fine. If *any* person maliciously burnt, or caused to be burnt, or aided or advised in the burning of any mansion, millhouse, boiling house, wharf house, or any ship, sloop, canoe, or any piece of sugar-cane, plantain walk, or any coffee, cocoa or cotton trees, he was adjudged a felon and if found guilty killed without the benefit of clergy. This law was clearly aimed at slaves as the most likely persons to protest against the inhumanity of slavery and the plantation system by such means. As the century wore on other laws were passed, including one enacted in 1785 to build a cage – the term used for a public prison for slaves and Blacks – in Carriacou 'to help preserve public peace'. This was eventually built, at a cost of £300 to the public, and placed under the supervision of the Magistrate of Carriacou; in 1789 another was built in St Patrick's and soon there were cages in every parish in Grenada and in Carriacou.[7] Laws were passed empowering every owner and employer of slaves to keep one white man for every 50 slaves. In Grenada, this was called 'An Act For The Importation of White Servants', but it was one of the many Deficiency Laws passed in the British West Indies in the 18th century to offset or counter-balance the relatively large Black population. These laws, however, failed in their object, as the ratio of Whites to slaves in Grenada fell significantly in the 18th century, from half in 1700, to 1:8 in 1753, 1:15 in 1771, and by 1783 to 1:24.

In 1789, laws were also passed prohibiting the sale of liquor to slaves. Another law, passed in the same year, was to ensure a more speedy trial and punishment of criminal slaves and to empower Justices of the Peace to appoint constables in cases of emergency. Also in 1789, all canoe and boat owners were ordered to take out licences, and ensure that their craft would not be used by slaves to escape or to be carried off from Grenada.

In 1825, all existing slave laws in Grenada were consolidated into one law. Slaves found off the plantation on which they were residing, without written permission (a pass) were to be taken up and apprehended. The apprehender, on conducting the slave home was to receive a gratuity of 9/- and mile-money of 3/- per mile; if the owner refused to pay, the required sum could be collected from the local Justice of the Peace who would then levy the same sum on the goods or tenements of the slave owner. Any slave absent from the estate for more than 48 hours without a ticket was deemed a runaway. Runaway slaves who remained at large upwards of six months, were, on conviction, sentenced to hard labour for life or to transportation. On a first conviction, a runaway could be whipped or sentenced to hard labour not exceeding three months; but, if adjudged an incorrigible runaway, he was to be treated similarly to a runaway absent for six months. Any person harbouring a runaway slave incurred a fine of £10 for each slave so harboured. Slaves who harboured runaways were liable to corporal punishment.

For a free person to sell, or give, arms to a slave was illegal. Slaves were forbidden to play drums or other hand instruments after 10 p.m. Any person carrying off, or attempting to carry off, another's slave was deemed guilty of a felony; if the culprit was white he was fined, whilst a slave was to be punished in an exemplary manner, not involving loss of limb or life. Slaves found between 9 p.m. and 4 a.m. in the town of St George's without a pass were to be apprehended and taken to the cage in the town; any slave found dancing in any public place in Grenada was to be arrested and imprisoned for the night. Swearing, uttering obscenities, committing indecent acts, gaming, drunkenness in tippling houses, cruelly whipping or beating of animals, furiously driving any cart within the precincts of the town, were, upon conviction, each punishable by 25 lashes.[8] It must be emphasized that in all cases of litigation, one white person's evidence was sufficient to convict any slave or group of slaves.

The practice of *obeah* was expressly forbidden, and punishable by death or transportation. The possession of poisonous drugs, pounded glass, parrot's beak, dog's or alligator's teeth, or any other material used in witchcraft constituted a felony in Grenada, and was punishable as such. One witchcraft practice was the drinking of human blood mixed with rum and grave dirt; this supposedly gave the user supernatural powers. Anyone found guilty of this act was punished by death.

Rebellion, conspiracy, murder, arson, manslaughter, burglary, armed robbery, committed by a slave, were all punishable by death or transportation; these sentences applied even during apprenticeship. John Phillip, of Upper Conference, was convicted in the August 1835 session of the Supreme Court of the crime of arson, having set fire to the Megasse House of Balthazar Estate. He was hanged and left to die in agony for one hour.[9]

In 1826 and 1827 Acts were passed to erect and regulate a treadmill in St George's town. This was a salutary mode of punishment but, according to the speed with which it was operated, could be converted into an instrument of torture. Forming part of the public gaol it was placed under Provost Marshal's control. Two or more Justices of the Peace could, upon conviction, send slaves to work on the treadmill for any time not exceeding 60 days, for any misdemeanour.

Once a person became a worker, the plantation system's harsh and oppressive disciplinary code applied irrespective of creed or colour. White indentured workers were subjected to equally inequitable conditions, but their lot differed from that of a slave in three respects: a) he was conceived in law as 'persona' and not 'res' as in the case of the slaves; b) his indentureship was temporary, i.e., for a fixed period of time, after which he was fully free; and c) he was paid a wage.[10] Also, in the case of vagrancy, for every day an indentured servant was absent he had to work for ten additional days at the end of his indentureship; anyone harbouring an indentured servant was fined 40/- for the first day and £5 for each day thereafter. An indentured servant guilty of trying to escape on board ship had to serve his master an additional three years at the end of his indentureship.

*Punishment on the treadmill in the 1820s*

During the period of slavery, in Grenada as elsewhere, society was rigidly stratified. The upper class – often referred to as the plantocracy – consisted of white planters, big merchants, top civil officials and military officers, and ministers of the Church of England. This group enjoyed all political power and exercised it in its own interest. Members of this class were either born in Europe, or if in the colonies of European parents, and invariably were white.

The middle stratum consisted of free Blacks and Coloured planters, small merchants, medium and small farmers, lesser professionals and artisans. The Coloureds and Free Blacks, though often wealthy, did not share equal civil and political rights with the Whites.

At the bottom of the class structure were the Black and Coloured slaves.

The basic principle underlying such stratification was that each group should remain in and accept the conditions of the class to which it was socially confined.

## The Judicial Pillar

There were two distinct and independent Courts of Laws: the Court of King's Bench and Grand Sessions of the Peace, concerned with criminal jurisdiction; and the Court of Common Pleas, restricted to civil jurisdiction. The former was established soon after the British arrived in 1763 and re-established in April 1784, while the latter was established in December 1791. The Justices were planter-appointed, the jury always planter-dominated; consequently justice was invariably perverted, especially in cases involving slaves and Whites. In October 1800, owing to its many imperfections, and to dissatisfaction with the personnel in the Court of King's Bench, the two Courts were amalgamated to become the Supreme Court of Judicature. The evidence of slaves was not admissible in courts of law until 24 November 1828, when their evidence was admitted, in all trials involving both civil and criminal cases, in the same manner as that of free persons.

An examination of the legal-judicial apparatus of the plantation system demonstrates that:

1. The authorities of the day were preoccupied with subversion and each slave was seen as a potential rebel or criminal.
2. Force and violence lay at the very heart of the laws promulgated. They were used to keep the slave in his stratum of society.
3. Control of every movement of the slave was necessary to reduce the incidence or eliminate the possibility of resistance.

4. The slave laws were but a comprehensive system of restrictions and had nothing to do with industrial relations between slave and planter.

## The Plantation as a Total Institution

'Total institutions are organised groups with well defined boundaries and a marked hierarchical structure approaching an internal caste system.'[11] Examples of these are inmates and staff in an asylum, prisoners and wardens, monks and abbots, nuns and mother superiors, slaves and masters. Characteristic of total institutions is that people enter them as already socially formed human beings with a culture and set of attitudes which must be reformed so that the inmate can be manipulated as a lunatic, monk, prisoner, or slave. Mechanisms are brought into play designed to effect a total break with the inmate's past, and to destroy his personality in order to establish a new personality, a new identity, a new set of attitudes to self and others.[12] For many slaves, once this new identity had been impressed on them, the more malleable and less prone to resistance, insubordination or rebellion, they became.

The first mechanism employed in Grenada and the British West Indies to destroy the Africans' personality was a process called 'breaking in', beginning with their experiences and suffering during the journey across the Atlantic. Packed in a ship, each confined to a coffin-like space, the future slave would see his other brothers and sisters fall sick, suffer, die and be thrown overboard. Some, unable to bear the sight of their suffering fellows, flung themselves overboard, preferring death to future torment. In an attempt to maximize their profits, slave traders frequently crammed the slave ships beyond their capacity, disregarding the health of the African.

The harsh treatment undergone by the African began to affect and transform his personality. That was the beginning of the 'breaking-in' process; the next step was the method of sale.

Slaves were sold in various ways. Sometimes the entire cargo would be consigned to a single planter; at others an agent sold them for a commission; or, more commonly, the ship's captain would hold a public auction called the *Vendue*. Families were often broken up during sale; slaves sharing a language or customs were often deliberately separated. Lastly, slaves were sold by a method called the *scramble*, which seems to have occasionally been used in Grenada. All maimed slaves would first be picked out and auctioned off; the healthy slaves were then sold for the scramble fee – a standard price for man,

*Slaves crowded on a ship bound for America*

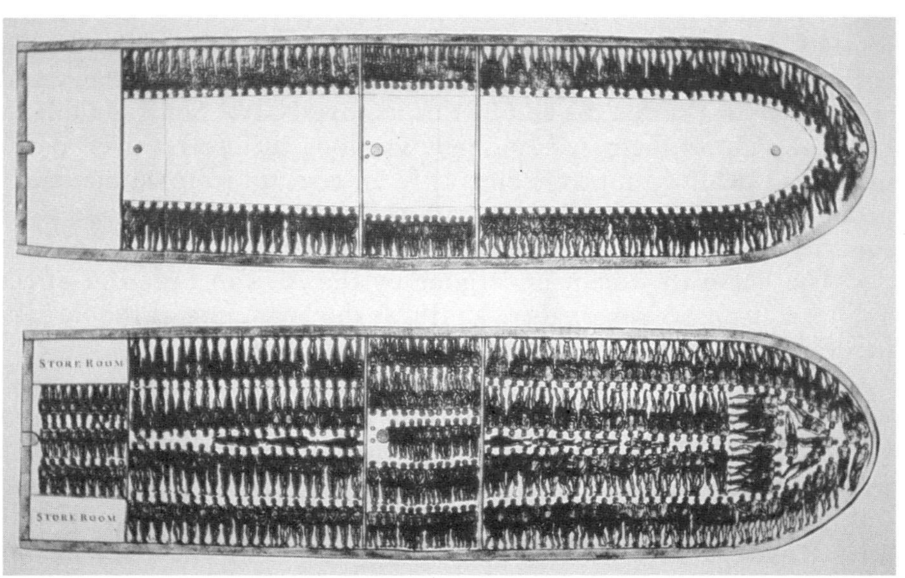


*Plan of slave ship, showing how slaves were packed like sardines for a capacity load*

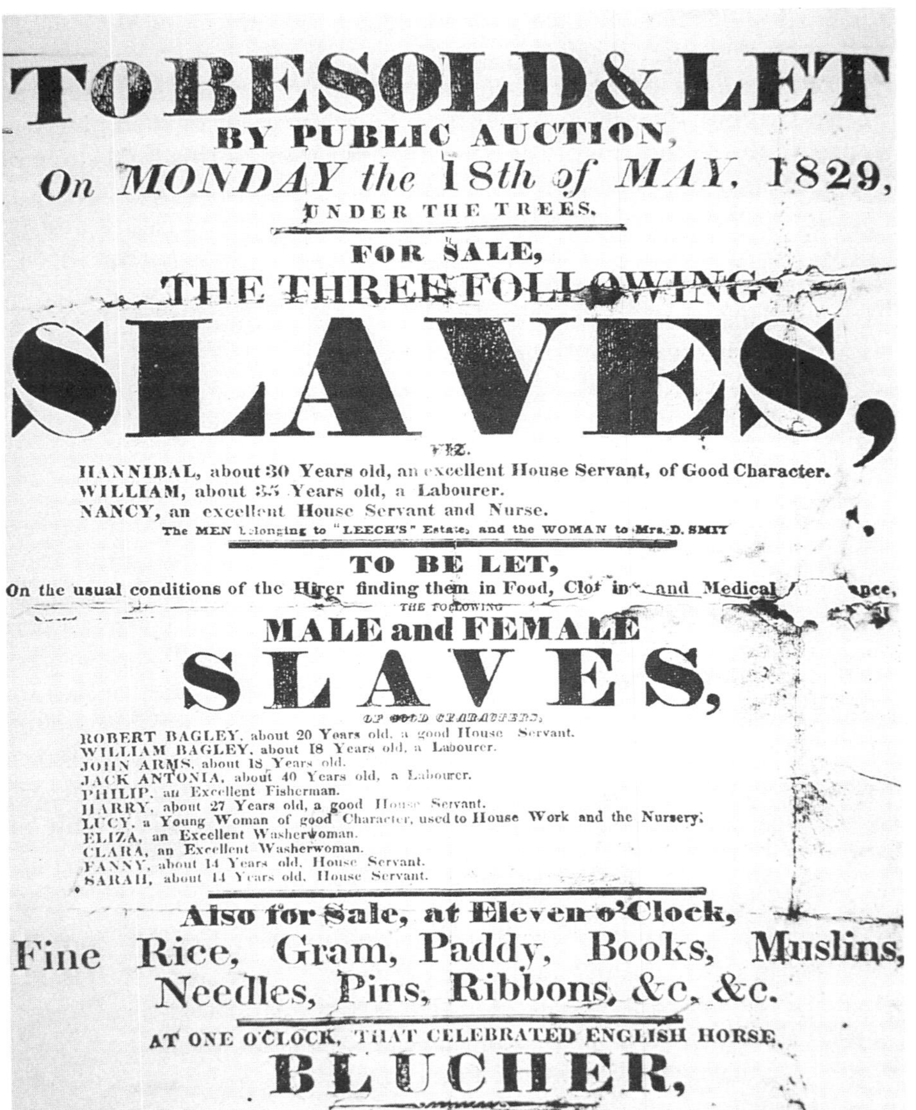


*Slave auction poster, 1829*

woman or child, previously agreed between slaver and buyer. The slaves were then herded into an enclosure and, at the sound of a bell, the buyers would rush in and scramble; whatever each person came up with was his. This crude method of slave buying was practised in Grenada as late as 1788; slaves from the ship *Alexander* were scrambled for in St George's that year,[13] and it is recorded that the female slaves were 'frightened out of their wits' by the onrush of the buyers and several of them climbed over the fence and ran about St George's as though they were insane.

Once purchased, slaves were taken to the plantation and prepared for field labour. The slave-driver was the main agent in such preparation, and the 18-hour workday the main weapon in this final stage of the 'breaking-in' or seasoning process.

Before long, the rigid organization of life on the estate and its oppressive discipline tended to destroy the individual personality of the African and created stereotypes of the Black slaves. The distinctive African identity gave place to plantation-type personalities: low self-esteem, self-hatred, inferiority complex, no cultural pride, contempt for others of one's kind, subservience, rejection of negroid physical features, and giving them the epithet of 'ugly'. The plantation with its physical and psychological violence recreated the African in its own image.

Work on the estate began at 5 a.m. and ended at 7 p.m. In harvest time a slave's working day was normally 18 hours despite poor food and clothing. A result of this virtual neglect was the very high mortality rate on the estates. In 1771 the slave population in Grenada was 26,211; between 1771 and 1808 more than 29,000 slaves were imported, yet by 1833, the slave population had declined to 23,536. In 1779 there were 35,000 slaves; between 1784 and 1787, as many as 9,752 more were imported, yet a year later the slave population was 26,775, or 18,000 fewer than it should have been assuming a zero rate of natural increase. The declining figures can be explained only by mortality rates.

By law, a Grenadian slave was entitled to:

- a portion of land to grow provisions to feed himself, and 28 working days, besides Sundays, between 1 May and 31 January each year, to cultivate such land; where the land was insufficient, each slave was to receive food rations;
- for each slave family, a good, comfortable house with one *cabannes* raised at least one foot from the ground;
- a weekly ration of salt and saltfish; and an annual quota of clothing.

Penalty in the event of default or negligence was £10; complaints were to be made to Justices of the Peace. Furthermore, each estate was required to have a hospital to provide medical care for the slaves; no slave was allowed to carry a cat-o'-nine-tails, whip, or other instrument denoting an emblem of authority.

The clothing allowance consisted of one *penistoun* or cloth jacket and three yards of *osnaburgs*, one hat, needles and thread, and a blanket once every three years; penalty for neglect was £100.

The sale of slaves' produce in the local market was rigidly controlled. When, in October 1784, markets were first re-established in the towns of Grenada, every day was market day. Later, Sunday market was abolished, and instead, Thursday was declared public market day; in December 1828, Thursday and Saturday were public market days. Any slave found selling goods on a Sunday had them confiscated. A free person guilty of the same offence was fined £5.

## How Many Slaves?

It is estimated that over 20 million Africans were transported to the New World to work as slaves on plantations. Apart from individual private traders, there were more than eight national slave trading companies, each enjoying a monopoly of trade bestowed on it by its home country; some were even financed by members of the royal family and the nobility. Britain had three national companies with a state monopoly of the slave trade at different periods of the 17th and 18th centuries; France two; the Dutch, Danes and Germans one company each. These companies were:

1. The Company of Royal (sic) Adventurers Trading to Africa, incorporated in 1663 for a period of 1,000 years (British).
2. The Royal (sic) African Company, formed in 1672 (British).
3. The British South Sea Company (British).
4. The French West India Company (French).
5. The French Guinea Company (French).
6. The Duch West India Company (Dutch).
7. The Danish West India Company (Danish).
8. The Brandenburg African Company (German).

In addition, thousands of industrial traders saw in the slave trade, and in the sugar trade, an opportunity for amassing wealth. Certain cities in Britain and France, for example Liverpool and Nantes, rose to prominence owing to the slave trade and the various monopolies enjoyed by their respective joint-stock companies. The motivating force in the trade was profits and more profits.

### *Slaves in Grenada*

Grenada shared in both French and British slave imports. It is estimated that between 1650 and 1808 the British West Indies received 1.9 million slaves, and between 1664 and 1830 the French colonies received 1.6 million. Figures on Grenada's slave imports are very fragmentary: she received 1,594 in 1763; 9,752 in the period 1784 to 1787; 2,190 in 1802–3.[14]

The heaviest importation of slaves apparently took place between 1735 and 1779, the period when sugar enjoyed its greatest prosperity and became the export crop 'par excellence' in the British West Indies, being produced on approximately 125 estates. Sugar remained the dominant crop through out the slave period. Table 8.1 records Grenada's slave population covering those years for which figures are available.

**Table 8.1 Slave Population 1700–1833[15]**

| *Year* | *Slave population* |
|---|---|
| 1700 | 525 |
| 1753 | 11,991 |
| 1779 | 35,000 |
| 1788 | 26,775 |
| 1799 | 30,000 |
| 1817 | 28,029 |
| 1820 | 26,899 |
| 1825 | 24,798 |
| 1830 | 23,878 |
| 1833 | 23,536 |

## Crop Distribution

The monoculture then characteristic of many British West Indian islands was, however, absent from Grenada, and coffee, cocoa and cotton were produced in significant quantities. Grenada's more diversified economic base ensured against an over-dependence on sugar, as Table 8.2 illustrates.

In 1805, of the 337 estates in Grenada, 36% were under sugar cultivation, 25% under cocoa, coffee and cotton; 18% cultivated provisions, and the remaining 21% consisted of wood, pasture and bush.

Two decades later, while the percentage of sugar estates remained unchanged that for coffee, cocoa and cotton fell from 18% to 16%, or from 23 to 11 cotton estates and 31 to 19 coffee estates. The number of cocoa estates remained more or less the same.

As Table 8.2 illustrates sugar was most extensively cultivated in St Andrew's followed by St Patrick's and St George's, with St Mark's as the least important sugar-growing parish. By 1824 most planters still largely depended on sugar for their livelihood. Whatever the planta-

**Table 8.2 Distribution of Estates in Grenada in 1805 and 1824**

| | *Sugar* | | *Coffee and cocoa* | | *Coffee* | | *Sugar and cotton* | | *Cotton* | | *Provisions, wood, pasture, bush* | | *Total* | |
|---|---|---|---|---|---|---|---|---|---|---|---|---|---|---|
| *Parish* | *1805* | *1824* | *1805* | *1824* | *1805* | *1824* | *1805* | *1824* | *1805* | *1824* | *1805* | *1824* | *1805* | *1824* |
| St George's | 16 | 24 | 3 | 3 | 18 | 13 | 4 | 3 | 16 | 5 | 18 | 32 | *75* | *80* |
| St John's | 14 | 11 | 7 | 8 | 4 | – | 5 | 1 | – | – | 9 | 21 | *39* | *41* |
| St Mark's | 11 | 10 | 6 | 6 | 2 | 1 | – | – | – | – | 12 | 15 | *31* | *32* |
| St Patrick's | 26 | 24 | – | – | – | – | – | – | 5 | 4 | 12 | 14 | *43* | *42* |
| St Andrew's | 43 | 40 | 3 | 3 | 5 | 4 | – | – | – | – | 43 | 44 | *94* | *91* |
| St David's | 14 | 14 | 2 | 2 | 2 | 1 | – | – | 2 | 2 | 35 | 37 | *55* | *56* |
| *Total:* | *124* | *123* | *21* | *22* | *31* | *19* | *9* | *4* | *23* | *11* | *129* | *163* | *337* | *342* |

Sources: 1805: *Grenada*, 1805. London, Cornhill R. Wilkinson, December, 1805.
1824: *Reference to the Plan of Grenada*, 1824, Garvin Smith, London, J. Miles & Co. 1882.

tion, its survival was partly dependent on demand for its produce and partly dependent upon management and organization of production.

## Layout and Organization of Work

The lands planted with sugar-cane were laid out in such a manner as to economize on transport costs, apportion task work, prevent the spread of fire, and facilitate crop rotation. It was generally divided into three to five large cane-fields, each of which was sub-divided into plots of five to 20 acres. Spaces of 12 to 18 feet were usually left between each plot to serve as a roadway for the ox-carts, which carried harvested canes to the mill. Sub-division of cane land also facilitated apportioning task-work such as holing, planting, dunging and harvesting.

Each plantation also had its provision grounds, woodlands, boiling house, distillery and grasslands. Normally, a centrally located 'works' was the main feature of the estate. On a 1,200 acre estate about one-sixth was in cane, one-eighth in pasture and three-quarters in woodland. The estate was well supplied with cattle and horses.

Over the years the system of cultivation and manufacture consisting of the sequence, vesting, crushing, boiling, curing and distilling, remained essentially unchanged. In the rainy season, from May or June to December, such agricultural operations as holing, dunging, planting, weeding, provision cultivation and maintenance work were carried out. In the dry season, from January to May, the canes were harvested, and the sugar and rum processed, the canes being cut and ground at the mill, then the cane juice boiled and clarified until it crystallized into sugar, while the molasses was generally conveyed to the Still House to be made into rum.

Trenching and holing were the two methods employed in planting the cuttings from the tops of canes. Trenching consisted of digging long trenches, in which a double row of cane cuttings were laid and then covered with soil. By the 18th century, holing was the commoner method. Holes five inches deep and five feet square were dug and one or two cane tops laid longitudinally in the centre of each hole and then covered. As the canes grew taller the hole was filled with compost and farmed into a mound. An able slave could dig about 60 to 80 holes in a ten-hour day.

The actual planting and harvesting of canes was done by three gangs on each estate: first gang, who did the heaviest work, consisted of able-bodied men and women; second, comprising older slaves, and third gang, composed of children and old female slaves, who did most of the weeding and looked after the provision ground.

When first planted in the West Indies, canes were harvested for as many as 15 years before the roots were grubbed and new cuttings planted; but in time the soil lost its fertility and the canes yielded less and less sugar. By the 1840s, therefore, there was widespread use both of imported and local fertilizers.

Between sugar planting and harvesting, corn, potatoes, peas and beans were cultivated in the provision grounds. Mill machinery, wagons, and miscellaneous equipment were repaired, and overseers directed gangs of slaves in the collection of supplies, gathering fuel and cleaning utensils.

The main apparatus of a sugar works was a three-roller cane mill, invented by a Sicilian in 1449. The roller, made of iron, stood upright and turned on pivots. Wind, water or cattle turned the middle one, which then turned the other two, each roller being filled with a cog and teeth for that purpose.

Two slaves fed the mill, one at the front inserted the canes into the rollers, the other at the back received the crushed stalks and passed them back to extract the remaining juice. In this way about 50–60% of the juice was extracted.

Boiling and clarifying the cane juice was the next operation. The juice was conveyed by means of lead pipes or a gutter to be temporarily stored in wood on stone cisterns in the boiling house. At the narrow end of the boiling house was a stone furnace into which was filled three or more copper boilers. The first and largest of these was four feet in diameter and three feet deep, the others were progressively smaller, with the

*Exterior (above) and interior (below) of an eighteenth-century West Indian boiling house*

last the 'teach' or 'tatch' measuring only 20 inches in diameter and 18 inches deep. Wood, coal and trash provided the main source of fuel.

In the boiling process, the raw juice was first conveyed from the cistern and strained in a basket lined with hair-cloth. It then went to the clarifying copper, to be boiled and stirred until the gross unctuous matter rose to the surface and was removed by a slave who operated a long-handled skimmer (wooden spoon). Lime water or 'temper' was added to the boiling liquid to speed the separation of the gross matter from the sugar liquor; this was then removed from the first copper, strained through a woollen blanket and placed in a wooden box full of holes. The slave who superintended these operations was called the boiler.

From the last boiler, the liquid sugar was cooled in wooden troughs or coolers until the surface had a sugary crust. This was then stirred, and the soft brown mass shovelled into earthen moulds of wooden hogsheads and again stirred. After standing for 13 or 14 hours the sugar cohered into a mass, the plug at the base of the moulds was then removed to allow the molasses to drain off. Steam from the coppers fouled the sugar, thus the curing process took place in a separate building – the Curing House – where the moulds were set upon earthenware pans – 'drips' – to receive the rest of the molasses. The moulds were then taken to the knocking room where they were turned upside down and the sugar removed. Each mould contained three different colours and quality of sugar: a brown top layer, a black bottom layer and a white, dry middle layer.[16]

*Planting sugar cane, West Indies (Antigua)*

We have seen how the plantation system terrorized the mind, and consumed the body of the African slave. Did slaves, then, accept their lot as the design of fate or the hand of destiny?

## Slave Resistance and the Grenada Maroons

Slaves developed many forms of resistance to the slave system. Many malingered in the field during the working day; some deliberately damaged property, burnt buildings, and killed plantation animals or treated them brutally. Many deserted the plantations and joined Maroon communities in the interiors of St John's and St Andrew's parishes. Running away, or vagrancy as it was popularly called, remained the main form of slave resistance in Grenada. By the 1790s established bands of Maroon slaves lived in Grenada; but so far no attention has been devoted to them in books. West Indian historians so far have restricted their discussion to the Jamaica Maroons and the Bush Negroes of Surinam. The impression is that the Maroon movement was confined exclusively to those territories, but this is not so.

As a result of the increasing number of slaves who successfully ran away from the plantation and remained at large, two distinct settlements developed in Grenada: one in the wooded interior of St John's parish and the other in the highlands of St Andrew's and St David's.

The Maroon settlements seem to have started towards the end of French colonial rule and to have expanded during the first three decades of British colonial rule. In 1765 Governor Robert Melville, writing to the Lords Commissioners for Trade and Plantation, mentioned the existence of runaway slaves in the hills. Later that year, writing to the planters of St John's, he described these slaves as the Grenada Maroons.[17] Who were they?

Numbering about 300, these runaway slaves inhabited the wooded mountains of Grenada in the second half of the 18th century, subsisting chiefly by depredations on cattle and provision grounds of the neighbouring estates. Their numbers were augmented by vagrant slaves from various parishes. According to Melville, soon after the constitution of Civil Government in Grenada in 1763 they became more audacious and did much damage to nearby plantations.

In 1765 Governor Melville offered them amnesty; when they refused to accept this he had two laws passed, on the 18 and 23 April 1765, authorizing their capture, trial and punishment if they persisted. Nevertheless, the Maroons continued to defy Melville and the

Government to the extent that by August 1765 the Governor feared a general Maroon uprising. He requested bayonets, muskets and cannon balls for the militia, and even suggested methods of killing Maroons to the planters, Justices of the Peace and militiamen.

By late 1765 the militia had captured many Maroons, among whom were some who had killed a Mr Farrel, an estate manager in St John's. They were punished with death, while the others captured were imprisoned. Many Maroons, nevertheless, had evaded captured by the militia and they retreated to the most inaccessible areas of Grenada.

As more and more runaway slaves joined their ranks the numbers of Maroons increased, and their sporadic acts of depredation continued. In the latter part of 1769 these were the cause of great alarm in St Andrew's. By 13 December 1770, the situation was such that Melville had to despatch an officer of the militia with 20 men to assist the inhabitants of St Andrew's, whom the Governor instructed to form groups and patrol the area in an attempt to suppress these 'internal enemies'. The Justice of the Peace in the St Andrew's area, William McIntosh, featured prominently in the organization of these activities.[18]

General sorties were carried out against the Maroons, resulting in the death of the St Andrew's group leader; many others were taken prisoner. The rest abandoned their base and retreated to St Andrew's mountains.

About this time there was great anxiety in Grenville, as it was thought that a general slave insurrection was imminent, but this never occurred. There was general unrest among the slave population, but some members of the plantocracy exaggerated this to induce enough new subjects to sign a petition summoning the Assembly. By 1771, however, tranquillity returned to Grenville.

But this was not the end of the Maroons; they appear again in the literature of the 1790s, and in 1793 they seem to have become quite active again.[19] Ninian Home, then acting Governor, sent a detachment of 30 armed slaves from various estates and six white militiamen to seek them out. Carrying food for three days, they were instructed to search every nook and cranny in the mountains. A militiaman's daily wage was then 4/1d or one dollar, but those who volunteered to seek the Maroons were paid 12/- a day plus £6 for every runaway slave or Maroon captured.[20] Bad weather prevented the detachment leaving on 26 September 1793; instead they set out to St Andrew's mountains on 17 October 1793, under the command of Lieutenant Horsford. Some Maroons were captured but most escaped, and despite persistent harassments, Maroons continued to live on in Grenada. Conceivably, by 1795 they formed part of the general rebellion against British rule, led by Fedon, for he had more than 7,000 men under arms.

The conflict with the Maroons is one example of the concept of divide and rule – of a colonial power dividing a colonized people and setting them against each other. For example, it was Black slaves who were armed and sent to track down the Maroons; the plantation slave driver was invariably a Black slave; in August 1795, during the Fedon uprising, the plantocracy recruited a Corps of Loyal Black Rangers who, commanded by a white officer, were sent to track down and kill Fedon and his men, and when the Fedon Rebellion was suppressed they were sent to track and capture runaway slaves. In May 1815, the Rangers recaptured 13 runaways; on 24 June three more were recaptured and in January 1821, a further 17, but these were only a small fraction of the many who had run away in November and December 1820. Between January and April 1821 some 67 more slaves were known to have become runaways.[21]

In many cases slaves fled Grenada, or even agreed to be abducted, so abhorrent was their enslavement. Many fell victim to dishonest men. In September 1765 23 slaves allowed themselves to be carried off by a Mulatto, D'Aurange, on the *Flag of Truce* sailing from Duquesne Bay.[22]

With the exception of the Fedon Rebellion, slave rebellions were few in Grenada; there were always rumours of slave uprisings, but none seemed to have materialized. In January 1794, acting Lieutenant-Governor, Ninian Home, arrested many Frenchmen who he believed had come to Grenada to foment trouble against the Government and to incite a slave insurrection. All militiamen in every parish, the harbour-master and customs' officers in Grenville and St George's, were put on full alert. Before martial law was declared, a French visitor, Alexandre Nevett, was imprisoned on entering Grenada and subsequently deported on suspicion of having come to foment trouble. Any sailor suspected of being in league with French emissaries was arrested and imprisoned. In January 1794 a 14-day embargo was placed on all ships in St George's harbour, and more Blacks were employed in the militia. These actions were precautions against the suspected slave insurrection.

Again in 1806 a similar insurrection in Carriacou was prevented. The Revd William Nash, whose sermons and activities had caused the slave population to become restless, was blamed for this. In 1816 slave insurrection was again feared as slaves were excited by the news of Bussa's slave insurrection in Barbados. On 24 November 1824, slaves on Duquesne Estate stopped work in protest over the driver who, contrary to an order of the Receiver, came to the field carrying a whip, with which he had struck two members of the gang and threatened to punish the rest. Immediately throwing down their tools, 23 slaves went directly to St Cyr, the residence of the Receiver, David McEwen, in order to lodge their protest.[23] Returning from St Cyr, on passing along Hermitage Estate, they saw the driver there flogging the slaves. They shouted: 'What a devil of a driver that is; if he continues flogging his master's negroes in that manner it will be his master's negroes who will bury them.'[24] The slaves' protest was investigated by McInnis and Simpson, magistrates in the area. Most of them were subsequently charged, tried and sentenced to be flogged by a specially assembled court presided over by McInnis, Simpson and Walsh, and three jurors. The Governor, reporting to the Colonial Office, described the incident as the 'Riot of Slaves on Duquesne Estate'.[25]

Slaves also managed to escape the plantations' forced labour regime by manumission. This was by way of purchasing his freedom, or the voluntary freeing of a slave by his master; in this latter case usually by will and testament. Manumission became commoner during the last two decades of slavery as the slave system was becoming increasingly uneconomic. Between 1817 and 1831, 1,226 slaves were manumitted, 443 (153 men and 290 women) between 1821 and 1825. Many women slaves were employed in an extravagant system of household management and to free them was a greater economy. According to the Registrar of Slaves at the time, most manumissions involved urban slaves. About 66% of those manumitted between 1821 and 1825 were from St George's town.

The price of manumission varied between about £300 and £26. Of 35 cases examined for 1821 to 1825, in only two cases did the fee exceed £300 (£330 and £400); in five cases it was £50 or less; in another five cases it varied between £51 and £100;[26] for the rest it was between £100 to £200. In addition to this, slaves being manumitted incurred other fees: £2.18s. to be paid to the Registrar, and £3.11s. to the Judge if the manumission was proved before him. Under the 1797 Guardian Act any person being manumitted had to receive an annunity of £10; therefore, he or she had to pay an additional £100 into the treasury, which then entitled them to the £10 annunity.[27] In 1806 the Guardian Act was amended to change the £10 annunity. In 1818 the £100 annuity payment was dropped, which explains the subsequent increase in manumission. From 1826 a record in the Registrar's office was sufficient evidence of manumission. Slaves manumitted between 1797 and 1806 continued to receive the annuity, but reduced to £4. In 1840 of the 44 persons who received pensions totalling £247, 40 had been manumitted between 1797 and 1818.[28]

## Demise of the Plantation System

The plantation system, which had dominated the economies of the West Indies since 1650, began to disintegrate in the late 18th century and this disintegration accelerated during the first three decades of the 19th century. The four factors accounting for this were:

1. The attack on West Indian monopoly by the industrial class in Britain.
2. The agitation of the humanitarians and its sequel, the anti-slavery public opinion.
3. The reform of the slave system by the Colonial Office.
4. Inexorable economic factors that made sugar production in the British West Indies expensive, inefficient and uneconomical. This process began as early as the 1780s, immediately after the War of American Independence, and, despite brief periods of recovery afterwards, continued into the 1830s and 1840s. Thus by 1830 the question was not if slavery would be abolished but when it would be abolished.

The abolition of the slave trade in 1807, of slavery in 1833 and protectionism in 1846 were all inseparably connected.[29] The vested interests built by the slave system had now turned around to destroy that system. British industrialists wanted an abundant supply of cheap sugar and scorned attempts to keep cheaper sugar off the British market, to kill competition, and to protect high-cost producers in the British West Indies.

On 4 May 1821 'the Manchester Chamber of Commerce presented a petition to the House of Commons deprecating a preference to one colony over another and in particular, a preference to a settlement of slaves over a nation of free men.'[30] In 1833, Manchester, through Mark Phillips, its representative in Parliament, advocated the admission of Brazilian sugar for refining.

Opposition to slavery also developed in the British industrial centre of Birmingham, and spread to Sheffield, the centre of the steel industry. In 1825 the people of Sheffield boycotted consumption of West Indian sugar and urged that East Indian sugar should replace it; this was intended to force Parliament to import East Indian sugar on the same terms as West Indian. In 1833 the Sheffield Anti-Slavery Society passed a motion calling for immediate and total emancipation instead of piecemeal freedom.[31] At the same time anti-mercantilist literature began to appear, condemning forced labour and showing the advantage of free labour. The popularization of books by Condor,

Hodgson and Naish[32] demonstrate why, by 1833, most industrialists were advocating an end to slavery.

In 1831, sugar refiners complained against both excessive duties on foreign sugar and West Indian monopoly. As a result Parliament passed annual acts to admit Brazilian and Cuban sugar into the British market, but for refining and re-export only. The refiners, however, remained dissatisfied, complaining that the West Indian monopoly was ruining their trade. Ironically, British capitalism was now biting the hand that fed it! When they depended on West Indian sugar, British capitalists ignored, and even defended, slavery, but once the West Indian monopoly became a hindrance to the expansion of their production and trade they were ready to use slavery as a first step to destroy that monopoly.

In 1820, the merchants of London and Glasgow presented a petition to Parliament demanding free trade, arguing that it was best for industry and commerce. In the same year the Glasgow Chamber of Commerce demanded that all restrictions on free trade be removed. The West Indian monopoly, they complained, was unprofitable and cost the British public £1.5 million to support it.[33]

The industrialists' position on the slavery issue gave support to the Anti-Slavery Society, a body formed in 1823 to fight for the mitigation and gradual abolition of slavery. Prominent on its list of agitators were Thomas Clarkson, James Ramsey and James Stephen, Snr, who succeeded in raising anti-slavery sentiments in Britain almost to the level of fanaticism. The movement was formed partly owing to the death of Smith, in British Guiana in 1823, the attacks on Shrewsbury in Barbados, and the vicious and violent campaign against Knibb in Jamaica. In all cases the malefactors were West Indian sugar planters who saw in these men threats to the security of their sugar interests. The main organ of the movement was the *Anti-slavery Reporter*, edited by Zachary Macaulay; this and some ten other newspapers[34] disseminated their aims and activities and exposed the evils of the plantation system. Between 1824 and 1833 their work helped to catalyse the passage of the 1833 Emancipation Act.

One immediate result of the Society's work was the British government's decision to liberalize the slave system, and accordingly, in 1823, they sent out their amelioration proposals, which were almost immediately implemented in the Crown Colonies of Trinidad and St Lucia but in those islands with Assemblies implementation was delayed. These proposals recommended to the West Indian governments: that the flogging of women be abolished; flogging of men be restrained; Sunday labour be prohibited; that a protector of slaves be appointed, and that slave's evidence be admitted in courts of law. The same period saw the removal of certain civil disabilities from the Free Blacks and Coloureds.

The most severe blow struck against the plantation system was the emergence of certain economic factors before which it was powerless.

The first was the effect of the War of American Independence on British West Indian economies. Eric Williams, in *Columbus to Castro*, concluded that this War caused starvation in the West Indies in the short run and ruination in the long run.[35] West Indians suffered both from the depredations of privateers who swarmed the area and from a shortage of supplies. The number of ships trading in the region fell by some 100 as Table 8.3 shows.

Insurance on produce-laden ships increased by some 23%, and freight rates soared, increasing by 25% in 1776 and doubling by 1781.[36] Duties on West Indian exports were almost doubled after the War. The shortage of goods and increased costs of insurance and transport led to a spiralling inflation during and after the War. In most cases prices rose by 100%, sometimes higher. The closing of the American markets and fewer freighters annually leaving for the British market increased the planters' hardships by the disastrous effects on the volume of exports (see Table 8.4).

'The decade 1783–93' according to Regatz, 'brought no relief to the planters; large numbers fell beneath the weight of accumulated distress.'[37] Between 1777 and 1791, in Jamaica, once the largest sugar-producing British West Indian colony, 30% of the estates went bankrupt; between 1799 and 1801, 65 plantations were abandoned

**Table 8.3 Sugar Trade Vessels 1774–78[38]**

| *Year* | *No. of vessels* | *Casks of sugar exported* |
|---|---|---|
| 1774–5 | 354 | 131,778 |
| 1775–6 | 329 | 115,571 |
| 1776–7 | 299 | 100,302 |
| 1777–8 | 243 | 76,700 |

**Table 8.4 Exports 1776 and 1780[39]**

| *Crop* | *1776* | *1780* |
|---|---|---|
| Cocoa | 653,000 lbs | 444,000 lbs |
| Coffee | 5,179,114 lbs | 2,075,600 lbs |
| Sugar | 1,656,624 cwts | 1,300,057 cwts |
| Rum | 3,341,020 galls | 1,617,808 galls[38] |

and 32 were sold under decrees of the Court of Chancery, and by 1807 there were suits pending against 115 estates. In 1808 a British Parliamentary Committee wrote: 'The West Indian planter is fast approaching crisis; nothing but inevitable ruin can be the consequence.' In 1832 another British Parliamentary Select Committee set up to inquire into economic conditions in the West Indies reported: 'Considerable distress had existed in the British West Indies for the past ten years greatly aggravated in the last three or four'.

Clearly, the plantation system was in decay and nothing could save it. The main mode of production – slavery – was proving to be too expensive; many slaves were unproductive; domestics numbered 13% throughout the British West Indies. Williams wrote: 'combined with a system of large estate owners the B.W.I had become a system of household management rather than a commercial plantation.' In Grenada, once productive estates were either abandoned or neglected. In 1805, 14, and by 1824, 18 of the 80 estates in St George's had become either bush, wood or pasture; of St Andrew's 97 estates, 22 were abandoned in 1824; of St David's 56, 28 were abandoned in 1805 and three more by 1824. Of Grenada's 342 estates in 1824, 86 were in bush and pasture.

The steady rise of international competition in the sugar trade also placed great pressures on British West Indian producers, who were slowly being pushed out of their traditional market. Between 1817 and 1831 British imports of sugar from Cuba increased 28 times; between 1827 and 1833 sugar imports from Singapore increased 6 times; they quadrupled from the Philippines and increased 22 times from Java.

The rapid increase in imports led prices both to fluctuate and decline, thus adversely affecting the West Indian producers who were now becoming high-cost producers. From 52/- per cwt in 1792 the price of sugar fell to 40/- in 1801; by 1814 it was 91/- per cwt, and by 1831, 24/4d (see Table 8.5).

**Table 8.5 Sugar Price Fluctuations 1792–1831**

| *Year* | *Price per cwt** |
|---|---|
| 1792 | 52/- |
| 1795–96 | 65/- |
| 1801 | 40/- to 30/- |
| 1814 | 91/- |
| 1820 | 33/- |
| 1831 | 24/4d |

* Excluding duty

The average Grenadian producer needed a price of 50/- to make a reasonable profit, but the Cuban producer needed only about 30/- to make a much larger profit. The Cubans produced sugar for at least 22/9d per cwt less than the most efficient West Indian producers. For the Grenadian sugar planter a price of 22/- per cwt meant losses and bankrúptcy. The 1808 British Parliamentary Committee had already indicated this. They stated that their investigations showed that in 1799 the average West Indian producer made profits of 10/9d per cwt, increasing in 1803 to 18/6d, but falling to zero by 1806.

In 1831, one of the best sugar estates in Grenada, producing about 100 hogshead (1,500 cwt) of sugar, and 40 puncheons of rum, made a profit of some £500 – then considered to be excellent. Twenty years before the estate could have been sold for £20,000, in 1831 if it fetched £5,000, it was lucky. This estate had 150 slaves, at a cost of over £1,000 per annum; its manager was paid £200; attorney's commission was £241; and, in 1831, its total expenses amounted to £3,017, against a total revenue £3,521. It made zero profits on the sugar side of its operations and only its revenues on rum provided its profits.

Between 1793 and 1829 some 60 financial houses which provided credit to West Indian producers went into liquidation, and ten more in 1831. The West Indian House of Manning and Anderdon, one of the foremost financial houses, suspended payments in July 1831. Debts outstanding to it totalled £374,372, with those of the West Indian estates alone amounting to some £224,000.[40]

## Reform of the System

With the disintegration of the plantation system in the 1820s, there was a simultaneous improvement in the conditions of life of the slave, and a liberalization of the system. Abolition in 1807 had forced the planters to care for whatever labour force they had or face acute labour shortage. In the 1820s positive steps were taken to increase the slave labour population. In Grenada, prizes were offered at the Agricultural Society's annual 'Ploughing Match' to the three mothers with the most slave children under 12 years of age. The mother with the most healthy children under 12 received a prize of £4 10s; the next received £36s and the third largest £25s. The Ploughing Match was a social festival for the plantocracy and was followed by a meal of turkeys, accompanied by wines, and dancing. It was rotated annually from estate to estate, and in 1826 was held on Paradise Estate. In that year, Jane Clair, a slave woman on Thuilleries Estate won the first

*Slaves dancing to their own music*

prize; Sylvia, on Mt Horne Estate, the second; and Derone, on Grand Bras Estate, the third prize.[41] By this means planters encouraged slave women to have large families.

In 1823 Lord Bathurst instructed the Legislatures in the British West Indies to pass laws ameliorating the slaves' conditions. Partly as a result of this, in 1825, the Grenadian Legislature passed an act consolidating all the slave laws then in force. It was now permissible to baptize and instruct slaves in the principles of the Christian religion; in the 18th century this had been forbidden. The work-day, from 5 a.m. to 7 p.m. was to include a half-hour break for breakfast and, from 12 midday to 2 p.m., a two-hour break for lunch. It was now illegal for masters to discharge old slaves on account of sickness, or to allow them to wander about seeking subsistence, on pain of a fine of £50. Punishments exceeding 15 lashes were to be administered in the presence of a free person and not more than 25 lashes were to be given on any one day; violation of this law carried a penalty of £10. Women slaves with five or more children were to be given 52 days each year to cultivate their own grounds. Children could no longer be separated from their parents nor was it permissible to separate married slaves. Laws were later passed admitting slave evidence in court cases involving other slaves and then, in all cases.

Both the Earl of Bathurst, Colonial Secretary, and Governor Sir George Murray were reasonably satisfied with the measures taken in Grenada to ameliorate slave conditions. On 25 October Bathurst wrote:

> Although after a full consideration of the Grenada Act I cannot but be sensible that it falls short of what has been recommended yet it deserves to be considered as an important improvement of the existing code.[42]

Sir George Murray commended the conduct of the Legislative Council and the Assembly in having adopted several measures for the amelioration of slaves by 1828. But it must be noted that what was written in law was often not adhered to by the planters.

In Grenadian society at large, many organizations were formed to advance the religious and social life of the slaves at this time. Most of these were under the auspices of the Church of England, which had openly supported slavery throughout the slave period. One such organization was the Society for the Education of the Poor, formed in 1824 with the Governor as chief patron, and including among its members ministers of the Church of England, prominent Assemblymen and planters. The Society started the Central School St George's for the children of Free Blacks and Coloureds. A Society for the Promotion of Christian Knowledge was founded in 1826, comprised of prominent members of the ruling and propertied class.[43] The Grenada District Committee for the conversion and religious instruction and education of the Negro slaves, was also formed in 1826, with the Governor as its chief patron, and membership similar to that of the previous body.

## The Churches' Role

Two years after Grenada was returned to Britain in 1783 laws were passed locally to provide salaries for Church of England ministers. In 1807 the Government divided Grenada into two Church of England benefices: the parish of St Mark, St John and St George, and the parish of St David, St Andrew and St Patrick. The Rector of each parish was paid £600 per annum by the Government; each parish also had a clerk and a sexton, each paid £100 per annum. In 1813 the Vestry of St George's was created, with full power and authority to regulate and direct all acts and matters related to the said town and parish of St George as far as it concerned the operation of the Anglican Church. The Vestry was composed of members of the Council, and members of the Assembly resident in the town and in the combined parishes of St George and St John, and the Rector of the parish.[44]

Control of the secular life of the Church of England in Grenada was in the hands of the politicians and the plantocracy. In 1825, in order to involve the Church more closely in the religious and social life of the slaves and people, the two benefices were divided into four: St George town and parish, St John and St Mark; St Patrick and St David and St Andrew. The number of Rectors was then increased to four at £660 per annum each, plus a housing allowance of £100 for those living outside St George. Thus with the liberalization of the plantation system under economic pressure, the Church of England, one of the pillars of that system, responded accordingly. In 1828 the Government granted a salary of £660 to the Roman Catholic priests in Grenada, and in 1832, to the Presbyterian ministers.[45] Thus, towards the end of the slave system all the clergy in Grenada were paid servants of the state. These clergymen now visited estates each week to instruct slaves.

From 1824, the children of the Free Blacks and Coloureds received religious instruction in the General School of St George's, and by 1828 128 such children were being taught. Every Sunday, between 9 a.m. and 10.30 a.m., the Catechist, headteacher and the four monitors of the Central School provided similar instruction to some 150 of the town's slaves. Additionally, the Catechist visited the estates in St George's parish to instruct slave children whom the manager assembled; on some estates even the managers assisted with the instructions.

The parish of St John and St Mark had their own Catechist, who on three days of the week ran a school in Charlotte Town for about 50 children, and visited estates in the parish to instruct the slaves and their children, on the other days.[46] The St David's and St Andrew's Catechist migrated to Antigua in 1828. Instructions were given by the proprietors and managers, or members of their families on estates not visited by a Catechist. On two estates, owned by the Honourable George Gun-Munroe, chapels were built and divine service held regularly.

According to an Anglican rector in Grenada at this time, the main barriers to the Church of England's programme of religious instruction were the Roman Catholic religion and patois. As many as 8% of the slave population and 65% of Free Coloureds were Roman Catholics.

In 1828 there was one Roman Catholic priest in Grenada; he celebrated three services each Sunday, at a central point in each of the three most populous areas of Grenada, with one sermon in French and two in English. He devoted two hours daily to catechetical work with the assistance of persons at his request. An average of 1,500–2,000 slaves received instructions from him. At the Sunday School, in St

George's, where he resided, some 304 children were taught, in both French and English, by eight men and eight women.

The reforms of the 1820s did not procure any revolutionary advance in the conditions of the slaves. Concessions, rather than changes, were made by the planter class; since they were simultaneously slave owners and law-makers they did not necessarily adhere to the letter of the law. Any judge who operated impartially was ostracized by the planters. For example, in the 1820s Chief Justice Bent battled with the plantocracy for three years – 1829–32. He and Father O'Hannon, the Roman Catholic priest, were close friends and popular among the slaves, Blacks and Free Coloureds for their frequent condemnation of the injustices of the ruling class.

In 1829 the President of the Council, Andrew Houston, suspended Chief Justice Bent because he persisted in summoning before him, under the Vagabond Act the Roman Catholic Vicar-General Le Goff and two other priests sent from Trinidad by Bishop McDonnel to replace Father O'Hannon. Although reinstated by the Secretary of State in November, Bent was suspended again, in April 1830, on a series of charges. Lord Goderich referred his case to the Privy Council, which in 1832, directed that he be reinstated, but the Secretary of State offered him the post of a Puisne Judge in Trinidad instead.

Bent's implacable criticism and exposure of their vile practices did not endear him to the plantocracy. Writing to Lord Goderich, on 25 January 1831, the Governor said that peace and tranquillity would never be restored to this once happy and united colony as long as Bent was allowed to preside on the bench of justice.[47]

## Free Blacks and Coloureds

During this period of liberalization the Free Blacks and Coloureds (3,318 in 1821, and 3,456 in 1824) demanded and received improvements in their social and political status. They were concentrated in the town of St George's as the figures in Table 8.6 (page 112) illustrate.

By 1828 there were 3,748 (1,507 males, 2,236 females) and, two years later 4,033, or close to 15% of Grenada's population.

On 19 December 1823, legislation was passed which bestowed upon them some of the rights enjoyed by white men.[48] These included:

1. That Free Blacks and Coloureds would receive the same penalty as Whites for unlawful practice as surgeons. The existing penalty (corporal punishment) for the Free Blacks and Coloureds was repealed.

**Table 8.6 Free Blacks and Coloureds 1821–24**

| | *1821* | *1822* | *1823* | *1824* |
|---|---|---|---|---|
| Town of St George's | 1,895 | 1,849 | 1,859 | 1,908 |
| Parish of St George | 316 | 307 | 366 | 285 |
| St John's | 177 | 203 | 241 | 271 |
| St Mark's | 87 | 92 | 94 | 107 |
| St Patrick's | 118 | 133 | 123 | 126 |
| St Andrew's | 303 | 305 | 290 | 326 |
| St David's | 185 | 193 | 189 | 211 |
| Carriacou | 237 | 262 | 226 | 252 |
| | *3,318* | *3,344* | *3,388* | *3,456* |

Source: *Home Correspondence*, Campbell to Bathurst, HO.65, 7 April 1826

2. Imposing a penalty of £20 for arson caused by negligence or careless behaviour. Formerly, the slaves and Free Blacks received the same punishment.
3. Imposing a penalty of £5 for stealing cows, plantains, etc. Formerly – as for slaves – the penalty was corporal punishment.
4. The right to serve summons on members of the Council and Assembly; formerly limited to Whites.
5. Giving the vote to all, conditional upon the qualifications outlined in the Election Act, and provided that the candidate was white.
6. The admission of evidence of two capable Free Coloured and Free Black witnesses as adequate for a person's conviction in court. Formerly, convictions were based on the evidence of two credible white witnesses.

Despite this the Free Coloured and Black population continued to be debarred from political office being still unable to stand as candidates at elections. In 1830, they were still dissatisfied with their status, and sent a letter to the Colonial Office complaining that:

1. The man of colour is most cruelly and unjustly held forth as an inferior being stigmatized and degraded by the local law and customs.
2. They were excluded from all civil rank and honour, these being open to Whites alone, many of whom had no personal merit.
3. Civil magistrates are exclusively Whites.
4. The Legislature was entirely confined to Whites.

In the same year, they voiced their grievances in a letter to the House of Commons. They complained that: although they possessed two-thirds of the property in the town; formed the greatest percentage of the free population; and their numbers filled the rank and file of the militia, their class was consigned to an inferior position; holding no rank in the militia; excluded from the Grand Jury and all offices of interest, except petty jurors and constables, lately granted more as a relief to Whites rather than a boon to the Free Blacks and Coloureds; and that they were not allowed to have a representative in the Legislature although the most uneducated Whites had recently been gaining seats on the Assembly.

In 1831, the Free Coloureds led by Frances Danglade, a Free Coloured woman, rioted through the streets of St George's in a demonstration against the inequities of their class and in open defiance of the magistrate. As a result Frances Danglade was imprisoned for 10 days, and later the Secretary of State was informed of the incident.[49]

On 22 December 1832, the local legislature was advised to pass laws, abolishing all civil and political disabilities from the Free Blacks and Coloureds. Thus they were allowed to give evidence, in all cases, and given the right to elect their own representatives to the Assembly and to be members of the Grand Jury.

## Officials and their Ownership of Slaves

During the slave period, many public officers, politicians and members of the clergy owned slaves, and few were prepared to liberate or manumit them; in fact, most of them continued to own slaves until 1833, including George Gun-Munroe who held the post of Assistant Judge and owned 3,317.[50]

Since these influential men were deeply involved in the sugar and slave business, any relaxation of the harshness of plantation life, and any improvements in the legal and constitutional status of the slaves, was obviously as a result of economic realities and not of political altruism.

NOTES

Full citations only given where work does not appear in the Bibliography.

1. Devas, *History of Grenada*, p. 85 and Ch. 10.
2. The St George's regiment consisted of 21 officers and 389 non-commissioned officers and privates; the St John's – 14 officers and 70 NCOs and privates; St Andrew's – 15 officers and 94 NCOs; St David's – 15 officers and 68 NCOs; Carriacou – 11 officers and 68 NCOs. In addition, there were troops of Light Dragoons consisting of 7 officers and 29 NCOs and 2 officers and 25 NCOs of the Loyal Black Rangers.
3. *Martin's British Colonies*, p. 47.
4. *Laws of Grenada 1763–1835* 'An Act for the better government of slaves', No. IV,

10 December 1766, p. 4; 'An Act to make slaves etc. real estate of inheritance', No. IX, 29 April 1766, p. 10.

5. Ibid. 'An Act for preventing and punishing those who shall wilfully fire, burn, or destroy canes, dwelling houses or any other edifices' No. XVI, 3 April, 1770, p. 19.
6. Ibid. 'An Act for empowering and appointing Commissioners ... to erect a cage in Carriacou' No. XL, 7 April 1785, p. 88; also No. LVI, 24 October 1879, p. 118.
7. Ibid. ... 'An Act to consolidate all the laws now in force relating to the slave population; 26 April 1825, p. 323.
8. *Grenada Free Press and Public Gazette*, Vol. ix, No. 500, 9 September 1835.
9. *Laws of Grenada*, 'An Act for the good government of servants' No. XVII, 30 April 1770, p. 21.
10. R.T. Smith, 'Social Stratification', p. 230.
11. Ibid.
12. Mannix, *Black Cargoes*, p. 129.
13. *Laws of Grenada*, 'An Act to consolidate ... laws'; The ration was 1/4 pound salt, 2 pounds saltfish and provision of 1/r acre of land.
14. Deerr, *History of Sugar*, Vol. II.
15. Ibid.
16. Sheridan, *Sugar and Slavery*, pp. 108–18.
17. *Letter Book 1765–66*, 'Melville to the Lord Commissioners', 13 September 1765.
18. Ibid. 1770, December 1770.
19. Ibid. 1793, 16 September 1765.
20. Ibid.
21. *St George's Chronicle and Grenada Gazette*.
22. *Letter Book, 1765–66,* 14 May 1765.
23. *Home Correspondence 1814–31*, 'Report of Board of Council on care of Duquesne Negros', Campbell to Bathurst, 31 May 1826.
24. Ibid.
25. Ibid.
26. *Grenada Free Press and Public Gazette*, Vol. 1, No. 4, 28 September 1826.
27. *Home Correspondence*, 'Return of Manumission within Government of Grenada', 24 December 1824.
28. *Laws of Grenada*, 'An Act to Repeal the Guardian Act' No. XCVI, 25 October 1806.
29. *Blue Book*, 1840.
30. Williams, *Capitalism and Slavery*, p. 156.
31. Ibid. p. 155.
32. Josiah Condor, *Wages or the Whip*, 1833; Adam Hodgson, *Letters to J.B. Say on the Expenses of Slave Labour and Free*, 1823; William Naish, *Advantages of Free Labour over Slaves.*
33. Williams, *Capitalism and Slavery* p. 156.
34. These other papers included: *Wesleyan Methodist*; *Missionary Herald*; *Edinburgh Review*; *Gentleman's Magazine*; *Monthly Review*.
35. Williams, *From Columbus to Castro*.
36. Ragatz, *Statistics*, p. 10.
37. Ragatz, *Rise and Fall*, p. 190.
38. Ragatz, *Rise and Fall*, p. 145.
39. Ibid. pp. 14–19.
40. Richard Sheridan, 'The West Indian Sugar Crisis'.
41. *Free Press and Public Gazette*, Vol. 1, No. 8, 8 October 1826; also, Vol. 1, No. 14.
42. Ibid. Vol. X, No. 282, 6 July 1836.
43. *Free Press and Public Gazette*, Vol. IX, No. 475, 1835. For example, Felix Palmer, Robert Newbold, Archibald Armstrong, Owsley Rowley, Henry Otway, William Snagg, Richard Gibbs, R.O. Smith, John Briscoe Gaff, Joseph Garraway, Robert McBurnie, Lewis Hoyes and J.C. Baker, all members of the Assembly, Council or colonial officials.
44. *Laws of Grenada* 'An Act to amend parts of an Act for providing a support for clergy of this government', No. CXXII, 8 March 1813, p. 277.

45. Ibid. 'An Act for granting a salary to Rev O'Hannan R.C. Clergyman', No. CXCIV, 24 November 1828, p. 366; 'An Act to provide a stipend for the clergyman of the Presbyterian Church' No. CCXLII, 21 December 1832, p. 1. (Supplementary laws.)
46. *Home Correspondence*, No. 14, J.C. Baker to Cambell, 10 December 1828.
47. Chief Justice Bent condemned many planters for ill-treating slaves, including: McEwen of St Cyr who ordered his slaves to be beaten for crossing a hill to make a complaint; the owner of Hope Valley who refused medicine to a slave whose leg had been chopped off, asserting he was a burden, and threatened to punish him because he could not bury a dead donkey owing to his disability. Accoring to Bent, the House of Assembly maligned him and accused him of improper conduct because he was uncompromising in such cases and imposed heavy penalties on the culprits. He reprimanded Magistrate Todd who attended a party held by some Coloureds in Carriacou solely in order to insult them and drive them from the house which a White resident had lent them. Bent was gratified that, instead, the Coloureds insulted Todd. Governor Campbell in a letter in March 1831 accused Bent of attending dinner parties with the lowest classes, and that at one of these two of Campbell's own negroes were present. Clearly, Bent's liberal behaviour was unacceptable to Grenada's ruling class. Bent even criticized the President of the Council, Andrew Houston, condemning his immorality and accused him of allowing his Coloured daughters to be concubines of his close friends – the Provost Marshal and his Aide-de-Camp. Bent wrote: 'There is no father with any feelings of religion ... who would not scorn the man who sanctioned the seduction and concubinage of his daughters as did the late Andrew Houston ...' (*Home Correspondence*, No. 14, J.C. Baker to Campbell, 10 December 1828).

    After his death, the House of Assembly voted funds to erect a monument to Houston's memory. Bent said he hoped this was for the same reason that there was a buoy on the Goodwin Sands – to enable others to avoid such conduct.

    The persecution of Bent showed that principled and impartial justice, even during the liberalization period, was intolerable to the plantocracy.
48. *Laws of Grenada*, No. CLIV, 19 December 1823.
49. *Grenada Free Press*. No. 226, 25 May 1831.
50. Owsley Rowley, Colonial Secretary and member of the Assembly owned 1,000; George Paterson, President of His Majesty's Council, 314; the Revd W. Sealey, Rector of St John's and St Mark's, 4; Rev M. Nash, Rector of Carriacou, 3; and Francis Mahon, Rector of the town of St George's, 15.

    The ministers of religion owned domestics, whereas the colonial officers owned domestic and plantation slaves. In 1830 all eight members of the Executive Council owned slaves: George Paterson, 314; John Berkley, 580; Owsley Rowley, 1,000; Archibald Armstrong, 135; George McLean, 979; Matthew Davies, 30; David Gibbs, 5; and John Hoyes, 220.

# 9

# *Emancipation and Apprenticeship*

## Emancipation

In sending out the Amelioration proposals the Colonial Office had hoped the West Indian Legislatures would use them to improve the lot of the slaves significantly. The half-way measures adopted by many colonies and the perfunctory manner in which these were implemented greatly disappointed the Colonial Office. As a result, in 1831, the House of Commons forthwith proceeded to devise means to abolish slavery throughout the British Empire.

Realizing the British government's policy towards slavery was now changing, the West Indians called all West Indian Assemblies to a congress, to be held in Barbados in February 1831, to discuss the impending question of Emancipation. Representatives attended from Barbados, Antigua, St Kitts, Nevis, Virgin Islands, Dominica, Demerara and Essequibo, Tobago, and St Vincent; Grenada's representatives were Robert Stronach and John Hoyes. A committee, chaired by John Hoyes, was appointed to draw up a memorandum to be sent to the British government. The text of the petition subsequently sent to the British government was as follows:

These colonies are now, and have been for some time past, labouring under multiplied difficulties and embarrassment.

1. War duties are still in existence 15 years after the war.
2. Advantage is given to foreign cultivators of sugar by their continuation of the Slave Trade.
3. The anti-slavery society and its activities would bring ruin and destruction to property; and we protest against any spoliation of or interference with our private propery.

4. The consequences of the Slave Trade are not now to be charged against the character of the West Indian colonists whose principal share in the transaction has been that of civilizing and bringing to order and comparative comfort persons brought into the colonies in a state of barbarism.
5. The existence of slavery and of property in or connected with and depending upon slaves in the West Indies having been thus created by Great Britain for her objects and benefit and having recognized and guaranteed by repeated Acts of Parliament and decisions of the highest law authorities, any attempt to injure or destroy property so sanctioned is a gross violation of every principle of law and justice, unless full and complete indemnification for all losses which may arise and all injuries which may be sustained by any changes in such property shall have been previously provided at the expense of the nation in general.[1]

The fifth clause of the petition indicated that the West Indian planters would be willing to accept Emancipation provided they were compensated for the loss of their property, that is, slaves. This was a far cry from their attitudes in the 1820s.

Grenada's planters were hostile to the intentions of the British government. At a public meeting of planters held on 29 June 1831, the chairman advised the colonists to resist to the utmost of their power any interference with, or injury to, their property. At that meeting, the planters passed three resolutions. One intimated that slavery could be abolished, as it existed in name only, but at the expense of the nation. The second called for full compensation to slave proprietors and all others who depended on slaves for a livelihood, as Emancipation, they said, would be followed by total ruin. The third suggested possible secession of Grenada from England. They demanded that 'they be absolved from all national obligation and left to look for other protectors who may appreciate the value of possessions which have contributed so much to British wealth and power.'[2]

The question of secession was again raised at a public meeting of planters and merchants on 5 July 1831. Those present resolved that, as the planters had been driven to the verge of desperation by gradual encroachments upon the island's institutions and domestic privileges, it was incumbent upon them to protect themselves.

If we are continually to be considered as aliens and outcasts; if our local privileges are forever to be disregarded, our constitutional rights trodden underfoot and the hard-earned produce of our estates fettered with rigorously unequal and ruinous imposition; if no merit is to be conceded to us for what we have effected in improving the moral conditions of our slaves; if by the measures which have already been put into force and others which ministers have declared in Parliament it is their purpose to adopt, we are in consequence to be more and more laid open to injustice and injury, and may even be exposed to imminent danger of our lives, and that without the smallest compensation being made to us, then the ties by which we are bound to the Mother Country must be considered as virtually severed and the duty of allegiance at an end.[3]

One of the most ardent advocates of secession was the planter James McQueen. He accused the Anti-Slavery Society of making the British electorate political slaves and of deliberately planning to destroy West Indian plantations. Despite all this the Emancipation issue had become part of British government's policy and the question was not whether slavery would be abolished but when and how.

Of the many plans for Emancipation drawn up and drafted by Colonial Office officials and Whig politicians – some as early as 1832 – three need special mention: one by Henry Taylor, legal clerk in the Colonial Office; another by Viscount Howick, and a third by Lord Stanley.

According to Taylor's plan, drafted in 1832, slaves were to be given Monday and Tuesday of each week; these days to be bought from him by his master, and, from the wages earned on these two days, the slave could buy a third day. Thus day by day other working days could be bought, thus a slave's freedom would be obtained.[4] The main weakness of Taylor's plan was that the slave would be half-free, half-slave; the psychological adjustment necessary to being a slave for three days a week and a free man for two was enormous. Taylor's plan also made no provision for the young, the aged, the sick and the disabled.

Howick's plan, drafted in 1833 and submitted to Cabinet in the same year by Lord Goderich, Secretary of State for the Colonies, proposed full emancipation, but recommended as a concomitant to Emancipation a tax of 40/- per acre on land cultivated for food. The object of the land tax was to prevent the newly emancipated from becoming peasants, and also, to enforce their dependence upon estate labour for a livelihood. Moreover, this tax on land was to be deducted from wages on estates. Each island's parishes were to be sub-divided into districts, each with a new police force or military establishment, to enforce the new regulations. Every labourer who left his district, except to go to church or market, was to be considered a vagabond and stiff penalties imposed. Absenteeism, slackness, insubordination, insolence, drunkenness, ill-use of cattle and the careless use of fire were also to be severely punishable. Howick's plan, criticized by Governors in the West Indies, members of the Anti-Slavery Society and fellow politicians, as reckless, violent and unrealistic, was rejected.[5]

Lord Stanley's plan, presented to the House of Commons on 14 May 1833, was in the form of six resolutions. One called for the freeing of all slave children under six years; all others were to be apprenticed until the age of 20 for females and 24 for males. Other slaves were to give three-quarters of a week as free labour to the planters, and be free to do personal work for the other quarter. Apprentices were to be under contract for 12 years; another resolution required Parliament to loan £15 million to the planters. Finally, District Magistrates were to be sent out to protect the freed men and to preserve peace. This plan was subsequently amended and provided the basis for formulating the Imperial Emancipation Act. The most important amendments included decreasing the apprenticeship period from 12 to 6 years and converting the £15 million loan into a compensation grant to the planters of £20 million.[6]

The Emancipation Act which was passed by Parliament was sent to the respective colonies with instructions that it be used as a guide to enable each Colonial Legislature to draw up its own corresponding Emancipation Act. No Legislature was to deviate from the principles embodied in the Imperial Act. The Colonial Legislatures were to draw up detailed regulations to govern the conduct of apprentices and the duties of Stipendiary Magistrates.

This was one of the salient weaknesses of the Imperial measure. As one historian wrote:

> It was a fatal flaw in the apprenticeship scheme that while it was based on one theory much of its operation had been left at the mercy of men who believed in and had recently practised a theory entirely different.[7]

The planters' legal advisers urged the Assemblies to take advantage of their legislative privileges to incorporate into their respective Emancipation Acts the strongest vagrancy laws and coercive enactments. Loitering upon a plantation in Barbados, according to the Barbados Act, was punishable by one month's imprisonment; in Jamaica, anyone threatening to run away from a plantation, on the evidence of one witness, could be imprisoned for one week by a Justice of the Peace; an act of vagrancy was defined in St Kitts as spreading false rumours or committing an act of insubordination, and conviction carried a penalty of 60 lashes or six weeks' imprisonment; in Dominica, making noise in the street constituted an act of vagrancy; in Nevis, an apprentice could have received as many as 90 lashes for any one offence; in Grenada, deliberate refusal to work, or peddling, huckstering or hawking without licence was considered vagrancy, and the offender was punished with one month's hard labour.[8] As George Stephen said:

> The apprentice remained an unemancipated prisoner on the estate to which he was attached, substantially liable to the same punishments and labouring under the same incapacity as before; the whip followed him at every step, hard labour at every turn.[9]

It would soon become evident that the law that ended slavery did not emancipate the slave. Slavery disappeared as a legal system, but it continued as a general system of industry. The apprenticeship system, which superseded slavery in 1834 and lasted until 1838, was nothing more than a form of neo-slavery.

In Grenada, the local Emancipation Act was passed on 11 March 1834, under the title of 'An Act for Carrying Into Effect the Provisions of an Act of the Imperial Parliament of Great Britain for the Abolition of Slavery'.[10] This law governed the social and economic relations of apprentices and planters in Grenada for the next four years.

For the purpose of administering the apprenticeship system Grenada was divided into six districts, with a police force in each, consisting of one special justice, one sergeant and ten privates. The gaols and cages in every parish were divided into apartments for male and female prisoners with separate stocks, cells for solitary confinement and machinery for labour. In each parish, there was also a culprit gang, composed of such apprentices who were confined to imprisonment with hard labour by the special justice.

The Act also stipulated that apprentices imprisoned with hard labour had either to work on the treadmill, or under some mark of disgrace on the plantations, or in cleaning, widening, mending or repairing public streets, roads and highways within the district.

Special magistrates were to go to any plantation in their district upon the application of the person in charge of the plantation, or of any apprentice, for the purpose of investigating complaints. They were required to keep journals in which they entered cases brought before them, and to provide relevant details of all cases from the date of the complaint to the decision taken and its implementation. If, however, a complaint was dismissed as frivolous, vexatious or malicious, an apprentice was to be whipped or imprisoned, but an employer was to pay a fine not exceeding £4.

The Act placed apprentices into three categories: praedial attached, praedial unattached and non-praedials. Each apprentice was registered in his or her respective category.

Apprentices were to receive an annual allowance of six yards of cloth or *pennistoun*, eight yards of *osnaburg*, and one hat or cap; triennial allowance of one blanket, a weekly allowance of two pounds of salted, dried or pickled fish. Where no provision grounds were provided, each apprentice was to receive eight pints of flour or six quarts of meal or grain weekly. If food was not provided, money equal to the marketable value of the food was to be given. Negligence of or refusal to provide these allowances was to carry a fine of £5 plus the value of the allowances. If provision grounds were granted, the labourers had to be given 14 full days over and above holidays and non-working time to cultivate such grounds.

No apprentice could be made to work from 6 p.m. on Saturdays to 6 a.m. on Mondays except in cases of emergency, for example, fires, floods, earthquakes, hurricanes and failure of machinery. Apprentices could lawfully be employed overnight provided they did not work for more than nine hours.

Each estate had to have a hospital, a medical practitioner and necessary medicines, and food for the sick had to be provided. Failure to adhere to the former regulation carried a penalty of £50 and to the latter, £5.

Another set of regulations in the Grenada Emancipation Act dealt with the incidence of vagrancy. Apprentices absent from work without cause were to work an additional two hours for every hour absent, provided this did not exceed 15 hours weekly. Those who absented themselves for nine hours in one week were adjudged deserters; those absent for two days were adjudged vagabonds; and those who stayed away for five days were called runaways. Deserters were to be given one week's imprisonment; vagabonds, not more than two weeks; and, runaways, not more than one month's imprisonment plus any number of stripes not exceeding 30. Those absent for seven days or more were adjudged notorious runaways and were to be given three months' hard labour and, if males, flogging not exceeding 39 lashes. These cases were to be investigated by stipendiary magistrates who would also execute the punishment.

If an apprentice performed his work indolently, carelessly or negligently, he was to give his master up to 15 hours' extra labour per week. If convicted a second time, the penalty was one week's solitary confinement in prison, with or without hard labour.

Wanton destruction to masters' property, ill-use of cattle or livestock, careless use of fire, carried a penalty of 15 hours' labour to the master or one month's imprisonment with hard labour. Wilful disobedience of masters' orders was similarly punishable. If three or more apprentices combined to resist the lawful commands of their employers they could be accused of a conspiracy and receive six months' solitary confinement in prison and a flogging not exceeding 39 lashes. Drunkenness, fighting, insolence and insubordination were all punishable crimes each carrying a sentence of one week's imprisonment or a flogging not exceeding 15 lashes.

The Emancipation Act expressly forbade the flogging of women. Instead, their penalties for offences committed were imprisonment, confinement in the public stocks and solitary confinement. The maximum time a woman could spend in the stocks was eight hours in any one day, between sunrise and sunset.

For any gang of apprenticed labourers to leave the estate to lodge a complaint before the special magistrate was unlawful. Instead, they were to select a person or a group not exceeding three who would then apply for a pass from the master. If this was refused, then the group could leave the estate unmolested, and the planter would be fined £5 for such refusal, or molestation.

It was the duty of Grenada's Governor to appoint inspectors in each district on 1 January each year to ascertain the work to be performed by apprentices on their respective plantations. If the tasks were excessive the inspectors were authorized to reduce them to a 'reasonable' and 'moderate' extent.

An apprentice guilty of a serious offence could be confined by his employer for up to 20 hours until he could be brought before a special magistrate. If, however, the apprentice was maliciously confined, the master was to pay a fine of £1. If an employer was found guilty of having whipped, beaten, imprisoned or confined in stocks, except as permitted, or otherwise maltreated an apprentice, the penalty was a fine of £5 or one month's imprisonment.

The Grenada Emancipation Act also made provisions for apprentices to reside upon the plantation to which they were attached. If they were found wandering beyond the limits of the plantation without a permit they could be detained by any free person and on conviction, be adjudged a vagabond and punished accordingly.

If a group of apprentices were to establish themselves as a community without lawful authority and habitually neglect to perform their duties, the community was to be dislodged and the houses destroyed. All sick, aged and infirm apprentices were to be cared for by the planters.

In order for the Grenada planters to receive their compensation money the Emancipation Act passed by the Legislature had to be accepted by the Colonial Office. This was necessary to ensure that local Emancipation Acts were consistent in all respects with the principles and general spirit of the Imperial measure. As a result, Grenada's Act of March 1834 was amended on 1 August of the same year.

The colony was divided into three, instead of six, divisions. The Governor was to appoint Justices of the Peace to assist the stipendiary magistrates sent by the British Government, and a stipendiary magistrate was to preside over each grand division. Sessions of the police court were to be held every Saturday in every grand division. Grenada's Emancipation Act was accepted and ratified by the Colonial Office in the latter part of 1834, and as a result, funds were transmitted to compensate planters for the loss of their slaves.

Slave owners in Grenada received a total of £616,255 compensation for their 23,638 slaves considered duly registered on 31 July 1834. The sum of £570,132 was paid for praedial attached, praedial unattached and non-praedials; £11,257 for the 1,309 aged and infirm, while £34,265 was paid for the 3,320 children.[11]

The basis for calculation of compensation was the status of the slave. The rates for 'head slaves' and 'tradesmen' were highest, while those on 'inferior field labour' and 'inferior domestics' were the least. Table 9.1 illustrates the scales of compensation.

The Emancipation Act created a half-slave, half-free status for the slaves, as they continued to live and operate under a similar comprehensive set of restrictions as before. Moreover, the various clauses of the Act showed that the planters were overtly preoccupied with ways and means of confining the apprentices to the places of their former enslavement. The laws made no provision for allowances which were customarily given but which had no statutory basis, for example, the provision of water carriers for field workers, the exemption of pregnant women, and women with more than four children from field labour, provision of cooks, etc.

In addition to the £616,255 cash compensation, Grenadian planters received compensation in the form of free labour, which, when quantified, amounted to £995,000. The average daily wage at

**Table 9.1 Rates of Slave Compensation**

| *Praedial slaves* | | *Compensation rates* | | |
|---|---|---|---|---|
| *No.* | *Class* | *£* | *s* | *d* |
| 1 | Head people | 41 | 5 | 7 |
| 2 | Tradesmen | 41 | 5 | 7 |
| 3 | Inferior tradesmen | 34 | 8 | 0 |
| 4 | Field labourers | 34 | 8 | 0 |
| 5 | Inferior field labourers | 20 | 12 | 0 |
| | *Non-praedial slaves* | | | |
| 1 | Head tradesmen | 41 | 5 | 7 |
| 2 | Inferior tradesmen | 34 | 8 | 0 |
| 3 | Head people on wharfs | 41 | 5 | 7 |
| 4 | Inferior people on wharfs | 27 | 10 | 5 |
| 5 | Head domestic | 34 | 8 | 0 |
| 6 | Inferior domestic | 20 | 12 | 10 |

Source: *Martin's Colonies*, p. 45

the time was 4d to 1/-; 18,500 apprentices gave free labour and worked for five days a week, 50 weeks annually for four years. As Eric Williams so aptly puts it: 'Those compensated were not those who suffered from slavery but its beneficiaries'. The ex-slaves received not a square inch of land, nor a shilling to help them now that they were soon to be on their own.

## The Neo-Servitude of Apprenticeship

The period of apprenticeship, in Grenada and elsewhere, can be seen as the last phase of slavery rather than the first phase of freedom.

Supposedly, apprenticeship was a transition period to allow apprentices and their masters to adjust, socio-economically, to full freedom. This was the British government's intention, but the planters saw it differently; to them it was a period during which they could extract the last drop of compulsory labour from the apprentices.

There were some 18,316 apprentices in Grenada – 8,826 males and 9,490 females. They were to be supervised by three stipendiary magistrates, one of whom, Thomas A. Sinclair, was present the day apprenticeship began, 1 August 1834. Eventually Grenada received its full quota of stipendiary magistrates, nine of whom served in Grenada from 1834 to 1838, each for differing lengths of time.[12]

The stipendiary magistrates were supposed to be the guardians of freedom. Their tasks were: to mediate in cases of disputes, essentially between planters and apprentices, and generally to help create a smooth transition from slavery to freedom; to visit every estate within their jurisdiction in Grenada twice a fortnight to hear complaints; to go to any estate to which they had been summoned, within 24 hours; to hold court each Saturday; and to submit weekly reports to the Governor who, in turn, transmitted them to the Colonial Office. A specially designated officer at the Colonial Office analysed these reports for the Secretary of State, who, in turn, reported on them to the House of Commons.

Stipendiary magistrates at first received £300 per annum but later, on 1 April 1835, they were given an additional allowance of £150 per annum. Each stipend included at least two or three horses as this was their main means of transportation.

Two weeks after the commencement of apprenticeship the Grenada Assembly appointed a committee (composed of Johns Wells, Louis La Grenade and Alexander Baillie) to enquire into and report upon the condition of apprenticed labourers. The committee came to the following conclusions in its report:

1. That since the commencement of the new system apprentices have shown less and less inclination to attend to their religious duties by absenting themselves from religious serices on Sundays.
2. That many of them have withdrawn their children from free schools and those above six discontinued their examination by Catechists appointed in the outer parishes.
3. That parents appear to have no control over their children.
4. That the laws now in force have not effected any improvement in the moral condition of the apprentices, nor have they in any way acted on them as an inducement to greater habits of industry. They generally seemed more inclined to spend their time in idleness and vicious pleasure, and in gratification of their passion for rum. Too large a portion of that class is addicted to rob and plunder their employers.
5. That the majority of labourers have too great a portion of land allowed them for their purposes.
6. That measures should be taken to enforce the attendance of the rising population as well as all classes of the apprenticed labourers at some place of worship at least once on every Sunday.

Thus, from the very inception of freedom, the Grenadian ruling class complained of four vices among the children of the working class. They complained that: a) they don't go to school; b) they refuse to go to church; c) they are disrespectful; and d) they steal a lot.

But these forms of behaviour were the logical outcome of a repressive system that held out little hope for the working people. Moreover, these reactions were simple manifestations of their lack of confidence in the ruling classes and a sign of contempt to the institutions that grew out of the oppressive polity they created.

The ruling class themselves had very little confidence in the newly emancipated, and continued to conceive of and treat them as rebels, thieves and mischief-makers. On the second day of apprenticeship they passed a law directed against two crimes: praedial larceny and burglary. The old distinction between petty larceny and grand larceny was dropped and every larceny, regardless of the value of the property stolen, was called simple larceny and subjected to the same law and similar penalties: two years' imprisonment or seven years' transportation. Male felons were to receive up to three whippings publicly or privately.

Every person convicted of burglary was to be executed. The mere intent to commit burglary if proven, was equally serious as the crime itself. Stealing money or valuables was punishable with four years' imprisonment.

In order effectively to implement the execution of these new laws, the Legislature passed an Act to Create a Local Police Force on 2 June 1836. The local police (43 constables and officers) were to supplement the local militia (826 non-commissioned officers and 97 commissioned officers). Police constables were stationed in five parishes and Grand Etang; in St John's and St Mark's there were five, plus the Chief Police Constable, Andrew Wilson; in St Patrick's three plus Charles Du Borg; in St Andrew's three plus the Police Chief John Neckles. Membership of the police force and militia in those days was restricted to Whites and Coloureds.

These laws reflected the continued paranoia of the plantocracy regarding the protection of property; the half-free Blacks were now seen as constituting a direct threat to the sanctity of that property. We have already seen how during the decade before emancipation, the local Legislature, acting in their own interests, tried to improve the slaves' day-to-day living conditions, as they were no longer able to replace dead slaves with the ease possible in the pre-1806 period. When, however, in 1834, the slaves were made to serve an apprenticeship, before receiving their freedom in 1838, the local Legislature passed numerous coercive pieces of legislation aimed at confining the ex-slaves to their former economic and social status, and rigidly circumscribing their movement; a clear deviation from the principle and spirit of apprenticeship.

One such Act was passed on 8 May 1836 entitled 'An Act to Provide for the More Effectual Suppression of Vagrancy and for the Punishment of Idle and Disorderly Persons'. A vagrant was described as any person who deliberately refused to work and who did not have any means of maintenance – every unlicensed huckster, peddler, hawker, every prostitute, every healthy person begging alms or encouraging children to so do. The penalty for vagrancy was imprisonment with a maximum of one month's hard labour. Persons suspected of committing theft and repeatedly thieving were also tried for vagrancy. Incorrigible rogues were given one year's hard labour. The law was an attempt to force men to continue labouring on estates, when it was feared that a mass exodus was impending.

In June 1835, the Legislature in Grenada drew up a scale of labour to regulate an apprentice's quantum of work, as there was the tendency either for defiant apprentices to go slow, or for unscrupulous planters to overwork willing or submissive ones. Where land had lain fallow for four years and was to be cultivated, there were to be 20 apprentices per acre; clearing and stumping abandoned cane fields: five per acre per day; holing land 20 inches square and 5 inches deep: 200 holes for every two apprentices per day; planting three plants to a hole: 450 holes to be planted per person per day. Where canes were weeded for the first time the rate was 200 holes per day per person; in the case of a second weeding, 250 holes per day per person. In cutting canes, each apprentice was to cut sufficient daily to produce 300 gallons of juice.

These tasks were very heavy, and the aim was to intensify labour not by lengthening the day, but by increasing each field worker's daily amount of work. It must be noted that this new scale of labour was in fact drawn up by the planters as it was their representatives who composed the Legislature.

Grenada was originally allotted three stipendiary magistrates but eventually received five, and in 1835, for the first time during the period, there were five stipendiary magistrates and one special justice.[13]

On 4 September, the Secretary of State, Lord Glenelg, instructed the Lieutenant-Governor to revoke the commission given to special justices. At the same time one stipendiary magistrate, T.A. Sinclair, was transferred to Carriacou after many complaints were made against him by planters in St Andrew's. A Mr Harford complained that Sinclair had prevented the removal of apprentices from Columbier Estate to L'Esterre, after two special magistrates had given legal sanction to do so in August 1835. T.A. Sinclair treated Harford rather harshly, and, as he was a planter of some standing, the plantocracy banded themselves together and actively sought Sinclair's dismissal or transfer. The Governor too, was displeased by Sinclair's behaviour, and consequently ordered his transfer to Carriacou. By November 1835, the stipendiary magistrates were H. Cayley, Sinclair, Ross and Garraway; in early 1836 Garraway was replaced by Fraser as special justice and in 1837 the latter received a commission as stipendiary magistrate. Each had jurisdiction over certain parishes or sections of the island, and heard, investigated and adjudicated complaints in their area. By August 1837 the stipendiary magistrates were: town and parish of St George, John Ross; St David, T. Cayley; St Andrew, L. Walsh; St Patrick and St Mark, C.S. Fraser; Carriacou and St John, T.A. Sinclair.

On more than one occasion during the apprenticeship period planters called parochial meetings to apply pressure on stipendiary magistrates whose impartial treatment and protection of apprentices ran counter to planters' interests. One such meeting, led by D. Logaw, Reid, and Polson, was called by planters of Carriacou in November 1837 to criticize and discredit T.A. Sinclair. Carriacou planters subjected their apprentices to particularly harsh treatment. At one time, in 1837, Sinclair was kept to busy for three weeks, hearing complaints, that he had to neglect entirely the St John's parish in Grenada. In most of these cases the planters found his decisions unacceptable, but the Governor found his work good and his performance in Carriacou to be above reproach. He wrote:

> The moral influence of that stipendiary magistrate over the apprentices was more than sufficient to keep them steadily and industriously occupied with their duties, and consequently there resulted so small a rate of crime or negligence in comparison with the population that it was unparalleled in any country.[14]

Some stipendiary magistrates in Grenada seem to have dealt very harshly with apprentices. In November, Lieutenant-Governor Mair expressed alarm, and complained that the amount of punishment given to apprentices had doubled in 1835. In August that year, Edward, an apprentice on Springs Estate, complained to the Governor about the harsh treatment he had received from Stipendiary Magistrate Cayley, having been ordered to work 20 days extra and receive 20 stripes for a small misdemeanour. Again, in February 1836, the Governor, alarmed by punishments meted out by Cayley, demanded a full report on the circumstances surrounding them. Cayley had sentenced labourers to 78 days' extra labour on estates.[15] Again, in 1837, Lord Glenelg, the Secretary of State, surprised at the high incidence of solitary confinement meted out to apprentices by Cayley and Fraser, instructed Lieutenant-Governor Mair to investigate the matter. In many cases apprentices were given from 30 to 90 days' confinement in the estate's workhouse; these were nothing but dungeons and as such, instruments of human torture. Lord Glenelg described such punishment as extremely severe and expressed grave doubts as to its effectiveness in disciplining or reforming recalcitrant apprentices.

In addition to the harsh treatment by the stipendiary magistrates, many apprentices were treated even more harshly by the managers and overseers. Some managers saw in apprenticeship a kind of short, partial reprieve before full Emancipation, when not only would they have to buy labour, but even worse, they would have neither jurisdiction nor control over the actions or industrial behaviour of their employees – so recently their slaves and apprentices. Thus, such men made apprenticeship a period of blatant exploitation, subjecting apprentices to all types of maltreatment and coercive acts.

A female apprentice, Elise of Beausejour, was sent to the estate hospital by Stipendiary Magistrate Cayley in July 1836; the following day the manager took her out of hospital and – sick, weak and scarcely able to walk – sent her to work in the field.

Sarah, a 60-year-old female apprentice of Mt Gay Estate, in New Year's week went to visit her godmother, two miles away, and fell ill. She reported to the manager but, as he was out, went instead to the overseer, who immediately put her in the stocks for two days and nights, for an act of vagrancy.

In March 1837 Betsy, an apprentice on Mt Reuil Estate was forced to work as a praedial though she was classified as non-praedial; an injustice so glaring that the Governor asked Stipendiary Magistrate Fraser to ensure that Betsy was treated justly by the manager, Leid. Subsequently, Lord Glenelg wrote complimenting Fraser's actions in the matter.

Agar was the manager of Mt Gay Estate, where Boy, an apprentice, worked. Going hunting one night, Boy passed near to Agar's house. On hearing footsteps Agar shouted, 'Who's there?' Boy answered, identifying himself and saying that he was going to hunt. Agar said, 'I'll hunt you instead', and pointed a gun at him. Boy turned and was walking away when Agar fired a volley shooting him on the arm and in the back. Agar was found guilty and sentenced to pay a fine. This incident illustrates the little value managers and planters placed on the lives of the workers at the time. Many treated their apprentices like animals, even shooting at them, as if they were human targets.[16]

The manager of Clarks Court Estate, Dr John Brown, a medical practitioner, habitually put slaves in the stocks, a punishment that was forbidden in those days. Brown, however, boasted of this, saying that he had been doing so for the last 20 years and that stipendiary magistrates Ross, and especially Cayley, approved of this mode of punishment.[17] He was also noted for confining apprentices to the estate hospital and administering seawater to them under the guise of medical treatment, but really as punishment. He was subsequently taken to court and prosecuted (in the Supreme Court) by the Attorney-General. Evidence against him was overwhelming, and his brutality was proven beyond a doubt, yet he was acquitted by the jury. The effect of this case, however, was to check such abominable practice on estates.[18]

## Premature End of Apprenticeship

It is by no means surprising that two years before expected the system of apprenticeship ended prematurely in 1838. As early as 1836 the Anti-Slavery Society, highlighting its ills, called for the system's abolition. The Parliamentary Committee set up in 1836 to enquire into the workings of the system raised seven objections:

1. There was too much punishment of apprentices.
2. The constitution of the valuation tribunal for manumission was defective.
3. There was no protection for stipendiary magistrates against vexatious lawsuits.
4. The flogging of females though forbidden, was still maintained.
5. The only legally accepted marriages were those celebrated by ministers of the Church of England.
6. The education of free children was sadly neglected.
7. The regulation of apprentices' working time was sadly lacking.[19]

From 1837 onwards a series of books and pamphlets were published, criticizing the system.[20] In December 1837 and January 1838 the Anti-Slavery Society carried the campaign against apprenticeship a step further; they held a series of 43 public meetings in Britain condemning the system. These meetings helped to spread opposition to the apprenticeship system among the public, and were very effective in bringing about its premature end. On 22 May 1838, Parliament voted 96 to 93 to end apprenticeship on 31 July 1838.

This system had attempted the impossible: compromise between slavery and freedom. As W.L. Burn said:

> At every turn it was dependent upon the existing judicial and administrative systems. Even with the best will in the world to support it, the wretched ineffectiveness of those crumbling systems on which it was built must have been constantly dangerous to it.[21]

It was over-dependent on the planter class and the inept judiciary; too many of its sanctions were left to be carried out by the very class and persons against whom they were directed.

In 1838, Lieutenant-Governor Doyle, when asked by the Governor-in-Chief of Barbados and the Windwards to make an appraisal of apprenticeship in Grenada, gave one of the most candid assessments. He said that although the system was intended to prepare the slave for unrestricted freedom he doubted whether they were any better off in 1838 than in 1834; and further wondered if they would be better off in 1842, or at least, at any future date, until everything such as coerced labour ceased, and the planters were forced by necessity to conciliate their labourers and pay them adequate wages to do their work.

It was not so much the abuses in the administration of the law, or actual infractions of that law, that had impeded the full and free working of the apprenticeship, but the manner in which every matter connected with the apprentices had been viewed by many older managers of estates. Apprentices were never considered to be free outside the time they were required by law to give to their employers, neither were they treated as such, which had been the intention of the law.

The inveterate prejudices against their race imbibed by the managers and overseers under the slavery system had not yet been eradicated. One great error lay with those proprietors of estates who continued to employ attorneys and managers who had been educated and brought up under the old slave system, and who were violently opposed to Emancipation. The effect of this was to create a crisis of trust between apprentices and overseers. This explains why the women, in particular, constantly refused to accept medical treatment and food for their free children; they were afraid that they would be trapped into apprenticing them to the plantation under some sinister scheme devised by these overseers. When, in 1837, a stipendiary magistrate suggested to them to apprentice their free children, they became very agitated and accused him of forcing them to sell their children as slaves.

Apprenticeship, an unhealthy compromise between slavery and freedom from the start, was destined to fail.

NOTES

Full citations only given where work does not appear in the Bibliography.

1. *Grenada Free Press and Public Gazette*. Vol. V. No. 267, 23 March 1831.
2. Ibid. Vol. V. No. 278, 15 April 1831.
3. Ibid. Vol. V, No. 282, 14 May 1831.
4. W.L. Burn. *Emancipation and Apprenticeship*, pp. 108–17.
5. Ibid.
6. Ibid.
7. Ibid. p. 162.
8. Ibid. p. 168.
9. Ibid.
10. *Laws of Grenada*. No. CCLI, 11 March 1834, p. 16 of supplement to main laws.
11. *Martin's Colonies*, p. 45.
12. These were: Thomas A. Sinclair (1833); Thomas Cayley (1834); R.S. Jephson (1835); J.W. Hay (1835); R.M. Sinclair (1836); J. Garraway (1835); Charles Fraser and L.J. Walsh (1837).
13. T.A. Sinclair, S.M. Jephson, John Ross, J.W. Hay, T. Hayler (stipendary magistrates); J. Garraway (Special Justice, appointed acting stipendary magistrate by the Governor.
14. *Miscellaneous Correspondence* 1835–41.
15. Ibid.
16. *Grenada Free Press and Public Gazette*. Vol. X, No. 530, 30 March 1836.
17. *Miscellaneous Correspondence* 1835–41.
18. Ibid. Lieutenant-Governor Doyle to Governor-General of Barbados, November 1838; *Grenada Free Press and Public Gazette*. Vol. IX, No. 506, August 1835.
19. Burn, *Emancipation and Apprenticeship*, p. 338.
20. Joseph Sturge and Thomas Harvey. *West Indies in 1837*; William Lloyd, *Letters From The West Indies*; and Thome and Kimball, *Emancipation in the West Indies*; followed by Sligo, *Jamaica under the Apprenticeship System* and the *Narrative of James Williams*.
21. *Letter Book 1838*. Doyle to Governor-General of Barbados, Circular Despatch, No. 17, 21 April 1838.

# 10

# *Free Labour in Grenada: 1838–65*

## The Newly Emancipated

Emancipation Day in Grenada and the rest of the British West Indies was 1 August 1838. Although slavery had been officially abolished since 31 July 1834, not until 1838 did slaves become fully free in the eyes of the law.

No act of violence or disorder marked the transition from apprenticeship to full freedom in Grenada; there was an atmosphere of peace and quiet. In the four months following Emancipation only one serious crime was recorded among the newly emancipated, and in only one quarter was a military presence required.[1] The majority of freedmen continued to work on the estates to which they had been attached during apprenticeship; some became independent peasant farmers, while others chose unemployment, rather than continue to labour in the place of their enslavement. As the years passed, the number of people residing and working on estates decreased while, concomitantly, the peasantry and village settlers increased.

All aged persons remained on the estates until August 1839 and received the same allowances they enjoyed during apprenticeship. After 1839 they steadily became neglected and abandoned, as they ceased to be the legal responsibility of their former masters. There were no lazarettos for the many lepers, no asylum for lunatics, and no legal provisions for the maintenance of destitute persons. These persons who had worked a lifetime for the planters were now being cast away from the estates, where, unsatisfactory as conditions were, there was still a minimum of food and shelter.

As early as May 1838 Lieutenant-Governor Doyle had advised the Governor-in-Chief Lionel Smith that firm steps would have to be taken to provide for the aged and the infirm who were unable to earn a living and whose maintenance would soon no longer be the liability of the planters. He was of the opinion that little would be done for this indigent class until its misery became extensive.[2] The aged and infirm continued to be neglected for many years after 1839, as the Legislature remained inactive and insensitive to their miseries. During the 1840s a few almshouses were established by private individuals acting out of philanthropic zeal. One was the Victoria Alms House, which catered for those persons of middle- and upper-class origin who had become poor and destitute through economic and other circumstances. There were also the General Alms Houses, which catered for members of the lower class unable to earn a living owing to age or infirmity.[3]

Very little was done by the Grenadian Legislature to help other classes of the newly emancipated to become economically functional after 1833; they continued to live at the whims and fancies of White Creole society. Medical attention and health facilities were deplorable; the one General Hospital – the Colony Hospital – was, in 1839, in a dilapidated condition. As a result of this neglect, together with ignorance and superstition, the poor were ravaged by disease. The churches at the time organized a few schools but as the emphasis was on religious education and the Bible, they had no perceptible effect on the economic problems and conditions facing the freed men.

In 1839, the civil, judicial and ecclesiastical establishment was maintained at a cost of £11,872 annually, and a further £11,000 per annum maintained the military establishment. Not a penny was voted for the insane, the disabled, the paupers, the children and the working adults. There was no cash vote for the Colony Hospital; the modicum of education that existed was financed by a grant by the imperial government. Many of the poor and indigent had to live on the streets of St George's or Hillsborough, or aimlessly tramp the country roads as beggars. In time the number of paupers and beggars increased; in 1859 there were 92 recorded paupers, and by 1864 and 1866, 147 and 174 respectively.[4]

With the commencement of freedom in 1838 some jurisdiction was required to be enacted, to ensure justice to the newly emancipated in civil and criminal cases, and the fulfilment of contracts by labourers and servants. The stipendiary magistrates were retained for many years after 1838, as part of the judiciary and to adjudicate in cases of industrial disputes. The judiciary to guide the colony during this first phase of freedom consisted of a chief justice, two assistant justices, five stipendiary magistrates, an attorney-general and a solicitor-general. Only the Chief Justice, John Sanderson, had any specialist training; he already had some seven years' experience as a judge in Grenada, and consequently was to be the main legal guide in the Colony. He was assisted by assistant judges L.J. Walsh and John Wells and by special justices C.J. Fraser, R.M. Jephson, Julien De Gourville and Phillip Staunton, who were appointed in December 1839.[5] In 1846 the number of special justices was increased from five to seven, one for each parish and one for Carriacou. This judiciary was to guide Grenada for the next two decades.

Immediately after 1 August 1838 a series of laws were passed to regulate industrial relations between planters and labourers and to ensure a continued supply of labour to the estates.[6] The first of these was entitled an 'Act to better adjust and more easily recover the wages of domestic servants in industry, and other labourers on estates.' All industrial disputes between planters and labourers were to be heard and determined by two justices; awards were not to exceed three times the existing wage rate; where workers were absent from work, part of their wages could be deducted. Misdemeanour or misconduct on estates was punishable either by imprisonment or by reduction in wages.

In order to discourage squatting and force the freed men to continue working for the estate, a law called An Act to Prevent Persons Taking Illegal Possession of Planters' or of Ungranted Land', was passed. Any illegal settler or squatter could be ejected forthwith by a Justice of the Peace; any person guilty of this offence a second time was adjudged a vagrant and punished accordingly. Another law, legalizing the ejection of tenants of up to seven years' standing, was also passed. Complaints had first to be made to a stipendiary magistrate who would decide upon the action to be taken. Together, these Acts were a concerted attempt to prevent the development of an independent peasantry, as such an institution would mean increasing labour problems for the estates.

On 2 December 1839, another Industrial Relations Act, entitled 'An Act for Regulating the Duties of Masters and Servants', was passed. By this law, contracts between planters and labourers were valid for a period of one year; all contracts had to be signed or made in the presence of a stipendiary magistrate; and such contracts could lapse without notice by either party after the stipulated time. Children aged between 10 and 16 could be apprenticed by parents in a trade but not as labourers on estates; such apprenticeship was not to exceed five years.[7]

## Four Types of Workers

Four types of workers emerged in Grenada during the first decade of full freedom.

### 1. *Tenants-at-will and the labour-rent system*

Labourers – also described as 'tenants at will' – who continued to work and reside on the estates to which they were attached continued to occupy the estate's cottages and to cultivate its provision grounds rent-free; in return, they agreed to provide the estate with a steady and continuous supply of labour. Those classified as first class were paid 8d and 9d per day; second-class tenants were paid 6d and 7d, while third-class tenants were paid 4d and 5d daily. Labourers who worked, but did not live on the estates, received wages varying from 10d to 1/- per day.[8]

Stipendiary magistrates, reporting in 1839, estimated that not more than 20% of all labourers worked for their employers at any one time. Referring to the parish of St David's they noted that not more than 12 to 14 people could be procured to cut canes in one area where the population was about 800; the resulting stoppages at the mill and boiling houses, and the loss of time to carters and mule boys were considerable.[9] Consequently, the planters had to find means to induce more freedmen to work for them. Free use of cottage and provision grounds was one such inducement. By 1850 the tenancy-at-will system had become widespread, as it was the only method which guaranteed a regular supply of labour to the planters. The 1844 Census revealed that some 6,373 freedmen lived on estates, roughly 33% of the apprentice population of 1838; labourers who worked for hire totalled some 10,196.[10]

### 2. *Early peasants*

The second type of worker to develop was the peasant. These peasants were ex-slaves who owned small freeholds, or rented or leased small lots of land from estates adjacent to where they lived. Occasionally they worked on the estates to earn money to supplement their income from the sale of their produce. In St Andrew's, peasants rented land for one to ten years at a rate of 10/- to 40/- per acre, while in St Patrick's they rented on an annual basis. After 1838 the peasantry grew in numbers from decade to decade. The dearest wish of the

*An old peasant outside his home c. 1899*

*Poor peasants in Grenada during the 19th century*

freedman was to have his own independent plot; this signified to him in a very real way his transition from slavery to freedom. Ownership of land, no matter how little, became the most important criterion of freedom to the Grenadian. Work on the estate, if and when it was done, was a necessary evil in that it provided some needed money. With the growth of the peasantry, village after village sprang up throughout Grenada, many of them taking the name of the estate in the area. Some of the first villages to spring up after 1839 included:

- Laura Estate settlement, Lower LaTante settlements and Belle Vue settlements in St David's;
- Chantimelle and La Mode in St Patrick's;
- Marquis, Munich, Harford village, Adelphi and Capitol in St Andrew's;
- Springs, Mt Aire, Paddock, Mardigras, Grand Anse, Mt La Croix, Annandale, Black Forest, Constantine, Mt Molinier, Mt Moritz, Vendomme, Mt Gay, Snug Corner, New Hampshire in St George's.[11]

The relatively larger number of villages in the parish of St George's was attributable to the following factors:

1. It contained many abandoned estates; plots from these were sold to peasants in the area.
2. The majority of the Free Coloureds lived in that parish and owned much land there.
3. The main town was in that parish and it was becoming slowly urbanized as people from the rural areas migrated to its environs.

By 1852, some 7,127 persons or 22% of the population were living in free villages in Grenada. Of 685 labourers in St John's and St Mark's in 1850, 413 owned freeholds or rented plots, 116 were metayers and 156 tenants-at-will.[12] These freeholds were not clustered together, but widely dispersed on the margins of the estates, which is how many villages in Grenada arose initially.

The peasant and village movements continued unchecked for the next decade. By 1863 11,400 persons were living in villages formed since Emancipation; three years later the number reached 14,693 and by 1870 stood at 16,000. By that year the parishes with the highest number of persons living in villages were: St Andrew's 6,450, and St Patrick's 3,350. Sixty percent of persons living in villages were then in those parishes and the amount of land they cultivated grew simultaneously. In 1852 some 4,954 acres were under peasant cultivation, increasing to 7,262 acres by 1858, but falling subsequently to 5,139 acres by 1866. Contrary to popular opinion among the employer class at the time, the ex-slaves did not abandon agriculture.

*The village of Beaulieu in the 19th century*

### *The metayers*

The metayer was the third labour type to emerge in Grenada. Metayage was a system of share-cropping introduced into Grenada around the year 1848 at a time when liquidity was scarce and it was difficult to pay wages in cash. This was soon after the passage of the Sugar Duties Act when the islands began to feel the adverse effects of the equalization of sugar duties. Moreover, about a decade after Emancipation many freedmen were becoming increasingly unwilling to work on the estates and, although many were still employed there, the supply of labour had declined. In 1834, 21,445 persons were employed on estates; in 1836, 16,835; by 1844, 10,196, and by 1852 it declined still further to 8,349. In 1852 some 13,500 persons were employed in agriculture as a whole, but some 8,200 labourers were on estates in 1871 and 7,000 other labourers; ten years later there were 12,500 agricultural labourers and 1,000 other labourers. However, over 3,000 of the 12,500 were peasants.

Although the number of labourers employed on some estates may have declined, the number employed in agriculture remained stable, at least for the three decades after 1852; by 1884 some 13,229 persons were still employed in agriculture. This shows that ex-slaves did not abandon agriculture but rather abandoned work in the estate's canefields and cocoa pieces. The 1881 Census gave a return of 12,483 agricultural labourers and noted that 3,000 of the adult males possessed lots from one acre upwards. Out of 4,255 married women (aged 20+) only 408 were returned as wives not employed. Some 7,000 women were involved in agriculture either as labourers or peasants.

Under the metayage system the estates provided machines, stock and carts and the metayer contributed his labour. The estate lands were rented to the metayer in allotments. When the canes were harvested they were transported to the estates' mills with the aid of the planters' carts and cattle, and when processed into sugar this was equally divided between planter (landlord) and the metayer. Usually the planter purchased the metayer's share at an agreed-upon price. It was normal to find metayers erecting houses on the allotment given them to farm.

The metayer system was at its height in Grenada from 1850 to about 1854. In 1866, out of a total of 140 sugar estates, 28 still operated under the metayage system; by 1868 this increased to 30, falling to ten by 1875, but rising to 17 by 1878.[13]

The metayage system was a temporary expedient adopted by planters to counter the economic exigencies of the time, but they were soon disillusioned with the system. Stipendiary magistrates, writing in 1854, reported that over 80% of the proprietors were opposed to metayage, as it prevented the general working of the estate and contributed to the growth and spread of idleness. They complained that tenants began work at 10 a.m., left in the early afternoon and spent the rest of the day idle. Planters were also dissatisfied with the metayer's negligence in performing his duty, while the metayer complained of the long delay in realizing the returns of his labour.[14] Under the system there was no protection for either landlord or tenant. Although the planters disliked it they found it difficult to change as the metayers refused to work for them as labourers. Two planters in St David's who attempted to abandon the system in 1852, soon changed their minds as the labourers threatened to leave.

Metayage, tenancy-at-will, and rent systems of land tenancy were a source of constant conflict and litigation between landlord on the one hand, and metayer, rentier and tenant on the other. Most of the offences, crimes and court cases during the 1850s and 1860s were in one way or another concerned with the workings of the various systems of land tenancy. The majority of the offences included the use of abusive and threatening language, and riotous and disorderly conduct. In 1850 there were 627 court cases: 155 for assault; three for felonies, 13 for theft; and 456 cases involved employers and labourers.[15] The majority of these was for the use of obscene and abusive language, illegal destruction of property, wage disputes, and the breaking of contracts. This was very much the pattern of things for the next 20 years.

One incident worth noting concerned a strike among estate labourers in the parish of St Patrick's, from 22 December 1847 to 11 January 1848. The main cause seemed to have been a reduction in their wages from 10d–1/- to 8d per day. Moreoever, they were threatened with the loss of the use of estate cottages and provision grounds if they refused to accept the reduction in wages. On 22 December Lieutenant-Governor Hamilton sent around a circular asking workers to be content with the moderate wages and to make fair agreement for their work, as they could not be allowed to reside in cottages and enjoy possession of grounds on estates without providing labour at a fair price to the estate or paying rent. Copies of this letter were given to the stipendiary magistrates who were instructed to read them to the workers. The workers did not believe that the Governor had written the letter, and thought instead that it was a conspiracy between stipendiary magistrates and their employers. On 11 January 1848, several hundreds of them assembled near the court house in St Patrick's where Stipendiary Magistrate Romney and local magistrates were conducting an investigation. They behaved in a violent and disorderly manner, attacking the constables on duty, storming the court house and eventually breaking up the stipendiary magistrates' meeting. They were subsequently dispersed when more constables arrived, but threatened to return on the following day with 2,000 other labourers.

Romney, fearing an insurrection, appealed to the Lieutenant-Govenor for assistance. A detachment of 50 miliary men was immediately despatched by boat for Sauteurs, but when they arrived on the morning of the 12th all was quiet. The Governor considered the matter sufficiently serious, and asked Romney to summon the headman of each estate in the parish to the court house on 13 January so that he could address them and explain the situation. This he did, in the company of the Roman Catholic priest, and the labourers then dispersed peaceably. By 17 January 1848, many had returned to work but some remained dissatisfied and were adamant in their decision not to return to work.[16]

Such persistent conflicts between planters and labourers were inevitable, as the interests of both groups were opposed to each other. The labourer wanted land and to be independent of estate labour, while the planter wanted a steady and continuous supply of cheap labour and thus wished the labourer to remain on the estate as its eternal hireling. Governor Keate expressed it well in his report on the 1853 Blue Book when he said:

> The planter must be well aware that every negro to whom he is paying wages has at heart a longing and determination sooner or later to possess a piece of land of his own or at all event to hire and occupy one which he can cultivate in his own way and at his own convenience and not at his employer's dictation.[17]

Keate further observed that the peasantry not only produced provisons, but also cocoa, coffee and sugar. Some had even set up small cane mills which were scoffed at by the planters, but the Governor saw it as a significant development among the peasants. He encouraged the metayage system as he saw it as a transition stage to farm tenancy.

## *Petty traders and artisans*

The fourth type of worker to emerge in Grenada after 1838 was the petty huckster, petty trader and artisan. Many freedmen abandoned the estate and took to various petty trades; some became carpenters, fishermen, masons, blacksmiths and wheelwrights. Others, mostly women, became hucksters, house servants, washerwomen and seamstresses.

Census returns of 1844 showed 300 hucksters in Grenada, of whom 167 were in the town of St George's, 44 in St Patrick's and 37 in St Mark's. In that year there were 389 fishermen, 1,036 house servants, 661 washerwomen and 1,409 seamstresses.[18] In addition some 4,498 other ex-slaves were employed in other trades and as handymen. About four decades later (1881) there were 5,200 seamstresses, washerwomen and domestics, accounting for 12% of the population. In addition there were 2,300 tradesmen, 1,093 porters and other labourers, and 472 fishermen and marines.

One feature of the slave-labour regime that continued into the free period was the incidence of child labour. During the decade immediately after 1838 there was a marked decline in child labour on estates. Many parents wanted their children to go to school rather than grow up in the planters' cocoa or cane field. But others saw in child labour a means of increasing the household's meagre income. Statistics on child labour are not very reliable as the magistrates did not record them with any degree of accuracy. According to the 1844 census there were 10,500 children under 16 years old, of whom 1,500 were in school, and the remaining 9,000 consisted of infants, unemployed and idle, and those employed on estates and in trades. The number of children employed on estates fell steadily after 1838 until it reached 271 by 1861. By 1866, however, it was 1,435, and 3,050 by 1878.[19] The increase in child labour during this later

*The village of River Road, famous for its laundresses' settlement*

*Laundresses at work in the 19th century*

*An essential feature of estate life was child labour. Here children are extracting cocoa beans from the pods*

period could be attributed to increasing financial hardship, shortage of money in the village, poor educational facilities and limited economic opportunities. The 1871 census showed that 11,265 children were not at school; by 1881 the figure had fallen, but not considerably.

## Marriages and the Newly Emancipated

Another feature that became well marked after 1838 was the number of marriages consecrated. Marriages increased from 30 per annum in the early 1830s, to 180 by the 1860s and 250 per annum by the 1870s. In 1871 there were 8,389 married people; by 1881, 9,986 – or 41% of the population over 15.[20] Despite this, illegitimate births, a social phenomena associated with the promiscuity of the plantation system, were still quite prevalent, and accounted for over 75% of all births between 1840 and 1881. As the century progressed the incidence of illegitimacy declined; between 1861 and 1881 61 out of every 100 births were illegitimate, and the average during the next 12 years was 52 out of 100.[21] The high incidence of illegitimacy in Grenada throughout the 19th century testifies to the relative domestication of women, many of whom were relegated to a life of continuous childbearing, in most cases, for different fathers. In spite of this the community remained an essentially religious one. It is typical of most communities that, when the prospects for economic improvement are remote and poverty becomes the order of the day, they find their rescue in religion.

## The Religious Denominations

There was considerable competition among the various religious denominations in Grenada after Emancipation for the souls of the newly emancipated. Chief of these was the Church of England, which sought to gain ascendancy over the Roman Catholics. There were four main denominations at the time – Church of England, Roman Catholic, Methodist, and Presbyterian or Church of Scotland. The Church of England was the most prominent in terms of physical facilities, buildings, lands, etc., while the Roman Catholic Church dominated numerically. By 1848 the Church of England had built seven churches and chapels in Grenada and one in Carriacou, and five resident clergymen serviced this church community. They also ran schools in St George's town and in every parish. For these they received a legislative grant of £380 annually, beginning in 1846.

The Church of Scotland had one church in the town of St George's, erected in 1832, partly with the assistance of a legislative grant and partly by subscriptions.

The Methodist Church had five places of worship and five schools in Grenada by 1848. Since 1846, this church establishment had received a legislative grant of £230 to help run its schools.

The Roman Catholic Church was the church of the working class throughout the 19th century, while the Church of England and Church of Scotland remained predominantly the church of the plantocracy. By 1848, the Catholic Church had seven places of worship to cater for the new class of freedmen. In every case where a RC church was erected the peasants and labourers contributed handsomely in cash and kind; the Legislature also gave some assistance; for example, in 1846, £750 was voted for erecting Roman Catholic Churches in the parish of St Patrick and in the unified parishes of St John and St Mark.

Despite the Church of England's activities to strengthen itself numerically, over 64% of the population remained Roman Catholic. Of a population of 28,903 in 1844, 18,523 were Roman Catholic, and 8,808 were Church of England. There were 328 Presbyterians, and 1,264 Methodists; also 34 Moravians, two Jews and four Muslims. The result of the 1851 General Census showed that the situation had remained virtually unchanged.[22]

By the year 1864 there were some 24 churches in Grenada catering for the spiritual development of the peasants and labourers: ten Church of England; eight Roman Catholic; four Wesleyan; and two Presbyterian. About 6,345 persons, or 18% of the population, attended church services on Sundays. Of these, 3,950 or 62% attended the Roman Catholic churches while 1,565 attended the Anglican churches. Methodist and Presbyterian church attendance was 690 and 140 respectively. By 1871 church attendance on Sundays increased further to 8,636 or 23% of the then population of 37,684, of whom 5,700 or 66% attended Roman Catholic churches.[23] The peasants bought special clothes – their 'Sunday best' – to wear for church services. On Sunday, too, they cooked the most sumptuous and delicious meal of the week.

## Commodity Prices and the Workers

The period 1840 to 1876 was generally one of stable prices and fixed incomes for the labourers. Wages, then 4d to 1/-daily in 1840 were basically the same 40 years later. Table 10.1 shows movements in the prices of certain basic items purchased by peasants and labourers from 1840 to 1876. These were considered by them to be essential items and were all imported.

A day's wage of 10d was equivalent at the time to 3lbs of rice, or 4-5 lbs of flour, or one cap of 5 lbs of muscovado sugar or 1 lb of beef. The price of rice remained unchanged for 36 years; where prices rose, the increase was marginal. In some cases, for example, milk and mutton, prices fell. Imported foods purchased by the peasantry were supplemented with produce from their provision grounds, by yard fowls, pigs and goats. Most of their demand for milk was satisfied by domestic sources.

As the villages increased and the size of the peasantry grew, the Grenadian sugar planters began to complain of a shortage of labour and the destruction of his sugar estates.

**Table 10.1 Prices of Selected Commodities 1840–76 (Grenada)**

| *Commodity* | *Unit* | *1840* | | *1845* | | *1855* | | *1860* | | *1865* | | *1876* | |
|---|---|---|---|---|---|---|---|---|---|---|---|---|---|
| | | *s* | *d* | *s* | *d* | *s* | *d* | *s* | *d* | *s* | *d* | *s* | *d* |
| Rice | lb | | 3 | | 3 | | 3 | | 3 | | 3 | | 3 |
| Flour | ″ | | 2 | | 2 | | 2½ | | 2½ | | 2 | | 2 |
| Saltfish | ″ | | 2 | | 2 | | 2 | | 2 | | 2½ | | 2½ |
| Sugar (brown) | ″ | | 6 | | 4 | | 6 | | 8 | | 8 | | 8 |
| Sugar (muscovado) | ″ | | 2 | | 2 | | 2 | | 2 | | 2 | | 2 |
| Cheese | ″ | 1 | 3 | 1 | 3 | 1 | 6 | 1 | 6 | 1 | 6 | 1 | 6 |
| Beef | ″ | | 6 | | 6 | | 8 | | 8 | | 8 | | 9 |
| Mutton | ″ | | 10 | | 10 | | 10 | | 10 | | 10 | | 9 |
| Pork | ″ | | 8 | | 8 | | 8 | | 8 | | 8 | | 8 |
| Butter | ″ | 1 | 0 | 1 | 0 | 1 | 0 | 1 | 0 | 1 | 0 | 1 | 0 |
| Milk | quart | | 4 | | 4 | | 3 | | 3 | | 3 | | 3 |
| Kerosene oil | gall | | – | | – | | – | 2 | 0 | 2 | 0 | 2 | 0 |
| Glengarry cap | one | | 9 | | 9 | | 9 | | 9 | 1 | 0 | 1 | 0 |
| Unbleached cotton | yard | | – | | – | | – | | 3 | | 3 | | 3 |
| Unbleached calico | ″ | | – | | – | | – | | 4 | | 4 | | 4 |
| Flannel | ″ | 1 | 0 | 1 | 0 | 1 | 0 | 1 | 0 | 1 | 0 | 1 | 0 |
| Ticklenburg | ″ | | 8 | | 8 | | 8 | | 8 | | 8 | | 8 |
| Linen checks | ″ | 1 | 0 | 1 | 0 | 1 | 0 | 1 | 0 | 1 | 0 | 1 | 6 |
| Head tie | one | 1 | 0 | 1 | 0 | 1 | 0 | 1 | 0 | 1 | 0 | 1 | 0 |

Source: Grenada, *Blue Books*, 1840, 1845, 1855, 1860, 1865, 1876; *Grenada Chronicle*, 27 December 1879

## Sugar Estates' Continued Decline Post-1850

Many factors contributed to the continued decline of the sugar industry after 1850; labour shortage was the least significant. The first and major factor was the high cost of production in Grenada and her consequent inability to compete. According to M.J. Higgins, a Grenadian planter who gave evidence before the 1848 Parliamentary Select Committee, the cost of producing a hundredweight of sugar, on 13 estates, increased from 9/5d, during the last three years of slavery and during apprenticeship, to 24/9d during the first three years of freedom.[24] By 1857 the cost of producing one hogshead (15cwt) was £13.15s, or roughly 18/- per cwt. In 1831–38 a good estate made a profit of $13.63 (£2.17/6d) per cwt; by 1839–47 the profits on the same estate had fallen drastically to $2.5 (10/-) per cwt. The following factors were responsible for the high production cost of sugar:

1. Heavy disbursements for salaries and for imported European stores and supplies.

2. Lack of implements and cost-saving devices. As late as 1876 there were only six ploughs and seven steam-engines on the 79 sugar estates in Grenada.
3. A high degree of absenteeism and the poor management of estates that developed as a result. By 1857 over 65% of Grenada's estates were owned by absentees; of a total of 152 planters in 1844, only 39 were resident in Grenada; the other 113 resided abroad and left the estates in the hands of attorneys and overseers.
4. Wastage and inefficiencies in the grinding and boiling operations.

As a result of the high cost of production, Grenadian sugar was uncompetitive after 1854, when it lost all preferential treatment in the British market. In 1841 the margin of protection afforded British West Indian sugar in the British market was 41/- per cwt, but by 1854 it was zero. 'All tubs then had to sit on their own bottoms.' The West Indian producers found it difficult to compete with the new sugar suppliers in the British market: Cuba, Brazil and European beet sugar producers. The rapid influx of foreign-grown sugar into England after 1846 led to a rapid decline in prices, and the bankruptcy of many estates in Grenada and the British West Indies. From an average of 40/- per cwt in 1839–43 sugar prices fell to 21/- by 1850–54 and 1860–69, and reached an all-time low of 13/- per cwt by 1884–90. Grenada exported little sugar either then or in the next few years.

The British West Indies virtually monopolized the British sugar market in the 1820s, supplying 3.9 million cwts or 89% of Britain's total imports out of annual imports of 4.4 million cwts. By 1857–60 British imports had increased to 8.2 million cwts, but the British West Indies supplied only 3.1 million cwts or 37% of total imports; three years later the West Indian share of the market fell to 34% (Table 10.2).

In the meantime, beet sugar's share of the market was gaining ground on cane. Moreover, since beet was produced by those European countries that purchased cane sugar, import substitution now became

**Table 10.2 Decline of BWI Share of the British Sugar Market 1820–63**

| | | *Million cwts* | |
|---|---|---|---|
| *Period* | *BWI* | *Foreign* | *Total* |
| 1821–30 | 3.9 | 0.185 | *4.4* |
| 1831–40 | 3.4 | 0.480 | *4.7* |
| 1841–50 | 2.3 | 1.260 | *6.0* |
| 1851–60 | 3.1 | 2.670 | *8.2* |
| 1861–63 | 3.4 | 4.600 | *10.0* |

Source: Leoni Levi, *On The Sugar Trade and Sugar Duties*, London, 29 February 1864.

a factor that adversely affected the re-export trade in cane sugar. In 1852–54 beet sugar imports into Britain accounted for only 5% of the market; by 1858–60 it was 8%, and by 1864–66 14%.[25]

The third factor which contributed to the decline of Grenada's sugar industry at this time was the indebtedness of the estates. Estates were indebted to the families of proprietors, to bankers, merchants and mortgagees; to receivers, trustees, legatees and annuitants. These debts retarded the rate of diversification in general and prevented the resuscitation of the sugar industry in particular.

The sequel to these problems was the abandonment of some estates and the sale of others. During 1838–56 some 47 estates were abandoned, and between 1856 and 1866 an additional 21 out of 142. Some abandoned estates were either divided into peasant lots or converted into cocoa production. By 1868, however, 34 sugar estates still lay abandoned; by 1875 the number had fallen to 22; but by 1878 had increased to 32.[26] Estate after estate was advertised for sale in the *St George's Chronicle* at this time, including Dougaldston, Revolution Hall, Mt Nesbit, La Force, La Vallete, Marli, Union, Clarks Court. During the first six months of 1867, 25 of the best sugar estates were put up for sale, including Tuilleries, Palmiste, Good Hope, Snell Hall, La Fortune, Duquesne, Samaritan, Mt Alexander, Observatory, Mon Repos, Hope and Telescope.

Obviously, the acreage under sugar cane simultaneously declined. Over the 14 years from 1852 to 1866 it fell from 7,105 to 4,988 acres. In 1853–57, 46.4m lbs of sugar (earning £395,781) were produced; by 1878–82, 16.8m lbs (earning £113,300) a decline of some 72%.[27] Clearly, the sugar industry in Grenada entered the final stage of its demise after the 1850s.

## Encumbered Estates Court Act 1854

The British government, well aware of the crisis in the sugar industry, especially the debt burden, passed a law in 1854, to facilitate the transfer of encumbered estates from illiquid planters to liquid merchants and investors; this was the Encumbered Estates Court Act. The imperial government realized the debt burden was hindering the economic development of the colonies and that steps had to be taken to transfer estates into the hands of new owners who could then develop the encumbered estates. The objectives of the Act were threefold:

1. To relieve the islands of insolvent proprietors and release estates from charges which rendered an outlay for cultivation improbable, and in many cases, impossible.

2. By facilitating the sale and transfer of encumbered estates it was hoped that machinery would be provided for obtaining a cheap rate of unimpeachable title to land.
3. Thus freed from debts estates would be free to develop under new ownership.[28]

A special court was set up in Britain, modelled on the Irish Encumbered Estates Court, to determine all matters concerning, or in any way connected with, claims on estates in the West Indies. Subsidiary courts were then set up in each island which placed itself under the Act.

The Legislature introduced the Act into Grenada in 1866, and until 1885, when the Act was repealed, 28 estates were sold by the Encumbered Estates Court. These amounted to 12,859 acres and were sold for £38,330 – a rate of £2.9 per acre and £1,368 per estate. In the British West Indies as a whole, the Court sold 290 estates totalling 181,323 acres for a sum of £445,950.[29]

Some of the first estates sold in Grenada by the Court included Bocage, Pearls, Boulogne, and Madeys, all owned by Theophilus Law and all sold in January 1867.[30] Others, sold in 1877, were Plains, Chambord and Mt Rich, in the parish of St Patrick's. Plains and Chambord were sold for £3,000, and were resold two years later for £4,885; Mt Rich was sold for £3,000 and resold in January 1880 for £7,360.

In 1884 the Encumbered Estates Court came up for considerable criticism before the Crossman Commission; by then it had outlived its usefulness. Two of the main criticisms related specifically to the Grenada branch of the Court. One was that the Court, sitting in Britain, was unjust to the poorer classes, and encouraged the monopoly of land ownership by the rich. The other was that the practice of establishing priority for consignee's lien over all previous or other charges was unfair.

The first objection related to Plaisance Estate in Grenada. The new owner, in order to clear his title legitimately, placed the estate before the Court. On the borders of the estate and intersecting with its boundaries were several plots owned by peasant proprietors. The estate, as presented before the Court, included many of these, and notices were served upon the proprietors that unless they appeared by Counsel before the Court in London by a certain date, their claims would be ignored. The conditional order, granting a clear title to all these lands within a declared boundary, was made absolute by the Court if no objection was made within the specified time. In the case of this particular estate one woman put forward in Grenada deeds proving that the 35 perches then in her possession had been purchased from the estate in the year 1851; but she was too poor to appear by Counsel before the Court in Britain; her protest in the island was of no avail to prevent the proprietor of the neighbouring estate, with its new title, absorbing without thought of compensation, her legally acquired freehold. Such persons forfeited their legally acquired land in the process of these transfers.

Regarding priority of consignee's lien on the corpus of the estate, it was argued that this made proprietors insolvent. Why was consignee's lien given priority? From earliest days consignee had figured prominently in estates in Grenada and elsewhere. The consignee had retained a strong hold on West Indian estates, acting as the agent for the sale of the produce and the supply of stores, machinery and capital. He became the natural channel for the advances of money required from time to time by the planter. When the Court was formed he came prominently before it; by its judgement the Court awarded priority to his claims on the corpus of an estate for all moneys advanced to carry on the estate. This priority was to take precedence over all mortgages, claims or charges.

Among the other objections raised against the Court were the following:

1. That estates were sold at prices insufficient to satisfy all claims sometimes not enough to satisfy consignee's claims.
2. That the owner of the estate, in the end was ruined by the system.
3. That the Act prevented an inflow of capital into the islands.

In the 1880s the Commission held the view that the Court was serving no useful purpose, that it had already served its purpose by clearing many West Indian estates of encumbrances. The Commission recommended abolition or reform of the Court.

Many witnesses who had given evidence before the Commission recommended the abolition of the Court in Grenada. In 1885 the local branch of the Encumbered Estates Court was abolished.

## From Sugar to Cocoa

While the sugar industry was experiencing all these adversities the economic base of Grenada underwent a gradual transformation from sugar to cocoa. The spread of cocoa cultivation was a direct result of the numerous crises that beset sugar.

Cocoa cultivation replaced cane on at least 12 estates during the 10 years from 1856 to 1866. Five of these estates were in St Mark's, and two each in St John's, St George's and St Andrew's; by 1860 most cocoa estates were in St Mark's and St John's. In 1846 there were 89 sugar estates and 52 cocoa; during the next ten years, although the number of sugar estates fell by 12, the number of cocoa estates went up by only two. During the next two decades, however, a transformation took place; by 1878 there were 73 sugar and 103 cocoa estates. In 1852 only 864 acres were planted in cocoa compared to 7,105 in

10.2 *A woman and her son employed on an estate*

canes; 12 years later the acreage in canes fell to 5,425 while cocoa increased to 4,464 acres. By 1878 cocoa cultivation had clearly surpassed cane cultivation. The acreage in cocoa amounted to 6,378 while that in canes 4,594 acres.[31]

The predominance of cocoa can also be seen from production and income figures. In 1853–57 total production amounted to 3.5m lbs increasing to 5.3m by 1856–62 and 10.8m by 1868–72. Finally, in 1878–82 production totalled 17.7m lbs.

The incomes from cocoa exports increased ten times between the period 1853–57 and 1878–82 – in the former period amounting to £56,906 and in the latter period to £617,169. By 1875 the most valuable estate in Grenada was a cocoa estate called Brothers in the parish of St John's, with some 588 acres under cocoa cultivation.

Another illustration of how and when cocoa replaced sugar can be drawn from comparative data on export earnings. In 1860 export earnings from sugar were £95,000 compared to £17,000 from cocoa; in 1880 earnings from sugar fell to £25,000 while those from cocoa rose to £125,000.[32]

Did the decline of the sugar economy affect the provision of social services for the newly emancipated in Grenada? What attempts were made to provide these social services in the first place even before this marked economic decline? The next chapter examines the provisions made for education in the period 1824 to 1885.

## NOTES

Full citations only given where work does not appear in the Bibliography.

1. *Grenada Gazette*, Vol. 13, No. 673, 2 January 1839.
2. Doyle to Governor-in-Chief, Barbados, No.20, 2 May 1838.
3. 'Report on the Blue Book for 1853', in *Outgoing Despatches* 1853.
4. *Blue Book*, 1850, 1864, 1866.
5. *Blue Book*, 1839.
6. *Laws of Grenada*, 13 August 1838 & 2 December 1839.
7. Ibid.
8. *Blue Book*, 1839, Grenada, 'Report of Stipendiary Magistrates for the first half of 1850' President Checkley to Governor Colebroke, No. 91, 27 September 1850.
9. *Free Press and Public Gazette* 25 February 1839.
10. *1844 Census*. Report of SMs for the year 1852, 1853.
11. 'General Report upon the appearance and progress of Cholera in Grenada'. Governor Keate to Governor Colebroke. No. 89, 6 October 1854.
12. Report of SMs for the first half of 1850. 27 September 1850.
13. *Blue Book*, 1868, 1875, 1878.
14. 'Report of SMs for the first half of 1852', Checkley to Governor in Chief. No. 74, 30 June 1852.
15. *Blue Book*, selected volumes, 1850 to 1870. Also Reports of SMs 1850–60.
16. Lieutenant-Governor K.B. Hamilton to Governor General Reid, 'Report on disturbances by agricultural labourers in St. Patrick' No. 125, 21 January 1848.
17. 1854, *Report on the 1853 Blue Book*. Enclosure No. 3 in Despatch No. 40.

18. *Census Returns*, 1844.
19. *Census Report of 1861*: *Blue Books*.
20. *Census Returns*, 1881.
21. *Blue Book*; figures were complied from Blue Books and Annual Reports of the Registrar of Births. Deaths, and Marriages.
22. 'Report of SMs for half year ended June 1852'. Checkley to the Governor-in-Chief of Barbados. No. 74, 30 June 1852.
23. *Blue Books*: selected volumes.
24. Deerr, *History of Sugar* Vol. I; Lobdell, 'Patterns of Investment'.
25. Williams, *From Columbus to Castro*.
26. *Blue Books*, 1838–78.
27. Ibid. 1878–82.
28. William Green, *British Slave Emancipation*, Clarendon Press, 1976, pp. 256–8.
29. *Report on the Encumbered Estates Court Act*, by Parliamentary Select Committee, 1885.
30. *St George's Chronicle*, issues for January 1867.
31. *Blue Books*, 1878.
32. Ibid. 1860 and 1880.

# 11

# *Education and the Working Class: 1824–85*

There was very little popular education in Grenada before Emancipation (1834). To the Legislature, and the rest of the ruling class, the more ignorant the slave the easier it was to control him; missionary groups' attempts to instruct slaves were interpreted as a move to subvert plantation life and the status quo. The teaching of Christianity to slaves, though not forbidden, was often violently resisted by the slaves' owners, because, according to one planter, as Richard Ligon noted, in 1657, 'once a Christian he could no more account him a slave, and so lose the hold he had on him as a slave'.[1]

After Emancipation, the ruling class and the educators saw in moral and religious instruction a means of integrating the ex-slaves into normal life. In the 1860s, a demand for popular, general, education was opposed by the upper class, on the grounds that not only was it unnecessary but potentially dangerous. Instead, they considered that an elitist-type secondary education was more beneficial to the community. By the late 19th century popular education was increasingly seen as a vehicle for upward social mobility. This conceptualization of the objective of education continued during most of the 20th century.

## Central School, St George's 1824

In 1823, there were 11 schools in the island (six in the parish of St George and five in the other parishes) mostly privately owned and catering for the children of the Whites and rich Free Coloureds. The Central School of St George's, established in 1824, founded by the Grenada Benevolent Society,[2] was the first major school in Grenada for children of the poor. Its stated aims were: 'To offer a plain education to all poor free children [Free Blacks and Coloureds] instructing them in their moral and religious duties and on the principles of the established Church of England'.[3] The School was opened on 29 November 1824 in a rented building, but early in 1825 moved to new permanent premises bought for £1,000. Most of this money, and money for operating the school, came from subscriptions of the Society's members and public-spirited members of the community; by 1825 £1,563 had been collected from these sources. The imperial government provided no assistance, but from 1829 the Grenada Legislature made three grants annually, totalling £89.[4]

In keeping with the values of the day the school had two sections; one for boys and one for girls. The principals – Horatio Turnbull of the boy's division and his wife of the girl's division – received £111 per annum each. Enrolment after one month was 19 – 14 boys and 5 girls; after one year it was 162 – of whom 107 were boys: 42 were from Carriacou and the outer parishes and 120 from the town of St George's.[5] All were children of Free Coloureds. In 1826 John McInnis, a planter in Grenada, was able to get one of his slaves admitted to the school – although this was against its rules – to be trained in order to teach other slaves on his estate; later that year the school made its facilities available to other proprietors who wanted to do likewise.

Dr Bell's education system was used in the school, as it was in the Central School, Barbados, where Horatio Turnbull was sent for training in this system. Religious books were invariably the tools for tuition,[6] and at first the curriculum essentially consisted of religious instructions and prayers. Reading, writing, spelling, ciphering and repeating arithemtic tables were introduced later. By 1832, 148 boys and 74 girls had graduated from the school, to take up a variety of occupations; 11 pupils had dropped out and nine were expelled for leading irreligious lives. By 1853, a total of 712 boys and 419 girls had graduated since the School's opening.[7]

For the 10 years preceding Emancipation and at least 10 years after, the Central School was one of the major institutions catering for the children of the poor. Since 1824, the Catholics had run a public school in St George's for the Free Coloured and slave children but there was no comparison between this school and Central School. There was also a third public school in Carriacou.[8]

## Schools in the Immediate Pre-Emancipation Era

Before Emancipation there were six private schools for the children of the white middle class; a Sunday School for the slave children and adult slaves; and a day school (held in the Anglican church) every Monday, Wednesday and Friday for slaves of all ages and sexes. The curriculum included fragments of the '3 Rs', as well as religious instruction.

In the town of Hillsborough, Carriacou, there was still only one public school by 1829; this provided education for 85 children both free and slave. The Bishop of Barbados, the provincial head of all Anglican Churches in Grenada, provided funds to operate this school. Most schools aforementioned were run under the auspices of the Church of England, then the established church of the State. During the years immediately preceding Emancipation, more schools were established in Grenada. A parochial school was established in St George's for all classes: in the combined parishes of St John's and St Mark's were two public schools, one for boys and one for girls, both in Gouyave. Finance for the establishment and part-operation of this school was from the Anglican bishop of the Diocese.

Three other schools were built during 1830–34: one in St Patrick's, one in St Andrew's (in 1833, the first for that parish); and a third in St David's. By 1836, in addition to schools for the children of Blacks and Free Coloureds there were 10 private schools for the children of the upper and middle classes; 12 estate schools for the children of apprentices; and Sunday Schools in almost every parish.

The Grenadian gentry assisted with the financing especially as the schools were under the aegis of the Church of England. In 1833, for example, the Central School received £87 grant-in-aid from the local government; St Patrick's parochial school received £50, while St Andrew's and St David's each received £30. Voluntary contributions in support of these schools amounted to £230 in the same year.[9]

It is apparent that at this stage Grenada's first schools were predominantly Church of England sponsored, and in fact the first teachers were usually married couples, members of the Church of England; set finance for building the schools came from the bishop of the Diocese, while three sources financed their operation and maintenance: the Diocese, the local government and voluntary contributions. The best financed and supported working-class school continued to be the Central School in St George's. With, in 1834, an enrolment of 180, it was the largest school in Grenada. By the beginning of Emancipation, although Roman Catholicism was the dominant religion, there were no established Roman Catholic schools in Grenada.

## Education During 1835–45

Resolution No. 5 of the 1833 Emancipation Act empowered the British, government to finance the education of freedmen in non-denominational schools in the West Indies on the principles of the British and Foreign School Society or the National Board of Ireland. Finance was to be provided upon 'liberal and comprehensive principles' and the education was to be moral and religious.

The British government had to decide whether the best agency to supervise this education scheme would be local government or religious bodies. According to the proposals embodied in the Negro Education Grant, £30,000 annually was to be made available to the religious denominations in the various islands for the first five years, then decreased by 20% each year until it was terminated in 1845. In addition, the Mico Charity Fund, a sum of £120,000, was to be used to set up other, non-denominational schools for the education of ex-slaves' children.

### *The Sterling Report: 1835*

In 1835, the Reverend John Sterling was sent by the imperial government to review the situation and make recommendations. Sterling found two opposing tendencies in British West Indian society: a) that the planters had conceptualized the Blacks as barbarous, indolent, vagrant, debauched, deceitful and ignorant; and b) that these Blacks were eager for knowledge and receptive to moral teachings.

Sterling summarized the many shortcomings in the existing system of religious education in Grenada and elsewhere as follows:

1. The methods used were of doubtful importance. There was too much rote learning and nothing was done to stimulate the mind. In one case he remarked that a child may learn the whole Bible and still be a heathen.
2. The period spent in school was too short – in most cases this was three to four hours per week.
3. Teachers were not trained and were totally inexperienced in pedagogy.

Nevertheless, he recommended that education should be in the charge of all religious bodies, and gave three reasons for not recommending the local governments: a) that if government was in control, religious education would disappear; b) that so far the churches had the most experience in popular education; and c) with the Government in control, the financial assistance from voluntary organizations and religious bodies would probably be withdrawn, and there was no assurance that government would provide these sums.[10] Thus, on 21 July 1835 the British government decided to make the grants available to religious bodies. Sterling's recommendation was influenced by the prevailing imperial conceptualization of Africans and Blacks as barbarous and uncivilized, and the civilizing and humanizing effect of religious education. The bedrock of imperial education schemes for newly emancipated West Indians was, therefore, religious instruction, and this continued to dominate most West Indian educational practices for the next century.

The imperial method employed to educate Blacks and Coloureds in Grenada after 1833 was almost a carbon copy of the British Dr Bell's system and the Irish National System. In both systems moral and religious training was dominant; religious training in the West Indies, however, was to be non-denominational. The Mico Charity schools set up in the West Indies after 1835 best fitted this role and function. In Grenada, by 1840, 12 Mico Charity schools had been set up by religious bodies; voluntary contributions supplemented the Fund's grants.

Additionally, under the Negro Education Grant separate schools were built for boys and girls, or where this was not feasible, the sexes were to be separated during classes. Schools established under the Negro Education Grant were to be regarded as the property of the religious bodies. The British government was to put up £250 to erect each school; if it had 200 pupils £100 would be granted for its maintenance. If the number on roll exceeded 200 then a further 10/- for each additional child would be given and vice versa.

These were some of the principles and guidelines which governed the disbursement of the Negro Education Grant. Working in close collaboration with the Colonial Office, the metropolitian missionary organizations, which were the primary promoters of the new schools, brought with them their own colour and class prejudices, especially their conceptualization of Blacks as barbarous and inferior.

The master/servant syndrome which had dominated Grenadian society for a century was reinforced by these teachers and thus continued unchallenged into the emancipation period under a different guise. Even a supposedly impartial observer such as Sterling referred to the newly emancipated 'as suffering under the combined influences of their barbarian origin'.[11] At that time the term 'barbarian' was also applied to planters, who were frequently accused of being crude, immoral, unlettered, and oafish.[12] James Stephen, in 1837, said he could think of no class more destitute of morals and more depraved than the West Indian planter class. Thus, vices that prevailed were not characteristic of Black workers alone but of the white planter class too. Understandably, the planters' interest and help in education was perfunctory; the development of education in Grenada in the post-Emancipation period must be seen with this in mind.

## *Negro education grant 1835*

Seventeen British territories in the Caribbean shared the first allocation of the Negro Education Grant of £18,200 on 8 December 1835; Grenada received £800, to be administered by the Society for the Propagation of the Gospel, and the Methodist Society.[13] Lieutenant-Governor Middlemore writing to the Governor-in-Chief (1835) drew his attention to the need for a more extensive system of education.

> The alteration in the condition of the working classes in Grenada renders the consideration of the state of education among that portion of the population more than usually important; although much has been done of late years by the establishment of day and Sunday schools in each parish a much more extended system of instruction should be brought to bear upon the whole community of apprenticed labourers and especially the young people under six years of age.[14]

Governor Middlemore recommended the establishment of a school for every four to five estates, which could be used as a chapel on Sundays.

At that time, St George's had two Central and six private schools, and a Sunday school; there were two public schools for St Mark's and St John's both in Gouyave; two public and two private schools in St David's and St Andrew's.[15]

Sauteurs had its first – Anglican – public school in 1835; later in the same year five proprietors built a school on Mt Gay Estate, which was discontinued soon after its inception, when the government started an infant school in St George's.

In 1835 the Church of England schools received a £220 Grenada government grant as well as £150 in voluntary contributions; these schools continued to be the best endowed. In St George's, the only public Roman Catholic school in Grenada received assistance from a few private individuals but none from government. The Catholic private school in Sauteurs, for moral and religious education, also received no government assistance. Of the two infant schools in Grenada, one, opened in 1836, was in St George's, the other, opened in 1835, was in Gouyave.

During the last two years of the apprenticeship period (1836–38) the Church of England opened four more schools in Grenada. The first, a Sunday school in the church, was in St George's; the second was a small school near Mr Ross' residence in Richmond Hill, built on lands donated by him; in 1837 he allowed a part of his home to be used as a Sunday School. The third was the Chapel School at Good Hope, St Paul's, erected in 1837 on lands donated by James Smith; the fourth was at Black Bay in St John's.

In 1838 the Methodists constructed and opened their first two schools; the Constantine Methodist and the Woburn Methodist, both in the parish of St George's. They were maintained by voluntary contributions, which in 1838 amounted to £150. In 1840 the Methodists built a third school, in St George's.

By the end of the apprenticeship period there were nine Anglican public schools (day and Sunday), two Methodist and one Roman Catholic, with a total enrolment of 1,234.[16]

## *Schools circa 1838–39*

Schools at this time were small, mostly consisting of fewer than 100 pupils. The Anglican Central School in St George's and the new Catholic school were the largest, their enrolment alone accounting for one-third of the entire school population in 1838. The infant school enrolment was also fairly large for the time. By 1838, however, no more than 10% of school-age children were attending school. This was due to the prevalence of child labour, the low level of parental interest in education, the negative attitude of the majority of the planter class towards popular education for ex-slaves, religious rivalries, and the patois/English language barrier.

In addition to the Anglican, Methodist and Catholic schools, in 1838 there were still eight private schools in the united parishes of St George's and St John's and two in the island ward of Carriacou. There were also twelve Mico Charity schools, one set up at Melville Street in St George's, another at Bacolet Estate and a third at River Antoine Estates. They had their own books, the Bible was their main source of teaching material, and they were non-denominational, open to all classes and both for children and adults. Attendance for adults was free, but each child paid 3d per week; all in excess of two from the same family were admitted free. In 1841, when the British government announced their decision to phase out the Negro Education Grant, the Mico Charity Establishment decided to do likewise.

The Catholics in Grenada at this time were the most inactive in the field of education, mostly owing to the lack of official assistance. Nevertheless, on 3 March 1838 they established another school, under the patronage of Lieutenant-Governor C.J. Doyle, an Irishman. The mode of instruction was based on the Irish National System.

Commenting on this the Reverend Thomas Coyle said: 'I feel gratified in saying that the system is the best that could be devised for giving liberal education to the masses of this island in point of utility and moral instruction'.[17] The school received no financial assistance from Government and depended largely on the generous contribution of Catholic parishoners. Its total enrolment of 176 boys and 73 girls made it the largest public school in Grenada in 1838.

## *La Trobe report: 1838*

The first major report on the progress of education in the British West Indies appeared in 1838. In 1837, Charles La Trobe, an inspector of schools, was sent by the imperial government to report especially on the Negro Education Grant during its first two years of operation.

He noted the absence of a system which combined the practical lessons of industry – agricultural work, manual labour and industrial skills – with the culture of the mind and that ex-slaves abhorred estate work while the planters cherished it for them: 'I have stated my conviction that the apathy and hesitation on the subject of education evinced by most of the planters chiefly hinges upon the idea of industrial training.'[18] To ex-slaves industrial training meant acquiring an industrial skill or becoming artisans; to the planter it meant a conditioning process that made the pupils amenable to estate labour.

Other obstacles to popular education La Trobe identified as;

- the patois spoken by the Blacks;
- the Roman Catholic religion (the religion of the majority);
- the few clergy;
- the discord between the various groups which needed to agree and co-operate on the question of education.

In his view, unless these matters were resolved the progress of education would be retarded. Nevertheless, education continued to be conceived of in Grenada as a conditioning process aimed at civilizing the children of the transplanted Africans, making them appendages of Anglo-Saxon culture, and teaching them their proper place in the social hierarchy.

In January 1847 the Colonial Office sent out a circular on a suggested scheme for Industrial and Normal Schools in the West Indies. The subjects on the curriculum were religious instruction, English, requirements of small farmers and relationship to authority. The last subject was intended to teach the relationship of the Colony to the Mother Country from an imperial perspective, and the domestic and social duties of the lower class of society.[19] Thus, the curriculum of the schools for the remainder of the century was to be guided by instructions in the three Rs, acceptance of one's social status and respect for the status quo.

## Educational Provisions and Developments: 1846–55

The Negro Education Grant was terminated in 1845, since the original intention had been that it was only temporary and transitory, and it was expected that the local Legislatures would follow it up by voting certain sums annually for education. By that time the Methodist Church had opened three more schools, one at La Baye, another in the town of St George's, and the third in Hillsborough (Carriacou). The Church of England also opened additional free schools in St George's.

With the termination of the Negro Education Grant the Grenadian government now had to provide finances to operate existing schools and to provide new ones. The Government's performance in this respect was disappointing; for the next six years there was no appreciable increase in educational expenditure and most schools experienced considerable hardships. In 1846 government continued to provide assistance for the schools of the two denominations it traditionally helped – the Anglicans and the Methodists, who received £230 and £117 respectively. Most of the money needed to run the Methodist schools, however, still came from voluntary contributions, which, in 1846 amounted to £235, or 66% of their total requirements.

In 1848 government made grants totalling £390, a marginal increase on its 1846 figure. By 1851 its contribution was £500; a meagre sum in view of the level of illiteracy, the size of the new school-age population and the need to educate the newly emancipated to take their places in Grenadian society. Meantime, the Anglicans continued to build and open more schools: two in Carriacou and one at Petit Martinique, and in 1855 another in Grenada, in Beausejour Valley. By that year the Catholics had considerably increased their number of schools. They ran three 'houses of instructions' for adults in St John's and St Mark's and two in the parish of St Patrick's. In addition they had at least seven established primary schools throughout Grenada, one in each parish, except St Mark's, and one in Carriacou. For each of these schools they received an annual grant of £30 from the Government.[20]

In 1855, 992 boys and 663 girls attended the various public elementary schools in Grenada; government assistance had almost doubled since 1851. With local government's responsibility for financing education, voluntary contributions began gradually to disappear. Despite the financial limitations Governor Robert Keate was pleased to observe the intellectual progress of the newly emancipated. He wrote: 'In close connection with the increase of the population is its advancement in intelligence and civilization. The grant made from public funds had been gradually augmented till it reached the sum of £1,060 in 1853.' The grant of £1,060 marked an increase of 100% on the 1851 figure. Prior to 1852 Roman Catholic schools had received little or no financial assistance from Government, but in 1852 they were allocated a grant of £190, and in 1853, £220. The remaining £840 contributed to the support of additional Church of England schools and the establishment of a Presbyterian school on Mt Rose Estate in the parish of St Patrick's.

The Government's increased education grant must be seen alongside the decline in voluntary contributions; from this standpoint the net increase for the schools was almost negligible.

## The Roman Catholic Church's Increasing Role

Owing to the increasing prominence of Roman Catholics in the educational field, the Church of England and Methodist schools were gradually falling behind. By the 1850s some 84% of the population were Roman Catholics, and as Roman Catholic schools opened, the population flocked to them. In 1852, of 609 new pupils admitted into schools in Grenada, 508 enrolled in Roman Catholic schools, 31 in Presbyterian and 80 in the Anglican and Methodist schools. There were ten Roman Catholic schools; 19 Church of England, four Methodist and one Presbyterian. In 1853 the RCs admitted an additional 119 students; the enrolment in the four Methodist schools increased from 276 to 338, and in the Presbyterian from 31 to 92; in the Church of England school, however, enrolment fell from 1,013 to 967. This was attributed to Roman Catholics transferring their children from the Anglican to the recently established Roman Catholic schools. Total enrolment in all schools in 1853 was 2,024 or 10% of the children of school age.[21]

Lieutenant-Governor Keate identified what he considered the two most serious obstacles to the success of popular education:

1. The prevalence of a 'barbarous patois' as the common medium of speech among the peasantry; hence the acquisition of a new language was to become a part of their elementary instruction; and
2. The division of the community into four religious sects – the Roman Catholics, Anglicans, Methodists and Presbyterians. The

desire of each sect to be established as the major religion exacerbated past rivalries, and led to duplication of claims on meagre resources. Keate saw the adoption of the non-denominational Irish National System as desirable, but almost impossible to introduce.

Keate considered that if education was to progress patois must be eradicated. He criticized the lack of good elementary textbooks, the use of the Bible as the only source book, and a method of teaching based on putting into children's mouths long, obsolete words and expressions rarely used in daily life. He recommended the establishment of a Central Teachers' Training School in the town of St George's, and the creation of a Board of Education to improve education administration.[22]

The Training School should be open to all persons of all denominations and, therefore, non-sectarian; its curriculum should be wholly secular; clergy and ministers should provide religious training but not within the school.

The Board of Education should meet monthly at stated times; ensure periodical inspection of all schools receiving government assistance; and require periodical reports from the ministers of religion who managed the Schools.

## The Education Act of 1857

Lieutenant-Governor Robert Keate's recommendations were to influence the Education Act of 1857, called 'An Act for Constituting the Board of Education and to Provide for the Due Instruction of the People in Grenada'.[23] The Act created the first Board of Education, composed of seven members (five Protestants and two Catholics) with the Governor presiding, and responsible for implementing the Act's other provisions. These included the appointment of a Principal for the Boys' Grammar School and the St George's Model School, and the distribution of the education vote. The Board was permitted to make bye-laws for the inspection of schools as long as these accorded with the spirit of the Act. In order to help carry out the provisions of the new Act the Government increased the education vote to £2,000 per annum.

Other essential aspects of the Act provided for the establishment of a Model School and a Normal School to train teachers, and a Grammar School for middle- and upper- class children. Before admittance to any of these schools a child's parents were required to pay a specific sum into the Treasury each quarter. A Principal and an assistant Principal, both appointed by the Governor, were required for the

Normal School; the Principal was also to be Principal of the Grammar School and Inspector of all grant-in-aid primary schools. Every parish priest was to be patron of his Church's school, and he was to select one person from his young volunteers for teacher training at the Normal School. Upon completion of training a teacher was required to return and serve in the school of his patron if there was a suitable vacancy, otherwise he or she could go to any other school with a vacancy and the school receiving such graduates would be most likely to receive assistance from the Board. Teacher training was financed by the Board but trainees were required to repay this when they started to work. The parents of a person who, once trained, no longer wanted to be a teacher, had to promise to repay the Board. The religion of no individual sect was to be taught in the Normal School. The Act was to be in force for three years (1857–60) after which progress would be reviewed.

In 1858 the Board established the Grammar, Normal and Model Schools at a cost to the Government of £600 per annum. There were 31 pupils in the Grammar School, 200 in the Model School and 12 pupil teachers in the Normal School. The Principal (J. Noble)'s duties included presenting an annual report on the functioning and progress of education in Grenada; in 1858 he presented the first comprehensive report on education, and the second of any kind in the Colony's history.

## The Noble Report 1858

Noble examined the operation, administration and personnel, the mode of teaching and learning, and the progress of the students in the schools already established.[24]

He was dismayed to find even children in the most advanced classes ignorant of the common arithmetic tables; he attributed this to unsuitable teaching, and recommended a more appropriate method of teaching. He also found that books used were of all kinds and that all the pupils, regardless of age or attainment, were being taught the same thing.

In Carriacou, children could read and write satisfactorily in only two schools. In many others children were unable to count to 20, name the days of the week or months of the year. These were the schools whose principals boasted of having trained teachers!

Most schools lacked books, maps and desks. Some schools had only two desks for more than 100 children; some had none. Most schools were dilapidated and too small to cater for different classes. In these conditions, Noble concluded, learning was impossible; moreover, it was incomprehensible why teachers did not abandon the struggle in despair. The physical difficulties were bad but the ingratitude and injustice were worse. Many people in Grenada, especially planters and Assemblymen, were still strongly opposed to popular education, claiming that so far it had succeeded only in making the newly emancipated averse to estate work and giving them strange ideas of their social status. Noble observed that this should not be construed to mean that ex-slaves had too much education but rather that they needed a good education.

The services of elementary school teachers were undervalued, mostly by the middle and upper classes. But Noble perceived the school teacher as an indispensable agent of change and progress. The upper class required teachers only to inculcate in the mass of Blacks respect for authority, acceptance of the status quo and subservience to his or her employers.

Many members of the lower class were also opposed to the education system, as they did not see how their children could benefit from it. Noble sympathized with them, as the system of education was meaningless, chaotic and futile. To remedy the situation, Noble made numerous recommendations covering all aspects of schooling: buildings, equipment, staffing and organization; and provided guidelines on curricula and attainment for each class from Standard I to Standard V.

The Assembly accepted the Noble report and subsequently, the Board of Education began to implement its recommendations, many of which were based on the syllabuses and the organization of classes in the Central School of St George's. But implementation was slow and by 1862 no significant effect could be observed. Governor Kortright, in a letter remarked: 'I regret to say that the system of education introduced by the Act of the Legislature in 1857 and continued by two subsequent Acts has not been satisfactory in its operation'.[25] An area that Noble failed to examine in detail was inadequacy of supervision, and the excessive work-load of the Inspector, who was not only headmaster of the Grammar and Normal Schools but also had to report on all schools in the Colony at least once every three months.

## The Struggle Continues

Under Noble's supervision the parochial schools improved, but apparently at the expense of the Grammar School. Resources were scarce, and Noble considered primary more important than secondary education as it involved the mass of the people.

The threatened closure of the Grammar School was resented by the Grenadian middle class and they accused the headmaster of inefficiency. Some still regarded the education of the lower class as unnecessary and to many it was a 'positive evil calculated to induce the educated portion of the poor classes to regard their fellow labourers as beneath them and to withdraw themselves from the class to which they properly belonged.'

This rigid class stratification now enunciated by the middle and upper classes in Grenada in the 1860s was a legacy of the plantation system bequeathed to Creole society. The social system of the classical plantation era began to take new shape in the late 19th century. The type of education at the time, the teachers, their prejudices and tendency to conform made challenge to this attitude impossible; education, on the contrary, reinforced it.

The headmaster of the Grammar School consequently resigned and the subsequent neglect owing to the Principal's work-load, plus falling attendance led, in 1862, to the closure of the Grammar School. In that year no education funds had been voted by the Legislature, resulting in much hardship for the schools; but credit is due to the clergymen of the several churches for keeping their schools running, and to the teachers who worked under financial pressure and at much personal sacrifice. Twenty-five schools, 25 teachers and 1,584 pupils were affected by this temporary cessation of the education grant. In 1863, however, the Legislature voted £500 for schools that operated in 1862 and a further £900 for those operating in 1863.

## The Grammar School Reopens, 1865

The Grammar School, reopened in 1865, together with the Normal and Model[26] School were the main institutions of further education at the time. The admission fee to the Grammar School was £4, £6 and £8 per term for the three different grades of students; the Model School fee was 1d, 2d and 3d per week. In addition to its usual pupils the Model School had six pupil teachers in training, each of whom received a small monthly allowance from the Board of Education. The cost of running the Model School and Grammar School amounted to £562.

Shortly after reopening, the enrolment at the Grammar School fell from 23 to 16. The Assembly was concerned at the poor attendance and a Commission of Enquiry was set up in June 1866 to look into the operation of the schools and the functioning of education.

The Commissioners found that tuition was satisfactory and the physical facilities were adequate, but suggested the exorbitant fees were probably the cause of poor attendance. A student studying one subject paid £4; if he studied three the fee was £6 or £8 depending on age.[27] The Commission suggested new rates of £1.5s for all subjects. Despite this, Grammar School enrolment fell to 16 in 1872, and by the middle of 1873 it again closed, to re-open in January 1874 with 36 students; by 1878, however, it closed for the third time.

## Schools in the 1860s and 1870s

In 1866 there was one secondary school, eight Church of England primary schools, seven Roman Catholic and five Methodist schools supported by Government, and receiving £1,200 in 1865 and £1,182 in 1866 in the form of grants.[28]

Not all schools in Grenada received government assistance; some were supported by funds of the Anglican bishop, and some Roman Catholic schools were privately endowed. The infant school in St George's was supported by an annual grant of £15 from the revenue of the lands of the Anglican Church. By 1878 there were 31 primary schools – an increase of about five since 1866.

The school population was 3,421, or 8% of the population and about 30% of the 5–20 year age group. In that year (1878) some 3,310 children were employed on sugar and cocoa estates throughout Grenada.[29] The government grant for education was £1,271, an increase of £210 over 25 years.

Although the number of students increased by some 60% (1853–78) the education vote remained virtually fixed for this period. The 31 primary schools in 1878 included 16 Anglican, five Wesleyan, and ten Roman Catholic. Of all schools the Grammar School had been the best endowed; it had eight pupils and Government made a financial contribution of £420. The Government allocated £37 for each child enrolled in the primary schools and £53 for each child in the Grammar School. Considering the number of children in need of elementary education such an allocation to the Grammar School was clearly injudicious.

In 1878, of the ten Roman Catholic schools one was a girls' secondary school (opened in 1876), St Joseph's Convent, run by the Sisters of St Joseph of Cluny, with, in 1878, 145 pupils.[30] It was maintained essentially by students' fees and by funds provided by the Roman Catholic Church.

## Education in the 1880s

The year 1882 saw the introducation of a New Education Code – adapted from the English Code – and the division of the schools into classes. In the same year, Governor Harley was instrumental in the promulgation of an Act designed to provide liberal aid to all schools in which the Christian religion was taught. This was the first systematic attempt to introduce a liberal system of educational grants in the Colony; formerly, Church of England schools had been particularly favoured. A far-reaching clause of the Act was the appointment of an Inspector of Schools responsible for the control and administration of funds vested in government and placed at the disposal of the Board of Education, and to administer examinations to pupil teachers.

The first Inspector under this new system assumed office on 1 January 1883. Reporting on progress under the New System, he stated that all schools had received a fair supply of furniture and equipment, and the teachers were certificated and the pupils arranged in standards in most schools; but he highlighted three areas for improvement: a) falsification of returns by teachers; b) poor knowledge of words by pupils; and c) poor results in promotional examinations, especially in arithmetic, geography and English history. He also drew attention to such deterrents to education as bad roads, long distances for students to travel and difficulty in crossing rivers without bridges.

The 1882 Code of Rules and Ordinance, subsequently strengthened by further Ordinances, defined the role and the extent of the Board of Education's powers, and had four main objectives:

1. Extension of primary education, to bring it within closer reach of the masses.
2. Unification and standardization of grants to schools of different denominations. This was a sequel to the disestablishment of the Anglican Church in 1874 and putting all Churches on an equal footing, vis-à-vis the Government.
3. Proper training of teachers.
4. To obtain the best results for funds disbursed.

During Governor Edward La Borde's administration (1883–85) popular education was largely neglected. But the next Governor, Walter Sendall, considered the £3,000 spent on education in 1885 to be inadequate and less than the resources of the Colony could justify. A Royal Commission to enquire into public expenditure etc. in 1882 had recommended a grant of £8,500 annually if Grenada was to develop an efficient system.

At that time one out of six children, or 2,191 out of a school-age population of 12,548, attended school. Sendall considered this unacceptable, but accepted the dual system of government schools and grant-in-aid schools. He promised to provide government schools in those areas not provided for by the churches, and during his administration government schools were established in many populous areas. These included: Concord Government (1885); Birchgrove Government (1886); and in 1887, Grand Roy, River Sallee, Hillsborough, Belvedere, and Hillsborough Government. Liberal building grants enabled new schools to be built, or old ones rebuilt, enlarged or repaired.

Meanwhile, two significant events in the history of education in Grenada occurred:

1. Implementing the Education Ordinance of 1888 which made primary education compulsory.
2. Publication of the Deighton Report in 1889.

### *The Deighton Report, 1889*

Horace Deighton, headmaster of Harrison College, Barbados, was employed by the Lieutenant-Governor to produce a report on the Colony's schools. Deighton found that the Board of Education had not, as required, drawn up rules for the regulation of government-aided schools, and consequently, every teacher followed his own inclinations; also that education had been reduced to a purely mechanical activity on the part of the students and teachers, and no teachers showed any real knowledge of school organization. He also lamented the absence of infant schools.[31] In the 1880s, only one-quarter of school-age children were enrolled in schools and of these approximately 50% only attended regularly; a state of affairs that continued for the rest of the century.[32] According to the 1891 census, out of 13,183 school-age children, 6,155 were enrolled in schools but only 3,246 or 23% attended.[33]

## Secondary Education: Expansion

By 1891 there were three secondary schools catering essentially for the children of the middle and upper classes: St Joseph's Convent, St George's Girl's High School, and the Grammar School (later the Grenada Secondary School).

The St George's Girls' High School (later Victoria Girls' High School) opened on 26 January 1891, was essentially a school for the daughters of middle-class Anglican families and was financed by private subscriptions. It received its first government grant of £2 a scholar per annum, not to exceed £100, in 1892, conditional upon: a) that its curriculum be subjected to government approval; b) that the school be examined annually; and c) that the Government be entitled to grant-free education in the school for two girls. School fees ranged from £3 to £5 per term. Overall responsibility for supervision and decision-making was in the hands of a governing body which met four times a year, and was responsible for appointing teachers.

The Grammar School (non-denominational) was opened on 2 February 1885 by private persons and incorporated as the Corporation of the Grenada Government School. Since the original Grammar School had been closed in 1878, many requests had been made for the establishment of a similar institution. The 1882 Royal Commission recommended that a Grammar School be immediately established, and that three scholarships annually should be awarded from open competition.[34] Governor Sendall supported the idea, but saw it as taxing the whole community for the benefit of a few.[35] However, the school was set up at the beginning of his administration, with 30 pupils and financed from a government grant of £250 yearly plus £5 for each boy who received half marks or above in the annual examinations, tuition fees, and private contributions. Fees were £2 per term and £1 6s 8d for boys in the preparatory classes. Eleven scholarships (six from government, five from the Governing Body) were available. Four government scholarships were available to girls, two each to St Joseph's Convent and St George's Girls' High School.[36]

In 1911, in accordance with the Secondary Education Ordinance of 1909 the Corporation of the Grenada Grammar School was abolished and the establishment and management of secondary schools under government provided for. The old Governing Board was replaced by the Board of Secondary Education consisting of the Governor, the entire Executive Council and two unofficial members of the Legislative Council. The Governor remained chairman of the Governing Body until 1924, when the ordinance was amended to make the President of the Council chairman. All aspects of the life of the school were rigidly controlled by the Governing Board; the Principal and staff had absolutely no autonomy – a distinctive feature of colonial rule at the time.

Thus reconstituted the Grammar School was reopened on 18 September 1911 in new commodious premises in Melville Street, St George's, with 38 pupils. Fees remained the same, but differentials between receipts and expenditure were taken care of by Government. Thus the school became almost totally financed by Government. In the ensuing years the number of students and the finances steadily grew.

In November 1915 new rules were drawn up for the operation of the school and embodied in the Secondary Education Ordinance of 1 December 1915. The name Grenada Grammar School was changed to Grenada Boys' School. (The name GBSS emerged during this post-1915 period.) On the Board's recommendation, decisions concerning appointments and dismissals of teaching staff were to be made by the Governor; lesser paid workers were to be appointed and dismissed by the Principal; the school day was to be opened and closed with prayers; the Principal had the exclusive right to choose all textbooks, subject to any revision of the Board; the former 39 teaching weeks were reduced to 37 and holidays increased from 13 to 15 weeks annually.

## Primary Schools at the Turn of the Century

By the turn of the century there were 37 primary schools in Grenada,[37] with a total enrolment of 7,128 and an average attendance, in 1896, of 3,527 – some 49% of the total. The £6,134 required to maintain these schools in the same year were covered by £5,792 from government and the remainder from school fees; voluntary contributions had ceased by 1890, except in the case of secondary schools.

Of 37 schools examined by the Inspector of Schools 30 were described as good in academic achievements, pedagogy, discipline and records, and seven not good. Attendance was still poor: in 1896 the Inspector attributed this to heavy rains, epidemics of mumps, measles and other diseases; additionally working-class parents' tendency to keep children at home to work in the house or the 'gardens' was probably a contributing factor.

## Conclusions

To summarize:

- Education in Grenada in the 19th century was religious-based, first dominated by the Church of England but later by the Roman Catholic church.
- It was perceived as a civilizing agent for Blacks both by the imperial government and the local legislature.

- The need for popular education was stressed but by the end of the century only 25% of school-age children attended school.
- No attempt was made to impart technical skills to the children of the labourers, workers and peasants.
- Provision was made, towards the end of the century, for solely elitist secondary education, with total enrolment of 140 for the three schools in 1896.
- A number of school teachers of both sexes did their best to develop the abilities of pupils in their care; these men and women devoted their lives to the children of the poorer classes.
- Teacher training was unsatisfactory and facilities for this were grossly inadequate. Government recognized the need for government-run primary schools and by the end of the century of the 37 existing they owned ten. The first government primary school was built in 1884.
- For most of the century learning consisted of memorized words and phrases, many of them unintelligible to the learner.
- The local legislature and the Grenadian gentry were unenthusiastic about popular education; some members of the plantation interest regarded it as unnecessary. Funds allocated for education from government revenues were, therefore, inadequate and fell short of what the economy could have afforded.

NOTES

Full citations only given where work does not appear in the Bibliography.

1. *Reports of the Society for the Education of the Poor, 1824–50*; also *Blue Book*, 1829.
2. Later named the Society for the Education of the Poor. Inaugurated in 1824, this Society was a major social welfare organization within the Anglican Church in Grenada.
3. *Reports of the Society for the Education of the Poor, 1824–50.*
4. Ibid.
5. Ibid. First Report, 1824.
6. Ibid.
7. Ibid, 1853.
8. Council Paper No. 12 of 1932, 'Report on the Education Department for 1931'.
9. *Blue Book*, 1833.
10. Gordon, *A Century of West Indian Education*, pp. 30–42.
11. Augier and Gordon, *Sources of West Indian History*.
12. Gordon, *A Century of West Indian Education*, p. 14.
13. Ibid.
14. *Outgoing Dispatches*, Governor Middlemore to Governor-General of Barbados, 16 April 1835.
15. *Blue Book*, 1836.
16. Ibid, 1838, 1840.
17. *Outgoing Dispatches*, 1838.
18. Gordon, *A Century of West Indian Education*, p. 30.
19. Ibid, p. 58; Augier and Gordon, *Sources of West Indian History*, p. 182.
20. *Blue Books*, 1846–55.

21. Keate to Colonial Office, in *Report on Blue Book for 1853*, September 1854.
22. Ibid.
23. *Letter Book*, 1855–60, 1857.
24. Ibid, 1858.
25. Kortright to Colonial Office, *Outgoing Dispatches*, No.59, 1862, 19 July 1862.
26. The Normal School had closed in 1859 and the two names were thereafter used interchangeably for the one institution.
27. *Blue Books*, 1865, 1866.
28. Ibid.
29. *Census of 1881*; *Blue Books*, 1878–81.
30. For details, see *Blue Book*, 1878.
31. Council Paper No.I of 1854, 'Report of Education Officer for 1852', 1854.
32. Annual Administrative Report, 'Report on Primary Schools for 1894', pp. 35–59.
33. Ibid. 'Report on Education' pp. 51–70.
34. Royal Commission, 1884, Vol.II, p. 61.
35. *Government Gazette*, 5 August 1885.
36. *Blue Book*, 1896.
37. Ten Government, seven Anglican, 14 Roman Catholic, four Wesleyan and two Presbyterian.

# 12

## *Health-Care Facilities and the 1854 Cholera Epidemic*

In any system of economic organization based on the exploitation of the worker, the health and well-being of the worker would be subordinated to that of the economic unit.

This was true of the era of plantation economy in Grenada that spanned the period 1763 to 1834; it was equally true for the era of Creole society (1838–85) and after. That the freed slaves, during the first two decades after Emancipation, were the main victims of the cholera epidemic which ravaged the British Colony of Grenada in 1854 was a direct result of neglect of health-care.

During the slavery period health facilities for slaves were provided by the estate hospital (or 'Hot House' as it was sometimes called), in which, as the health of the worker was of no importance to the planter, only a modicum of medical attention was afforded the sick and the infirm.

### The Immediate Post-Emancipation Period

After Emancipation, one of the first provisions for health-care in Grenada was the passing of an Act in May 1835 to establish Boards of Health. The Governor was to appoint suitable persons as members of the Boards for the town of St George's, for the parishes and for Carriacou.

The members of these Boards were to visit each parish under their jurisdiction and give directions to clean up garbage and clear drains, and to inspect houses to ensure that cleanliness was observed. To obstruct any Board member in the performance of his duties was punishable by a fine of £5. The Act made it illegal to throw carcases in the streets, on pain of a fine of 30/-, half of which would be paid to the informer; also keeping pigs in the town was illegal under the Act and carried a penalty of a £2.5s fine or imprisonment.[1]

The water works in St George's were begun in the same year that Boards of Health were established, and completed in 1837. In 1841 additions were made in order to provide better accommodation for shipping in the harbour. By the 1850s the estimated useful life of the pipes had been far exceeded; minor repairs were continually effected, but by 1854 they were completely worn out and recommendations were made for their replacement.

It cost government £1,840 in 1835 and 1837 to furnish and lay down the pipes that provided the town of St George's with water; the extension in 1841 cost an additional £1,115. Water rates for houses with pipeborne water were 2% of the rental value of the house; vessels paid a rate of 2d currency per ton, increasing in 1843 to 2d sterling, while the domestic rate was reduced to 0.5% of the rental value of the house.[2] Between 1835 and 1854 it cost government £2,647 to operate the water works, including the cost of building the reservoir and laying the pipes in 1841; revenue collected from the rates during the same period amounted to £3,977.

Apart from these measures, there were very few provisions for health-care. Apprentices continued to be provided for in the estate hospital until about December 1838; the General Hospital on Hospital Hill was the only one for the public, and at Richmond Hill (where today is the prison) was a military hospital for the regiments and militia.

## The Colony Hospital circa 1850

The Colony Hospital, founded in 1734 when the island was under French rule, was placed in the hands of a religious order and supported by charitable subscriptions and profits from a sugar plantation in St George's which had been purchased with the institution's funds. After cession of the island to the British in 1762 the charity was administered by trustees appointed by the Governor. In 1798 an Act to incorporate the trustees of the Colony Hospital was passed, with the Governor as Chancellor and the sole visitor of the Charity. The number of directors was limited to 19, to be appointed by the Governor, with the Chief Justice, the Speaker of the Assembly, the Attorney-General and the Rector of St George's as ex-officio directors.

This constitution remained essentially unchanged for the next three decades.[3]

The Colony Hospital was situated on the south side and lower part of Hospital Hill, with, by 1850, about five acres of provision or garden ground for the surgeon's use.

The hospital itself was described as disorganized, needing repair, filthy, and furnished with neither bedsteads, bedding, nor utensils, except two or three urinals and two small shelves with a few bottles of medicine; the atmosphere was permeated with a revolting stench of filth and decay. The average number of patients in the hospital at any one time was about 18; there was accommodation of sorts for 48 patients. The Surgeon of the Hospital managed and lived in the institution; there was also a Secretary/Treasurer to the hospital corporation; each of these officials was paid £40 per annum. The fee for patients admitted to hospital was 21/- (one guinea)

Funds for running the hospital in the period after Emancipation were from three sources: rents from lands owned by the Corporation; donations: and grants of the Grenada legislature (see Table 12.1).

The legislature's annual grant of £200 was to assist with maintenance and to ensure that proper services were provided, but the control of finances and general management of the hospital degenerated so much that an inquiry into its operation and condition was instituted in 1850.[4]

All the hospital inmates were found to be drunkards, and both the surgeon and the Secretary/Treasurer too. The report of the inquiry concluded that both men were unfit for their duties, in that they had ignored the unkind treatment meted out to many patients, and were responsible for the abysmal waste of the hospital's resources and its maladministration.

Government's first grant of £200 to the Hospital Corporation was in 1845 and this annual sum remained unchanged for the next 13 years, even though the Colony Hospital was the only one to serve

**Table 12.1 Revenue and Expenditure of the Colony Hospital Corporation**

| | *1846* £ | *1847* £ | *1848* £ |
|---|---|---|---|
| Expenditure | 430 | 404 | 375 |
| Rents of lots paid | 206 | 259 | 86 |
| Donations | 17 | 6.10s | 10 |
| Grants by Legislature | 200 | 200 | 200 |
| Arrears – rents of lots | 223 | 463 | 380 |

Source: *Papers Connected With Inquiry Into The Colony Hospital,* 1850

28,923 people. In 1858, however, the hospital was transferred to the military barracks at Fort George which had been renovated for the purpose, and the grant was increased to £500 per annum. In 1866 it was again increased to £800, an additional £300 was granted to the Directors for the care of sick and indigent unindentured immigrants. In that year running expenses of the hospital were £1,271 and revenues amounted to £1,293.

An alms house and a lunatic asylum were established at this time, in the town of St George's, but were later transferred to the officers' quarters of the military barracks at Richmond Hill. The asylum, supported by a government grant of £300, was under the superintendence of a government officer, assisted by an under-keeper. The same superintendent, assisted by a matron, was in charge of the alms house (poor house), under the direction of a Board of Guardians appointed by the Governor; government granted £500 annually towards its support. There was also the Victoria Alms House, in St George's, supported by voluntary contributions to provide 'respectable' women, who had become destitute, with board and lodging free of charge.

The paltry provisions for health-care and health education, before 1854, exposed the labouring classes to the full violence of disease, pests and epidemics, and this, plus their superstitious beliefs, made them easy prey to the ravages of disease and pestilence. The majority of victims of any epidemic were, therefore, of that class – as was the case with the cholera epidemic in Grenada, in June 1854.

## Cholera in the West Indies

Between 1850 and 1856 a series of cholera epidemics swept through the islands. Jamaica was the first to be attacked, in 1850–51, and some 32,000 persons died; in 1852 it was the Bahamas, and in 1854 the eastern Caribbean. In Barbados alone 20,000 persons were said to have died of the disease, and in Trinidad, 4,000. In Grenada, between June 1854 when the epidemic struck and September 1854 when it was brought under control, it had devastated the island's population with some 12% of its 32,000 people dead.

These recurrent epidemics are clear manifestations of the almost complete absence of sanitation and hygiene throughout the West Indies in general and in Grenada in particular. It is ample evidence that the plantocracy had abdicated responsibility to colonies where the mass of the population had just been freed, and merited the accusation of Henry Taylor that they were 'eminently disqualified from the great task of improving a people newly born into freedom'. The devastation

*The old lunatic asylum on Richmond Hill*

wrought by the 1854 epidemic in Grenada was a direct result of the imperial government's negligence and the open refusal of the Grenadian plantocracy to ensure that the newly emancipated population was properly housed and educated, and lived in healthy surroundings.

Immediately it became known that Asiatic cholera had broken out in Barbados, steps were taken to clean up the town of St George's as it was presumed the danger was most imminent there. The Board of Health ordered the removal and burning of all filth and garbage; in addition, trees were cut down and other barriers to the free circulation of air removed. These measures proved to be ineffective and Grenada, nevertheless, remained vulnerable to an outbreak of cholera.

## *Cholera in Grenada*

The disease broke out on Saturday 10 June 1854, among the artillery soldiers quartered in the barracks at Fort George, and spread to the 69th Regiment, which had recently arrived from Trinidad, and subsequently to the rest of the island's population.[5]

The disease had first appeared in Jamaica in 1851, and was probably carried to the other islands by inter-island vessels. Barbados was attacked before Grenada and indications are that it spread from there to Grenada. The outbreak of cholera coincided with the first wave of Asian immigration, and it seems likely that it could have been carried to the West Indies by one of these immigrant vessels.

In May 1854, ships coming to Grenada from Barbados were quarantined for seven days; but according to Lieutenant-Governor Keate, the quarantine regulations were established more with a view to meeting prejudices and preventing panic than to keep out the disease. The Governor, however, was apparently sceptical that the disease had been introduced into Grenada by inter-island shipping, owing to the volume of traffic between Grenada and Barbados. He stated, 'While quarantine was in force, as it was for the space of five weeks, only three or four vessels became liable to detention.' It is worthwhile to note that the first victims, the soldiers at Fort George, had previously been stationed in Barbados; medical opinion seems to have been convinced that this was the source through which the disease was introduced.

Despite the measures taken to clean up the town of St George's before the epidemic, when it finally broke out, the deficient machinery of the Board of Health and the generally unhealthy surroundings in which the lower classes lived rendered precautionary measures ineffective; as the Governor wrote: 'The predisposing causes are attributable to the impossibility of eradicating in so short a time, longstanding habits of neglect and individual indifference to sanitary precautions.[6] This was prevalent both in urban and rural areas and reflected the relative neglect of the social conditions of the working people after 1838. Governor Keate failed to appreciate this fact, and instead blamed the peasants themselves. He wrote:

> The negro peasantry of this island are not only, generally speaking, unable to appreciate the benefits of cleanliness, but either by nature or the force of circumstances, they are so miserly and penurious in their habits, that it was found impossible to induce even those among them who were known to have means, to expend the smallest sums to improve their dwellings or to procure good food or medicines, and when the epidemic reached them, they appeared to prefer death either by disease or starvation to the outlay of a single shilling of their hoarded treasure.[7]

This observation applied more to the independent settlers in the hills and valleys than to the inhabitants of the town and the labourers located on estates. In this despatch, however, the Governor revealed himself as guilty of oversimplification of the social situation.

As part of the precautionary measures, houses and other dwellings were disinfected with lime. According to one doctor, however, houses and cottages in many places, though carefully limewashed outside, were left untouched inside with all its dirt and filth. The absence of active and intelligent supervision, as well as the haphazard approach of officials of the day to the health of the poorer classes, were responsible for this neglect.

Discovering that conditions at Fort George were extremely unsanitary, the troops there were removed to an airier place, at Richmond Hill. This in no way affected the spread of the disease, since it not only devastated the artillery men but wreaked havoc among members of the 69th Regiment also stationed at Richmond Hill. By 4 July, when it seemed to have been brought under control among the troops, the disease spread to the civilian population; the first to be infected were seven inhabitants in the Morne Jaloux area, a mile or two windward of St George's. The crowding of the neighbours into the cottages of those attacked, and the holding of 'wakes' over the bodies of the dead, led to an increase in the virulence of the disease. Measures were, however, taken by the police, the magistrates and the clergy of all denominations to persuade people to stay away from wakes.

## *The epidemic spreads*

After this initial outbreak cases began to appear sporadically in the town and parish of St George's, from the healthiest to the swampiest areas. Though these cases were few, they appeared simultaneously in so many different localities it became obvious that the one doctor who, in those days, served the parish of St George's could not cope. The disease had not yet reached epidemic level when a Dr Huggins arrived from Trinidad on private matters and did much to help. At this time the disease broke out on Calivigny Estate in south-east St George's. Panic among the estate workers was aggravated by the reaction of both the manager and overseer who promptly fled the estate, leaving the workers to the mercy of the malady. In the meantime, the Board of Health for the parish of St George's had instituted house-to-house visitation and distribution of medicines.

It took these visitors some time to reach Calivigny Estate to appraise conditions there. When they did it was to find many dead, some from want of care, others from starvation, but most from cholera. All work had ceased and the labourers made no attempt to obtain food after being abandoned by their employers. 'Many had fled and the remainder had huddled themselves together in their huts with every breath of air carefully excluded, awaiting death with apathy and despair.'[8] The spectacle of dead bodies lying unburied among their bewildered and despairing fellow workers must have been terrifying.

When the police arrived they buried the dead, and burnt the surrounding bush as well as those cottages made inaccessible by the high bush and narrow pathways. On the arrival of Drs Huggins and Aquart it was decided to convert the estate's dwelling house into a hospital. The estate attorney ordered a part of the estate's stock to be killed to furnish meat for the inmates of the hospital. These measures, especially burning the bush and huts, did much to bring the disease under control there.

Many agents were actively involved in the campaign against the 1854 cholera epidemic. Some estate managers co-operated by taking the necessary preventive and precautionary measures; and members of the clergy, medical men, house-to-house visitors and distributors of medicines, police and the members of the several Boards of Health, worked tirelessly.

Because of the acute shortage of doctors, a cholera hospital was set up in St George's, under Dr Huggins, so that the limited medical resources could serve the greatest number. The hospital, housed in barracks at Fort George, became the Colony Hospital after the eradication of cholera.

It is noteworthy that about 30 prisoners in St George's gaol escaped infection. This was attributed to the 'cleanliness of the institution and to the regular and wholesome diet furnished to its inmates'.[9]

By the middle of July 1854, many people had died of the disease, both in the town and parish of St George's and Grenada was in the grip of an epidemic. By 10 July 132 deaths were recorded by Drs Aquart and Huggins; they also confirmed that the disease was the same as that in Barbados in all respects. Assistance was sought from Trinidad and a Dr France was sent to help.

It became necessary to seek burial sites for the mass of dead. A piece of land in the leeward of St George's was obtained from the Colony Hospital Corporation for this purpose; this is the present Cemetery Hill. In rural areas, churchyards, estates' lands and peasant plots were all used as burial grounds. In many cases the number to be buried was so great that the regulatory six feet depth was not followed, nor were the graves properly covered. During the six weeks that the malady raged in St George's there was an average of 16 deaths per day, and by 25 July 1854, the total of 374 deaths had occurred in St George's. The epidemic took a heavy toll along the banks of the River St John (River Road today) which were inhabited by a colony of washerwomen who fell early victims to the disease.

The epidemic then spread from St George's to St David's, but in a mild form, and it was hoped it would soon diminish. This hope, however, proved to be in vain, as soon afterwards it broke out in St Patrick's with ten-fold violence, both in the town of Sauteurs and on several estates in the parish simultaneously. The three doctors in the parish, together with the clergy, managers, overseers and members of the St Patrick's Board of Health, all fought actively to bring the disease under control, but, by the time they had succeeded the mortality rate in St Patrick's was estimated at 25% of the population.

The Roman Catholic Chapel and an old block house formerly used by the militia were converted into temporary hospitals, used more to accommodate the abandoned and neglected rather than as a means of arresting the spread of the pestilence. Although cholera was most severe in St Patrick's, providentially its duration was the shortest. Of 1,720 persons attacked by the disease there 1,250 died.

St Mark's, St John's and St Andrew's parishes, which initially had not been affected, now also fell victim to the epidemic; St Andrew's first. The Board of Health's precautions, in this, the largest parish with only one medical practitioner, seemed adequate. House-to-house visitations were organized at the earliest stages of the outbreak, although many areas remained neglected. The disease here took a virulent form similar to that in St Patrick's, but many people recovered, having been sought out and treated in the earliest stage. By 31 August 1854, there were 1,559 reported cases of cholera, resulting in 616 deaths.[10]

Next the parishes of St John's and St Mark's were attacked. The timely arrival of Dr Mercer from the Colony Hospital at Port of Spain, Trinidad, helped to alleviate the situation, as there was no resident doctor in either of these two parishes. The disease appears to have been the least rapacious in these two parishes, partly owing to their relatively small size, and partly to the ubiquitous energies of Dr Mercer and his aides. Dr Mercer was in Grenada for only a few weeks as he had to hurry back to Trinidad where cholera had broken out. His main contribution was the implementation of a small-scale plan of preventive medicine.

In St David's parish the epidemic maintained its hold to the last. The epidemic's progress was slow and reached its peak so late that the last phase of the disease in Grenada was seen in St David's.

Cholera first appeared in St David's parish on 27 June in a boy at Charlotte Vale, who had on that day just come from the town of St George's; on 29 June two other cases were discovered: one at Laura Land and the other on Lower La Tante lands. By 1 July the disease had spread throughout the parish, and appeared last on Requin and on La Sagesse Estates. Few people escaped infection, but those who received proper treatment as soon as they were affected invariably recovered; in many of the cases where people died there was wanton neglect in applying for remedies. The disease killed both young and old, those living in clean, as well as those in dirty surroundings, the intemperate and negligent as well as the provident, but mortality was heaviest in the dirtiest and most unhealthy areas. Additionally, the outbreak of the disease here coincided with heavy rains and this helped to increase the rate of infection.

The unhealthy conditions under which the labouring population lived assisted the full development of the disease. Notwithstanding the frequent exhortations of the Board of Health to the people to adopt sanitary measures, a negligent and lackadaisical attitude prevailed. Such measures in health education, proper housing, etc. should, of course, have been undertaken since 1839. It took an epidemic to move the authorities to action. There was considerable dirty and stagnant water around the houses; the high bushes in front of houses were not cleared; the whitewash was applied to the outside instead of the inside of houses; bedrooms remained dark and unventilated; in many cases the sick were placed on the cold ground as the first step in their treatment of the disease.

During the course of the disease in St David's the medical doctor was assisted by the house-to-house visitors, who distributed medicines, and by the managers and attorneys of estates.[11] Various treatments were applied to the cholera victims: Dr Stevens' consisted of the application of large doses of calomel and opium, quinine and chloroform; Dr Ayres' consisted of a warm bath, a large blister put over the stomach and liver, and a pill of 3g calomel, 0.5g Dover's Powders and 0.25g camphor to be administered every 15 minutes in a tablespoonful of water until the vomiting ceased, then 2g of calomel every 30 minutes until the patient's tongue had become moist.

By 9 October the epidemic had killed 193 of St David's population of 2,581; 110 of the victims were 40 years and over.

The island of Carriacou remained free from the disease until 6 July 1854 when the first cholera death occurred. The cholera was carried by passengers aboard two sloops, the *Recovery* and the *Rose Ann*, both of which had come from Grenada. The first victim was a man who was landed from the *Recovery* in an advanced stage of the disease and who died while being carried to his house. The second case was a boy from the same sloop, found almost dead on Harvey Vale Estate and given medicine. He responded to care but in the absence of the nurse drank an inordinate quantity of water whereupon the symptoms were renewed and he died; a man who attended him on the estate died soon afterwards.

The *Rose Ann* arrived with all her crew in an apparently healthy state; however, within 24 hours everyone except the Captain was dead. The town of Hillsborough was, therefore, the first area to be attacked. From there the disease spread rapidly throughout the island and in some areas it was particularly malignant. In the village of

Bogles, with a population of about 400 persons, nearly 20% died. In Petit Martinique mortality was considerable, and such panic followed that the remaining community fled and sought refuge in Carriacou. That the island had little water and few doctors could explain the disease's spread there. In a report of 1854, Dr Maynard, Carriacou's resident physician, alluded to the morbid unwillingness to be visited or treated for the disease by the inhabitants of both Carriacou and Petit Martinique.

In Carriacou many local medicines were used to treat the disease; mention was made of a certain 'Bitter Bush' which seemed to have been very effective. Superstitions led many people to use other methods, the efficacy of which was doubtful. Two of these included drinking a mixture of brandy and pepper, and the application of hot stones to the prostrate body of the sick. Some 1,000 out of Carriacou's population of 4,000 were infected; out of these 386 died and the remainder recovered.

## Extent of Mortality Resulting from Cholera

By 25 August 1854 the cholera epidemic had almost completely disappeared from Grenada, lingering only in the parish of St David's. By early September 1854, however, it was completely eradicated. In all, it lasted some 12 weeks, infecting 6,788 people of whom 3,788 died. Table 12.2 shows the extent of the mortality between 21 June and 15 September 1854 among the different age groups on a parish to parish level.

**Table 12.2 Deaths from Cholera**

| | | *Deaths from cholera* | | | | | | | | |
|---|---|---|---|---|---|---|---|---|---|---|
| *Population* | *District* | *0–10 yrs* | | *11–40 yrs* | | *40+* | | | *Total* | *Total* |
| | | *M* | *F* | *M* | *F* | *M* | *F* | *M* | *F* | *M&F* |
| 4,567 | St George's Town | 35 | 24 | 63 | 89 | 56 | 12 | 154 | 275 | *379* |
| 5,413 | St George's Parish | 42 | 33 | 108 | 83 | 78 | 81 | 228 | 197 | *425* |
| 2,876 | St John's | 18 | 17 | 58 | 55 | 35 | 54 | 169 | 178 | *347* |
| 1,738 | St Mark's | 13 | 12 | 33 | 31 | 43 | 50 | 89 | 93 | *182* |
| 5,160 | St Patrick's | 136 | 147 | 257 | 219 | 213 | 215 | 606 | 581 | *1,250* |
| 5,635 | St Andrew's | 19 | 42 | 99 | 106 | 175 | 175 | 293 | 323 | *616* |
| 2,581 | St David's | 6 | 13 | 31 | 33 | 55 | 55 | 92 | 101 | *193* |
| 4,401 | Carriacou | 30 | 5 | 141 | 105 | 52 | 53 | 223 | 163 | *386* |
| *32,671* | | *299* | *293* | *790* | *721* | *707* | *795* | *1,854* | *1,861* | *3,778* |

Source: Despatch No. 89, 1854: Lieutenant-Governor Keate to Governor Colebroke, Grenada, Report on Appearance and Progress of Cholera in Grenada, 6 October 1854

St Patrick's was the hardest hit of all parishes, losing 25% of its population. The greatest number of recoveries was in St Andrew's: 943 out of 1,599; the recovery rate in St John's and St Mark's was also quite high, 337 out of 724 and 113 out of 295 respectively. Of the 122 who were admitted into the Cholera Hospital from 9 July to 22 August 80 died and 47 recovered. The under-10-year-olds were the least severely affected.

The 1854 cholera epidemic in Grenada showed the undoubted need for improved sanitation and better medical attention among Grenadians in general, and the labouring population in particular, and both Doctors Parkin and Huggins suggested various sanitary improvements to obviate unhealthiness. The need to change the constitution of the Boards of Health was also highlighted. Closer co-ordination of activities between the Central Board of Health in St George's and the other Boards in the outlying districts was essential. It was also necessary to transform these Boards from debating societies into functioning organs of the Colony's health system. Lastly, the epidemic showed the need for an increase in funds allocated by the local government to the various Boards of Health to enable them to embark upon schemes of preventive medicine and community health education among the peasantry.

As a result of the epidemic Dr Huggins made the following recommendations to the Board of Health in October 1854, aimed at improving the cleanliness of the environment in the town of St George's:

1. Scavenger carts be employed to convey rubbish and filth to an isolated spot near a neighbouring estate to be made into manure.
2. Measures be adopted to have all rubbish collected in casks or boxes ready to be thrown into the carts and put into the streets on such days as may be decided upon by the members of each section of the town.
3. Means be adopted for deodorizing the collection at the refuse dump in order to facilitate its removal to the estate and lands of the settlers.
4. Measures be taken to keep the streets free from grass as it grew in such thick clumps that the flow of water after showers was impeded.
5. Vacant lots in the town be immediately cleared of weeds and the collection removed at once.
6. Inspections be made weekly of the different yards as they were so constructed to ensure that accumulation took place on levels that were made for the convenience of the tenants.
7. Inspections be made weekly of the different drains running under the flooring of houses to ensure that they were kept clean and that no water accumulated in them.[12]

Immediately after the cholera epidemic a doctor was appointed for each district, that is, the town of St George's, St Mark's, St John's, St Patrick's and St David's. His duty was to vaccinate all children, and to attend and furnish medical and surgical aid and medicines to the poor and destitute who needed this attention. A dispensary was also established in Hillsborough (Carriacou) and the Health Officer of that island was authorized to vaccinate all children and attend to the poor and destitute. There were no public hospitals or asylums in any of the parishes except in the capital, St George's, and thus the sick, lunatics and paupers were received from the other parishes into the hospital, alms houses and lunatic asylums there.

## Expanded Medical Facilities Post-1854

With the commencement of Indian indentured immigration in 1858 the need arose for expanded medical facilities in Grenada. Medical facilities on the estates were very poor and consequently the General Hospital was given a grant of £300, as mentioned before, to provide for the care of sick and indigent immigrants. This provision did not work too well owing to the limited space and facilities in the General Hospital. In 1866, Act No. 230 was passed to regulate conditions pertaining to immigrants. According to this, each estate had to provide hospital accommodation, medical assistance, a sick nurse and medicines before they could receive Indian immigrants. As a result numerous estate hospitals emerged. By 31 March 1867 some 31 estates which had received Indian immigrants, had their own estate hospital and a nurse, and had arranged for visits by a doctor. Others, which did not have hospitals of their own, made separate arrangements. The Protector of Immigrants who made an inspection of all these facilities in 1867 found only six to be in good condition; the majority of estates had hospitals, but the state of the buildings was far from satisfactory.

Indian immigrants infected with serious diseases were transferred for treatment to the Colony Hospital. Thus, by 1867, the major institutions that provided health-care were the Colony Hospital and the estate hospitals. In 1877, the £800 annual grant to the Colony Hospital was, after 12 years, increased to £1,000; the grants to the lunatic asylum and the alms house were simultaneously increased to £700 each; the dispensary in Carriacou received a grant of £150 at the same time.

By 1883, the year before the Royal Commission visited Grenada, there were two hospitals in St George's, one central lunatic asylum, one leper asylum and two alms houses, all supported by Government.

The lunatic asylum received patients from the other Windward Islands and these colonies contributed to its upkeep. There was also one hospital in St John's parish, opened in August 1882, one in St Patrick's, opened in May 1882, and one in St Andrew's, opened in March 1882. These hospitals, originally reserved for Indian immigrants, were opened to the public in 1882. There was one medical officer serving each parish and one serving Carriacou and Petit Martinique; the Colonial Surgeon headed the medical department.

A Yaws Hospital was opened in 1881 at Marine Cottage. There were 17 patients at the beginning of 1882 and 81 in all were admitted during the year. An average of 21 patients was in the hospital daily; each remained for about 68 days. The health of the island was described as 'tolerably good' at the time. The death rate was 3% of the population while the infant mortality rate was 19% of total deaths or 338 out of 1,146. The main causes of death were zymotic diseases, diseases of the digestive system and of the respiratory organs.[13]

The 1883 Royal Commission recommended that a Chief Medical Officer head the Department of Health, with a staff of 17 District Medical Officers in towns and country districts. It also recommended a complete series of government dispensaries under qualified dispensers, and a Board of Visitors in each district where there was a hospital. The Commission showed great concern over the prevalence of yaws in Grenada and the other islands.[14]

## Yaws: Another Pestilence

Yaws was prevalent throughout Grenada but more widespread in the parishes of St Andrew's, St David's and St George's. The prevalence of the disease in severely affected areas was due to the unclean habits of the people and overcrowding of residences, and not to climatic or ecological factors. No connection was found between the diet of the people and the spread of the disease; it was limited almost exclusively to the labouring population although there were a few cases among the upper class. Quack doctors in Grenada proposed strange cures for yaws, one being to feed the patient for months on the flesh of the armadillo only, mysteriously cooked with herbs and then suspended for hours over pots of some boiling infusion.[15]

In St David's in particular, where the disease was rampant, the hygienic conditions of the houses of the labouring class and small proprietors were appalling, greatly overcrowded, frequently with as many as nine persons occuping two rooms neither larger than 10ft × 12ft; bedrooms were often devoid of air or sunlight; five-sixths of the sleeping room was occupied by a large four-poster bed, beneath which was the receptacle for all household belongings as well as 'tensils' to defecate in. Frequently, neither the bedroom nor outer room was floored and the ground was often saturated with all kinds of filth; thus once a disease was introduced into the house, an ulcer or skin abrasion readily led to infection with yaws or leprosy.

In St David's was a bay called 'Yaws' Bay' where the patients bathed. By 1896 the disease was still prevalent and some 88 cases were treated in the Yaws Hospital, the majority of which were sent in by the Medical Officers of St David's and St George's.

*

To summarize: an examination of health provisions showed that little was done to provide adequate health-care for the newly emancipated and the labouring population before the cholera epidemic, but this event aroused a recognition in some people that action was needed and, as a result, health-care facilities were extended; above all, more attention was paid to the sanitary conditions in the town. By the 1870s the main hospitals in Grenada catering for the labouring population were the Colony and estate hospitals. Most of these estate hospitals, which catered primarily for the indentured labourers, were opened to the general public in 1882. By that year the labouring people's health conditions were still far from satisfactory, and they continued to fall easy prey to epidemics and debilitating fevers. Their housing was abominable; pipe-borne water was non-existent in the rural areas (Les Avocats waterworks was opened in 1885).

Soon after Emancipation the Grenadian working class and labouring population were joined by increasing numbers of immigrants who came as indentured workers. The Liberated Africans were caught on the high seas and distributed on estates; the Indians, Portuguese and other Africans came under an imperial Indentured Immigration Scheme. Their arrival, as we shall see, markedly changed the demographic structure of the island, as well as influencing the social and cultural patterns of Grenadian society.

NOTES

Full citations only given where work does not appear in the Bibliography.

1. *Laws of Grenada*, 'An Act for establishing Boards of Health', 18 May 1835.
2. Keate to Colebroke 'Forwarding Blue Book 1854', Enclosure No.6 in Despatch No. 61 of 1854, 22 May 1855.
3. *Blue Book*, 1866.
4. *Papers Connected with an Inquiry into the State of the Colony Hospital of Grenada, 1850.*
5. Despatch, No. 89 of 1854. 1854. Keate to Colebroke. 'Report on the appearance and progress of Cholera in Grenada.'

6. Ibid.
7. Ibid.
8. Ibid.
9. Ibid.
10. Ibid. 'Enclosure No. 6 in Despatch No. 89'.
11. Ibid. 'Enclosure No. 3 in Despatch No. 89'.
12. Ibid.
13. *Census of 1881*, 1881.
14. *Royal Commission, 1884*, p. 54.
15. Governor to Secretary of State. 'Dr. Nicholls Mission to the Windward Islands' S.S. 390/91. 18 August 1891.

# 13

## *Indentured Immigration Scheme: 1834–85*

The Indentured Immigration Scheme to Grenada was the sequel to a general panic which spread among the West Indian planters, especially the Jamaicans, resulting from a combination of the abolition of slavery in 1834, and the Colonial Preference System which operated from 1846 to 1854. The expenses of this immigration scheme were a heavy burden on Grenada's scarce resources.

Grenada was no longer a major sugar producer, and compared to St Kitts, Barbados or Trinidad, production was insignificant. The period of indentured immigration, in fact, coincided with a most significant decline in Grenada's sugar industry. In 1833 the island produced 10,203 tons of Muscovado sugar for export; by 1853 only 4,683 tons – less than half the 1833 figure – was produced; by 1873, after 15 years of Indian immigration, production declined to 3,168 tons. Based on Noel Deerr's book, *History of Sugar*,[1] it would appear that by 1883 Grenada was producing no sugar for export; minimal quantities, varying from 77 to 110 tons only, were exported in selected years afterwards.

### Liberated Africans

In 1836, the HMS *Vestal* captured three slave ships off the coast of Grenada – two were Portuguese vessels, *Negrinha* and *Phoenix*. The cargo of the three ships, consisting of 1,250 African slaves – the so-called 'Emancipados' destined for Cuba or Brazil – were apprenticed out to planters, in September of that year.[2] The following year, when

HMS *Harpy* captured another slaver in Grenada's waters, an additional 280 Liberated Africans were similarly apprenticed.

Measures were immediately effected to protect these Africans and they were treated similarly to apprentices. On 19 April 1837 an Act was passed for the protection, and promotion of the industry and good conduct, of Africans who had been transhipped to Grenada. All expenses incurred between arrival and indenture were paid for by the public treasury; employers who wanted African indentures were required to pay the public treasury £1 currency for every African allotted to them. Fit and proper persons were to be chosen to implement this scheme, and provisions had to be made for religious instruction, and for the health of the indentured.

Indentures were initially for three years, after which they could be renewed if the worker wished. Wages were to be 5d per day during the first year, 10d during the second and 1s 3d for the remainder of the term.[3] Stipendiary magistrates were given jurisdiction over these Liberated Africans; if an African was maltreated the guilty person was to forfeit the indenture and pay a fine of £5 to the person affected.

Liberated Africans who came to Grenada were not part of any organized immigration scheme but a result of the British attempt to end the slave trade after its 1807 abolition of slavery Act, which, as a British imperial measure conferred jurisdiction only in those territories that were part of the Empire. Spain and Portugal gave their assurances of co-operation with the British in this regard, but nationals in their countries continued to engage in the slave trade between West Africa and Brazil and Cuba on a fairly large scale. Not until the third quarter of the 19th century was the slave trade abolished in the empires of these two metropolitan powers: 1852 in the Portuguese, 1870 in the Spanish.

## Labour Shortage: Real or Imaginary?

During the period of sustained indentured immigration (1846–55) Grenada did not experience any really severe labour shortage. The sugar-cane industry had already entered a stage of decline, and cocoa cultivation did not require the same intensive techniques as did sugar-cane. The population seemed to have been quite adequate to fulfil the labour demands of the period, provided that employers were prepared to pay reasonable wages (1s 6d to 2s 6d per day).

Lieutenant-Governor Keate, in a circular letter to Governor Colebroke of the Windward Islands, dated 16 March 1854, wrote:

'The cocoa and coffee estates throughout the island are managed almost without exception upon the metairie system and with success.'[4]

In the immediate post-1838 period and as late as 1854, like their Jamaican counterparts, the Grenadian planters raised cries of ruin and impending disaster upon realizing that ex-slaves were now in a position to bargain over their terms of employment. Almost invariably, they blamed the decline of the sugar industry on a deficient labour supply owing to: the negro's natural proneness to idleness; an abundance of vacant lands in the island which facilitated independent freeholds; the inducement of higher wages in Trinidad; and the rapid expansion and facility of squatting as a system of land tenure.

More realistically, the decline of the sugar industry in Grenada was due to: a) a shortage of capital and hence the slowness to modernize technology; b) antiquated methods of production, estate management and organization; c) growing inability to compete internationally; d) low prices on the world market; and e) estate indebtedness.

Available evidence suggests that, contrary to popular belief, the Grenadian freedmen did not abandon estate agriculture and the cultivation of the land after 1838. Some became independent peasants, others tenant farmers; but many continued to sell their labour to the estates. According to the 1851 census, 13 years after full freedom, 13,502 workers or 65% of the adult population over 15 years of age were employed in agriculture on estates; over 50% of these were women, partly because women outnumbered men by 17.4% in the 15-plus age range.[5] As late as 1881, 56% of the adult Black population between the ages of 15 and 65 were actively employed on estates,[6] again with a prevalence of women. In 1848, as a result of the liquidity constraints and the poor financial situation in which Grenadian planters found themselves, the metayage system of land tenure was introduced (see pages 132–4). Planters experienced increasing difficulty in finding liquid funds to pay for labour, and consequently estate lands were leased out to workers on a share rental basis; if independent farmers used estate machinery to grind sugar, the estates claimed 50% of the produce as a fee.

Unable to hire labourers on a continuous basis, with a persistent decline in the production of the main staples, and freedmen steadily aspiring towards an independent status and no longer malleable, the planting interest found it expedient to embark upon elaborate immigration schemes with the hope that foreign immigrant labour could be more easily coerced than Creole labour.

The indentured immigration scheme into Grenada was a luxury the colony could ill-afford; consequently, any disbursement of funds on immigration was a misallocation of scarce resources. That the

Grenadian workers were taxed in order partially to finance the cost of immigration was not only unjust but a clear manifestation of the degradation of black freed-men in the eyes of the landed gentry, as, effectively, he was called upon to help finance a measure that was aimed at depressing his wages. James Stephen, Under-Secretary in the Colonial Office, had, since 1840, opposed such taxation as it imposed exceptional hardships upon the emancipated class.[7]

## Immigration: Overall View

During the period of indentured immigration – 1838–85 – 7,142 immigrants arrived in Grenada, comprising 164 Maltese, 3,205 Indians, 601 Portuguese (Madeirans) and 3,072 Africans.[8] (See Table 13.1.) Of the total number of immigrants to the West Indies, 8.03% Portuguese, 30.9% Indian and 53.9% African went to the Leeward and Windward Islands, and Grenada received 1.46% Portuguese 0.74% Indian and 7.81 African immigrants out of the total number.[9]

### *Maltese and Portuguese*

After the arrival of the first Liberated Africans in 1836 and 1837, the first immigrants to Grenada under an organized indentured scheme were 164 Maltese, in 1839, on the ship *Inglist Naprin*. In August of that year a House of Assembly Committee on Immigration was set up to supervise the proposed scheme of Maltese immigration. A loan of £6,000 was to be raised to cover the following expenses: a) transportation from Malta to Grenada, £2,730; b) advances to immigrants,

**Table 13.1 Indentured Immigration to Grenada 1834–85[10]**

| *Period* | *Indians* | *Africans* | *Portuguese* | *Maltese* |
|---|---|---|---|---|
| 1834–40 | – | 1,530 | – | 164 |
| 1846–50 | – | 1,057 | 589 | – |
| 1851–55 | – | – | – | – |
| 1856–60 | 940 | 192 | – | – |
| 1861–65 | 1,089 | 293 | – | – |
| 1866–70 | 264 | – | – | – |
| 1871–75 | 274 | – | – | – |
| 1876–80 | 466 | – | – | – |
| 1881–85 | 172 | – | – | – |
| *Total* | *3,205* | *3,072* | *601* | *164* |

£1,200; c) payment to Maltese clergymen as interpreters, £150; and d) expenses of agency advances to immigrants, £1,920. When the Maltese immigrants arrived they were distributed among 15 estates: Brizan, Morne Jaloux, Upper Mt Parnassus, in the parish of St George's; Bailles Bacolet, Upper La Tante, in the parish of St David's; Mt Rose Point, Morne Fendue, Mt Alexander, in the parish of St Patrick's; Upper Gouyave, Palmiste, in the parish of St John's; and Grand Etang, Noel's Hall, and Grand Anse, in other parishes.

According to the *Grenada Handbook* these Maltese immigrants were totally unsuitable and in 1841 their contracts were dissolved. They apparently abandoned estate labour soon after arrival and instead became hucksters, petty traders and porters. The 1851 census noted that the relative decrease in huckstering was because the Maltese immigrants had driven most hucksters out of the trade.[11]

After the failure of Maltese immigration, efforts were made to obtain Portuguese immigrants from Madeira, and from 1846 to 1850, 591 came, 436 in 1846.[12] The Portuguese too, quickly abandoned estate labour to become shop-keepers and assistants at sugar mills. They seldom remained long in any one place; of the 100 in St Patrick's at the beginning of 1852, 48 left over the next six months.

The limited supply of African labour from the Mixed Commission Courts of Brazil and Cuba, as well as its non-dependability, led to increased interest in the possibility of developing a contract labour scheme between West Africa and the Caribbean. Governor George Hill of Trinidad had recommended such a scheme in 1835.[13]

## *African indentured immigrants*

There was much opposition to such trans-Atlantic migration schemes, predominantly from the Anti-Slavery Society in Britain and the Under-Secretary of State for the Colonies, James Stephen. The former maintained that such a traffic would approximate the abolished slave trade, and James Stephen considered that it would lead to a further degradation of the Caribbean colonies. Nonetheless, by 1840 the Colonial Office, under pressure from the West India interest and Caribbean planters, conceded to the opening up of the Sierra Leonean indentured immigration scheme, and on the 25 February 1843, Lord Stanley announced the imperial government's intention to 'administer a systematic migration of African labourers to the three large West Indian Colonies'.[14] By consenting to the scheme, the imperial government not only acceded to the planter interest but, more importantly, acted in its own self-interest. The profitability of the plantation economy under a system of paid labour was part of the imperial government's grand experiment in post-1834 West Indies. Failure of that experiment would be a kind of humiliation, hence the persistent attempts to sustain the tottering edifice of the planter-class society with various economic palliatives.

By 1849 Grenada received her first shipment of Africans under the imperial government's scheme, and in that year and in the following, 1,057 arrived in the ships *Ceres* (from St Helena) and *Clarendon*, *Brandon* and *Atlantic* (from Sierra Leone),[15] and were distributed among 31 estates in St David's and St George's, 10 in St John's and St Mark's, 49 in St Patrick's and St Andrew's and one in Carriacou. By December 1853 only 463 of the 1,039 African immigrants on estates remained there after their term of indenture had expired; the others either returned to Africa or became independent settlers.[16] African immigrants worked under conditions similar to those of Creole labourers and went to those estates which paid the highest wages. Many in St Patrick's left their original estate and went to others either in the same parish or elsewhere. Other immigrants joined their countrymen of older residence in Grenada to form small villages procuring a livelihood together by cultivating provisions, and manioc which they processed into farine, cassava, bread and starch; they also made and sold considerable quantities of charcoal.

Of the 226 originally allotted to planters in St Andrew's only 90 were still in the parish on 31 December 1853; the remainder had gone to other parishes and some had migrated to Trinidad. The employers in St Andrew's spoke very commendably both of the adults and minors.[17] According to one member of the planting community: 'Apart from the actual labour they gave, the competition [they provided] had a good effect on the other labourers of the colony.'[18] By the end of 1851 the Black African population in Grenada (as distinct from the Black Creole) was 2,405, predominantly from Sierra Leone, Kroo Coast and St Helena. The planters continued to request the importation of more Africans and were supported in this by the stipendiary magistrates.

After his one year contract had expired the African indenture became either an independent landowner or a squatter. Those who had to be repatriated seemed to have over-stayed their stated term, because the repatriation of small numbers of immigrants was difficult to organize. The Lieutenant-Governor openly expressed his displeasure with the former situation, as the differences between African and Creole upheld as advantageous to the Colony now diminished as both groups became integrated socio-economically and began to develop common patterns of behaviour and to act in unison.

## The Contract Under Indentureship

A central issue relating to immigration to Grenada and elsewhere in the British West Indies, was whether indentured workers should be contracted for one year, or for a longer term. The local planting interest wanted longer contracts while the British government was hesitant, lest the system developed into a form of neo-slavery. The original intention, in September 1838, was that all contracts were to be for one year only.[19]

In 1846, however, with Gladstone as Secretary of State, three-year contracts were permitted, but for Madeirans only – a compromise that was unsatisfactory to the West Indians. Gladstone's rationale lay in conceding that these workers were capable of protecting themselves against unscrupulous employers, and thus he could find no valid grounds for objecting.[20] In 1849, with Earl Grey as Secretary of State, three-year contracts with Africans were permitted, provided they were imported at the expense of the Colony. Compulsory contracts, however, were not to exceed one year.[21] The next decade saw increasing demands for five-year contracts and these demands increasingly rejected by the imperial government. But in 1862, with Newcastle as Secretary of State, five-year contracts were permitted.

Original indentures into Grenada signed one-year contracts, as did Liberated Africans; but Africans introduced at the Colony's expense signed three-year contracts, as did the Portuguese from Madeira. After 1850, Africans signed three-year contracts regardless of circumstances of entry, and immigrants who came after 1862 were allowed to sign five-year contracts. The 1869 ordinance on immigration, however, reduced the contractual term to three years.

### *East Indian immigrants*

Close to 50% of Grenada's immigrants in the period under consideration consisted of East Indian indentures. Between 1857 and 1885 ten shipments of East Indians arrived, totalling 3,205 (see Table 13.2 on page 198). The first arrivals landed on the 1 May 1857 from the ship *Maidstone*; 375 had left Calcutta, 283 arrived, giving a mortality rate in passage of 25%. In subsequent shipments the mortality rate was considerably lower.

As the Population Report of 1862 revealed, of the 1,856 East Indian immigrants into Grenada, most were distributed to estates in St Patrick's (797) and St Andrew's (680) – comprising 80% of the Indian population resident in Grenada. The fact that these parishes contained

**Table 13.2 East Indians Entering Grenada 1857–85[22]**

| *Year* | *(Ship)* | *No. on arrival* | *Transportation cost (approximate) (£)* |
|---|---|---|---|
| 1857 | (*Maidstone*) | 283 | 3,464 |
| 1858 | (*Fulwood*) | 353 | 4,321 |
| 1858 | (*Jalawar*) | 304 | 2,967 |
| 1862 | (*Accrington*) | 414 | 5,528 |
| 1862 | (*Ganges*) | 311 | 4,994 |
| 1862 | (*Athletae*) | 364 | 5,300 |
| 1866 | (*Countess of Ripon*) | 264 | 3,081 |
| 1871 | (*Sevilla*) | 274 | 3,197 |
| 1878 | (*Hermione*) | 466 | 5,670 |
| 1885 | (*Poonah*) | 172 | 2,007 |

the majority of cocoa, nutmeg and sugar-cane estates possibly accounted for this distribution. Only 50 immigrants were allocated to estates in other parishes.[23]

During the period of indentureship in Grenada Indian immigrants failed to reproduce themselves; between 1866 and 1879 the rate of natural increase was negative. The absence of Indian women among the immigrants was partly responsible for this. After 1880, however, although the birth rate remained low, there was a marked change in the rate of natural increase. For the 30 years 1866 to 1896, a total of 1,084 births of Indians in Grenada was recorded, and 891 recorded deaths; a natural increase of 193 – approximately 6 per annum.

Poor hospital care, and disregard of the legal dietary prescription for hospital patients resulted in a high mortality rate in the early period. For example, of the 225 who arrived on the *Countess of Ripon* in 1866, 32 or 15% had died by the following year. The improvement after 1880 was partly owing to the vigilance of the local authorities in ensuring that medical facilities and other necessities were made available to the immigrants. Also, the threat of legal proceedings against delinquent overseers and estate owners apparently resulted in some recognition of their responsibilities towards the immigrants.

Most Indians who came to Grenada were from Calcutta and Madras. They signed five-year contracts to work on estates, and were required to work nine hours a day for six days a week; they lived on the estates in free accommodation, and were given weekly food rations for which 4d weekly was deducted from their wage. They were not to wander more than two miles beyond the estate without a pass;

if and when found they were liable to arrest and imprisonment. If an immigrant deliberately failed to report for work, this was considered a criminal offence, punishable with imprisonment.

In 1858 an American observer, George Sewell, visiting Grenada, found the laws in Grenada were very liberal towards the East Indians. He said that:

> Every estate was to have clean and good-sized living houses for immigrants with separate apartments for males and females. There was to be a medical doctor whose job it was to make visits to each estate and give medical attendance to the Indians for which the estate would pay 1/- per immigrant per day. Wages were paid every month and the employers were not permitted to deduct anything from the sum given without the consent of the indenture.[24]

Sewell was apparently enumerating the provisions, written on paper, but not observed. His visit took place only one year after the Indian Immigration scheme was initiated – too short a time to appraise the scheme fully or give any critical assessment.

Sewell's picture of relatively good conditions was at variance with the high mortality rate of Indian indentured workers during the first 25 years of the scheme. This was attributed partly to the immigrants' living and depressing working conditions, and partly to the system of servile labour; some immigrants, disillusioned by general neglect, became vagrants; on many estates no provisions were made for medical attention; when a worker fell sick he was left to die. The following description of a hospital on Observatory Estate for about 20 Indians depicts the unhealthy and unsanitary conditions that existed: 'A thatched cottage consisting of two rooms, no furniture, poor ventilation ... no classification nor division of the sexes could be made. There is no bedding.'[25] The Lieutenant-Governor himself at the time noted that:

> The unfortunate and rapid decadence ... in this, as a sugar producing colony may, I suspect, in some measure to be attributed to the irritating measures resorted to in reference to the coolies and if persevered, it may not ultimately prove very creditable to the chief actors.[26]

In 1863, 45 Indians were admitted into the General Hospital as opposed to seven Africans. Indians remained for 2,388 days at an average of 8.74 per day while Africans remained for 371 days at an average of 1.26 per day.[27]

In 1866, 10 years after the arrival of the first Indians, a Commission of Inquiry was set up consisting of the Immigration Agent, George Gun-Munroe, and the police magistrate of the Western District, George Palmer, to investigate the severe mortality rate among the Indians on Mt Alexander Estate in the parish of St Patrick's. The Committee was given eight specific terms of reference. They were to ascertain:

1. Whether provisions for medical care for the Indian immigrants were made.
2. The cause of death of several immigrants who had died since the month of February 1866.
3. The distance of the doctor from the estate.
4. Whether the high death rate was attributable to any local cause.
5. The cause of the apparent neglect to provide the person who died from lock-jaw with medical assistance.
6. The number of Indians on the estate.
7. Whether any competent nurse was placed in charge of the coolies sent from an estate to the hospital.
8. Whether the regulations for the general treatment of Indian immigrants made by the Governor-in-Council on 18 September 1856 had been enforced.[28]

The Commission's report condemned the existing facilities on the estates wholesale: poor sanitary conditions, lack of medical care, the widespread defecation of the Indians around their huts, and the disregard of statutory provisions relating to the care of the immigrants.

The Commission found that there had been considerable sickness and mortality among the Indians on the estate, and one man with lock-jaw had received no medical attention. Of the 17 Indians allocated to Mt Alexander Estate in February 1866 seven had died by July; this fact was responsible for the authorities becoming concerned, and had led to the subsequent inquiry. These deaths were found to have resulted from lack of proper hospital and medical care, disregard of regulations regarding their diet, and the state of their dwellings.

Additionally, the manager of the estate was found to be guilty of culpable neglect; the doctor who was required to visit the estate twice weekly relaxed his duties due to the healthy state of the parish; the Indians washed their sores in a pond on the estate where they also drank water; their houses measured 12 ft × 9 ft, and two Indians occupied one room. In one case 13 Indians placed on the sick list remained without medical assistance for 14 days. Under such conditions infectious diseases were easily transmitted. The Commission found that one doctor was inadequate for the parish of St Patrick's and that the hospital building was too dilapidated to be of any use; they condemned the system whereby doctors prescribed medicines, leaving the overseers and managers to administer them. In short, they found that absence of hospital care and lack of proper food were mainly responsible for the high mortality rate.[29] Other estates where Indians were similarly mistreated included Calivigny and Clarks Court in the parish of St George's. As a result of the Commission's report, in 1867, the Indians left Mt Alexander and were either relocated or migrated to British Guiana and on the advice of the Immigration Agent, eight Indians from Calivigny Estate and four from Clarks Estate also migrated to British Guiana.[30] According to the June 1867 half-yearly report of the Immigration Agent, on only 19 out of the 53 estates where East Indians were located were they in good health.

As a result of the 1866 Commission's Report the Lieutenant-Governor, Major R.M. Mundy, demanded quarterly reports from estates employing Indian immigrants, indicating if and how managers and owners complied with the 1856 Act. He made it emphatically clear that after 5 September 1866 legal proceedings would be immediately taken against all persons in charge of estates on which immigrants, indentured or not, were located, who failed to provide such estates with a proper hospital, furniture, medicines and nurses.

The incidence of Indian vagrancy was apparently of concern to the authorities, as many vagrant immigrants became destitute and eventually died. On 18 August 1866, the Governor made enquiries from the Protector of Indians about numerous Indians seen wandering aimlessly in the St Andrew's area, most of them in an emaciated condition;[31] he wanted to ascertain whether their vagrancy was deliberate or whether it was caused by the general condition of neglect.

By 27 November 1866, despite the Lieutenant-Governor's threat, Diamond, Piedmont, Bocage, Grenville Vale, Woodford and Madeys estates not only had no hospitals, but had made no provisions for medical attendance for the Indians. Towards the end of 1867, however, conditions appeared to have improved. The Colonial Secretary for Grenada, in his 1868 report, mentioned that living conditions among the immigrants were far more satisfactory than those of the previous year. (Appendix 5, page 486, is a return for 1867 showing provision made on various estates for Indian immigrants.)

## *Immigration laws*

By 1868 ten pieces of legislation had been passed to govern indentured immigration to Grenada, including Act No. 230 to alter the laws of contracts; Act No. 284 to improve the laws regulating immigration to Grenada; Act No. 380 to authorize payment from the Immigration Fund to return passages to India of certain immigrants, and to permit such immigrants to accept a bounty in commutation of such passages; and Act No. 390 to provide for the payment of bounties to resident Indians who agreed to prolong their term of service.

In 1869 all these laws were superseded by the consolidated Immigration Act, which contained 114 clauses and governed every aspect of immigration from recruitment to repatriation. The Act provided for the appointment of an Emigration Agent abroad at a salary of £280 plus £150 allowance; there was to be one interpreter for every 100 Indians; private persons who imported Indians would receive one-half of the bounty for such immigrants; upon arrival of the immigrants the ship and cargo were to be inspected and sick immigrants removed to the Colony Hospital. Allotment of immigrants was to be made by the Government at its own discretion; those who received Indians were to pay indenture fees; children under the age of 15 were not to be separated from their parents. Immigrants who were not indentured upon arrival were to be cared for at the expense of the Immigration Fund. Each immigrant had to have a certificate of indenture signed by the Immigration Agent, and each employer was to keep a list of indentures. To employ children of less than seven years of age was not permitted.

A series of clauses also dealt with contracts. Those made outside Grenada were invalid unless they carried the consent of the imperial government; contracts made with Chinese for five years or less were considered valid if attested; other contracts made out of the Colony had to be for less than three years. Portuguese immigrants were to be indentured for not more than three years, as were immigrants from India, China, and Africa and first-class Liberated Africans. Verbal agreements or contracts were to be valid for one month and renewable thereafter on a month to month basis and the penalty on an employer for a breach of verbal contract was one month's salary. No one was permitted to cancel an indenture without the consent of the Government.

Every employer of indentured workers had first to pay to the Treasury half of the passage or bounty money of every indentured immigrant, then £1 down-payment plus three promissory notes, each for one-third of the balance plus 6% interest. Where an immigrant reindentured himself, the employer had to pay £10 for every adult and £5 for others. Any immigrant who completed his term of indentureship was entitled to demand a certificate of industrial residence from the Immigration Agent, possession of which was evidence that the immigrant was released from the obligation to perform further service. Any immigrant could, however, reindenture himself for a further term of five years if he wished and be paid £10 as bounty. When immigrants from different estates married, the wife was reindentured to the proprietor of her husband's estate, and her original proprietor received compensation of either £10 or £8 dependent on whether the marriage took place in the first or second year of indentureship.

Estates that hired indentured labour were to provide comfortable and adequate accommodation, proper hospitals, hospital furniture, medicines and nurses, and arrange for a licensed medical officer to attend the sick regularly. In the event of negligence or default the proprietor was to be fined £4 plus a similar sum for every 14 days' default.

The Immigration Agent was empowered to visit any estate at any time and anyone obstructing him was to be fined £10. He was required to visit every estate in January and July each year, and at other times as the Governor directed.

A number of clauses also dealt with estates' discipline of the immigrant and the restriction of his movements. An immigrant who was found more than two miles away from the estates without a ticket of leave or industrial residence was to be apprehended by the police or rural constable without warrant. The indenture was to work for nine hours every day except Sunday, Christmas Day, Good Friday and New Year's Day which were holidays.

The Governor had the right to discharge an immigrant on the grounds of ill-usage, neglect or breach of contract by employers. Breaking contracts, wilful disobedience, and insolence were punishable by either forfeiture of wages or by a term of imprisonment not exceeding 30 days. Where an indenture endangered property by the careless use of fire, or cruelly used, or through negligence caused damage to cattle, he was to be fined £4 and imprisoned for not more than 30 days.

The sum of £300 was to continue to be paid to the Colony Hospital to defray the expenses of medical treatment, care and maintenance of unindentured immigrants who would be admitted therein.

The last series of clauses of the Act dealt with repatriation. After an immigrant had received a certificate of industrial residence he could take out his passport and leave whenever he wished, at his own expense. If, however, his agreement gave him the right to a return passage provided he came after 1 January 1858, and completed five years of Industrial Residence and ten years of Actual Residence, this was to be paid from the Immigration Fund.[32]

Many at this time, such as a certain Dr Horsford, considered the presence of the Indians to be a kind of cultural and social pollution of the society. Witnessing the steady inflow of East Indians, Horsford argued:

> An increase of population by Coolie immigration in particular would lead in time if numbers of them do not return at the expired term of service to their over-running the country; and just in proportion as they preponderate and remain in barbaric ignorance, they will become nuisances to the community by fostering heathenism in our midst and by their innate tendency to crime.[33]

He then cited the case of one Chutterjorn who had committed a most callous murder on Marli Estate. The contention that the East Indians in the region displayed a high propensity to crime, and lived in the 'shadow of the jail' was an exaggeration for Grenada. Apparently most serious crimes committed by the Indians were crimes of passion – wife-murders – stemming from deep-seated and uncontrollable jealousy and not from any innate instinct to kill. This is well illustrated by the case of Gopaul who most cruelly murdered his wife, Jummoonha, in 1878. Gopaul believed his wife was unfaithful. According to his daughter who witnessed the crime, he had stopped taking food prepared by his wife for over a year, and repeatedly accused her of poisoning his rum. The last few months before the murder he was unable to sleep and talked to himself, sometimes all night, calling the names of men with whom he believed his wife was involved. Gopaul was sentenced to death on 6 June 1878 and executed on the 18th. In 1867, Kumly, on Gouyave Estate, was murdered by her husband, Bissesseur; Jethun, on Telescope, was strangled by another man due to jealousy over a woman.

This was such a distinctive feature of Indian life in Grenada that the Immigration Agent's report form had a section: *Abstract of murder of women*, with a sub-section devoted specifically to wife-murders. One factor which contributed to the murder of women, and particularly wives, was the numerical imbalance between the sexes. In 1867 there were 1,301 Indian men to 557 women, a ratio of 2.3. In other colonies there were even fewer women to men, because estate owners found them unacceptable as they were unable to work as hard as the men. Laws had to be passed by the imperial government to control the sex ratio, as the paucity of women was leading to all kinds of immorality. In 1857–58 the ratio was set at 1:3; the following year it was decided that the number of men should not exceed twice that of women, but in 1860 the ratio was relaxed to 1:4 to placate the planters. In 1868 a high incidence of women murders resulted in raising the ratio to 1:2.5 but owing to the difficulty in recruiting women the proportion of women was again reduced in 1878 from 40% to 25%.[34] In 1881 there were 959 men and 613 women but the 1921 census recorded 1,313 men and 1,379 women.

Despite the scarcity of Indian women there was no evidence of any marked consorting between Indian men and Black women. The East Indians, according to Donald Wood, 'were isolated from the other inhabitants by language and customs and the Hindus were bound together by sanctions of their caste and religion to band endogamy.'[35] Indians also found the Africans unattractive as the latter did not satisfy their concept and criteria of beauty. When those who returned to India were asked by the Protector of Immigrants their opinion of the Africans, they spoke with great disgust, referring to such physical attributes as their coarse woolly hair, describing them as resembling monkeys more than human beings.[36] The Indians in Grenada seemed to have developed little or no sexual relations with Black women. Miscegenation was a marked feature of West Indies history; practised by the Spaniards, French, English and Dutch, but the Indians were the exception – although of course, they came as colonized and the other as colonizers. Nonetheless, in Grenada Indians formed a closed community for the first 25 years of indentureship. Changes occurred afterwards as a result of the Presbyterians' and Anglicans' increasing Christianization of the Indians.[37]

## *Neglect of the immigrants*

In spite of the consolidated Ordinance of 1869, the provision of estate hospitals, and greater supervision of the indentured, the Protector of Immigrants, J.P. Denham, found the conditions of the immigrants to be such that in his 1878 annual report he wrote:

> I regret to say that the opinion I have come to is that East Indians ought not to be sent to this island and what is more those who arrived by the 'Hermione' in March 1878 ought to be sent away to Demerara or Trinidad where they will be properly treated and looked after.[38]

Denham found estate managers in Grenada unfit to have charge over Indians: they were contemptuous of the need to care for them, and refused to pay them sufficient to enable them to obtain the common necessities of life. They grudgingly and reluctantly provided medicines and rations for them when they were sick, as according to law they were required to do. They worked them so hard, even before they were accustomed to the work, that it was difficult to conceive how they would survive their five years' indentureship. Denham observed that by December 1877 some 2,000 Indians had been imported, but that a mere 112 were located on estates, thus testifying to the fact that conditions there were so deplorable the Indians abandoned them at the earliest opportunity. Many migrated to Trinidad, some set up settlements in different parts of the island, others returned to India. Denham himself described the treatment they received on the estates as iniquitous, 'kicked-off as soon as they became ill', and allowed to die in the road of yaws and other diseases.

Three planters – William Shears, Fred Kent and John Langdon – were particularly insensitive to the Indians' conditions. These men owned and managed most of the estates in St Patrick's and behaved as if they were doing the Government a favour by applying for Indians. The attitude of overseers was the same, as they behaved in a manner to please the proprietors and attorneys. The lot of Indians on Beausejour Estate was so insupportable that Denham transferred them to other estates. All the indentured Indians there were laid up with fever for over a month; the manager refused to supply them with the necessary maintenance as provided under the Immigration Act, instead he beat them as he would draught animals in order to get them to work. One Indian died under the pressure and another had to be removed to the Colony Hospital. On 17 August, the manager was fined 10/- by Acting Police Magistrate Sinclair for his crimes. He was subsequently charged by Denham for violation of the Immigration Law. In his inquiry Denham concluded: 'There is no doubt that the so-called proprietors are not in a position to employ East Indian immigrants and are unable to fulfill their part of the contract.[39] According to a report by the next Protector of Immigrants, Phillip C. Cork, by 1882 conditions seem to have improved. The report stated that Indians were granted hospital accommodation and medical treatment when sick for which the employer paid 1/-per day; cottages were provided, kept in repair and white-washed. Initially, each estate had to make its own hospital provisions, but after 1866 sick Indians were usually sent to the General Hospital, St Andrew's and St Patrick's Hospitals. In 1882, 186 were accommodated in these hospitals; of these 54 were suffering from ulcers, 29 from fevers and 50 from yaws; 162 were cured, three died and 21 were still in hospital by the end of that year.[40] Improved conditions were reflected in the considerably reduced death rate; in 1882 it was 1.68% or eight in all.

## *Working conditions*

The 243 Indian men and 95 women indentured in 1882 worked, on average, three and a half and two and a quarter days per week respectively. This seems to have been the general state of affairs after 1867, and one that most planters found highly unsatisfactory. Of the 30 indentures brought to trial in 1882 three were for desertion, seven for refusal to work, seven for absence without leave and two for refusing to finish work.[41]

Wages were paid both in cash and in kind: men received 1/- per day and women 9d; in addition, the sick received 1/- per day for hospital accommodation and medical treatment. The Indians were allowed garden plots on which to grow vegetables; they could also raise livestock on the estates and were given free access to fruits and some vegetables. Thus, with the exception of buying clothes[42] indentured Indians had no need to spend their monthly wage, most of which was either remitted to India or used to buy land in Grenada.

In 1869 232 Indians reindentured themselves, first for two years and then for a further five years. Bounties were put aside for indentured labourers – £2 per annum for five years for men, and £1 per annum for women, conditional on their remaining in the Colony. The bounty of those who chose to remain permanently in Grenada was converted into land grants at the rate of £1 for 2 acres. Thus, an immigrant entitled to a bounty of £10 would, if he became a Grenadian, be entitled to 20 acres of land.

## *Repatriation and emigration*

Of the 3,205 indentured Indians in Grenada, 380 were said to have returned to India, as Table 13.3 illustrates.[43]

Many of the immigrants returned with sizeable savings. The Indians themselves were noted for thrift. The 102 adults who returned to India on the *Pandoras* in 1872 had £1,609 in cash.

During the last quarter of the 19th century many Indian workers emigrated from Grenada to other islands, mainly Trinidad and British Guiana. Ten Indian workers left Grenada for these islands in 1875. In 1876–77, 86 more migrated, while in 1872–73, 208 had gone to these parts. The main attractions were the prospect of better economic opportunities, and that these areas were beginning to become headquarters of Indians in the Caribbean. Until 1901, however, the majority remained in Grenada. Of a total Indian population of 1,572, the

**Table 13.3 Indentured Indians Returning to India**

| *Period* | *Indians returning* |
|---|---|
| 1866–70 | 76 |
| 1871–75 | 102 |
| 1876–80 | – |
| 1881–85 | 29 |
| 1886–90 | 95 |
| 1891–95 | 78 |

Source: *Blue Books, Letter Books*, and Roberts and Byrne

1881 census recorded 1,056 who had completed their indentureship and were still living in Grenada; by 1921 out of a total Indian population, in the Caribbean, of 2,692, only 181 had completed indentureship and were resident in the Island.

### *Christianization of East Indians*

A significant change among the immigrants in Grenada was their rapid conversion to Christianity. In 1871, Hindus and Mohammedans constituted four per 1,000 of Grenada's population of 37,684; in 1921 the population was 66,302, and Hindus and Mohammedans numbered one per 1,000. Of the 1,572 Indians in the colony in 1882, 94 were Mohammedans, 821 were Hindus, and 655 were Christians (121 Roman Catholics, 534 Anglican),[44] 41.8% of the immigrants having that year been converted to Christianity. The 1891 census revealed that the Christian religion predominated in the Indian community. The 'denigration of his religion, his isolation from India and the proselytization of the Christian churches', were possibly responsible for this,[45] with Presbyterians, beginning around 1884, being influential in this regard. In 1891, of Indians in Grenada, 509 were Hindus; 72 Mohammedans; and 1,501 were Christians (1,151 Anglicans, 185 Catholics, and 165 Presbyterians).

## The Financing of Immigration

East Indian and African immigration was basically financed from:

- loans, raised locally and abroad;
- taxes, levied on imports and exports;
- receipts from planters; and
- votes of the local Legislature.

An Immigration Fund was started as early as 1850, with revenues from the same sources, to defray the costs of importing immigrants. One-third (later, one-quarter) of the revenue collected on the consumption of rum and other selected imports went into this fund. The fund was to provide for: hospital fees for immigrants, wages to the Protector of Immigrants and to interpreters, bounty in lieu of return passages, and financing return passages. Revenue for the last two items came predominantly from those planters who employed indentured workers.

In 1850 the Immigration Fund stood at £1,706 1s 6d; in 1851 £1,489 8s 8d and in 1852 £2,393 14s 6d, falling to £1,544 14s 6d in

1853. Between 1855 and 1889 approximately £133,000 was spent on immigration, equal to the revenue raised during the period. In 1858 to finance immigration a £7,000, 4% guaranteed Imperial Loan was raised locally. In 1872, another private loan of £1,800, and in 1879 £10,000 at 5% interest for 10 years were raised from a local financier and merchant. In 1890 the Immigration Fund was converted into a special fund; the balance was increasingly reduced during 1890–99, and by 1895 had fallen from £1,963 in 1890 to £256.

How much did Indian immigration cost Grenada? Appendix 9 shows the various amounts disbursed in the period 1855–95, on immigration purposes; it also shows the sources of revenue for the various years during the period.

## Indian Immigration Ends

Indian indentureship in Grenada officially ended in 1890. In that year the 172 who had arrived in 1885 had served their five-year term of indentureship; some, however, renewed their indentureship for another term, due to end in 1894. But the acting Protector of Immigrants' report for 1893 stated there were no indentured immigrants in the Colony. This was because an Indian repatriation ship was leaving St Lucia in September of that year and so few wished to return to India from Grenada that the two islands agreed to share the cost of repatriation. In fact 14% of those who had come had forfeited bounty or return passage. Indian indentureship to Grenada, therefore, effectively ended in September 1893. Those who chose to stay bought lands with their bounty money and deposited their savings in the local banks.

A few years before the end of indentureship, the Minister of the Church of Scotland (Presbyterian) started a Mission for Indian Immigrants, with the main objective being to open schools to educate Indian children and teach them Christian worship. By 1893 there were two day schools, one at Samaritan, with 70 Indian children enrolled, the other at Belair, with an enrolment of 75 Indian children out of a total of 130.

## The Relative Impact of Indians in Grenada

Indian immigration had no marked economic impact on Grenada. By 1860, a few estates about to be abandoned were retained in cultivation and some that had been abandoned were reclaimed. Even supposing a mild return to prosperity in the period it would be difficult to isolate indentureship as the causal factor. On the other hand it had socio-cultural effects. Its most marked influence was on the racial composition of the population, especially in the parishes of St Patrick's and St Andrew's.

Indians worked predominantly on the sugar plantations and sugar production and exports fell from 4,938 tons in 1858 to 77 tons in 1888. Conversely, cocoa production increased from 477 tons in 1864, to 1,050 tons in 1871, and 2,767 tons in 1884. In 1878 cocoa exports amounted to 21,864 bags, increasing to 53,387 bags (over 100%) in 1901. Coffee production fell to an all-time low of 244 lbs by 1900. The expansion of cocoa production was due to demand and to soil fertility, rather than to Indian indentureship, which was an insignificant supplement to the labour force on such estates, where the ratio of Black workers to Indians was 26.1%.

The period 1855 to 1895 was by no means one of prosperity. In the 1880s Grenada experienced a severe depression, and sugar virtually went out of production. The cost of indentureship, borne by the Colony, was simply in response to the erroneous judgement of the planters, who, in turn, were quick to blame their problems on labour shortage – artificial in most cases – and who failed to appreciate that the blame lay in their technological backwardness, capital shortage, poor management, lack of specialization, changing market situations and the international division of labour.

## NOTES

Full citations only given where work does not appear in the Bibliography.

1. Deerr, *History of Sugar*, p. 199.
2. *Blue Book*, 1836, also *Grenada Handbook*.
3. *Laws of Grenada* 1837.
4. *Letter Book 1854*, 'Lieutenant Governor Robert Keate to Governor Colebroke', 16 March 1854.
5. *Report of the 1851 Census*, 'Population', 1851.
6. *Blue Book*, 'Population', 1881.
7. Green, 'James Stephen and British West Indian Policy' p. 49.
8. Drawn up from *Blue Books, Letter Books, St George's Chronicle and the Grenada Gazette* and *Free Press*; also Roberts and Byrne, 'Summary statistics'.
9. Roberts and Byrne. 'Summary statistics'.
10. Ibid.
11. *Census Report*, 1851.
12. *Grenada Handbook*.
13. Mixed Commission Courts were those set up in Sierra Leone, Loanda, Havanna and Rio by the British government, regulated by treaties between Britain and foreign powers, to try slavers captured in American waters and in the Atlantic. This was part of Britain's attempt to crush the international slave trade after its abolition in the British Empire in 1807. The human cargoes on these slavers were confiscated and the slaves – so-called 'emancipados' – were indentured out for seven years. This indentureship turned out to be more brutal than

slavery. Liberated Africans indentured in Cuba were known to have been subjected to notorious abuse, sometimes being transferred surreptitiously into actual slaves. C.O. 295/106 No. 8 Hill to Aberdeen, 3 March 1835; The Lieutenant-Governor of British Guiana, Carmichael Smythe, made a similar request in 1836.

14. Green, 'James Stephen and British West Indian Policy', p. 48.
15. *St George's Chronicle and Grenada Gazette*, Vol. VI, 30 April 1852.
16. *Return of African Immigrants*, for half year ending December 1853–54.
17. Ibid.
18. *St George's Chronicle and Grenada Gazette*, Vol. VI, 30 April 1852.
19. Great Britain, *Parliamentary Papers*, Vol. XXX, pp. 445, 751.
20. K.O. Lawrence, 'The Evolution of Long Term Labour Policy', *Journal of Caribbean History*.
21. C.O. 318/182, Minute by Grey, 25 July 1849; Great Britain, *Parliamentary Papers*; Grey to Berkly, 31 July and 15 December 1859, Nos. 80, 129.
22. *Blue Books* 1857–85 inclusive.
23. *Annual Report on Indentured Immigration* 1889.
24. Sewell, *Ordeal of Free Labour* p. 89.
25. Ibid.
26. *St George's Chronicle and Grenada Gazette,* 25 October 1863.
27. *Chronicle,* 14 June 1866.
28. Ibid.
29. *Indian Mortality for half year ended 30th June*, 1867, p. 186.
30. *Letter Book*, 3 July 1867.
31. *Chronicle*, 18 August 1866.
32. *Laws of Grenada*, 'An Act to Consolidate and amend the law relating to immigration' 1869.
33. *St George's Chronicle and Grenada Gazette*, 29 March 1862.
34. Weller, *The East Indian Indenture in Trinidad*, p. 4.
35. Wood, *Trinidad in Transition*, p. 137.
36. Ibid. p. 138.
37. Steele, 'East Indian Indenture' pp. 34–5.
38. *C.O. Despatch*, 'Immigration' to Lieutenant-Governor G. Dusidas from H.W. Hurley. 14 October 1878.
39. Ibid.
40. D.G. Garraway, *Special Report Compiled from the 1881 Census*
41. Ibid.
42. Ibid.
43. G.W. Roberts and J. Byrne gave figures of 278; but from the various records in the *Letter Books* and *Blue Books* it would appear that the number was 380. Roberts had omitted the return of 102 statute adults in 1872.
44. *Eighth Report of the Registrar-General of Births, Deaths, etc*, 1882.
45. Steele. 'East Indian Indenture, p. 35.

# 14

# *Political Elitism, Continued Oligarchy: 1838–1930*

The emancipation of the Blacks in 1838 raised the fundamental issue of the form of government that would develop in the West Indies. Would it be a continuation of oligarchy under the planter-dominated Assembly, or would the structures change to accommodate the 500,000 newly emancipated Blacks into the political decision-making process? In the British Colonial Office's view either of these would lead to dictatorship. A continuation of planter domination would mean an intensification of the dictatorship of the few over the majority, while for ex-slaves to dominate would mean a dictatorship of the majority Blacks over the minority Whites. The Colonial Office solved the problem by recommending the dictatorship of the Governor and it was left to the imperial government to find an opportunity to introduce this change.

In Grenada the political dominance of the plantocracy was prolonged until 1877, when Crown Colony government was introduced. The few merchants who entered the Assembly shared similar views with, had similar interests to, and belonged to the same class as the planters. Thus, between 1838 and 1877 a tiny élite of planters and businessmen dominated Grenada's political life.

## Constitution of Government

In 1833, for the second time since secession in 1763, Grenada ceased to have a separate government and was included under a common administration with St Vincent, Tobago and Barbados. The Governor-in-Chief was to reside in Barbados, a Lieutenant-Governor in Grenada; the first Governor under this revised constitutional government was Sir Lionel Smith and Grenada's first Lieutenant-Governor was Major-General George Middlemore. In addition to these two officials, Grenada's government at the time of Emancipation consisted of an Executive Council of nine, and 26 members forming a House of Assembly. The constitutional provisions applying to the executive and legislative functions of government during the slave period continued to apply during the post-Emancipation period.

The Lieutenant-Governor, the Chief Justice, and the Attorney-General were all ex-officio members of the Council. Councillors were nominated by the Governor and appointed by a mandamus from the King; they held office at the monarch's pleasure. The Council's main function was to advise the Governor. It sat as a Court of Error or Appeal and corresponded generally to the House of Lords; it also rendered judgement on all Acts passed by the Assemblies.

The House of Assembly had privileges equivalent to those of the House of Commons in Britain. It had the sole power to levy and distribute taxes, but had no control over differential duties (a permanent revenue of a few thousand pounds to the Crown). The Assembly had many permanent Boards performing executive duties, and a Commission of Correspondence which maintained communication with Grenada's agent in London.

The House of Assembly was a semi-representative body with elected members. Membership was restricted to adult males who owned a plantation or estate, or were joint owners of 50 acres of land with a house thereon rented for not less than £40 per annum; or a lessee of a plantation comprising not less than 100 acres, of which 30 must be under cultivation; or the recipient of an annual income of £200 derived from a profession or trade. In short, a combination of White and Coloured bourgeois-plantocracy.

Equally selective and discriminatory conditions governed the eligibility of voters, who had to be adult (aged 21 years or over) males who owned ten acres of land, of which five must be under cultivation; or a dwelling house and adjoining land bringing in £10 annually in one's own name or in the name of one's wife; or a payee of rent as a lessor or rentier of any plantation; or a creditor of a sum of not less than £20 per annum. These provisions excluded the mass of ex-slaves; many who qualified never really bothered about being enfranchized, as bureaucratic hurdles would certainly have frustrated their efforts to participate in government.

## General Elections 1837–77

The first of the seven elections of members of the Grenadian Assembly held between 1837 and 1877 was in 1837. The Assembly was elected for a term of seven years with members elected in five electoral parishes. Throughout this time the voting population was consistently less than 1% of the adult population of Grenada, that is, only one out of every 100 adults voted. In 1837, 136 voters elected the 26-member House of Assembly – the number of voters included the 26 representatives.

The united parishes of St Mark's and St Patrick's returned six members, elected by eight voters, of whom six were themselves candidates. In 1850 there were 7,952 males aged 21 years and over, yet, in the elections of that year, only 141 were on the electoral roll; of these 99 voted to elect the 26-member House – a mere 1.2% of all males over 20 years of age. This pattern typified every election from 1837 to 1877. There was nothing representative about the House in either the pre- or post-Emancipation periods. Its composition, the franchise, and the exercise of that franchise, were an anachronism in an age when slaves had become citizens, if not socially and politically at least legally. In the following pages elections to the House in the 1837–77 period are reviewed. Details of the elected candidates in some of these elections are to be found in Appendix 4.

The electoral districts in 1837 remained unchanged from those of 70 years before. The number of Assemblymen, however, had increased from 24 to 26 since 1766, because the number of representatives for the combined parishes of St George's and St John's had been increased from five to seven.

The constitution of the Assembly and the continued maintenance of large electoral districts after 1837 indicated the plantocracy's unwillingness to give representation to the newly emancipated. By retaining the constitutional structures of the slavery period they denied them not only representation but also an active voice in the government of Grenada. Thus, despite emancipation and the enfranchisement of more Grenadians, the plantocracy was intent on monopolizing political power.

In the 1850 elections, 12 persons elected in 1843 were all re-elected. Three Assemblymen (Alexander Baille and Alexander Horne for St George's town, and Richard Gibbs for the combined parishes of St George's and St John's) were elected three times for the same parish from 1837 to 1850. Adam Reid, who also served throughout, was twice elected for St Patrick's and St Mark's and once for Carriacou.

Throughout 1833 to 1876 a common practice, fairly widespread in the post-1850 period, was for representatives to change constituencies; there were a few similar cases before 1850.

Three of the six candidates for St George's and St John's and three of the six for St Mark's and St Patrick's returned in 1843, were elected again in the 1850 elections. The turnover of candidates was by no means as slow in the 1837–50 period as afterwards, but in certain areas some candidates tended to monopolize representation over a considerable period; for example, Henry Garraway and John Aird served as Assemblymen from 1843 to 1869, and William Simmons served from 1856 to 1877.

The constitution of the Assembly and the large electoral districts, combined with the plantocracy's promotion of an élitist and narrow franchise explains how, in the 1850 general election, 26 candidates came to be elected by 99 voters, including the 26 candidates themselves (see Table 14.1).

Throughout this period there were frequent by-elections to fill casual vacancies; many seats went uncontested. In one case, early in 1853, a member was elected by the vote of one elector.

In the 1856 elections the number of eligible electors increased to 229, the number who voted to 155, but the percentage of those eligible who did vote fell from 70% in 1850 to 67% in 1856. Of 50 voters in the town of St George's, 33 elected four representatives; 35 out of 67 in St George's and St John's elected seven representatives. In Carriacou, only 17 out of 61 eligible voters elected three representatives. In the parishes of St Patrick's and St Mark's, 24 out of the 31 registered voters elected six representatives.

For elections between 1862 and 1876, the number of electors and voters doubled but still represented only a tiny percentage of the adult population. In the 1862 elections 482 out of 655 registered electors

**Table 14.1 Political Franchise 1850**

| *Parish* | *No. of electors* | *No. voted* | *Representatives returned* |
|---|---|---|---|
| Town of St George's | 36 | 32 | 4 |
| St George's and St John's | 44 | 33 | 7 |
| St Patrick's and St Mark's | 15 | 10 | 6 |
| St Andrew's and St David's | 24 | 17 | 6 |
| Carriacou | 22 | 7 | 3 |
| *Total:* | *141* | *99* | *26* |

Source: *Blue Book,* 1850

voted – an increase on the number in 1856 of over 200%. During the next 15 years, however, the numbers declined.

In the 1869 elections, out of a total of 506 electors, 412 voted; in Carriacou, the number of electors had fallen to 14, of whom 12 elected three members; by 1876 the number of registered voters had increased to 75 but only eight actually voted in the elections. The 1862 elections were the most popular of all, as the number of electors and voters far exceeded those in other elections, with a 75% turn-out. This contrasted sharply with the 1876 elections – the last before the beginning of Crown Colony government – with the number of representatives reduced to eight, one in each parish and one for the town of St George's, and one for Carriacou. Out of a total of 575 registered voters 265 elected the eight representatives – a 46% turnout, the lowest for the 50 years after Emancipation. The resident Whites' apathy towards the Government of the country – as a result of declining fortunes, economic recession and losses in the operation of estates – was mainly responsible for this.

Despite the emergence of new interest groups, the Grenada Assembly continued to be dominated by a narrow group of planters and attorneys. There were no established political parties then, but there were loose political groupings; the chief one was in St George's, which convened meetings immediately before elections to choose candidates to represent the group.

At one such meeting, convened at the home of Joseph Orgais on 17 January 1856, five persons stood, from among whom four had to be selected; three were selected unanimously and the fourth by a vote of 14 to 8. The unsuccessful fifth candidate nevertheless contested the election in the town of St George's, and lost. Six candidates stood in St George's town from whom the electors had to choose four. Significantly, the four successful candidates were those whose nomination had been endorsed by this town group.[1]

On many occasions in elections at this time candidates were returned unopposed. Even when seats were contested the range of candidates was so restricted that there was virtually no contest. In the 1856 elections ten candidates stood for the combined parishes of St George's and St John's from among whom voters had to choose seven; that was considered a remarkable contest. For St David's and St Andrew's combined, the electors had to elect six representatives from among seven candidates; for St Patrick's six from among eight candidates. This situation was similar to that in the 1862 and 1869 elections: in 1862 for the town of St George's electors had to choose four out of five candidates; the four successful candidates were the same four who had been elected in 1856. In St Patrick's, in the 1869 elections six representatives were to be chosen from among seven candidates; in the town of St George's four out of five candidates, and in St John's and St George's, seven out of eight. The classic case was that of the constituency of Carriacou where their three candidates were returned unopposed; in fact, in no less than three elections (1856, 1862, 1869) Carriacou's electors had to choose three representatives from three candidates.[2] In the combined parishes of St David's and St Andrew's, William Wells, Alexander Bain and William Whiteman were elected for three consecutive terms during the 20-year period 1856 to 1876. They dominated political life in St David's for that period.[3]

At that time elections were held at the Court House in the town of St George's, at Grenville, Sauteurs; and at Hillsborough, on five different days and presided over by the Provost Marshal who performed the job of returning officer.[4] The constituencies consisted of three combined parishes – St George's and St John's, St Andrew's and St David's, St Patrick's and St Mark's – the island of Carriacou, and the town of St George's.

One interest group that increasingly won seats to the Assembly was the rising class of merchants in the various towns of Grenada. These men not only owned commercial houses, but were now becoming the owners of bankrupt and abandoned estates in Grenada.[5]

Next were the powerful attorneys for St Andrew's, outstandingly William Shears and John Langdon who, in addition to being attorneys of the majority of estates in that parish also owned estates themselves in that and other parishes. In St Patrick's, there was Jonathan Date, attorney of Belmont, Mt Rose, Morne Fendue, Plains, Chambourd and Mt Alexander estates and owner of Carriere and Conference estates; in addition there were the lesser attorneys, such as William Whiteman, of Tuilleries and Grand Bacolet; Hall Alexander of Mt Reuil and River Salee; Felix Preudhomme of Dougaldstone; William Date of Belmont and Mt Rose and William McEwen of Mt Rodney. Lastly, there was an amorphous group of men who had at one time or another between 1840 and 1877 held public office in Grenada.[6]

These new groups, far from replacing the plantocracy, helped strengthen it for, although some were professionals, public officers and merchants, they had invariably bought up estates of absentee planters as well as other bankrupt estates, and as such, could most appropriately be called the new planting interest. Their presence ensured the continued dominance of the plantocracy in Grenada's political life.

Seven conclusions can be drawn from the elections of that period:

1. Candidates were elected on a very narrow franchise to an extent that at times it was possible for a candidate to elect himself.
2. The elections made a mockery of representative government and

the system is more appropriately referred to as unrepresentative rather than semi-representative.

3. A closely knit group of planters and merchants, consisting mostly of a few families or a total of about 200 persons, governed Grenada from Emancipation to the coming of Crown Colony government.
4. It was inconsistent that in 1869 the number of registered voters was 100 less than in 1862, particularly as the voters' list increased by 186% between 1856 and 1862. Such anomalies were possible in a planter-dominated society where the *fait accompli* typified political activities and élitism predominated.
5. The rigid income and property qualifications were aimed at restricting representation, keeping out the newly emancipated Blacks and limiting participation in the politics of the country to the new merchant/planter class.

After 1838, and especially after 1850, many representatives were merchants from the various towns of Grenada and Carriacou. The vacuum created by the exodus of White planters and attorneys was now being filled by the rich Coloureds, the merchants and the professional men.

## The Bankruptcy of the Old Representative System

A notable feature of the period, not only in Grenada but also in other islands with Assemblies, was the irregular attendance at meetings both of Councillors and Assemblymen. On 25 April 1846 the *Grenada Chronicle* attacked this apathy. The editor wrote: 'It would be far preferable and decidedly more honest in honourable members if their private business clash with their public duties to resign their seats.' The Governor of Grenada, writing four years later, raised similar concerns: 'At present, there is little interest in the election of members. In all cases the infrequency of uncontested elections and the small number of votes usually polled was very observable.'

He was of the opinion that there was insufficient material in the Colony for the formation of a Legislative Council of 35 members (nine in the Council and 26 in the Assembly). He expressed the hope that the new Election Bill would increase the number of electors by changing the qualifications; he remained convinced, however, that a smaller body would more efficiently carry out the country's business. Furthermore, the Executive was entirely unrepresented in the Lower House and had no means of initiating measures there, except by advice and suggestions conveyed in opening speeches and messages.

The Governor suggested that the Assembly and the Council amalgamate into one body, two-thirds to be elective and one-third nominative, and consist of 17 instead of 35 members. The nine nominated members could, therefore, represent the Governor's views, in so far as they coincided with their own; as a minority they would have no constitutional influence on the passage of laws distasteful to the community. Much valuable time would be saved and the measures introduced fully discussed, unlike the situation in an assembly from which all those conducting the Colony's official business absented themselves, and whose most useful members were from time to time withdrawn to fill vacancies in the Council. Moreover, as the Legislative Councils were composed of the same persons and all heads of departments had seats at the Council Board and not in the Assembly, neither the heads of department nor a Council thus formed could act as a connecting link between Executive and Assembly. The Governor recommended that a separate Executive Council be set up, comprising members of the Council and Assembly. By these means the officer administering the government would be in direct communication with the Assembly. Members of this small Executive Council could be responsible for laying an annual estimate of revenue and expenditure before the Assembly, after it had been prepared in the Executive Council, and thus eliminate the practice at that time of voting appropriation of public money on the motion of any individual member. However, nothing came out of this suggestion.

In 1854, in order to escape the shortcomings of an apathetic Assembly, Jamaica created an Executive Committee to manage the financial affairs of the island along the lines advocated by the Governor of Grenada. Many islands followed suit; St Vincent adopted the Jamaican plan of an Executive Committee in 1859.

Although Grenada rejected the Jamaican model of reform the defects of the Grenadian constitution led, in July 1855, to the suggested formation of a General Assembly for the Windward Islands; this, however, was rejected. Without doubt, the House at that time was an unfit and politically inept body, consisting of 16 planters, seven merchants, two magistrates and a journalist, who represented their own interest groups and could not be considered as a general representative body. Their political restrictiveness and insularity were the reasons for their rejection of the idea of a General Assembly for the Windwards.

In 1856 the Constitution was changed to create a ten-man Executive Council, comprising members from the Legislative Council and General Assembly; this was an attempt to give the Governor a voice in the Legislature's debates. In 1859, this measure was discarded and the traditional arrangement of an Executive Council appointed by the Governor exclusively outside the Assembly again adopted. Many colonies had moved to form executive councils or committees for the purpose of obtaining financial assistance from Britain; when this was not forthcoming they abandoned their experiments.

The quality of the Assembly continued to degenerate with unprecedented apathy and ignorance among many members. Dr Orgias described the Assembly of 1869 as composed of ignorant people who for most of the time, engaged in personal abuse. The *Grenada Handbook* referred to the Legislature of 1871 as utterly unfit to govern to the extent that the Governor and other thinking members of the community became greatly concerned. Meetings of the Assembly were characterized by personal invective and the subordination of public to private interests. The administration of the Government was a series of struggles to induce the Legislature to act upon matters affecting the well-being of the colony; more often than not this resulted in failure.[7] Clearly, the *Handbook* concluded, a sweeping change was necessary, and to this end, all Grenadians who had the interests of the country at heart, directed their attention.

## Crown Colony Status: A Backward Step

In 1876 an Act was passed to create a single Legislative Chamber consisting of 17 members: nine nominated and eight elected. This single body was to replace the Legislative Council and the House of Assembly. The Act passed by a majority of five in the House of Assembly, and received unanimous approval in the Council. Consequently, on 7 January 1876, the Governor-in-Chief, John Pope-Hennessy, dissolved the 112-year-old legislative bodies.

Most members of the Grenadian intelligentsia considered this to be an improvement in the Constitution; there were, however, obstacles to its efficient functioning. One was the paucity of interest in public affairs demonstrated by the educated class in particular. They were quite satisfied to allow government to be inefficiently conducted, and quite content that power remain in irresponsible hands. Additionally the new constitution had created an Executive Committee to be paid from the revenues of the Colony, but in its then impoverished state many questioned its ability to meet that requirement.

The Legislative Assembly convened for the first time on 9 February 1876, and Charles Simmons, an elected member, introduced a motion to place government entirely in the Crown's hands. The motion passed the House by a vote of 12 to three: the Grenadian House had voted voluntarily to become a Crown Colony. Only Dr William Wells, Speaker of the House of Assembly for 15 years, prominent politician and medical practitioner of long standing in the parish of St David's, protested. His contemporaries, however, considered it unwise to support him, but posterity praised his progressive political outlook. Wells stated that the new constitution had cast aside the undoubted rights of the people to have a voice in the making of the laws by which they were governed.

When Emancipation had overnight created some 25,000 citizens in Grenada and about 600,000 in the West Indies, the Colonial Office had had to face central political questions: how to avoid the possibility of dictatorship in the Caribbean? how to avert the impending political dominance of the newly emancipated? and how to curb the existing dictatorship of the plantocracy-bourgeoisie? Henry Taylor, as early as 1837, had advised that the answer was to make the Governor supreme. The Morant Bay Uprising of 1865 was just the opportunity for which the British government had waited in order to create a dictatorship of Governor. Beginning with Jamaica in 1866, almost all the colonies with representative government reverted to the inferior status of Crown Colonies. Grenada decided to abolish elections and to adopt Crown Colony rule in 1877. An Imperial Order in Council on 3 December 1877 proclaimed a Crown Colony.

Under the new constitution the Grenadian government comprised the following:

- a Governor – appointed by Her Majesty's Government;
- a Lieutenant-Governor – appointed by Her Majesty's Government;
- an Executive Council – appointed by Her Majesty's Government;
- a Legislative Council – also appointed by Her Majesty's Government.

The Executive Council was composed of four officials and three unofficials with a purely advisory function, as the Governor was the main executive and also President of the Executive Council. In 1877, the composition of the Executive Council was as follows: Samuel Mitchell, Colonial Secretary; A.A.M. Sheriff, Attorney-General; F.M. Chadwick, Public Treasurer; and three unofficial members – L.F. Marrast, W. Shears, and John Langdon. The Legislative Council was composed of the same six men. Its function was essentially to ratify decisions made or taken by the Governor; and to assist the Governor in passing laws. It had no initiative of its own.

## The Search for Political Unity

Towards the end of the 19th century, in an attempt to rationalize its administration, the British government suggested schemes for political unity. On 14 January 1876 the Governor of Barbados, speaking to the House of Assembly, proposed the consolidation of certain administrative departments for Barbados and the Windwards, including: a common Auditor-General; exchange of prisoners; a common lunatic asylum; a Chief Justice for the Windwards; and together with centralization of the judicial system in Barbados, a police force for the Windwards. The Governor was proposing changes to the Constitution that could have had far-reaching effects on the future of the colonies; but the insularity of the Barbadians, principally, frustrated this early attempt at unity. The House of Assembly in Barbados, in rejecting the proposal for the consolidation of departments, stated:

> The House of Assembly ... wishes to bring before your Excellency that they have no intention to consent to become one of a political Federation of the Islands, in any shape or upon any conditions incident to such a Federation – or to merge the independent separate Legislature of this island ... in a Federative legislature.[8]

Some members of the Barbadian plantocracy even told their employees that Federation would mean a return to slavery; others said it was a scheme to reduce Barbados to a Crown Colony. On this occasion, though reluctant at first, the Windwards supported the idea of closer unity.

In 1884, consequent upon the failure of the 1876 scheme, the British government proposed a Federation of St Lucia, St Vincent, Grenada and Tobago, as in that same year, the government of Barbados was separated from that of the Windwards. On 26 January 1885, Sir William Robinson visited Grenada and placed this scheme for Federation before the Council. After the House adjourned that day a public meeting (presided over by William Sayer Commissiong) was called outside the St George's Court House to discuss the 'Federation proposals' and to take a decision. Many people spoke – some in favour of closer union, others opposed to it. Finally, R.J. Sergeant moved that the meeting authorize unofficial members of the Legislative Council to accept the offer of the Home Government regarding confederation, provided that the Treasury of the Confederated Islands be not a common one. This motion was seconded by G.W. Smith; as an amendment to this motion J.D. Glean moved that:

> ... in the opinion of this meeting Federation having proved a failure in the Leeward Islands, this meeting failed to see what benefits can in any form accrue to this colony from the proposed union of the islands. It is therefore the desire of this meeting that the scheme be rejected by the Legislative Council.[9]

To which J.J. St Bernard added: 'This meeting further respectfully request Her Majesty's Government to concede to the people of Grenada representative institutions and control over political affairs.'[10] The meeting voted unanimously in favour of these two amendments.

During February 1885, there were meetings in each parish to rally the population against confederation, and in each of these meetings a resounding 'No' was given to the confederation scheme. The St David's meeting not only opposed confederation but, like St George's, demanded that Grenada have its own Governor and a Legislature composed of an equal number of nominated and elected members.[11]

The House reconvened on 23 February 1885 and when the five unofficial members unanimously opposed the confederation motion, Governor Robinson withdrew it. The reasons for Grenada's rejection of the scheme given by one unofficial member, C.M. Browne, as he addressed the House that day were:

1. The proposals put forward showed no tangible benefits that would accrue to Grenada, except that Grenada would be the seat of government (St Lucia objected to Grenada being the capital).
2. The difficulties of inter-island communication would interfere with the regular attendance of members at meetings of the Legislature.
3. It would be impracticable to arrange to enable each island to act singly and independently of the others.

None of the above reasons, seen in retrospect, was a strong enough basis for opposing unity; the real basis for opposition was island insularity as manifested by Barbados in 1876. Subsequent opposition in St Vincent and Tobago and St Lucia led to the scheme being totally abandoned.

## Crown Colony Rule: Early Dissatisfaction

Soon after the introduction of Crown Colony government into Grenada, in 1877, former members of the Assembly who had advocated its introduction began to criticize its method of execution. H.B. Beckwith, ex-President of the Council and long-standing member of the then-defunct Assembly, severely criticized Governor Harley for his conduct of the affairs of the Government under the system of Crown Colony rule. In a letter to the Secretary of State in July 1878, Beckwith complained that since the assumption of government by Colonel Harley the peace and quiet of the community had been disturbed; moreover, the high-handed and illegal way in which the new constitution was operated by the Governor had brought a great measure of discredit to a system of government which he and others had laboured to procure under Lieutenant-Governor Graham, and which, if carried out with prudence, economy and justice, would have secured the well-being of all classes of the community.[12]

Governor Harley himself was of the opinion that the reactions of Beckwith and his supporters were the result of them not having been invited to be part of the Governor's chosen Executive and Legislative Councils; the unpopularity of Crown Colony government was regarded by Harley as a minority view held only by Beckwith and his group.

In 1878 Beckwith and William Simmons started a newspaper – the *New Era* – for the express purpose of criticizing the Lieutenant-Governor and the manner in which he was executing government. The Governor described the paper as libellous, exciting discontent, infamous and disgraceful. *New Era* seems to have been short-lived, in that it failed to win the support of the upper class, main readers at the time.

Beckwith's actions since 1877 were described by the Governor as an attempt to make all government impossible in Grenada.[13] Between 1878 and 1880 Beckwith called a series of public meetings to protest against several government measures and to organize support for his attack on the administration of Crown Colony; unfortunately, these meetings were poorly attended. A meeting advertised for weeks beforehand in the *Chronicle*, to be held in the Commercial Room in St George's in August 1878 had to be held elsewhere, as the Executive Council ordered that the door of the Commercial Room be closed and the entrance surrounded by a cordon of policemen. Many persons who ordinarily would have attended the meeting were deterred because of this apparent show of force by the Establishment, and only 16 people were present. This meeting condemned the intimidatory actions of the Governor, and many measures introduced by the new Executive, and called for a return to representative government.

In November 1881 Beckwith and two colleagues drew up a petition protesting against Crown Colony government and against a series of fiscal measures instituted by the Lieutenant-Governor. The petition was signed by 467 persons, predominantly planters and merchants, but also shopkeepers, medium and small proprietors and artisans. The petitioners requested that the Secretary of State give the taxpayers the right to select and send representatives to the Legislative Council in lieu of the present exclusive system of nomination by the Governor of an unofficial section of the Council. Beckwith and his colleagues were not opposed to Crown Colony government as such, but they were dissatisfied with those appointed to the Councils and the method the Governor used to make such appointments.

Crown Colony status meant that Grenadians had no effective voice and no popular representation in the government of Grenada. In 1876 Beckwith had supported the change from representative to Crown Colony government and was one of the politicians who strongly advocated it. Now, in 1881, he was demanding the opposite. Beckwith and the leaders of his group were individualists and political opportunists and, as such, lacked a clear political outlook. Nevertheless, their petition, in designating some of the new taxes as oppressive, defended (perhaps conveniently) the interests of the rising class of small proprietors and peasants.

The next series of attacks on Crown Colony government appeared in a memorandum by William Galway Donovan and 18 others, submitted to the Crossman Commission of 1883. They wrote:

> We would like to draw your attention to the strong feeling which pervades the entire community against the present system of government. To express ourselves in the mildest language, the thing is simply odious. We are thankful for the solicitude which this supposed Crown Government manifests on our behalf; but we beg to assure you that no one can be more solicitous for our well-being than ourselves. We know the people of England entertain very crude notions respecting our condition. Because we are negroes or mulattoes must we be ignorant? Does God give intellectual power and reasoning faculties only to Whites? We cannot submit to be ruled like serfs when we consider ourselves to be free-born Britons. We therefore ask you to make such representations as will secure us a share in the management of our own affairs.[14]

The memorandum went on to outline areas of neglect and extravagance of the Government, both of which reflected an insensitivity of the Executive to the wishes and needs of the people.

There is no doubt that by 1885 the majority of the intelligentsia and monied class in Grenada were firmly opposed to Crown Colony government. Donovan continued to attack this system mercilessly in the *Grenada People* of which he was both editor and owner. His slogan was, 'A naked freedman is a nobler object than a gorgeous slave.' Unfortunately, as a result of a libel suit against him by a judge of the Circuit Court, whom he had attacked in the *Grenada People*, he was imprisoned and his paper was closed down in February 1885 by orders of the Court, although he testified that what he had written was the truth. At that time the *St George's Chronicle* had the following to say: 'Notwithstanding the violent and objectionable tone it [*Grenada People*] adopted at times, it nevertheless by its fearless demeanour did much to expose the rottenness of Crown Colony government and to educate the British people on our affairs'.[15]

*William Galway Donovan, early advocate of self-government*

In Britain, prior to 1843 any unfavourable material – true or false – published by anyone was, according to law, libellous. After the introduction of Lord Campbell's Act in 1843, however, once what was written was proven to be accurate, there was no libel. This Act was introduced into Grenada soon after Donovan's imprisonment, and he was then released.

On 9 May 1885 Donovan gave notice that the *Grenada People* would resume publication, and indicated that the policy of the paper would be the same as before – only more so. He emphasized:

> I shall continue in my journal to advocate the right of the people of Grenada to representative government. I shall criticize freely men and measures, believing as I do that the people of the Colony are qualified to manage through their representatives all local affairs and that until this fundamental right is restored to the people neither the prosperity of the colony nor the contentment of the people will be ensured. I shall most strenuously advocate the abolition of Crown Colony and the restoration of self-government. I seek to make the people thoroughly dissatisfied with any system of government which virtually denies their existence and defiantly and insolently tramples

their right. Without representation political liberty is destroyed. No intelligent people, nor people possessed of self-respect and not having surrendered the dignity of their manhood would consent to be branded as political slaves – tamely submitting to see their money expended without regard to their wants and in wanton and insolent defiance of their wishes.

To obtain justice you must obtain representation.[16]

The arbitrary nature of Crown Colony rule and its insensitivity to the sentiments of the common people were well exemplified by the passage of the Bonfire Act and its sequel, the Bonfire Riots of 1885 in St George's.

## Bonfire Riots of 1885

In early November a law was passed prohibiting, from the 5th day of November, lighting bonfires and discharging fireworks in the market square and other public places to commemorate the anniversary of Guy Fawkes. Working-class inhabitants of the town rejected this arbitrary attempt to deprive them of their right to festivities. From Wednesday, 4 November, tar-barrels were surreptitiously lighted at a late hour in various parts of the town and, the police, in trying to put them out, were pelted.

On Thursday 5 November the poor classes in the town – women as well as men – showed a determination to riot and to resist the police. The authorities forthwith strengthened the force by swearing-in 100 'special constables' to act as police-aides. About that time, printed slips of paper were circulated throughout the town stating that a number of persons of the poorer classes intended to assemble for the purpose of creating disorder.

Squads of reserve police were despatched during the early evening to patrol various streets of the town. About 8.30 p.m. however, bricks, bats, stones, bottles, and every imaginable form of missile began to be hurled indiscriminately from certain houses of the poorer classes, from vacant lots and from alleys in St John, St Juille, Hillsborough, Melville, Grenville and Halifax Streets, as well as from the market square. All street lamps in these areas were broken and total darkness enveloped the town. Several constables were struck and many severely injured. E.W. Begrie (Inspector of Schools) was injured by a blow on the head, several other urban middle-and upper-class members were also injured, and the windows of some houses and businesses in the market square were smashed.

The disturbances continued until about 11 p.m.; police reinforcements were sent out to quiet the disturbance and pick up the injured constables; by midnight the situation was under control. The performance of the police aides was hardly satisfactory, as they hid themselves for hours, leaving the injured to fend for themselves. It was believed that this riot was encouraged by certain 'respectable' young men of the town who apparently were dissatisfied with the unrepresentative and dictatorial nature of Crown Colony rule (Donovan perhaps).

The authorities anticipated a continuation of the riot on the following night and more inhabitants of the town were summoned and sworn in as special constables. During that night around eight companies, each consisting of 50 constables, patrolled the town. There were, however, no disturbances that night and by 10 p.m. the companies were dismissed.

Speaking on 6 November, the Governor blamed the disturbances on the police and their rough and uncivil manner towards the people. He said, 'We cannot but express the opinion that it was due in a very great measure to the want of tact on the part of the police as well as the rough and uncivil manner that too often characterises their dealings with the people.' An incident on Thursday 5 November clearly substantiated this accusation. On that afternoon, as the special constables were assembling, a man who had been arrested was brought in. He was immediately attacked by a policeman who dealt him several blows about the shoulder with a stick, saying at the same time, 'You are the fellow who escaped from me, take that'. Other policemen present followed his example. Donovan, editor of the *Grenada People*, interposed himself between the man and the police and he also received some blows. Livingston Payne, another witness who tried to shield Donovan was severely injured on the hand; George Otway who also intervened was dealt a blow on his head with a truncheon and knocked unconscious.

During the night of the disturbances the police themselves threw showers of stones at the crowd and used their truncheons quite indiscriminately; so much so that the Governor remarked, 'When so-called peace officers behave this way, what can be expected from the lower classes?'

## Walter Sendall's Administration 1885–89

The administration of Governor Walter J. Sendall, between 1885 and 1889, seems to have neutralized much of the ill-will built up against Crown Colony government during previous administrations. After a short interval to familiarize himself with local circumstances, Sendall met the Legislative Council on 31 July, and in his opening speech outlined the policy he would pursue for the next four years. Emphasis was to be placed on road construction, public works, the creation of

*A plantation Great House: Chantilly's Estate, late 19th century*

local authorities to look after parish and town affairs, improvement and extension of primary education, better collection of government revenue, reorganization of the prison and post office, and the establishment of a botanical garden for the promotion of improved methods of agriculture and the introduction of new plants. The Councillors, planters and citizens at large, warmly welcomed the new plans.

Two years later, Sendall was severely criticized in the *Chronicle* by one 'Lobby' for having failed to fulfill any of these promises. He was accused of distrusting most people except his personal clique; of taking no interest in the people; treating some visitors to Government House without respect; being void of common courtesy to the ordinary people; being afraid to move among the people he governed; and deliberately refusing to have audience with Jerome Robert Fletcher who had made an appointment to see him, because he was a Black man.

By the end of his administration in November 1889, however, he had succeeded in implementing quite a few reforms, and the *Chronicle* noted, that, for 20 years before 1885, £50,000 of taxpayers' money had been wasted on roads which at that time were still totally inadequate; the stinted measure of primary education had been a mere burlesque, while secondary education had been resolutely and imperiously denied by the local executive; the crude and oppressive character of the excise laws had resulted in widespread smuggling throughout the Colony; and the abuses that had crept into various public departments had become the norm. In highlighting Sendall's successes, the *Chronicle* observed that the policies he had enunciated in that first address had been substantially realized. Public roads were in a satisfactory condition by 1889; the highway from St George's to Grand Etang was well macadamized and reconstructed. The system of primary education had been considerably improved; grants were increased, and government schools had been established in several populous centres; a measure of local autonomy had been accorded to the people in the form of local parochial boards; the prison and the Colony Hospital were vastly improved; the objectionable excise laws had been removed; a large area of ten square miles between St David's and St George's had been supplied with water; a tunnel connecting the Carenage with the market square had been constructed; a Hospital Board, a Botanical Garden Committee, and an enlarged Education Committee, three times the size of the previous one, were all established and functional.[17] The *Chronicle* concluded that when Grenadians compared the past four and a half years of their political life with the period they lived under Lieutenant-Governor Harley and Administrators Thomas Kerr and Edward La Borde it was difficult to believe that the same system of Crown Colony government had been in operation.

W.S. Commissiong expressed the feelings of the Legislature towards Sendall's administration in the following words addressed to the Council: 'The news that the colony was about to lose the services of so able, wise and liberal a ruler as Your Excellency has proved to be sad and was received with profound regret throughout the entire community.'[18] Strenuous efforts were made to have Governor Sendall's term of administration extended but these proved unsuccessful.

Sendall had succeeded in allaying most of the fears of the opponents of Crown Colony government and in reducing the concern of those who criticized but were not opposed to it. His administration had many lasting and beneficial effects on the Colony.

Improved relations in the community with the Executive, however, were due not to any changes in the structure of Central Government nor to fundamental changes in Crown Colony government, but solely to the personality and reforms of Governor Sendall. The basis for political discontent – the dictatorial nature of Crown Colony rule – still remained.

Above and below *Grenadian planter-class life in the late 1880s*

*The Queen's Park Bridge before the present Green Bridge was built, late 1890s*

*The Market Square, St George's, 1899*

Despite the successes of the Sendall administration, W.G. Donovan, foremost opponent of Crown Colony rule, continued to advocate the involvement of the people in political affairs and their right to elect representatives to the Legislature, and to attack the arbitrariness of Crown Colony rule. In two memoranda – in April and August 1893 – to the Secretary of State, the Marquis of Ripon, he stated unequivocally that the present system of governing Grenada was repugnant to its inhabitants. The Executive Government, he claimed, was looked upon as the public enemy, if not by a large majority of the people, at least by a powerful educated minority. He recommended that the existing Parochial Boards be extended to parochial councils, with greater autonomy and with responsibility for repairs and maintenance of streets, roads and all public places within the area; and for sanitary matters, poor relief, water supply, lighting, and for the establishment of schools of secondary education where this was found to be necessary. To perform these duties they should, in addition to property tax in town, be allowed to impose and collect revenue from the licences on wheeled vehicles, porters, jobbers, and on dogs. They should also be allowed to impose, collect and administer the land tax and other purely parochial rates and taxes.[19]

## District Boards: An Attempt at Decentralization

The Parochial Boards that Donovan was seeking to reform were first instituted in October 1886 under a system of local self-government. A local Board was created in each of the six parishes in Grenada and in the island of Carriacou; half the members of each Board was nominated by the Governor and the other half was elected by the ratepayers of each parish.

Certain powers formerly vested in the Government, such as levying and disbursement of local rates, the control and management of the town, the upkeep of the by-ways, and other purely local matters, were delegated to these Boards. The first election of members to the respective Boards was on 12 November 1886, and the community showed great interest and participated widely. In 1891 an ordinance was passed converting Parochial Board into wholly elected bodies; five years later the 1896 Commission on Boards recommended that the parish be made the unit of local administration; this took effect in 1900. In the same year another ordinance was passed, abolishing the wholly elected Parochial Boards and instead creating Town Boards and reintroducing the semi-elective system; this system was still in operation in 1933. District Boards, subject to the Governor's

*St Andrew's District Board circa 1920*

approval, had the power to frame bye-laws in order to carry into effect the powers conferred upon them.

The importance of the Parochial Board was that it placed the running of the local affairs of the parish in the hands of the people of the parish. It was democratic in the sense that those who paid rates elected their representatives on the board. Every male over 21 who paid rates of 10/- on freehold or leasehold or who rented property of £20 or more per annum, or who received income of £140 per annum, qualified to be an elector. These Boards, by affording participation and control, were supposed to act as a kind of counterweight at the parish level to the autocracy of the Governor. But this function was limited by the fact that many members of the Governor's unofficial hand-picked Legislative Council were elected to these Boards and held dominant positions on them; for example, John Stuart Martin, Francis Gurney, Frederick Harford, Domingo DeFreitas who were all members of the Legislative Council in 1903 were simultaneously prominent members of the parochial Boards. Moreover, these Boards were invariably dominated by the wealthy, Coloured upper and middle classes. The presence of Legislative Council members on these Boards, meant:

1. They carried great influence as they were invariably made Chairmen.
2. The Governor's voice and influence were also imposed by their very presence.

The foregoing dimensions reduced somewhat the impact of people's power and control at the local level which had been the original intention of the Parochial Boards. Nonetheless, the executive and decision-making functions of the Boards made them a far more respectable body than the hand-picked Legislative Council.

## Legislative Council: A Powerless Body

As the years progressed the number of members on the Legislative Council increased, but it remained solely an advisory body devoid of any executive power. In 1882 the Executive Council was reduced from six to four members, while the Legislative Council was increased from six to ten members. All members of the Executive continued to belong to the official side of the Legislative Council.[20]

In August 1896 the number of councillors in the Legislative Council was increased by four – two official and two unofficial – and the unofficial members were to hold office for six years. By the end of the decade the amended Executive and Legislative Councils consisted of five and 13 members respectively.

Some councillors served in political office for more than 20 years. It was the pattern in the period of appointed legislatures for a member, once nominated by the Governor, to serve for decades. On many occasions the country was in the hands of one man and sometimes of four or five men.

In 1920 the Legislative Council consisted of an equal number – seven each – of nominated and official members; the latter formed the Executive composed of three ex-officio members: the Colonial Secretary, the Attorney-General and the Colonial Treasurer; and three others appointed by the Governor, who was himself President of the Executive Council. The term of office for Executive members who sat on the Legislative Council was three years, while other, unofficial, members served a six-year term. The aims of the local representation in both Executive and Legislative Councils were to develop greater co-operation and working-togetherness of the two bodies, to minimize effort and time, and to increase communications between these two levels of Government.

Despite concessions, political power under Crown Colony government remained firmly in the hands of the Governor until the early 1950s. Some members of the educated class continued to oppose it, but the mass of the population – over 60,000 – who had never been part of the political life, remained detached and politically unaware. As opportunities for emigration appeared many migrated to escape the social, political and economic vacuum in which they found themselves.

NOTES

Full citations only given where work does not appear in the Bibliography.

1. *St George's Chronicle and Grenada Gazette*, 26 January 1856.
2. Ibid. Vol. 8, 20 February 1869 and 22 February 1862.
3. Ibid.
4. Ibid. Vol. 7, 15 February 1862.
5. Such men as: Richard Gibbs, who served on the Assembly from 1843 to 1856; Alexander Baillie (1843–56); Samuel Cockburn (1850–62); Charles Simmons (1862–77); William Simmons (1856–77); Hall Alexander (1856–77); Lucius Dill (1856–62); John Desbat (1869–76); William Steel (1862–69); John Gay (1862–69); Felix Renwick (1869–76); and the druggists, H.B. Beckwith (1862–76) and Clarke Christy (1856–62).
6. These included: Alexander Turnbull and Robert Gentle (teachers); John Aird (1843–76); H. Garraway, W. Sinclair and L.B. Otway (police magistrates); George Gun-Munro (immigration agent); David Davidson, the editor of the *St George's Chronicle*; medical officers Dr P. Orgias and Dr William Wells; the Coroner of St David's, John Wells; the medical attendant of St George's gaol, John Brown, John Wells also served as Speaker of the Assembly; so well did he serve the parish that in 1882 he was honoured for his services by the community.
7. *Grenada Handbook*, p. 48.
8. *Outgoing Dispatches*, 15 January 1876.
9. *St George's Chronicle and Grenada Gazette*, 31 January 1885.
10. Ibid.
11. Ibid.
12. Lieutenant-Governor Harley to Dundas, No.154, 3 August 1878.
13. Governor Hurley to Secretary of State, No.256, 28 November 1881.
14. West Indies, *Report of Royal Commission*, Part II, 1884, p. 58.
15. *St George's Chronicle and Grenada Gazette*, 8 February 1885.
16. Ibid. 9 May 1885.
17. Ibid. November 1889.
18. Ibid.
19. Ibid. 9 August 1893, 6 April 1893. Letter to Secretary of State from W.G. Donovan, Grenada, 9 August 1893.
20. *Blue Book*, 1882.

# 15

# *Demographic Factors, Religion and Housing Conditions: 1844–1921*

The Grenadian population grew steadily from 1844 to 1891, but then the rate of growth declined, as Table 15.1 (page 238) illustrates.

The decline in growth rate during the first two decades of the 20th century was due to large-scale emigration. Between 1911 and 1921, 12,045 people had probably emigrated. The census enumerator in 1921 observed that: 'Not only was the whole natural increment wiped out by emigration but there was a further draft on the population of 1911 to the extent of 448'.[1]

## Migration

Grenada's emigrants at the time went mainly to Trinidad, Panama, Cuba, Brazil and Venezuela, in search of employment and new economic opportunities. In 1906, the year of the first large-scale emigrations, 1,534 Grenadians migrated to the Panama Canal Zone, and in the same year 813 returned; many had died on the Isthmus. From 1911 to 1916, 450 Grenadians migrated to the Canal Zone; throughout the 1911–22 period 871 arrivals from the Canal Zone to Grenada were recorded.[2]

In the late 19th century (post-1871) young men from the parish of St David's went to caratal, Venezuela to dig for gold; many were successful and returned to the parish to invest their earnings in land and home-steads.

**Table 15.1 Population Growth Rates 1844–1921**

| *Year* | *Population* | *Percentage* *Increase* | *Decrease* |
|---|---|---|---|
| 1844 | 28,923[2] | – | – |
| 1851 | 32,671[3] | 14.0 | – |
| 1871 | 37,684 | 18.0 | – |
| 1881 | 42,403 | 12.5 | – |
| 1891 | 53,209 | 25.5 | – |
| 1901 | 63,438 | 19.0 | – |
| 1911 | 66,750 | 5.0 | – |
| 1921 | 66,302[4] | – | 0.67 |

The period 1910–23 witnessed a number of departures for Brazil and Cuba (as well as a number of arrivals). These involved Grenadian workers recruited to work in the sugar plantations of American companies in Cuba, and the coffee plantations of Brazilian *hacendados*. There was apparently regular recruitment of labour in Grenada to work on foreign farms at this time; for this reason, in December 1899, the Government of Grenada passed the Emigration Regulation Ordinance authorizing licensed persons only to collect, recruit or

*Members of the Grenada Volunteer Corps, some of whom fought in the First World War*

arrange for the engagement of emigrants outside Grenada. This Ordinance was superseded in October 1927 by the Emigrants Protection Ordinance which was amended in 1930. The principal ordinance made it compulsory for every recruiter of emigrants to take out a permit and to be registered annually. It also drew up a number of clauses pertinent to the welfare of the emigrants thus recruited. For example, a condition of contract was that recruiting agents made no deductions from the wages of recruits: agents were required to pay 10/– into the Treasury for every recruit; the person recruited had to pay 2/- into the Treasury. Both the agent and the emigré were required to deposit 25/- to finance repatriation in the event of unexpected circumstances, and to save the Colony bearing such expenses.[6] Funds collected by the Treasury in this period were consolidated into a Distressed Emigrants Fund.

For every 100 men who emigrated during the decade 1911 to 1921 there were 57 women emigrants. The highest proportion of male emigrants – 70% – was from the parish of St Mark's and the lowest – 51% – was from St Andrew's. The emigrants, as would be expected, were in the most productive period of their lives.

Emigration to Panama continued until about 1916 and then petered out, but as late as the mid-1920s some were still returning to Grenada. Emigration to Trinidad has been a constant feature of Grenada's history from the immediate post-1807 period to the present day. Emigration to Cuba to cut sugar-cane prevailed essentially during the periods 1900–10 and 1920–30. At a later date emigration to the Netherlands Antilles of Curaçao and Aruba occurred. Table 15.2 (page 240) shows the flow of migrants to and from Grenada recorded during the period 1911 to 1928. Unrecorded migration was quite significant as the discrepancy between intercensal population changes, the natural increase of the population and the actual net recorded outflow of migrants reveal.

Large sums of money were remitted by the emigrants to dependants and relatives in Grenada. The Post Office showed money orders from the Canal Zone and Cuba from April 1911 to December 1920 amounting to £64,861; the estimated amount that flowed into the Colony from the same places through other authentic and reliable sources was about £100,000. The money order business with Trinidad amounted to £14,000.[7] These remittances constituted valuable capital inflow of great benefit to the country. Much of it went to purchase lands, construct houses, and open retail shops and other commercial enterprises.

During the 1930s and 1940s the majority of Grenadians migrated to Trinidad as usual. For 16 years examined in the period 1928 to

**Table 15.2 Movement of Migrants to and from Grenada 1911–28**

| *Year* | *Arrivals* | | | | | *Departures* | | | | |
|---|---|---|---|---|---|---|---|---|---|---|
| | *Barbados* | *Cuba* | *Panama* | *Trinidad* | *Total** | *Barbados* | *Cuba* | *Panama* | *Trinidad* | *Total** |
| 1911 | 375 | – | 87 | 2,668 | 4,101 | 630 | – | 166 | 2,388 | 4,122 |
| 1912 | 654 | – | 114 | 2,986 | 4,876 | 1,116 | – | 74 | 2,977 | 5,280 |
| 1913 | 592 | – | 180 | 3,023 | 5,084 | 740 | – | 168 | 3,320 | 5,345 |
| 1914 | 500 | – | 216 | 3,160 | 5,101 | 367 | – | 47 | 3,189 | 4,599 |
| 1915 | 495 | – | 100 | 2,664 | 4,484 | 377 | – | 9 | 3,245 | 4,670 |
| 1916 | 594 | – | 21 | 2,316 | 4,739 | 470 | – | 6 | 1,962 | 4,572 |
| 1917 | 512 | – | 31 | 2,546 | 3,760 | 526 | – | – | 3,034 | 4,532 |
| 1918 | 395 | – | 20 | 2,679 | 3,702 | 310 | – | – | 3,341 | 4,331 |
| 1919 | 642 | – | 1 | 3,298 | 5,092 | 782 | – | – | 3,898 | 5,622 |
| 1920 | 609 | 12 | 29 | 3,802 | 5,324 | 696 | – | – | 3,836 | 5,771 |
| 1921 | 371 | 135 | 35 | 3,666 | 4,886 | 409 | 348 | – | 4,268 | 5,693 |
| 1922 | – | 53 | 37 | 3,329 | 4,925 | – | – | – | 3,561 | 4,498 |
| 1923 | 422 | 69 | 6 | 3,294 | 5,101 | 433 | 215 | – | 3,835 | 5,377 |
| 1928 | 493 | 532 | – | 3,363 | 5,160 | 371 | 324 | – | 3,213 | 4,528 |
| | *6,654* | *801* | *877* | *42,794* | *66,335* | *4,907* | *887* | *470* | *46,067* | *68,940* |

Source: Grenada, *Report and General Abstract of the Registrar General*, 1911–1922
* The totals will not add correctly as the category 'Other' has been omitted.

1953 there was a total of 77,169 departures to, and 73,695 arrivals from Trinidad, revealing the net official outflow of Grenadians to Trinidad to be 3,474. A schooner trade had always plied between Grenada and Trinidad, so that most of those enumerated as departures, returned and showed up as arrivals. The net figure gives an indication of the level of official emigration for those years.

In the decade 1940–50 hundreds of Grenadians travelled to Curacao and Aruba to work for the Lago Oil Company in its oil refineries that were being installed in these areas, and, in search of better employment opportunities. The majority of these returned to Grenada in the 1940s and in subsequent decades.

Throughout the 20th century there was always a constant flow of migrants to and from the USA and the UK. In the pre-war years the volume was low; but it increased markedly in the post-war era and especially in the period 1950 to 1970.

This emigration of Grenadians did much to reduce the growth rate of the population and exerted downward pressure on both growth of the labour and the level of unemployment.

## Birth and Death Rates

From 1871 to 1921 the rate of natural increase was steady. The death rate declined from 27.4 per thousand in the 1871–80 decades, to 19.8

**Table 15.3 Rate of Natural Increase of Grenada's Population 1867–1979**

| *Period* | *Population range* | *Birth rate* | *Death rate* | *Rate of natural increase* |
|---|---|---|---|---|
| 1867–70 | 35,993–43,807 | 41.5 | 25.2 | 16.3 |
| 1871–80 | 38,423–43,807 | 44.0 | 27.4 | 16.6 |
| 1887–92 | n/a–53,209 | 45.4 | 24.9 | 20.5 |
| 1891–1900 | 54,062–65,523 | 42.7 | 21.1 | 21.6 |
| 1901–10 | 64,288–75,274 | 38.4 | 21.6 | 16.8 |
| 1911–20 | 67,848–75,216 | 35.7 | 19.8 | 15.9 |
| 1921–30 | 66,957–76,967 | 33.1 | 17.3 | 15.8 |
| 1925–34 | 70,184–83,588 | 32.3 | 16.0 | 16.3 |
| 1934–39 | 83,588–89,415 | 31.2 | 14.5 | 16.7 |
| 1939–48 | 90,085–74,719 | 28.5 | 14.7 | 13.8 |
| 1948–56 | 74,140–88,600 | 39.2 | 13.8 | 25.4 |
| 1961–70 | 88,677–92,775 | 32.5 | 8.6 | 23.9 |
| 1971–79 | 98,743–108,907 | 26.1 | 6.7 | 19.4 |

Sources: Grenada, *Census Reports* 1861–1970; *Blue Books*; *Reports and General Abstracts of Births, Deaths and Marriages* 1867–1979, selected years.

per thousand in the 1911–20 decade, and 13.8 per thousand in the period 1948–56.[8] The birth rate also declined over the same period, sometimes faster than the death rate.

The decline in the birth rate during the Second World War was due to the exodus of large numbers of young adults to Trinidad to seek employment.

## *Illegitimate births*

In the decade 1881–91 illegitimate births accounted for 53.4% of total births; 1891–1901, 49.1%; 1901–11, 49.2%; and between 1911 and 1921, 54.8%. In 1928 out of a total of 2,507 births, 1,529 or 61% were illegitimate, and by 1949 out of a total of 2,746 births 1,859 or 67.7% were illegitimate. In 1979 77.48% of total births were illegitimate.

One reason for the relatively high incidence of illegitimacy was that the majority of the population were unmarried. In 1881, only 34% of all adults over 15 years old (less widowed) were married; in 1891, the figure was 36%; it was 42% in 1911; and 38% in 1921.

In many cases these children were fathered by different men on the same woman, and were rarely supported by the fathers. The women concerned thus had to perform the role of both breadwinner and housewife.

**Table 15.4 Birthplaces of Sections of Grenada's Population 1871–1921**

| | *1871* | *1881* | *1891* | *1901* | *1911* | *1921* |
|---|---|---|---|---|---|---|
| Grenada | 52,525 | 32,469 | 40,719 | 51,206 | 55,218 | 56,207 |
| Carriacou | – | 5,056 | 6,024 | 6,680 | 6,829 | 6,837 |
| Trinidad | 2,146 | 1,180 | 462 | 395 | 482 | 461 |
| Barbados | – | – | 1,835 | 1,802 | 1,456 | 1,068 |
| Other BWI | – | 1,397 | 2,122 | 1,938 | 1,917 | 1,131 |
| Africa | 1,135 | 807 | 593 | 342 | 136 | 39 |
| India | 1,344 | 1,052 | 1,017 | 631 | 406 | 181 |
| United Kingdom | 178 | 163 | 134 | 140 | 91 | 110 |
| *Total population* | *57,684* | *42,403* | *53,209* | *63,458* | *66,750* | *66,302* |

Source: *Census Reports*

### *Population born within and outside Grenada 1871–1921*

According to the 1871 census 86% of Grenadians were native-born; 5.7% were born in Barbados and Trinidad; 3.6% in India, and 3% in Africa. As immigration drew to an end, however, few Grenadians were born outside the country. In the census of 1921, 95% of the population were recorded as native-born; 2.3% in Barbados and Trinidad. In the same year Indians who had been born in India numbered 181 or 0.27% compared to 1,344 in the 1871 census; African-born Africans numbered 39, compared to 1,135 in 1871; and Britishers numbered 110 or 0.14%, compared to 178 in 1871 (see Table 15.4).

## Age Distribution 1871–1970

A feature of Grenada's population throughout the century (1871–1970) was its relative youthfulness: some 60–65% of the population were always below 25 years of age and some 80% were below the age of 40 years (see Table 15.5).

Three factors were responsible for the relative youthfulness of the population:

1. the low average life expectancy especially during the earlier decades and as late as the 1946 census;
2. the constant flow of emigration part of which consisted of the middle-aged;
3. the fall in infant and overall mortality. Most changes in the percentage of the population under 40 years in 1946, 1960 and 1970 can be explained by this third factor.

**Table 15.5 Distribution of Grenada's Population by Age 1871–1970**

| *Census year* | *1871* | | | *1881* | | | *1921* | | | *1946* | | | *1960** | *1970** |
|---|---|---|---|---|---|---|---|---|---|---|---|---|---|---|
| *Age* | *M* | *F* | *Total* | *M* | *F* | *Total* | *M* | *F* | *Total* | *M* | *F* | *Total* | *Total* | *Total* |
| Under 5 | 3,143 | 3,076 | 6,219 | 3,535 | 3,522 | 7,057 | 4,912 | 4,875 | 9,787 | 4,691 | 4,971 | 9,662 | 17,595 | 12,401 |
| 5–9 | 2,466 | 2,580 | 5,046 | 3,086 | 3,045 | 6,131 | 4,622 | 4,484 | 9,106 | 5,501 | 5,189 | 10,690 | 13,942 | 16,144 |
| 10–14 | 2,109 | 1,952 | 4,061 | 2,694 | 2,545 | 5,239 | 4,611 | 4,602 | 9,213 | 5,115 | 5,056 | 10,171 | 10,731 | 15,176 |
| 15–19 | 1,798 | 1,907 | 3,705 | 1,932 | 2,203 | 4,135 | 3,249 | 4,159 | 7,408 | 3,750 | 4,284 | 8,034 | 7,794 | 10,418 |
| 20–24 | 3,094 | 3,400 | 6,494 | 1,542 | 1,933 | 3,475 | 2,112 | 3,884 | 5,996 | 2,210 | 3,330 | 5,540 | 6,257 | 6,755 |
| 25–30 | | | | 1,452 | 2,036 | 3,488 | 1,454 | 3,044 | 4,498 | 1,509 | 2,595 | 4,104 | 5,030 | 4,202 |
| 31–40 | 2,270 | 2,387 | 4,657 | 2,239 | 2,606 | 4,845 | 2,236 | 4,462 | 6,698 | 2,852 | 4,585 | 7,437 | 8,021 | 7,157 |
| 41–50 | 1,590 | 1,659 | 3,249 | 1,654 | 1,803 | 3,457 | 2,314 | 3,311 | 5,625 | 2,403 | 3,927 | 6,330 | 6,734 | 6,808 |
| 51–60 | 850 | 1,021 | 1,871 | 959 | 1,137 | 2,096 | 1,724 | 2,192 | 3,916 | 1,654 | 2,861 | 4,515 | 5,740 | 5,583 |
| 61–70 | | | | 539 | 757 | 1,296 | 973 | 1,370 | 2,343 | 1,227 | 2,063 | 3,290 | 3,756 | 4,693 |
| 71–80 | 960 | 1,422 | 2,382 | 270 | 424 | 694 | 451 | 680 | 1,131 | 657 | 1,134 | 1,791 | 2,094 | 2,275 |
| 80 and over | | | | 172 | 318 | 490 | 189 | 392 | 581 | 265 | 558 | 823 | 983 | 1163 |
| *Total* | *18,280* | *19,404* | *37,684* | *20,074* | *22,329* | *42,403* | *28,847* | *37,455* | *66,320* | *31,834* | *40,553* | *72,387* | *88,677* | *92,775* |
| 0–24 | | | 60.0% | | | 61.4% | | | 63.0% | | | 61.0% | 63.5% | 65.6% |
| 25–39 | | | 20.3% | | | 19.6% | | | 16.8% | | | 15.9% | 14.7% | 12.2% |
| 0–39 | | | 80.3% | | | 81.0% | | | 79.8% | | | 78.9% | 78.2% | 77.8% |

Source: Grenada, *Census Reports* 1871–1970
* A breakdown of males/females is not available for these dates.

## Racial Composition of the Population

During the period 1881–1921 Blacks increased by 20,000; Coloureds by 2,000 and Whites and Orientals by 70 and 1,000 respectively. By 1970, Blacks constituted 84.3% or 78,226 out of a population of 92,772; Coloureds comprised 10,332 or 11.1%; East Indians 3.4% or 3,183.[9] One reason for the low percentage of Coloureds in the 1881 and 1921 censuses (22.8% and 17.5% respectively) was that many persons of mixed blood returned themselves as Whites.[10] A further factor involved was emigration which the 1921 census reported as affecting this group more than any other racial groups. Subsequent decline in the numbers of Coloureds was also for the same reason and increased absorption into the Black group as a result of intermarriage and miscegenation, plus the practice of family planning.

## Occupations

As Table 15.6 amply illustrates, by 1921 the pattern of industrial occupations had not changed markedly since the 1844 census.

The 1891 census divided the working population into six occupational classes (see Table 15.7).

Lastly, there was the unoccupied class, which was practically negligible in the rural areas; most were in the town and parish of St George's and numbered not more than 11 per 1000 in 1891.

The predominant occupations among men, by 1921 and until the mid-20th century, were field labour, shopkeeping, artisanal trades,

**Table 15.6 Major Occupations in Grenada 1844–1921**

| *Category* | *1844* | *1851* | *1881* | *1891* | *1921* |
|---|---|---|---|---|---|
| Planters and large proprietors | 490 | 392 | 505 | 708 | 1,951 |
| Agricultural labourers* | 10,198 | 13,110 | 12,483 | 13,938 | 15,455† |
| Merchants and shopkeepers | 426 | 394 | 418 | 816 | 808 |
| Artisans | 1,711 | 1,854 | 2,320 | 2,681 | 1,403 |
| Fishermen | 389 | 467 | 472 | 698 | 393 |
| Seamstresses | 1,409 | 1,795 | 2,667 | 2,695 | 3,566 |
| Domestic servants | 1,036 | 1,005 | 1,665 | 2,736 | 3,962 |
| Washerwomen and laundresses | 661 | 634 | 879 | 1,140 | 1,140 |

Source: *Census Reports*
* Mainly women, i.e., 132 to every 100 men.
† Including peasants.

**Table 15.7 Working Population: 1891 Census**
(Total adults 31,420)

| *Class* | *Total number* |
|---|---|
| **Professionals**: public officers, doctors, lawyers, clergymen, engineers, teachers, police, photographers | 413 |
| **Commercial** | 1,887 |
| **Agricultural**: resident proprietors (441) estate managers (267), labourers and peasants owning five or less acres (2,500), workers (13,938) | 17,146 |
| **Industrial**: mainly carpenters, masons, joiners, sailors, blacksmiths | 2,681 |
| **Domestic**: servants, laundresses, seamstresses | 6,571 |

crafts and fishing and those among women included field labour, domestic work, sewing and laundry work. Small numbers of the workforce remained unemployed, with young people constituting the majority.

### *School attendance*

Of the population of 53,209 enumerated in the 1891 census, 21,789, or 41% of the total, were children; of these 12,431 or 57% did not attend school. Of the remainder, 258 per 1000 attended government-assisted denominational schools, 811 per 1000 attended government schools, and 91 per 1000 private schools. Of the 1921 population of 66,302, 27,265 or 42% were enumerated as children, 13,186 of whom were not attending schools. Of the remainder, 9,429 attended assisted schools, and 2,343 and 3,057 attended government and private schools respectively.

## Decline of the African and Indian Population

The phasing out of African immigration by 1865 (see Table 15.8), and Indian immigration by 1890, obviously resulted in a decreased number of these nationals in Grenada.

In 1881 there were 1,572 Indians in Grenada, and the 1891 census recorded 2,118. Between 1881–91, 121 had returned to India, but many Indians from other West Indian islands, especially St Vincent, chose to migrate to Grenada. The greatest number of Indians was in St John's and St Patrick's, where the majority of cultivated cocoa lands

**Table 15.8 Decline of the African Immigrant Population 1844–1924**

| *Census year* | *Africans* | *Total population* | *Africans as % of population* |
|---|---|---|---|
| 1844 | 2,285 | 28,923 | 8.0 |
| 1851 | 2,425 | 32,671 | 7.4 |
| 1861 | 1,432 | 35,000 | 4.1 |
| 1871 | 1,135 | 37,684 | 3.0 |
| 1881 | 807 | 42,403 | 2.0 |
| 1891 | 593 | 53,209 | 1.1 |
| 1901 | 342 | 63,438 | 0.5 |
| 1911 | 136 | 66,750 | 0.2 |
| 1924 | 39 | 66,403 | 0.05 |

Source: Grenada, *Census Reports* 1844–1921

were to be found. There were also 15 mature producing nutmeg holdings. Those Indians not employed in the agricultural sector were proprietors of smallholdings, or comparatively larger acreages, and some were engaged in business.

By 1921, the Indian population in Grenada had increased to 2,672, the majority of whom were in St Andrew's and St Patrick's. However, more and more Indians moved into St John's and St Mark's and from 1891 to 1921 their numbers increased by 588% and 297% respectively in these two parishes. The presence of Presbyterian Mission Stations in these two parishes and the establishment of at least five Indian Mission Schools partially accounts for this. The relatively high number of Indians was due to immigration of Barbadians to fill posts in the teaching profession and the lower echelons of the Civil Service.

## Religion

In 1871, 21,000 out of the population of 37,654 were Roman Catholic; in 1881, 23,884 out of the population then of 42,403; in 1901, 36,437 out of 63,438; and in 1921 39,594 out of 66,302. Thus, over the years 1871 to 1921, 57–59% of the total population were Roman Catholics. Over the same period Anglicans accounted for 33–35% of the total population and Wesleyans 4–6%. The remaining population subscribed to a variety of other religious sects. In 1970 the Roman Catholics accounted for 64% of the population and Anglicans 21.7%.

## Housing Conditions

As the population grew throughout the period 1871–1921 the number of houses – albeit of poor quality – also increased. Between 1891 and 1901 the number of houses increased by 1,940 or 18%, while the population increased by 10,000 or 20%; during the decade 1901 to 1911 houses increased by 1,580 or 12.4%, while population increased by 3,000 or 5% and from 1911 to 1921 houses increased by 6%, while population fell marginally.

In the 1920s, 75%, or 49,995 out of 65,696 of the population lived in one-or two-room wood-and-wattle – *roseau* – houses. Out of a total of 14,210, 12,865 or 90% were wood-and-wattle houses. The The considerable overcrowding in these poorly structured, small dwellings made them unfit for the promotion of healthy family life.

The poor housing conditions, the prevalence of contagious diseases, the lack of proper education, and the low income of the labouring population, made the working class during the first half of the 20th century the neglected, indigent, exploited and oppressed group in Grenadian society.

NOTES

Full citations only given where work does not appear in the Bibliography.

1. *Report and General Abstract of the Census of 1921, St George's.* 1922, p. 8.
2. *Administrative Reports.* 'Report and General Abstract of the Registrar General', 1910–23 inclusive.
3. *Census of 1844*
4. *Census of 1851*; also *Report on the Blue Book of 1851.*
5. *Reports and General Abstracts of Censuses of, 1871, 1881, 1891, 1921.*
6. *Laws of Grenada 1933.* 'Ordinance to regulate the emigration of persons from Grenada'. No. 30, 1927, No.4 of 1930.
7. *Census of 1921.*
8. *Abstract of Births, Deaths and Marriages* also *Vital Statistics* 1871–1960 inclusive.
9. *Censuses.* 1921, 1946, 1960, 1970.
10. *Report and General Abstract 1921 Census*, p. 10.

# 16

## *Growth of the Peasantry and the 1951 Social Revolution*

Modern West Indian history begins without a peasantry and this is of particular interest because in tracing it we trace the birth and development of an entirely new class which had profoundly affected the foundation of West Indian society.[1]

The term *peasantry* refers here to anyone who owned up to 10 acres of land and whose livelihood depended largely on the cultivation and produce of this land. 'Peasantry' refers to persons variously described as peasant farmers, small farmers and peasant proprietors; in law it denoted 'a small holder engaged in the cultivation of an area of land not exceeding 10 acres in extent'.[2] Closely related to this group was the proto-peasantry: tenant farmers who worked under a system of share-wage or share-rent, and estate labourers who supplemented their wages with the produce of small lots, either owned, rented or given to them free of charge by large proprietors. Whereas in the earlier chapters they were referred to separately as labourers, tenants-at-will and metayers, throughout this chapter, unless otherwise specified, the term 'peasantry' will be used to designate all of these.

During the first half of the 20th century the peasantry constituted a significant proportion of Grenada's working population, the main source of labour, and the predominant agents of domestic food supply. Despite this they existed on the fringes of Grenadian society, especially in terms of income distribution, overall economic status and general social conditions. No radical change took place in their conditions of life; such change that did take place can be explained as superstructural rather than substructural, superficial rather than fundamental, being merely accommodations to the existing system of ownership of wealth, production of goods, and distribution of income rather than attempts to develop a more egalitarian system. The social and economic conditions under which peasants and workers lived were a product of the economic structure and organization of society. A system that breeds exploitation and neglects workers' real needs develops irreconcilable contradictions that form the basis of class struggle; and in that struggle the ruling class will be prepared to go to extremes to defend its vested interests.

By 1950, despite the proliferation of land settlement schemes, the upgrading of wages of agricultural workers seven times in the previous ten years,[3] the persistent disbursement of funds under CDW, and the replacement of large export dealers in the nutmeg industry by a producer co-operative, Grenada remained a society dominated by a tiny clique of planter-merchants and professionals, who controlled both Legislative and Executive Councils of government, as well as the civil service and who owned most of the fertile land and wealth in the country. The compensation for those who tilled the soil was in no way commensurate with the labour expended. It was this condition that provided the seeds of the 1951 uprising.

In 1930, relatively speaking, Grenada was a very populous country, with a population of 76,967, and a density of 578 per square mile. With a birth rate of 32.6 and a death rate of 15.8 per 1,000 its population was increasing at a rate of 16 per 1,000, assuming an equality between immigration and emigration as was the case in 1930.[4] For every person there were 1.1 acres of land space and 0.80 acres of cultivable land – a decrease of 0.79 and 0.20 acres respectively since 1921. Thus, a rapidly diminishing land/man ratio had become a reality as an increasing population continued to exert its pressure on Grenada's limited size.

As we saw in the previous chapter, the population was particularly young; 77% aged 40 and under; 62% were aged 24 and under. Seventy-eight percent of the population was aged 5 to 59, and 52% between 15 and 59 years of age. As child labour was still prevalent, it can be asserted that over 65% of Grenada's population was physically active. Racially, Blacks (76.9%) were predominant; Coloureds composed 17.5%, East Indians 4.1% and Whites 1.4%. The latter together with some Coloureds comprised the dominant class, notwithstanding the fact that a portion of them was made up of the poor Whites of Mt Moritz. According to the 1921 census, 84.17% of the population were rural dwellers. An estimated 42.7% of those over five years were illiterate, with the highest percentages in St Mark's and St Andrew's: 51.7% and 46.1% respectively. Peasants who owned small plots numbered 9,257 in 1900; 10,688 in 1905, 11,568 in 1910.

In short, the Grenadian peasantry was: one of the largest in the Caribbean relative to size; young; predominantly Black; largely illiterate. Generally there was no rigid sexual division of labour, rural women performing similar agricultural activities to men in addition to their domestic chores.

In the early 20th century peasants were enticed into debts by loans from their richer neighbours – merchants and large proprietors – who, at the first sign of any defaulting in repayment, would secure a writ of execution from the Court and sell or acquire the peasant lands. Many peasants became debt peons working to pay debts that never seemed to end. Whereas peasants had previously borrowed such sums interest free, at this time they were charged 8–10% compound interest half-yearly, or sometimes quarterly; in addition provision was made for a commission of 2.5% to 5%, if the amount of produce the borrower had undertaken to deliver as repayment fell short.

According to a Commission of Enquiry (headed by F. Gurney) appointed in 1908 to look into this and other related matters,[5] the peasants denied that they had pledged to deliver any specified quantity of produce from any crop whereby commission on account of shortage became payable and that they had ever contracted to pay interest on advances. They also expressed dissatisfaction with the price they were paid for their produce.

The peasants worst affected were those of Concord, Mon Plaisir and Grand Roy, and their main grievances were against two moneylenders whom they accused of exchanging accounts with the aim of possessing themselves of the borrower's holdings. The Commission concluded that it was difficult to ascertain the veracity of these accusations against the local proprietor-financiers. But Frank Gurney and other members of the Commission were planters, councillors and members of the same financial class thus accused.

The Commission found that year by year the amount of peasants' produce delivered to their creditors had decreased. The debtors explained that this was owing to the rapid unproductiveness and depletion of the soil; other factors were poor soil preparation and fertilization. The Commission also found that the peasant proprietors did not cultivate as much provisions as had their ancestors. The peasants, however, maintained that within recent years they had been deprived of gardens they had held on various estates, and that they were not permitted to open up new land.

Simultaneously, a large number of shops had been opened in the districts and the peasants began to do business with many of these.

Lacking foresight and caution they soon became heavily in debt to these merchants, with the result that the latter levied their property.

The Commission recommended that: more plots be established, particularly in Concord, Grand Roy and Mon Plaisir districts; depots be established in suitable localities where all cocoa could be sold by public auction; a Government Land Bank be set up to assist the peasants in the cultivation and improvement of their holdings.

For every £1 earned by the peasants at the time £13/2s; was earned by estate proprietors. For every one acre owned by the peasants, 3.5 and 6.2 were owned by large proprietors in Carriacou and Grenada respectively.[6]

## Grenadian Peasantry 1930–50

An examination of the role and activities of the Grenadian peasantry shows that by 1950, it had considerably modified the character of the pure plantation economy of 1838, as elements of the plantation staple economy became juxtaposed with elements of peasant subsistence economy.[7] The West India Royal Commission that visited Grenada in 1939 noted this, and was particularly impressed not only by the size of Grenada's peasantry, but by 'its ability to alleviate distress' caused by slumps in the international markets for Grenadian staples. The Commission wrote:

> It may be noted that the adverse effects of the slump in cocoa on the ordinary worker is somewhat mitigated by the prevalence of peasant proprietorship and the consequent opportunity for a large proportion of the population to supplement their cash earnings by home-grown foodstuffs.[8]

The peasantry had, in some respects, initiated the part-conversion of the plantation economy into pre-modern communities by bringing into existence villages and markets, causing schools and hospitals to be built and initiating the local co-operative movement. By 1930, even though politically impotent and economically weak, they were a force to be reckoned with.

In 1930, there was a total of 15,319 peasants in Grenada; the majority of whom – 12,924 or 84.4% – owned less than 2.5 acres of land each; 1,802 owned between 2.5 and five acres and the remainder between five and ten acres. Out of a total of 15,983 proprietors, 95.8% were peasants; 2.6% could be classified as medium-sized proprietors owning between ten and 100 acres; 1.6% were estate owners. In 1930, the majority of land in Grenada was owned by 138 proprietors.[9]

This was exemplified in the nutmeg industry; in 1940 there were 6,264 producers, of whom 6,070 or 97% owned less than ten acres; 95 or 1.5% owned between ten and 20 acres, 8% between 20 and 50 acres and 0.7% more than 50 acres.[10] Out of a total of 63,000 acres of land under cultivation then, intermittent peasant cultivation comprised 17,650 acres, or 29%, leaving 72% of the cultivable land in the hands of large proprietors.[11] Thus, about 95.8% of the land owners owned about 28% of the cultivable land, and 4.5% of them owned about 72%.

Nonetheless, the evidence reveals a steady growth in the size of the peasantry in the 1930–50 period. Three factors were responsible for this:

(a) the breaking up of heavily encumbered estates
(b) the government-sponsored ‘Land Settlement Schemes’; and
(c) labourers purchasing of land on the extremities of estates.

By 1949 there was a total of 19,592 peasants, an increase of 4,273 or 27.8% on the 1930 figures (see Table 16.1).

Table 16.1 shows that by 1945, of the total number of holdings in the island, peasants’ holdings had increased to 97.4%. There is no indication that this increase had in any significant way changed the system of land tenure or the structure of ownership. There were still 130 estates varying in size from 100 to 1000+ acres; the number of estates had declined by eight over the previous 15 years, but these were the derelict, bankrupt and heavily encumbered estates abandoned because there were no willing buyers to continue operating them as estates.[12] The estate system, therefore, continued intact despite the numerical increase and aggregate size of peasant holdings.

**Table 16.1 Size and Numerical Growth of the Grenadian Peasantry 1924–61**

| *Year* | *<2.5 acres* | *2.5–5* | *5–7* | *7–10* | *10–100* | *100+* | *Total* |
|---|---|---|---|---|---|---|---|
| 1929 | 12,924 | 1,802 | 402 | 291 | 426 | 138 | *15,983* |
| 1932 | 13,946 | 1,700 | 320 | 210 | 407 | 134 | *16,717* |
| 1936 | 14,367 | 1,731 | 314 | 206 | 404 | 130 | *17,212* |
| *Year* | *<10 acres* | *10* | *11–50* | *51–100* | *100–1000* | *1000+* | *Total* |
| 1939 | 18,259 | 54 | 337 | 66 | 126 | 1 | *18,843* |
| 1940 | 18,456 | 54 | 337 | 66 | 124 | 1 | *19,038* |
| 1945 | 19,592 | 47 | 267 | 69 | 130 | 1 | *20,106* |
| 1956 | 12,067 | – | 458 | 53 | 95 | 1 | *12,674* |
| 1961 | 13,444 | – | 518 | 42 | 92 | – | *14,096* |

Source: Grenada, *Blue Books*, 1925–61

Undoubtedly, the government-sponsored land settlement scheme of the 1930s and 1940s contributed to this significant expansion of the peasantry, but the scheme's lack of clear objectives and the absence of complementary institutions militated against the achievement of its optimal potential.

This was not the first attempt at land settlement in Grenada. The scheme dates back to 1904, when, during the following four years, Beausejour Estate in Carriacou was distributed and resettled. 'In fact the first five areas to be resettled under this scheme were in Carriacou.'[13] The other four areas referred to were Harvey Vale, Retreat, Belair and Bellevue (North). Between 1908 and 1921 six settlements were formed in Grenada, including Morne Rouge (1909), Old Westerhall (1918), Mt St Cyr (1918), Mt Pleasant (1919), New Westerhall (1919) and Calivigny (1921). No further settlement took place until 1933. The resurgence of land settlement schemes in the 1930s was due to:

- insufficient or insecure tenure: unsatisfactory relationship between landlord and tenant;
- insufficient and intermittent employment;
- inadequate social facilities and services;
- the deep-seated impression among certain classes that ownership of land was, in itself, a social advancement.[14]

This land settlement scheme is often referred to in the literature as the genesis of land reform, but it was not land reform, it was land transfer, that is the redistribution of land *per se*, with total disregard of the redistribution of economic power. In most cases, the system of land transfer operated when the owner of an estate announced his desire to sell but failed to find a purchaser. The schemes were effected by the sub-division of the land into smaller plots and its resale on an installment/purchase system to persons of various occupations, many of whom, judging by the results, had little or no intention of practising any systematic form of agriculture. None of the institutional structures that accompany land reform – credit facilities, subsidy schemes, marketing organizations, economic and social infrastructure – were set up.

By 1940 there were 20 land settlement areas under the government-sponsored scheme – 14 in Grenada and six in Carriacou. In all 4,274 acres were resettled – 2,309 in Carriacou and 1,965 in Grenada. Eight of these settlements were established in Grenada and one, Limlair, in Carriacou during the decade 1930–40. The eight included Fraze, Mt Cassel, St Cloud, Point Salines, Mt Nesbit, Plaisance, Belair, River Salee, comprising 1,021 acres and cut into 540 lots ranging from three poles to three acres each.[15]

Six of these settlements (Fraze, Plaisance, Mt Cassel, Belair, Mt Nesbit, Limlair) comprised 891 acres, divided into 366 lots, and purchased at a total cost of £10,618; by 1936 306 had been sold and £664 collected from the allottees – 6.2% of their total cost. The selling price per acre varied from £5 to £36. By 1949 only £890 or 8% of the original costs were still outstanding.

The policy of government was to recover all monies expended plus a 5% interest charge and a 15% commission. The terms of payment were 8.5% cash down, with the balance to be paid in 15 years. The estates were purchased with the assistance of a £15,000 loan for land settlement from the Colonial Development Advisory Committee.[16]

By 1945, ten years after settlement, 41% of the areas were not completely paid for; 59% were. Of the original 200 allottees, 36 were ejected and 97 were living on the lots. By 1948, the arrears for seven of the eight areas settled in Grenada in the 1930s, plus Limlair in Carriacou were £8,896 – 75% of which was accounted for by Limlair. In the following years it was £1,546, with 15% accounted for by Limlair. In 1949, the settlers of Limlair apparently liquidated a large portion of their outstanding financial commitments. One reason for these 1948 arrears was that 39 more lots were created on existing settlements after 1945.

By 1945, of the various land settlements established under the government scheme the following observations obtained:

1. 60–75% were partly worked; 35% were unworked.
2. There was no financial assistance to enable settlers to work the lands to their best advantage.
3. Many lots were uneconomic in size and incapable of maintaining a family of six.
4. There was an outstanding lack of skilled agricultural supervision.
5. Certain areas were of very low fertility.
6. There were many absentee settlers; all lands did not necessarily go to peasant labourers.
7. Between 33% and 60% of production was consumed at home while the rest was disposed of in the nearest market.
8. All in all the peasants honoured their annual financial commitments.[17]

The West India Royal Commission realized the shortcomings enumerated and, in recommending an expansion of the existing scheme, suggested more acres of fertile land be acquired to settle 750 peasants, and the provision of the necessary supportive institutions.

In 1945, the year when the Commission's report came out, the Director of Agriculture in Grenada was asked to carry out a thorough examination of the scheme and to make recommendations. Among his recommendations were the placing of the Agriculture Department in full control of the scheme and the setting up of complementary infrastructural facilities. Until 1949 nothing further was done. During that year a grant of £25,000 from CDW was approved for the implementation of a three-year scheme for the rehabilitation of existing land settlement areas, many of which had become almost derelict by that time.[18]

It would appear that the land transfer system lacked clear economic objectives; the main idea behind the purchases in many cases seemed to be ownership of land for ownership's sake. There was, apparently, no planned scheme of agricultural development for the small holders. Many areas were unsuitable for small agricultural development; little, if any, attention was given to topographical conditions; those who made a genuine effort to cultivate received no assistance and guidance. Consequently, productivity fell and the yield was not an adequate compensation for labour expended. In his 1945 report, the Director of Agriculture concluded 'that the scheme had done little good, if any, to the settlers; they have been a net loss to the community'. A government committee set up in 1947 to report on Grenada's agricultural policy, having examined the land settlement schemes, reached the following, somewhat bitter, conclusion: 'Experience has shown that land settlements which have been initiated merely as a result of popular demand – or for the purpose of relieving unemployment have invariably led to disappointment and failure.'

## The Proto-Peasantry

Another group of peasants, related to the first but requiring separate consideration, comprised labourers who both sold their labour to the estates, and owned or rented land.

With the increase in the number of peasants fewer people sold their labour to estates on a consistent and continuous basis; with rising unemployment in the 1930s, partially caused by the adverse conditions facing export crops, estates gave out land to their former employees on a rental basis or occasionally free of cost, to plant food. This group of peasants numbered 12,937 in 1939 and occupied 15,078 acres; some of them, as would be expected, were included in the group discussed above, and worked two or three days per week on the estates. They grew food crops on their rented or free land, either for subsistence, or for the local market or both. There was no clear distinction between peasant farmer and estate worker; estate work was seen by small owners as a means of procuring ready cash to meet their domestic needs and to supplement their meagre income from the freeholds. This group was in the transitional stage between estate labourer and self-sustaining peasant – in fact, the period 1921 to 1949 marked this transition period in Grenadian history.

In 1921 there were 17,717 agricultural labourers whose daily wage ranged from 10d to 1/–; in 1930 there were only 15,000, comprising 20% of the total labour force (21.2% were unemployed), and 70% of all persons employed in the principal industries of the country.[19] By 1949 their number had declined to 5,323 but they still accounted for 64% of persons employed in the principal industries. This decline in the number of estate workers between 1930 and 1950 is indicative of the simultaneous expansion of the peasantry.[20]

A third group of peasants was the tenants, who operated under a system of share rent. These were to be found both in Grenada and in Carriacou, but on a more organized and institutionalized basis in the latter territory, where they formed part of the 'Metayer System'; few estates in Grenada operated on this system. In most cases there was no restriction on the crops grown by the tenant, his side of the contract was fulfilled as long as he gave one-quarter or one-half of the produce to the landlord. A number of estates in Grenada, for one reason or another, refused to rent or give land to their labourers, fearful (as the 1939 Commission speculated) that they would thereby lose the services of the labourers, who might become independent of estate labour. In the immediate post-emancipation days, not only in Grenada, but in Jamaica, Guyana, Antigua and Barbados, planters vigorously resisted the peasant movement. It is distressing to note that 100 years later some planters in Grenada were employing the selfsame tactics.

The metayer system itself was introduced in Carriacou during the depression of the 1880s when, finding it no longer feasible to export sugar, the absentee owners of the sugar estates leased their estates to persons resident there who would later sub-let them to tenants. Realizing that this system was not viable owing to the tenants' increasing debts the alternative of working land on the basis of tenants giving an agreed portion of the produce in lieu of rent – the metayer system – was tried.[21]

The prevalence of this system in the 1930s testifies to its success during the 50 years after its initiation. A four-man committee appointed to examine the system in 1935 found that: 'From the point of view of the labourer there can be no question of the fact that in conditions obtaining in Carriacou, a system of sharing produce is fairer and more advantageous to him than a rental system.[22]

There were two types of metayer system: the poling and the Craigston. Under the poling system the tenant cultivated a piece of the landlord's land, usually one to three acres, on the understanding that the produce was to be shared between them in certain proportions; the agreement was neither written nor verbally defined but based on custom and convention, and might be for one year or for an indefinite period. The tenant was obliged to grow cotton and corn; in addition he might grow some pigeon peas, cassava and okras. The owner supplied the cotton seeds; the peasants, the corn seeds, the cassava slips and, most important, the labour. Upon harvesting, two-thirds of the corn went to the tenant and one-third to the owner, while the other produce was divided equally between peasant and owner.[23]

The Craigston system was introduced about 1917 and differed from the poling in the method and proportion of sharing the produce. The tenant was allowed to keep everything except one barrel of corn in the straw per acre and two-thirds of the cotton, which was the owner's share. All the harvesting was the tenant's responsibility, but he was paid 50¢ per 100 lbs for picking the owner's portion of the cotton. The poling system seems to have been the more popular with the peasant, as under the Craigston system he was made to bear most of the risks, including failure to get his full one-third of the cotton, and no credit for fractions of a pound. Unlike the peasants, landlords apparently preferred the Craigston system and opposed tenants' attempts to revert to the poling system.

The metayer system as a whole had many other defects. The highly insecure tenure conditions did not encourage proper cultivation of land, and resulted not only in low productivity per acre but per man/day of labour. Given conditions of drought in Carriacou, the system worked invariably in the landlord's favour, especially under the Craigston System, and for that reason the 1935 Committee recommended a return of the poling system.[24]

## Peasants' Contribution and Exploitation

The ruling class and landed gentry of the day, in Grenada or Carriacou, rarely acknowledged the economic contribution of the peasants who provided all the labour in the cultivation of both export and cash crops; a constant supply of vegetables, provisions and meat for domestic consumption; increasing portions of the colony's output of cocoa and nutmegs, which still remained the oligopoly of the big estates; and additionally, initiated and supported the co-operative movement. Three outstanding examples of this were:

1. *The Su-su*, a system of short-term co-operative savings based on mutual trust among the savers. It remained one of the outstanding manifestations of peasant understanding and co-operation.
2. *The Marketing Co-operative*, among small farmers and allottees of land under the Settlement Scheme which was started in the cane belt settlements in 1950. It developed into a large organization, which, by 1951, was marketing some 9,000 tons of peasants' cane.[25]
3. *The Friendly Societies*, voluntary organizations established for the mutual aid of members in times of financial need, occasioned by sickness or death. The author's concern is not with secret orders, who considered themselves to be the guardians of esoteric knowledge on the occult, but with ordinary Friendly Societies. There were 66 of these in 1935 with a total membership of 12,135 and net assets of £9,157. By 1947 the number had increased to 99 with a total membership of 19,946 and net assets of £137,357.[26] This spectacular rise was, according to Leonard Fletcher, due to increased confidence in the movement as well as increased wartime prosperity.

Not only was the peasantry's economic contribution not recognized by the ruling class in the 1930s and 1940s, but neither were they well compensated for their labours. Many factors accounted for this.

1. The nature of the international specialization of production whereby Grenada and other developing countries were forced to specialize in the production of raw materials, namely, agricultural staples, with very weak income-demand elasticities.
2. The system of international pricing between centre and periphery countries whereby oligopolistic pricing obtained in the centre and exclusively competitive pricing in the periphery – Grenada was, and still is, in the periphery.
3. In addition to this the productivity gains from international trade in these export products were appropriated in the UK and, to a lesser extent, Canada and the USA which had a highly developed infrastructure in international production and a developed industrial sector. As the price of Grenada's exports stagnated or declined, and concomitantly her earnings, the prices of her imports rose. This is the phenomenon of deteriorating terms of trade.
4. Additionally, there were cases of linkages and value-added, most of which accrued to businesses in the UK, and to a lesser extent elsewhere. In the period 1944–50 Grenada sold £17 million worth of nutmegs and their by-products abroad. Assuming that this represented 10% of its total final value, its total value-added would be

£170 million; £153 million of this accrued to producers and manufacturers abroad. Thus, the plight of the Grenadian workers and their economic conditions in the 1930s and 1940s were partly related to the structural weaknesses of the Grenadian economy, and partly to the maldistribution of income and the poor returns to labour as a means of production.

In Grenada in the 1930s and 1940s the productive processes were labour-intensive; labour was thus the most important factor of production. The incomes to labour or the wage of the labourer should then have been positively related to the value of the product; however, in a labour surplus economy with weak unionization of the worker, the worker's wage will be a traditional one and bear very little, if any, relationship to the value of the product. For example, in 1935, the value of Grenada's four major exports was £200,000; there were about 6,000 labourers, each working for approximately 100 days per year at an average of 1/- per day; the gross income to labour, therefore, was £30,000 or 15% of the export value of the four major exports.[27]

The exploitation of peasant labourers took place on two levels: a) locally, through the low wages, and b) internationally, through the low prices obtained for Grenada's staples and the accruing of their value-added abroad.

Both the 1937 Committee, and the 1939 West India Royal Commission found that wages paid for estate work were below subsistence level. Evidence revealed that the daily wage for an estate labourer in 1935 was still 10d or 1/- as it had been in 1840 (two years after Emancipation). The Commission of Enquiry set up to investigate the economic conditions of wage earners in 1937 recommended – with great reluctance – that a minimum wage be fixed at 1/3d per day per man, and 1/- per day per woman, after earlier in its findings admitting that the minimum wage should not be less than 1/6d per day.[28] The Commission's recommendations were implemented the following year. Although this was a 25% increase, it was unsatisfactory in view of the annual increase in prices of some 14% according to the consumer price index at the time.

Even during the apprenticeship period (1834–38) many workers received as much as 1/6d per day – even higher than wages in 1938. In the 1940–50 period there were seven wage increases, and by 1950 the statutory minimum wage was 82¢ for men and 68¢ for women.[29]

The sudden wage increases in the 1940s, after 100 years of virtual stagnation, were by no means a spontaneous display of planter altruism, but occurred as a result of both the Moyne Commission's recommendations and the spread of violent demonstrations among

Caribbean workers in the period 1934–39 against intolerable working conditions.[30] The demonstrations mentioned were:

1. May–July 1934: Disturbances on sugar estates in Trinidad.
2. January 1935: Disturbances on estates in St Kitts.
3. January–May 1935: Strikes of stevedores in Falmouth, Jamaica.
4. 1935: Revolt in Kingstown and Camden Park, St Vincent.
5. September–October 1935: Disturbances on estates in Guyana.
6. 1937: Oilworkers' strike and general disturbances in Trinidad.
7. 1937: Disturbances on From estates in Jamaica.
8. May–June 1938: General disturbances in Jamaica and the famous Westmorland riots.
9. February 1939: Disturbances on Leonora plantations and other estates in British Guiana (Guyana).

The Grenadian estate owners, the employers of agricultural labour, who were spared these holocausts took heed of the saying 'when your neighbour's house is on fire, wet yours'. It was solely for this reason that there were voluntary agreements and co-operation with the authorities whenever they recommended a wage increase. It was to assuage the feelings of discontent simmering among the Grenadian workers who, disorganized as they were, found themselves at the mercy of the planter and merchant middlemen, who were simultaneously legislator and employer.

These wage increases were simply palliatives to the workers' needs; concessions that employers were willing to make in order to protect their own self-interest. Indeed, the unions of the day worked in close collaboration with the planters and they had no desire to challenge the colonial status quo, being quite satisfied with crumbs that fell from the table of the landed rich. In the meantime, the workers' grievances increased but could find no outlet for expression. Grenada in the 1940s was a society rife with prejudices and class contradictions.

To be socially acceptable one had to have either fair skin, straight hair and 'good looks', or a reasonable amount of wealth. Blacks, who for most part had 'bad' hair and 'bad' looks, and those who were poor, were socially ostracized and consigned to the lowest social strata.

The dominant class along occupational lines consisted of merchants, professionals, politicians, estate owners and civil servants. This group enjoyed economic prosperity, owned most of the wealth in the country and monopolized whatever political power was afforded under the constitution of the time. This class made use of whatever education they had, plus their mastery of the English language, to tighten its grip on the mass of workers and consolidate the prevailing class distinctions. The mass of workers and peasants remained essentially subservient, and their economic reward was restricted to one of mere subsistence.

## The GCNA and the Grenada Sugar Factory

The operation and structure of the nutmeg industry in Grenada as well as the Grenada Sugar Factory can be used as prototypes of the above relationship. There were 6,264 nutmeg producers in Grenada; among these there were 6,070 small producers, 99 large producers, and 99 medium-sized producers (10–20 acres). In 1942 a number of nutmeg producer-exporters, under the leadership of Norman Gay, decided to form a producer co-operative for the marketing of the island's nutmegs and mace. The main aims of the promoters were to make the co-operative the sole exporter of nutmegs thereby eliminating the cut-throat competition of independent exporters, whose price bargaining leverage was weak, and to take the profits of the export trade out of the hands of the middlemen and into those of the producers.[31] Formerly, the large producers prepared and exported their produce themselves, but the average peasant sold his nuts green to small dealers who cured them (often under unsatisfactory conditions) and then sold them to the large export dealers – the merchant middlemen of St George's who then processed them for shipment. Thus, the peasant producer had to pay the middlemen to export his produce, and two sets of distributors profited from the labourers.

The formation of this co-operative provoked a storm of opposition from the middlemen, the Grenada Nutmeg Producers' League, and numerous members of the Legislative Council. Open conflict ensued between the divergent vested interests of two wealthy groups: merchants and large producers. Peasants' interests were incidental; nonetheless they stood to benefit more from the formation of the co-operative. In 1950, the Honourable T.E. Noble Smith moved that a Commission be set up to examine the affairs of the Association. The Commission found the conduct of the Association's affairs to be satisfactory and recommended the retention of the legal monopoly bestowed upon the GCNA (Grenada Co-operative Nutmeg Association) by government.

The GCNA remained a large producer co-operative with small producers knowing little or nothing of it, far less being able to participate – their participation was limited to selling their produce in the local pool. The nutmeg estate workers prepared the land for cultivation, planted, harvested, separated the mace from the nuts, dried and bagged the crop, and in return received nothing but a subsistence wage; small producers supplemented estate produce with their own. Between 1919 and 1950 these workers helped to contribute £8.5 million to Gross Domestic Product in this industry alone, while their wages for these 30 years were £3 million, that is, 28% of the value of output of one industry alone.[32]

Small producers had little or no voice in the running of the GCNA. Membership of the Board reflects the dominant position of the large producers and other members of the upper class, and shows the locus of decision-making powers as well as control.[33] On a nine-member Board, the 6,070 small growers had only one representative.

In the sugar-cane industry too, small producers were numerous but had no power and control, as an examination of the structure and performance of the Grenada Sugar Factory will illustrate.

The small cane suppliers numbered 171 but control was in the hands of seven shareholders. The Grenada Sugar Factory was a public corporation set up in 1936 to produce sugar and rum. The Honourable C.F.P. Renwick owned 4,500 of its ordinary shares given to him for services rendered and to be rendered to the Corporation. W.L.Innis, a Barbadian, was given 1,000 as promoter's share; the remaining 1,200 shares were divided among five of the original subscribers to the 37,600 8% preference shares. The company received a $43,200 loan at 4% from the Grenada Co-operative Bank – one of the two peasant banks in the island. Most of the canes processed were procured from the Company's four estates at Woodlands, Hope Vale, Calivigny and Bardia. The last was purchased from C.F.P. Renwick in June 1941 for £8,736; in addition 171 peasant producers, two estates and a few contractors delivered canes to the factory.[34]

From 1936 to 1945 the company processed 102,860 tons of cane, an annual average of 11,400 tons; 11,509 tons or 11% came from the peasant farmers, while the remainder came from other estates, company estates and contractors; $496,697 were disbursed in payments and $44,933 or 9.04% were paid to peasant producers. There seems to have been a great disparity in the prices paid to the various suppliers of cane. In 1942, whereas the company's estates received $6.03 per ton of cane, other estates received $5.40, and peasants $4.30. In 1945 the situation was similar: $5.88 was paid for the company's cane, $5.72 for other estates and $4.88 for the peasants.[35]

The company stated that the reason for higher prices for the company's cane was that it wished to show a profit on the operation of its estates; this was an intra-company transaction and simply a book entry. But that does not explain the disparity between prices paid to other estates and peasant producers, which, in fact, was that by paying the large producer a higher price the company could attract his canes.

At least 5,850 tons of cane from other sources was needed for the company's target production of 1,600 tons of sugar to be attained. From 1943 to 1945, other estates and peasants supplied 4,500 tons per year; 80% of its normal external demand. Between 1936 and 1945 the company made profits of $181,999 on sugar and rum produced.

The peasants and workers not only did most of the hard labour for little pay but also had to pay most of the local taxes in Grenada. In 1948 51.9% of local revenue came from customs duties and 15% from income taxes. In that year cocoa and nutmeg exporters received a gross income of $4.022m most of which went to large proprietors. Income tax paid was 9.74% of these earnings; notwithstanding the fact that most of this income tax would have been paid by public officers. Large proprietors paid little or no tax and those locals who bore the brunt of financing government expenditure were the consumers – of whom 95% were peasants and labourers. Between 1944 and 1950 the gentry received $11m for cocoa and $17m for nutmegs exported; this was essentially tax-free, as estate owners who received the bulk of this $28m paid very little income tax.

## Conditions among the Peasantry

Clearly by the end of the 1940s the workers and peasants of Grenada were not only living in a state of economic exploitation but of social degradation too. The housing conditions of the peasants and labourers continued to be grossly inadequate and provisions for their health continued to be neglected by the local and imperial governments.

Some peasants' houses were built of imported deal boards or shingles, on small supporting piles to compensate for the uneven foundation and ground on which they stood. They were small with one bedroom and one living room – each about ten feet by eight feet. Their roofs were either thatched or shingled. The houses of labourers and poorer peasants were made of mud and wattle, with cane straw thatched roofs; poorly ventilated and with mud floors.

The District Medical Officer of St Mark's had the following to say on housing in his parish in 1938: 'housing conditions are appallingly bad with little protection against rain storms. Houses are over crowded, ventilation is inadequate. The children eat, sleep, play on the same floor.'[36]

It was common at the time to find as many as 15 persons living in a two-room house; as is evidenced by medical officers' reports. One referred to the houses in his district as ramshackle or delapidated straw, mud or wooden structures between 12 and 15 feet square with as many as ten persons living in one house. The average number in a one-bedroom house was six.

Working-class housing had not changed in any way since the 1921 census, or, one may speculate, since the census of 1871. The census compiler for 1921, commenting on houses, reported that: 'Many houses were occupied by a far greater number than they were probably capable of accommodating with anything like a proper regard to health, comfort and decency.'[37]

The census recorded over 100 one-room houses with as many as ten occupants each; it also recorded some 143 two-room houses with as many as 11 to 19 occupants each.[38]

The Commission of 1938 appointed to look into economic conditions of wage earners in Grenada concluded: 'The housing of the agricultural labourer is disgraceful. It is impossible to use any other word to describe it. Houses little larger than small bicycle sheds are made of beaten out kerosene tins or old packing boxes.'[39] It referred to the *roseau* houses made of wattle and daub, prevalent among the rural poor, as nothing but rickety structures. Very often these consisted of one room in which the labourer, his wife and children were herded together. The children slept on the floor; cracks were stopped up at night to prevent the entry of mosquitoes, draughts, and 'evil spirits'. Obviously, under such living conditions, tuberculosis and other diseases were rampant.

In 1946 the Slum Clearance and Housing ordinance was enacted, specifically to provide proper houses for persons of the working class, to eradicate slum areas and to repair or demolish insanitary dwellings. By 1949, the Central Planning and Housing Authority (the executive authority established by that ordinance) had built 12 houses, and these were for persons who lost their homes during the 1945 floods. The sum of $19,200 was provided as housing loans – repayable over 10–15 years – to 20 working-class persons in St David's. Clearly, the Housing Authority was inadequate and had little impact. By the end of the 1940s, 86% of the houses in Grenada were still wood, wattle and mud; 80% were either one- or two-room dwellings with no privacy for adults.

The absence of adequate housing was compounded by the virtual lack of domestic sanitation. Dr Spearman, in his 1938 report, said:

It is doubtful if one peasants' house in a hundred is provided with latrine accommodation. Soil pollution was, therefore, gross and the struggle against flies, flyborne and intestinal infections, such as the enteric and dysentric group of diseases and helminthic infections such as ankylostomiasis and round worms, is rendered infinitely more difficult.[40]

Defecation in the open was common and this increased the incidence of fly-borne and air-borne diseases. Spearman advised that many more latrines were required throughout Grenada, together with long-term propaganda to make the average worker 'latrine-minded' and so prevent the then widespread soil-pollution and its consequent effects on public health.

The standard of peasant infant care was very low. Between 1935 and 1950, an annual average of 400 children born in the hospital went home fat and healthy only to return in a few months in an advanced state of marasmus due to neglect and improper and insufficient feeding.

Economic conditions at the time forced mothers to work in the fields or elsewhere, and they invariably had to leave small children and babies to fend for themselves as best they could during the day. In many cases the women were unmarried, and in the majority of cases the father of these children (sometimes fathers) neither lived with them nor contributed to their upkeep. In cases where a woman was 'married by repute' the situation was different.

Generally children were given an excess of starchy foods and insufficient protein-rich foods. Because some areas lacked a milk supply, and some peasants believed it caused worms, children's diets rarely included this important food. Hundreds of school children commonly breakfasted on 'bush-tea', sweetened with wet sugar and a bit of bread, and their midday meal seldom consisted of more than a piece of cold roasted breadfruit – often nothing at all. Many children had nothing to wear except rags or 'shirt-tails' and many were kept away from school due to lack of adequate and proper clothing.

The 1938 Commission on Economic Conditions among Wage-earners described the peasants' housing as disgraceful, his clothing as wretched and his body as emaciated by hookworms, veneral disease and tuberculosis. His children were ravaged by yaws and gastro-enteritis. These conditions still prevailed by 1949. In that year the Labour Commissioner reported that the anti-yaws and venereal disease units were busily occupied, and that these diseases were under control in St John's parish alone. The same report spoke of protein, vitamin B, calcium and iron deficiencies in the diet of workers and their children.

*Children playing cricket in 'shirt tails' – the team is the 'Young Ranjits'*

## Social Revolution 1951

These were the underlying economic and social conditions in Grenada by 1950; and these conditions made possible the emergence of E.M. Gairy's Grenada Manual and Mental Workers Union (GMMWU) as the voice of the working class, and accounted for his subsequent meteoric rise to political power. The appearance of the GMMWU was the match that ignited the discontent which had been simmering for decades among the Grenadian peasants and workers.

Previously, estate workers were represented by two trade unions: the St John's Labour Party, with a membership of 3,000, and the Grenada Workers' Union (GWU). These two unions constituted the Trades Union Council. These unions had never been really genuine workers organizations; they worked within the existing colonial framework and were thus prepared to compromise with the employers. In addition, the members of the executive were invariably colonial-minded Grenadians who had developed a great reverence for class and colour status. By 1950 both unions came to be viewed as almost synonymous with the employers of labour in attitudes, values and beliefs, even by the very workers they represented. In his 1951 report the Labour Officer stated how the executive of these unions had to 'lie low' because of violent hostility displayed towards them by their former members during the 1951 uprising. This showed the extent to which these executives had lost credibility in the eyes of their rank and file, and the extent to which the workers had accepted the GMMWU as their main bargaining body.

The 1951 uprising was undoubtedly a workers' and peasants' movement aimed at settling the social injustices of the last 125 years. The participants were the proto-peasantry and the road workers, ably supported by small peasants. Together, these constituted the class that for more than a century had laboured under social, political and economic disabilities. The GMMWU was formed specifically to represent this class economically and politically.

Membership of the union, which was open to all sections of the working community, increased rapidly and reached 2,070 within the first three months of its registration.[41] The workers predominantly represented were estate labourers and daily-paid government workers.

Within one month of its registration the GMMWU addressed a six-point demand to the management of the Grenada Sugar Factory Ltd, demanding *inter alia*, a 50% wage increase to workers employed by the company with retroactive effect from 27 July 1950; time-and-a half for work done in excess of eight hours daily, 14 days' annual vacation on full pay to each worker who worked 200 days in each year; full pay on public holidays and double pay if required to work on such days; establishment of better relationships between the supervisory group and the workers; and the installation of water pipes in convenient places for drinking and domestic purposes.[42]

On 17 August the company replied that the matter had been placed before the Board of Directors but no final decision had been reached. On the morning of 24 August 1950 the union called a strike of the workers employed on the estates and in the Sugar Factory, involving at that time some 496 labourers. Simultaneously, 15 workers employed on the nearby Grand Anse Estate stopped work bringing the total number of strikers to 511. On the following day the remaining 65 workers on the Grand Anse Beach Estate went on strike bringing the total to 576. Between Thursday 31 August and Friday 1 September, a total of 430 workers on 12 estates joined the strike in sympathy with the strikers in the cane belt; they also demanded higher wages for themselves. The widespread acts of violence, intimidation and larceny during the strikes were controlled by police called in from St Lucia.

After persistent attempts by the Department of Labour to get the opposing parties to reach an accord, the Sugar Company gave an undertaking to His Excellency Governor Arundell to meet the union, provided the workers returned to work before the negotiations began. After the union had settled many minor problems in the strike-affected estates, work was eventually resumed on 15 estates between 4 and 7 September 1950.

On 7 and 12 September respectively, two meetings were held between the Directors of the Sugar Factory and the representatives of the union, with the Labour Officer acting as chairman. The company argued that due to its poor financial position it was unable to award a wage increase without further assistance from government, either in the form of an increased subsidy or by permission to increase the selling price of sugar by 1¢ per lb. It was obvious that if permission for the latter was granted the workers themselves would be called upon to subsidize their wage increase by 1¢ on every pound of sugar they bought.

The union opposed the proposal on the grounds that the workers themselves provided the existing subsidy by way of taxation and that the price of sugar was already too high. The union then proposed that part of the company's profits, which had been utilized during the past two years to liquidate its mortgage debt, be used to pay higher wages. The company refused on the grounds that the mortgage debenture did not permit this. It was agreed by both parties to refer the matter to arbitration as provided by Section III of the Trade Disputes Ordinance, 1943 (No. 5 of 1943). Four points were submitted to the tribunal for determination: the 50% increase, the 14-day annual vacation on full pay, pay on public holidays, and the installation of water pipes in the cane belt.

The Arbitration Tribunal was subsequently set up by the Governor, and after consideration of the various points submitted, the following awards were made on 4 November 1950:

1. An increase of 25% in the wages payable to all workers, with retroactive effect from 27 July 1950; the price of sugar of $7.00 per 100 lbs increased to $8.00 per 100 lbs; and the price paid for sugar-cane increased to $11.85 per ton.
2. Workers who work for 200 days or more for the company in any one year were to be given 7 days' holiday with full pay effective 1 January 1950.
3. Double pay was to be given to workers who work on public holidays.[43]

The Tribunal, in awarding the 25% wage increase, were, in fact, calling upon workers to subsidize that increase by 1¢ on every pound of sugar they bought. Nonetheless the decision of the Tribunal ended – at least for the present – the unrest in the cane belt.

From this point onwards the GMMWU became a *béte noire* to the employers of agricultural labour and was considered anathema by the members of the ruling class in general. Consequently, the Grenada Agricultural Association tried to ignore the presence of the GMMWU, now giving added recognition to both the Grenada Workers Union and the St John's Labour Party as the bargaining body it recognized for the estate workers; a letter addressed to it by the GMMWU on 22 August 1950, demanding a 20% wage increase, was thus rejected. The Association instead proceeded to sign a different agreement with the GWU and the SJLP on 24 October on behalf of the same workers represented by the GMMWU. The main points dealt with in the agreement included *inter alia*:

1. The retention of the existing statutory minimum wage of 82¢ and 68¢ respectively – but a payment of a bonus of 3.75% of the statutory minimum wage for every 10¢ increase over and above the basic local price normally paid for cocoa by dealers in the local market; for the purpose of fixing the bonus the local selling price norm was taken as 20¢ per lb.
2. The subjecting of these bonus rates to revision at the end of each quarter.

The effect of the agreement was to fix the total emoluments at 94¢ and 78¢ respectively for the quarter ending 31 December 1950 and upon examination of the prices paid for cocoa in the local markets it was decided that the bonus for the quarter ending 31 March 1951 should be 11.25% of the statutory minimum wage, or 9¢ for men and 8¢ for women. This brought the wages for men and women for that quarter to 91¢ and 76¢ respectively, a decrease of 3¢ and 2¢ on the wages paid during the previous quarter, i.e. October to December 1950.[44]

This agreement was ratified after the GMMWU, on 22 August 1950, had addressed a letter to the Grenada Agricultural Employers Society demanding a 20% increase and a meeting for the settlement of a 'few general grievances'. The Grenada Agricultural Association's disregard of this letter, and their subsequent agreement, on 24 October (effective from 1 October) with the Grenada Trades Union Council incensed the leadership of the GMMWU. This not only initiated the battle of the unions but it made it unlikely that the main unions representing the agricultural workers could develop a common front, and widened the gap between the GMMWU and the employers of agricultural labour. It relegated rapprochement between the worker and employer to an illusion. It was 'divide and rule' tactics, whereby the Agricultural Association and the Grenada Agricultural Employers

Society hoped to enter into a separate agreement with the Grenada Trades Union Council and thus weaken the strength of the GMMWU by endorsing the former union as the only bargaining agent for agricultural workers. In this way they were guilty of a monumental error in judgement, and catalysed the very development they were trying to forestall. It manifested a gross ignorance of class struggle and the existing class structure in Grenada, together with the position of existing unions in that milieu. The GMMWU, seeing its first request ignored, addressed another letter to the Society on 16 October 1950. It made eight demands:

1. An increase of 46.5% on the statutory minimum wage viz. a wage of $1.20 and $1.00 for male and female respectively.
2. Payment at the rate of time-and-a-half for work done in excess of eight hours.
3. Payment of time-and-a-half for work done on Sundays and public holidays in excess of 8 hours.
4. Payment at the rate of double time for work done on Sundays and holidays.
5. Seven days' holiday with full pay to each worker who worked 200 days in any year.
6. Fourteen days' annual sick leave on half-pay.
7. The institution of a better system of supervision for the benefit of the industry of the community.
8. The institution of a better system of transport of produce from field to estate yard – the union was opposed to women carrying heavy loads when donkeys, mules, etc. could be provided.[45]

On 30 October 1950 the Society replied stating that an agreement providing for the payment of bonus dependent on the local price of cocoa had been entered into with the Trades Union Council, and that this agreement was operative from 1 October. The Society promised to put the union's proposal before a joint meeting of the Grenada Agricultural Association and the Grenada Agricultural Employers Society.

It appeared that the union was again ignored on this score, as the decision of the joint meeting was never communicated to it. The meeting was, however, held on 10 November 1950, for the press reported the decision that the existing agreement with the Trades Union Council could not be broken.[46] At that meeting the employers decided to fall in line with the Arbitration Tribunal (which dealt with the sugar disputes) and agreed to grant seven full days' paid holiday for workers who worked 200 days or more annually.

Interestingly, the St George's Workers Union in its memorandum to the 1948 Wages Committee had demanded basic wages of $1.20 and $1.00, the same wages that the GMMWU was demanding in 1950, yet it was prepared to enter into an agreement which retained the existing statutory minimum wage of 82¢ and 68¢. The other Union had demanded wages of $1.00 and 84¢.

In January the Trades Union Council (GWU) requested the Society to alter the agreement by providing that, for any fall below 59.5¢ per lb in the local market, the society should regard the price of cocoa as 59.5¢ per lb.[47] This request was made less out of concern for labourers than out of concern for the internal peace of the colony and the health of the union. They stated that, as the price of cocoa had fallen below 59.5¢, the bonus payable would consequently fall to 3.75% of the statutory minimum, and that sugar-cane workers and seamen had recently received increases of 25% and 15%, that any fall in wages might lead to more disturbances and the present situation was disturbing enough.[48] In its reply on 17 July, the Society considered it inadvisable to alter the terms of the agreement since the first change in the rate of bonus had been responsibly accepted.

Displaced by the estate-owners' disregard of the GMMWU's demands, on 29 January 1951, the President-General of the GMMWU, Eric Gairy, turned up at La Sagesse Estate, called workers together and spoke to them. The owner and manager intervened to enquire about the workers' grievances; they were told that these would be forthcoming in due course. A stoppage of work occurred from this date and lasted until the end of the island-wide strike which will be discussed shortly. On 8 February 1951, at a meeting on this estate, attended by the Labour Officer, the union leader demanded a 45% wage increase from the owner. The owner replied that as a member of the Agricultural Employers Society he was bound by the agreement the Society signed with the Trades Union Council.

In the meantime workers continued to lay down tools ... Since 30 January 1951 workers on the Hope Estate had refused to work; on the same day workers on Belmont Estate struck after a visit by the President-General, but work was subsequently resumed on the instructions of the union leader. On 13 February workers on Grand Bacolet Estate struck. Realizing that estates were going on strike one after another, employers of estate labour convened a joint meeting between the Agricultural Association and the Agricultural Employers Society on 8 February. The members passed a resolution reaffirming the Society's loyalty to the agreement entered into with the Trades Union Council.[49] The Labour Officer was aware that a mass industrial upheaval was imminent but felt helpless to prevent it. As a last resort he delivered three broadcasts on 16 and 17 February on the subject of trade unionism; but that was futile and it could not have prevented what was by then a virtual *fait accompli*. On 18 February the heads of the four leading religious denominations issued a joint appeal to their congregations in a last effort to prevent the island-wide strike due to start on the following day.

On 16 February HMS *Devonshire* was instructed by the Commander-in-Chief to get ready to proceed to Grenada. On 19 February 1951 the Grenada Manual and Mental Workers Union called an island-wide strike of agricultural and road workers. On the same day police reinforcements were requested from St Lucia, and an experienced police officer from Trinidad. By the end of that week almost all estate workers and road gangs had ceased work.

The general strike which ensued lasted four weeks, from 19 February to 19 March, and involved all agricultural and road workers throughout Grenada, resulting in the loss of 124,226 man days. A state of emergency was declared on 22 February and lasted until 5 March. The GMMWU's leaders, Eric Gairy and Gascoigne Blaize, were detained aboard HMS *Devonshire*. During their absence Messrs Lowe, McKie and Williams assumed leadership of the workers' struggle.

The two-months-old strike threw the entire planter society into a state of panic and hysteria, which not even the reassuring words of the Acting Governor were able to allay. Damage was done to estates including livestock to the value of £195,000; there was widespread arson as government buildings went up in flames, resulting in a loss of more than £18,000. Four persons were reported shot and killed by policemen, and there were countless cases of looting, violence, intimidation and wounding. At the end of the strike the GMMWU emerged victorious, and for the next 28 years the President-General, E.M. Gairy, became the arbiter of the political fortunes of Grenada; afterwards, the mere mention of his name conjured up for most people scenes of violence, arson, intimidation and death. Three of the men who died were killed by policemen in La Tante, who fired on a hostile crowd that assaulted them as they went to the assistance of a shopkeeper whose shop had just been looted. The crowd was on its way to the St David's Court House to demand the release of their colleagues, eight of whom had been arrested the previous day for picking cocoa on Marlmount Estate, the property of J.B. Renwick. The fourth person killed – Allick Andrews of Upper Capital – was shot by policemen when he attacked the Mt Pleasant watchman with a cutlass. He was with a group of workers that clashed with the police who had gone to protect the property from raiders.

There were essentially two classes involved in the 1951 uprising: the oppressors and the oppressed. In a famous Market Square meeting on 22 March, as E.M. Gairy said, 'There are no longer 7, 8 or 10 classes in Grenada today. There are only two classes, those belonging to the oppressors and those belonging to Gairy's movement. We form a *Mibone* nest!' The Administrator, the Executive and Legislative Councils, estate owners, merchant class and the civil service comprised the oppressors, for whom the local police force was the tool, existing essentially to protect their interests. The oppressed comprised the mass of agricultural workers, road workers and other members of the rural poor, including independent small farmers. The GMMWU merely provided leadership for this group.

At the outbreak of the strike the Governor, Sir Robert Arundell, was away, and the Administrator, George Green, acted for him. He was eventually criticized for his incompetence in dealing with the situation and for over-reacting. The Acting Governor was pushed into declaring a state of emergency and detaining GMMWU's leadership by both the Agricultural Employers Society and the Executive Council. The Legislature passed four 'anti-subversive' ordinances, and tabled a fifth, to help deal with the crisis. These were:

1. The Public Order Ordinance, No. 2 of 1951.
2. The Criminal Procedure Amendment Ordinance.
3. The Public Utility Undertaking and Public Health Services Arbitration Ordinance.
4. The Sedition Ordinance.

The fifth, which was not passed, was the Importation of Publications Ordinance.

The aim of these ordinances was not only to protect the interests of the employers but to crush the workers' struggle by fettering the leadership of the trade union movement. Gairy, in a Market Square meeting on 21 February 1951, attended by thousands of workers from all over the country, said that the Legislative Council had met to 'pass laws to bring them back into slavery'. He also made it clear that 'their fight was not against the police but against the employers whom they will hunt out if anything happened'. The ruling class was, by then, armed and prepared to use violence; Green had conceded to their demand for extra force. In a meeting with Governor Arundell on 11 March, planters, on the verge of hysteria, boasted how they went about armed and were in fact armed at the meeting. Lieutenant-Colonel H. DeGale gave the warning that

> unless Government is prepared to rule, we, the planters and the merchants will have to take the Government into our own hands, and we hope that you will given us the licence which you have given to these communistic hooligans when we do act.[50]

T.E. Noble Smith told the Governor that he always travelled with two guns, and intended to use them. G.S.W. Smith hinted that communists had taken possession of the land; that they were telling the people that their land was taken away from them 100 years ago and the time had come to get it back, even if at the cost of bloodshed. Denis Henry informed the Governor that 'Gairyism is not only a trade union, it bears all the hallmarks of communism'.[51]

The ruling class in Grenada was convinced that these disturbances were no genuine wage dispute but a well-guided communist plot designed to overthrow society. On 19 February the Superintendent of Police, Colonel A.A. Donald, told the Executive Council he was convinced that this was a 'deepseated communist plot against constituted authority' and that he had taken due precautions to handle the situation. His solution was simply to shoot all those who misbehaved; in fact, he had given orders to that effect. Governor Arundell said of Donald: 'I have never had any confidence in Donald. He appears to be prematurely senile, is rather uncouth and one of the stupidest men I have ever had to deal with.'[52]

Gairy's association with Butler in Trinidad and Bustamante in Jamaica was apparently the basis for the allegation of a communist plot as both men were branded communists at that time by the ruling class. In those days of the McCarthy witch-hunts in the USA any association or involvement in the social and economic cause of the working class was interpreted as communism. On 3 March 1951 one Lucius Mondezi, a member of the Workers Freedom Movement in Trinidad, was ordered to leave Grenada, one day after his arrival, on suspicion that he was a Bolshevik, in league with Gairy and Gascoigne Blaize. In a confidential report to the Colonial Office dated 1 March 1951, the Acting Governor said that the planters had stated, quite unequivocally, that the present situation was not 'merely a wage dispute but was a communist uprising organized by Gairy'. There is no doubt that the 1951 disturbances were a class confrontation, but that they were an organized communist plot spearheaded from outside was rather far-fetched. W.E. Julien, a leading merchant of the day, described them as a class-war: 'Instead of a strike we find in every direction bitter class hatred, the haves against the have-nots. Some of the biggest estates are abandoned today and gangsters are reaping the produce.'[53] He went on to say:

> I am one of the men in Grenada who feel that there would never have been a Gairy if what I call the 'plantocracy' and other employers of labour in Grenada had forgotten their selfishness and had gone down to making some arrangement whereby the labourers would receive some of the benefits which war and the aftermath of war have brought to the owners of land. Some of them have definitely brought it on themselves.[54]

The more the situation deteriorated between 22 February and 4 March, the less able was the executive authority to reconcile the differences. The Governor, who hurried back to deal with the situation, arrived on 5 March 1951 accompanied by the labour adviser to the Secretary of State, E.W. Barltrop, sent by the Colonial Office to mediate. The Governor immediately convened a meeting of the Executive Council whereupon it was decided to end the state of emergency and to release both Gairy and Blaize. This embittered the planting interest and they accused the Governor of abdicating his responsibilities. The entire country was in a state of violent ferment with 10,000 workers up in arms and acting on their own in retaliation to the arrest and detention of their leaders. Upon his release Gairy assured the Governor that the violence would cease, as it had arisen primarily because of his arrest and detention. Between 8 and 22 March he addressed a series of meetings in which he called for peace, and outlined the ills of the society which had to be eradicated. The mood of the people, consequently, became less and less violent.

The Governor in giving his personal appraisal of the situation saw it as a confrontation between organized labour and the employers of labour. He condemned the planters for behaving as if a general strike had never occurred elsewhere. He wrote: 'They have become hysterical and their jumpiness and constant rumours have not helped.'[55] Both the Governor and E.W. Barltrop considered the crisis as not simply a labour dispute, but a social revolution, with unpredictable repercussions. The class structure of Grenada had been overturned; for the first time in its history, the Blacks had successfully asserted themselves and successfully revolted against their status of *peonage*.

The Governor described the President-General of the GMMWU as: 'an egoist, ambitious for power and with an inferiority complex apparently because of his dark colour, determined to show the world that he can rise above birth and colour to political leadership of his people.'[56] But he admitted that Gairy had established a remarkable ascendancy over the working class; had become their *de facto* leader, and his detention and arrest had immortalized him in their eyes; the Governor had been ... reliably informed that Gairy has been hailed as the reincarnation of Fedon, and has been heard to have said that Grenada needs a blood purge.'

Thus in Grenada of the 1950s members of the ruling class saw Gairy as the representative of the forces of evil; while members of the working class tended to see him as a heavensent leader.

Gairy, meantime, continued to paint the struggle in terms of class and to further consolidate their allegiance to him. In a meeting in the Market Square on 15 March he referred to some individual members of the ruling class and used them to represent their class and its relationship to the 'poor Black people' of the country. Referring to Denis Henry, he said he illustrated how his class lived apart from the community and used its wealth to foster its own position.

> He called me a 'filter'. He is a man who has lots of money. He went to England to study law; he returned to the Colony and up to now he has not contributed anything to the community. He refused to sit at the same table with me. But I will stand in Grenada and see him ask me to take a seat with him.[57]

He told the crowd to boycott Gerald Smith's business: 'I do not want you people to patronize Gerald Smith store. This is the first store I am speaking against – and if you know any shops that buy from him do not buy from these shops.'[58]

Of H. DeGale he said he 'had shot a man for intimidating workers on his sister's estate. What had government done about that? Was DeGale arrested?' (Crowd: 'No!')[59] Referring to Norris Hughes he analysed how workers had to pay taxes to protect the ruling class, but received no protection themselves. He asked:

> Why do we have to pay taxes in order to get policemen and marines to protect a $20,000 house belonging to Mr Hughes' son? That is unfair. Why should not Mr Hughes and his son live in good grace with the people so that they would have no fear at all?[60]

In all meetings throughout the strike, five main issues were enunciated again and again in order to show the masses, clearly and precisely, their class interests. They were:

1. That Grenada was ruled by one class, the upper class. This had to end as that class did not have the interests of the rural poor at heart.
2. Poor housing was widespread in the country. People needed decent homes and some privacy.
3. The Nutmeg Bill, though opposed by most people in Grenada, was passed owing to the power of the landed gentry; Grenada's main

industries, cocoa, nutmeg and sugar, were owned and totally controlled by them.
4. Colour prejudice was rampant in the labour market; persons were employed in business and in the civil service on the basis of colour and class affiliations. A system of favouritism prevailed instead of a system of meritocracy. This had to be abolished.
5. Workers had always been exploited by being overworked and underpaid.

On 19 March the general strike ended and workers returned to work with the assurance that settlement would be reached between 19 March and 4 April 1951. By then Gairy's position was firmly entrenched. In the face of the unanimous support he was able to mobilize, plus the allegiance of 40,000 rural poor, the ruling class had no choice but to capitulate. A wage agreement, negotiated between the Grenada Agricultural Employers Society and the GMMWU, with Barltrop as mediator, was reached on 4 April 1951. In the eyes of the workers this was a major victory for Gairy as the union's demands were met. The main points of the agreement were:

1. The statutory minimum wage for all agricultural and road workers was to be $1.20 and $1.00 respectively for men and women. This was to take effect from 1 January 1951.
2. Seven days' annual holiday on full pay must be given to workers who had worked not less than 200 days in any one year, commencing 1 January 1951.
3. A Reference Board was to be set up with the object of promoting good will between employers and workers and for the purpose of determining any dispute with regard to wages or conditions of employment.
4. The agreement was to remain in force for one year as from 4 April 1951 and would be deemed to continue beyond that period until determined by either party giving three months' notice in writing.[61]

The workers received back pay at the foregoing rates for every day they worked, beginning 1 August 1950, deducting what they had already received. This payment was made on 27 April 1951.

The 1951 labour unrest was a belated attempt by the Grenadian working class to catch up with the development of similar movements in the rest of the Caribbean. It provided a leap forward in the consciousness of the worker, and 100 years of docility and subservience seemed to have evaporated overnight. A social revolution had occurred that marked the apotheosis of the estate labourers' post-Emancipation struggle.

This social uprising coincided with the granting of adult suffrage; thus the mass of the workers who previously had no say in government became enfranchised overnight. That signified the end of plantocracy and the rise of a new leadership. The GMMWU formed its own political party in 1951, the Grenada's People's Party, which subsequently became the Grenada United Labour Party and was the party of working class – the peasants, proto-peasantry, rural-poor and estate labourers – and as such its success in the 1951 elections was inevitable.

E.M. Gairy thus became not only the undisputed trade union leader in the country, but the political arbiter of Grenada's future. He had successfully seized political power from the plantocracy, but the economic structure, which had created the contradictions of 1951, remained intact. A permanent contribution of the 1951 social uprising was the recognition of the power of organized labour and the 'strike' as its weapon to obtain from the employer class acceptance and respect for the legitimate demands of the workers.

NOTES

Full citations only given where work does not appear in the Bibliography.

1. Lewis, *Evolution of the Peasantry*, p. 1.
2. Council Paper No. 8, 1938, *Commission of Inquiry into the Economic Conditions of Wage Earners in Grenada*. 1938, p. 11.
3. Grenada Department of Labour, *Statistics on Wage and Income*. Special compilation.
4. *Blue Book*, 1930, p. 112.
5. *Report of the Peasant Proprietary Commission*, 3 December 1907.
6. Auchinleck, 'Peasant Agriculture in Grenada'.
7. Marshall. 'Notes on Peasant Development'.
8. West India Royal Commission, Report, 1939, p. 412.
9. *Blue Book*, Agriculture, 1930.
10. *Report of the Inquiry into the Nutmeg Industry of Grenada*, 1951, p. 1.
11. *Grenada Handbook*, 1946, p. 104.
12. *Blue Books*, 1929–45.
13. Fletcher, *Development of a Policy Towards Land Reform*.
14. Council Paper No. 9, 1938, *Report of the Agricultural Dept for 1937 and 1938*, pp. 10–17. Council Paper No. 14, 1945, *Report by the Director of Agriculture on Land Settlement in Grenada*, 1945, p. 13.
15. *Report by the Director of Agriculture on Land Settlement in Grenada*, pp 8–9.
16. *Report of the Agricultural Department*, 1933, 1934.
17. *Report by the Director of Agriculture On Land Settlements in Grenada*.
18. *Agricultural Report*. 1951, p. 23.
19. *Blue Book*, 1930.
20. *Blue Book*, 1949. Council Paper No. 1, 1951. *Report of the Labour Department*, 1949, 1951.
21. Council Paper No. 12, 1935. *Metayer System in Carriacou*, 1935. p. 1.
22. Ibid.
23. Ibid.
24. Ibid.
25. *Report of the Agricultural Department for 1957*.

26. L. Fletcher, 'The Decline of Friendly Societies in Grenada', p. 101.
27. *Blue Book*, 1935.
28. *Report of the Commission appointed to enquire into the economic conditions of wage earners; Report of the Agricultural Department for 1937 and 1938.*
29. By the 1940s the British Caribbean Currency Board currency was the British Caribbean dollar which had an exchange rate of BC$4.8: £1 sterling. It was pegged to the £; that remained until 1976 when the sterling peg was changed to a US dollar peg.
30. *West India Royal Commission Report*, 1939. p. 402.
31. *Report of Inquiry into the Nutmeg Industry*, 1951, p. 1.
32. Ibid.
33. GCNA membership: F.M. Henry (barrister and large farmer); S.H. Smith (small grower and managing director of Johan Browne & Hubbard – the largest firm in Grenada); Charles DeGale (large grower); Herbert Neckles (small grower, prominent member of local planting class); Hon. A. Williamson, OBE (medium-sized grower and member of Legislature); F.C. Noel (large grower and export dealer); Hon. G.H. Adams (Colonial Treasurer); A.I. Thompson (manager and part owner of a large dry-goods store – nominated by Governor to sit on Board); Wilfred Denny (small grower); F.C. Hughes (Chief Executive Officer and prominent member of the upper class).
34. Council Paper No. 13, 1945. *The Grenada Sugar Factory Co.*, C.Y. Shepherd, 1945, p. 2.
35. Ibid.
36. Council Paper No. 4, 1938. *Economic Conditions of the Grenada Peasantry*, Report of Dr B. Spearman.
37. *Report of General Abstracts of Census of 1921*. Grenada, p. 32.
38. Ibid.
39. Council Paper No. 8, 1938. *Commission of Inquiry*, 1938.
40. *Economic Conditions of the Grenada Peasantry*, Dr B. Spearman.
41. Council Paper No. 4, 1954. *Report of the Labour Department for 1951.*
42. Council Paper No. 6, 1951. *Report of the Labour Department for 1950.*
43. Ibid.
44. Ibid.
45. Council Paper No. 4, 1954. *Report of the Labour Department for 1951.*
46. Ibid; *The West Indian*, 12 November 1950.
47. *Report of the Labour Department for 1951.*
48. Ibid.
49. Ibid.
50. Minutes of meeting at Government House, 7 March 1951.
51. Ibid.
52. Telegram: Governor of Grenada to Secretary of State, 16 March 1951.
53. Meeting at Government House, 7 March 1951.
54. *Grenada Disturbances*. Report of the Governor to Colonial Office, No. 117, 5 April 1951.
55. Ibid.
56. *Grenada Disturbances*. Appendix xix, 'Minutes of a meeting, held by E.M. Gairy in the Market Square, St George's'. 15 March 1951.
57. Ibid.
58. Ibid.
59. Ibid.
60. Ibid.
61. *Grenada Disturbances, February–March 1951*. A special compilation by the Governor's Secretary. The Governor, Sir Robert Arundell, was out of the island at the time; the President of the Council, George Green, acted as Governor in his absence.

# 17

# *Development of Organized Labour: 1940–60*

The first period of trade union activity in the Caribbean – 1899 to 1920 – was centred mostly in the larger territories and left Grenada relatively unaffected. After a lull in the 1920s, the 1930s not only witnessed increased trade union activity, but frequent labour unrest and in some cases mass uprisings of the workers; again, Grenada remained relatively unaffected.

In the larger territories, almost all leaders of popular movements who had arisen by the end of the Second World War and had initiated active combat with the propertied ruling class, initially utilized trade unionism as their main forum of struggle. Almost invariably these trade union leaders later became prominent political figures. In Jamaica, Alexander Bustamante was undisputed leader of the Bustamante Industrial Trade Union; in Trinidad, in 1919, the Trinidad Workingman's Association was led by A.A. Cipriani, who was followed in the 1930s by Tubal Uriah 'Buzz' Butler who polarized the working-class protest; in Barbados, Grantley Adams, an Oxford-educated lawyer, led the Barbados Workers' Union. In Antigua, in the early 1940s, V.C. Bird led the Antigua Trades and Labour Union; in British Honduras there was George Price and the General Workers Union, and in St Kitts there was Robert Bradshaw.[1]

The purpose of this chapter, however, is not to demonstrate the relationship between trade unionism and politics, between the union and the party, but to trace the development of the trade union movement in Grenada from the 1940s to the 1960s, and to see the extent to which it was preoccupied with changing the established order.

## Main Hypotheses on Trade Unions

It is suggested that the pre-1940s trade unions (the Grenada Trades Union, the Grenada Workers Union, the General Workers Union and St John's Labour Party) all followed a policy of co-operation, accommodation and collaboration with the main employers of labour. These were pseudo-working class organizations with only a superficial appeal to the workers. Their activities provided palliatives to workers' and labourers' grievances, rather than any attempt to effect a radical transformation in their conditions of work and general mode of life.

Despite the wage increases and peripheral socio-economic changes in the 1940–60 period, no fundamental change occurred in the relationship between the labourers and the forces of production. The aspirations of the unions of the 1940s were frustrated by the social relations between the unions' executives and the employers of labour, in addition to their policy of rapprochement. The GMMWU, which arose in July 1950 and emerged as the indomitable voice of the working class, was soon to subordinate trade unionism to party politics; the Grenada People's Party (later, the Grenada United Labour Party) grew out of the GMMWU and took precedence over it. This is a potentially healthy development, provided the leadership of the mass movement can do two things: a) seize political power; and b) use it to transform the mode of life and social relations of the labouring population and simultaneously create structural transformation in the archaic and inequitable relationship between the worker and the forces of production.

The GMMWU leadership succeeded in the first, but not in the second.

The initial successes of the GMMWU were not consolidated as a trade union organization, but rather as a political organization; thus, by the mid-1950s its pre-eminence in the trade union field was lost. The GMMWU's ascendancy had simultaneously relegated the St John's Labour Party, the General Workers Union and the Grenada Workers Union – previously the main bargaining agents of the labouring population – to oblivion. The GMMWU was able to polarize Grenada's class structure in the early 1950s, revealing those who identified with their interests and those who were opposed to them; in this way the movement's leadership succeeded in projecting into the minds of the working class and rural population the image of a working-class saviour.

This had immense political appeal and was responsible for the subsequent success of the political movement which emerged from the union; but the mass of the labouring population, though retaining a strong identification with the union and unreserved admiration for its leadership, saw the union less and less as a main vehicle for promoting their interests and satisfying their aspirations as workers. Their membership became nominal, and the seriousness of purpose characteristic of their early union activities was dissipated.

The Grenada Seamen and Waterfront Workers Union, an offshoot of the Grenada Workers Union, was however an exception. Since its inception in 1952 it worked as a union with a seriousness of purpose such that, by the end of the 1950–60 decade it emerged as one of the strongest bargaining agents for workers in the Colony. Other unions, for example the Commercial and Industrial Workers Union and the Technical and Allied Workers Union, were moving in a similar direction as that of the GSWWU but they still had to prove themselves.

## Socio-economic Conditions of Workers

In 1940, about 9,000 persons were employed in the principal sectors in Grenada. Of these, 5,306 were employed as agricultural labourers on estates, 2,634 of whom were women; the remaining 3,694 were engaged in varying proportions in the following occupations: domestic servants, clerical, official, commercial, and the building and construction industry; estates labourers and government road workers were the least well off. The findings of the 1937 Commission of Enquiry into the economic conditions of the various classes of wage-earners in Grenada with special reference to the agricultural industry, revealed that the agricultural labourer's wages were grossly inadequate, as was his housing, clothing and health-care.[2] Tuberculosis, yaws, hookworm, malaria, gastro-enteritis, and venereal diseases were widespread among the working people and their families, and, by 1940, the infant mortality rate exceeded 115 per 1000. In addition, socially and economically deprived, the labourer was ostracized politically.

It would, however, be misleading to say that in the 1930s no attempts were made by public authorities to increase peasants' holdings in the island. In the 1930–40 decade, as we have seen, at least eight areas were apportioned among peasants under the government-sponsored land settlement scheme, but the average acreage of 1–1.5 per lot was totally insufficient to maintain a family of five.[3] By 1940, estates had allotted 15,078 acres to 12,937 persons to work on a share-rental basis, as estates could not provide their labourers with five days' work weekly; of 5,306 persons employed on estates in 1940, only 1,549 were employed continuously.

Grenadian working women were burdened with a high percentage of illegitimate children, but they shrank not an inch from their responsibilities. Sixty-six percent of all children born in Grenada were born to these women; 66% of these had either no support, or at best meagre support from their fathers.

## Class Contrasts

Such were the conditions under which the working class laboured around 1940. Fundamental contradictions existed between the life of the labourer and that of the main employers of labour: employers' extravagance opposed to employees' poverty; employers' general literacy opposed to employees' illiteracy; many social activities for employers opposed to few for employees; employers' master-image, and labourers' subservience (an attempt to prolong the slave-planter syndrome); upper-class prestige opposed to working-class degradation; employers owned most of the wealth and enjoyed all social privileges as opposed to workers' exploitation and state of social atrophy; employers developed a superiority complex by virtue of their education, their money and, at times, even their physical appearance, while, lacking these, workers developed an inferiority complex.

Despite labour unrest elsewhere in the Caribbean, the Grenadian worker neither clenched a fist, brandished a cutlass nor threw a stone. Contradictions existed and conditions were ripe for the working class to assert itself but a catalyst was lacking – a leadership to weld the various elements into a coherent whole. But also many factors neutralized the contradictions from time to time. For example, labourers' privileges, or indulgences on estates for some workers; frequent wage increases, seven between 1940–49 (none of significance); the tranquilizing effect of the colonial regime; and reverence and a degree of fear for the 'nice-Governor', the so-called 'Buckra', and his pillars of support – civil service, police and courts.

The 1939 report on labour commented that relationships between employers and employees were of a friendly nature. It was not that workers had no grievances, but that there was no outlet for them; they remained submerged and simmering. In 1940, there was no organization they could depend upon to represent them and their interests.

## Unions in the 1940s

Between 1940 and 1949 three trade union organizations came to the fore and tried to represent the worker.

1. The St John's Labour Party/General Workers Union.
2. The Grenada Trade Union.
3. The St George's Workers Union, later the Grenada Workers Union.

In addition six ordinances related to employer-employee relationships were passed: two of 1934, two of 1939 and one of 1940:

1. The Department of Labour Ordinance (No. 6 of 1940): promulgated in order to constitute a department of labour for the first time in the Colony, outlining its functions and those of its officers. It provided for the payment of minimum wages to agricultural workers and the regulation of hours of work.
2. The Tenants' Compensation Ordinance of 1939: this regulated the conditions and provisions of land tenancy as well measures to reconcile disputes between landlord and tenant.
3. Recruitment of Workers Ordinance of 1939: this regulated the recruitment of Grenadian workers for work overseas, for example, Curacao, Aruba, USA, and so on.
4. The Employment of Women, Young Persons and Children Ordinance of 1938.
5. The Workmen's Compensation Ordinance of 1934.
6. The Trades Union Ordinance of 1934.

The last three are of particular relevance here and need to be discussed in some detail.

One legacy of slavery that became accepted practice was the employment of women and minors without any special conditions attached. The ordinance of 1938 sought to regulate the employment of these categories of workers. Two major rulings were:

1. The legal age for the employment of young persons and children was raised from 12 to 14 years.
2. The employment of women and children/young persons at night was made illegal.

The Workmen's Compensation Ordinance was directed towards compensating any worker accidentially injured in the course of employment, and for any injury resulting in partial or total, temporary or permanent, disablement. The provisions of this Ordinance were:

1. Where death resulted from the injury the sum equivalent to 30 months' wages or £250, whichever was less, had to be paid to his next of kin or dependants.
2. Where there was permanent total disablement, a sum equivalent to 42 months' wages or £350, whichever was less. In the case of a minor a sum equal to 84 months' wages or £350, whichever was less.
3. Where permanent, partial disablement resulted then a percentage of what was paid in the case of permanent disablement was to be paid; the percentage would depend on the percentage loss of earnings capacity caused by the injury.
4. Where temporary disablement, partial or total, occurred, a half-monthly payment every 16th day of the month for a period of five years or during the period of incapacitation, whichever was shorter, was to be made.[4]

The Trade Union Ordinance, passed in 1934, provided for a registrar of trade unions, registration of all trade unions, the unionization of juniors (16–21 year olds), an annual return of trade unions, and the amalgamation of workers. This ordinance was amended twice between 1934 and 1951.

Apparently neither the Workmen's Compensation Ordinance nor the Trade Union Ordinance were more than paper directives. From the literature concerning the first ten years of the ordinance's existence, it was either disregarded or there were no cases for compensation. The first trade union to be registered – the Grenada Trades Union – came into being in 1937 and four years later was defunct.

A main criticism by the Moyne Commission that visited Grenada in 1939 was the virtual absence of trade unions in a country with so many agricultural labourers. The Commission recommended that provisions be made for the representation of rural workers, as these were generally neglected in the Caribbean at large.[5]

The period 1940–50 marked the genesis of the trade union movement in Grenada with the establishment of a Department of Labour, and the added provisions made for trade union registration and functioning. As was noted above, in 1937 there was one registered trade union, the Grenada Trades Union. Though the St John's Labour Party/General Workers Union had existed since 1929 it was not registered until 1941. The Grenada Union of Teachers had existed since 1913, but became a registered union only in 1960.

The St John's Labour Party (later called the Grenada Labour Party/General Workers Union), founded in November 1929 and based at Gouyave, had the following objectives:

- to promote measures to foster and protect the interests of workers;
- to defend and uphold the rights and privileges of workers;
- to try and avoid unnecessary litigation between employers and employees; and
- to settle disputes by means of arbitration if possible.

In 1940 its membership stood at 400.

The organization was both a trade union and a Friendly Society; in 1930 it began to provide sickness benefits for its members, and in 1932 set up the Grenada Cooperative Bank Ltd, aimed at encouraging thrift among workers and mobilizing their savings. In the 1940s the bank loaned the Grenada Sugar Factory Ltd $43,200 and $28,000 in mortages bearing 4% and 6% interest respectively.[6]

Throughout the 1940s this union – though not limited to representing agricultural workers only – together with the Grenada Workers' Union, was frequently involved in negotiating wage agreements with the Grenada Employers Association on behalf of estate workers.

The Grenada Trades Union was formed in the latter part of the 1930s and in 1939 was the only registered union in the island. There were signs of its early demise in 1942, when it failed to comply with the law, in so far as book-keeping was concerned, and also neglected its annual returns. Every opportunity was given to its executive to put matters right but this was to no avail; subsequently the union was dissolved. The Registrar of Trade Unions gazetted the following on 8 July 1942: 'Take notice that I have this day cancelled the Registration of the Grenada Trades Union as it has ceased to exist – violation of the law by the union before it became defunct being incidental.'[7]

Thus, by 1944 the St John's Labour Party and General Workers Union became the workers' sole bargaining agency. Although it was described as performing useful pioneer work and receiving the full support of the Labour Department, the Labour Officer was not satisfied with the general pace of the trade union movement's development and in 1944, with a view to encouraging the formation of more trade unions, he addressed a meeting in St George's under the auspices of the Forester's Social Welfare League, and another at Grenville. Two years later the St George's Workers Union was founded, representing both urban and rural workers, but predominantly urban-based; its headquarters was in St George's.

Throughout the latter 1940s, both the General Workers Union and the St George's Workers Union were involved in wage negotiations on behalf of the agricultural workers; the St George's Workers Union represented stevedores and store clerks. Both Unions were at that time amalgamated into the Grenada Trades Union Council and more or less worked in unison from then onwards.

From 1938 to 1950 agricultural workers were awarded nine separate wage increases; the first five had been fixed by the Governor-in-Council; the last four were as a result of negotiations between the unions and the Agricultural Association of Grenada.[8] During that time daily wages were increased from 30¢ for men and 28¢ for women in 1938, to 82¢ + 9¢ bonus for men and 68¢ + 8¢ bonus for women in 1950.

Since the formation of the St George's Workers Union (the Grenada Workers Union), in 1946, at least four wage agreements were reached between the union and the Grenada Shipping Agents on behalf of the stevedores; and one wage agreement between the union and the commercial business sector on behalf of the clerks.

Despite these increases, in calculating workers' real income in 1947 on a 1939 base it was found that it had stagnated. In 1940 men received 34¢ and women 28¢ per day respectively, in 1947, 72¢ and 60¢, an increase of some 110% in both cases. According to the consumer price index at the time there had been an increase of 106% over the same time span; thus, a worker's real income had increased by a meagre 4% or 5% per annum over seven years.[9]

On 15 January 1948, in an attempt to break the impasse between the unions and the Association, the Grenada Legislative Council unanimously carried a motion to appoint a committee, chaired by the Labour Officer, to examine rates of pay, hours of work and conditions of employment of agricultural labourers.[10] Soon afterwards, before the Committee made its recommendations, the Assocation approved by resolution a daily wage of 78% and 66¢ respectively for men and women labourers. The Department of Labour established this as the statutory minimum wage in 1949, with effect from 26 September 1949.

The committee on agricultural wages held 11 meetings during which a total of 94 witnesses gave evidence.[11] In its report the committee stated they had been handicapped by the planters' reluctance to give evidence. The memorandum submitted by the Agricultural Association was considered as sufficient evidence by the planters, thus making it unnecessary for them to appear before the committee individually. In this memorandum the planters recommended the substitution of existing rates of 72¢ (men) and 60¢ (women) daily, by a wage of 10¢ and 8.5¢ per hour in respect of an eight-hour working day. Since their main complaint was that it was impossible for them to get a fair day's work, due to workers' relaxed attitudes, they saw in the proposal a means whereby to increase workers' industriousness. Thus, they were guided by their own economic self-interest, as only they stood to gain by increased industriousness of the worker. The proposal was, however, rejected outright by the committee.

The St John's Labour Party advocated a daily wage of $1.00 (men) and 84¢ (women) in an attempt to bring the labourers' earnings more in line with the cost of living. The St George's Workers Union recommended a daily wage of $2.00 or 8s 4d to be paid as: $1.20, daily cash wage; $0.80, wage in kind from gardens, the raising of live-stock and purchases at reduced rates from estates. The union considered $2.00 as the minimum wage necessary to maintain a man and an average-sized family.

The Agricultural Wages Committee recommended 82¢ (men) and 68¢ (women) daily, in view of two considerations: a) the wage required to enable a man to live in minimum comfort; and b) the ability of the agricultural industry to pay.[12]

In addition the committee also recommended that the present statutory description of 'day's work', 'task work' and 'piece work' remain. It rejected the submission of the Agricultural Association with respect to the substitution of hourly work for day's work; it suggested that estates make more of the so-called 'indulgences' available to their employees, and see to it that workers were decently housed and thus induce a sense of pride in their home and develop a clean and healthy outlook.[13]

> To this end the estate management should regard the barrack as a blot on the estate and should provide instead ... small buildings suitable to the needs of the individual family with the modern amenities which the labourer expects and to which he is entitled – buildings, which must provide privacy for a man and his wife with separate rooms for his children of different sexes; buildings that will materially assist in lessening the incidence of immorality and disease.[14]

Upon publication of the Wages Committee Report, the Agricultural Association elected a committee to examine it. Early in December 1948 this committee submitted its report and on 9 December 1948 a general meeting was convened to examine the recommendations. The Agricultural Association committee stated categorically that the wages of 78¢ and 66¢ should not increase, primarily because the agricultural industry was unable to pay more. The report was adopted unanimously.[15]

By the end of 1949 no steps had been taken to implement the recommendations of the Agricultural Wages Committee, although its report had been before the Legislative Council since November 1948 (Council Paper No. 12 of 1948). On 18 January 1950 the Legislative Council passed unanimously a motion to the effect that 'the recommendations of the Agricultural Wages Committee be implemented forthwith' and from that day the following minimum wages became law: men 82¢ per day; women 68¢ per day. (A day = eight hours.)[16]

Why had 15 months elapsed between submission of the Wages Committee Report to the Legislative Council and its final implementation? Possibly it was an attempt to assuage the planters' feelings or simply delaying tactics by the planter-dominated Council. Even had the Governor ratified the report, the approval of the Legislative Council was required before it could become operative. Under the Department of Labour Ordinance 1940 (No. 16 of 1940) the Governor-in-Council was empowered

> to make provision 'inter alia' for the fixing of rates of wages in any industry or occupation and all order made by the Governor-in-Council under the authority of this Section shall not become operative until approved by resolution of the Legislative Council.[17]

Either way the delay was probably owing to the planters' resistance.

The first agreement between the St George's Workers Union and the shipping agents on behalf of the stevedores was on 12 December 1945 and effective for one year. The main points of the agreement were payment of wages at the rate of 30¢ per hour and fixing the duration of the working day. Previously, the wage rate had been 20¢ per hour; this new wage comprised a basic wage of 22¢ plus 8¢ per hour cost-of-living allowance. The agreement was the climax of industrial action taken by the stevedores earlier that year when they struck for approximately two hours while unloading a ship.

On 24 January 1947 another agreement between both parties was ratified. According to this the duration of a working day was from 7 a.m. to 4 p.m., while overtime was to be paid from 4 p.m. to 7 a.m. The practice of fixing wage rates based on the cost-of-living index figure was discontinued in favour of a 'flat rate'; wages were increased from 30¢ to 34¢ an hour and overtime was to be paid at the rate of time-and-a-half.[18] In April 1949 this agreement was superseded. The principal amendments on the 1947 agreement were: a) an increase of 4¢ per hour for winchmen, guymen and gangwaymen; b) double pay for work on holidays; c) an additional 7¢ per hour for handling cement, manure, caustic soda and explosives.[19]

This agreement expired in 1950 and a new one came into effect on 13 December 1950. The main points of this agreement were an increase from 38¢ to 44¢ per hour for hold-men; and an increase for tally clerks bringing their rates to 54¢ for a senior, 56¢ for the chief and 46¢ for a junior. These rates were for an eight-hour day, from

7 a.m. to 4 p.m.; overtime was to begin from 12 noon on Saturdays instead of from 4 p.m.[20] Some key personalities negotiating for the stevedores at this time were: George B. Otway, Bertie Johnson, Leonard Green, E.A. 'Doc' Mitchell, and W. Nicholson.

A spirit of amity and co-operation seems to have existed between the St George's Workers Union and the shipping agents Geo. F. Huggins, Jonas Browne and Hubbard and Thompson Hankey and Co. On no occasion in these various negotiations from 1946 to 1950 was there a deadlock. This exemplified the inability of this worker organization to resist the status quo, as well as the preparedness of its leaders to be satisfied with minute concessions made to them by the employer class. The tendency, at times, to conform to colonial institutions made the leadership of the organization into establishment figures, incapable of resisting the powerful merchant class in St George's.

In 1951 the Grenada Workers Union became the bargaining body for the longshoremen and immediately initiated bargaining for wage increases for these workers. The negotiations continued well into 1952. In the past longshoremen had been hired by an independent contractor, but, as a result of agitation for increased wages, the shipping agents expressed their willingness to enter into an agreement with the union.

The union demanded a 50% wage increase retroactive from 27 November 1951, plus a cost-of-living allowance. Five meetings were held under the Chairmanship of the Labour Officer, and agreement was reached on hours of work, waiting time, and stoppage of work due to acts of nature, but not on wage rates and cost-of-living allowance. An arbitration tribunal was set up consisting of Sir Clement Malone (chairman), N. Crinchlow (union representative) and H.O. Culhane (representative of the Shipping Agents).

By 1952 the union had reduced its demands for wage increases to 33.5%. In addition it demanded a cost-of-living allowance of 0.5¢ per hour for every five-point increase, using as the base the time when the agreement was entered into. The tribunal made the following awards:

- time and-a-half for overtime from Monday to Friday;
- time and-a-half for overtime from 11 a.m. on Saturday to 7 a.m. Sunday;
- double pay for work on Good Friday, Christmas Day, Sundays and Bank Holidays;
- an increase of 15% on basic hourly wage retroactive from 24 January 1952;
- a cost-of-living allowance of 0.5¢ per hour for every five-point rise in the index when it exceeds 258 points (the index for October 1951).

These negotiations resulted in a virtual defeat for the workers and the union representing them, on their two major points: wage increase and cost-of-living allowance.

In the same year the GWU signed a new agreement with the shipping agents on behalf of the stevedores – the fifth since the war – with the following increases per hour: foreman, $1.15, 112% increase; winchman and gangwayman, each 0.69¢, 50%; holdman, 0.55¢, 25%; tally clerks: Chief, 0.67¢; Senior, 0.65¢; Junior, 0.55¢, representing a 20% increase each.

A new post, that of Chief Stevedore, was also created, with a wage of $1.50 per hour plus an overtime rate of $2.00-$3.00 per hour. He was to act on behalf of the shipping agents to engage stevedores to load or unload cargo, to submit time sheets, and receive money for work done and make prompt payment to each stevedore. He was required to be present on the docks at all times while work was being done.

The period 1939–49 sharply highlights the pro-status quo attitude of the existing union executives and their readiness to be accommodated within the established order rather than to challenge it. This is why ten years of trade union activity in Grenada passed with hardly any major case of industrial dispute. Those minor disagreements that did arise needed only the appearance of the Labour Officer to be settled. The first major disputes to arise were in 1950. It is noteworthy that although the Trades Disputes Ordinance had existed since 1943, it was resorted to for the first time only in mid-1950.

In spite of their shortcomings, however, by 1949 both the Grenada Workers Union and the St John's Labour Party had helped consolidate the trade union movement in Grenada. The Grenada Workers Union had five branch organizations, including a clerks' union, with a total membership of 2,434. The St John's Labour Party had two branch organizations with a membership of 517. At that time the total number of people employed in the agricultural and commercial sectors together with government-employed workers was 8,265. Thus, some 3,000 out of 8,265, or 38% of all persons in regular paid employment had been unionized.

## Labour Disputes 1950–51

The industrial disputes of 1950–51 involved none of the existing unions, but the Grenada Manual and Mental Workers Union (GMMWU) which, in three months, had catapulted itself to the position of the main bargaining body for the agricultural working class.

In 1950, the year in which the GMMWU was formed and registered, there were at least five cases of industrial disputes, of which the most significant was that between the GMMWU and the Grenada Sugar Factory Ltd, as has already been noted. A review of the 1950 disputes reveals a total of 5,673 man-days lost because of strikes. Three trade unions now represented agricultural and other workers, with paid-up membership as follows: St John's Labour Party (General Workers Union) 593; Grenada Workers Union 2,600; GMMWU (30 September 1950) 2,070. Of the 8,494 workers employed in the colony, 5,340 were employed in agriculture, 517 in the spice industry, 140 in the sugar industry; 1,400 were government workers, and 1,097 were workers in the business or commercial sector.

Another salient feature of the year 1950 was the number of cases of awards under the Workmen's Compensation Ordinance. The industrial disputes of 1950 were a dress rehearsal for those of 1951.

The 1951 general strike and the defeat of the employers and the proestablishment unions has already been discussed. Suffice it to say that 1951 marked a watershed in Grenada's history in general and in trade union development in particular.

While a spirit of confrontation marked the relationship between the employers of agricultural labour and the GMMWU, a spirit of accommodation and co-operation existed between these employers and the Grenada Trades Union Council (General Workers Union, Grenada Workers Union).

## The GMMWU

On 13 April 1951 the Grenada Agricultural Employers Society entered into an agreement with the Grenada Trades Union Council in terms identical to those entered into with the GMMWU on 4 April. This superfluous gesture exemplified the close affiliation between the Grenada Trades Union and the employers of labour, and represented a final attempt by the employers to legitimize the now moribund General Workers Union and the Grenada Workers Union. Each union boasted a membership of 600 and 3,000 respectively – on paper – but the majority of the agricultural members had struck under the leadership of the GMMWU and by then were staunch members and supporters of that union, which in 1951 had 5,000 members plus the support of non-members. In his 1951 report, the Labour Officer said of the unions that formed the TUC:

> These unions negotiated jointly in the past with the Grenada Agricultural Employers Society on questions affecting rates of pay of agricultural workers. At the time of the 1951 disturbances such an agreement was in existence but subsequent events proved that the great body of agricultural workers were no longer prepared to accept them as their representatives for purposes of negotiations.
>
> Moreover, these workers showed hostility towards the officers of these unions and they were obliged to 'lie low' towards the latter part of the year.[21]

The GMMWU recognized this weakness and stated categorically that the Trades Union Council should cease its activities and be dissolved. Indeed, the position of these two unions was steadily becoming anachronistic.

The second success of the GMMWU and its leadership was the launching of its political party: the Grenada People's Party. In the first general elections held under adult suffrage, towards the end of 1951, they won six out of eight elected seats to the Colony's Legislative Council.[22]

The GMMWU's successful challenge to the plantocracy and monied class also affected other sectors of the labour market. In 1951 the Civil Service Association, on behalf of all employees who received cost-of-living allowance, applied to the Government for an increase of 100% on existing rates with retroactive effect from 1 January 1950. The committee appointed by government to look into this, in submitting its report, recommended the acceptance of a 100% increase on the cost-of-living allowance, but to take effect from January 1951.[23] The General Workers Union, on behalf of the clerks and shop assistants, also demanded higher wages, and, when it was felt that there was nobody with whom to negotiate, threatened strike action. The Labour Officer intervened to avoid this and a Clerks' Wages Council was set up which finally submitted wage regulation proposals to government; and early in 1952 their proposals were ratified by the Governor. These provided the following monthly wages for clerks: $40.00 in St George's town; $35.00 in Grenville town; $30.00 in Sauteurs town; and $25.00 in all other places. Shop assistants were to receive $30.00 per month in the town of St George's, $30,00 in Grenville, $25.00 in Sauteurs, Victoria, Gouyave and Hillsborough, and $20.00 in other places.[24]

The activities of the GMMWU not only injected some dynamism into the GWU but apparently influenced workers' consciousness in other sectors not necessarily under the GMMWU's aegis. Individual estate workers were going on strike and taking other industrial action without directives from the executive of their union.

On 27 March 1952, 90 workers on the Calivigny Estates refused to work under a newly appointed overseer; on 31 March workers on Woodlands and Hope Vale Estates joined their strike in sympathy, but on the advice of the union they returned to work on the 1 and 2 April respectively.[25] On Calivigny Estate work was eventually resumed on 30 July 1952, on the instructions of the union, which eventually had supported the workers' claim. The estate was unable to harvest 1,320 tons of canes valued at $12.85 per ton.

On 19 August 1952 workers again took unilateral action; this time 30 workers on Petit Etang Estate went on strike in protest against the dismissal of one of their members. The union subsequently intervened and accused the employer of victimization, rejecting the idea that it was part of the estate's systematic retrenchment plan. On 25 August 1952, the union called a strike of all estate workers in the Parish of St David's in sympathy with the workers at Petit Etang; 392 workers on 12 estates, plus those on the Ashenden Government Agricultural Station, responded. Work was eventually resumed on 9 September. Approximately 2,140 man-days had been lost as a result of this industrial action.

Other disputes followed:

- On 2 May 1953 a worker on Bocage Estate was fired by the manager; on 4 May the workers struck, demanding his re-instatement.
- On 30 April 1953, on Diamond Estate, a worker was dismissed for encouraging a cocoa gang to refuse its allotted task, and using threatening language to achieve this purpose. The union instructed the 60 workers to strike on the following Monday, and on that day they gathered at the GMMWU office in Victoria. When news reached Tufton Hall of what was going on 45 workers 'downed tools' in sympathy. They eventually returned to work on 11 May 1953.
- On 4 May 1953 the owner of Waltham Estate, Phillip Brown transferred two watchmen from Belmont to Waltham. Their presence and especially the firearms they carried, infuriated the 136 workers on Waltham Estate, and they forthwith demanded their immediate removal. Sticks and cutlasses were brandished and the watchman were subsequently removed in the interests of peace and quiet.

The events of 1951 led to a number of novel statutory provisions being passed. The Public Utility Undertakings and Public Health Services Arbitration Ordinance (No. 3 of 1951) was passed to ensure that the essential services of the community would not be dislocated by action resulting from trade disputes; it also provided for the setting up of an Arbitration Tribunal to settle such disputes. There was the

Wages Council Ordinance, to set up a Wages Council to look after the regulation of workers' wages; and the Wages Council (Clerks) Order, 1951 (No. 58 of 1951), to regulate wages of persons employed in the wholesale and retail trade. Formerly wages were fixed by the Labour Advisory Board which made recommendation to the Governor-in-Council, who then made a minimum wage order under the authority of Section 10 of the Department of Labour Ordinance 1940. The order became operative when approved by resolution of the Legislative Council.[26] This method of wage-fixing was replaced in 1951 by collective bargaining; review by government of its employees' wage rates and the Clerks' Wages Council.

An important change in 1951 was the repeal of the Trade Union Ordinance and Trade Disputes Ordinance (No. 6 of 1943, No. 5 of 1948) and their replacement by the Trade Unions and Trade Disputes Ordinance of 1951 (No. 20 of 1951). The purpose of this Ordinance was to amend and consolidate the law relating to trade unions and trade disputes. The main change was that trade unions were required to submit their accounts to the Registrar before 1 April each year.

As a result of an agreement between the management of the Caribbean Tobacco Company and the Grenada Workers' Union, 1952 witnessed continued wage increases in other sectors. As unions and workers continued to make demands on employers, workers received a 25% wage increase and an annual bonus amounting to four months' salary. Initially the union had demanded a wage increase of 150%, but later changed it to 100% for workers employed 10 years or more and 75% for workers with less than 10 years' service. Workers in the Grenada Sugar Factory, as a result of negotiations between the GMMWU and the management, were granted wage increases from $1.02s and 68¢ to $1.20 and $1.00 respectively, thereby bringing their wages on par with other workers in agriculture.[27]

## Labour Dispute 1953

Towards the end of 1953 the GMMWU addressed proposals relating to increased wages and other conditions of service to both the Sugar Company and the employers' union who, between them, employed all agricultural labour in the colony – some 6,000 workers. However, negotiations broke down and all parties agreed to have the matter brought before an Arbitration Tribunal. The tribunal rejected the wage increases but awarded overtime at the rate of time-and-a-half for work on Sundays and holidays; it also modified the holiday provisions as follows: five days' holiday for 150 days' work per annum; six days' for 175; and seven days' for 200.[28] The GMMWU's request for free access to the estates at all times and for collecting dues was denied. The employers' union and Grenada Sugar Factory accepted the tribunal's decision – indeed, it was very much in their favour. The GMMWU, however, rejected the decision on the grounds that the three arbitrators could not reach a unanimous agreement, and that the chairman, who was to exercise his prerogative in such circumstances, was partial in his decision.

Despite the rejection of the tribunal's awards, the various parties agreed to the revival of the Reference Board – a body created after the 1951 disturbances, consisting of employers and worker representatives – to determine any dispute with regard to wages and conditions of work.[29] Five meetings were held by this body, three between July and September 1953 and two between October and December. Matters discussed were:

1. The appointment of a committee to investigate the circumstances leading to the dismissal of four workers on an estate.
2. The appointment of a panel of arbitrators to whom points of difference could be referred in the event of disagreements after all reasonable efforts at settlement had failed.
3. The various complaints by worker representatives.
4. The procedure to be adopted to determine disputes arising between individual employers and members of the Grenada Manual and Mental Workers Union.
5. The rejection of the GMMWU's request to enter estates of certain employers and objection to its collecting of dues on certain estates.[30]

None of the GMMWU's proposals met with approval, so on 26 November 1953 they called a strike of all agricultural workers except those in the sugar industry. About one-third of the estimated 6,000 agricultural workers stopped work – many through fear of violence or intimidation – but by the week before Christmas the vast majority had returned, except for those in St Mark's and St John's. The Labour Officer wrote: 'Whenever this Union takes strike action all agricultural workers whether members of the union or not are expected to obey and this obedience has in the past been enforced by violent action if necessary.'[31]

In early 1954 the strike was extended to incorporate the sugar workers. The arson, violence, stone-throwing or intimidation in 1951 had been directed at employers, for the confrontation was between employers and workers, but in 1954 it was between strikers and those determined to work. Such disturbances, however, were confined to St John's and St Mark's. The Labour Advisory Board discussed the situation, commenting on six areas and arriving at the following conclusions:

1. The Labour Advisory Board at a meeting held on Monday 7 December 1953 reviewed the history of a trade dispute between the Grenada Agriculturalists Union and the GMMWU which originated in 1950 and which after conciliation had failed was eventually determined by an Arbitration Tribunal which both parties requested His Excellency the Governor to set up.
2. The Board noted with deep regret that the Manual and Mental Workers Union failed to honour the tribunal's award.
3. The Board was appreciative of the efforts made to set up machinery – in the form of the Reference Board – aimed at providing groundwork and harmonious relationship between the employers and the union.
4. The Board then proceeded to give consideration to the circumstances leading to the current strike of agricultural workers which commenced on 26 November.
5. It noted that:
   - Prior to the commencement of the strike the GMMWU was reminded by the Labour Officer that a formula had been worked out by the Reference Board for the purposes of determining issues in dispute.
   - At the commencement of the strike no issue in dispute and no complaints had been brought to the notice of the Labour Officer, the Reference Board or the employers' union.
   - The reasons for the strike were unknown.
   - After the commencement of the strike the Workers Union referred the Labour Officer to a letter which the former had addressed to the employers' union in May last in which it was stated that the parties should come forward to discuss the same questions once more.
6. The Board, after mature consideration of all the relevant factors, was of the opinion that:
   - The repudiation of the tribunal's awards was a regrettable breach of moral obligation on the part of the union.
   - There was no merit in the reference by the GMMWU to its letter of May 1953.
   - the Government had taken every reasonable step to bring about a state of industrial peace by

     a) attempts at conciliation; b) setting up of an arbitration tribunal; and c) providing chairman, secretary and clerical staff for the smooth functioning of the Reference Board.

- Having provided the highest tribunal known in these parts at great expense to the State no encouragement should be given any attempt at reopening the issues in dispute so soon after determination by the tribunal.
- The real purpose of the strike appeared to be a drive to stir up unrest for reasons unknown to the Board, while claiming the protection of laws offered trade unions.
- In actual fact the workers concerned were regretably illiterate and ignorant of the purpose of the strike.[32]

The Board condemned the 1953–54 strike and stood solidly behind the Governor. In one sense they were defending vested interests; in another they could not see the reason for the industrial action. The strikers themselves were at a loss to know the real reasons for the strike. Understandably, then, by the end of February 1954, it had petered out. In all, some 55,000 man-days were lost.

On 28 April, two months after the strike ended, the Agricultural Employers Society announced a voluntary increase of 24¢ for men and 20¢ for women, bringing the daily basic wage to $1.44 and $1.20 respectively. In addition they stated that the customary indulgences and perquisites would be still enjoyed by workers. This was a belated attempt to meet some of the GMMWU's demands but given in such a way as to demonstrate that the employers had not given in to the union. The last thing employers wanted to see were strikes, for these not only upset the status quo and generally disturbed the peace, but were psychologically and economically damaging to the planter class and the tradition of gentility to which they were accustomed.

Apart from minor negotiations and sporadic disputes, the 1954 imbroglio was the last major industrial action by the GMMWU on behalf of its members in the decade 1950–60. The pre-eminence of the GMMWU in the trade union field entered a stage of decline, and its financial membership started to dwindle. In his report at the end of 1954 the Labour Officer stated that the union's financial membership was at its lowest ebb since 1950, but emphasized that a large percentage of workers, while refraining from paying fees, remained loyal to the President-General. This loyalty was to continue and have its real impact on the political fortunes of the movement. By 1955 it had become evident that the GMMWU's leadership was more preoccupied with politics than with trade unionism, and that its main forum of struggle had shifted to the Legislative Council. Such trade union activities as did take place after 1955 were subordinate to the political struggle; by 1955, politics had dethroned trade unionism.

## The Seamen and Waterfront Workers Union

After severing its branch membership with the Grenada Workers Union in May 1952, the Seamen and Waterfront Workers Union, representing stevedores and longshoremen, was registered on 22 July 1953. The main personality behind this 1952 secession was G.B.W. Otway. He had been a member of the Grenada Working Man's Association since 1928, an organization that included in its ranks such personalities as T.A. Marryshow, Arnold Williamson, John Fleming, L.B. Berkley, and E.A. 'Doc' Mitchell.

The first agreement signed by the Grenada Seamen and Waterfront Workers Union on behalf of the stevedores was on 1 January 1954. It provided for wage-increases of between 5% and 15% for the various categories of stevedores and longshoremen. This agreement was to have expired in 1955, but owing to the devastation of Grenada's economy by hurricane Janet in September 1955, it remained valid until 1957.

By 1956 the Union seems to have commanded great respect from the Labour Officer and the shipping agents. The Labour Officer wrote: 'The business of the union appears to be conducted along constitutional lines and in the field of collective bargaining it has earned a reputation for conducting its affairs with sound and accepted Trade Union principles.'[33] By this time it had secured affiliation with the International Transport Workers Federation, started a credit union among the workers and initiated an educational programme for its members. The membership was not large – 550 in 1960 – but though fifth in numerical strength it was first in financial strength – $6,194.00. In 1957 its hold in the waterfront was increased by securing membership of lightermen; and in that year employment on the waterfront was closed to non-union members. By 1958 they were the most highly organized, cohesive, industrious and serious trade union in the country.

## End of the GWU and the SJLP

By 1955 both the Grenada Workers Union and the St John's Labour Party existed more as friendly societies than as trade unions. The GWU still appeared to be unable to gain the workers' confidence after the dramatic setback it suffered at the birth of the GMMWU. The few who had retained their membership in the hope of financial assistance in sickness or death, neither belonged to any single trade nor had any stable mode of employment. Consequently, as a bargaining power, even for its financial members, the union was ineffective. It was affiliated to the International Confederation of Free Trade Unions and received financial assistance from that source.[34]

## Other Unions 1956–58

In 1956–58 four more unions appeared; two of these, the Commercial and Industrial Workers Union, registered in 1956, and the Grenada Technical and Allied Workers Union, were to become strong in the trade union world. By 1960 there were 13 trade unions (see Table 17.1) in Grenada, a massive increase since the 1950s. The GMMWU had by then changed its name to the Grenada Trades Union.

**Table 17.1 Registered Trade Unions in Grenada circa 1960**

| *Name of union* | *Registration date* | *No. of members* | *Filing of last return* | *Financial strength $* |
|---|---|---|---|---|
| Grenada (St John's) Labour Party/General Workers | 24 July 1941 | 657 | 1952 | 1,417.32 |
| Grenada Workers | 9 October 1946 | 400 | 1955 | 1,719.66 |
| Grenada Union of Teachers | 6 December 1960 | 400 | 1960 | 1,094.48 |
| Grenada Trades (Grenada Manual & Mental Workers) | 7 July 1950 | 8115 | 1960 | 674.66 |
| Grenada Seamen and Waterfront Workers | 22 June 1950 | 550 | – | 6,694.74 |
| Grenada Trades Union Council | 4 May 1955 | – | 1959 | 183.49 |
| Amalgamated Workers | 15 August 1956 | 53 | – | – |
| Commercial & Industrial Workers | 12 December 1956 | 402 | 1960 | 941.10 |
| Grenada Taxi & Motor Drivers | 1956 | now non-existent | 1955 | 84.42 |
| Grenada Agriculturists | 25 October 1952 | 141 | 1959 | 391.89 |
| Grenada Technical & Allied Workers | 2 June 1958 | – | 1958 | – |
| Grenada General Labour | 8 July 1958 | – | 1958 | – |
| Grenada Civil Service Association | 3 January 1959 | 164 | 1959 | 2,122.75 |

Source: Grenada, Ministry of Labour, *Special Compilation from Returns*, 1960

## Summary Conclusions 1940–60

During these two decades many significant events in the life of the working people in Grenada can be identified.

1. The traditional omnipotence of the employers of labour in Grenada was not only effectively challenged but broken.
2. The wage rate for the mass of workers increased from 34¢ and 28¢ per day for men and women respectively in 1940, to $1.56 and $1.40 per day by 1959. This represented a total increase of 360% and 400%. It may be argued that this was no significant achievement as workers' wages in a labour-surplus economy like Grenada often represent subsistence or sub-subsistence wages rather than the true value of the workers' labour. Nevertheless, this can be seen as a remarkable change since for 100 years prior to 1940 workers' wages had remained essentially static. Between 1939 and 1959 the consumer price index increased by 200%; thus, the real income of the labourer had increased by 160% and 200% respectively, representing some improvement in purchasing power.
3. Child labour (the employment of persons under 14 years old) was prohibited and compulsory education was introduced.
4. Workers' servility and subservience to employers was on the way out; workers prestige had clearly emerged.
5. The death rate among the population fell from 14.5 per 1,000 in the period 1934–39, to 13.8 in the 1948–56 period; the birth rate increased from 31.2 per 1,000 in the former period to 39.2 in the latter. This must be largely attributed to the campaigns conducted by the World Health Organization and UNICEF for the eradication of prevalent diseases, as well as programmes for better child care.
6. In 1939, about four laws only were concerned with protecting the worker, but by 1960 there were 14 laws specifically designed for this purpose.[35]

The foregoing analysis on the development of the trade union movement reveals the following:

1. The labour movement in Grenada was slow to develop; during the first ten years no major dispute or confrontation arose; this was certainly not due to the absence of working-class grievances but to the strategy of the existing unions in the 1939–49 decade.
2. The unions of the 1940s were prepared to work for change only within the existing colonial system using the means sanctioned by the establishment.
3. The appearance of the Grenada Manual and Mental Workers Union (GMMWU) in 1950 radicalized the trade union movement in Grenada and with it the strike became the institutionalized tool of workers' protest as well as the undisputed aid to bargaining.

4. The GMMWU rapidly rose to the pinnacle of pre-eminence in the trade union field, but by 1955 there were signs of its decline, mainly because politics began to take precedence over trade unionism within the leadership.
5. In terms of worker cohesion and solidarity, organization skills, seriousness and bargaining power, the Seamen and Waterfront Workers' Union took the previously pre-eminent place of the GMMWU.
6. Although by 1960 Grenada had 13 trade unions, the agricultural worker's lot was the worst of all the workers; he was still at the bottom of the income ladder, and the disparities between his standard of living and that of other workers, industrial, clerical and commercial, had barely been narrowed. Moreover, if the disparities between the living standards of the labourer and those of the estate owners had been minimized in any way, it was quite insignificant.

Changes occurred in working-class consciousness, in the willingness of the worker to fight for his cause, in social factors affecting his life, but there was no fundamental change in the relationship between the worker and the forces of production. Despite the industrial upheavals of 1950–51, he remained essentially a man dispossessed; the surplus value of his labour was appropriated both by local employers and foreign purchasers of Grenada's staples. The protection of unemployment benefits, insurance schemes, health plans, sickness benefits schemes, were virtually absent from his union's concerns, neither were employers asked to contribute to or initiate such schemes. In short, as has already been observed, the work of the unions and their achievements by 1960, significant though they were by and large, were simply palliatives to the real causes of working-class distress. These comprised not only employers' reluctance to award pay increases to workers, but a set of structural, historical and institutional factors that constitute the substructure upon which Grenada's economy and polity were built. Despite all the changes, 1960 saw the Grenadian worker still struggling to find his place in the sun. It was, therefore, hardly surprising that hundreds of workers migrated – especially in the two decades after the Second World War – in order to seek for better opportunities and for economic and professional improvement.

## Trade Unions and Industrial Disputes 1960–69

In any economic system where wages lag behind prices and workers have to finance fully all goods and services for themselves, a fundamental basis exists for constant employer-employee conflict and general industrial unrest.

In the 1960s four trade unions were particularly active: the GMMWU, the Grenada Technical and Allied Workers Union, the Commercial and Industrial Workers Union and the Grenada Seamen and Waterfront Workers Union. For the five years 1962 to 1967, the GMMWU's President-General, E.M. Gairy (who was Chief Minister in 1961 and whose government was dissolved in 1962 as a result of the 1961 report of a Commission of Enquiry into Public Expenditure in Grenada), made constant representations on behalf of workers. He was less interested in the welfare of the workers he represented than in exploiting their genuine grievances to satisfy his own selfish political aims and help him regain political power. He used the strike weapon as well as other forms of industrial action to harass the Government of the Grenada National Party, and their supporters and agents in business and industry, in order to deny them the opportunity to capture any significant portions of his supporters.

The significance of the industrial disputes in the 1960s lay neither in the scale nor in the prominence they assumed – and none reached the intensity or broad mass appeal of the 1951 general strike – but in the regularity and persistence with which they occurred. All unions were involved in one way or another, but the industrial activities of the GMMWU were by far the most ubiquitous, especially between 1962 and 1967. Since the mid-1950s the GMMWU leadership had subordinated the interests of the workers to its political ambitions; now out of power they once more turned to the union as a springboard to political prominence.

Employers generally were minimally concerned about the social and economic welfare of their employees. Workers existed essentially to produce goods and services and to promote the profit-maximizing motive of businesses, and when this was threatened by industrial disputes workers were seen as expendable, and conceptualized and treated merely as tools. Most employers in Grenada in the 1960s did not even entertain the idea of an escalator clause and unions' demands for cost-of-living allowances were obstinately resisted. Moreover, the social treatment of the worker, often spoken to and treated as a subhuman species, contributed to the unions' agitation for improved working conditions in the 1960s.

In the decade 1960–70 the GMMWU's prime targets were basically the GNP government; the Grenada Sugar Factory, of which the owners and managers were strong GNP supporters; and the owners of some large estates, who were hostile to the GULP, Gairy's party.

The GMMWU was particularly active between 1962 and 1967.[36] Gairy loved to rule but he was now out in the cold, and his only trump card was the union. The primary motive for his prolific industrial activities during these five years was to ensure his return to power in the 1967 elections. The improvement in workers' conditions as well as gaining redress for wrongs committed against union members were by and large secondary and generally incidental; it has often been alleged that Gairy used most of the union's funds at this time for his personal purposes.

In 1961, while still in power, there was only one recorded case of industrial dispute involving the GMMWU. From June to December 1962, however, there were five cases of industrial dispute between the union and employers. After the dissolution of the GULP government in 1961 over the misuse of funds, and after its recent defeat at the polls, it was leaving no stone unturned in building up its support. The non-fulfilment of the Unitary Statehood promise of the GNP provided the GMMWU with the opportunity to feed upon both the discontent and disappointment of workers.

On 29 January 1962, there was a spontaneous strike by 19 workers of Windsor Estate against the supervisor's ill-treatment of workers; the GMMWU immediately stepped in and supported the workers. Attempts by the Labour Department to settle the dispute between management and union failed; after one week, however, the workers returned to work of their own volition.

During the first quarter of 1962 the GMMWU submitted a draft agreement for higher wages and better working conditions for all agricultural workers. Five meetings were held under the chairmanship of the Labour Commissioner; full agreement was reached on many issues but none on wages. It was subsequently agreed that government be asked to set up a Commission of Enquiry to study and advise on the economy of the agricultural industry, with reference to its ability to pay higher wages. This Commission was set up only on 22 April 1963, and its enquiry completed on 29 June.

The Commission found that 50% of the estates made an average profit of 32%; 25% made less than 12.5% but greater than 2.5%; and 25% operated at a loss. As a result, an increase in wages from $1.80 to $1.91 for men and from $1.50 to $1.59 for women was recommended. The Commission's recommendations were based on the fact that whereas revenue had increased by 6% wages had remained stagnant over the same period.

The GMMWU had to call a one-day strike of its members at the Grenada Breweries in support of its claim for recognition and its wish to commence wage negotiations. After the Labour Department had been called in to verify the union's claim that the majority of workers were members it was recognized by the company. A wage agreement was eventually signed on 18 October 1962, along with agreements on clothing and equipment allowance, retroactive pay, vacation, sick leave and overtime for employees.

On 15 June 1962, IMEC Bahamas dismissed five workers. The union claimed that this was a lock-out and called out the other three workers, but promised to let the men return provided they were all re-employed by 20 June – an edict that IMEC complied with.

Cape International had built the Grenada Beach Hotel; the GMMWU alleged that the company intimidated its members and called all 58 workers out on a strike that lasted for 21 days. The company eventually agreed to apologise and the workers returned to their jobs.

The GMMWU's industrial activities became even more widespread during the next four years. For more than two years it was in open confrontation with the Grenada Sugar Factory, which was situated in the heart of Gairy's constituency, over wages and various cases of alleged victimization. In addition to the factory some 20 estates, the Agricultural Society of Grenada, and the Farmers' Union were also in constant conflict with the union over wages, pension schemes and dismissal of workers. In each case there was some form of industrial action; often, both sides were adamant, for political rather than industrial reasons.

There were also numerous disputes between the GNP government and the GMMWU. From 1964 to 1966 there were no fewer than 18 cases of industrial action and disputes involving the union and government. Most of these involved pay increases and improved working conditions for the daily paid workers in the various government departments, and also some monthly paid workers, for example, plant protection officers, employees in the Mental Hospital and of the District Boards. Gairy's main objective was to pressure the Government continuously so that workers would feel his interest was in helping them, and thus give him their vote in 1967; he also wanted to deprive the GNP of winning over daily-paid government-employed workers who had traditionally supported the GMMWU.

With victory at the polls in 1967 and the GULP back in power, the GMMWU's industrial activities were once more submerged and the proliferation of disputes subsided. Having achieved his aim, Gairy was no longer interested in the workers' struggles.

One particularly significant dispute occurred in 1968 involving the Grenada Farmers' Union (GFU); this too had a political dimension as the leadership of the Farmers' Union had strongly opposed Gairy in the 1967 elections.

In 1968 the GFU and the Society of Agricultural Employers merged. In the same year the 1966 agreement between GMMWU and the Society expired, and the GFU wrote to the GMMWU to inform it of the merger and requested a meeting to review the 1966 agreement in light of the new minimum wage law. The GMMWU ignored the request and in December 1968 the GFU sought once more to have the meeting called. It was eventually convened in January 1969 by the Minister of Labour but at the same time disturbances flared up on the Mt Rich and Mt Reuil estates and the GFU resorted to lock-out action. The matter was resolved eventually through arbitration. In many cases where disputes emerged and the lesser echelons in the unions could not solve them, a private intervention by Gairy, or at times the use of some political muscle usually brought about agreement.

The second very active union in the 1960s was that of the Technical and Allied Workers. In this decade its major confrontations were with two multinationals – the Grenada Electricity Services Ltd (CDC) and Geest Industries – and with the Government of Grenada. Between 1961 and 1967 there were no less than 40 cases of industrial dispute between this union and various employers. In addition to those already mentioned, the majority of these involved BWIA, Texaco, Cable and Wireless, and a few hoteliers: Grenada Beach, Calabash, Blue Horizons. Ten of these cases went before arbitration tribunals, nine of which involved the multi-nationals, Geest Industries Ltd, and Grenada Electricity Services Ltd.

A typical case of company obstinacy was the 1965 dispute between the Technical and Allied Workers Union and Grenlec. In a letter dated 22 October, the union informed the Administrator that a dispute was impending over the renewal of an agreement governing the working conditions of the technical workers in the Electricity Company. The Labour Commissioner called both parties together and each made its position clear. The union concluded that the Labour Commissioner failed to conciliate and that the matter should be referred to a tribunal in accordance with the Public Utility Undertakings Arbitration Ordinance No. 246.

The original tribunal was composed of A. Date, D. Knight and A. Norris Hughes; however, both parties, in a joint letter to the Administrator, suggested that the tribunal be changed to C. Renwick,

D. Richardson and D. Knight. The tribunal began its hearing in February and submitted a report signed by two members. The third member, representing the union, on seeing the report prepared by the chairman, withdrew, but his resignation from the tribunal was not received until some time after the receipt of the award. The union subsequently rejected the award as invalid, as the tribunal went outside its terms of reference. The union gave written notification to the company on 24 March that its members had been instructed to go slow as from that date. The company maintained that the award was valid and binding both on it and the workers, and declared its intention to implement the award on 7 May 1965; when the company attempted to do so the union instructed its workers to strike. At this point, the Government intervened and persuaded both parties to refer the matter to the court for a ruling. The court first ruled that the matter was valid, but upon appeal it was considered invalid on the grounds that three persons instead of five were appointed to the tribunal. Eventually the union's demand for a 30% wage increase was implemented.

Collective agreements in the 1960s were reached only after long and protracted discussions, and at times after confrontation between union and employer. There were two exceptions to this: a) the Seamen and Waterfront Workers Union and the shipping agents; and b) the Commercial and Industrial Workers Union (CIWU) and Everybody's Stores Ltd. There was always minimum delay in effecting an agreement between the latter parties. Moreover, of the 20-odd cases of industrial disputes from September 1961 to March 1966 between CIWU and employers, not one reached an arbitration tribunal. The relationship between the managers/owners of these businesses and the union's bosses partly accounted for this; a second factor was the bargaining leverage of dockers and the varied pressures they could apply to get their demands met.

Examples of protracted disputes were:

- government and CIWU for higher wages and improved working conditions of attendants: 1.5 years (1965–66);
- Geest Industries and TAWU for clerical staff (9 months);
- BWIA and TAWU for clerical staff (9 months);
- Grenlec and TAWU for wages for electricity workers: 2 years (1964–66).

The fewest cases of confrontation in the 1960s were between the Grenada Union of Teachers and government, the Civil Service Association and government, and the SWWU and the shipping agents. Confrontation in these cases was invariably over the question of victimization.

The long list of disputes in the 1960s attests to the fact that industrial peace is difficult to attain in a polity where the mass of workers do not have a workers' government to represent them – not in name but in practice. When a symbiotic relationship exists between government and employers as it did in Grenada in the 1960s and later in the 1970s, it is increasingly difficult for the worker to achieve significant gains.

The term 'Labour Party' in government means nothing. It is just a label, and a useless one; unless that party defends the interests and upholds the economic and civil rights of the working class it is simply a label. Workers' interests can be consistently and truly defended only when a genuine workers' and farmers' government emerges, one devoted to the workers' cause and aligned in no way to big business, the *nouveaux riches* and big merchants and planters.

## Tubal Uriah Butler

One Grenadian who made an invaluable contribution to the workers' struggle and left a permanent mark on the trade union movement in the region was Tubal Uriah Butler (Buzz); he was born in Grenada in 1891 and died in Trinidad in 1978. In the First World War he served in the West India Regiment, and greatly admired its Commander, Captain Andrew Cipriani, who, in 1918, started the first serious trade union in Trinidad, The Trinidad's Workingman's Association. When Butler returned to Grenada he joined the Grenada Representative Government Movement and in 1919 founded the Grenada Union of Returned Soldiers. These men had laid their lives on the line to fight for king and empire, but on their return to Grenada found themselves neglected, unemployed and regarded with contempt by the Grenadian upper class whose lives they had gone to war to protect.[37]

While serving abroad many of these ex-servicemen had come into contact with progressive literature and thought, and probably this influence, combined with a steep rise in the cost of living at this time sparked off their unrest. In January 1920, this group openly protested against the conditions under which they and the poorer classes in Grenada lived. This protest culminated in a series of disturbances and an attempt to burn down St George's. Simultaneously, there were numerous burglaries in St George's; many persons were sent threatening letters by a body calling themselves the 'T.T.T. Gang'.

Rewards of £100 and £250 were offered by the Government and by representatives of the Associated Fire Insurance Co respectively, to anyone providing information leading to the arrest and conviction of the guilty persons. A body of special constables was immediately enrolled, mainly from the staff of government departments, principal firms and offices. At the same time measures were taken to increase the police force by 50, thus restoring it to its former strength.[38] The Food Control Committee was also re-established to control the prices of foodstuffs, mainly those consumed by the poorer classes.

In the following year, Butler, like many other Grenadians, migrated to Trinidad. He found work in the oil belt, but in 1929 was injured and permanently lamed in an industrial accident. He joined the Trinidad Labour Party (TLP) led by Cipriani, but soon found his approach to be unacceptable. In 1930 Butler led a 60-mile hunger march from the oil belt to Port-of-Spain, as a challenge to Cipriani's constitutional approach to articulate oppressed workers' grievances. Convinced that Cipriani's methods were gaining little for the workers, Butler left the TLP and formed his own party – the British Empire Workers and Home Rule Party.

In 1936 and 1937 Butler went up and down the oil belt, rallying people to his banner. He was a magnificent, impassioned and down-to-earth orator. His ability to arouse the masses was supreme. A charismatic leader of genuine working-class background, far more intimately linked to the masses than Cipriani, he spoke their language and articulated bread-and-butter issues with passion. Butler also had a very strong religious and messianic style. He believed that God had appointed him to lead the people out of the wilderness of oppression and often used religious metaphors in his speeches. Addressing a mass gathering of workers on one occasion he said:

> After years and years of weeping and groanings, untold miseries and complainings, prayers and petitions, the toiling masses of this colony prayed to the God of Justice and Fair Play, Freedom and Liberty, the God of their ancient and incomparably glorious African forefathers, to send them a leader. He came in the name of the Spiritual Lion of the tribe of Judah, the Great King Jesus, in a new political organization known as the British Empire Workers and Citizens Home Rule Party of Trinidad where he took evidence of the sufferings of his people. Let us hope that God in His mercy will not desert his suffering black children.

Butler told his listeners that unemployment and low wages were the work of the evil white men who controlled the Colony – above all, the oil magnates. But he agreed to take strike action only after all alternatives had failed – that is, appeals to the Governor (whom he begged on his knees to intervene with the oil companies) and to the employers. Only when Butler became convinced that British fair play was not extended to loyal citizens of the Empire did he yield to the demands for an oil workers' strike; even then the plan was for a peaceful sit-down strike to paralyse the oilfields. It was the blunders and insensitivity of the police and employers that transformed the peaceful strike of 19 June 1937 into a violent and bloody confrontation in which 14 people were killed and 59 injured.

The underlying causes of the strike and riots were economic, racial and political. Undoubtedly, however, they had been invoked by Butler's activities in the oilfields that served to crystallize and articulate the workers' grievances and to mobilize them for joint action. His arrest was a clumsy reaction on the part of the authorities, since it served only to immortalize him in the eyes of his followers and of generations to come.

Butler was tried and convicted for sedition and sentenced to two years in prison. He was released early in 1939, and interned at the outbreak of the Second World War, but again released in 1940. He then tried to regain leadership of the working-class movement, and especially of the Oilfields Workers Trade Union (OWTU), formed in 1937 by Rienzi. He felt that the OWTU's leadership was denying him the power and glory which was rightly his, and in 1941 he engineered a strike to discredit the union. As a result he was again detained (1941–45), as the colonial government considered that he was endangering the British war effort by jeopardizing vital oil supplies. His long years in jail added to his popularity – he was a martyr in the workers' cause – but his absence during the crucial years meant that leadership inevitably passed to others.

He was released at the end of the War, and offered a top post by the OWTU, but he was more interested in leadership. In 1946 he again organized a general strike in which his followers stormed the Red House; the OWTU expelled him as it considered these actions to be anti-union.

Butler then formed a loose organization known as the Butler Party, which contested the 1946 elections (the first held on universal suffrage in Trinidad) and won three seats. After 1946 he tried to forge political links with the Indians, and in the 1950 elections his party won six seats, four of which were won by Indian candidates.

But although the Butler Party was the only group in the Legislative Council, by a piece of constitutional engineering it was denied a single seat in the Executive Council. The British officials, and moderate politicians such as Gomes, were concerned to deny Butler the legitimacy that office would have given him; they considered him to be too uneducated and lacking in administrative skills, to take office. 'Butlerism' became a spent force. The alliance between him and Indian politicians fell apart. Butler was in Britain for much of the

*Tubal Uriah 'Buzz' Butler*

period 1950–56 and his movement was decisively defeated in the 1956 election. Eric Williams and the PNM had arrived in the political arena and that arrival eclipsed the Butler Party.[39]

Butler's role in 1937 was one of the great historical significance not only for Trinidad but for the entire British West Indies. He was not a great constructive political leader but his actions helped to bring the working class on to the centre stage of national life.

NOTES

Full citations only given where work does not appear in the Bibliography.

1. Henry, *Labour Relations and Industrial Conflict,* pp. 36–37.
2. Council Paper No. 8, 1938. *Report of the Commission appointed to enquire into the economics of the various classes of wage earners with special reference to the agricultural labourer*, 1937, p. 7.
3. Council Paper No. 14, 1934. *Report of the Commission of Enquiry on the conditions of children and young persons,* 1938.
4. *Laws of Grenada*, Vol. II. pp. 2240–2261.
5. *West India Royal Commission's Report*, 1945, p. 321, also pp. 190–213.
6. Council Paper No. 13, 1945, *Report of the Committee set up to look into the Grenada Sugar Factory Ltd.* 1945. Report and enquiry were done by Dr. C.Y. Shepherd.

7. Council Paper No. 16, 1945, *Report of the Labour Department for the years 1942 and 1944*, 1945. This union was first called the St John's Labour Party/General Workers Union. Its headquarters was in St John's.
8. *The West Indian*, Vol XXXLV, No. 214, 24 November 1948. Council Paper No. 1, 1950. *Report of the Labour Department for 1948*, 1951.
9. *The West Indian,* Vol. XXXLV, No. 214, 24 November 1948.
10. *Report of the Labour Department for 1948*, 1951.
11. *West Indian,* Vol. XXXLV, No. 214, 24 November 1948.
12. Ibid. Nos. 214 and 215, 24 and 25 November 1948.
13. Ibid.
14. Ibid.
15. Ibid. Vol. XXXLV, No. 226, 12 December 1948.
16. *Report of the Labour Department for 1949,* 1951.
17. Ibid.
18. Council Paper No. 6, 1951, *Report of the Labour Department for 1950–51.*
19. Ibid.
20. Ibid.
21. Council Paper No. 4, *Report on the Labour Department for 1951.*
22. Ibid.
23. Council Paper No. 4, 1954, *Report of the Labour Department for 1951.* Council Paper No. 6, 1954, *Report of the Labour Department for 1952.*
24. Ibid.
25. Ibid.
26. Council Paper No. 4, 1951, *Report on the Labour Disputes for the year 1951.*
27. Council Paper No. 6, 1954.
28. Council Paper No. 7, 1954. *Report of the Labour Department for 1954,* 1956.
29. Ibid.
30. Ibid.
31. Ibid.
32. Ibid.
33. Council Paper No. 10, 1958, *Report of the Labour Department for 1956.*
34. Council Paper No. 9, 1957, *Report of the Labour Department for 1955.*
35. 1. Department of Labour Ordinance 1940 (No. 6 of 1940) and subsequent amendments and regulations.

 2. Wages Council Ordinance 1951 (No. 4 of 1951). The Wages Regulation (clerks) Order 1960 and the Wages Council Order (Minor Industrial Undertakings) 1960 (SRO No. 32 of 1960) and amendment SRO No. 36 of 1960.

 3. Recruiting of Workers Ordinance 1939 (No. 17 of 1939) and subsequent amendments.

 4. Workmen's Compensation Ordinance of 1934 (No. 19 of 1934) and amending ordinance 1954.

 5. The Employer and Servants Ordinance 1936 (No. 8 of 1936) and a subsequent amendment.

 6. Employment of Women. Young Persons and Children Ordinance 1934 (No. 8 of 1934) and subsequent amendments.

 7. Trade Union and Trades Disputes Ordinance 1934 (No. 20 of 1951) and Trade Unions Rules 1952 (SRO No. 8 of 1952).

 8. Accidents and Occupation Disease Ordinance 1951 providing for the notification to the Labour Department of accidents and occupational diseases.

 9. The Public Utility Undertakings and Public Health Arbitration Ordinance 1951 (No. 3 of 1951).

 10. Trade Disputes Ordinance (No. 5 of 1943).

 11. Licence (Amendment) Rules 1958 (SRO No. 13 of 1958).

 12. Labour Clauses Ordinance, 1960.

 13. Factories Ordinance 1958 which provided for the promotion of the health and welfare of persons employed in factories.

14. The Labour Commissioner was empowered to see that the provisions of these laws were observed and was vested with the authority to enforce them through the courts.

36. *Reports of the Labour Department 1955–68.*
37. In December 1920, the Governor dissolved the Central Contingent Committee established in 1918 to assist ex-servicemen, as no provision had been made in the 1920 Estimates for the Committee's work.
38. *Government Gazette*, Vol. 38, No. 14, 19 March 1920.
39. *Caribbean Emancipators*, 1976.

# 18

# *Expansion of Education in the 20th Century: 1900–60*

## School Enrolment and Attendance

One problem that plagued education in Grenada in the 19th century and continued to do so for much of the 20th century, was the low level of attendance in schools. This, when added to the already small number of children of school age on roll, meant that not more than one-third of Grenadian children were receiving an education (see Table 18.1).

By 1931, 59 out of every 100 children were not receiving any education, and average attendance for the first quarter of the 20th

**Table 18.1 School Enrolment and Attendance 1871–1931**

| *Year* | *Population age 5–15* | *No. on roll* | *Average attendance* | *No. on roll as % of age group 5–15* | *Average attendance as % of 5–15 population* |
|---|---|---|---|---|---|
| 1871 | 9,400 | 2,529 | – | 26 | – |
| 1881 | 11,000 | 2,106 | 1,401 | 19 | 13 |
| 1891 | 13,500 | 6,155 | 3,246 | 46 | 24 |
| 1901 | 17,000 | 9,731 | 4,744 | 57 | 28 |
| 1911 | 17,900 | 9,724 | 4,594 | 54 | 25 |
| 1921 | 17,700 | 9,435 | 5,847 | 53 | 33 |
| 1931 | 20,000 | 13,250 | 8,260 | 66 | 41 |

Source: Grenada, *Education Reports and Census data*, 1871–1931

century was generally about 50% of the number of students enrolled, increasing to about 60% during the period 1901–30 – an average annual rate of less than 2%. The percentage of average attendance increased between 1881 and 1931, but it was still unsatisfactory. The improvement over the 1920–30 decade could be attributed to the effects of the 1920 Compulsory Education Ordinance, which made it mandatory for all children aged 6 to 14 to attend school.

## Continued Dominance of the Church's Role

Whereas during much of the 19th century the Church of England controlled the majority of primary schools, by the first quarter of the 20th century the Roman Catholics controlled the greater number – some 50% – of all schools in Grenada. In 1900 there was a total of 40 primary schools: 18 Roman Catholic, nine government and seven Church of England. Fifty percent of the children enrolled, and a little less than 50% of those attending were in the Roman Catholic schools. Three decades later the situation was virtually unchanged: of a total of 58 schools (18 more than in 1900) 27 were Roman Catholic, 10 were government and 14 were Church of England. Of the 13,250 students enrolled, 6,656 were in the Roman Catholic schools, and of the 8,260 actually in attendance some 4,026 were attending Roman Catholic schools.

Although government's contribution to these schools increased absolutely from £5,807 per annum in 1900 to £8,787 by 1930, its average contribution per child remained the same: about £1/1s per annum (see Table 18.2) During these 30 years the number of government schools increased by one; Catholic schools by nine; Anglican schools by seven; Wesleyans by one, and Presbyterians none at all. The Wesleyans ran five schools and the Presbyterians two. Their role in the field of education had become static, but the equally static role of the government was more serious as it limited the success of the school system and helped to nullify many of the new measures government itself had taken for popular education.

**Table 18.2 Government Contribution to Education per Child[1]**

| | | | |
|---|---|---|---|
| 1901 | £1 4s 5d | 1920 | £1 10s 5d |
| 1905 | £1 3s 2d | 1925 | £0 19s 2d |
| 1910 | £1 1s 3d | 1930 | £1 1s 2d |
| 1915 | £1 3s 5d | | |

## Education Changes in the Early 20th Century

Among the many measures taken were those aimed at improving the performance of students and teachers. Teachers, in addition to fixed salaries, received incentive bonuses to help encourage high attendances. By 1900, in addition to their regular wages (£40 for a first-class teacher, £30 for a second-class and £20 for a third-class), they received 6/- per child in the preliminary standard who had made 200 attendances per annum, a grant of 2/- per pass in each subject in Standards 1 to 2, a grant of 2/- per pass in Standards 3 to 7 – the whole amount of school fees collected. School principals continued to receive £15 per annum for house rent, or free quarters in denominational schools.

In 1906, an Ordinance was passed to amend and consolidate the law relating to primary education; this failed to recognize infant schools, and only teachers in government schools were allowed to apply for a pensionable allowance, thus causing great dissatisfaction among teachers in the denominational schools. A protest was lodged through Archbishop Flood and, as a result, the Ordinance was suspended the following year. Another objection raised against it was that it took the power of appointing and dismissing staff away from those managers who were ministers of religion and gave it to the government. In 1907 this Ordinance was superseded by another. Infant schools were recognized as grant-in-aid and a reclassification of all primary schools was made in order to promote a healthier system. The new classification consisted of Combined, Lower Division and Infant. The salaries of principals were now related directly to the kind of school in which they taught. Bonuses were given to principals for successfully training pupil teachers and for successful examination results.[2] The 1907 ordinance also provided for a pensionable allowance for all teachers except those in infant schools; this was welcomed by principals, particularly in the denominational schools.

The conditions of service of primary school teachers and those of the secondary schools reflected the class structure of Grenadian society at the time. Not only did secondary school teachers enjoy more social prestige in the community but they were well remunerated for their services. For example, in 1910, with only 26 pupils, mainly sons of rich Coloured and middle-class families, the principal of the Grenada Boys' Secondary School received a salary of £200 per annum plus a number of allowances. In 1911 the school was reorganized and as a result the number of pupils rose to 70.

The principals of the other secondary schools, though less favourably treated, were nonetheless better off than the best-paid principals in the primary system; these were still dependent on voluntary contributions to operate. St Joseph's Convent Secondary School received an annual government grant of £100, while the Victoria Girls' High School received £50. The latter was closed in 1911, reopened in January 1912 under the name of the Grenada Girls' High School, closed again in 1916, and later reopened under the directorship of the Church of England and given the name the Church of England High School (CEHS). Again, in 1946 under new management, it was renamed the Anglican High School.

Among the many events in the field of education in the 1911–20 decade four are worthy of mention.

1. The inclusion of religious instruction in schools for the last half-hour of the pre-luncheon session; initiated in 1913, this has continued to this day.
2. The establishment, in 1916, of the annual Grenada Scholarship to the value of £175 tenable for five years at any university in the British Empire. The successful candidate was chosen from the results of the University of Cambridge Senior Examination; suspended on 1 January 1924, this scholarship was restored in 1926 on a biennial basis, and the age limit raised from 10 to 19.
3. In November 1915, the Grenada Boys' Secondary School was brought under total control of government and new rules to govern its management were drawn up. This has already been detailed.[3]
4. The abolition in 1917 of all gratuities and result grants and the payment of better monthly salaries to elementary teachers.

These new increases carried with them certain conditions and obligations which, if not fulfilled, could lead to a partial loss of salary. The school had to ensure that the number of pupils eligible for an examination was 50% of the number on roll; that the number present for examinations in extra subjects was 15% of the total; that there was a 90% pass rate in the three 'Rs'; and that there was a 60% pass rate in other subjects. These conditions became a source of constant protest as many of the circumstances that affected the achievement of these targets were outside the control and ambit of the teachers. These conditions were subsequently changed.

## Education in Grenada After 100 Years

The period 1924–30 marked the end of a 100-year attempt to provide education for the mass of the Grenadian working people. An examination of the 1927 census reveals that out of a population of 56,515 aged five years and above, 29,944 were able to read and write, 4,710 to read only. The approximate number of illiterates was, therefore, 31,811 or 56% of population aged five years and over.[5] Thus the achievement of 100 years was very limited.

By 1930, education was seen as one of the three vehicles for vertical class mobility; in order of priority these were: colour and Caucasian features, income and wealth, and, lastly, education.

Education was dominated by middle-class ideals, and thus largely academic, as the aspirations of sons of the middle class, and consequently the whole population, were geared towards either law, or medicine, or business – the three professions with the highest potential for class mobility. Technical education was considered to be inferior and moreover, *infra dig* for the sons and daughters of the Grenadian middle class, many of whom were forced by social pressures to follow careers for which they had neither inclination nor ability. For many, to complete their training was a hard struggle, but once attained, the certificate conferred and not the ability to do the job was the key to economic power, political influence and social prestige. In essence, for the next 25 years, education continued to foster élitism and to glorify the ideals, values and traditions of upper- and middle-class Grenadian society.

The principles governing colonial education were generally accepted but from time to time some people expressed dissatisfaction with many of its aspects. Recommendations submitted by committee after committee were never implemented, usually for financial or sectarian reasons.

## The 1928 Education Committee and the New System

In 1928, a committee appointed by the Governor to consider the possibility of reorganizing the educational system recommended the establishment of five government and three denominational senior schools in all the main centres of Grenada. Other recommendations included incremental salaries for head teachers, higher salaries for other teachers, the abolition of separate infant schools, and a new system of staffing.

This report was rejected by the wholly denominational Board of Education, which, on 31 May 1929, produced an alternative report entitled *Views of the Board*. This report recommended that all senior schools except those in St George's – where it was proposed to set up one Anglican and one Roman Catholic mixed senior school – should be removed from government control. The salary scales suggested by the committee were modified and pensions were demanded for headmasters of denominational schools.

Government accepted these proposals, except in so far as it insisted upon setting up a senior schools of its own in St Andrew's. There was a violent campaign against this decision but the Government stood firm, pointing out that to establish a Roman Catholic senior school in St Andrew's would mean additional expenditure. Father R. Devas and Canon Fowler each asked to have denominational senior schools in St Andrew's in order to prevent the government setting up a senior school. This meant that the Anglicans' combined school at St Giles would have to become a junior school, as would the Catholics' combined school at Munich. With great reluctance the Board agreed to this proposal provided that the Wesleyans retained their combined school: the government also agreed to this compromise. Thus in the 1930s the Government met stiff resistance from the various denominations when it attempted to play a more dominant role in education and to increase its control over schools. Father Devas had demanded a senior school, only in order that Catholic children in the upper standards of three large Catholic schools would not be compelled to continue their education in a government school.

The new system of education agreed upon between government and the various denominations was passed by the Legislative Council on 13 March 1931. The scheme provided for denominational senior schools in St George's, the Anglicans being asked to reduce their combined school at St Paul's to a junior; similarly the Catholics were asked to sacrifice Morne Jaloux. There were to be two denominational senior schools in St Andrew's, the Anglicans having had to reduce St Giles and Holy Innocents to a junior status, and the Catholics, Munich, La Fillette and Mt St Eryan's. The classification of schools after the 1931 ordinance was as follows: 1. Manual Training Centres. 2. Senior schools. 3. Combined schools. 4. Junior schools. 5. Advanced junior schools. 6. Assisted schools. 7. Infant schools.

1. The manual training centres, established in important centres of population, gave practical instruction in handicraft, agriculture and other industrial occupations.
2. In the senior schools classes were held for more advanced pupils who had passed qualifying Standard III examinations. The average attendance of these schools was to be not less than 75%.
3. In combined schools, in addition to provision for junior students, separate classes were conducted for more advanced pupils. The

pupils left this school at age 14 unless they passed the Standard IV examination.

4. In junior schools, reading, writing and arithmetic and other subjects prescribed in the code were taught up to Standard III to pupils aged 6 to 14 years of age.
5. Advanced junior schools, by permission of the Director of Education, in addition to the tuition prescribed for a junior school provided further instructions as prescribed in the code.
6. Assisted schools were those which had received a grant in the previous year and in which the average attendance for the year ended 30 September was below the minimum required for a junior school but not less than 30. The mode and type of instruction in this school was similar to that in the junior school.
7. Infant schools provided instruction to children between the ages of four and nine.

Table 18.3 shows the numbers of schools in Grenada in 1931. In that year, the long awaited Head Teachers' Pensions Ordinance was passed by the government,[6] and many head teachers who had been in teaching for more than 40 years took this opportunity to resign.

**Table 18.3 Schools in Grenada 1931**

| | | | | | Total |
|---|---|---|---|---|---|
| Government | – | 4 Junior | 5 Combined | – | 9 |
| Anglican | 2 Senior | 7 Junior | 4 Combined | 1 Infant | 14 |
| Roman Catholic | 2 Senior | 10 Junior | 9 Combined | 8 Infant | 29 |
| Wesleyan | – | 1 Junior | 3 Combined | 1 Infant | 5 |
| Presbyterian | – | – | 2 Combined | – | 2[7] |

## Education in the 1930s and 1940s

About this time, the *Royal Reader*, the main reading text since 1883, was replaced by the *West Indian Readers*. The Director of Education observed that:

> It is pleasing to record that the old Royal Reader is gradually creeping out of our schools to the great advantage of both teachers and pupils. An old bogey here and there still persists in trying to retain this incubus, but for the most part the progressive headmasters are adopting the West Indian Readers.[8]

Education in Grenada benefited from the Commission of Enquiry carried out in 1932, from 11 to 18 December, by A. Mayhew of the Colonial Office and F.C. Marriot, Director of Education in Trinidad. The report for Grenada, which was laid before the House on 10 May 1933,[9] condemned the salaries paid to teachers as totally inadequate to maintain a status appropriate to their profession and as inconsistent with their qualifications. The Commission went on to recommend that: Grenadian teachers should be trained in Trinidad instead of at the Rawle Institute in Barbados; a modern secondary school should be established; a domestic science centre should be set up; manual training centres should be expanded; and primary schools should be properly inspected. In 1935 the last Grenadian teacher was trained at the Rawle Institute. By 1936 some of the recommendations were being implemented. From that year all teachers were sent for training to Trinidad. By that year, too, three more training centres were set up: the Sauteurs, Birchgrove and the St John's Centres. These, plus the St George's Centre, which had been set up in 1931, brought the number of such centres to four.

There were now 250 teachers (60 headteachers, 53 assistant teachers, 118 pupil teachers and 19 monitors) catering for 66 schools (29 Roman Catholic, 16 Government, 14 Anglican, five Wesleyan and two Methodist). School attendance was similar to that of the 1920s; out of a total enrolment of 13,343 the average attendance was 8,253 or 62%. The Roman Catholic schools accounted for 50% of both enrolment and daily attendance.

The four secondary schools catered for 478 pupils; the Grenada Boys' Secondary School (GBSS) was the outstanding boys' school, and St Joseph's Convent the outstanding girls' school. The Model School catered for children whose parents preferred not to send them to the free elementary schools but were unable to pay the fees of the other secondary schools. The children of the poor were deprived of secondary education, as government gave very few scholarships – 20 per annum, eight for boys tenable at the GBSS and 12 for girls, six tenable at the Church of England High School and six at St Joseph's Convent. These schools continued to cater predominantly for the more privileged classes in Grenada.

An Island Scholarship, which provided for education at a British university, was awarded every two years to the pupil who obtained the best grade in the London Matriculation, and later the Higher School Certificate. Despite the fact that children from the lower classes were outnumbered in the secondary schools, 50% of the Island Scholarships awarded between 1930 and 1951 were won by boys from the lower classes, three of whom were from very poor homes.

The remaining 50% of these scholarships were awarded to middle- and upper-class children, 70% of whom studied law and medicine, professions noted for their social and financial prestige.

In the 1930s secondary school pupils wrote three external examinations, set and graded by Examination Syndicates in the Universities of London and Cambridge. They included the Cambridge Junior (dropped in 1948) usually written by students in Form 4, Cambridge Senior, by Form 5, and the London Matriculation – replaced by the Higher School Certificate (HSC) in 1946 – by the upper forms. In 1964 both SC and HSC were replaced by the GCE 'O' and 'A' Levels.

In the 1930s and 1940s only those secondary school pupils who passed a qualifying examination were allowed to enter for the external examinations. Despite this, the aggregate results were not significantly better than they are today when rigid screening is no longer observed. Additionally, the size of classes, the general atmosphere and the teacher-pupil ratio were all much better than they are today.

In 1933 there was a 46% pass rate from the three leading schools in the Cambridge Senior and 50% in the Cambridge Junior. In the 1935 Cambridge Junior there was a 37.5% pass rate from these three schools, and a 55% in the Cambridge Senior; in 1936 56% passed the Cambridge Senior and 41% the Cambridge Junior level, and five out of seven passed the London Matriculation, with Sydney Gun-Munro of GBSS awarded the Island Scholarship. Ten years later there was a 64% pass rate in the Junior, a 61% in the Senior and an 88% in the HSC.

Despite an apparently steady performance at the secondary level in the 1940s, most children were still not receiving a meaningful education. Not only were secondary schools exclusively academic, preparing their students for the professions of law, medicine, engineering and education, but only about 2% of primary school children reached secondary schools. Most school children were immersed in the Three Rs, learning by rote and regurgitating material, of which much was irrelevant and unintelligible to them.

By the 1940s education in Grenada had made no significant impact on the social life of the people. There was a Board of Education but it seldom met; there was the Director of Education, who in late 1937 became Chairman of the Board when the post of Director became obsolete; four schools had been built in 1936–37 (Hillsborough Government, Petit Martinique RC. St George's Methodist and St Paul's Government) but these were open buildings with no separate classrooms. Teachers often had to shout against each other to be heard in class. The schools were disorganized, the curriculum was irrelevant, but most of all education lacked a clear perspective.

Many teachers were untrained and academically poor. Pupils were often absent from school helping with household chores or working to help support the family, as children were generally abandoned by their fathers, and mothers had to be both housewives and breadwinners.

In 1939 there were 29 class I headteachers, 20 class II and 4 class III, assisted by 100 assistant teachers of whom most were untrained and used the whip as their greatest teaching aid. There were also 146 pupil-teachers and 30 monitors, the majority of whom were largely from Classes VII and VIII and had to write four local examinations: 1st, 2nd, 3rd and 4th year – to become certificated; but this did not mean they had received teacher-training. An average class consisted of 50–60 children, presenting a formidable task for untrained teachers, and leading to the destruction of any inclination to learn for the majority of students, with school representing a life of torture.

At the turn of the century one or two teachers were sent to Rawle Training College in Barbados; by late 1940s they were sent to the Government Training College in Trinidad; usually the candidate who won first place in the 4th year teachers' examination was sent.[10] This provision for training was grossly inadequate.

## The Hammond Report

This was the situation S.A. Hammond, Education Advisor to the Comptroller for Development and Welfare, found when he visited Grenada in 1942. The British government, influenced by the general sentiments of the 1939 Royal Commission, had set up a Colonial Development and Welfare Fund to assist the British West Indies to build up a social infrastructure. Hammond's area was educational policy and administration. He carried out an investigation and made the following recommendations:

1. Schools should be divided into three categories, according to age:
   (a) pre-school, i.e. those children below 6 years for whom play centres should be organized with the help of the community;
   (b) age group 6–12; this should be made the compulsory school age;
   (c) age group 12–16; this should be classified as the voluntary school age for which senior schools or departments should be provided.
2. There should be secondary school courses for prospective teachers from 15 to 18 years of age.

3. A student-teacher system should be initiated.
4. The number of pupil-teachers should be increased in order to reduce the size of classes and to permit them to study for half of the working day.
5. Vacation courses should be organized for pupil-teachers.
6. Supervising teachers should be appointed to assist pupil-teachers.
7. Schools should be reorganized in such a way as to ensure that after age 12 students would be in the senior department.

## *Colonial Development and Welfare and Education*

Funds for the implementation of the Hammond recommendations were provided by the Colonial Development and Welfare (CDW) organization. A sum of £1,258 was given to cover the cost of the Education Officer's salary, travelling allowance, pension, passage for family and other incidentals. A grant of £14,355 was given for the Grenada Teachers' Training Scheme, of which £2,019 was spent in 1945. This was to cover the cost of training five supervisory teachers and two additional teachers for the customary two years at the Government Training College in Trinidad; in 1946 CDW sponsored training for four out of nine teachers in Trinidad. It was also to finance the cost of 16 boys and girls' entering the local secondary schools as free scholarship holders; the money covered maintenance allowances, the provision of free books and special tuition at the GBSS to prepare them for pupil teacherships leading to first class teachers. The cost of an extra master at the GBSS for this purpose was also covered.

In 1945 eight boys entered the GBBS for the three-year course to become Intending Teachers; two girls were at the Anglican High School and six at St Joseph's Convent undergoing similar training. Six supervisory teachers returned to Grenada in 1945, five of whom were placed one in each of five pupil-teacher training centres around the island.

In 1946 there were 100 extra pupil-teachers in training, half of the cost (£1,500) being met from CDW funds. In 1947 a sixth pupil-teacher training centre was established. The CDW also sponsored and subsidized seven adult education institutes; a school building programme; the institution of vocational training; and the grant of a medical scholarship valued at £1,785 for five years. CDW also made a grant of £6,980 for such school supplies as books, stationery and minor pieces of equipment.

The ten-year education plan which came out in 1946 helped to put the contribution of CDW into a framework and to give it a perspective. According to the Education Officer, the plan was to cost the government £305,750. Among its many aims were: the provision of a sufficient number of teachers and elementary schools for the 6–14 age group; the provision of vocational and professional training; and the provision of opportunities for adult education. The plan as outlined made provision for:

- £13,000 for Education Officer and staff;
- £16,000 for books and stationery;
- £50,000 for teacher-training – nine teachers in Trinidad, 48 Intending Teachers at Secondary Schools, and seven Supervising Teachers. It planned on training 400 teachers between 1947 and 1952;
- £130,000 for school buildings to house 12,000 children of school age;
- £30,000 for secondary school buildings;
- £10,000 for a Technical High School;
- £31,250 for school farms;
- £2,500 for vocational training;
- £10,000 for adult education;
- £21,000 for woodwork and machine shop;
- £3,000 for library services;
- £2,000 for visual education.

This plan was to be submitted to the Secretary of State for his approval. By 1949 approval was still awaited. Very few of the plan's projections were ultimately realized.

Meantime a model school and farm – the Grand Roy school – built under the CDW Scheme at a cost of £11,400, based upon the recommendations of Hammond, was completed. With 11 acres of land attached, it was given £5,000 under CDW to establish and run the school farm. It was the first school of its kind in Grenada, and in opening it, the Governor, Sir Arthur Grimble said:

> The curriculum of the school will establish a determined breakaway from the black-coat and white collar ambitions which historically have restricted, biassed and misdirected educational policy here no less than elsewhere in the empire. The main object of this new educational instrument will be to turn out boys and girls both keenly aware of the dignity of the land, the home, the workshop and prepared to use to their own and their country's best advantage the opportunities which nature herself has set at the door of every rural community.[11]

It was proposed that five more school farms, based on the Grand Roy model, should be built during the ensuing years at a cost of £31,250.

In 1948, owing to old schools being renovated and new ones built there were 2,270 more places available in the elementary schools. In that same year the training scheme of the extra pupil-teachers matured, as 46 pupil-teachers passed their 3rd year examination thereby qualifying as student-teachers, as the pupil-teacher was to be replaced by a student-teacher system and the CDW Scheme for producing qualified student-teachers was gradually reduced (see Table 18.4).

Thus, by 1952 there were to be no more CDW Intending Teachers in secondary schools provided for by CDW funds, but it was hoped that local government would continue to award scholarships to the secondary schools to children of post-primary age (14 years and over).

During the CDW Scheme's first five years some £300,000 were spent on educational schemes in Grenada. Its main impact was to considerably strengthen Grenada's educational infrastructure, but the impact was minimal in areas such as curriculum development, liberalization of secondary school education, educational values and elitism.

## Expansion of Secondary Education in the Late 1940s

During the same period secondary education facilities expanded, but on the initiative of the Church not the government. In 1945 a coeducational secondary school, St Andrew's Anglican Secondary School, was opened in Grenville as a private venture under the auspices of the Anglican Church. In January 1947 the Presentation Brothers College was opened in St George's under the principalship of Brother Gregory Sheehan, with 96 students on roll during its first year. The previous year the GBSS had been transferred from Melville Street to the army barracks in Tanteen; there were 310 boys on roll at the

**Table 18.4 CDW Scheme for Student Teachers**

| *Year* | *No. of Intending Teachers in secondary schools* | *No. of extra pupil-teachers in training* |
|---|---|---|
| 1947 | 48 | 150 |
| 1948 | 48 | 100 |
| 1949 | 48 | 75 |
| 1950 | 32 | 50 |
| 1951 | 16 | 25 |
| 1952 | nil | nil |

time. The boys in the senior forms were now being prepared for the HSC which had been introduced in 1946. In 1952 a new Catholic Convent school for girls was opened at Grenville.

## Teacher-Training

The basis of any progress in education rests on the quality of training the teacher receives, the material he is taught to impart and the method of presenting it; thus, teacher-training lies at the heart of any effective education system. With the end of the CDW Scheme of training in secondary schools, the CDW continued to assist teacher-training, in the area of in-service training, with the existing in-service programme intensified and broadened. By 1959 the emphasis was placed on training teachers in particular areas of the school system, for example, Infant Education and Home Economics. An Infant Education Organizer was appointed in the early 1960s. After the end of the Intending Teachers scheme in 1953 an average of four teachers annually were sent for training to Erdiston College, Barbados; this continued until 1963.

In 1960 the primary schools were divided into infant, junior and senior departments, and a qualified or experienced teacher was placed in charge of each department. In the same year Dr Quincy Danda and C.V.D. Hadley visited and discussed the setting up of a teachers' college for the Windwards in St Vincent. The failure of Federation in 1962, however, meant an end to this. In the same year Grenada set up its own Teachers' College, which opened in September 1963, in temporary quarters. Dr R.O. Staples, whose services were supplied by the External Aid office, Ministry of External Affairs, Government of Canada, was the first Principal, assisted by two full-time staff members of Grenada's Department of Education, and six visiting tutors. The college operated on funds made available under the British Colonial Development and Welfare Scheme, No. D5469, as part of a three-year scheme. In its first year, 18 (ten men and eight women) enrolled for a one-year course. Twelve students (five men and seven women) entered from secondary schools in January 1964. The work of the college was in special relationship with the Institute of Education, University of the West Indies. The college, therefore, was the result of the joint enterprise of the Grenadian, Canadian and British governments (in students, staff and funds) and the University of the West Indies (academically).[12]

## Conclusion

During the early 19th century education was conceived of as essentially a civilizing agent: to bring the Grenadian ex-slave community into the mainstream of civilization. Later, added to this was the idea of education as a means to vertical class mobility, an idea reinforced rather than challenged by the educational system. A few colonials were educated to fill various civil service posts once held by British expatriates; others entered the commercial field, mostly as clerks in the distributive sector. Thus, the civil service and business sectors together with law and medicine, became the established avenues for upward mobility.

The colonial economy was a dependent economy, and by making Grenadians dependent for their livelihood on a narrow range of agencies and activities, the colonial education system reinforced the Colony's dependency status. Education was not concerned to develop and diversify local production, technical skills and various forms of indigenous technology. The system practised resulted in the majority of Grenadians being largely unemployed and unemployable. Many emigrated and others undertook forms of subsistence self-employment using the rudimentary skills at their disposal, and living on subsistence agriculture or trade. As the colonial system was not based on education for production and employment it was not only generally irrelevant but often wasteful.

Education in the early 20th century taught the Grenadian to adore and even deify the British. Beginning in the 1920s, however, a few exceptional, educated Grenadians began to challenge this state of affairs, as we shall see in the next chapter.

NOTES

Full citations only given where work does not appear in the Bibliography.

1. *Blue Books* 1900–31: all data were compiled from the *Blue Books* and the annual education reports for the period.
2. *Reports on the Department of Education 1906*, 1907.
3. *The Secondary Education Ordinance, 1915*.
4. *Blue Book* 1917; *Annual Report of the Education Department for 1917*.
5. 'Report and General Abstracts', *Census of 1921*, 1921. Compiled by D. Julian Garraway.
6. *Head Teachers Pensions Ordinance* 1931, 13 March 1931.
7. *The Primary Education Ordinance of 1931*, 13 March 1931.
8. *Council Paper No. 3 of 1932*, 'Report of the Education for 1931'.
9. *Council Paper No. 7 of 1933*, 'Proposals of the Education Commission relating to Grenada'.
10. Ministry of Education, *A Review of the Historical Development of Education in Grenada*, 1973.
11. *Address by Sir Arthur Grimble at the Opening of the Grand Roy School and Farm*, 1947.
12. *Masters and Mistresses Journal*, St George's, Grenada Publishers Ltd. 1967, pp. 15–16.

# 19

# *Agriculture and the New Mercantilism: Economic History 1950–82*

In common with other colonies in the Caribbean and elsewhere, Grenada's economic history has, since earliest times, been marked by openness, dependency and a maldistribution of its income and wealth. The economy was largely dependent on imports to satisfy much of its domestic demand for food; its currency was either the same as, or pegged to, that in the metropole. Much of the income generated from the exploitation of the land accrued in various forms in the metropole, for example, taxes, import duties, value-added, profits, interest. The little that returned or remained in Grenada was enjoyed by an élite that constituted the wealthy, propertied, ruling class.

Grenada's dependency status was further reinforced in that almost all economic activity revolved around the production and export of two or three staples: cocoa and sugar in the 19th century, and cocoa, bananas, and nutmegs in the 20th.

## The Cocoa Industry

The cocoa industry has replaced sugar as the mainstay of Grenada's economy since the 1880s. The nutmeg industry became prominent around the turn of the century, while the banana industry became commercially significant about 1934. From 1930 to 1982 these three crops formed the substructure of the island's economy as directly or indirectly they have generated much of the income and employment in the country.

The expansion in the cocoa industry, which had become well marked by the 1880s, continued uninterrupted for the rest of the century. By 1904 the island recorded its largest crop ever, some 67,225 cwt bags; this was double the 1884 crop.[1] Despite heavy rains in certain years the annual crop continued to increase, to 90,987 cwts by 1929.[2] Most of the cocoa was produced on the estates; although peasants produced some cocoa their share of production was small and of inferior quality.

In the late 1920s experiments were conducted to improve cocoa yield, including examining yield per acre, and per tree, under different conditions. In 1936 another series of experiments were conducted to determine the types of manures best suited to different types of soil in Grenada.[3] These tests were carried out on some 13 estates in the colony, and the results of these investigations redounded to the industry's benefit.

About 1936, too, the practice of interplanting cocoa with bananas began, and this led to improved agronomy. The main disease from which the cocoa trees suffered was 'thrips', but it was not widespread.

A major programme, the Cocoa Industry Improvement Scheme, financed by the Colonial Development and Welfare Fund, aimed to expand the acreage under cocoa cultivation, was undertaken in 1944. Between 1950 and 1955 $500,000 was spent on this scheme.[4]

The emphasis on the rehabilitation programme was not only on increased planting but also on improved varieties and greater production of pods per tree. Increased cultivation was slow at first and only an additional 1,074 acres were planted in the ten years 1944 to 1954. The uprooting of old trees by hurricane 'Janet' as well as loss of relatively young plants created the impetus for accelerated rehabilitation. Consequently, there was considerable expansion after 1955, and by 1962 some 7,000 acres had been planted in cloned cocoa trees.[5]

For the five years (1950–55) prior to the hurricane the average annual production was 5.68 million pounds; in the next two years (1956–57) it averaged only 1.9 million pounds owing to the damage caused by the hurricane. By 1956, however, the success of the rehabilitation programme was revealed by production reaching 5.2 million pounds.

In 1951 the Cocoa Rehabilitation Board was established by statute (Sec 6 of the Cocoa Cess Ordinance, Ch. 59 of 1951) to improve the quality of the product.[6] It applied the funds of the Cocoa Cess account, advised the Ministry of Agriculture in all matters affecting the improvement scheme, and assisted in arrangements for the purchase, preparation, handling, grading and marketing of cocoa.

By the early 1960s, this Board had become redundant as most of its functions were carried out by the Ministry of Agriculture, and the

Grenada Cocoa Industry Board (GCIB) which had superseded the Rehabilitation Board, was responsible for marketing. This Board had been set up under the Cocoa Industry Ordinance of 1964, which established the Grenada Cocoa Association. The GCIB was set up to control and manage the affairs of the Association. It consisted of nine members, six elected by members of the Association and three nominated by the government.[7]

The Association's functions were to encourage improvements in the standard of quality of cocoa prepared and exported; to ensure that the most favourable arrangements were maintained for the purchase, sale, handling, grading, exportation and marketing of cocoa; to encourage improvements and replacements of existing fermentation and drying installations and the provision of additional installations; to encourage co-operative enterprise in the receiving and preparation of cocoa.

The Board was authorized to issue licences to persons to export cocoa, which no one was permitted to do without the Board's consent. The Association has grown from strength to strength and today is the sole exporter of cocoa from Grenada. It has become the farmers' co-operative in the receiving and marketing of cocoa.

By 1962 the cocoa industry was still predominantly in the hands of large estates; in other words, there had been no appreciable change in ownership and control since the 1930s. In 1962 there were 8,430 cocoa farmers, of whom 7,870 had 10 acres and less each, and produced 10% of all cocoa exported; 89 owned more than 100 acres each, and produced 20% of all cocoa exported, while the 471 medium-sized growers produced the remaining 70%.[8]

In the immediate post-war years there was a marked increase in the price of Grenada's cocoa. From 6.37% per pound in 1938 it rose to 12.8 cents by 1944 and 54 cents by 1950. Thereafter, and for the next 20 years, prices fell and reached a low of 58 cents per pound.[9]

Throughout these years the main beneficiaries of Grenada's cocoa were neither the producers nor the Colony, but the manufacturers and distributors who enjoyed the value-added at each stage of processing.

## The Nutmeg Industry

While the cocoa industry has been of economic importance for over 200 years, the nutmeg industry has had commercial significance for less than 100 years. The nutmeg plant was first introduced into Grenada from Banda, a small island in the East Indies, by one Frank Gurney around the year 1843. In the decade 1840 to 1850 some

Grenadian planters were apparently recruited to help with the sugar industry in the East Indies, and no doubt this contributed further to the early introduction and sporadic cultivation of the product.

Not until 1860, however, was its cultivation on a commercial basis seriously considered. This coincided with the decline in the sugar industry and the simultaneous search for other economic crops to replace sugar. By 1878 production totalled some 470 cwts at a value of £2,116, and production slowly increased until by 1910 exports were 8,489 cwts, representing 14% of world exports; by 1929, 22,666 cwts were exported, or 22% of world exports.[10] In 1918 it had in fact accounted for 33% of world exports, but this high share of the market was owing to a decline in production in the Dutch East Indies as a result of the war.

The early decades of the 20th century witnessed a remarkable expansion of cultivation and production. By 1950 exports had reached 62,000 cwts and earned £667,000. In the interim prices, which had doubled by the mid-1920s, fell by some 79% in the 1930s, then rose again to 53.5¢ per lb by 1947. In September 1955, however, most trees (80%) were destroyed by hurricane 'Janet'.

From 1975 onwards, it emerged as the economy's number-one industry, despite the devastation wrought by the hurricane. In 1973, it accounted for 38% of Grenada's domestic exports and almost 50% in 1975. It is thus the major earner of foreign currency – the currency Grenada most needs to finance imports of goods and services. In 1976 it brought in US$5.5 million and as the industry has a low import content, its net benefit and contribution to Grenada's balance of payments by far surpassed that of cocoa, bananas and tourism.

In March 1942 a number of local nutmeg producers had decided to form a co-operative which should be the sole exporter of Grenada's nutmegs.[11] In a circular despatch from the Governor to the Secretary of State on 16 January 1945, the following reasons were given for the formation of the Grenada Co-operative Nutmeg Association (GCNA):

1. To secure the stablest prices for local producers by ending the cut-throat competition among independent local exporters.
2. To put more of the profits of the export trade in the hands of producers rather than in the hands of middle-men.
3. To increase the demand for Grenada's nutmegs by setting standards of quality.

A planning committee was appointed to draw up legislation to govern the Association. The original bill was drafted by a legal practitioner, and presented as an official bill to the Legislative Council. The

Council passed it; but certain features were unsatisfactory both to the Governor and the Secretary of State. A revised Bill was later introduced in 1946 and passed as the Nutmeg Industry Ordinance (No. 8 of 1946), which made the GCNA sole exporters of nutmegs.

The GCNA came into being on 27 March 1947, and began receiving nutmegs on 1 October 1947. Ordinance No. 8 of 1946 made it possible for dealers to be members of the Association, but advances to dealers for nutmegs purchased were less than those given to producers who dealt with the Association directly. This disparity was deliberately created to encourage producers to support the Association. Local dealers protested vehemently and persuaded their supporter (the Hon. J.B. Renwick) to introduce a motion in the Legislative Council on 21 July 1948 to force the GCNA to pay the same advances to dealers as to producers. The motion was defeated. On the same date another motion was introduced, designed to dissolve the Association's monopoly position in buying and exporting nutmegs and to replace it with a Statutory Board with the power to give licences to dealers, as well as control local and export prices. Consequently the industry was divided into two camps, those who supported, and those who opposed, the GCNA. A committee was set up to effect a compromise; but to no avail. The efforts of J. Beasley, of the CDW in the West Indies, to settle the dispute also failed.

Government then intervened and passed the Nutmeg Industry Amendment Ordinance No. 10 of 1949. The main provisions were as follows:

1. To organize and effect the holding of area meetings so as to educate producers in the principles of co-operatives.
2. To ensure proper auditing of the Association's Accounts.
3. To compel the Association to build up an adequate Reserve Fund.
4. To appoint a Manager as Chief Executive Officer.
5. To allow the GCNA to use the services of any export dealer on a commission basis.
6. To allow the Association to appoint buying and processing agents.
7. To provide for the distribution of earnings to producers during the year rather than at the end of the disposal of a year's crop.

The export dealers' opposition to the Association was due to the fact that its existence had meant an end to their middle-man privileges. Their defenders were the Hon. J.B. Renwick and the Hon. F.B. Paterson, but by 1949 legislative actions and motions of both men to protect the vested interest of the independent exporters were defeated in the Legislative Council.

Rumblings and dissatisfaction over the monopoly power of the Association continued throughout 1949 and 1950, mostly from an obscure association of middle-men. The Grenada Producers Protective League, which even brought in Sir Algernon Wharton from Trinidad to argue their case. The issue was finally settled in 1951 when a Commission of Enquiry set up by the Legislative Council in 1950 recommended to government the continuation of the Association's monopoly position in receiving and exporting nutmegs, a position that has so far remained unchanged. By 1970 out of a total of approximately 6,000 producers, 4,000 were members of the Association.[12]

By 1977 there were some 21 receiving and processing stations around the country, of which 18 mostly specialized in receiving nutmegs and mace, though they did a limited amount of drying. The other three stations, one each in Gouyave, Grenville and Victoria, specialized in the drying, curing and final preparations of nutmegs and mace before export.

## The Banana Industry

Bananas have been grown for more than a century in Grenada, but in terms of economic importance their cultivation as an industry began in 1954. In 1934 the Canadian Banana Company signed a contract to buy Grenada's bananas, and three years later production and exports had increased from 16,600 stems to 157,000 stems.

During the second half of 1953 keen interest was aroused in growing this fruit when the possibility of securing a long-term contract with a United Kingdom firm for the supply of Lacatan bananas arose. During the last five months of 1953 suckers were imported from Jamaica and Dominica, through the agency of the Grenada Agriculturists Union,[13] for direct distribution to growers for the establishment of nurseries. In September of the same year the Agriculturists Union successfully arranged trial shipments with Geest Industries Ltd; and until the end of the year regular fortnightly shipments were made both of the Lacatan and Gros Michel varieties. An interim price of 4.5 cents per pound was agreed upon by the Union and the Company at that point.

Negotiations for a long-term contract with Geest Industries, which began in late 1953, were concluded and signed in 1955; the contract covered the purchase and export of fruit over a ten-year period. In 1954 the Banana Ordinance, which set up the Grenada Banana Co-operative Society, was passed. According to this all bananas grown in the counry and intended for export should be delivered to the Society and none should be exported except by the Society or such person or persons as may be authorized by them under licence. The Ordinance placed firm control over production and export of bananas in the hands of the Society. This control included the regulation of prices to growers, grading and selection of fruit, disposal of rejects and the imposition of a cess for leaf-spot control.[14]

In 1955, in common with cocoa and nutmeg production, the banana industry suffered as a result of hurricane 'Janet'. Large-scale production was subsequently achieved as a result of the Agricultural Rehabilitation Programme.

Because of the relatively short growing season (nine months) and the ready export outlet, the industry provided farmers with a quick and relatively high return on investment; at the same time it blended admirably into a rehabilitation programme aimed at re-establishing the cocoa and nutmeg farms.

In 1958 exports reached a total of 948,000 stems at an average of 27.7lbs per stem as compared with 49,863 stems in 1953: this marked an increase of some 2,000%. Thus, the period 1953–58 marked the beginning of the banana industry on a commercial and economic scale.

Out of a total of 13,056 acres in bananas in 1958 84% represented interplanting of cocoa and nutmegs; in these areas the banana trees were used as a temporary shade for the young plants. The remaining 2,088 acres were in pure stand bananas. The guaranteed market which the Geest contract offered was a major factor in creating the initial incentive to expand banana production (see Table 19.1).

During 1957–59 the average price received by the Association per pound of bananas fell from some 8¢ in 1957 to approximately 5.5¢ in 1959. It seems unlikely that this drop in price would have been occasioned by a similar drop in the wholesale price as the latter has always

**Table 19.1 Banana Exports 1953–59**

| *Year* | *Stems exported* | *Average weight each* | *Value EC$** | *Average price per lb.* |
|---|---|---|---|---|
| 1953 | 40,863 | – | 51,089 | – |
| 1954 | 108,900 | – | 189,237 | – |
| 1955 | 92,243 | – | 139,500 | – |
| 1956 | 67,115 | – | 138,500 | – |
| 1957 | 568,841 | 30.8 | 1,387,778 | 7.9 |
| 1958 | 947,893 | 27.7 | 1,752,340 | 6.6 |
| 1959 | 1,151,543 | 26.8 | 1,755,596 | 5.6 |

* Eastern Caribbean dollars

Source: Grenada, *Five-Year Development Plan* 1964–68

displayed upward movement. Noteworthy is that while the GBCS was paid an average of 6.3 cents by Geest Industries Ltd, sellers of bananas on the world market received an *f.o.b.* price of 7.3 US cents or approximately 14.6 EC cents.

One amazing feature of the banana trade is the extent to which prices paid to the Society have remained static throughout the first 18 years of Geest's trading relations with the GBCS. During the first ten years of the Geest contract, the price of bananas fell from 8¢ per lb in 1957 to 5¢ in 1960 and remained around that level until 1965. Only once, in the 14 years 1958 to 1972, did the price exceed 6¢ and that was in 1962 when the price was 6.3¢. The average price received during the entire period was 5.6¢ per lb. The average *f.o.b.* price received by sellers of fruit from any origin on the world market at the same time was 15.4 US¢ per kg or 14 EC¢ per lb.

Obviously the opportunity cost of the Geest contract was quite high. Based on the fact that world prices exceeded Geest's contract by an average of 8.4¢ per lb the net opportunity cost of the Geest contract on the 571m lbs exported between 1958 and 1972 was EC$45.7.

After 1973 the average price per pound received by the Society increased steadily from 11.1 cents in that year to 22 cents in 1975 to 28.6 cents in 1978 and to 40 cents in 1980. The price increase during the commodity prices boom of 1973–74 by far exceeded that of the years 1977–80. The favourable movements in prices in the 1970s were all related to the expansion of incomes in the developed market economies, the income elasticity of demand for bananas, and to changes in the tastes and preferences of consumers in these economies.

Table 19.2 presents the average of the prices received by the Society for various shipments during each year. The price varied from shipment to shipment, due to the variability of the Green Market Price (GMP) for fruit, the extreme variability of UK fixed costs, West Indies

**Table 19.2 Average Price Received for Bananas Exported 1970–80**

| *Year* | *Price (cents) per lb* | *Year* | *Price (cents) per lb* |
|---|---|---|---|
| 1970 | 5.40 | 1976 | 22.0 |
| 1971 | 4.95 | 1977 | 26.4 |
| 1972 | 5.80 | 1978 | 28.6 |
| 1973 | 11.10 | 1979 | 32.1 |
| 1974 | 15.90 | 1980 | 40.3 |
| 1975 | 22.10 | | |

Source: *Abstract of Statistics*, 1979

(WI) fixed costs, and the constant upward rise in UK variable costs and West Indies fixed costs and freight charges.

For 21 shipments examined for 1974, freight costs rose from £21 per ton to £36 per ton, an increase of 71% in one year. In January 1978 freight charges were £57.6 per ton; two years later they were £90 per ton, an increase of 56%. UK variable costs rose by more than 50% during the same period; at the same time WI variable costs increased by 34%. The GMP for 3 December 1975 shipment was £180; by the 20th of that month it fell to £174 and by 10 January 1976 it fell further to £169; however, by March 1976 the price rose to £178; by November 1976 it had risen further to £200; however, by December it was down again to £178. This was the general pattern with the GMP.[15]

The GMP represents the selling price of green bananas sold in the UK to green ripeners, delivered to their depots. The green ripeners are independent firms who handle about 20% of Windward fruit, and Geest depots (11 in all) which handle 80%. The GMP is negotiated weekly by Geest and Winban; the factors affecting this negotiated price are the volume of fruit on the market, the demand at a particular price, weather conditions and seasonal factors. Thus, the gross wholesale price of ripe bananas is used as the marker or reference from which the GMP is ultimately derived. This price is based on an *estimate* of the average wholesale price per box of all ripe fruit sold throughout the UK to secondary wholesalers and directly to multiples. The average wholesale price per box is then multiplied by 76 (to ascertain price per ton) allowing four boxes or 5% for shrinkage during ripening and wastage.

In 1973 a new agreement between Geest and Winban came into effect. Under this agreement the Society assumed responsibility for expenses incurred in the provision of a) cartons and associated materials; b) hurricane insurance; c) export taxes; and d) bonuses payable to growers. These were then included in the basic price paid by Geest to the GBCS. Previously these expenses were met by Geest and recovered from the Society by deduction from the contract price.

After 1973 the increase in prices by Geest to Winban far exceeded world market prices for bananas.[16] The 1973 price of 11 cents was a 91% increase on that of 1972; world market price rose from 16.1 US¢ per kg in 1972 to 16.5¢ in 1973, an increase of 2.4%. The 1975 price of 22.1¢ marked a 100% increase on 1973; world prices increased by 49.6% from 16.5¢ to 22.1¢ per kg. Between 1972 and 1978 the price received by Winban rose by 393%; world prices during the same period increased by 95.6%. Despite this, by 1978 world prices exceeded the price paid by Geest (see Table 19.3).

**Table 19.3 Comparison of Price Movements: Winban and World Prices**

| *Year* | *% Increase in price received by Winban* | *% Increase in world prices* |
|---|---|---|
| 1972 | – | – |
| 1973 | 91 | 2.4 |
| 1974 | 43 | 11.5 |
| 1975 | 39 | 34.2 |
| 1976 | 0 | 4.0 |
| 1977 | 20 | 7.0 |
| 1978 | 8 | 14.5 |

Banana production expanded initially in 1957, reached a peak by 1959 and then levelled off over the ensuing three years. The cocoa rehabilitation programme, which picked up in the 1960s, the opening up of feeder roads, improvement in existing cultural practices and better irrigation played a major role in the marked expansion of the industry by the mid- and late-1960s, as Table 19.4 illustrates.

The falling-off of production in the 1969–72 period was due, *inter alia*, to three consecutive drought months in 1969 and 1970, followed by six successive months in 1971(see below).

| | 1968 | 1969 | 1970 | 1971 |
|---|---|---|---|---|
| March–June (rainfall in inches) | 6.4 | 5.6 | 4.8 | 2.4 |

**Table 19.4 Banana Exports 1961–80**

| *Year* | *Exports (million lbs)* | *Year* | *Exports (million lbs)* |
|---|---|---|---|
| 1961 | 25.943 | 1971 | 31.537 |
| 1962 | 22.120 | 1972 | 28.027 |
| 1963 | 32.599 | 1973 | 24.232 |
| 1964 | 32.643 | 1974 | 19.578 |
| 1965 | 47.164 | 1975 | 30.103 |
| 1966 | 46.081 | 1976 | 35.018 |
| 1967 | 58.506 | 1977 | 31.956 |
| 1968 | 59.938 | 1978 | 31.473 |
| 1969 | 50.576 | 1979 | 30.909 |
| 1970 | 42.066 | 1980 | 26.481 |

Source: *Abstract of Statistics*, 1979

The main factor accounting for the 45% increase in exports between 1973 and 1976, and the recovery in 1975 was the Banana Rehabilitation Programme which began in 1973 and ended in 1976. Two schemes constituted the programme: the Replanting Assistance Scheme (RAS) and the Shot-in-the-Arm Assistance Scheme (SAAS); additional financial aid was provided to the industry through a government-sponsored CDB Loan.[17]

Both the RAS and the SAAS were financed by the British government under a programme of emergency aid to the Windward Islands Banana Industry. Under the schemes the Society was supplied with fertilizer, weed-killers and pesticides free of cost; fertilizer and weed-killers were supplied to growers at half-price, and pesticides free of cost. The amount collected in 1973 and 1974 under both schemes was $125,000 and $131,000 respectively, and in 1975 and 1976 $149,000 each.

In 1975 the Grenada government raised a loan of $1,185,000 at 4% from the Caribbean Development Bank, with the Society as executing agency, as part of the Banana Rehabilitation Scheme, which was used, among other things, to finance essential inputs. Repayments of principal were to be made annually over a ten-year period commencing 31 May 1978. The loan was in two instalments, one in 1975 and the other in 1976. As of 31 December 1980 the balance on the loan was $414,501.[18]

The rehabilitation programme aimed to replant 1,000 acres of bananas between April 1973 and April 1975. By May 1974, 364 acres accommodated some 218,982 plants, between May and August 1974, 150 acres were approved for planting for small farmers and 200 for large, making a total of 291 approved holdings amounting to 876 acres. The distribution by size of holdings was: 20–50 acres: seven; 10–20 acres: three; 5–10 acres: 14; 0.5 acres: 267. Banana exports from project holdings from April 1974 to July 1975 represented 19% of the total or 17,320 tons.[19]

Unfortunately no evaluation nor cost-benefit analysis was made for this programme; these could have assisted and informed later strategy for the industry. Rough calculations showed that more than $1.739 million were spent on inputs and various forms of subsidy; by July 1975 the increase in production was roughly 17,320 tons.

In 1977 the Banana Five-Year Development Plan began and took the place of the Rehabilitation Scheme. Under this Plan the British government provided funds to the governments of Dominica, Grenada, St Vincent and St Lucia for a wide-based programme of development in the banana industry. The various associations were responsible for implementing the main components of the plan with

Winban providing specialist assistance in research and fruit technology, and Winban's manager as overall co-ordinator of the plan.[20]

The plan was implemented in June 1977 with the payment of subsidies on inputs. A subsidy of nine cents per pound was paid on every pound of fruit sold by growers up to a maximum of 15 tons per grower per year. By June 1978 this aid amounted to $1.7 million. Growers were able to use this money, together with the input cess they had accumulated, to buy fertilizer, weed-killer, insecticides, nematocides, blue diothene or any other Winban-recommended input.

The growers direct receipts, as a percentage of the Society's revenue, would be much greater when subsidies are added – especially for the last half of the decade. For example, during the first eight months of 1981 the average price per lb received from Geest was 38.6 cents. The average price received directly by growers was 18 cents, but when the Association's subsidy of 23.7 cents per lb is added the total receipts by growers would be 41.8 cents or 3.2 cents in excess of the Society's revenue.

Despite the favourable prices for bananas post-1973, with the exception of 1975–76, production failed to respond to these changes; one can only assume that supply was price-inelastic. In fact, its elasticity coefficient is negative. This is incredible as most supply curves

**Table 19.5 Growers' Price as a Percentage of Average Selling Price 1969–81**

| *Year* | *A Exports (million lbs)* | *B Revenue (million $)* | *C Direct growers receipts (million $)* | *C as % of A* |
|---|---|---|---|---|
| 1969 | 50.0 | 2.916 | 2.56 | 88 |
| 1970 | 42.1 | 2.269 | 1.97 | 87 |
| 1971 | 31.5 | 1.561 | 1.48 | 95 |
| 1972 | 28.0 | 1.63 | 1.26 | 77 |
| 1973 | 24.6 | 2.73 | 1.43 | 52 |
| 1974 | 19.6 | 3.12 | 1.45 | 46 |
| 1975 | 30.1 | 6.64 | 2.54 | 38 |
| 1976 | 35.0 | 7.70 | 3.27 | 42 |
| 1977 | 31.9 | 8.43 | 4.69 | 56 |
| 1978 | 31.5 | 9.00 | 4.98 | 55 |
| 1979 | 30.9 | 9.93 | 5.44 | 55 |
| 1980 | 26.5 | 10.67 | 5.75 | 53 |
| 1981 | 23.5 | 9.27 | | |

Source: GBCS, *Accounts of the Association* 1969–81

have a positive coefficient. A variety of factors may be responsible for this: lack of knowledge and information, poor commercial practices, non-scientific (i.e. non-economic) approach to production and the subsistence approach to agriculture by many farmers.

## The New Mercantilism

A continuing phenomenon of economic history and world trade is the transfer of wealth from countries on the periphery of the world economic system – including Grenada and those countries described as developing or Third World – to countries at the centre, that is developed market economies. This export of wealth can take place in one or more of five forms:

1. The loss of a country's value-added to the countries where its agricultural or mineral raw materials are processed or manufactured.
2. The experience of deteriorating terms of trade as a result of oligopoly pricing for the products of the centre countries and perfect competitive pricing for the products of the periphery countries.
3. The dominance of foreign direct investment at the periphery; this involves an initial inflow of capital and a subsequent outflow of management fees, consultancy fees, interest payments and of course profits. The outflow is considerably greater when there exist cases of transfer pricing and over-invoicing between a parent at the centre and a subsidiary branch or affiliate in the periphery.
4. The presence of portfolio investment whose interest-rate structure has a built-in profit component.
5. The 'brain drain' from the periphery to the centre which reduces periphery countries' potential for developing technology and for achieving technological transformation. In addition, the country loses income extending over the entire useful life of the human asset.

The first, second, third and fifth forms are particularly relevant to Grenada. Here, however, only the first will be examined and analysed, beginning with the following propositions in relation to Grenada:

1. No country is really poor; instead countries are made poor. Poverty and riches are processes and not immutable states of nature designated by the gods. The constant use of the term 'poor' has a psychologically damaging effect. It contributes to a certain paralysis of the will and to a fatalistic view of the future.

2. Grenada's contribution to the wealth of developed market economies has been massive, especially in consideration of the period 1674 to 1979 as a whole.
3. The continued export of wealth will make Grenada less and less capable of providing adequate health-care, more and better education for the population, more employment for the unemployed, higher incomes and improved standards of living for the working class and better social services in general for the people.

Let us examine the first export crop – nutmegs. The nutmeg industry provides income and employment fully or partially for approximately 5,300 producers and their families and some 475 workers involved in processing and administration. Thus, some 28,000 persons are dependent on the industry for a livelihood partially or fully, and this industry is one of the pillars of the economy.

Between 1966 and 1979 inclusive, Grenada exported 53 million pounds of nutmegs and seven million pounds of mace. The total final value of the nutmegs was estimated at EC$1,022m; this is not inconceivable when one considers that one ounce of ground and bottled nutmeg, imported by a popular supermarket in Grenada, cost $3.80 (1979). Out of this EC$1,022m final value, the Grenada Co-operative Nutmeg Association, the marketing agency for all Grenada's nutmeg exports, received $104 million, from which the nutmeg producers and farmers received $66.3m or 6% of the total final value of nutmegs exported during the 14 years under examination. The remaining EC$918 million is a measure of Grenada's contribution to the wealth of the developed market economies on the export of her nutmegs alone. This took the form of income, employment, interest, profits and rents and went to the agents, brokers, millers, manufacturers, wholesalers and retailers abroad. Table 19.6 shows the marketing and distribution system for nutmegs as well as the value-added for each stage of that system. The conversion rate is 2lbs green to 1lb dry.

**Table 19.6 Marketing and Distribution System for Nutmegs 1976**

| *Stage of production* | *Quantity* | *EC$ value* | *Value-added: EC$* |
|---|---|---|---|
| Local producer | 2 lbs (green) | 1.28 | 1.28 |
| GCNA | 1 lb (dry) | 1.89 | 0.61 |
| Agent broker | 1 lb | 5.67 | 3.78 |
| Miller | – | – | – |
| Wholesalers | 1 lb | 16.56 | 10.89 |
| Retailers | – | 22.68 | 6.12 |

Note: No significant chemical transformation involved.
Source: Drawn up from company accounts, price data and *Spices*, by ITC, 1975

The conclusion to be drawn from Table 19.6 is that 8.33 cents out of every dollar value-added in the nutmeg trade went to the producer country and 91.67 to businesses and persons in the developed market and non-market economies.

If Grenada could bypass the agents and millers, and grind, blend and package the nutmegs itself, its earnings on the 23 million pounds exported during these four years would have been $130 million instead of $58 million.

In recent years spice traders have been organizing themselves into cartel-like bodies. In Germany, there is the wholesale purchasing association of food chains; in France, there are six spice trade associations, the largest of which is the Union Interprofessionelle de Poivre et des Epices; in the USA the American Spice Association consists of 22 brokers, 25 importers and 70 grinders and processors; in Canada the importers, brokers, packers and flavour houses are all members of the Canadian Spice Association of the General Produce Brokers Association. The dominant firms are McCormick Foods, Schwartz Spices and British Pepper and Spice Company Ltd. Some resistance by these associations to the penetration of processed nutmegs and spices into the developed market economies is envisaged, but such resistance is not insurmountable.

The situation in the cocoa trade is similar. Production and distribution of cocoa consists of three stages: the production of raw cocoa, the manufacture of cocoa intermediates, and the manufacture of cocoa products. At each stage the value-added is considerable. Moreover, the presence of various middle-men in the distribution of the raw material has contributed to an increase in value-added. The process is as follows: the Grenada Cocoa Board sells its product through brokers and dealers, who, in turn, sell it to specialist roaster-grinders and manufacturers who sell to wholesalers and retailers. Thus, by the time a pound of cocoa reaches the refined stage, its value could be as high as ten times what it was traded for on the international market.

Preliminary calculations show that, for example in 1967, £143 of edible cocoa was, after processing, valued at £408. Manufacturers' price was three times the price of intermediate cocoa.[21] When roasting of beans, grinding and manufacture of cocoa liquor, marketing of cocoa butter and cocoa powder, wholesaling and retailing of the chocolate products are included, obviously a value-added ten times the original price received by the producing country is realistic. There is also the added factor of the 'Futures Market' where there can be significant differentials between spot and market prices. Between 1976 and 1979, Grenada exported 21.3 million pounds of cocoa for EC$62.5m; the total value-added on this was approximately

EC$625m. Thus, in those three years Grenada contributed EC$562 million to the wealth of the developed market economy countries. The main cocoa-liquor importers are the USA, USSR and France. Cocoa liquor, the paste obtained by grinding the nibs of the cocoa beans, and cooled to produce hard blocks, contains about 55% of fatty matter called cocoa butter; this is separated from the liquor by a process referred to as hotpressing. Cocoa powder is the unsweetened cocoa produced by pulverizing cocoa cake. Twenty-five percent of the cocoa exported from developing countries is in the form of cocoa intermediates; the possibility of manufacturing these cocoa intermediates is well worth attention by our technologists.

Most of the above-mentioned value-added is enjoyed by nine major chocolate manufacturers around the world, some of which employ more people than the population of Grenada. The turn-over of some of them on chocolate products alone exceeds Grenada's GDP tenfold. These multinationals include: Nestlé and Interfood (Swiss), Cadbury, Schweppes, Rowntree, Mackintosh, and United Biscuits Holdings (British), and Hershey Foods Corporation, Mars Corporation, W.R. Grace and General Foods Corporation (American).

The third case illustrative of the export of wealth through the loss of value-added, concerns bananas. An UNCTAD study entitled *Marketing and Distribution System of Bananas*, published in 1975 and updated in 1978, has demonstrated that 11.5% of the final value of bananas accrues to the exporting country and 88.5% to the foreign enterprises involved in the banana trade from the shipping stage to the retail stage. Based on these findings the value-added to UK enterprises during the 1955–80 period was extraordinary. Table 19.7 illustrates the findings of UNCTAD's study.[22]

During 1957 to 1980 inclusive the Grenada Banana Co-operative Society sold a total of 824m lbs of bananas to Geest Industries Ltd; in exchange the Society received $90.8m. This represented 18.7% of

**Table 19.7 Distribution of Value-Added in the International Banana Trade 1978**

| *% Distribution* | *Activity* | *Area* |
|---|---|---|
| 11.5 | Returns to growers | Producing country |
| 26.1 | Others: including packing, transport, taxes, loading, stevedoring, etc. | |
| 11.5 | Freight and insurance | Foreign enterprises |
| 19.0 | Ripeness gross margin | |
| 31.9 | Retail gross margin | |

EC$495m, the total final value of bananas exported during these years.

A total of $404.2m, roughly £81m sterling, accrued to individuals and enterprises in Britain involved in the marketing and distribution of Grenada's bananas, the greater part to Geest Industries Ltd, as this is the major enterprise involved in the West Indies-United Kingdom banana trade. Geest Industries transported the fruit in its own ships, ripened them in its own depots, and then wholesaled to multiples, greengrocers, etc. This vertical integration and marketing concentration explains why Geest enjoyed a considerable share of the value-added involved in the banana trade. When Geest began its operations in 1954 it had to charter ships but eventually it was able to buy its own fleet, and its significant share of the value-added enabled it to do this.

The international banana trade, like the cocoa trade, is controlled by a few large companies, including United Brands, Standard Fruit, Del Monte (US), Sumitomo (Japan), Geest (Britain), and Noboa (Italy). In some cases there is a tendency towards market concentration and vertical integration. This is the situation where one firm is involved in more than one of the following activities: transporting the fruit in its own ships, insuring them with its own company and ripening them itself; its level of sales and its profitability will thus be considerably enlarged.

Fundamentally, exports pay for imports. Consequently when goods are sold abroad, it is not so much the value of the earnings that is important but the volume of the goods these earnings can purchase. For example, if Grenada and the United Kingdom exchanged cars for nutmegs the situation would devolve more or less as follows.

In 1970 Grenada sold 3,030 lbs of nutmegs and was able to pay for one British-made car, meantime the British economy enjoyed the value-added on the 3,030 lbs nutmegs. In 1977 Grenada had to sell 6,349 lbs of nutmegs, even though their price had doubled, to pay for a similar car. Thus, the British economy was able to enjoy value-added on 6,349 instead of 3,030 pounds, whereas in return, Grenada received the same one car. In this case the net export of wealth was the additional 3,000 pounds of nutmegs Grenada had to give up to obtain one car, plus the value-added on the 6,349 pounds. In 1975 double the quantity of cocoa was required to buy the same quantity of fertilizer as in 1974.

In the 18th century Grenada exchanged sugar and coffee for wines and horses. The sugar was then processed in Britain. That was the era of the old mercantilism. Today, the structure is the same, all that has changed is the form: sugar becomes cocoa and nutmegs, and a horse becomes a car. This is the era of the new mercantilism.

From the foregoing, it is evident that *Grenada is not a poor country*, but *a country made poor*. The challenge in 1982, in the present, and in the future is to develop strategies individually and collectively, with groups of countries in a similar position, to reduce this export of wealth and enable the working class to enjoy the fruits of its labour. It is in answer to this challenge that the old élite was challenged for political power in 1951 by Gairy; but Gairy and his régimes eventually betrayed the cause of the peasants, labourers and other workers; and it was as a result of such a betrayal that the Gairy regime was challenged, opposed and eventually overthrown. This is the theme of the next chapter.

NOTES

Full citations only given where work does not appear in the Bibliography.

1. *Blue Books*, 1904.
2. Ibid, 1929.
3. *Annual Report of the Department of Agriculture*, 1936.
4. *Five Year Development Plan (1964–68)*, 1965.
5. Ibid.
6. *Laws of Grenada*, Cocoa Cess Ordinance, Ch. 59 of 1951.
7. *Laws of Grenada*, Cocoa Industry Ordinance, 1964.
8. *Five Year Development Plan*, 1964–68.
9. *Abstract of Statistics*, 1979.
10. Council Paper No. 6 of 1933, 'Report of the Spice Commission'.
11. *Report of the Inquiry into the Nutmeg Industry*, 1951.
12. *Report of the Commission of Inquiry into the GCNA*, September 1971.
13. *Report of the Agricultural Department for 1953*, Government Printery, 1955.
14. *Laws of Grenada*, Banana Ordinance 1954, 1954.
15. GBCS, *Price Schedules*.
16. UNCTAD, *Marketing and Distribution System for Bananas* (1975).
17. GBCS, *File of the Banana Association*, 1973–79.
18. Ibid.
19. Ibid.
20. Ibid.
21. UNCTAD, *Marketing and Distribution System for Cocoa* (1975), p.83.
22. Ibid.

# 20

# *From Crown Colony Rule to Revolution*

Agitation to change Grenada's Crown Colony constitution began in 1915 with the establishment of the *West Indian* newspaper by T.A. Marryshow and a local lawyer, C.F.P. Renwick. From its formation until 1934 the paper consistently advocated two political changes: a) reform of Grenada's Crown Colony status; and b) the creation of a Federation of the British West Indies.

By constantly advocating these changes, those in the vanguard of this movement for political reform began to receive the support of the community, especially the better educated sector. One gesture of supportive action came from the St George's District Board, which, at its meeting in August 1917, approved a resolution demanding a measure of representation in the government of their country and called on the Board to transmit this sentiment to the Governor. Marryshow himself argued that the time was ripe and the climate appropriate for Grenadians to make such a demand.

In September 1917, a meeting of all the District Boards was called to discuss the issue. This meeting resolved that a committee be formed to prepare a petition requesting representation from the imperial government. Later that year, as a result of this meeting, and of the general importance of the issue to the Colony as a whole, the Grenada Representative Association (GRA) was formed. This association comprised both militant and reformist elements. The militant group, led by William Galway Donovan and A.A. Richards, demanded full representation, that is, a wholly elective Legislative Council; the reformists or moderates, led by Domingo Sebastian DeFreitas (a planter from St John's and a member of the Governor's Legislative Council since

1895), demanded a partly elective, partly nominated Legislative Council.

Domingo S. DeFreitas was elected the first President of the Grenada Representative Association, thus marking the ascendancy of the moderate element, as DeFreitas was not only a member of the plantocracy, but also a leading advocate of limited constitutional reform. T.A. Marryshow played the role of arbiter between the two groups in attempting to reconcile their differing views.

In 1919 the Association began to hold meetings in the main towns of Grenada to inform people on the issue and whip up support for its cause; on most of these occasions the main speaker was Marryshow. Resolutions demanding an effective voice for the people of Grenada were passed in each of these meetings. Donovan continued to advocate full representation while DeFreitas supported only limited representation. Marryshow compromised by stating that the time was premature to decide how much representation was needed. Eventually, at an executive meeting of the Association at which both Marryshow and Donovan were present, a compromise was reached. It was agreed that the following specific demands be made to His Majesty's government:

*Outstanding advocate of Caribbean unity and an opponent of repression, T.A. Marryshow*

- an equal number of elected and nominated members in the Legislative Council;
- exclusion of the Governor from the Council;
- the right of the Legislative Council to introduce all types of bills including money bills;
- the right of elected members to sit in the Executive Council;
- the qualifications for Legislative Council elections be the same as that for elections to the District Boards.

In November 1920 the Association submitted a petition to the Secretary of State, Lord Milner. It was signed by 25 planters, 19 merchants, all the lawyers, all the elected members of District Boards, two newspaper editors, members of the Board of Education and Justices of the Peace. The actual petition submitted was less specific than had been agreed, consisting instead of a general statement requesting representation and an end to Crown Colony government. This, in essence, was another victory for the Reformists/Moderates.

The Governor of Grenada, George Haddon-Smith, who held the same view as the Reformists, opposed the idea of a wholly elected Legislative Council but acceded to a limited number of elected representatives, and this was the basis of his recommendations to the Colonial Office. The Governor's recommendations were accepted by the Secretary of State and in 1921 he replied to the Grenada Representative Association's petition, recommending a Legislative Council composed of the Governor, six officials, three non-officials and four elected members.

The GRA's militants, Donovan, Richards, Fleming, Renwick and now Marryshow, found this unacceptable and continued to agitate for a more just reform of the Legislative Council. At the same time, other islands began to make similar demands, with the result that the British government sent Colonel E.F.L. Wood to conduct an enquiry into constitutional government in the British West Indies.

Wood's enquiry began in December 1921 and ended in February 1922. On 22 January 1922 the GRA, led by Marryshow, met Wood and presented its memorandum on constitutional government for Grenada, proposing among other things:

1. A wholly elected unofficial side.
2. That if nominated members were included on the unofficial side, they should be nominated from names submitted by the District Boards acting jointly.
3. No unofficial member of the Legislative Council should, at the time, be a member of the Executive Council.
4. A Federation of the British West Indies.[1]

Wood recommended a Legislative Council composed of the Governor, seven officials, three nominated and five elected members. These recommendations were accepted and, in 1924, an Order-in-Council outlining the new constitutional provisions was sent to Grenada. The constitution gave the Governor considerable, even autocratic powers, and although it conceded limited representation, the official and nominated members, who were the mouthpiece of the Governor, were in the majority. The Governor retained full control over all financial matters; moreover, he had the power to assent to, reject or reserve for the imperial government's ruling, any Bill passed by the Legislative Council.

The constitution also prescribed a restrictive franchise similar to that of the mid-19th century. To qualify to vote in the 1925 elections one had to be male, British and 21 years and over, or a British subject, or a female 30 years and over, with an income of £30 per annum or more, or ownership of property valued at £150. This excluded the mass of peasants and protopeasants. Candidates had to be male with an income of £200 per annum or own property in the constituency of £500 and resident in the constituency for the 12 months preceeding the elections. Women were given the franchise under the 1925 constitution for the first time in the country's history.

Thus, on 30 November 1924, the old Legislative Council came to an end and the constitution of 1876 was fundamentally revised. The new constitution provided for the election of five members to the Legislative Council. General elections were restored – they had been abandoned 50 years previously. The new Legislative Council was to consist of three nominated members and five elected members on the unofficial side; and seven members, in addition to the Governor who would serve as President, on the official side. The seven members were to include not more than four ex-officio members, among whom were the Attorney-General, Colonial Secretary and Treasurer.[2]

For the first general election in the 20th century Grenada was divided into five electoral districts and voters' rolls for each district were prepared as shown in Table 20.1:

**Table 20.1 Electorate in Grenada 1925**

| | |
|---|---|
| St George's | 508 |
| St John's and St Mark's | 259 |
| St Patrick's and Carriacou | 886 |
| St Andrew's | 349 |
| St David's and South St George's | 157 |
| Total | 2,159 |

Grenada's total population according to the 1921 census was 66,302. The voting population was 3.25% of the total population and 7.08% of the total adult population above the age of 21 (30,488). Thus by 1925 an electoral franchise as restrictive and élitist as in the year 1850 existed in Grenada. The following persons were prohibited from becoming elected members of the Legislative Council:

- a person according to the 1925 constitution who holds any office of emolument under the Crown or under a municipal corporation;
- a minister of religion;
- a returning officer;
- a female person.[3]

In the electoral districts of St George's, St Mark's and St John's, and St David's, no contest took place and the candidates were elected unopposed. In the St Patrick's electoral district three candidates contested the seat, and two contested the seat for St Andrew's.

Between 1925 and 1933 there were three elections under the 1925 constitution. Both elected members and nominated members served a two-year term up to 1927, when it was extended to three years. The successful candidates in the 1925 elections were T.A. Marryshow, D.A. McIntyre, Charles F.P. Renwick, Charles H.W.G. Lucas and Fitz Henry Copland. All five were re-elected in 1927; in the 1931 elections only Marryshow was reelected. Four new members joined the Legislative Council that year: George E. Edwards, John F. Flemming, Willan E. Julien and F.B. Paterson. (The full composition of the Legislative Council for these years is given in Appendix 1.)

## Demands for Self-Government and Federation in the 1930s

The period 1930 to 1936 witnessed demands for further constitutional advancement; but these demands were juxtaposed with demands for a West Indies Federation. The Grenadians saw Federation as an institution that would ensure the future success of self-government.

Meanwhile, the British government began to put its own views on the subject together. Instead of a Federation they advocated Closer Union. This Closer Union was an attempt to rationalize the cost of administering the islands as separate entities by combining these territories into one unit and establishing a central administration. Thus, whereas Marryshow and the West Indians saw Federation as a step to self-government, the imperial government saw it as a means of rationalizing the cost of administration.

In March 1931, in a motion to the Grenada Legislative Council, Marryshow called on the Secretary of State to set up a Commission to look into the issue of self-government for Grenada; but the Secretary of State recommended an amendment to the motion to include Federation. By this, however, he meant closer union of the Windwards and Leewards with Trinidad and Tobago. These were the terms of reference of the Closer Union Commission when it was subsequently set up; the Grenadians were not happy with this.

In the meantime, the depression was having political after-effects on Grenada that manifested themselves in two ways.

1. The demonstration of about 10,000 people led by Marryshow and the Grenada Workingman's Association over the Customs Amendment Order of 1931–32.
2. The resignation of the five elected members of the Legislative Council in 1932 over the passing of the Budget Bill of that year and the Governor's disregard of the recommendations made on that Bill.

As a result of these mass resignations there were by-elections in all five electoral districts on 14 March 1932. All members were returned unopposed. On 1 June 1933 there was a by-election in St Andrew's on the retirement of George Elmore Edwards, and T.E. Noble Smith was elected in his place. The Legislature in 1933 consisted of:

1. The Executive Council: the Colonial Secretary, the Attorney-General, the Colonial Treasurer, the Chief Medical Officer and three members.
2. The Legislative Council: six unofficial members, three nominated unofficial members and five elected unofficial members, three nominated unofficial members and five elected members ensured an automatic majority for the Governor in the Legislative Council.

## *Demand for Constitutional Change 1932–36*

When the elected members had returned to office after the 1932 by-elections they sent a delegation (comprising Marryshow and Elmore Edwards) to Britain to demand some effective control in the government of the country, but, unfortunately, they failed to get their proposals on constitutional change and self-government accepted.

Meanwhile, the Closer Union Commission was carrying out its investigation; this began in 1932 and ended in 1933. The Commission found that the people interviewed in the various islands wanted self-government and were not in favour of closer union *per se*. They recommended that the Windwards and Leewards be administered as a single political unit, and a simultaneous reform of the constitution to allow for more popular representation in the affairs of the colony. This, they argued, could be achieved by abolishing the Governor's official majority in the Legislative Council and replacing it with a majority of elected and non-official members. They suggested, however, that the Governor should retain his veto powers and be given the power to pass laws that may be opposed in the legislature. By so doing, the Commissioners ensured the Governor's continued control of the decision-making process while giving the locals additional voices in the legislature.[4]

When these recommendations on Closer Union were published in 1933, they met with strong opposition in Grenada. Marryshow was in the vanguard of this protest and wrote numerous articles in the local newspaper condemning the recommendations and putting forward alternative proposals. In October 1933 he moved a motion in the House stating that the unofficial members were opposed to the report; this was passed by a vote of five elected to three nominated members. An attempt to have the recommendation passed in March 1934 proved futile, as both the elected and nominated members voted against it. Eventually the Colonial Office decided to abandon the scheme.

The Secretary of State, instead, proposed a few constitutional changes, including the abolition of the Governor's official majority in the Legislative Council; the creation of an unofficial majority of elected and nominated members; and the giving of reserve powers to the Governor to pass any measure in the interest of the good government of the Colony.

The nominated members recommended an increase in their number from three to four; Marryshow and Paterson opposed this and instead demanded an elected majority; but on 15 May 1935 Paterson moved a motion in the Council calling on members to accept the recommendations of the Secretary of State. The motion was accepted. These constitutional changes came into effect in 1936; it was not a new constitution but merely a modification of the one of 1925. The legislature was now composed of a Governor (with a casting vote), three ex-officio officials (Colonial Secretary, Attorney-General and Colonial Treasurer), four nominated and seven elected members.

On 17 December 1936 the old legislature was dissolved. The next general election under the new constitution was held on 18 March 1937. The new Legislature, convened on 25 March 1937, consisted of four nominated members and four ex-officio members – the Governor, the Colonial Secretary, the Attorney-General and the Colonial Treasurer and the seven members elected in the general election.

As reorganized, the 1936 constitution reduced the number of official members from seven to three and increased the number of unofficial members from three to four nominated and from five to seven elected.

## *The Moyne Commission*

The next significant constitutional change occurred in 1951, notwithstanding the fact that the office of Administrator was constituted in place of the Colonial Secretary in 1945.

The changes in the 1950–51 period were a result of the West India Royal Commission report of 1945. Coming in 1951 these changes were somewhat belated in view of the fact that the Moyne Commission took place in 1938–39, and the report was submitted then. Two factors explain the delay in the implementation of Lord Moyne's recommendations. One was the outbreak of the 1939–45 war and the other was the division of views at the local, regional and imperial level on the Federation question and its corollary, constitutional advance.

The Moyne Commission was set up in response to the social upheavals in the British West Indies and the mobilization of the working class by various trade union leaders to demand social, economic and political justice in the 1930s. The Commission made a number of recommendations on various aspects of life in the British West Indies. On the question of constitutional advancement, Moyne recommended that:

1. The Executive Council should include elected members as well as representatives of major interest groups in the society.
2. There be introduced a better system of nomination so as to ensure that the Legislature was representative of all significant interest groups in the community.

In the meantime, two meetings related to the issue of constitutional advance took place, one at the local level and the other at the regional level. The former was a meeting of the unofficial members of the local legislature and the latter a conference of West Indian legislatures held in Grenada in January 1945. Both meetings agreed upon the following constitutional changes:

- that there be an elected majority in the legislature;
- that the Governor should no longer be the President of the Council;

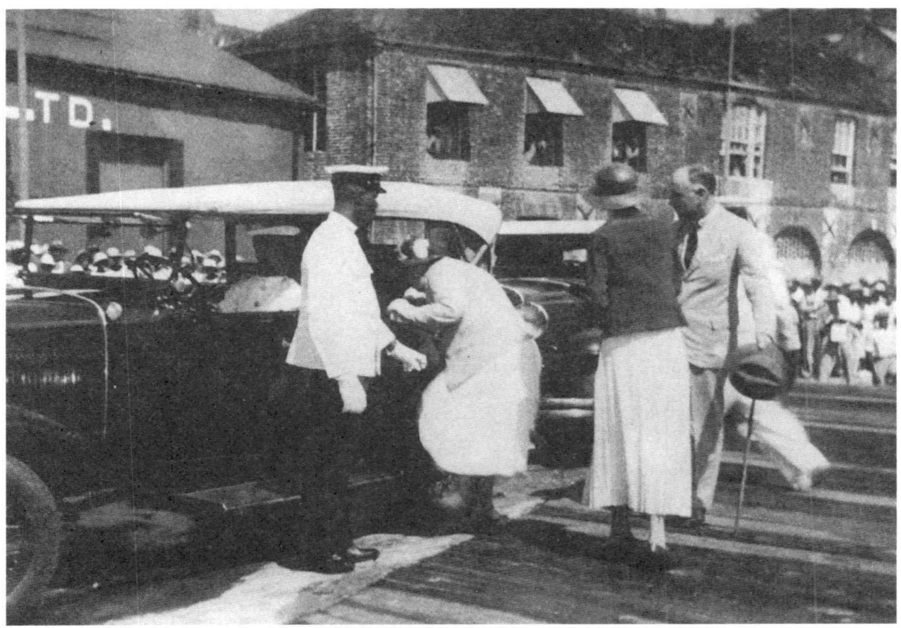

*Governor Edward Heape, c. 1948*

*Parade marking the visit of the Prince of Wales*

- that there be a reduction in the number of official and nominated members;
- that advisory committees comprised of elected members be set up at the executive level; and
- that universal adult suffrage with a literacy test be introduced.[5]

These meetings were followed by the St Kitts Conference on Closer Union, in 1947, with Marryshow, Paterson and Renwick representing Grenada. This meeting discussed a plan for the union of the Windwards and Leewards. This Closer Union issue was, however, superseded in the same year by the Montego Bay Conference on Federation. A Federation of the British West Indies was agreed upon, with individual units retaining full autonomy over those areas not delegated to the central government of the Federation. This conference coincided with the beginning of decolonization within the British Empire, as three former British colonies, India, Pakistan and Ceylon (now Sri Lanka) became independent territories in 1947 and 1948. This significant constitutional advance for Indian colonies clearly meant that the British had to accede to some of the constitutional demands of the West Indian colonies.

In April 1949 Sir Robert Arundell announced at a meeting of the Grenada Legislative Council that the imperial government had agreed to constitutional changes for Grenada. The provisions of this new constitution took effect in September 1951 and included among other things:

1. Universal adult suffrage for all persons 21 years and over.
2. £15 deposit for a candidate, which would not be refunded if the candidate failed to get one-eighth of the votes in his constituency.
3. A legislature comprising: eight elected members, three official members with the Administrator allowed to vote, and three nominated unofficial members. Thus, out of a voting legislature of 12 members, there were now eight elected members.

In order to restrict and curtail the power of the elected majority the imperial government allowed the Governor to retain his powers, 'in the interest of good government and public order'. For example, the Governor had power to pass any Bill that the Legislature rejected; he could refuse assent to bills passed by the Legislature; he could recommend the Secretary of State to veto a particular Bill or measure. Thus, the only real constitutional advances were the extension of the franchise and the abolition of the income and property qualifications for candidature at elections. The reserve powers of the Governor ensured the continued dominance of this official's, and of the imperial government's, views. Committees on economic development and social services were also set up, each comprising legislators and a civil servant. These were established by the Legislative Council before the 1951 constitution came out.[6]

The year of these constitutional advances (1951) marked the entry into the political arena of Eric Gairy, an ex-schoolteacher and migrant worker who had just returned from Aruba. The mass of newly enfranchised stood firmly behind him. After a successful strike, from February to April 1951, which threw the planter, local merchant, and local middle class into complete disarray, he contested the October 1951 elections and he and his Grenada United Labour Party completely swept the polls. This victory was so overwhelming that the Governor could not help but invite the leader, E.M. Gairy, to help form the Executive. The entry of 'Uncle Gairy', as he was popularly called in 1951, ushered in a genuine social revolution in the lives of the working class, and, as was expected, his name became anathema in almost every upper-and middle-class home in Grenada. A new dimension was added to Grenada's politics.

## The Committee System

At a meeting of the Legislative Council on 20 December 1954, the Acting Administrator announced the imperial government's decision to introduce the committee system into Grenada. This system had been in operation in the Leewards and St Vincent for the previous two to four years.

The main rationale for this change was to prepare Legislative Council members for their role of decision-making in the planned West Indian Federation by acquainting them with the machinery and operation of government correspondence and business, and by increasing their knowledge of government administration and finance.

According to the scheme, unofficial members of the Legislative Council were divided into three committees: a) Trade and Production; b) Communications and Works, and c) Education and Social Services.

Each committee was composed of four members and was responsible for discussing subjects pertinent to its portfolio and reporting on such matters to the Administrator, Finance Committee and Executive Council. The functions of these committees were neither legislative nor executive but purely advisory. This system became operative in 1955 and was superseded by the ministerial system of government in 1960.

## Ministerial Government and Squandermania 1959–62

On 21 December 1959 new constitutional provisions for Grenada again came into effect. These provided for an Administrator to administer government and represent the Queen. They also provided for an Executive Council with a Chief Minister, appointed by the Administrator, who was to be an elected member who commanded the confidence of a majority of the elected members. In addition, there was to be a minister without portfolio and an ex-officio member, the principal law officer.[7] H.A. Blaize became the first Chief Minister in 1960, G.E.D. Clyne became the second Chief Minister, and Gairy's party, the GULP, formed the second Ministerial Executive. In 1957 Gairy himself was suspended from the Council and from taking part in elections for five years (1957–61) for breaking up a meeting of his opponents in the 1957 elections. In the 1961 elections Joshua Thorne contested Gairy's seat on his behalf. When the suspension expired, Thorne resigned and Gairy contested and won the seat in a by-election. Shortly afterwards he was appointed Chief Minister and Minister of Finance.

Under the ministerial system of government the Legislative Council was to consist of ten elected members, two nominated members and one ex-officio member. There were many other provisions of the 1959 constitution which dealt with the structure and operation of the public service under the ministerial system. The 1959 constitutional provisions, except those relating to the Legislative Council, came into effect on 1 January 1960; the provisions relating to the Legislative Council came into effect in March 1961.

The 1959 constitution was suspended on 18 June 1962 as a result of the report of a Commission of Enquiry into the control of public expenditure in Grenada in 1961. On 22 January 1962 a Commission was issued by the Administrator, James Monteith Lloyd, appointing as Commissioners Justice Frank Field, Louis Blache-Fraser and E.Howard Hollis, to enquire into the spending of public funds in Grenada during the financial year commencing 1 January 1961 and subsequently, and to report and make recommendations. The enquiry began on 5 February and ended on 2 May. Halfway during the proceedings Fraser resigned for business reasons and was replaced by Harold Watson. In all, some 37 persons gave evidence, including 23 civil servants and a number of other persons representing a variety of interests in the community.[8]

The Commissioners found that in 1961 and after the statutory and other controls over public expenditure were totally disregarded by the Minister of Finance at the time, E.M. Gairy, and by others who took orders from him. Expenditure in excess of the estimates was often incurred without the authority of a warrant; warrants were issued in excess of the amounts permitted by law or without the required approval of the federal government. Payments were made for the sole purpose of using up balances which would otherwise have lapsed, and other payments which were due were deferred until the following year because no provisions had been made for them.

Expenditure was incurred by officers not in control of votes, without the consent or even the knowledge of those appointed to control them, and payments were made by the Treasury on unsigned vouchers. The circumstances, or rather the manner in which irregular payments were made or directed to be made, proliferated and became significant when Gairy assumed the office of Minister of Finance in 1961. He made it quite clear that he did not need the services of a Financial Secretary; and those public officers who did not yield to the Minister's demands or who incurred his displeasure, were humiliated, victimized or antagonized, politically or personally.

Having browbeaten most of the public servants into subservience, the Minister of Finance embarked on a series of financial adventures which, in every case, involved either a waste or misuse of public funds. Moreover, this was done in ignorance or with total disregard for the laws and regulations governing public finance in Grenada. The Minister also drastically curtailed the functions of the Tenders Board.

Prior to 22 November 1961, contracts for public works not exceeding $1,500 were awarded by the Director of Public Works; contracts involving larger sums were to be awarded by the Tenders Board. After this date the Director's power was restricted to works costing $25 or less; contracts for works costing between $25 and $5,000 were to be awarded not by the Tenders Board as was formerly the case, but by its chairman. The chairman was no longer the Financial Secretary but the Principal Secretary to the Minister of Communications and Works. He was accountable to that minister and that minister took instructions from the Chief Minister who was at the same time Minister of Finance. What this meant was that the award of contracts was now the prerogative of Gairy, and any criticism by the Treasury through the Financial Secretary or by the technical officers through the Director of Public Works was silenced.

The Commission itemized many instances of work done by private persons at public expense, plus many cases of wasteful and extravagant expenditure. One example of the latter was the refurnishing of Mt Royal, the residence of the Minister of Finance, at a cost of $17,250 without the approval of the Tenders Board. This included a piano costing $3,500, a radiogram costing $1,450 and two radios. In addition, there were countless cases where payments amounting to thousands of dollars were made gratuitously and unnecessarily. Lastly, there were instances of questionable expenditure, involving the purchase of lands on Minorca Estate, the purchase of Sapco building, the purchase of lands from Bardia Estate, the purchase of lifeboats, cement, cold storage rooms and the insurance of government vehicles.

The estate (Bardia) is a classic in graft. It comprised 165 acres and was sold in 1961 for $40,000; government then bought 30 acres from the new owner for $20,000 or at the price of $666 per acre, despite two separate and independent valuations of $320 and $340 an acre. The Commissioners noted that, having regard to the two independent valuations and to the price of $240 that was paid by the new owner, it was difficult to understand the willingness of government to purchase at $666 per acre.[9]

After carrying out their examination the Commissioners concluded that the Minister of Finance had disregarded and contravened the laws and regulations governing the control of expenditure. The Commissioners accused the Government and Minister of Finance of financial mismanagement and wasteful expenditure.

- The Executive had deliberately destroyed the morale of the civil service by an undesirable interference with administrative duties and by threats to officers' security.
- The civil service had been induced by this interference and these threats to commit or condone improprieties or irregularities in the expenditure of public funds.
- Expenditures had been incurred wastefully or unnecessarily through failure by ministers to seek or refusal to accept the advice of the civil servants.[10]
- The main actor and arch offender in this regard was the Minister of Finance, E.M. Gairy. This misuse and misappropriation of government funds has been described in local parlance as 'Squandermania.'

Gairy himself has always had a dubious history when it came to debt and finance. Between 1952 and 1965 there were some 17 debt cases brought against him in the High Court in its original jurisdiction alone. These were as follows:

1. McIntyre Bros. vs Gairy: action for $787 for goods sold in 1952.
2. George DeFreitas vs Gairy: action for $510.55 for goods sold to him in 1952.
3. Barclays Bank vs Gairy: action for $407.45 for money lent in 1954.

4. Simeon Francis vs Gairy: action for amount of money spent by Gairy in 1954.
5. Everybody's Stores vs Gairy: action for $360 owed for rent in 1955.
6. Everybody's Stores vs Gairy: action for $1,178.50 for goods sold in 1954.
7. Everybody's Stores vs Gairy: action for $966 for goods and rent in 1956.
8. Everybody's Stores vs Gairy: action for $390 for rent owed in 1958.
9. Government of Grenada vs Gairy: action for $6,278.87 borrowed by Gairy from the coalition government of 1954–57. Action taken in 1958.
10. Hankey's vs Gairy: action for $284.86 for goods sold in 1959.
11. George DeFreitas vs Gairy: action for $2,162.00 for money lent in 1960.
12. Hankey's vs Gairy: action for $747 for goods sold in 1963.
13. Nick's Ltd. vs Gairy: action for $385 for goods sold in 1963.
14. Government of Grenada vs Gairy: action for $1,504 lent in 1962.
15. Armand Williams vs Gairy: action for $500 lent to Gairy in 1965.
16. Lennard Sargeant vs Gairy: action for $300 lent in 1965.
17. Lennard Sargeant vs Gairy: action for $250 lent in 1965.[11]

After the suspension of the constitution in 1961 the Administrator was given wider reserve powers, including that of appointing an official Minister of Finance. General elections followed on 13 September 1962, and these were won by the Grenada National Party (GNP). H.A. Blaize, leader of the party, was asked by the Administrator to form the government; his party won six out of the ten seats, while the GULP won four.

The Federation of the West Indies, which came into being in 1958 and ended in 1962, did not have any effect on Grenada's constitution. Four years later, however, the constitution underwent significant and fundamental changes.

Within the given colonial structure, the GNP government of 1962–67 was a reformist government. Its period was one of political and economic stability. Some economic and social reforms were carried out but there were no structural economic or social changes. If anything, the urban bourgeoisie and rural gentry became more entrenched as their party was now in power.

The GNP government declared that its constitutional objective was towards entry into a unitary state with Trinidad and Tobago. In fact, this promise had accounted for a large measure of its success at the polls in 1962. This declaration of intent was subsequently reaffirmed in Throne-speeches of 1962, 1963 and 1964. As a result of this stated aim Grenada did not participate in the deliberations of the Regional Council of Ministers of the other Windward and Leeward Islands who were then considering the formation of an Eastern Caribbean Federation of the remaining Windwards, the Leewards and Barbados. This subsequently proved to be abortive.

In the meantime fact-finding Commissions appointed by the Prime Minister of Trinidad and Tobago visited Grenada to examine the implications of unitary statehood with respect to economic, fiscal,

*E.M. Gairy*

administrative and legal matters. Missions from Grenada made similar trips to Trinidad. Eventually this scheme was abandoned owing to intense opposition by the people of Trinidad and Tobago.

In January 1966 the Grenada constitution as provided for in Orders-in-Council of 1959 and 1962 and in Royal Instructions of 1959, which had been suspended in 1962, was restored. This restoration relieved the GNP of many constitutional disabilities under which it had laboured during the last four years.

The GNP government carried out many reforms in the fields of agriculture, education, health and communications. Some of these included the initiation of a Fertilizer Subsidy Scheme, the establishment of the Agricultural Bank, the setting up of a scheme to propagate economic crops, the construction of primary schools, the expansion of water supply, the extension of teacher-training facilities and the construction of the Commercial and Domestic Arts Institute.

During this period the Colonial Development and Welfare (CDW) grants remained the major source of finance for development expenditure in the public sector. The Colony's CDW allocation for the three-year period – 1 April 1963 to 31 March 1966 – was EC$720,000. In 1965 the UK government revised Grenada's allocation and provided funds amounting to $2.313 million for the three-year period ending 31 March 1968.[12]

During the GNP administration, the business of government was conducted by the following departments: Administration, Agriculture, Forestry and Land, Audit, Education, Electricity and Telephones, Labour, Legal, Medical, Police, Post Office, Prisons, Public Works and Treasury.

The Legislative Council passed, instituted and numbered bills and presented them to the Administrator for assent. Unless it was otherwise expressly provided such bills became law when the Administrator had assented thereto in Her Majesty's name and on Her Majesty's behalf, and signed the same in token of such assent and notification to that effect had been published in the *Gazette*. Unless he had been authorized by the Secretary of State to assent thereto, the Administrator must reserve for signification of Her Majesty's pleasure any Bill which appeared to him, acting in his discretion, to be inconsistent with any obligations of Her Majesty or of Her Majesty's Government in the United Kingdom toward any other State or power or any international organization, or to be likely to prejudice the royal prerogative, or the maintenance of law and order in Grenada, or the efficiency of the judiciary or the public service or any part thereof, or which was in any way repugnant to or inconsistent with the provisions of the Orders-in-Council. Any law assented to by the

Administrator might be disallowed by Her Majesty through the Secretary of State.

There was a Legislative Council Standing Committee on Finance, consisting of all members of the Council, except the Speaker and the Attorney-General, of which the Minister of Finance was Chairman. All votes entailing expenditure from public funds for which the sanction of the Legislative Council was necessary were required to be considered by the Standing Committee on Finance before they were submitted to the Council for acceptance. No item of expenditure which had not been approved by the committee could be submitted for the consideration of the Council unless a motion was made to that effect.

There was also a Public Accounts Committee of the Legislative Council consisting of three members, none of whom was to be a member of the Executive Council; they were elected by the Legislative Council as soon as possible after the beginning of each session on a motion by the Minister of Finance. It was the duty of this committee to examine the audited accounts of expenditure from public funds and such other accounts laid before the legislature as the Council might refer to the committee together with the Principal Auditor's report thereon.[13]

Local government was under the Ministry of Trade and Production. The island was divided into the municipal borough of St George's and the districts of St David's, St Andrew's, St Patrick's, St Mark's and St John's. For the purpose of local government, the municipal borough of St George was placed under the St George's Corporation, and each of the several districts under a District Board. The St George's Corporation and District Boards were bodies corporate. The former was constituted under the St George's Corporation Ordinance 1961 (No. 3 of 1961), the latter under the District Boards Ordinance Cap. 99 of the Revised Laws of Grenada.

The islands of Carriacou and Petit Martinique were included in the Carriacou District created by the Carriacou District Ordinance of 1904.

The St George's Corporation was run by a council consisting of the mayor, four aldermen and eight councillors. The councillors were elected by the burgesses and the council elected the aldermen. Both aldermen and councillors held office for three years. The District Boards had an equal number of elected and nominated members. The largest was St Andrew's, with 14 members, and the smallest was St Mark's with eight. St John's and St David's each had ten, while St Patrick's had 12. The life of each Board was three years.

The restoration of the 1959 constitution in 1966 freed the GNP government from any restraint in discussing proposals on further constitutional advance in 1966, which were to lead to associated statehood with Britain and to full self-government.

## Associated Statehood

With effect from 3 March 1967 Grenada became an Associated State of Great Britain and as such, was given a new constitution, which provided for:

1. A Governor who was to be the representative of the Queen.
2. A legislature composed of:
   (a) *The Senate* which consisted of nine members, five appointed by the Governor on the advice of the Premier; two appointed by the Governor on the advice of the leader of the Opposition; two appointed by the Governor on the advice of the Premier after he had consulted interest groups.
   (b) *The House of Representatives* consisting of such members as corresponded to the number of constituencies.
3. An Executive: this was to consist of a Premier, and such other ministers as may be established by the Legislature or by the Governor acting on the advice of the Premier. There was also to be a Cabinet consisting of the Premier, all ministers and the Attorney-General or an ex-officio member.

The Legislature was given full control of all Grenada's affairs except defence and external affairs, which were still controlled by Great Britain.[14]

The first Premier under the new constitution was H.A. Blaize, but later in 1967 his party was deposed in the general elections by E.M. Gairy and the Grenada United Labour Party by a seven to three margin. Grenada was governed under this constitution from 1967 to February 1974 when she became a fully independent country within the Commonwealth.

Between 1950 and 1972 a total of seven general elections was held to elect members to Grenada's House of Representatives. The results of some of these are shown in Appendix 3. The elections showed that it was possible for a party to poll less than 50% of the votes cast and still govern; this was the system of 'first past the post.' Under a system of proportional representation, where the allocation of seats in the House reflects the relative numerical proportions of the votes cast, the situation would have been different. In none of the five elections won by the GULP, Gairy's party, did it receive more than 50% of the registered votes. Many seats, in fact, were won by the

GULP because too many candidates opposed the GULP and thus split the votes. In these elections the electorate's ignorance was constantly exploited by politicians who indulged in all kinds of trickery to win votes.

- In the 1951 elections the electorate numbered 34,133; 21,203 unspoilt votes were cast, of which GULP received 12,781, or 37% of the electorate and 60% of the votes cast.[15]
- The electorate in the 1954 elections numbered 36,846 and cast 22,476 unspoilt votes. The GULP polled 10,937 votes or 29% of the registered voters and 48% of the votes cast. In St Patrick's the victorious GULP candidate polled 1,138 votes compared to a total of 1,875 for the other two candidates. In St Andrew's South, again, the successful GULP candidate polled 1,363 votes compared to 1,982 cast for his four opponents. In St David's the GULP candidate polled 1,055, while his four opponents polled a total of 1,488. In all three constituencies there were more voters opposed to the GULP than there were in favour.[16]
- GULP lost the 1957 elections. The electorate numbered 37,738, out of which 24,710 voted. GULP polled 9,975 or 26% of the registered votes and 40% of the votes cast. In the constituency of St David's the GULP candidate polled 983, his nearest rival polled 960, but there was a third candidate who polled 585. Had it been a two-way fight the GULP candidate would certainly have lost, as 1,500 voters opposed him – 600 more than those for him.[17]
- In 1961 out of an electorate of 41,087, 21,754 voted. GULP polled 11,606 or 28% of the registered voters and 53% of the unspoilt votes. They won 80% of the seats in the House of Representatives with only 28% of popular support. The other parties had 24% of popular support but obtained only 20% of the seats. This clearly demonstrates the fallibility of the first-past-the-post system relative to 'government by the people for the people'.[18]
- The GNP won the 1962 general elections by a six-to-four margin and formed the Government for the next five years. The electorate numbered 31,766 and 21,107 unspoilt votes were cast. GULP secured 30% of the electorate and GNP 36%. GULP polled 46% of votes cast while GNP polled 54%. GNP obtained 60% of the seats and GULP 40%.[19]
- In the 1967 elections 29,017 voted out of a total electorate of 38,800. Of these the GULP polled 15,827 votes or 41% of the electorate; the GNP polled 13,190 or 34%. GULP received 54% of the unspoilt votes cast but 70% of the seats while GNP with 46% had 30%.[20]

- The 1972 election was a classic example of the inadequacies of the electoral system. The electorate numbered 41,529 and cast 34,241 unspoilt votes. GULP polled 20,155 or 48% of the electorate and 59% of the unspoilt votes cast, yet they received 87% of the seats. GNP received 14,086 votes or 34% of the electorate and 42% of the unspoilt votes cast, but received 13% of the seats.[21]

Gairy's defeat at the polls in 1962 was a hard blow, one he found difficult to live with. While out of power he lived in virtual penury, waiting for 1967 when he could make a bid to return. He won the elections in that year and was back in power. Despite the 1962 defeat he was still able to build up considerable mass popular support.

He ruled Grenada with an iron hand during the next 12 years, making himself financially prosperous in the process. In these 12 years Gairy utterly disregarded the principles he had upheld in 1951, violated the very workers' rights he had campaigned for in 1951, and destroyed some of the people he fought for in that year. In 1951 he had defended the working class and won their trust, but from 1967 to 1979 he increasingly exploited them for his own ends and betrayed them. By what he did and supported he became increasingly anti-working class.

## Political Debacle and Constitutional Violations

The history of Grenada between 1968 and 1979, but especially between 1973 and 1979, illustrates Gairy's hopes that after 1967 he could perpetuate himself in power, even against popular wishes, by essentially three strategies:

1. By making as many people as possible economically dependent upon the Government and upon himself in order to control them politically.
2. By crushing dissent and by making it difficult if not impossible for Parliamentary Opposition to operate and perform. By 1979 Parliament had become his personal property.
3. By creating a highly centralized bureaucracy where decision-making depended on the Cabinet which, in effect, was Gairy himself.

In the process there were many occasions on which people's constitutional rights were violated.

One of the first actions taken in a bid to operate these strategies was the passing in 1968 of the Firearms Act a few months after Gairy was returned to power. The significance of this Act was more in its unwritten political intent than in its written clauses. Although applicable to all firearms' owners, the aim was to call in all licensed firearms from those persons who were opposed to the Government. It was an attempt to control the population by ensuring that the Government and its supporters controlled the means of violence.

The second calculated effort to control the population, this time by controlling the means of their existence, was the spate of land acquisitions in 1971 and 1972 under the Government's programme of land for the landless. The last year when estate lands were acquired was 1963, when Pointzfield 'B' in St Patrick's was appropriated. In 1971, 14 estates were taken over by the Government, and in 1972 seven more. By 1978 over 30 estates had been acquired under this scheme.

What is revealing is that in many cases the owners of these estates were opponents of the Government. In some cases, especially for those appropriated after 1972, payment was not made. Many estates thus acquired were not sub-divided to give land to the landless. The object instead was to break the economic power of those medium and large landowners opposed to the Government, and to control the workers on these estates by making them directly dependent on the Government for their livelihood.

A similar effort to undermine the economic independence of Grenadians was the government seizure of producer co-operatives – all statutory bodies – by abolishing those Boards elected by growers and replacing them with government-nominated interim Boards. The producer co-operatives seized between 1972 and 1975 were: a) The Grenada Cocoa Industry Board; b) The Banana Co-operative Society; and c) The Grenada Co-operative Nutmeg Association. The last, the largest, and the most significant, was the Nutmeg Board. In June 1975 the elected Nutmeg Board was dissolved by an Act entitled Nutmeg Board Dissolution Order Validation Act 1975. Clause 4 of the Act read as follows:

> Notwithstanding the provisions contained in the principal law or any other law to the contrary the Board referred to in Section 3 above is hereby declared to be lawful and is confirmed as on the 4th day of July 1975 and until such time as a Board declared elected under the provision of the principal law is constituted.

After the creation of an interim Board the Government appointed a Commission to inquire into the financial affairs of the Association for the period June 1969 to 4 July 1975.

H.R.P. Dennison of Guyana was appointed Sole Commissioner and evidence was heard at sittings lasting from 29 October to 5 December 1975. At the beginning of the sittings the members of the dissolved Nutmeg Board indicated, through their legal representatives, their unwillingness to participate and give evidence unless certain demands were met. These demands were not granted by the Commissioner, and the persons concerned then filed an application with the High Court for an injunction to restrain the Commission from sitting. On 1 December judgment was given against the application. An appeal against the judgment was subsequently filed by Counsel for members of the dissolved Board but the appeal was dismissed in a decision given by the High Court on 25 July 1976.

While the Commission was holding its hearings, however, an originating motion was filed in the High Court on 30 October 1975, in the name of Bornston Hamilton, F.J. Archibald and the other members of the dissolved Board, by their solicitor, Maurice Bishop, seeking, *inter alia*

- a declaration that the Nutmeg Board (Dissolution) Order 1975 made by the Governor-General on 4 July 1975 was *ultra vires*;
- a declaration that the interim Board was unconstitutional and *ultra* vires;
- an order to restrain the interim Board from sitting.

The matter was heard in High Court during April 1976, and on 28 July the Court upheld the motion. The presiding judge, Justice Archibald Nedd, in presenting his findings stated that the Act passed by Parliament in an attempt to validate the dissolution order was null and void, that the dissolution was bad law, a breach of the constitution and could not be validated. Thereupon the interim Board appealed the decision. The Appeal Court upset Justice Nedd's decision and the matter was subsequently the subject of an appeal to the Privy Council.

According to the Nutmeg Industry Ordinance, 'If the Board is dissolved after March 31st in any year the persons appointed shall perform their duties up to the 30th June next when the New Board shall be constituted.' The Nutmeg Board was dissolved in June 1975, yet by March 1979 the elected Board had not been reconstituted. There were some 6,000 nutmeg producers, about 3,000 cocoa producers and approximately 2,000 banana producers; to control these Boards was to control the area of decision-making of over 10,000 producers and their families and consequently to control them politically.

The fourth tactic was the victimization of persons employed in the Public Service by means either of transfer, termination of employment or some other form of pressure. The examples made of such persons demonstrated to others that they were economically dependent on the Government and would suffer a similar fate if they opposed the ruling party or showed any strong leanings towards the Opposition. Those who had families to feed, mortgages to pay or other financial encumbrances to discharge, understood this tacit message only too well. Some public officers were afraid to speak or give an opinion lest they be reported, others behaved hypocritically and played the game.

The process was one of total emasculation of public officers. Many were filled with resentment, but could say nothing lest they be victimized. This was the lot of many public officers from 1970 to 1978. The main sanction for what the Gairy government interpreted as political misdemeanour was victimization or the threat of it. Hiring and firing of persons in the public service was decided by Cabinet and in Cabinet Gairy was boss: the Public Service Commission was, therefore, reduced to a mere rubber stamp.

Gairy's fifth tactic was to give concessions and monopolies to certain businesses and other supporters. By doing so he ensured that the political wheels were constantly greased; often such persons would be reminded that their privileges would be withdrawn if they failed to live up to expectations.

Then came the beating of the six members of the New Jewel Movement on 18 November 1973. That single act destroyed Gairy politically, as his régime was then conceived, especially by the young, as the epitome of brutality and callousness. The mere mention of Gairy's name among the 15–30 age group was sufficient to evoke revulsion and even hostility. The young had nothing to remember him for; some of their parents (especially the poor) who lived through and benefited from the 1951 'social revolution' idolized him, and his popularity among them fed upon this first impression. But the young, who lived through the 1970s, could remember only inflation, unemployment and acts of brutality, sometimes sporadic, sometimes widespread. Gairy's name became anathema to the young; in politics he was their *béte noire*.

The vanguard party for the youth, the anti-Gairy elements, and increasingly, the workers, was the New Jewel Movement. Already its precursor organization JEWEL (Joint Endeavours for Welfare, Education and Liberation) had won nationwide recognition, when on 21 January 1973 it organized a People's Trial of Lord Brownlow, an Englishman who had deprived the people of St David's parish of access to the La Sagesse beach. For over 100 years the people had used the roads, playground and beach on the La Sagesse Estate freely: when the estate was owned by Sir Joseph De LaMothe, from about 1900 to 1950, the roads and beach were used freely. The first commemoration

*The Trial of Lord Brownlow, La Sagesse, 1973*

of the World War Armistice in 1919 was celebrated at La Sagesse recreation ground. The grounds were also used for horse-racing, scout jamborees, camps, athletic meetings, and cricket and football matches. Louis Strauss, who owned the estate from 1950 to 1955, never prevented anyone from using these facilities, neither did DeGale and Henry who owned it from 1955 to 1960. The people continued to use the facilities unobstructed until Lord Brownlow bought the property; then, all roads leading to the beach were declared private and the people thus deprived of access to the beach. On 21 January 1973 at the People's Trial of Lord Brownlow he was found guilty and the participants then proceeded to execute sentence – breaking down the gates and the re-establishment of access to the La Sagesse beach. The Government sent out large numbers of police, headed by Innocent Belmar, but they only observed the proceedings quietly. Forty persons were, however, subsequently charged with destruction of property and disorderly conduct. Among the 40 were Maurice Bishop, Unison Whiteman, Teddy Victor and Sebastian Thomas. Most of the persons charged were members of Jewel and MAP (Movement for Assemblies of People). The charges were eventually thrown out.

The New Jewel Movement (NJM) was formed on Sunday 11 March 1973, when, at a joint meeting in St David's, the 'Jewel' organization of St David's, and MAP of St George's merged into one political group. The leaders of the 'Jewel' organization were Teddy Victor, Unison Whiteman and Sebastian Thomas. The leaders of MAP were Maurice Bishop, Unison Whiteman, Franklyn Harvey and a few other professionals. Unison Whiteman was the main link in the merger of the two organizations.

Papers were presented by both groups analysing the political situation and presenting strategies for moving forward. It was agreed to mobilize the masses around the burning issue of the day – independence – and to that end, a People's Convention on Independence was arranged for 6 May 1973. Assemblies of the people were proposed as the new governmental structure for society. At that meeting it was agreed that Maurice Bishop and Unison Whiteman should be the joint co-ordinating secretaries for the movement. The organ of the Jewel organization in St David's, *Jewel*, now became the organ for the new movement and its name was modified from *Jewel* to *The New Jewel*. At the same time the slogan of that paper was changed from 'Let's join hands to build a better land' to 'Not just another society but a just society' and 'Let those who labour hold the reins'. In its first publication *The New Jewel* referred to that historic meeting as *The Great Merger*.

The philosophy of the movement as well as its thinking on various social, political, economic and legal issues were well enunciated in its manifesto for *Power to the People* published later that same year. It called for a whole range of far-reaching programmes: agricultural reform, agro-industries, free secondary education, curriculum reform and freedom schools, a national health insurance scheme and preventive medicine campaigns, social planning, new tourism, the nationalization of banks, the phasing-out of foreign insurance companies and the establishment of a government-owned National Insurance Company, to mention a few. The manifesto called for an end to party politics and the institution of People's Assemblies as the political structure that would ensure participatory democracy and the permanent involvement of all the people in decision-making.[22]

From the time of the merger onwards members of the movement worked indefatigably to organize the people into cells at their places of work or residence and to educate and mobilize them for political action. Much of this political work took place around the issue of independence. On 6 May the People's Convention on Independence was held at Seamoon, and attended by thousands of Grenadians from all walks of life. The Convention called for people's involvement in the independence constitution, as well as the initiation of positive and concrete steps to cure national, social and economic ills. The NJM never opposed independence. It was critical of 'flag and anthem' independence and an independence full of trappings but without substance for the people and their ills; this was a meaningless independence and this it disregarded. Instead it supported a meaningful, real and genuine

*Selwyn Strachan, Maurice Bishop and Bernard Coard, in 1979*

*Maurice Bishop*

*The NJM People's Congress, 4 November 1973*

independence. It could not see that type of independence being achieved either under the GULP or the GNP. It called for independence under a new progressive, imaginative, honest and hard-working leadership. It demanded independence projects not celebrations, it demanded negotiations with the British for partial reparation for wealth exported to them from Grenada during the three centuries or so of British rule.

During the period of agitation many of the NJM's followers were intimidated, brutalized and even murdered. On Sunday 22 April, Jeremiah Richardson was murdered by secret police; the following day there were mass demonstrations in St Andrew's, the home parish of the deceased, and Pearls Airport was shut down; police were called in and opened fire on the demonstrators, wounding at least ten. On Monday 30 April, Mathew Joseph, another NJM supporter, was shot by a police officer; on 26 May, Hamilton, another supporter, was beaten by the secret police, and Goodrich Antoine was brutalized by the Mongoose Gang.

Gairy returned to Grenada from the first independence talks on 27 May, and many Jewel supporters who went to the airport on his arrival were beaten by the secret police. The following day, Leonard Greendige, another NJM supporter, was beaten on the Esplanade by Gairy's Mongoose Gang, and on 1 June, Alston Williams was 'chopped up' by the secret police for selling NJM newspapers. On 9 June, Clarence Ferguson was savagely beaten and 'chopped up' by the Mongoose Gang; his daughter, a high-school student, who was with him, was stripped naked in public. Ferguson had to be immediately hospitalized.

As both local and regional support for the NJM grew, the brutality of the Gairy regime and its para-military personnel was intensified. On almost every occasion when there was an incident between the NJM supporters and Gairy's para-military, the former was invariably on the receiving end. This was the pattern up to independence.

Then, on 4 November, NJM held a People's Congress at Seamoon. No fewer than 8,000 Grenadians attended, despite searches and a massive show of guns by the Government. Twenty-seven charges were read out against the government and for every one the people shouted unanimously: 'Guilty!' This resolution was called the *People's Indictment*. Copies of it were sent to Gairy and other members of government as well as senators, calling on them to resign with effect from 18 November 1973. The following is the full text of the indictment.[23]

Whereas a government can only rule with the consent of the people AND WHEREAS a Government is the servant (and not the master) of the people and is under a moral duty to carry out the wishes of the people AND WHEREAS the PEOPLE elect a Government to provide them with material benefits and to improve the quality of their lives AND WHEREAS the PEOPLE have a sacred right to work in order to feed themselves and their children, house and clothe themselves and obtain proper, adequate and cheap medical attention

AND WHEREAS the people are ALWAYS entitled to withdraw their consent and to remove a Government when it becomes clear that the Government is unable or unwilling to carry out their minimum wishes and supply them with their basic demands

AND WHEREAS the present Government of Grenada has demonstrated beyond any reasonable doubt both its unwillingness and its inability to carry out the wishes of the people, many of which were stated in the Manifesto issued by the party of the Government in the last elections

AND WHEREAS conclusive proof of the inability and unwillingness of this Government to carry out its mandate to govern us according to our wishes and instructions is provided by the following MAJOR CRIMES COMMITTED by the Government against the people to wit:

1. The Gairy Government encouraged and openly condoned the murders of our citizens: viz Bro. Jerry Richardson, Bro. Cummings, Bro. Lester Richardson and Bro. Alister Saunders among others.

2. The Gairy Government ordered or condoned the shooting of the ten peaceful and unarmed demonstrators who were protesting the murder of Jerry Richardson by a member of the Police Force.
3. The Gairy Government has been carrying out its plan to rule the people by fear thus hiring known criminals to brutalize people who are bold enough to oppose its corrupt Government.
4. The Gairy Government has been using the method of malicious arrests and arbitrary searches as a means of provoking and harassing opponents of its criminal Government in an attempt to stifle dissent.
5. The Gairy Government has squandered and continues to squander the people's money on dream projects employing political Civil Servants and squandering millions on unnecessary travel, arms and secret police while people are 'ketching hell' to make a living.
6. The Gairy Government has abused our laws in seizing the people's co-operatives viz: the Banana Co-operative and the Cocoa Association.
7. The Gairy Government has confiscated the people's Radio Station, and turned it into a propaganda machine for its personal satisfaction and glorification.
8. The Gairy Government has not accounted for the spending of people's money in the G.M. & M.W.U. from 1951 to today.
9. The Gairy Government must answer for the arbitrary dismissal of the brave and gallant nurses who protested against the appalling conditions which obtained at the General Hospital in 1970.
10. The Gairy Government victimized hundreds of persons in the Police, Civil Service, Estates, and among citizens generally since 1967 when it resumed office.
11. The Gairy Government has destroyed the Police Force, and turned it into a band of Legalized Criminals. It is Gairy who has sent known criminals to associate with the Police, to spy on them, and commit acts to belittle and embarrass them.
12. The Gairy Government destroyed Agriculture in the State. It did so by the acquisition (through spite) of highly productive estates and cutting them up into land for the landless scandal. It destroyed our Agricultural Stations, and Westerhall Farm bears testimony to this.
13. The Gairy Government has sold out all Government lands and buildings. Quarantine Station is gone. Even the Mental Hospital and Alms House lands are up for sale.
14. The Gairy Government has destroyed our Hospitals, and has endangered our health and lives with poor medical facilities; doctors are now afraid to remain in Grenada. There are no resident doctors in Carriacou, St. David's and Gouyave.
15. The Gairy Government has acquired people's property in an effort to deprive political opponents of their livelihood.
16. The Gairy Government has refused to hold public enquiries into the wanton shooting of our citizens, and into other national disasters such as the sinking of the City of St. George, and into conditions in the Police Force, Civil Service and Prisons.

17. The Gairy Government has destroyed our roads. Our main roads are deplorable. Feeder roads can now be remembered.
18. The Gairy Government has conspired with Brownlow and others to take away people's rights to La Sagesse and other beaches.
19. The Gairy Government has refused to pay its dues to Secondary Schools and the Universities. It has insulted youth by demonstrating that secret police came before youth.
20. The Gairy Government has transformed our democracy into ruthless one-man dictatorship. Gairy's dreams are our plans. The entire country is now as his private estate.
21. The Gairy Government has shown its complete contempt of and disregard for the people's wishes by its approach to the question of Independence.
22. The Gairy Government has enriched itself among other ways by taking bubul [salaries for which little or no work was done] salaries for the entire clique.
23. The Gairy Government has done nothing to reduce the scandalously high cost of living and by its policy of raising taxes on the essential foods and other items like rice, flour and kerosene, it has increased the level of poverty in the island.
24. The Gairy Government has increasingly been giving away our best lands to foreigners.
25. The Gairy Government was BORN IN BLOOD, BAPTIZED IN FIRE, CHRISTENED WITH BULLETS, IS MARRIED TO FOREIGNERS AND IS RESULTING IN DEATH TO THE PEOPLE.
26. The Gairy Government has made no effort to provide us with a sense of direction and worthwhile sense of values.
27. The Gairy Government has consistently neglected throughout its years in office from 1951 onwards the basic needs of the people for decent housing, adequate clothing, reliable transport, cheap and high quality medical facilities, a better quality of education for all our children, the development (instead of destruction) of our Agriculture for us to feed all our people and the denial of the opportunity to work and earn a livelihood of over half of the people. These are the gravest crimes of which any Government can stand accused and be proved guilty.

AND WHEREAS the people of Grenada have now decided that for the reasons given above we must decide on the best course of action now open to us to save Grenada.
NOW THEREFORE BE IT RESOLVED that a Congress of the People meeting at Seamoon on the 4th day of November 1973 has democratically and collectively agreed to take the following actions:

a. To pass a verdict of guilty on the charges laid against this Government and to condemn this Government for irresponsibility, corruption, incompetence, inefficiency, breach of contract, and to pass a vote of no confidence in the Government.

b. To call upon this Government to resign with effect from 18th November, 1973.
c. To appoint a National Unity Council from among persons present at this Congress charged with the responsibility of implementing the decision taken at the Congress to remove this Government from office and to constitute a provisional government of the people pending the call of New Elections by the Governor to elect a new popular Government.
d. To agree to use the New Jewel's Manifesto for power to the people as the basis of a new plan that the new Government will operate to run the country.

AND BE IT FURTHER RESOLVED THAT COPIES OF THIS Resolution of the PEOPLE'S WILL be forwarded to the Governor, Premier and Cabinet as official notice of our decisions taken today.

It was agreed that if the Government refused to resign there would be a general strike to shut down the country until the Government did resign. Gairy now became afraid that all these moves by the NJM would seriously hinder his plans for gaining independence. He called a meeting on 4 November in Grenville Market Square to counter the effect of the NJM's recent mobilization. Some NJM supporters who attended this meeting were beaten and brutalized by government supporters, with Gairy himself identifying some persons for beatings.

The fatal error was that, being under pressure from opposition forces and witnessing an erosion of his support, Gairy thought that the only method of neutralizing the situation was through violent intimidation and force. But his methods were all counter-productive; moreover, it showed that as far as dealing with opposition was concerned he was politically immature. He never, in fact, understood the type of opposition he was up against. On Thursday, 8 November, he broadcast on the radio and promised to bring 54 charges – including sedition and treason – against the NJM. Then came Sunday 18 November 1973, when a reign of terror was unleashed on six members of the NJM who had gone to Grenville to hold a meeting. They were mercilessly beaten by a crowd of secret police under the supervision of Inspector Belmar, some almost beyond recognition. The six were Maurice Bishop, Unison Whiteman, Kenrick Radix, Selwyn Strachan, Simon Daniel and Hudson Austin.

Of all the events outlined, 'Bloody Sunday', as it was called thereafter, was one of Gairy's most expensive errors, one from which he was never to recover. Unwittingly, he had committed political suicide. The beating of the six NJM members in 1973 was purely a case of Gairy's over-reaction to the call by the Jewel for a general strike if he, Gairy had failed to resign within two weeks for the 27 reasons stated. Indications were that the strike might not have succeeded; but Gairy lost his head; said he knew 54 reasons why the NJM should be tried for treason; unleashed an onslaught on 18 November, and thus made living martyrs of New Jewel Movement leaders. In fact, the beatings precipitated the very strike they were intended to prevent. For one month in January 1974, the island was locked in a general strike and the streets were filled with thousands of Grenadians young and old demonstrating and chanting: 'Gairy must go!' The Governor, Hilda Bynoe, overwhelmed by the massiveness of the demonstrations, resigned and migrated to Trinidad.

Initiative in those demonstrations was provided by the Seamen and Waterfront Workers' Union and the NJM; but the strikes and demonstrations failed to force the Government to resign, even though at one time they were on the brink of it. Gairy called up his secret police to Mt Royal on Monday 21 January. After the meeting, assisted by armed police, they proceeded to unleash terror on the demonstrators, causing serious injuries to many including women, to break up the demonstrations. Rupert Bishop was shot and killed and businesses in St George's were looted, first by Gairy's supporters, then by others. The population panicked. They wanted one thing – security; no group was able to give them that – not the unions, not the Committee of 22, not the NJM – as none was sufficiently prepared. There was no answer to the Government's guns and force. Independence came with the usual flag-waving and anthem-singing ceremony.

The coming of independence in Grenada differed from similar experiences in the then five other independent Caribbean countries. In Grenada, it was marked by periods of bitter rivalry between government and opposition forces from early 1973 to February 1974. The overriding consideration in all this was the question of political power. Opposition groups sought power; the Government intended to keep it and was prepared to defend it relentlessly. The Opposition claimed, and with justification, that it wanted to protect Grenada from an incipient dictatorship which would be catalysed with the political autonomy independence would bring. The Government claimed that it had a mandate to govern, and that it was the only fit body to do the job of nation-building. Independence was used as an issue around which to settle the more critical and overriding question of which political group in society should enjoy power and what it would use it to do. The NJM was clear on the question of power; it was inseparable from the people and it must be used to transform the lives of the working people.

From about April 1973 to February 1974 the issue was contested at all levels – diplomatic, regional, legalistic, and violent. There were the mass demonstrations referred to; the shut down of Pearls Airport (May 1973); the closure of the Port and shutdown of the island for

Above and below *Anti-government demonstrations, January 1974*

approximately one month; there was the formation and efforts of the Committee of 22; there was looting of businesses in St George's; the shooting at demonstrators by the Police and the murder of one of them, Rupert Bishop, who died protecting school children from police guns. The demands on the Government to resign had proved futile. The Governor resigned but the Government remained. Independence came on 7 February 1974 and Gairy became the first Prime Minister.

Both the statehood and independence constitutions had one weakness which, if exploited by a dominant figure in the Executive could result in the subversion of Parliament. That weakness pertained to the undemocratic structure of the upper house or Senate. Both constitutions made it possible for the ruling party to have an automatic two-thirds majority in the upper house.

Under the statehood constitution, seven members of the nine-member Senate were government-appointed. Thus, government could always count on a guaranteed majority in the upper house. If Cabinet was dominated by a powerful figure, as long as his colleagues were prepared to obey his dictates, then he could get all Bills that require an ordinary majority to pass the lower house and subsequently become law. Gairy hand-picked his Senators and no one dared disobey; in fact a Senatorship was a kind of patronage bestowed on his underlings and stooges.

With a majority in the lower house and a guaranteed majority in the upper house, Parliament can be effectively controlled by a dominant individual. This is precisely what happened in Grenada, to a lesser extent in the period 1967 to 1974, but to a greater extent in the period 1974 to 1979. The independence constitution facilitated the final emergence of Gairy as a dictator. It unleashed his hitherto restrained tendency towards dictatorship. But be that as it may, with the killing of Rupert Bishop by the police, Gairy had compounded the difficulty of his situation and created an image that was beyond repair in the eyes of Grenadians. And this is where the subsequent Chilean connection can be seen in its true perspective. Realizing the possibility of an unconstitutional seizure of power, Gairy sought and received the assistance of Chile from 1975 onwards to help build up his military apparatus. Every step in this direction increased his vulnerability inside as well as outside Grenada. Gairy wanted to control the NJM and, while the methods he employed helped him in the short run, in the long run they destroyed him politically.

Then came the report of the Duffus Commission which took away from the Gairy regime any shred of credibility it had left. The Commission was set up on 6 December 1973 to enquire into the circumstances leading to the arrest and charging of the six NJM members on Sunday 18 November 1973, the alleged brutality by the

*The funeral of Rupert Bishop, Maurice Bishop's father, gunned down in January 1974*

police on these persons, and to ascertain whether there was a breakdown of law and order in the State and whether constitutional rights were infringed upon by the operation of the police force, the police aides and the magistracy during the 11 months leading up to 18 November 1973. Subsequently, the relevant period of the enquiry was extended from 18 November 1973 to 29 March 1974. The Commission commenced sitting on 17 December 1973 and ended on 16 May 1974. Over 30 persons and many organizations and bodies gave evidence.

On the matter of breakdown of law and order the Commission stated that it found ample evidence of the occurrence of several incidents during the relevant period pointing clearly and unmistakably to such a breakdown. There was also clear evidence of infringement of the constitutional rights of citizens both by the regular police and the police aides, who acted on behalf of the Government.[24]

As regards the arrest and charge of the battering of the six NJM members, the Commission came to the following conclusions based on the findings of fact:

1. The six members of the New Jewel Movement visited Grenville on 18 November for the sole purpose of attending the meeting of businessmen. (Gairy had claimed that they had gone there to organize a takeover of the Government.)
2. The meeting was called for the purpose of discussing participation by the business community at Grenville in the general strike proposed by the New Jewel Movement, in the 9 November 1973 issue of its paper.

3. There was no intention by the six members of the New Jewel Movement to seize control of the Grenville Police Station by armed attack or otherwise.
4. There were no reasonable grounds for A.S.P. Belmar to apprehend a dangerous attack on his person or on the Grenville Police Station by the six men.
5. There were no reasonable grounds for apprehending the possibility of such an attack.
6. There was no credible evidence to support the allegation that a rifle and ammunition were found in the possession of the six men.
7. The action taken by the police was not justifiable.
8. The action taken by the police was in all the circumstances a breach of the constitutional rights of each of the six men.
9. The actions taken by the members of the police force were not genuinely designed as a countermeasure taken by the Government to meet any reliable allegation of a threat to the security of the State by the NJM or any of its members; but was instead forcible action taken to suppress political opposition which was genuinely believed to be likely to retard the progress of Grenada towards political independence.[25]

With regard to the incidents of early 1974 the Commission concluded that Gairy believed the demonstrations were aimed at preventing or delaying independence, and that he was so committed to leading Grenada to independence that the possibility of delay by recurring demonstrations, as on 19 January, the Saturday preceding 'Bloody Monday', deeply disturbed Gairy; he could not stand 25,000 people tramping the streets against him. He recalled the police aides – all the violent men – and personally supervised their selection. His intentions were clear, he had to curb or crush the activities of the demonstrators. This he partially succeeded in doing on Monday 21st when the police aides clashed with the demonstrators, and, with the assistance of police, tear gas and rifle shots, terrorized thousands of peaceful demonstrators. The Commission recommended:

1. The complete disbanding of the police aides who had inflicted such unspeakable atrocities upon many citizens of Grenada.
2. A thorough reorganization of the police force, including the removal of A.S.P. Innocent Belmar from that force and his preclusion from holding any office in the public services.
3. The removal of certain magistrates from office due to their failure to discharge their judicial duties with fairness and competence.
4. An inquiry into the conduct of the Solicitor General with a view to removing him from office.

5. The speedy processing of all criminal charges concerned with violent incidents during the relevant period which have been disclosed before the Commission.[26]

The Duffus Report constituted an indictment against the Gairy regime and called into question its legitimacy to govern. The report exposed, both regionally and internationally, the legal and constitutional ills of the Government. Its international image, now considerably tarnished, was irreparable. Gairy had driven another nail into his coffin.

Belmar was removed from office but in the general election of the following year he was asked to stand as a GULP candidate for the St Andrew's North-West constituency. He won the seat, and Gairy saw this as a moral victory; but Belmar's victory at the polls and his presence in the House was simply a deliberate act of contempt by Gairy towards the Duffus Commission.

Another attempt by Gairy to control the population and destroy the voice of dissent was made through the passage in 1975 of the Newspaper Amendment Act.[27] By that Act the deposit required of anyone publishing a newspaper was increased from EC$900 to EC$20,000. The real aim of this was to close down the New Jewel's newspaper which was started in 1973 and, within two years, had built up a circulation of some 10,000. The paper was both educational and agitational, and guided by three principles: truthful information, use of the vernacular and simple language, and emphasis on relevant political and economic issues.

This newspaper was building up the NJM and Gairy knew that, or was so advised. To counter the political impact of the paper he had to pass the Newspaper Act. In so doing he struck a blow at three fundamental freedoms – freedom of the press, the right to dissent and criticize, and freedom of speech. Gairy thus attempted to dictate what political material should or should not be read.

Then came the election of 1976. The Government was accused by the Opposition of massive pre-election rigging. But worse were the conditions under which the People's Alliance was forced to conduct its campaign; sometimes with no public address system, as they were refused many times permission to use it, at other times being granted permission for a mere two hours. This was clearly an attempt to reduce the Alliance's potential gains at the expense of Gairy's GULP. Despite these odds the People's Alliance won six seats as against Gairy's nine; this did not satisfy Gairy as he had expected a much larger margin of victory and he was anxious to decimate the new parliamentary opposition.

With six Opposition members in the House of Representatives instead of one, as in the former House, the population expected to see Parliament functioning vibrantly once more. In this they were to be disappointed as Parliament soon degenerated into a one-man, one-party affair. The convening of Parliament was in essence a theatrical act with Gairy always the leading actor. There was little or no debate; the extent of participation by members of the ruling party was to laugh and say 'Aye'. The Opposition would vote the expected 'No'. A good example of the farce of parliamentary proceedings was evident in the meeting of 18 February 1978, when in one sitting some 16 Bills were passed by the House of Representatives, each carried through three readings.

On some occasions the Opposition walked out in protest against the manifest rape of Parliament. For the Government, the object of their control of Parliament was to hurl personal invective, ridicule the Opposition, kill debate by giving insufficient notice of bills, and deny the Opposition the use of the radio. The Grenada parliament had become a caricature of the West minister model and, moreover, reflected the inherent weaknesses of that model.

Parliament and the House of Representatives became Gairy's own sounding board. If he was boss in Parliament, he was the maximum leader in Cabinet. He built up a highly centralized bureaucracy and succeeded in stripping the civil service of all autonomy in decision-making. Every matter was to be dealt with in Cabinet – from the hiring of a janitor to the building of a school – and in Cabinet, Gairy's voice was supreme and his word law. Thus the Cabinet's energies were dissipated on trivial matters that could have been adequately handled lower down in the bureaucracy, and so was unable to spend enough time on such matters of major importance as curbing inflation and unemployment, stabilizing the balance of payments, restructuring education and stimulating growth. By building up such an over-centralized bureaucracy with the lower echelons impotent, Gairy sowed the seeds of his own demise and catalysed his downfall.

The ban on loudspeakers, which had been rather perfunctory during the 1976 election, was reintroduced in late 1977 and made permanent. This time the issue was the dispute between the Government and the Public Services Association – the Grenada Union of Teachers, the Technical and Allied Workers Union and the Civil Service Association – over the recommendations of the 1977 Salaries Revision Commission. The ban on the use of public address systems was a vindictive act by Gairy aimed at preventing the unions from informing their membership on the salaries issue. In a series of meetings on the salaries impasse held throughout the island in December 1977 and

January 1978, union leaders had to use their unaided voices to address mass gatherings even inside union headquarters.

The issue was one of bread-and-butter and totally a non-partisan one. The Commission had recommended increases of 83% on the average for the 1977–8 period in view of the fact that the public officers had received no salary increases since 1974. When negotiations between the union leaders and the Minister of Finance broke down, Gairy took the matter over and stubbornly decided that Government was not going to pay the recommended increases. The unions called a strike and Gairy responded by addressing the nation on Friday 26 January 1978. Many threats were made and the stage was set for a display of violence. On 28 January, the government held a big rally in St George's. Posters with the names of union leaders were displayed before a hostile crowd. The crowd itself called on the Government to 'let go the lion.'

At this stage the lives of the union's executive officers were at stake and the issue was no longer one of industrial relations but a political one. Worse, all this was occurring only a few weeks after the fatal shooting of a minister, Innocent Belmar. Gairy associated the impending strike over wages with the shooting as politically motivated by his opponents who intended to unseat him. He made it clear that in 1974 he had been caught napping, that was the last strike that the union leaders would call, and boasted that he was well prepared. This was said emphatically three times in the presence of certain heads of churches who were trying to mediate a couple of days before the intended strike. At this stage, the options were money or executive lives.

Faced with the possible price of continued militancy, the unions had no choice but to accept under violent duress what Gairy's government was willing to offer, as they could not protect those whose lives were threatened against that violent onslaught – far less conquer it. It was a bitter pill for the unions and a sad day for organized labour. What the event showed, as one participant wrote shortly afterwards, was that in Grenada in 1978, gun-and- terror tactics had become the fatal arbiter in any major dispute involving any significant portion of the public and Gairy's government. This was again demonstrated nine months later when a NJM rally, called for 19 November 1978, had to be called off in the face of similar threats. Needless to say, both incidents lost Gairy a lot of political support.

In the meantime, the NJM's influence in the trade unions had been growing, especially as some of their top members were given executive positions in the Commercial and Industrial Workers Union, the CSA, the Grenada Union of Teachers, and the Seamen and Waterfront Workers' Union. Simultaneously, Gairy was striving to get his union, the GMMIWU (Grenada Manual, Mental, Maritime and Intellectual Workers' Union) to represent as many workers as possible. Many new businesses were given franchises on the understanding that Gairy's union would be the bargaining body for its employees. Gairy was becoming very worried by the Jewel's support in the unions, as well as the extent of the anti-Gairy sentiments within the ranks of organized labour.

The beginning of 1978 witnessed more active and concrete steps being taken to counter the Jewel threat in the trade union movement. In February 1978 the Government passed two pieces of legislation: (a) the Essential Services (Amendment) Act 1978, and (b) the Grenada Port Authority (Amendment) Act 1978. The Port Authority Act established an authority necessary to provide and maintain efficient port services. This of course would affect the nature and settlement of industrial disputes involving the SWWU and the Grenada Shipping Agents. It would considerably weaken the strike weapon previously used on the docks since, during strikes and goslows, the Authority would be able to devise alternative arrangements for the loading of cargoes. The Essential Services Act made provision for the settlement of disputes in essential services solely by arbitration. This Act effectively made any strike action in the essential services sector illegal.

The political motive of these Acts was to preclude possible success of any shut-down that could be politically motivated to bring down the Government. With the growing influence of the Jewel movement in certain unions this possibility was seen as a real threat.

One cannot avoid noting a parallel between these provisions and similar steps taken in 1951 to control and curtail industrial action by the GMMWU (Gairy's Union). These steps were taken by the establishment of the day – the Legislative Council, the Governor and the Colonial Office acting in unison.

The 1978 provisions, according to Gairy, were designed 'to safeguard against electricity strikes, closed ports, telephone strikes and other such industrial activities'. After passing the Public Utility Undertakings and Public Health Arbitration Ordinance of 1951, the Acting Governor, George Green, said 'The object was to ensure that the Essential Services should not be dislocated by action resulting from trade disputes.' This ordinance was passed to suppress Gairy's industrial activities then. The House proceeded to pass one other piece of anti-subversive legislation: The Public Order Ordinance No. 1 of 1951. Another, introduced but not passed, was the Sedition and the Importation of Publications (Prohibition) Ordinance. In 1978, a similar ordinance was passed by the Grenada government.

In a mass meeting on 22 February 1951, Gairy indicated to his followers that the 'Legislative Council was meeting then to pass laws to bring them back into slavery. But we shall stand together and we shall die together.' This was greeted with rapturous applause. Whereas in 1951 Gairy fought against forms of legislation inimical to justice and freedom, by 1978, in order to preserve political power, he had become the architect of the same kind of legislation which had been odious to him 27 years before.

## The Grenada Revolution 1979

On 13 March 1979 Gairy's government was overthrown in an armed seizure of power: the overthrow was organized and executed by the New Jewel Movement and sanctioned by the thousands who rallied to its banner. At a victory rally on 25 March 1979, the People's Revolutionary Government suspended the constitution of 1974 with effect retroactive to 12.01 a.m. on 13 March 1979. This was the essence of People's Law No. 1. The actual law reads as follows:

> The Constitution of Grenada is hereby and has been suspended as of 12.01 a.m. on March 13th, 1979. All acts or deeds by or under the authority of the People's Revolutionary Government are hereby deemed and declared to have been legally done.

In the preamble to People's Law No. 1 the People's Revoutionary Government (PRG) pledged to observe fundamental rights and freedoms of Grenadians. The appropriate section reads as follows:

> The PRG pledges to observe the fundamental rights and freedom of our people subject to certain measures necessary to:
> the maintenance of stability, peace, order and good government;
> the final eradication of Gairyism; and
> the protection of the People's Revolution.

People's Law No. 7 established a People's Revolutionary Army and members of the army were vested with the same powers of arrest and search as those vested in members of the Royal Grenada Police Force.

With the suspension of the constitution, government became essentially one of governing by decree. The PRG passed many laws to enable it to begin the reconstruction of Grenada. This was a period of transition which preceded but not precluded a return to constitutional government. This was stated with the declaration of the Grenada Revolution. The said declaration also stated in Paragraph 3 that the PRG pledged to return to constitutional rule at an early opportunity; that a Consultative Assembly would be set up to consult with all the people for the purpose of the establishment of a new constitution which would reflect the wishes and aspirations of all the people of Grenada; that the new constitution would be submitted for popular approval in a referendum. In 1980, some observers asked why there had not been a return to constitutional government. Many reasons for this delay were given by the PRG including: (a) the problem of national security, especially the possibility of an invasion externally generated by Gairy or other forces which still existed in a real sense: (b) the need to get the economy on a sound footing after years of economic mismanagement.

By 1980 the PRG had decreed some 63 People's Laws. People's Laws Nos 46 and 47 repealed the following laws of the old régime:

- Importation of Publications (Prohibition) Act, 1965;
- Public Order Act of 1974;
- Essential Services Act of 1978;
- Essential Services (Amendment) Act of 1978;
- Newspaper (Amendment) Act of 1975 & 1976.

All anti-worker laws were repealed in all their forms. Law No. 29 provided for the compulsory recognition by employers of trade unions that represent a majority of workers. Law No. 43 amended the Nutmeg Industry Ordinance, and introduced a new section into the principal ordinance entitled 86A. According to this section:

> The Association (G.C.N.A.) may make such allowances and pay such expenses as may be approved by the Minister of Agriculture and all such allowances and expenses that have been approved by the said Minister. The Association may provide loans to meet the partial cost of establishing and developing approved agro-industries on such terms as may be agreed upon by the Association and the Minister of Agriculture.

The interim Board of 1975 set up by the former government was dissolved, and a new interim Board appointed, pending the election of a Board as provided under the principal ordinance.

People's Laws Nos 17 and 21 provided for the establishment of Preventive Detention. Under this law the Minister of National Security could order the detention of anyone whom he had reason to believe may act in a manner prejudicial to public safety or public order or defence of Grenada or with a view to subverting or otherwise sabotaging the PRG. Persons detained under this law would be allowed no bail; the writ of *habeas corpus* would not lie in the case of any person denied bail by or under this law, and the Supreme Court under any rule of law or other authority had no jurisdiction to grant such bail. No such detention could be called into question in any court.

Despite the seemingly major issues and problems that surrounded a return to constitutional government since the 'overthrow', it would be accurate to say that many Grenadians still anxiously awaited such a return, primarily to give weight to whatever major national decisions may have been taken and to give them a sense of constitutional security. Even up to 1983 they had such expectations, but realized that they had been duped and fooled.

## NOTES

Full citations only given where work does not appear in the Bibliography.

1. Emmanuel, *Crown Colony Politics*, pp. 54–70
2. *Census* of 1921. Constitutional Order in Council 1924.
3. Constitutional Order in Council 1924, March 1924.
4. Emmanuel, *Crown Colony Politics*, p. 117.
5. Ibid, p. 128; West India Royal Commission 1938–39, Cmnd 6607, 1945.
6. Ann Spackman, *Constitutional History*, p. 209.
7. Constitutional Order in Council, 1959.
8. *Report of the Commission of Enquiry into the Control of Public Expenditure in Grenada during 1961 and Subsequently*, 1962, p.1.
9. Ibid, p.8.
10. Ibid, pp. 9–10.
11. *The New Jewel*, Vol. 1, No. 36, 9 February 1973.
12. *Grenada, 1965–66,* Government Printery, 1968.
13. Ibid.
14. Associated States Constitution 1967.
15. *Report on the Legislative Council General Elections for 1951*, 1952.
16. Council Paper No. 3, 1955, *Report on the Legislative Council General Elections of 1954*, 1955.
17. Council Paper No. 4, 1958, *Report on General Elections of 1957*, 1958.
18. Council Paper No. 13, 1961, *Report on ... General Elections of 1961*, 1961.
19. Council Paper No. 3, 1963, *Report on ... General Elections of 1962*, 1963.
20. *Report on the General Elections of 1967*, St George's, Government Printery, 1973.
21. *Report on the General Elections of 1972.*
22. The New Jewel Movement, *Manifesto for Power to the People*, November 1973.
23. *The New Jewel* 9 November 1973.
24. *Report of the Duffus Commission*, p. 6.
25. Ibid, pp. 136–7.
26. Ibid, pp. 231–5.
27. *Newspaper (Amendment) Act 1975*, 'An Act to Amend the Newspaper Ordinance', Cap. 197.

# 21

# *The Revolution Self-Destructs*

In 1981 I was in conversation with Jacqueline Creft, a member of the People's Revolutionary Government and later Minister for Education in the same government. She inquired about the central thesis of the book, *Grenada: Island of Conflict*, the first edition of which was in manuscript form at the time. I told her that it analysed five conflicts in Grenada's history; and that each one of these conflicts was reconciled violently. She further inquired, which was the last. I answered, the 1970–79 conflict, between the Gairy dictatorship and the anti-Gairy forces. She retorted, 'I hope that one will be the last.' Little did she know at the time, that the seeds of a sixth conflict were being sown; that the conflict would be reconciled violently, once more; and that she would be one of its ill-fated victims.

## Hypotheses Summarized

History has been particularly harsh and unkind to Grenada, especially during the period 1970–83. Grenada's experiences during that period can be described as unparalleled among the countries of the Commonwealth Caribbean. It is the only country in this grouping to have had so many years of dictatorship, both of the extreme right and extreme left.

Grenada experienced massive popular demonstrations, against the right-wing totalitarian government of Eric Gairy, that brutalized its people; saw the violent overthrow of that government in 1979; went through four and a half years of revolutionary government; witnessed the suspension of the constitution and its replacement by government by decree and by the gun.

*Jacqueline 'Jackie' Creft, Minister for Education in the PRG 1979–83, executed with Bishop 19 October 1983*

It later saw the self-destruction of that same government, the execution of the Prime Minister, three ministers and many others, the occurrence of a *coup d'etat*, a popular military intervention by a superpower, and a full-scale three-day war, all in October, 1983.

It experienced the restoration of democracy in 1984, but five years later saw the virtual self-destruction of the very government that was at the centre of this restoration. There is no simple, nor is there a single, explanation for this web of political events extending from 1970 to 1989.

The Gairy government of 1970–79 used a combination of fear, terror, force and patronage to govern. The 1973 constitution which ushered in independence for Grenada in February 1974 facilitated the dictatorship of Gairy; it enabled him to brutalize unofficial opposition and emasculate the official opposition, thereby reducing Grenada to a modern-day plantation, ruled by a tyrannical overlord. This bred its own reaction and an irreconcilable conflict developed, settled later when Gairy himself was given a dose of his own medicine, and was violently overthrown on 13 March 1979.

Whereas the Gairy dictatorship was a dictatorship of one man, the People's Revolutionary Government (PRG) which succeeded him was a dictatorship of a party élite, and Grenada became the classic one-party state, without its Parliament and highly militarized. A rigid ideological path was pursued, based on the principles of Scientific Socialism. This created its own internal and external reaction, resulting not only in deep conflict, but also in the cannibalization of many children of the Revolution, and ultimately the self-destruction of the People's Revolutionary Government itself.

The PRG's performance in the fields of infrastructure and social services was impressive; however this was insufficient to provide a counterbalance to the adverse effects on the working people, of worsening economic conditions in the important sectors of agriculture and tourism. Consequently, these very worsening economic conditions helped fan the flames of growing ideological conflict within the ruling party of the New Jewel Movement and the Government.

The People's Revolutionary Government inherited a severely handicapped and poorly managed economy; one that was virtually raped during the previous 12 years (1967–79) of the Gairy dictatorship. This situation was compounded by the various structural weaknesses and economic deformities characteristic of a small, highly open and dependent micro-economy. The Grenadian economy, with a population of some 93,000, lacked the critical mass to support any meaningful domestic industry. The intrinsic limitations of Grenada's small economy therefore made it highly vulnerable to external shocks.

With decline in the agricultural export markets, stagnation and decline in the tourism industry, and with the absence of the ingredients for self-sustained growth, economic pressures mounted and invariably manifested themselves in rising discontent among farmers, peasants, workers and the rural poor. This helped to erode popular support for the Revolution, drastically affected attendance at and support for mass rallies and mass organizations – dominant features of the Grenada Revolution. Coupled with this was the increasingly negative attitude to the Revolution as a result of its undemocratic practices and its infringement of peoples' fundamental rights and freedoms, in particular its practice of 'detention without trial', its anti-Church attitude and its labour camp. This increasing decline in popular support for the Revolution threw the upper echelons of the party and government into a state of crisis and panic. They tried to find various scapegoats, but each step along that path further compounded the anomaly of their situation; finally the Prime Minister, Maurice Bishop, was made into the ultimate scapegoat; all the ills at the time were blamed on him, from pot-holes in the roads to the various crises facing the Revolution by 1983. The very people he fed and helped, turned around and treacherously bit the hands that fed them, and savagely betrayed him. This is the case of the Louison brothers, the Austins and the Stranchans.

His end reminds one of the fate of Maximillien Robespierre, one of the architects of the French Revolution of 1789–93. Robespierre was an arch-revolutionary; he was instrumental in the invention of the guillotine as the supreme place of justice; thousands, especially the bourgeois, perished at the guillotine in the name of justice and equality; finally in 1793 Robespierre himself perished at the guillotine, an artifice of his own inventive mind.

What is the lesson to be learnt? Rigid ideological formulae are irrelevant to peasant societies in the Commonwealth Caribbean; any attempt to superimpose them on its people will result in failure; political doctrines must be flexible in their application and adaptable to varied socio-economic circumstances and cultures. If not they will ossify, be relegated to oblivion, and fade away. The application of rigid theories of Marxist Leninism to the management of the State by the PRG was perhaps its most monumental error, one from which it was never to recover. This was never accepted until perhaps many years later. But what good is there in being wise after the fact?

## Economic Malformations

Politics in countries like Grenada involve bread-and-butter issues. In his very first address to the nation on 13 March 1979 Maurice Bishop hit the nail on the head when he said 'People of Grenada, this revolution is for work, for food, for decent housing and health services and for a bright future for our children and grandchildren.'[1] He proceeded to give Grenadians the following assurances.

> Let me assure the people of Grenada that all democratic freedoms, including freedom of elections, religious and political opinion, will be fully restored to the people. The personal safety and property of individuals will be protected.[2]

He even promised free elections in six months.

Grenadians lived to see these promises broken, and the assurances given, destroyed. I have no reason to doubt the sincerity of those words of Bishop on the morning of 13 March; but as the Revolution matured, and the communist hard-liners consolidated their hold on the Government, the social democratic stance of Bishop and the Revolution gave way to the ideological purity of the true Marxist-Leninists. Worst of all, the failure of Maurice Bishop to hold General Elections as promised led to the substitution of military rule and government by decree for constitutional government. This failure was the most costly since it contributed to the mayhem of October 1983, the massacre of Maurice Bishop and his colleagues, and the ultimate destruction of the Revolution.

Moreover, despite their commendable efforts, the failure of the People's Revolutionary Government to successfully tackle and overcome the economic constraints of high dependency, small size and narrow resource base, as well as its inability to create conditions for self-sustained growth, helped erode its economic base and thereby contributed to significant political fall-outs.

The PRG's view of these economic constraints was subjective, narrow and ideological. While recognizing the contribution of scholars and of regional and international organizations to these economic constraints, in their view the fundamental cause of these problems was imperialism.

> The problem of smallness of economies, land sizes and resources of developing third world countries like Grenada is a problem that has been addressed on several occasions by several eminent people over the years. It is a matter that has been looked at exhaustively in the United Nations, in the Organisation of American States, the Non-Aligned Movement and several other international fora. We contend, comrades, that the real problem is not the question of smallness *per se* but the real problem is the question of imperialism.[3]

Such an analysis and its conclusions were extremely partial. Even if the problem of dependency can be related to imperialism, the problem of small size is a characteristic intrinsic to small islands and is a function of geography and nature rather than imperialism. Good economic management is a product of pragmatism and objective reality and is simply not derived from ideological purity and political extremism. Being deluded by the latter the very objectives of providing work, food, housing, health, and a bright future for the people of Grenada, Carriacou and Petit Martinique eluded the PRG's grasp and contributed to growing disillusion towards the later part of the régime.

## The Dependency Syndrome

Grenada suffered and still suffers from at least five forms of dependency, viz:

1. Dependency on external grants to finance most of its capital budget annually, due to little or no public-sector savings.
2. Dependency on foreign trade and a narrow range of exports for most of its economic activity, and for most of its foreign-exchange earnings.
3. Dependency on foreign know-how and foreign technical expertise.
4. Dependency on foreign direct investment due to low levels of national savings.
5. Dependency on a high level of imports to satisfy national consumer demand and production inputs.[4]

This condition has persisted from the era of pure plantation economy to the present. Few structural changes have occurred during these four centuries; most changes that occurred were changes in form, rather than changes in matter and structure.[5] Consequently, this dependency reduced considerably these states' ability to withstand external shocks. As Maurice Bishop often said, 'When North America sneezes, countries like Grenada catch pneumonia.' Thus the openness and dependency of Grenada in the international economy made it highly susceptible to external shocks and pressures. Robert Looney described the situation as follows:

> Small countries peg their exchange rate to those of their major trading partners with the net result being that global growth, recession, and inflation, are transmitted directly and immediately to their domestic economies. This vulnerability to shocks from the world economy has been demonstrated in terms of relatively poor micro-economic performance in the long run and relative instability in the short run.[6]

What is unquestionable is that international factors influenced domestic performance during the era of the PRG.

Grenada's balance of visible trade worsened every year during the 12 years 1976–88; from a deficit of EC $32m in 1976 to one of EC $161m in 1988. The Government depended on external sources for varying quantities of support in order to finance its entire capital budget during the revolutionary period; the economy's degree of openness, measured by the ratio of exports plus imports to GDP, rose from 102 in 1981 to 126 by 1984.

The pegging of the EC dollar to the US dollar meant that Grenada was subjected to changes in the terms of trade over which it had no control. Fiscal, monetary, prices and income policies, with the People's Revolutionary Government's best intentions, could not have been too independent, but were constrained by considerations of the monetary union of which it was a part. So there were international factors that were beyond the control of the People's Revolutionary Government. The adverse domestic consequences of some of these influenced attitudes towards the Revolution and helped undermine domestic support.

## *Small size*

While dependency posed one series of problems for the Revolutionary Government, small size posed other challenges.

Grenada can be described as a classic example of a small state and a micro-economy, with a population of 93,000, a domestic market size of less, a land base of 344 sq km and few natural resources. A consequence of this is that a number of economic activities are rendered non-viable, as domestic demand is insufficient to support them. Carl Stone puts it this way:

> Small economies, with limited domestic markets, resource endowments, and populations, are unlikely to increase their living standards beyond very modest horizons, if they fail to develop a minimal threshold of per capita export or hard currency earnings.[7]

The PRG's management and planning were incomparable. But that could not compensate for instabilty of earnings in the export sector. This, more than any other economic factors, was what defied the planning and management talent of the People's Revolutionary Government.

Grenada is an agricultural society; any self-sustained growth must be based on the proper utilization and development of land-and sea based resources. Any significant improvement in the living standards of Grenada's rural population depends on the proper management of these resources. This challenge again defied the PRG.

During the two decades 1961–81 both farm acreage cultivated and the number of farmers fell by almost one half (Table 21.1): In 1981 the average age of the farmer was 57 years. The period witnessed a horrendous decline in the principal sector of the economy – agriculture – a decline which had repercussions in many related areas

**Table 21.1 Comparative Farm and Farmer Statistics 1961–81**

| *Year* | *Farm acreage* | *Adjusted farm acreage* | *No. of farmers* |
|---|---|---|---|
| 1961 | 60,197 | 50,693 | 15,319 |
| 1975 | 46,577 | 38,942 | 12,565 |
| 1981 | 34,243 | 34,243 | 8,202 |

Sources:
1961: WI Agricultural Census, *Grenada*, 1961
1975: *Abstract of Statistics*, Grenada, 1979
1981: *Grenada Agricultural Census*, 1981.

of national life, both social and political, since agricultural earnings carry a high multiplier effect.

Successive governments failed to harmonize the desire for land by the landless class, with the economic objective of boosting agricultural production, consolidating agricultural diversification, and reducing the level of food insecurity. Land and land-use policies were used to serve narrow political objectives at the expense of promoting necessary land reform and economic development. This was equally true for the abortive 'Land for the Landless' policy of the Gairy régime and for the 'State Farm Program' of the People's Revolutionary Government, which will be considered later in this chapter.

If the economic constraints discussed above posed difficulties for the PRG, the poor performance of the principal sectors of the economy bedevilled and frustrated them, and undermined popular support for the Revolution. Added to this, by 1983 the PRG stood discredited in the eyes of the Church, particularly over its human rights record, both among the clergy and the majority of the laity. This caused considerable political fall-out in a country rooted in its religious tradition and practices.

## Economic Strains Bring Political Pains

### I

The economic strategy of the PRG, as articulated in many speeches, policy statements and reports and as manifested in concrete activities, could be synthesized into the following goals:

1. The rehabilitation of existing infrastructure and an increase in Grenada's Gross Domestic Capital formation.
2. The stimulation of productive investment both in the private sector and in new public-sector projects and enterprises.
3. Improvement in the efficiency of the public sector (including state enterprises) and the maintenance of sound public finances.
4. The placing of the development emphasis on agriculture, agro-industries and tourism in order to cure unemployment, stimulate growth and raise the standard of living.
5. The development of a policy of export promotion to overcome the limitations of a small domestic market.[8]

The soundness of these policy objectives is beyond question. The failure to achieve most of them was not due to a lack of managerial skill or failure to mobilize resources, but to the government's inability to control the behaviour of international markets and its blind adherence to the doctrine of Scientific Socialism and, relatedly, the principles of central planning.

Undoubtedly the Government was committed to an economic transformation of Grenada, so that Grenadians could enjoy a measure of social and economic security. In this regard the development of agriculture, tourism and manufacturing was critical. But the development of these sectors in itself required a general expansion of infrastructure and technology, a raising of educational standards, the creation of a technically skilled and highly motivated work-force, and the creation of a climate for private-sector initiative and the flowering of entrepreneurship. These were all negated by the People's Revolutionary Government's blind adherence to the theory and practice of Scientific Socialism.

The Government failed to realize that successful export promotion is private-sector led and not public-sector led. In any highly open economy this is the *sine qua non* for growth and success.

An open economy is usually placed under considerable pressure when the performance of the export sector is weak. That was precisely the situation in the period 1979–83. The major export items had difficult trading experiences in that period. The sector came under three distinct types of pressures: unattractive prices, restricted markets and declining sales, and rising costs of imported inputs. The effect in each case was a severe reduction both in farmers' earnings and in government revenues derived from export taxes. Throughout its four years the People's Revolutionary Government developed no serious response to these; neither in policy formulation nor in implementation.

Export earnings declined by an average of 13% per annum during the 1979–82 period (see Table 21.2). The two commodities most severely affected were cocoa and nutmegs, the crops the majority of farmers and rural folks depend on for their livlihood. The drop in banana earnings was marginal.

With a farmer population (full time and part time) of some 10,000 and an average family size of four persons, a total of 40,000 persons out of a population of 90,000 at the time depended on agriculture directly and indirectly for their livlihood. Agriculture provides the highest level of direct employment and accounted for a large percentage of GDP and foreign-exchange earnings.

The cocoa industry had 7,000 registered producers at the start. The industry was affected mostly by unfavourable prices. Export prices of 1979 were virtually halved by 1982; the decline was sustained over three years. The spot price of a ton of cocoa on the

**Table 21.2 Earnings, Production and Export Data for Cocoa, Banana, Nutmeg and Mace 1979–82**

| | *1979* | *1980* | *1981* | *1982* |
|---|---|---|---|---|
| *Cocoa*: | | | | |
| Production (lbs) | 5,788,633 | 4,689,180 | 5,546,416 | 4,024,432 |
| Exports (lbs) | 5,382,667 | 4,013,609 | 55,891,872 | 4,995,649 |
| Price EC$ | 5.07 | 4.52 | 3.24 | 2.69 |
| Value EC$ | 27,318,780 | 18,162,136 | 19,114,667 | 13,454,061 |
| *Bananas*: | | | | |
| Production (lbs) | 30,909,000 | | | |
| Exports (lbs) | 30,909,000 | 26,481,000 | 26,497,000 | 22,031,000 |
| Price | 0.32 | 0.40 | 0.373 | 0.40 |
| Value | 9,932,000 | 10,688,000 | 9,886,000 | 8,920,000 |
| *Nutmeg & Mace*: | | | | |
| Production (N) | 5,128,778 | 5,486,294 | 5,300,836 | 6,157,754 |
| Mace | 625,467 | 647,672 | 532,129 | 502,905 |
| Exports (N) | 4,533,499 | 3,970,239 | 3,572,700 | 4,210,664 |
| Mace | 576,350 | 665,915 | 491,640 | 695,345 |
| Price (N) | 2.38–2.88 | 2.48–2.98 | 2.27–3.41 | 1.95–3.48 |
| Value (N & M) | 12,453,067 | 11,389,998 | 9,786,726 | 10,640,716 |
| Total earnings $ | 49,703,847 | 40,690,134 | 38,787,393 | 33,014,777 |
| % Change | – | –18.2 | –4.7 | –15 |

Source: *Financial Statements*, GCNA, GBCS, GCIB, 1979–82

London market averaged £2,000 per long ton in 1978–79; by 1982 the price had fallen to a low of £900 per ton.

Simultaneously with this price decline there occurred a persistent depreciation in the price of sterling which led to a further erosion of earnings in the industry and of income to farmers (see Table 21.3).

The average for 1982 compared to the average for 1983 showed an improvement that appeared encouraging. Despite this, the industry was far away from the very favourable position it had in 1979, when earnings were at an all-time high of EC$27m. The extreme price variability for internationally traded commodities makes it difficult for the

**Table 21.3 Effect of Exchange-Rate Changes on Export Earnings**

| | *National export* | *Price* | *£/$EC** | *Earnings in $EC* |
|---|---|---|---|---|
| 1979/80 | 1 ton cocoa | £2,000 | 5.6 | 11,200 |
| 1982 | 1 ton cocoa | £ 900 | 4.0 | 3,600 |
| 1983 | 1 ton cocoa | £1,400 | 4.3 | 6,020 |

* US$1 = EC$2.70

public sector to plan accurately, as unanticipated shortfalls can often jeopardize well-designed plans.

Both in 1981 and 1982 the Board of the Grenada Cocoa Association had to dip deep into its reserves to keep up payments to a reasonable level to farmers. As a result, retained earnings had fallen in this industry from EC$12.2m at the end of 1980 to EC$6.9m at the end of 1982. The industry continued to be plagued by low yields and this was felt most in periods of price decline.

Although the price of bananas rose during the period under review, exports fell by 26%. The main causes were the high and rising cost of inputs and the inability of the price paid by Geest Industries Ltd to respond to the rising cost of the inputs. These costs made expanded production most difficult. Twenty-five cents out of every dollar earnings had to be spent on boxes alone. In 1982 the cost of producing and shipping a pound of bananas including subsidies was 43.5 cents; the average revenue per pound was 40.54 cents; thus the loss was 2.96 cents on every pound exported. This amounted to EC$638,899 on exports for 1982.[9] The situation was not dissimilar in 1980 and 1981.

This situation explains the accumulated deficit of EC$2.334m on operations by the Grenada Banana Co-operative Society in 1979, 1980 and 1981. The challenge which this industry faced was to increase yield per acre, rationalize costs and ensure a better return to the 1,300 farmers involved.

In the case of the nutmeg industry the main problem was marketing difficulties and a build-up of involuntary stock. Whereas the level of stock in the 1976–78 period averaged 3.1m lbs, in the period 1980–82 it averaged 6.1m lbs. In other words there was an average of 3m lbs of nutmegs available for sale for which markets could not have been found. In 1982 the level of stock reached an all-time high of 7.786m lbs.[10] The nutmeg industry is Grenada's premier agricultural industry.

**Table 21.4 GCNA: Comparative Statements of Trading and Surplus (EC$m)**

| | *1977* | *1978* | *1979* | *1980* | *1981* | *1982* | *1983* |
|---|---|---|---|---|---|---|---|
| Gross income $m | 15.3 | 16.1 | 12.4 | 11.8 | 9.7 | 10.6 | 11.7 |
| Operating income $m | 3.3 | 3.8 | 2.5 | 1.8 | 0.3 | < 0.1 | 0.2 |
| Trading surplus $m | 4.1 | 4.1 | 2.8 | 2.1 | 0.5 | < 0.1 | 0.2 |
| Price per lb. $ | 2.2 | 2.4 | 2.4 | 2.5 | 2.3 | 2.0 | 1.6 |
| Sales-volume (m lbs.) | 4.8 | 6.1 | 4.5 | 4.0 | 3.6 | 4.2 | 5.9 |
| Production (m lbs) | 6.7 | 4.4 | 5.4 | 5.4 | 5.3 | 6.2 | 4.8 |
| Surplus payments | 4.0 | 4.0 | 4.4 | 4.0 | 3.1 | 1.0 | 1.2 |

Source: GCNA *Financial Statements*, 1977–82

The year 1983 was the fourth that this industry had been under persistent pressures; so much so, that some farmers were beginning to question the viability of continued production. Table 21.4 shows the picture vividly.

The problem was neither one of falling prices nor low production but rather one of declining volume of sales and revenues with a simultaneous growth in production. The result was an involuntary rise in inventories. One of the challenges faced by this industry was to convert a percentage of its stock into oil, and contract sales for it internationally with the major pharmaceutical firms. Seven thousand registered farmers depend on the industry. The significant fall in the annual bonus from $4m in the 1977–80 period to $1m by 1992 helped to shatter farmers' confidence, and that of the rural working class, in the People's Revolutionary Government, as 28,000 out of a population of 93,000 depended on this industry totally or partially for their livelihood. (This figure excludes those who depended on it indirectly, who range in the thousands.) Nutmegs to Grenada are as oil is to Trinidad and Tobago, bauxite to Jamaica, and tourism to Barbados.

It was an unfortunate coincidence for the PRG that the critical period for them was the very period when commodity prices remained depressed: international commodity prices excluding oil fell by 15.5% in 1980–81 and by a further 15% in 1981–82.[11] The world price index for cocoa fell from 100 in 1980 to 66.9 by 1982. As Oyow analysed it:

> The success of OPEC in virtually dictating oil prices raised the possibility that more commodity producers would follow suit and organize themselves into cartels. Raw material dependent states rationalized as a result. Waste was reduced and recycling became the order of the day. Companies intensified research into the use of plastics and synthetic materials. These measures coupled with recession and subsequent changes in the structure of the economies of the industrialized world led to a drop in demand for raw materials in the 1980's and to collapse in prices.[12]

## II

The manifest weaknesses inherent in a narrow agricultural export base forced the Government to move to diversify the export base, to include non-traditional exports. The performance of these was encouraging. In 1979 they accounted for 7% of commodity exports. Three years later (1982) they accounted for 37% (see Table 21.5, page 403). Yet this could not have compensated for the decline in the traditional export sector.

**Table 21.5 Non-traditional Exports 1979–82 (percentage of all exports)**

| | *1979* | *1980* | *1981* | *1982* |
|---|---|---|---|---|
| Traditional exports | 93.0 | 85.4 | 73.6 | 63.4 |
| Non-traditional exports | 7.0 | 14.6 | 26.4 | 36.6 |

The non-traditional exports included fruits and vegetables, clothing, flour and wheat products, furniture and agro-industrial products. Exports of fruits and vegetables increased from EC$1.4m in 1981 to EC$4.5m in 1982 – an increase of 315%. The existence of the Marketing and National Importing Board as a marketing outlet for fruits and vegetables contributed to the increase in production in this area. However benefits were felt by a small number of farmers and were not widespread among the rural community.

The export of clothing also showed encouraging growth in the three years 1980–82. The most striking years were 1980 and 1981 when earnings grew by 139% and 147% respectively (see Table 21.6). For the period earnings increased at an average of 100% per annum. Like fruits and vegetables, the benefits from this were limited to two companies and were not spread among the population. Furthermore the cost of imported inputs accounted for a large share of the final value and value-added was not considerable.

Flour and wheat products increased their earnings from $1.784m in 1981 to $1.935m in 1982. This represented an 8% increase and was very encouraging for an industry that was only about three years old. Again all material inputs were imported and valueadded was limited. At any rate this industry's growth was constrained by the fact that it was essentially based on import-substitution.

Earnings from furniture exports also increased by almost 100% during the years 1981–82 (Table 21.7, page 404). Export earnings in this industry increased at an average annual rate of 55% in the period 1979 to 1982. This again was very encouraging as it was a line of export that had begun to develop only recently. Its macro-economic impact, like the others outlined above, was very limited and restricted, even if its value-added exceeded the others previously mentioned, proportionally.

**Table 21.6 Clothing Exports 1979–82**

| | *1979* | *1980* | *1981* | *1982* |
|---|---|---|---|---|
| Export earnings (EC$m) | 0.991 | 2.373 | 5.857 | 6.554 |
| % of growth | – | 139 | 147 | 12 |

**Table 21.7 Exports of Furniture 1979–82**

| | *1979* | *1980* | *1981* | *1982* |
|---|---|---|---|---|
| Export earnings (EC$m) | 0.365 | 0.975 | 0.570 | 1.003 |
| % change | – | +118 | –30 | +76 |

Agro-industrial products were even more recent developments. These products were produced in one of the 35 state enterprises – Grenada Agro-Industries. In 1982 nectars, jams, condiments, etc. worth some EC$805,000 were produced, EC$382,000 worth of which were sold abroad. The existence of the plant and its demand for fruits created a market for many farmers who now sought to supplement their income from traditional crops by the production and sale of fruits. This was what a World Bank survey had to say:

> The development of agro-industries offers promise. Grenada has an abundance of fruits and vegetables which are often lost through spoilage because of the very short harvesting period for these perishable products. The establishment of the Grenada Agro-Industries provides a market for these products to be processed into jams, sauces, jellies and nectars. It gives incentives for many full time and part-time farmers to produce more because of the ready market it provides.[13]

Some industrial products remained stable while others showed a marginal decline (Table 21.8). The agro-industrial potential of Grenada was largely unrealized, although credit had to be given to the PRG for starting serious agro-processing. The Government published an investment code which included a section on various forms of fiscal incentives to the manufacturing sector. Manufacturing for external markets was very favourably treated in the *Investment Code of the People's Revolutionary Government.*

The Government advocated an industrialization approach based on import substitution and export promotion, both of which involved

**Table 21.8 Selected Industrial Production 1978–81**

| | *1978* | *1979* | *1980* | *1981* |
|---|---|---|---|---|
| Rum (gallons) | 72,800 | 78,800 | 72,500 | 77,100 |
| Beer (gallons) | 286,000 | 36,800 | 306,000 | 270,000 |
| Cigarettes | 133,900 | 113,000 | 101,000 | 99,000 |
| Malt (gallons) | 89,000 | 106,800 | 119,000 | 136,000 |
| Edible oil | 63,800 | 67,700 | 54,000 | 69,000 |
| Sugar (tons) | 583.000 | 524.000 | 493.000 | n.a. |
| Poultry Feed | – | – | 1,253,000 | 2,766,000 |

as much as was possible 'the greater utilization of natural and human resources'.[14] The strategy involved establishing clear intersectoral linkages between agriculture, industry and tourism so that they become mutually complementary and self-reinforcing.

As far as the traditional export crops were concerned, the intention was to expand production and generate greater foreign exchange through greater raw material export. Given the depressed nature of the commodities market, and the volatility of price to international demand-and-supply conditions, the future of this was very uncertain. Most of these activities were either in the planning stage or in their initial stages and were not sufficiently advanced to impact significantly on people's standard of living: Laudable in themselves, but their macro-economic impact for the time being was very limited.

Despite the PRG's interest in, and emphasis on, manufacturing, the sector remained relatively small; there was considerable unused capacity in many production lines, resulting in wastage of plant and equipment (Table 21.9). The manufacturing sector did not have the economic impact that the PRG expected and urgently wanted.

The manufacturing sector itself had many problems during the era of the Revolution, including:

- limited sources and availability of credit;
- limited levels of technological skills;
- constraints of infrastucture;
- low efficiency levels of import substitution industries;
- import bias of distributors and consumers;
- product quality – inferior in some cases;
- lack of aggressive export promotion.

## III

Loans and advances of commercial banks in 1979 were 47.5% of total liabilities/assets. By 1982 the figure had fallen to 44.4%. In 1978 the manufacturing sector was able to command 5.4% of loans and advances; this fell to 4.2% by 1982. In the interval there was stiff competition for funds with the distributive trades, the public utility sector, and government and statutory bodies. Public utilities which had loans outstanding in 1979 of EC$5.30m had increased their quantum to EC$5.526m by 1982.

Government and statutory bodies increased their share likewise from EC$9m to EC$13m in the same interval. Both sources accounted for 60% of the increase in loans and advances. At the same time manufacturing amount fell from EC$6.5m to EC$5.8m. Thus, the

**Table 21.9 Levels of Consumption and Plant Under-Utilization in 1982**

| | | *Consumption* | | | | *Capacity sq. ft.* | | | | |
|---|---|---|---|---|---|---|---|---|---|---|
| *Product classification* | *Unit* | *Total cons.* | *Imports 1982* | *Local prod.* | *Local prod. % cons.* | *Total cap.* | *Utilized cap.* | *Utilized cap. % cons.* | *Total cap. % con.* | *Ess cap.* |
| 1. Tomato catsup | kg | 65,700 | 50,000 | 15,700 | 24 | 122,000 | 15,000 | 13 | 186 | 86 |
| 2. Coffee* | ″ | 18,900 | 12,200 | 6,700 | 35 | 27,000 | 6,700 | 25 | 143 | 43 |
| 3. Spices | ″ | 3,600 | 3,400 | 200 | 6 | 10,900 | 1,100 | 10 | 303 | 203 |
| 4. Cigarettes | ″ | 27,200 | 4,500 | 22,700 | 83 | 26,000 | 22,700 | 63 | 132 | 32 |
| 5. Macaroni† | ″ | 107,000 | 107,000 | n/a | n/a | 40,000 | n/a | n/a | 37 | – |
| 6. Liquid Detergents | litre | 26,800 | 23,500 | 3,300 | 12 | 32,500 | 3,300 | 10 | 121 | 21 |
| 7. Aerated Drinks | ″ | 747,800 | 286,200 | 461,600 | 62 | 1,480,000 | 461,600 | 31 | 198 | 98 |
| 8. Rum | ″ | 86,000 | 8,400 | 78,000 | 90 | 300,000 | 78,200 | 26 | 346 | 246 |
| 9. Plastic Bags | kg | 162,000 | 137,000 | 25,000 | 15 | 200,000 | 25,000 | 13 | 123 | 23 |

Sources: Central Statistics Office 1982
Independent Manufacturers Data 1982
M. Julien, *Constraints to Industrial Development*, 1983
Notes: * Roasted and ground coffee only
† Production commenced September 1983.

manufacturing sector was 'crowded out' from sharing in the increase in loans and advances outstanding between 1979 and 1982. A possible explanation for this change in loan portfolio mix is the scepticism about the viability of manufacturing concerns as shared by some commercial bankers. They often lament the fatality rate among infant industries in the region, the poor marketing skills of investors, inferior manufacturing techniques and the high level of long-term loans for new manufacturing concerns.

Another possible explanation was that the 20% special deposits of 1982 reduced the liquidity base of the banks by EC$21.6m, which in fact had meant a reduced ability to create credit, and consequently, tighter terms on the remaining funds available. Conversely, the ratio of banks' net foreign assets to total deposits fell from 26% in 1981 to 4.6% by December 1982. Thus, a public-sector borrowing requirement on the whole which totalled ed EC$34m by 1982 contributed to a liquidity squeeze and in the aggregate placed constraints on private-sector access to credit. The result in effect had meant the persistence of contractionary monetary policy on the banking side and expansionary fiscal policy on the central government side.

In such a situation the Grenada Development Bank should have come to the rescue. But, as this institution was for some time under-capitalized, it has had to operate a precautionary lending policy. Loans requested from 1979 to 1982 totalled EC$4.727m; approvals amounted to EC$1.35m or 29% of applications.[15] The caution with which funds were lent can be seen from the securities received and held. The security-to-loan ratio was 2:1 throughout, which meant that for every $1 lent $2 were held.[16] The weakness with this is that more loans tended to go into those areas where collateral was most easily obtainable, and less into those areas where it was less available, despite the feasibility of a project in the latter.

**Table 21.10 Grenada Development Bank: Analysis of Loans to the Manufacturing Sector**

| *Period* | *Authorized loans* | *Security received* | *Total security held* | *Security to loans ratio* | *Security investment ratio* |
|---|---|---|---|---|---|
| 1979 | 96,000 | 113,000 | 209,000 | 2:1 | 7:1 |
| 1980 | 274,800 | 306,200 | 581,000 | 2:1 | 6:1 |
| 1981 | 102,000 | 118,675 | 220,675 | 2:1 | 7:1 |
| 1982 | 878,000 | 975,000 | 1,853,000 | 2:1 | 6:1 |
| Total | 1,350,800 | 1,513,575 | 2,863,675 | 2:1 | 6:1 |

Source: The Grenada Development Bank

## IV

Whereas the manufacturing sector did show signs of bouyancy and promise under the People's Revolutionary Government, the tourism sector, another pillar of the economy, declined. Cruise-ship visitors declined from 139,000 in 1979 to 62,000 in 1982; stay-over visitors also declined from 32,000 in 1979 to 23,000 in 1982, a decline of 28%. Even in decline, tourism contributed about 50% of Grenada's foreign-exchange earnings in 1981.

This decline can be attributed principally to three factors:

1. Adverse publicity abroad, consequent upon the outbreak of the Revolution.
2. Recession in North America which adversely affected expenditure on income-superior goods and services, as holidays.
3. The difficulties which visitors experienced in getting to and from Grenada.

Tourism affects the livelihood of hundreds of hoteliers and other hotel workers, farmers, fishermen, craft workers, vendors and entertainers. Its decline, like that of agriculture, had a negative impact on the People's Revolutionary Government.

Indeed, the importance of tourism had been underlined by the creation in 1982 of a separate Ministry of Tourism. A public relations campaign was launched in 1982, and the promotions budget was increased by 300% to EC$700,000. The development and expansion of tourism presupposed a sound infrastructure; without it the benefits of an expanded industry cannot be harnessed. Given the work to be done on the infrastructure and the requirements for growth, the infrastructural activities at the time, though considerable, were still insufficient, as it had been estimated that full development of the infrastructure would cost approximately EC$600m.

## V

The most important of the infrastuctural investments were:

1. The construction of the international airport.
2. The building of the eastern main road.
3. The construction of feeder roads to bring rich agricultural lands into production.
4. The establishment of a new telephone exchange system.

5. The housing construction programme.
6. The acquisition of new electricity generators for Grenlec.

The cost of the international airport was estimated at EC$191m and completion was expected by 1984. Investment by the state sector amounted to EC$149m between 1979 and 1981, and a further EC$101m was planned for 1982. By 1982 over 40 miles of road had been constructed, both main and feeder. In 1982 a housing construction programme, involving two schemes and 32 houses, began and was completed. In the same year another scheme comprising 289 low-cost houses commenced; the first phase involved constructing 50 houses at a cost of EC$2.3m.[17] The Sandino Plant – a gift from the Republic of Cuba – which arrived in 1982 to construct farm buildings and storage facilities could have produced 500 houses a year. Since 1980 over EC$1.3m had been disbursed through the National House Repair Programme, to low-income householders, either as grants or as 'soft' loans. Added to this 1,506 housing units were repaired. (Table 21.11 shows the capital expenditure of goverment during the period 1978–82.)

The central government improved upon financial and budgetary management. There were tighter controls and almost day to day monitoring of expenditure. Expenditure limits were set monthly and departments were expected to remain within these limits. The budget, which was in deficit for decades, was said to have experienced a surplus in 1979 and 1982. The figure for the latter year was significant (Table 21.12). The surplus in the latter year went towards the closing of the financing gap which had arisen as a result of the massive capital expenditure programmes.

**Table 21.11 Estimated Capital Expenditure (in EC$m) by Central Government 1978–82**

| | *1978* | *1979* | *1980* | *1981* | *1982* |
|---|---|---|---|---|---|
| Expenditure | 3.9 | 41.5 | 31.4 | 76.2 | 101.5 |
| % change | – | +964% | –24% | +143% | +33% |

Source: Ministry of Finance, *Report on National Budget 1982, 1983*

**Table 21.12 Revenue and Expenditure (EC$m) 1978–82**

| | *1978* | *1979* | *1980* | *1981* | *1982* |
|---|---|---|---|---|---|
| Revenue | 44.8 | 54.9 | 58.0 | 62.6 | 74.0 |
| Expenditure | 53.1 | 53.9 | 59.6 | 63.8 | 67.5 |
| Balance | –8.3 | +1.0 | –0.7 | –1.2 | +6.5 |

Source: Ministry of Finance, Budget Data 1978–82

**Table 21.13 Estimated Growth Rate of GDP (EC$m) 1979–82**

| | *1979* | *1980* | *1981* | *1982* |
|---|---|---|---|---|
| Nominal GDP | 196.6 | 231.7 | 261.5 | 298.4 |
| Real GDP | 144.2 | 148.6 | 153.0 | 161.5 |
| Deflator | 136.3 | 155.9 | 171.0 | 184.8 |
| Rate of growth (%) | 2.1 | 3.0 | 3.0 | 5.5* |

Source: Report on National Budget, 1983; World Bank Report, *Econ. Memo.*, No. 3825-GRD, August 1982
* The 5.5% was adjusted downwards to 3.0% by the World Bank.

The net effect of all economic activities, despite problems and reverses, had been a modest but steady growth rate of GDP since 1979 (Table 21.13). The main productive sectors did not account for this growth; mainly new capital projects accounted for this.

The growth rate averaged 3.4% over the period 1978–82, with the highest rate occurring in 1982. The main contributors have been the construction sector, the manufacturing sector, distributive trades, and fruit and vegetable production.

The growth rate did not have a significant impact on people's living standards; the time-scale was too short, as most of the activities accounting for it were infrastructural. However, the social programmes of the PRG did have some impact on quality of services. A comparison of the indicators in Table 21.14, showing physical quality of life, will show this to some extent.

**Table 21.14 Physical Quality-of-Life Indicators in 1978 and 1981**

| | *1978* | *1981* |
|---|---|---|
| Death rate (per 100) | 7.00 | 6.80 |
| Doctors per 1000 of the population | 0.23 | 0.35 |
| Nurses per 1000 of the population | 1.51 | 3.15 |
| Cost of doctor's visit in institutions (EC$) | 10.00 | 0.00 |
| Dentists per 1000 of the population | 0.04 | 0.07 |
| Clinics per 1000 of the population | 0.29 | 0.30 |
| Infant mortality per 1000 | 29.00 | 14.80 |
| Literacy rate % | 85.0 | 90.0 |
| Teachers per 1000 of population of school age | 32.0 | 28.5 |
| School enrolment ratio (primary) % | 82.0 | 90.0 |
| School enrolment ratio (secondary) % | 32.0 | 41.0 |
| Students in university on scholarship | 35.0 | 250.0 |
| School fees (secondary & tertiary) – EC$ | 45.0 | 0.0 |

Source: CSO, Statistical data 1978 & 1981; *Abstract of Statistics*, 1979

## VI

The achievement of the People's Revolutionary Government in the social sphere was commendable. They embarked on a major low-income housing program in 1981, building 32 units, and embarked on a 289-unit program in 1982. They imported the Sandino Housing Plant in 1982 and projected to commission it in 1983; after 1980 over EC$1.3m was spent to repair 1,506 homes under a National House Repair Programme (see page 409). Health care was made free for all and the health delivery system at the hospitals and clinics was inproved; milk, butterfat and rice were distributed to expectant low-income mothers at some 63 centres throughout the country; all primary and secondary education was made free; Common Entrance places to secondary school were increased from 302 in 1978 to 1,032 by 1980 thus raising secondary enrolment ratio from 32 in 1978 to 40 by 1980–1. A book and uniform assistance program was initiated for children of low-income parents. The People's Revolutionary Government introduced a system of work/study throughout the education system with the slogan 'Every student a worker, every worker a student'. At the tertiary level the State provided over 223 scholarships for university training in Cuba, UWI, German Democratic Republic, and the USSR. An Adult Education Programme was started in 1980, with registration of over 3,000; though the effort was praiseworthy, its success was restricted and limited and its impact almost negligible.

Despite the successes in the social field and in some infrastructural areas, the performance of the major sectors of the economy during the PRG period was disastrous. Undoubtedly this poor performance helped to undermine the régime and create the conditions for internal disaffection and internecine party rivalry and conflict. Consequently, the social programme and infrastructure work mentioned above would have been shortlived, as they were based on subsidies and gifts and did not proceed from any genuine, self-sustained surplus in the budget. The weaknesses of the main sectors would ultimately have compounded this. It was a fundamental error in the fiscal and economic plan.

Prices rose more steeply in 1979 and 1980 than in 1981 and 1982. The rate of growth in the last two years was significantly lower than in the preceding two years. Nonetheless the purchasing power of the dollar declined from January 1979 December 1982, to 56% of its value.

Of course, wages rose during the same period. In 1981, 1982 and 1983 public workers received increases of 17.3%, 10% and 12.5% respectively – a compounded increase of 45.13%. The cumulative increase in prices for the same period was 34.3%. Wages exceeded prices by some 11% for these categories of workers. In 1981 agricultural workers received increases of 11.5%, manufacturing workers 12.5% to 17.5%, bank employees 15% to 22% and workers in the commercial sector between 7.5% and 32%.

## VII

Since 1979 the People's Revolutionary Government had stated that part of its strategy was the creation of a mixed economy consisting of a private sector, a co-operative sector and a dominant state sector. The latter was a novel experience for the country. However, a huge state sector, far from strengthening the PRG, helped to paralyse it, by forcing the régime to spend millions on subsidizing loss-making ventures, and therefore carried with it a huge opportunity cost, a cost the régime could not afford.

Government employed 10,000 workers in state enterprises and public service; this accounted for 30% of the work force.[18] There were some 43 state enterprises at this time, with some 29 classified as directly productive. These employed 2,333 persons and produced income in 1981 and 1982 of EC$26m and EC$36.7m respectively. However, the net margin in 1982 was only EC$0.828m (about 2% of sales). Some enterprises which made a loss were the Grenada Farms Corporation, Grenada Sugar Factory, National Fisheries Co., National Transport Service, and the Grenada Resorts Corporation. These were goods- and service-producing sectors. Those which made profits were the Central Water Commission, National Inporting Board, Grenada Telephone Company, Grenada Electricity Services Ltd, National Commercial Bank, and Grencraft. The commitment of the People's Revolutionary Government to a large state sector led to a massive resource misallocation and a significant welfare loss. Examples of this include:

1. The Grenada Farms Corporation – an agricultural state-owned company. The Grenada Farms Corporation comprised 37 state farms accounting for 2,997 acres, and employed about 800 persons. In 1982 these farms made a net loss of EC$1m and had to be subsidized. The net income of 21 farms was examined for 1983. Their aggregate net income was EC$20,000; only two of the 21 farms had a positive net income – of EC$4,000 and EC$16,000 respectively.[19]

2. The Grenada Agro-Industries was a good project idea. It was a fruit canning plant, employing 47 persons, and it purchased produce from about 800 farmers. During its three years of operation (1981–83) it made a net loss every year, totalling $60,000.[20] In 1983 the following major problems were identified by a senior People's Revolutionary Government official who studied its operations:
   - inexperienced staff;
   - insufficient working capital;
   - poor quality packaging material;
   - unreliable electricity supply;
   - frequent breakdown of equipment.

   Loss on operations did not include depreciation, unsaleable inventory, and storage charges. When these were considered GAIL accumulated a total loss to the Government of approximately EC$2m in less than three years.[21]
3. The Spice Island Coffee Processing Plant, another state enterprise, made a net loss from 1980 to 1983 inclusive, totalling some EC$50,000. Its total sales for these four years were valued at a paltry EC$389,523.
4. The Grenada Sugar Factory made an accumulated loss of EC$250,000 in the four-year period 1980 to 1983, on sales of some EC$7.8m.
5. The National Fisheries Co. Ltd itself made a loss of EC$570,000 for its period of operation, April 1981 to December 1983. This excluded depreciation and interest expenses. Revenue from its fleet operation covered only 42% of cost, while that from fish processing covered only 54% of cost.
6. The Forestry Development Corporation also recorded a loss for its two years of operation. The FDC was a large money-loser, with losses of $271,353 in 1983 and EC$296,611 in 1982. Recurrent government grants of EC$189,000 were even insufficient to cover the losses.

The interesting point is that most of these state enterprises were expected to make profits *but the outcome in almost every case went directly opposite to the expectations*. Not only did this upset many senior members of the party and Government, they became the subject of serious internal criticisms within the upper echelons of those institutions.

The People's Revolutionary Government maintained loyalty to its ideology on the issue of state enterprises; however, their performance was an economic and financial disaster in the majority of cases and helped to discredit the very philosophy the Government was committed to selling to the people of Grenada. In that regard they suffered an uncalculated defeat.

The decline of the traditional export sector and its accompanying woes forced the PRG to request the IMF in 1983 to give it a Structural Adjustment Programme. This is the most convincing piece of evidence to prove that their macro-economic policies did not work and taken overall, did not succeed in putting Grenada on a path of self sustained growth. This speaks volumes.

By 1983 the public sector was unable to generate a level of surplus sufficient to service debt, subsidize loss-making state enterprises and finance the various social programme of the PRG. The Government had no choice but to go to the IMF. By that time the population had by far exceeded its taxable capacity; the high level of both direct and indirect taxes was beginning to produce a disincentive to effort.

In July 1983 the IMF approved an extended arrangement for the Government authorizing purchases of up to the equivalent of SDR13.5m or approximately EC$40m over the next three years,[22] in support of the Government's economic and financial programme. Grenada's outstanding obligations to the fund up to then, excluding Trust Fund Loans, was equivalent to SDR4.3m.[23]

External debt as a percentage of GDP grew from 13.5% in 1979 to 33.5% in 1982. In 1981 consumption was 98% of GDP; in 1980 it was 100%. Debt-service ratio – debt repayments as a percentage of exports – also increased from 1.6% in 1979 to 10.5% in 1982.

The People's Revolutionary Government's good economic management and a number of sound policies did not prevent their overall economic failure, for the system they aimed to build ... was alien to the experiences of Grenadians, and like any bitter substance, they vomited it up. By 1983 the Government had lost the confidence of most of the people and were in deep economic and financial crisis.

By 1983 adherence to ideology had reached cult proportions among the leadership of the New Jewel Movement (NJM) and the

**Table 21.15 Total Public Debt 1979–82**

| | *1979* | *1980* | *1981* | *1982* |
|---|---|---|---|---|
| External debt (EC$m) | 21.7 | 36.6 | 69.5 | 100.2 |
| Domestic debt (EC$m) | 31.9 | 32.3 | 35.9 | 65.5 |
| Total public debt (EC$m) | 53.6 | 68.9 | 105.4 | 165.7 |
| External debt as % GDP | 13.5 | 18.7 | 31.1 | 33.5 |
| Debt-service ratio % | 1.6 | 3.0 | 3.7 | 10.5* |

Source: World Bank Econ. Memo.; CSO, Trade Statistics.
* Projected figure.

*The first rally of the PRG, 18 March 1979*

*Members of the first PRG, 1979. Seated left to right: Norris Bani, Rupert Ambrose, Bernard Gilleus, Pamala Buxo, Lloyd Noel, Lyden Ranidhanny, George Louison, Bernard Coard, Maurice Bishop*

PRG. This passionate commitment to Marxism-Leninism blinded most of the leaders to the folly of economic policy rooted in ideology. The economic reality was by then quite evident, but ideological passion could not bring them to accept it and revise the doctrine. In light of the crash of Communist régimes in the Soviet Union, Eastern Europe, Nicaragua and elsewhere, later, this folly of the People's Revolutionary Government is now fully apparent. At the time their path was not just the only pure and correct one, it also represented the ultimate in political truism itself. Some of their staunchest members at the time were prepared to die for their ideology or kill in defence of it. To a few the Grenada Revolution had reached the level of a fanatical cult by 1983.

## Marxism-Leninism Rules: The Pitfalls of Ideological Cultism:

The People's Revolutionary Government which governed Grenada from March 1979 to October 1983 aspired to build, or create, a Marxist-Leninist state in Grenada. The term 'Marxist-Leninist' is used in this context to define a system of government that embodies the concepts of state ownership of the commanding heights of the economy, the governing of a country by a single vanguard party, dictatorship of the proletariat, and the principles of democratic centralism and proletarian internationalism.[24]

The rigid adherence to these very concepts and principles led to deep ideological conflicts within the ruling party and government; worsening economic conditions in Grenada in 1981–82, but more particularly in 1982–83, fanned the flames of ideological division and led to the self-destruction of the PRG regime in October 1983.

Mass political rallies which were one of the dominant features of the Revolution in 1980–81, became fewer and fewer later and became almost non-existent by 1983.

By 1983 the People's Revolutionary Government had almost completely alienated the churches and by the same token most of their followers. The political effects were particularly devastating as Grenada is a country that was almost 100% religious. The PRG treated the churches collectively as an organization in alliance with international and regional imperialist and reactionary forces. The churches and their leaders were subjected to close surveillance by the Government with assistance from the Cubans and Nicaraguans.[25] Their tactics included:

- monitoring all sermons by the parish priests and pastors;
- monitoring of all meetings of churches' hierarchy;

- monitoring elements of society that pay regular visits to the hierarchy of the churches;
- tapping the telephones of so-called counter-revolutionary church leaders;[26]
- closing down of the *Focus*, a newspaper printed by the Catholic Church;
- spying on members of the clergy, considered to be counter-revolutionary;
- denying certain priests and pastors a work permit.

In a top-secret report by Michael Roberts, of the Special Branch, written on 15 March 1983, and sent to Major Keith Roberts, it was stated that the Roman Catholic, Anglican, Methodist and Seventh Day Adventist Churches were all hostile to the New Jewel Movement and that the Catholic Church was the most important, because of its size and internal discipline. The PRG's concern over the Church had become so bad that by July 1983 Major Keith Roberts had to write to Maurice Bishop and others saying:

> In the medium term if serious measures are not taken we can find ourselves faced with a Poland Situation ... we see the church in the immediate period as being the most dangerous sector for the development of internal counter revolution.[27]

Roberts recommended extreme and desperate measures indicating a state of sheer panic: Some of these included

- removal from primary schools of all deeply religious principals, by whatever means, in two weeks' time;
- introduction of political education in every classroom;
- political education for all teachers;
- cut-back on all religious programmes on the State Radio;
- opening Marxist-Leninist bookshops in all parishes;
- getting Marxist-Leninist literature into all schools.[28]

The Revolution clearly recognized its vulnerability as far as the churches in Grenada were concerned, as Roberts wrote in his top-secret letter of March 1983.

> It is safe to say that there is no left religion in Grenada. But the broad masses of churchgoers are to varying extent supporters of the Revolution. This cannot be said of the leaders of the churches in Grenada.[29]

As early as February 1980, the PRG expressed grave concern over the ideological content of many tracts and religious literature which were being distributed among the masses. In a top-secret report sent to

Maurice Bishop on 11 February 1980 the following was said about the Roman Catholic Church:

> A series of publications are being put out by the Catholic Church. Most of those published so far aimed at showing that communism is atheistic and should be feared and that the New Jewel Movement is Communist.[30]

The human-rights record of the People's Revolutionary Government angered not only the churches but the Grenadian public at large. The New Jewel Movement condemned Gairy's terrible human rights record; however, in office they made Gairy look like a saint.

Grenada, during the Revolution, was a classic one-party state. There was one functioning political party, the ruling New Jewel Movement. Parliament was suspended: The *Free West Indian* was the only newspaper, and it was the voice of the People's Revolutionary Government. Similarly, radio and television were both state-owned and totally government-controlled. During these times a foreign radio station 'Radio Antilles' continued to represent the voice of truth.

Man is material, social and spiritual. All parts must be addressed. The People's Revolutionary Government was concerned mostly with the material and disregarded the spiritual. It was a fatal flaw in a predominantly religious Grenada.

## *The Russian connection*

There is no doubt whatsoever that the PRG's intentions were to impose a communist dictatorship upon Grenadians, by transforming Grenada ultimately into a small Russia in the Caribbean.

One strategy used to facilitate this was to form Grenada into one big armed camp and govern her by fear, terror, and the gun. Five military assistance agreements were signed, three with Russia, one with Cuba and one with North Korea. These agreements were to give Grenada guns, guns and more guns. In April 1979 Cuba provided the following weapons:

- 3,400 Russian and US rifles with 3 million rounds of ammunition;
- 200 machine guns, with half-a-million rounds of ammunition;
- 100 pistols with 66,000 rounds of ammunition;
- 100 shoulder-fixed rocket launchers with 4,000 rockets;
- 12–82mm mortars with 4,800 mortar shells;
- 12–75mm cannon with 600 shells;
- 12–12.7mm anti-aircraft guns with 237,000 rounds of ammunition.

Furthermore the five agreements referred to above provided the following deliveries.

*Major Ewart 'Headache' Layne leading the troops*

*A section of the People's Revolutionary Army on parade*

- 10,000 assault and other rifles – Soviet AK47 Czech M-52/57 guiper rifles and Casbenes;
- 4,500 submachine guns and machine guns;
- About 11.5m rounds of 7.62 ammunition;
- 294 portable rocket launchers with about 16,000 rockets;
- 84 82mm mortars with more than 4,800 mortar shells;
- 12 75mm cannon with some 600 cannon shells;
- 60 crew-served anti-aircraft guns with 600,000 rounds of ammunition;
- 15,000 hand grenades;
- 7,000 land mines;
- 30 76mm 215 field guns with almost 11,000 rounds of ammunition;
- 30 57mm 215 anti-tank guns with about 10,000 rounds of ammunition;
- A number of armoured cars.

By early 1983 a great quantity of these weapons had already been landed in Grenada; some were in use, but most were stored in armed camps across the country.

The ammunition was sufficient to outfit the entire male population above 21 years. While Grenada was investing in arms and in instruments for state violence, countries like St Lucia were investing in banana cultivation. After four years (by 1984) the situation was clear. While St Lucia was earning EC$56m from the export of bananas and St Vincent EC$30m, Grenada was earning EC$8m. This is one of the clear examples of the subordination of agricultural interests to military interests during the People's Revolutionary Government.

## *The Hope Vale prison camp (Grenada)*

The People's Revolutionary Government, in the footsteps of Russia and Cuba, created its own concentration (prison) camp, at Hope Vale. Most of the inmates were members of the Rastafarian sect – a sect that was very supportive of the PRG, and its take-over in the early days of the Revolution. There were detainees of other persuasions also at Hope Vale particularly those who were singled out for special pressure and humiliation. Conditions at Hope Vale were unsanitary, resulting in much illness; detainees were subjected to long and arduous hours of work; they slept under a leaking roof in a building suitable for pigs, with mattresses, containing 'faeces and blood', which were taken from the mental asylum.

This is the kind of inhumanity that was practised upon the Grenadian people.

### *Preventive detention*

The laws establishing preventive detention were brutal in that on mere suspicion hundreds of innocent persons were jailed for unlimited periods of time. Over three thousand persons were arbitrarily arrested at one time or another and held in detention without trial.

## Gairy's Autocracy and his Self-Destruction

When members of a party witness wrongdoing within a party and fail to condemn, resist and advise against it, they are contributing to the very destruction of the party by their inaction and silence, as much as by their active support.

During the Grenada United Labour Party (GULP) régime, stooges of Gairy's government sat by and allowed Gairy to do all sorts of wrong without criticism. The results of this were violence in the streets and around the country, and ultimately the overthrow of Gairy himself. Reference to a few of these incidents will be sufficient to illustrate the point:

- the slaying of Jeremiah Richardson by police on 20 April 1973 and the failure to hold a coroner's inquest;
- shooting down of demonstrators at Pearls on 23 April 1973;
- Bloody Sunday beatings and disfigurings of 'the NJM Six' on 18 November 1973 at Greenville;
- The murder of Rupert Bishop, father of Maurice Bishop, on 21 January 1974;
- the savage beating of Edwin Cudjoe on 24 November 1974;
- the slaying of 27-year-old Ralph Gibbs on 5 October 1976 by policemen with no inquiry after;
- the shooting of Georgiana Armstrong of River Road on 7 March 1977 by a Gairy thug;
- the killing of Allister Strachan following the 19 June 1977 Market Square shootings by Gairy's forces.

The gun that was turned against other people all along with Gairy's ministers sitting by and saying nothing, was now turned against them, when in January 1978 Innocent Belmar (an MP) was shot and killed. It was not a full 15 months later when Gairy's government itself was overthrown in the armed seizure of power, with three officers losing their lives and many ministers being imprisoned.

Autocratic rule, where allowed to proceed unchecked, usually ends up devouring the autocrat, his stooges and the country. The same is true of the People's Revolutionary Government régime. Gairy's régime was autocracy of the right; the People's Revolutionary Government was autocracy of the left. Gairy's government was a dictatorship of one man; the PRG was a dictatorship of an intellectual élite.

## Abuse of Human Rights Helped Destroy Bishop

Four abuses in particular helped undermine credibility in the PRG, created increased alienation of the people from them, and helped to hasten the end of the PRG.

1. Torture of detainees, though not widespread in the 1979–83 period, as has been alleged, did in fact take place in a number of cases. Some detainees were beaten, while others were chopped even in the presence of and under the instruction of high-ranking PRG officials. In one incident a government minister actually pushed a lighted cigarette in a detainee's nose and on another occasion a minister supervised the battering of other detainees. Burning detainees' skin with iron rods and cutting their testicles with razor blades are two other forms of torture known to have taken place.
2. The murder of Ralph Thompson at the hands of the People's Revolutionary Government is one of the crimes that is still crying to heaven for vengeance. Thompson was one of the foremost activists for the NJM and one of the PRG's strongest early supporters. When his lawyers Tillman Thomas and Lloyd Noel applied for a writ of *Habeus Corpus*, those who represented the PRG in order to argue against his getting his freedom were Heyliger and Radix. He later died in prison in pain and torment. Even when he asked for special medical attention he was denied it.
3. The murder of Ethelbert John is yet another crime also crying to heaven for vengeance. John also died in detention in 1981 at the hands of merciless persons.
4. The execution of Strachan Phillip on 19 June 1980, allegedly for a crime he never committed, is a deed that lives to haunt every PRG member. The murder of Strachan Phillip was clearly a case of the shedding of an innocent man's blood. The security forces and the Central Committee who sent them were judge, jury and executioner, all in one. While the assault on Strachan Phillip's home was in progress, Prime Minister Bishop was on the radio addressing the

nation saying, 'At this moment the security forces are now at the home of the chief of counter-revolutionaries in St Paul's, Strachan Phillip.'

It was alledged that the soldier who actually shot and killed Strachan was one of the persons executed by the RMC at Fort George on 19 October, along with Bishop.

The point to note is that all of this blood-letting seems to have been openly supported by Bishop, the Louisons and others. The very evil they encouraged returned to destroy them later. The very wolves Bishop helped to feed and breed turned around and devoured him, once they had enough strength.

The People's Revolutionary Government lived in constant fear of foreign invasion by foreign counter-revolutionaries assisted, as they claimed, by US imperialism. This preoccupation with foreign invasion made the Government paranoid, so much so that they became afraid of their own shadow. This was the basis for many phantom plots forcefully constructed by army intelligence and the resulting detentions of many innocent persons.

But there were attempts to overthrow the PRG through violence. This made them even more paranoid, as they were supported by the manuoevres of US/Caribbean forces in the region – a kind of clearly designed psychological warfare. The 19 June bombing is perhaps the most telling piece of evidence of a violent attempt to wipe out the People's Revolutionary Government leadership and destroy the Revolution.

On 19 June 1980 thousands of PRG supporters and Grenadians gathered in a mass rally in Queen's Park to commemorate two Grenadian heroes – Tubal Uriah Butler, outstanding Grenadian Trade Unionist in Trinidad, and Allister Strachan, an NJM activist who was murdered in the anti-Gairy struggle in 1973.

During the rally there was a massive explosion, so loud, that it was audible up to three miles away. A bomb had gone off below the speakers' platform, on which the Prime Minister and five of the six PRG ministers were seated. The thick cement of the platform deflected the force of the blast; instead the explosion went outside the platform killing three young women and injuring scores of other persons. This bomb was found to be a sophisticated time device, a technology previously unknown to the majority of Grenadians.[31]

All fingers were pointed at Strachan Phillip, the former PRA Sergeant who was entrusted with building up the People's Revolutionary Army (PRA), before 13 March 1979, and the Budhlall brothers. In a tabloid put out at the time, allegedly by the

*Mass rally in St George's town, the day after the 19 June bombing*

Budhlalls, called the *People's Cry*, Strachan Phillip was described as the first hero of the Revolution. Clearly that was no basis for Phillip's guilt. The PRG interpreted this as 'The first hero of a planned new revolution'; however, what was meant was that Strachan Phillip was the first hero of the 13 March 1979 Revolution, as he commanded the forces that stormed the barracks of Gairy's soldiers on the morning of 13 March. As mentioned before, Phillip's home was stormed and he was killed by security forces who went directly to his home at Mt Airy and opened fire on him in his barricaded quarters. Even today he is regarded as an innocent man; in fact, it is known that he loved Maurice Bishop dearly, but became disillusioned by the trend the Revolution had taken. Moreover, during the trial his name was never even mentioned. In 1978 the garage of an Englishman, Dr Davies, the then manager of Barclays Bank in Grenada, was blow up by a bomb. This was foreign to Grenada; the PRG knew who had the skills to make that bomb at that time.

What is striking is that a week after the Queen's Park bomb-blast, on 26 June 1980, another bomb exploded, in the woods near

Belmont in St Patrick's; the carrier, who was completely dismembered, was a 'Rasta' who was linked by the security forces to the Budhlall group. The security forces claimed that the device was similar to the one used in Queen's Park.

These events confirmed PRG fears that local counter-revolutionaries were in league with imperialism to destroy the Grenada Revolution. They became even more suspicious, so much so that peculiar movements of persons were interpreted by them as plots to unseat them.

The Revolution became paranoid after 19 June 1980; and from then on national security became the number one consideration even more than formerly.

5. The most brutal of all the incidents, if one may venture a comparison, is the butchery of the Stanislaus brothers, young Stephen Lalsee, a student at the Institute for further Education (IFE), and two other young men, by PRA soldiers in Plains, St Patrick's in 1980. They were all murdered in cold blood; some say their car was mistaken for another; but the most distasteful pill was the cover-up of such a brutal deed by the authorities.

   Worst yet, in order to placate the wrath of St Patrick's, the Government sent PRA soldiers into the hills to execute a few Rastas from the Mt Rich area. About three were brutally slain.

These incidents depict nothing less than a nightmare to which Grenadians were subjected; a nightmare in which the hands of some people who are walking around now playing innocent, are fully bloodstained.

The execution of Bishop and others on 19 October was part of this nightmare of evil that was stalking the land of Grenada. Bishop helped to create a monster, which went out of control in 1983 and devoured him and many of his colleagues.

Some of the PRG activists were a treacherous lot; often they shouted and cheered Bishop, when he served their purpose; yet when he was no longer deemed necessary, they turned on him. Like Christ, they shouted, 'Hosanna' during the rallies, but on 19 October, some shouted 'Crucify him'. Almost everyone who attended the extraordinary meeting of the Central Committee from 14–16 September 1983 came out to crucify Bishop.

The minutes of the meeting quoted George Louison as saying '*That having listened to a number of comrades – L. James, P. Coard, McBarnette, Layne, Cornwall, Ventour – he agreed that there is a lot of problems in the leadership*.' Louison was the number-two ideological man, after Coard; such a statement from him was tantamount not only to a condemnation of Bishop, but a signing of Bishop's death warrant.

At the Extraordinary General Meeting of full members on Sunday 25 September 1983, the minutes quoted Einstein Louison as saying 'on Cde. Bishop concerns, what is clear is that Cde. Bishop lost touch with the reality around him.' He also said that 'this is true for Cde. Fitzroy Bain'. He pointed out that Bishop had been failing to supervise his work and thus he criticized him for this slackness. He went on to say that the Central Committee comrades who did not vote for the decision (i.e. joint leadership) but had previously agreed to all the analyses of the crisis and problem reminded him of what Marx said of some philosophers – 'They only interpret the world; the point is to change it.' Thus he criticized Central Committee members who voted against joint leadership thereby agreeing fully to it, and condemning Bishop to be disgraced.

To contribute to the death of a man, and then come back and want to form an organization in his name, is the model of treachery, deceit, hypocrisy and opportunism. Such behaviour can only be described as shameless and unrepentant.

What was evident is that by 1983 the PRG and the Revolution were discredited in the eyes of the Grenadian clergy and the vast majority of the laity. To them, detention, failure to hold elections and undemocratic practices were totally unacceptable. Again Roberts, writing in 1983, said:

> The fact that the large percentage of Grenadians have very deep trust in the Church and also taking into account the weaknesses in all our mass organizations and therefore our influence over the masses, we see this development as a dangerous one.[32]

The pillars of the Revolution were crumbling beneath it.

## Concerns of Socialist International

One other such pillar was the support given to the Grenada Revolution by Socialist International: By 1983 the Socialist International was polarized into the Democratic Socialist camp and the Scientific Socialist camp. The People's Revolutionary Government came in for constant criticism, by 1983, from the Democratic Socialist camp. At a meeting of the Socialist International in Switzerland on 4 November 1982 there was outspoken criticism of both the New Jewel Movement and the Sandinistas.[33]

Then there was the secret regional caucus of five political parties in the Caribbean and Latin America affiliated to the Socialist International, which met on 6–7 January, 1983. The report of the meeting noted a resolution drafted by Hector Oqueli of the MNR (Movimiento Nacional Revolutionario) of El Salvador, and subsequently submitted to the Socialist International. This document showed that the New Jewel Movement was fundamentally opposed to the democratic ideals of the Socialist International; that the NJM worked closely with the Cubans to undermine the effectiveness of the Socialist International; and that the NJM's greatest concerns over the Socialist International was the latter's insistence on democratic institutions and democratic elections.[34]

## Economic Strains and Political Pains Continued

While all these events were happening the economic pressures continued to take its toll. The Central Committee meeting of 13–19 July concluded:

> While our economy has continued to grow we are experiencing extreme difficulties in mobilising external finance, and in receiving already promised amounts: This has led to a serious cash flow problem, which has slowed down and even is threatening to halt key capital investment projects, caused limited lay-offs and has *shaken the confidence of broad sections of the masses.*[35]

At this point an explanation is necessary lest it be (mis)construed that there is an inconsistency between the economic growth referred to and the general depressed economic situation. The sector contributing to this growth was construction – in particular, airport and road. But this infrastructure had not yet had time to contribute to the increased production of goods and services. The situation in the main productive sectors remained quite depressed; and it is these sectors that impacted directly on living conditions among the masses.

The same Central Committee report in reviewing problems and difficulties faced by the Revolution listed the following:

1. The continued weak performance of the productive sectors – agriculture, agro-industries, fisheries and tourism.
2. The failure of one of our most strategic sectors to get moving i.e. export marketing.
3. The fact that 1983/84 would be difficult years.
4. The negative effects of severe cash flow problems on key capital projects.[36]

The People's Revolutionary Government's response to this was twofold: (a) maximum effort on the economic front; and (b) stepping up of its ideological work.

The latter posed a problem, as by 1983 the party and Government lacked ideological homogeneity. As early as October 1982 this was recognized at an extraordinary meeting of the Central Committee, which the leadership attended except Bernard Coard, who had resigned from the same committee. The Central Committee concluded that the party stood at the crossroads: either the party took the easy petty-bourgeois route to social democracy or continued on the communist route. The Central Committee reaffirmed the position taken by the General Meeting of 12 and 13 September 1982 that the party must be placed on a firm Leninist footing.

The Committee at that time agreed on an assessment of individual members of the Central Committee. One of the criteria was their ideological level. It is interesting to note that out of a possible 5, Maurice Bishop scored 1 less than Liam James, Ewart Layne, Phyllis Coard, George Louison, and Selwyn Strachan. Fitzroy Bain and Unison Whiteman scored 1 and 2.5 respectively. Those with low scores lacked ideological clarity, while conversely those with high ones had that clarity. By 1983 the New Jewel Movement had two camps, those who were ideological hardliners, and those who were ideological 'softliners' and social democrats.

Economic prosperity could blunt the sharpness of the conflict and ideological divide between groups; for once the bread-and-butter issues of workers and the masses are addressed their confidence and perhaps allegiance invariably will remain. However economic difficulties can shake their confidence and shift their allegiance to a position of neutrality, or even opposition. This can help to sharpen the ideological divide and polarize the sides.

The People's Revolutionary Government considered workers to be socialism's sovereign class, and workers were made to feel so. But the purchasing power of workers' dollars fell between 1979 and 1982, and organized labour sought restoration of lost earnings for its membership.

In 1980 three trade unions, representing some 7,000 old public workers, were caught up in an industrial dispute over wages with the Government. The Government took a hard stand and so did the unions until they were forced to take industrial action; the Government accused the workers of sabotaging the second anniversary of the Revolution and treated the unions with contempt and sheer arrogance. Senior union officials were victimized. The unions were incensed; and although the issue was settled in 1981 with government moving from its stand, the entire impasse left a bitter taste in the mouths of organized labour and did the PRG incalculable harm. This was one of the major nails the People's Revolutionary Government put into its coffin. Their treatment of the unions in 1980–81 cost them much support among the Public Workers Union from that time. Although the workers came off better, the damage was already done.

The poor performance of the major sectors of the economy from 1979 to 1982 led to widespread but quiet discontent and disillusionment among the farming community, which accounted for close to 50% of the population. By 1982 the situation was such that the morale of the vast majority was broken. The response was growing disinterest in and lack of support for the PRG. Three other factors inflamed the situation. The first was the refusal of the PRG to hold General Elections, which they promised the people on the morning of 13 March 1979 and which they said would be held in six months; the second was the banning of news papers, including the *Focus*, the newspaper of the Roman Catholic Church, the most dominant religion in Grenada; as Bishop said 'If the workers take over the Torchlight Newspaper we watch and say nothing, but if the Torchlight move against the workers, we jail the Torchlight.' The third was the detention of innocent persons, some on suspicion and others on mere rumours. These were three burning issues which the régime never addressed and which undermined their support in a way they themselves never imagined was likely.

## The Self-Destruction of the PRG: A People Betrayed

It is against this background of serious economic and political uncertainty that a major conflict developed within the upper echelons of the People's Revolutionary Government in September 1983. No single issue precipitated that conflict; it was a build up of many factors, most of which have been outlined above.

Evidence supports the idea that it was the widely felt sense among members of the Politburo and Central Committee that the Revolution was disintegrating, together with the ideological cultism of Bernard Coard, that triggered the power struggle. The factors seem to have been personal, ideological and systemic.

The minutes of the Central Committee meeting of August 1983 suggest that a number of Politburo members were convinced that the Revolution was facing a 'dangerous crisis'. In that meeting Hudson Austin claimed that the masses were 'in a state of demoralization'; Selwyn Strachan, Minister of Mobilization, asserted that 'sections of the party had begun to rebel against the higher organs'. Liam James concluded that this was the 'beginning of the disintegration of the party'. Bishop himself agreed that the party faced 'the threat of disintegration'.[37]

The crisis, systemic in nature, was accompanied by a factional struggle between Bishop's and Coard's protegés. This struggle had both a personal and ideological aspect to it. While Coard dominated the party, Bishop was dominant and popular with the masses, despite his shortcomings. Bishop was charismatic and warm, Coard was cold and calculating. Grenadians always mistrusted Bernard Coard. He was never a man of the people, and perhaps was secretly jealous of Bishop's amazing popular appeal, which sometimes verged on humiliating him in public.

Ideological differences seemed to have been the key to explaining the crisis. Both Coard and Bishop espoused Marxism-Leninism. They both had as their goal the socialist transformation of Grenadian society. By 1983 Coard and his supporters had become extremely impatient with the pace of change; Bishop and his supporters tended to favour a long-term and rather circuitous route, one that involved anaesthetizing the population. Coard's impatience can be judged from his resignation from the Central Committee.

## *The power struggle and joint leadership*

After the resignation of Bernard Coard from the Politburo and Central Committee, Bishop was known to have remarked that 'a power struggle was well under way'. In the meantime Coard, being fully conscious of Bishop's sensitivity, refrained from any severe criticism of his weaknesses and shortcomings, lest he be accused of undermining Bishop in a bid for the leadership of the party and the country. But Bishop remained convinced that the resignation of Coard was aimed at bringing pressure on him and was an oblique attack on the quality of leadership he provided to the Revolution.

The first sign of real strain and tension surfaced at the emergency meeting of the Central Committee convened on 28 August to discuss a report by Leon 'Bogo' Cornwall, Ambassador to Cuba, who had returned recently. Cornwall reported that upon his return he had found a disturbing state of affairs in the party and country. In short, the Central Committee was not performing; and there was widespread demoralization among senior cadres of the party and Government. Cornwall was supported by many other Central Committee members. In fact, Liam 'Owusu' James observed 'we are seeing the disintegration of the party'. Christopher 'Cojo' DeRiggs noted that 'the heart of the crisis was the Central Committee'. As a result of this, an emergency meeting was scheduled for mid-September. Bishop summed up the proceedings of the meeting and tried to temporize.[38] As Thondike wrote in his book *Grenada*, the stage was set for confrontation.[39] Certainly the lines between the pro-Bishopites and his critics were drawn.

The Central Committee meeting of 14–16 September 1983 laid the basis for much that was to follow. If it was not the genesis of the October crisis, it certainly acted as its catalyst. At the very outset Bishop's critics seized the initiative by rejecting his agenda and substituting it with 'Chalky' Ventour's alternative, an agenda which they felt went to the heart of the matter. It was three-fold:

1. To assess the work of the Central Committee.
2. To analyse the present state of the party and Revolution.
3. To determine the way forward.

As usual the meeting of 14–16 September was at Bishop's home in Mt Wheldale. A scathing, cold-blooded and calculated attack was unleashed on Maurice Bishop by each of the members of the Central Committee who spoke, as if programmed and rehearsed.

Layne observed that the public had become despondent, that dissatisfaction was rife, and that the Revolution was in the greatest danger since 1979. He referred to the low morale among party members, the formalistic approach of the Central Committee, and the fact that the Committee was on a path to 'right opportunism'. He made a clarion call for the creation of a Vanguard party, to lead the way to revolutionary change.[40] Ventour claimed that the party 'was facing disintegration'. Cornwall asserted that the 'honeymoon period' for the Revolution was over; Tan Batholomew spoke of the 'timidity' of the leadership, and poor quality of leadership of the mass organization; Phyllis Coard referred to the 'demoralized masses'. Bishop in an attempt to regain control of the meeting intervened by admitting that the main problem was the Central Committee. He referred to increasing non-attendance at zonal and parish council meetings.[41] Most of the speakers laid the blame on the Central Committee; but they never stopped to ask why the masses were not responding to the People's Revolutionary Government. The fundamental reason was that Marxist-Leninist ideology and all it entailed was alien to the Grenadian character. The ideologues in the party insisted on an ideological line; the people at large were not interested; and with the advent of all kinds of economic pressures, their lack of interest became even more pronounced. In other words the basic cause of the crisis was misplaced and misunderstood.

Louison agreed to this lack of contact with the masses, but thought that the situation was being exaggerated. Whiteman felt that they wasted too much time on small issues and neglected the 'fundamentals', such as the Church. Bishop, in summing up the day's proceedings, was the only one who came close to the concerns of Grenadians and hence the root of the crisis. He said:

> The 'deep' crisis in the party and revolution was due to the poor functioning of the Committee, compounded by the weakness of the material base; e.g unrepaired roads, electricity outages and 'retrenchment' of workers.

However no meaningful solutions were arrived at. His critics did not agree with him and on the second day again went on the offensive, to place the blame squarely on Bishop's shoulders. Liam James put it this way: 'The most fundamental problem is the quality of leadership of the Central Committee and the party, provided by Cde. Maurice Bishop.'[42]

Bishop was accused of 'right opportunism' and leading the party to social democracy. James concluded that the three qualities needed to push the Revolution forward were lacking in Bishop. These were:

1. A Leninist level of organization and discipline.
2. Great depth in ideological clarity.
3. Brilliance in strategy and tactics.[43]

The clearly expressed view was that those qualities he lacked were precisely those qualities Bernard Coard possessed. The criticisms of Bishop were supported by Strachan, Ventour, Layne, Phyllis Coard, Cornwall, McBarnette, DeRiggs and Batholomew. Bishop faced a situation he had never faced before; for the first time he was severely criticized and challenged; his supporters on the Committee tried to come to his rescue but to no avail. The die had been cast.

The critical moment came when Liam James proposed a model of joint leadership to marry the strengths of Bishop to those of Bernard Coard, brilliant in theory but unworkable in practice, due to the frailties of human nature. Bishop was to concentrate on international affairs, and with work among the masses, while Coard would take responsibility for strategy and tactics and party organization; he was also to chair the Politburo. Nine members voted for the proposal, George Louison and Whiteman opposed it, and Bishop, Austin and Bain abstained.[44]

According to Thorndike, at that meeting the severest attack came from Phyllis Coard. She said: 'Bishop was disorganized very often; avoided responsibility for mistakes and was hostile to criticism. He had opposed both the closure of the Torchlight, decided in his absence, and the prosecution of the "gang of 26".[45]

Bishop concluded by assuring the Committee that he had never had a problem sharing power or accepting criticisms; but his concern was how this joint leadership would operate; he was also concerned about how it would be explained, as well as about people's perception of it. His feeling was that the public and the world would see this as a power struggle and as a vote of no confidence in him as political leader and Prime Minister. He called for more time to reflect on this.

## *Bishop in turmoil internally*

When this was explained to Coard, his reaction was that the party needed 'a fundamental package of measures' to survive. He further assured members of the Committee that what was proposed was attainable.[46]

Bishop refused to attend the Extraordinary Meeting of full members of the New Jewel Movement carded for 25 September, on the grounds that he needed more time to reflect. In the circumstances Coard considered it inappropriate to attend also. The meeting, almost unanimously, moved that Bishop attend – by a vote of 46 to 1. Bishop showed great reluctance but eventually he came.

He explained that he was 'confused' and 'emotional'; he questioned the real meaning of the Committee's decision. He complained: 'I am suspicious that Comrades have concluded that the party must be transformed into a Marxist-Leninist party and I am the wrong person to be leader.'[47] He considered it unprincipled and he wanted to know 'the genuine substantial preference of the Comrades'. Liam James, one of Coards main protegés, reacted swiftly: he criticized Bishop for disrespecting the Leninist principles of democratic centralism, and proceeded to accuse him of showing contempt to the Central Committee, and of imagining conspiracies to unseat him. Whiteman spoke up in support of Bishop; however the overwhelming opinion was against Bishop and in support of the Central Committee's decision of joint leadership. Both Coard and Bishop spoke at the conclusion of the meeting. Coard spoke about the sincerity of the Central Committee members and of their commitment to build socialism and communism. He pledged to work with Bishop for the party, the Revolution and the Grenadian working class. Bishop in his summation accepted the criticisms and pledged to 'fulfill[sic] the decision in practice'. It is interesting that after Coard spoke, Bishop demonstrated comraderie and embraced him. The meeting ended with the singing of the

*Internationale*; and the general feeling was that the crisis was over, and the Revolution was saved.[48] But that was not to be.

It was clear from the meeting of the 25th that Bishop, Whiteman and Louison were not fully convinced about the merits of joint leadership. The odds however were stacked against them in the Committee. The central question at this juncture, according to Valenta, was 'whether Bishop like Khrushchev in the June 1957 Soviet Leadership Crisis could outmaneuver his opponents at the Central committee and transform a hostile Politburo majority into what Khrushchev had called a mere arithmetic majority.'[49] Bishop failed to do that.

## *The Eastern European interlude*

Bishop left the next day for Czechoslovakia and Hungary, heading an economic aid mission to these countries; he was accompanied by Louison and Whiteman. This was a tactical error; unless of course, it was clear in his mind that the crisis was over, even though he had some misgivings about joint leadership. Considering the later developments it was a definite error to absent himself from the country, days after his party's deepest crisis in four years. Worst of all he left behind no able lieutenant. On his return he admitted to Julian Rizo, Cuba's Ambassador, that he never imagined that things would become so serious in his absence.

While abroad, in conversation with his aide, he again spoke of the crisis as a power struggle, and somehow concluded that it could not work. It is generally believed that he was influenced by Louison to reconsider and reject it, for Louison himself in addressing Grenadian students in Hungary referred to the issue of joint leadership as unsettled, and as one that would 'mash up the Revolution' if accepted.

## *The polarization of camps*

Bishop returned to Grenada on Saturday 8 October. Unlike previous fanfares in welcoming back the leader, only a shabbily dressed Selwyn Strachan went to the airport to welcome the leader back. They returned via Cuba; it is said that while in Cuba Cletus St Paul, Bishop's top and trusted security aide, contacted Grenada to say that 'Bishop had rejected joint leadership' and hinted at violence.

On Monday 10 October the Central Committee met in yet another emergency session. The Committee took a firm decision not to re-open the issue. By this time the New Jewel Movement branch of the People's Revolutionary Army passed a resolution standing firmly behind the Central Committee, and called on the Central Committee to expel anyone who failed to submit to the collective decision of the Committee. Even the army was standing firmly behind the principle of Democratic Centralism, the cornerstone of Revolutionary Socialist government.

The Central Committee met again on Wednesday 12 October in the Operations Room at Fort Rupert. By this time the situation was deteriorating rapidly; after criticizing the Central Committee for some minor improprieties, Bishop outlined his case and finally informed them that his mind was made up: he was now against joint leadership. He appeared to be convinced that Coard and his clique were using this as a scheme to displace him.

## *Bishop's house arrest*

In the meantime the meeting was adjourned in order to deal with a rumour which was spreading in St George's Town that the Coards were planning to kill Bishop. Investigations carried out by the intelligence division concluded that the rumour was spread by St Paul and George, Bishop's security, on the instructions of Bishop himself. The meeting was reconvened and both Bishop and St Paul were questioned by the Central Committee. St Paul denied the charge and was placed under arrest and taken to Fedon's Camp at Calivigny; then later he was transferred to Fort Frederick. Bishop was ordered to make a public denial on radio; he refused and left the meeting. At that juncture he was ordered to be placed under house arrest. That was Wednesday 12 October 1983. The crisis had reached a point of no solution, and the demise of the Revolution a point of no return.

The news of Bishop's house arrest was announced at a meeting at Coard's home the following morning. Coard supported Bishop's house arrest and insisted it was a logical consequence of his actions. He was blamed for the entire crisis, and in Coard's view should be penalized. A meeting of full members was arranged for the evening of the same day. Bishop was carried to the meeting and was called upon to answer questions about the 'spreading of the vicious rumour'. He denied it; but George his security aide was called in to confront him. George admitted that the rumour was spread, and at the instructions of Bishop. Bishop was embarrassed and gave no further response in his defence. The general opinion was that he was guilty. The meeting denounced Bishop as a 'disgrace to the party, and as a man beyond redemption'.[50] Bishop's house arrest was then announced as well as the expulsion of George Louison from the party. The Revolution had had a 'heart attack', which would prove to be fatal. Many members held the view that even then what was still required was a resolution of the crisis and not an escalation.

Days of mediation ensued between Louison and Whiteman on the one hand and Coard and Strachan on the other. The two sides were intransigent, displaying both machismo and arrogance. Eventually both agreed that a compromise had to be fashioned by 18 October.

Meanwhile news of Bishop's house arrest spread among the population. The people accepted this with disbelief, horror, fear and great trepidation. By this time Kenrick Radix was busy among the people condemning Coard as being power hungry (he was one of Bishop's closest friends). Later that day when Strachan went to the Free West Indian in downtown St Georges, and announced that Coard was Prime Minister, the people's reaction was quick and decisive: 'No Bishop No Revolution'; 'Coard stands for Communism'. The Grenadian masses were beginning to speak. They welcomed revolutionary change; but a change in the direction of communism was anathema to them. The ideologues, finally, had learnt a lesson: 'You can bring a horse to the water, but you can't force it to drink.' The conclusion was unmistakably clear, Revolution? Yes! Communism? No! The public reaction to Strachan forced the immediate resignation of Coard, on the grounds that he had no ambition to be Prime Minister. His wife Phyllis also resigned. A spate of other resignations followed – Whiteman, Louison, and Jackie Creft. The collapse of the Revolution was in process.

### *The masses take over*

With public support mounting for Bishop, his allies in the party and Government were reinforced and they began organizing for street protests. Unison Whiteman and Vincent Noel were particularly active, and so was Kenrick Radix. They were all fearless. Fidel Castro himself showed considerable concern over the split in the party, and over the quick deterioration of affairs, as it appeared that there was no one who was able to have the crisis resolved. Austin was directed to make a broadcast to the nation on Sunday the 16th to allay fears and seek calm – but that was to no avail; by Tuesday 18 October, demonstrations had begun in the town of Grenville; schools had to be closed as secondary students were in the vanguard of these demonstrations shouting 'No Bishop! No School!'

Meanwhile George Louison made many unsuccessful attempts to contact Bernard Coard to try to work out a compromise; he later resigned his post, started to mobilize people, and was arrested. Whiteman continued to be active, eluding the security forces and planning mass demonstrations for Wednesday 19 October. He was ably assisted by trade unionist Vincent Noel.

In the meantime Michael Als of the People's Popular Movement of Trinidad and Tobago and Rupert Rupnarine of the Working People's Alliance of Guyana, were working around the clock to hammer out a compromise and solution. The Central Committee eventually decided on them, at a meeting at Coard's house, which was directly opposite, and contiguous to, Bishop's residence, the very place of his house arrest.

The compromise consisted of the following. Bishop would be reinstated as Prime Minister and political leader in charge of the entire process,[51] on one condition, that in a public broadcast he admitted 'to his error of spreading the rumour about the Coards, and stating that the Central Committee was the most important political institution in the country'.[52] He was to appeal for calm and give the assurance that a settlement was in sight. The popularity of Bishop and his mass base had triumphed momentarily. Certainly the Central Committee, in working out that compromise, admitted this and succumbed. It marked the triumph of the personality cult over the organized analytical mind. But this triumph was but a temporary interlude in the midst of the crisis.

It was the view of the Central Committee that if the compromise failed, the last resort was a declaration of 'martial law'. A delegation consisting of Layne, Austin and Batholomew was to present the proposals to Bishop. Bishop asked for time to reflect, but agreed in principle to the broadcast; although he needed Whiteman and Louison to help him draft the text. He also agreed to meet with Bernard Coard the next day, and give his final answer. That day was to be 19 October.

During these days of crisis and tension, Bishop was known to have smoked profusely, obviously under considerable stress, heartaches, and pain. In conversation with his mother, moments before the fateful day he was known to have said, 'They killed my father and if they kill me, I am satisfied.'

## *Bishop's last address*

Bishop did make a public broadcast on or about Tuesday 18 October. He did not accept responsibility for spreading any rumour; obviously the statement itself was part of the grand compromise. Here is the gist of that statement, the last public statement of Maurice Bishop:

Sisters and Brothers, the Central Committee of the New Jewel Movement has been made aware of the spreading of a vicious rumour calculated to project an image of disunity and infighting in our party and to create confusion among our people. The Central Committee of the New Jewel Movement wishes to let the people know that this rumour is a complete and utter lie. Given the dangerous nature of this rumour the party immediately called in the Security Forces to identify its source. The Security Forces are vigorously pursuing the investigations and one person has been detained. The Central Committee therefore takes this opportunity to warn our people against being taken in by counter revolution. The Central Committee of our party wishes to reaffirm that the New Jewel Movement Party remains as firm as it has always been and continues to press ahead with the task of building the revolution and the country, and bringing greater benefits to our poor and working people.[53]

This was a most incredible broadcast. Why? Because there was a rumour that there was a plot by the Coards to kill Bishop; and the rumour originated on the instructions of Bishop. Now he read a statement in his own voice condemning the rumour and describing it as 'a complete and utter lie', knowing fully well that he had created it. Of course he never admitted that he created it; but this was part of the grand attempted cover-up. This was not the first time the party and Government were involved in a cover-up. Moreover, it shows that the New Jewel Movement was prepared to use any means including lies, deceit, and fabrication, to achieve whatever ends it set itself. That is why Teddy Victor, one of the founders of the New Jewel Movement in 1973, and a detainee of the Revolution, said many years later, 'The New Jewel Movement was born in deceit, it thrived on deceit, and it died in deceit.'

## October 19th: That Fateful Day

On 19 October 1983, that fateful day, thousands of Grenadians, including workers, youths and school children from all across the country, in a mass demonstration led by Unison Whiteman, Vincent Noel and two businessmen, marched to and converged on Mt Wheldale, rescued Bishop from his captors, and freed him from house arrest. He asked to be taken to Fort Rupert, while thousands more awaited his appearance in St George's Market Square. That took place at 10:35 a.m. on the morning of 19 October. During the assault on Mt Wheldale, the soldiers were given firm instructions not to fire at the people but to fire in the air. That's why there was no fatality during the storming of Bishop's place of captivity by the masses.

During the storming of Fort Rupert, the soldiers were instructed not to fire on the crowd that stormed the fort – a military installation and the headquarters of armed forces. At any rate the soldiers did

*A section of the large crowd that built up in the Market Square, St George's, to await the appearance of Prime Minister Maurice Bishop after he was freed from house arrest by the masses, 19 October 1983*

not fire and gave up their weapons on Bishop's orders to the base commander, Captain Stroude.

Attempts were made by the armed forces to establish communications with Maurice Bishop and Unison Whiteman, to continue negotiations for a peaceful solution, and to persuade them to let the civilians leave the Fort. That could have been a trap by the armed forces to isolate the political people from the masses and then to subject them to revolutionary discipline.

As the drama unfolded, Bishop was advised by Lester 'Goat' Redhead, Stroude's Deputy, to negotiate. Bishop refused and instead demanded the arrest of the PRG leadership. In response to the request by the other side at Fort Frederick for a peaceful solution, Whiteman responded on Bishop's behalf: He shouted 'No Compromise! No Negotiations! We want manners for all of you.'[54]

In the meantime Bishop announced that Hudson Austin was no longer commander of the People's Revolutionary Army, and that he was now replaced by Einstein Louison. Louison was given the keys to the armoury and soon the distribution of arms began to supposedly trained civilians in the crowd. Stroude all along made sure that his military superiors on Fort Frederick were kept informed on these developments, especially the distribution of weapons. The same Louison, days after the intervention, proceeded to condemn Bishop, in his own arrogant and unrepentant voice, for taking over Fort Rupert. He said:

> Maurice asked me to take command, right. And to deal with 'them men' and the party members, right; and for that matter, he even asked me to get myself back in greens; ... The first shot came from the other faction, and not the army; and to mob the army headquarters and to take it over in that context is 'dread', right; and to me, that was a wrong move by Maurice and them ... It was completely wrong for them comrades to mob the headquarters of the army; completely wrong...[55]

This was the man with whom Bishop chose to replace Austin, who was placed in charge on Fort Rupert, the army's headquarters, and who is recorded as one of the two persons present when weapons were distributed to civilians on the morning of 19 October at the army headquarters.

The take-over of Fort Rupert, the Military Headquarters of the People's Revolutionary Government, was considered totally unacceptable to the military and political leadership and other members of the Central Committee. They formed the distinct and clear impression that orders had been given by Bishop to eliminate them, to arrest the Central Committee, and to mount an armed assault on Fort Frederick. The distribution of arms to the civilians on Fort Rupert by Noel and others in charge was ill-advised, indiscreet, and an incalculable error, as it convinced the Coard faction that an armed assault was ordered on them at Fort Frederick. This more than anything else was responsible for all the violence that followed.

## *To kill or be killed*

The Coard faction now faced the prospect of either being eliminated by an armed popular uprising in support of Bishop, or being incarcerated or themselves killed. It was to them a case of 'live or die'. In the circumstances they panicked and decided on a course of action dictated by 'Leninist discipline', to use their jargon. To them it was now a struggle between 'Leninist Forces' and 'right opportunists' or 'counter-revolutionaries' as was the case in 1903–24 in Russia, 1921 in Mongolia, 1956 in Hungary, 1968 in Czechoslovakia, 1980–81 in Poland, 1979 in Afghanistan with Haffizulah Amin, and 1981 in South Yemen with Mohammed Ali.

The assault on Fort Rupert by the contingent of the People's Revolutionary Armed Forces from Calivigny occurred at about 1 p.m. on the afternoon of 19 October. It was led by Captain Conrad

Mayers, a Grenadian in the US Army, who had returned to join his secondary school mates, who were then senior officers in the People's Revolutionary Army. As the three armoured cars arrived, shooting began from the crowd: three officers were killed, Captain Conrad Mayers and officers Dorset Peters and Raphael Mason. Orders were then given to the armoured-car personnel to fire their way through. Volleys of rocket shells and bullets followed for about five to ten minutes. Bishop was heard to have shouted, 'My God, my God, they are using the guns on the masses.' This is to contradict an assurance given to the people by the Revolution since 1979 – that is, 'never will the guns be turned on the people'.

Twice before in history Grenadians were confronted with a choice of throwing themselves over a cliff rather than face oncoming guns. This brutal choice was to face them once again on 19 October. Those among the crowd, who had run up to the highest section of the Fort, mortified by the gunblast and rain of bullets, rather than face, what they thought was oncoming bullets, threw themselves over a wall more than 50 feet high. They preferred to chance the uncertainty of a headlong plunge to the certainty of approaching gunfire.

After this initial assault had quietened down, Maurice Bishop, Jacqueline Creft, Unison Whiteman, Fitzroy Bain, Norris Bain, 'Brat' Bullen, Evelyn Maitland and 'Pomphead' Hayling, were all captured, taken to the upper courtyard, lined up against a wall and summarily executed. When they were asked to turn around and face the wall, Bishop refused, saying: 'They shot my father in his back; if they are going to shoot me, I want to look at my executioners in their eyes.' That was a supreme act of stoical courage; and he displayed a will-power of steel.

Maurice Bishop's family was dogged by tragedy. He lost his father violently in January 1974; and he lost his closest friend Jackie on that same fateful day, 19 October 1983, when he himself suffered a most violent death, with bullets from his executioners, the splitting of his skull and the chopping-off of his fingers to steal his ring. Twelve years later, his son Vladimir Creft suffered a violent death in Canada, a country thousands of miles away from Grenada. Bishop must have been destined to experience this human trauma and tragedy; the reason evades the author's mind. But 19 October 1983 will never be forgotten and will leave its indelible imprint on the annals of Grenada's history.

Grenada had witnessed its darkest hour and its most tragic and painful moment in centuries. A white flare was fired from Fort Rupert as if to signal to the Central Committee leadership that the job was completed and that the mission was accomplished.[56]

## *The formation of the RMC*

Two hours later General Austin made a radio broadcast to the nation, placing the blame for what had happened on the indiscretion of Bishop and his colleagues, his alliance with so-called counter-revolutionaries, and at the same time placing the entire country under house arrest. Austin sounded like a man caught 'between the devil and the deep blue sea'.

He announced the formation of a Revolutionary Military Council, among other things:

> The People's Revolutionary Army has of 3:00 p.m. today established a Revolutionary Military Council, which will form the government of the country until normality is restored. Let it be clearly understood that the Revolutionary Armed Forces will govern with absolute strictness. Anyone who seeks to demonstrate or disturb the peace will be shot. All day and all night curfew will be established for the next four days ... No one is to leave their house; anyone violating this curfew will be shot on site ... all schools are closed and all work places except essential services until further notice.

The Revolution had committed suicide, and the rigid adherence to ideology proved to be its self-inflicted deadly wound.

The Revolutionary Military Council realized that all the conditions existed for a military intervention. Grenadians felt so terrorized and were in such a state of shock and fear, that they were prepared to welcome assistance from 'Satan' himself.

So when on 25 October US forces landed at the invitation of regional governments (OECS) the nation breathed a sigh of relief and some 93% of the population welcomed the American armed forces with open arms. The very invasion the People's Revolutionary Government had imagined for years, they invited on 19 October 1983 by their own ideological paranoia. In so doing they played right into President Reagan's hands. He seized the opportunity and Grenadians for a while idolized him. Grenada secured for him his re-election at the polls. He secured for Grenadians a freedom they yearned for, and a rescue from the jaws of a monster. Bishop and his colleagues created a monster they could not tame; it went wild and devoured them all.

## *The lessons of 19 October*

October 19th was a classic epic confrontation between revolutionaries from above and a revolution from below; a confrontation between the popular leader and the masses, against the ideologue Bernard Coard and an élite officer corps; between populist forces and a totalitarian

*US Marines patrolling the streets of St George's, October 1983*

*US Marines landing by helicopter at the Greenville landing zone*

*US troops guarding Cuban and Grenadian prisoners at Point Salines*

Leninist clique; between the party and the people. The outcome suggests that no side was victorious. The drama holds many lessons for the region and indeed many Third World Countries.

1. Rigid ideological ideas are irrelevant to the Commonwealth Caribbean. It is political suicide to attack or alienate the Church in a predominantly Christian community.

2. Marxist-Leninist régimes with their emphasis on militarization, ideological purity, democratic centralism and Bolshevik staunchness inevitably produce popular resistance, disillusionment, and factional bloodshed. Worst yet, it is difficult for such régimes to survive in predominantly peasant agrarian societies.
3. Stripped of its ideological aberration and lunacy, many of the social and economic programmes of the People's Revolutionary Government were good and could help develop self-reliance in our people and attack the disease of dependent underdevelopment.
4. No people can be satisfactorily governed from a textbook and by abstract theoretical ideas. The stark reality is that 'man does not live by bread alone'. Revolutionaries in Grenada heard this cliché all their lives, but never once reflected upon its correctness.
5. Peasant agrarian societies like Grenada have certain characteristic features which can be utilized in the development process, but which when ignored or deliberately submerged can prove suicidal to those who govern.
6. Parliamentary democracy with structures for popular consultation and participation is still the best governmental form for Commonwealth Caribbean countries. The abolition of the 1973 Grenada constitution by the People's Revolutionary Government, and the failure to reconstitute Parliament made Bishop a victim of the Central Committee and Politburo. There was no constitutional counterweight to those party organs and he suffered tragically and paid the price expressly for this.
7. The 1979–83 Revolution devoured at first elements it considered hostile to it, then elements opposed to Leninism, then Bishop's supporters, then ultimately Bishop himself, which supports the dictum that revolutions tend to devour their own children. It is reminiscent of France in 1789–93, 200 years before, when Robespierre the architect of the guillotine during the French Revolution, and leader of the Jacobin Party, was sent to the guillotine to be executed in 1793, an artifice of his own creation.

## Conclusion: Main Political Periods 1763–1983

There were at least seven broad stages in Grenada's historical development from 1763 to 1983; these can be summarized as follows:

1. The old Representative System: 1763–1876.
2. The classic Crown Colony Government: 1877–1924.
3. The modified Crown Colony Government: 1924–51.
4. The Responsible Government: 1952–67.

5. Self-Government: 1967–74.
6. The Pre-Revolution and Independence era: 1974–79.
7. The Revolutionary era: 1979–83.

In none of these stages did ordinary working people play a continued and dominant role in the political process: Grenada's constitutional experience manifested four major characteristics: political inequality of opportunity; external dependence on an imperial centre; no clear outline of a path to development, and the dominance of élitist groups in the economic, social and political life of the country. This unequal distribution and balance of power and opportunity bred irreconcilable conflicts that culminated in the Revolution of 13 March 1979.

The period of old representative government had its heyday during the slavery era and was based on the British imperial maxim that, 'Colonies were individual Societies with their own lives to live within the imperial matrix.' It was generally recognized that in colonies such as Grenada, the British expatriate population could be accorded a measure of representative government, as they were considered capable of governing themselves responsibly. There the underlying conflict was between the élitist British and the mass of Frenchmen treated as second-class citizens and the oppressed slaves.

After the mass of Blacks had become free as a result of the Emancipation Act of 1833, the British government sought every opportunity to prevent representative government from falling into the hands of Blacks; consequently, they went along with the local White population in obstructing the enfranchisement of the newly emancipated. Faced with an impending 'Black threat', Crown Colony government was introduced into Grenada and elsewhere as the best preventive to that threat. According to Ann Spackman, Crown Colony government came to Grenada and to the West Indies as a result of the irresponsibility and obstructionism of the Assemblies, and the fear of opening representative institutions to Coloured and Black men.[57]

Thus, it was essentially the impending entry of the Black man into the realm of politics, and the fear of his seizure of power, which forced the British to establish the dictatorship of the Governor, through the system of Crown Colony government. This development must be seen against the background of the simultaneous development of responsible government and the achievement of Dominion status in White areas of the empire. In 1840, on the recommendations of the Durham Report, Canada was given full representative government, and in 1867 attained full self-government (Dominion status). In 1850 the British government passed the Australian Colonies Government Act, which granted Australians the privilege of having responsible government; Queensland followed suit in 1859. New Zealand achieved responsible government in 1857, and by 1907 was a Dominion. Thus, while the White areas of the Empire forged ahead constitutionally, the Black areas either remained stagnant or regressed.

The object of the Crown Colony government was to enshrine political decision-making in the hands of the appointed British Governor, and as such, to create a semi-permanent 'trusteeship' over the Blacks. This then created the conditions for the continued dominance of the élite groups that possessed economic power. There was no doubt that the political structure of Crown Colony pushed Governor and Councils further away from the people, and consequently created in these masses a basic mistrust of politics, politicians and government. The West Indies was imbued during the process with an essentially 'anarchist' approach to politics, or if not that, a totally apathetic and nonchalant attitude to the political process. The underlying conflict during this long period was between the Blacks and the local Whites, Mulattos, merchants and planter class.

Crown Colony government in Grenada passed through many stages. At first the Executive Council was entirely official, with an essentially advisory function and the Governor had power to reject its advice. During this period the Legislative Council was partly nominated and partly official, with three members each; the Governor presided and could cast his vote if there was any deadlock. In the 1880s the Legislative Council had a majority of unofficial (nominated) over official members. This was the period of classical, or pure, Crown Colony rule in Grenada. Although the Legislative Council took part in formulating laws, the Governor had ultimate power to make laws for the 'peace, order and good government' of Grenada. The Governor himself, even until 1967, had full responsibility for civil and military services.

The next stage of Crown Colony government was the election of five members to the Legislative Council and the creation of an unofficial majority; seven officials to eight unofficials, with the Governor presiding. At this stage, there was the possibility of the official side being defeated when Bills were voted upon. To counter this, the Governor was given the additional power of certification to pass as law Bills rejected by the Council. This was in addition to his powers of assent, and the power to reserve a Bill for the imperial government for its disallowal after the Governor had given his assent. Thus, granting an increase of representation in no way altered the process of decision-making under the system of modified Crown Colony government. It must also be remembered that the nominated members on the unofficial side of the Legislative Council normally identified and voted with the officials and were rarely in conflict with the Governor. Even the elected members (with the exception perhaps of T.A. Marryshow) rarely challenged the Governor or the parliamentary status quo.

In 1937 a balance between the elected members of the Legislative Council and other members was created. Following this was the stage when the elected members had a clear majority on the Executive Council; the advent of elected members on the Executive, plus an elected majority in the Legislative Council, was the first significant challenge to the power of the Governor under Crown Colony. This was partly owing to years of fighting by reformers such as T.A. Marryshow for more representation and self-government. Soon after this the Executive became the chief instrument of public policy and as such the Governor was obliged to consult and act upon the advice of the Executive; however, he had the right to reject and not to consult; if he did, a dissenting member had the right to record his reasons for rejecting.

This stage is usually associated with the committee stage. Elected members on the Executive now had departments with which they were associated. They were given subject areas and expected to propose policies on those subjects given them by the Governor, and to explain and defend such policies in the Legislature. The elected members were not heads of departments; the heads remained the career civil servants who were responsible to the Governor and invariably were non-Grenadians. The committee system was introduced in Grenada in 1955. The unofficial members were divided into three committees: (a) Trade and Production; (b) Communications and Works; (c) Education and Social Services. Each committee elected its own chairman, discussed policies and made recommendations relative to the functioning of its departments. Recommendations were ratified by either the Executive or the Legislative Council.

During this stage, elected members came to enjoy a clear majority on the Executive. The Cabinet stage followed in 1960, and full internal self-government was achieved in 1967. Both these stages marked the final demise of the Governor's political power and the entrenchment of all responsibilities for internal affairs in the hands of the elected Executive and Legislative Councils. Independence in 1974 was the final stage. It took Grenada 100 years after Canada and 70 years after Australia and New Zealand to become independent, although constitutionally, in 1838, Grenada was more advanced than any of these territories. But such was the fate of colonies which in the imperial matrix were treated as forgotten outposts of the Empire; they became the victims of imperial negligence once they had served their purpose.

The conflict in this period was between individual self-seeking politicians and businessmen and the mass of exploited peasants under the banner of a vanguard party that advocated People's Power.

Thus the Grenadian people and working class passed through five stages: the slave stage, from 1650 to 1834; the half-slave, half-free, from 1834 to 1838; the stage of peonage when the majority of ex-slaves were still dependent to a certain extent on estate labour; then dependent peasants, owing land but still dependent on others for additional income; finally, independent peasantry, which existed for most of the 20th century.

The challenge is now faced by Grenadians both in and out of Grenada to develop genuine people's involvement in government and politics and to eradicate the lingering stereotype of politics as selfish and dirty, and to transform the achievement of 1974 from essentially one of 'flag and anthem' independence to a people's independence. For in the final analysis the real test of difference between constitutional developments and provisions during the 207 years of British colonial rule and those provisions two or three decades afterwards would be whether in the latter period Grenadians achieve any real sovereignty over their human conditions, their existence and future lives, whether democratic institutions are set up to enable Grenadians to participate in the decision-making process at all levels and so become masters of their destiny, or whether they continue to be victims of external agencies and internal élitist groups.

The Revolution held out promises to many Grenadians and to Caribbean peoples. But in the final analysis it failed because it destroyed itself. There were many achievements and there were many setbacks and failures. In the process a nation and a people's psyche have been wounded. Do Grenadians have the strength, the resilience, the true grit of character to heal the wounds, to build on the contributions and achievements of the past and so honour the ashes of our forefathers, and the temples of our God?

Sacrifices have been made by generation after generation; the legacy is but a foundation; it has to be built upon and bequeathed to generations unborn.

NOTES

Full citations only given where work does not appear in the Bibliography.

1. Maurice Bishop, *Selected Speeches, 1979–81*, Havana Casa del las, 1982, p. 4.
2. Ibid, p. 4.

3. Ibid, pp. 189–90.
4. William Demas, 'Situation and change' in *Caribbean Economy*, ed. G. Beckford, ISER, UWI, 1975, p. 62.
5. Lloyd Best & Kari Levitt, 'Character of Caribbean economy', in *Caribbean Economy* p. 37.
6. Robert Looney, 'Macro-economic consequences of the size of third world nations,' *World Development* Vol. 17, No. 1, 1989, p. 70.
7. Carl Stone, *Problems and Policies in Small Economies*, Jamaica, Easle Publishers, 1980, p. 69.
8. Grenada, *Report on the National Economy for 1982 and the Budget Plan for 1983*, Ministry of Finance, February 1983.
9. G. Brizan, 'The banana industry in Grenada' (unpublished), 1983.
10. GCNA, *Financial Statements* 1982.
11. Carlos Fortin, 'Magnitude and impact of price fall on LDC exporters', *Courier*, No. 116, August 1989, p. 58.
12. A. Oyowe, 'Commodity prices and development of the third world', *Courier*, No. 116, p. 56.
13. World Bank, *Econ. Memorandum on Grenada*, 1982.
14. Cepal/Carib 81/3, *Industrial Development Strategies in Caribbean Countries*, Grenada, Anthony Boatswain, Jan. 1981, p. 17.
15. Grenada Development Bank, *Financial Data*, 1979–82.
16. The security-to-investment ratio represents the value of security required by the GDB as a factor of the investor's equity. The investor's equity is calculated at 15% of the total project cost.
17. Ministry of Planning, *Summary of Major Developments in the Economy, 1979–82*, Sept. 1982.
18. Ministry of Planning, *Preliminary Report on the Unemployment Census*, 1982; Trevor Farrel, *Unemployment Survey*, Grenada, 1980.
19. *Agriculture in Grenada: A critical assessment*, Washington DC, DAI, pp. 17–20.
20. Ibid, p. 51.
21. Ibid, p. 50.
22. SDR is the Special Drawing Right (ISDR = C.US$1.16-1.20)
23. *IMF survey*, 'Stand-by and extended arrangements', 5 Sept. 1983.
24. *Fundamentals of Marxism-Leninism*, Moscow, 1962.
25. *Grenada Documents: An overview and selection*, Washington DC, September 1994, p. 4.
26. Ibid.
27. Document No. 5; Ministry of Interior, 12 July, 1983, p. 4.
28. Ibid, p. 5.
29. Ibid, p. 2. The term 'left religion' was used to describe an almost church religious fervour felt for the leftist cause.
30. *Grenada Documents*, Document 3, 11 February 1980.
31. *Grenada, the Peaceful Revolution*, NY, Epica Task Force, 1982, p. 68.
32. *Grenada Documents*, Document 5, July 1983, p. 4.
33. *Grenada Documents*, p. 12.
34. Ibid, p. 14.
35. Grenada, *Central Committee Report on Plenary Session*, 13–19 July, 1983, p. 2.
36. Ibid, p. 10.
37. Minutes of the Emergency Meeting of NJM Central Committee, 26 August, 1983.
38. Ibid, p. 5.
39. Tony Thorndike, *Grenada*, London, Francis Printer, 1985, p. 143.
40. Ibid.
41. Extraordinary meeting of Central Committee of NJM, 14–16 September 1983, in *Grenada Documents* p. 10.
42. 'Extraordinary meeting of the Central Committee, NJM,' 14–16 September 1983, in *Grenada Documents*.
43. Ibid.
44. Ibid, p. 34.

45. Thorndike, *Grenada*, p. 145.
46. Central Committee Meeting, NJM, 23 September 1983.
47. Extraordinary General Meeting of full members, NJM, 25 September 1983.
48. Thorndike, *Grenada*, p. 152.
49. Jiri Valenta and Virginia Valenta, *Leninism in Grenada*, p. 18.
50. Thorndike, *Grenada*, p. 156.
51. Ibid, p. 158.
52. Ibid.
53. Grenada, Radio broadcast of Prime Minister Maurice Bishop, 18 October 1983.
54. Thorndike, *Grenada*, p. 160.
55. Voluntary interview of Einstein Louison, late 1983.
56. The question which remains unanswered in all of this is, since the Cuban and Grenadian Revolutionary Governments were fraternally close, and since Maurice Bishop had become like a son or brother to Fidel Castro, why didn't Castro help to settle the crisis of October 1983 and avoid the massacre of October 19th, 1983?

    As Castro was so close to Bishop and apparently did not act at that crucial moment, can it be concluded that the rest of the Central Committee by that time had come to view Fidel Castro as part of their problem? Could it be that by October 1983 a serious rift was developing between Castro and the Grenadian ideologues on the Central Committee? Interestingly and ironically, after the massacre Castro called for exemplary punishment for members of the Coard faction, who are supposed to be his Marxist-Leninist colleagues. Evidently, he wanted them, later called the Grenada 17, to be completely eradicated, more so than even his enemy, the USA.

    Another question which arises is, did difference between the leadership styles of Castro and Bishop contribute to the problem? It is a fact that Castro was the maximum leader '*par excellence*' in Cuba; but Bishop was only part of a collective political leadership in Grenada. As Prime Minister, and as Chairman of the Central Committee, he was *primus interpares* first among equals, despite his charismatic appeal. Some analysts say Bishop was not the main architect of the Grenada Revolution. Moreover, collective leadership was at the very foundation of the New Jewel Movement since its inception in 1973, as both Maurice Bishop and Unison Whiteman were elected joint co-ordinating secretaries of the New Jewel Movement from its inception.
57. Ann Spackman, *Constitutional Development of the West Indies*, 'Preface' and 'Introduction'.

# *A Postscript*
# *The Modern Era and the Human Resource Factor*

Education, like other social services, can be a contributor to, as well as a product of, growth and development. It is fundamentally an investment in human capital formation; it therefore behoves small dependent countries like Grenada, with scarce limited resources, to allocate and use their resources on education efficiently in order to obtain optimal benefits.

Psacharopoulos, Tan and Jimenez in a recent World Bank paper argued that the social returns to investment in education in Latin America are substantial; and in other parts of the world they are highest at the primary level. Even university education had a 16% rate of return, which is far in excess of any criterion discount rate (10%). This suggests that the expansion of any level of education in the country would be a good social investment.

Moreover, these measures are likely to be under-estimates of the true social rates since they do not reflect non-market effects, which can be substantial. Not only does the society gain from having a high literate and numerate population, but the indirect effects on health and fertility can be substantial, though immeasurable in money terms.

It is from this standpoint that this chapter undertakes an analysis of education in Grenada in the 1970s and 1980s, its progress and pitfalls, and submits for consideration certain reforms which will help to improve the internal efficiency of the education delivery system. Given the centuries of crisis and conflict, the development of the human-resource factor will be the best guarantee of political stability and the resolution of political conflicts.

## Why the Emphasis on Education

There are four other main considerations which justify an ongoing analysis and evaluation of the education sector in Grenada.

1. Education is one of the pillars of the Grenadian economy.
2. Today Grenada is experiencing high and rising unemployment; consequently a well-planned and managed education plant can contribute significantly to reducing the magnitude of this problem.
3. The rapid rate of development of science and technology and its widespread use and application suggests that any country which fails to keep up will remain in the dark ages.
4. Human resource in Grenada is the most abundant and precious resource; prudence dictates that she develops that resource through judicious investment in human capital formation.

## *Pillars of the economy*

Grenada's economy stands on at least six main pillars. These are:

1. The agriculture sector.
2. The tourism sector.
3. The small industrial sector.
4. Infrastructure.
5. The financial sector.
6. A well-trained, skilled and healthy labour force.

Education is concerned essentially though not exclusively with the last pillar, producing skilled workers, professionals, managers and creative artists, to service the goods- and services-producing sectors and progressively improve the quality of life in the country.

## *High and rising unemployment*

The most serious problem in Grenada in the 1970s and 1980s was high and rising unemployment. In 1970, unemployment was estimated at 2,880 or 10.1% of a labour force of 28,682. Ten years later this rose to 17.4 % – 5,768 unemployed in an economically active population of 31,640 persons. In 1987, unemployment was estimated at 11,600 or 29.0% in a labour force of approximately 40,000; thus unemployment has exhibited secular growth despite periods of reduction or slow growth due to seasonal and cyclical factors.

Recognizing the severity of high unemployment and the threat it posed to the country's peace and social stability, the post-intervention government in its 1984 manifesto had the following to say: 'Unemployment is a source of social instability. The opportunity of every Grenadian to have a job must be our Government's first priority.'

By 1987, the Government claimed that it had created some 7,400 jobs in the two-year period 1985–86. Evidently these were not all permanent jobs; a great number constituted the temporarily employed – road-workers (2,400 in 1985 and 1986); those employed in 1985 and unemployed in 1986, and private-sector job-leavers). Consequently, the figure was closer to 3,500 and not 7,400. This was substantiated by the fact that proposed employment in projects approved in 1985 and 1986, but which commenced operations in 1986, totalled 1,709; and this was for all sectors of the economy. Thus unemployment was far more critical than it was made out to be.

Even the National Economic Council in its July 1986 Report admitted that unemployment was high and was in fact the most pressing problem to be addressed at that time:

> It is estimated that the unemployed make up about 25 percent of the work force. At this rate unemployment remains high and constitutes the most pressing problem to be addressed within the development strategy.

It is undeniable that the incidence of social disease is positively correlated with high levels of unemployment. Violent crimes have been on the increase in Grenada in recent times, and these include rape, murder and armed robberies. The use of hard drugs, in particular cocaine, and drug-related social malformations, has increased to an extent that has made concerns both universal and all-pervasive. The contribution of education in addressing these issues cannot be under-estimated.

### *Living in the science and technology age*

Yet a third consideration which invites this critical assessment of education is the rapid rate of development of science and technology and its widespread application to our daily lives. Today micro-electronics, genetic engineering, biotechnology and sophisticated forms of communication, have ushered in a veritable Technological Revolution. Some argue that this development would be socially and economically disruptive; others hope that this vast productive potential can be harnessed to raise living standards and help eliminate poverty. Despite the conflicting emotions, one thing is clear, and that is that countries like Grenada cannot afford to remain detached from such developments, the consequences of which are far-reaching and fundamental.

Moreover, traditional production technologies are rapidly becoming obsolete in light of recent technological changes; in order for countries like Grenada to compete now and in the future, they would have to modernize their production techniques. This is inescapable. Failure to do so could mean loss of trade, loss of income, even higher levels of unemployment, social atrophy, and violent upheavals. Here again it is education that offers a promise of survival.

## *The colonial and neo-colonial legacy*

During the two centuries of British colonial rule (1763–1967) and the decade or so of neo-colonial rule, the education sector in Grenada was essentially an enclave in an economy which was itself nothing more than an appendage of the British economy.

The dominant economic principle was one of staple production for export to the metropole. The number and variety of economic activities were limited and restricted by the very nature of the relationship between the Colony and the metropole – the UK. There was no processing of raw materials into finished products, and very little diversification of the economic base during all these years; no incentive was given to promote indigenous technology; there was no inventory of resources and hence no strategy to develop them or find possible uses to which they could have been put. Evidently the range of skills to be produced by the education sector was limited since the economy, which was deliberately kept primitive, did not require much skilled personnel.

One group of students (a tiny élite) who completed the primary cycle and was fortunate enough to get into the secondary cycle and complete it, became professionals i.e., lawyers, doctors, businessmen. In fact these were the only professions accorded any value and upon which any status was bestowed. Another small group filled posts in the civil service and some entered the commercial and financial sectors, first as clerks, then subsequently worked their way up to middle management positions. But the mass of Grenadians who left the school system at various points, many before completing the appropriate cycle, were unemployable; some migrated, while others undertook forms of subsistence employment using the most rudimentary skills at their disposal. Many also joined the ranks of the unemployed. This in essence was the situation right up to the 1970s. It is only in recent times that attempts have been made to break that syndrome.

The curriculum in the schools themselves, both primary and secondary, was in general academically oriented and narrow; consequently it appealed to the aptitude and interests of only a small percentage of the school-age population. The school was often popularly called a 'gaol' and learning was not enjoyable for many weak students. In their case it was a burden. The school therefore failed to recognize at first a diversity of aptitudes and interests and as a result did not cater for such variety. In the process, the slow learner academically was stigmatized as 'dunce' or no good and indeed treated as a failure. It is incredible, but this pernicious system was in place right up to the 1980s. Clearly the education system was geared towards producing on the one hand a majority of dropouts and failures and on the other a minority of academic successes.

Moreover as the orientation in schools was in the main academic, parents and teachers geared children towards 'white-collar' jobs from a very early age. In the primary school the brightest students worked towards the all-important 'scholarship' and Common Entrance examinations which gave access to secondary school. Those who were left behind were virtually consigned to an inferior status and left school educationally underdeveloped. A similar syndrome occurred between those who succeeded at 'O' level and those who failed to make it. The very structure and operations of the education system had a built-in mechanism to facilitate wastage. Further those who passed 'O' and 'A' levels were confronted with the reality of only a limited number of white-collar jobs available. As a result many remained unemployed.

Whatever little practical work there was, was allocated almost strictly along the lines of sex and academic achievement. Boys were offered Woodwork and Agriculture while girls were offered Cookery and Needlework. This was unfortunate as it predisposed children into believing that certain forms of work are for men and others are for women. Worst of all, the students who were put to do these subjects were those who were academically weak and who were slow learners. The result is that this work is looked down upon and the subjects themselves have had very poor status.

Additionally, colonial and neo-colonial governments exhibited a manifest neglect for mass education for most of the period 1763–1979. The first government elementary school was established in 1884, 121 years after the commencement of British rule; the first government secondary school was established in 1885 and remained the only one for the entire (206) years of British rule. Nowhere is this most manifest than in the state and quality of the physical plant.

There have been changes, qualitative and quantitative since the colonial era; however these changes were not fundamental enough to impact significantly on the country's development.

## Trends in Education Development

### *Enrolment at primary and secondary levels*

An examination of schools' enrolment data over the 15-year period 1970–85 reveals a drop in primary enrolment and a simultaneous increase in secondary enrolment. In 1970 a total of 30,522 students were enrolled at the primary and all-age schools; by 1984–85 enrolment had dropped to 19,939, a decline of some 10,000 during that 15-year period.

A partial explanation for this drop is the increase in secondary enrolment, which went from 3,039 in 1970 to 6,508 in 1984–85. The other causal factors for the decline were lower fertility rates, net emigration, and the transition from junior secondary to full secondary.

The number of students receiving a secondary education in 1985 was double the figure for 1970. The number of secondary schools themselves had increased from 12 in 1970 to 18 by 1985. This indicated a quantitative improvement in secondary education, and was further substantiated by the movements in enrolment ratio. This was a relic of the Revolutionary era.

Infants 1 to Junior V was 64%; in other words 64 out of every 100 students aged 5–17 were in Infants 1 to Junior V. The ratio for all students 10 to 17 in both secondary and all-age was 38.9%. By 1979 the enrolment ratio for all students from Infants to Senior 11 in the primary and all-age categories was 65.3% or 22,861 on roll out of a 5–17 age cohort of 35,028. Secondary enrolment proper, i.e. all children 10–17 plus in secondary schools had a ratio of 22.4%. The total enrolment ratio for the age cohort 5 to 17 plus in the entire school system stood at 74.8%. The fact that Common Entrance places increased from 190 in 1970 – or 7% of all those sitting the exam – to 1,032 in 1980 – or 32% percent of all those sitting – was further testimony of this quantitative improvement.

## *Teacher-pupil ratio*

One estimate of the internal efficiency of the school system is the pupil-teacher ratio. This had fallen from 1:38 in 1970 to 1:26 by 1984–85. Thus the average size of classes had been reduced by 32% during the period. This is a qualitative improvement. At the same time average attendance had not improved during those 15 years; it was 84% in 1970, averaged about that for the decade, and was still 84% in the 1984–85 school year. A number of factors were responsible, viz. dropout, repetition, uninteresting nature of teaching and learning, little work on curriculum improvement, lack of dynamism in pedagogy, and the economic status of certain students.

## *Education wastage*

Pupils who enter a given cycle of education are expected to complete that cycle; if they leave before completion at an intermediate stage, they are referred to as ‘dropouts’ and they constitute an element of educational wastage. In cases where students repeat a grade additional resources are used up and this is another element of wastage. Both repetition and dropouts have a regressive effect on equity in an educational system. The economic profiles of dropouts and repeaters in Grenada showed that they were invariably from low-income families and from economically depressed areas. W.F. Fernando in his 1974 study on Grenada found that the bulk of the pupils leave school before graduating at the secondary cycle and they can be considered as having failed the goals of the system.

Children who leave school before completing the primary cycle fail to achieve a minimum of functional literacy and therefore constitute a real burden to a society with scarce resources. Over the years there has been some improvement in this area.

## *Teacher qualification*

The most important prerequisite for internal efficiency in the school system is the level of teacher-training and years of experience of the teaching force. In 1970 only 260 out of 806 primary school teachers or 32% were trained; in 1980 the percentage was the same; it increased between 1976 and 79 then fell again. A UNESCO Mission writing in 1982 said Grenada's formal education system did not yet seem to offer a systematic, specific and worthy learning alternative for all those pupils who do not want or cannot continue preparation for GCE and CXC.

When one considers a primary enrolment in 1970–80 of 18,700 producing an upper secondary enrolment of 2,000 and an 'A' level enrolment of not more than 200 one can readily appreciate the extent to which the system was failing to achieve its end. Nor had this changed by 1987.

In 1983, 16,541 at the primary level produced 955 in Form V and a similar 180 at 'A' level as in 1979–80. By 1984–85 the percentage of trained teachers had increased to 50%, a result of in-service and in-college training during the previous five years. The fact that 50% of teachers were still untrained spoke of teacher fluidity, as a result of frustration, lack of motivation, and poor renumeration. The high attrition rate at both primary and secondary levels was indeed the most crippling element facing education at the time. Of the 242 secondary teachers in 1984, 145 or 60% were untrained, or below what is considered a proper level for secondary teaching. Although the teacher/ student ratio was 1:21, the trained teacher/student ratio was 1:155. The deficiency lay not in the number of teachers but in the level of qualification and experience. It was not uncommon to find theoretical areas required in secondary schools being taught either by primary school teachers or untrained undergraduates.

The following factors adversely affected teaching conditions in Grenada.

1. There was a lack of textbooks; as a result up to 50% of teacher-time was taken up with transcription or dictation.
2. School attendance was low, on a daily (80% shorter day), weekly (Friday problems) and seasonal (rainy and crop season) basis.
3. Classrooms were overcrowded, inadequate and defectively built.
4. All teaching was subordinated to the needs of CEE.
5. Parents and pupils took little interest in the achievement of good grades.
6. There was an absence of sufficiently detailed teaching guides.

## *Schools output*

Performance in external exams is one quantitative criteria to judge the quantity and quality of our schools output. In 1970, 944 students wrote the school leaving exam, 206 (22%) passed it; out of the 852 who wrote the exam in 1981, 70 passed (8%); this improved in 1983 to 23%.

As regards GCE/CXC exams, results were still quite poor. In 1970, 3,867 subjects were offered, 1,417 passes were recorded (43%). In 1985 and 1986, there was a total of 13,194 subject entries, while subject passes recorded totalled 4,247 (32%).

The GCE pass rate overall for 1985/86 was the same for 1979/80. A total of 13,381 subjects were entered then; 4,259 pass credits were secured – three for every ten subject entries on average. Poor output represents considerable loss of teachers' time, materials, plant depreciation, examination fees and the cost of keeping a student in school for one year. The quality and quantity of schools' output during the period (with exceptions) were generally disconcerting.

**Table 1 GCE and CXC Pass Rates in 1985 and 1986**

| | *1985* | | *1986* | |
|---|---|---|---|---|
| | GCE | : CXC % | GCE | : CXC % |
| English | | 35 | 30 | 34 |
| Maths | | 46 | 18 | 37 |
| Chemistry | | 100 | 38 | 100 |
| Physics | | 45 | 52 | 22 |
| Biology | | 16 | 23 | |

## *Physical plant*

Whereas the physical condition of schools is not all there is to learning, nonetheless it can either facilitate learning or militate against it. At the time a large number of the schools in Grenada were in a state of disrepair with many beyond repair and having to be replaced by completely new structures.

Between 1966 and 1972, 27 new school buildings were put up, financed mostly by the British Development Division and the Canadian International Development Agency, to the tune of EC$6.6m. By 1984 the condition of most of these schools was deplorable as they had deteriorated through years of neglect by both the Gairy government and the Denominational Boards. Some refurbishing was done under USAID financing but a lot still remained to be done.

In 1980 a survey was conducted of the physical state of the 66 primary and all-age schools. It was discovered that 51 needed repairs badly, and that some of these needed to be replaced entirely. Some of the more common ills included leaking roofs, damaged toilets, broken partitions, absence of doors and windows, and poor water facilities. The cost of putting all the schools into proper condition was estimated then at EC$6.5m (at 1980 prices).

A similar survey of school furniture at the time revealed that 7,665 children had little or no seating or writing facilities, this represented 36% of the then school enrolment. There was need also for 295 teacher's desks and 195 cupboards. Though there was some relief in later years, in 1990 the situation was still far from satisfactory.

## *Administration*

Education administration is not an end in itself but a means to an end. The administrative structure and managerial procedures of the late 1980s were not conducive to the necessary improvements required either in learning, educational output, or school programming. Simply changing the organigram meant nothing, and in fact was incidental to these issues. What was needed was a reorientation of the overall purpose of educational administration, the nature of its functions and criteria to achieve quality education.

The administrative structure did not at that time seem to take fully into account the four generally accepted lines of action with which it had to concern itself:

*Infants Department, St Mary's Junior School, St George's*

*Teacher and pupil, St Mary's Junior School*

1. Communication with bodies of higher, equal or subordinate responsibilities.
2. Administration of issues related to personnel, materials, repairs and maintenance.
3. Management of major levels or types of education: early childhood, primary, secondary, teacher-training and adult education.
4. Technical activities of a horizontal nature: curriculum development, evaluation criteria, planning, research and statistics.

## Quality Education: The Way Forward

It is obvious from the foregoing that education must be well-planned if Grenada hopes to achieve identifiable goals. Given the country's weak resource base, rising cost of education and yet the need to achieve national goals, a medium-term educational sector plan needs to be designed, appropriately, preferably by divisional heads and technical staff. The plan which forms the sector's working document to guide its education work for the medium term should consist of six discrete parts:

1. Principles and policies to guide education development.
2. Goals to the beginning of the new millenium.
3. Specific goals of each sub-sector by priorities for the medium term.
4. Analysis of the present situation.
5. Strategies to achieve the goals.
6. Budget and financing by priorities.

Four caveats need to be mentioned.

1. As innovations with a qualitative purpose are costly, resources should be identified before the decision is taken to implement them.
2. Qualitative reforms should be carefully planned and should be programmed for gradual implementation.
3. Qualitative improvements cannot be reduced to one action.
4. Single changes in education must never develop in isolation from the other parts of the system.

An analysis of Grenada's educational progress and pitfalls suggests a number of worthwhile – and in fact necessary – goals, if education is to play its role in the development matrix.

### *Opportunity for all*

The first goal is the expansion of educational opportunity for all and the eradication of illiteracy so that each Grenadian is at least functionally literate. To achieve this the following measures are envisaged:

- the zoning of primary schools;
- the expansion and zoning of secondary schools;
- provisions of adequate learning facilities for the physically handicapped and mentally retarded.
- expansion of adult education with an emphasis on functional literacy, upgrading of workers' existing skills, and the imparting of new skills.

### *Universal primary and secondary education*

The second goal is the attainment of universal primary and secondary education, and improved learning facilities for the 13 plus age group, in the all-age schools which comprise about 15% of the entire primary and all-age school population. Primary enrolment is about 90% while secondary enrolment stands at 40%. To attain universality Grenada has to carry out the following.

1. Improve on and increase the enrolment ratio for children of pre-primary school age.
2. Raise the primary enrolment ratio to 100%.
3. Raise secondary enrolment ratio to about 75% in the medium term, and simultaneously improve on the internal efficiency of the school system.
4. Consolidate the movement towards comprehensive secondary schools. These institutions should provide a mixed curriculum consisting of academic education – with a strong science base and bias – together with technical education, cultural education (creative arts) and sport.
5. Build at least four new comprehensive secondary schools, one each in St Andrew's, St David's, St Patrick's and Carriacou.
6. Increase progressively the number of Common Entrance places until finally there is easy passage from primary to secondary level.
7. Establish at least seven skills training centres, one in each parish.

### *An integrated system*

Thirdly, Grenada's education system must ensure full passage. Individual rungs of the education ladder should be linked together forming an integrated and cohesive whole, as illustrated in Figure 5 (page 467). The various levels of the education system should hold together internally as a cohesive whole. There should be easy movement from one cycle to the other, the system should not be closed at any point, thus enabling the learner to begin at the first cycle of first level and end at the last cycle of the last level. The tools to ensure full passage comprise the following:

1. All education should be government-financed and free of charge. So far:
   - Primary education is free.
   - Secondary education is free.
   - Technical education is free.
   - Pre-university education (IFE) is free.
   - Education in post-secondary institutions is free – Teacher-training; agricultural schools; nursing education.

   This was a legacy of the Revolutionary era.
2. Educational wastage at both student and teacher levels – i.e., repetition, dropouts, absenteeism and an untrained teaching force must be eliminated. The first two can be eliminated by the development of a comprehensive and poly-technical curriculum at both the primary and secondary levels. By exposing students to a variety of skills and offerings, it is much easier to captivate their interest and aptitude, than by restricting them to a narrow set of academic options most of which are badly taught. To consolidate the wider choice now available and ensure that the desired effect is obtained, those who teach must know *what they have to teach and how best to teach it*. Pedagogy becomes the invaluable complement to curriculum. Pedagogy is dynamic and must not be restricted to a training situation.
   - Subject teachers in primary and secondary schools should meet monthly to examine and discuss the effectiveness of pedagogical approaches in their respective subject areas. They should come up with new and interesting methods of presenting concepts and knowledge.
   - Staff meetings should be devoted sometimes to a review of pedagogy in subject areas where achievement is low.
   - Secondary Schools Subject Associations should concentrate from time to time not only on the relevance of content but on the effectiveness of methods to teach that content.
   - The Ministry must produce and replicate modular audio-visual units which can assist primary school teachers to present content in a way that can excite the students. Areas that are worthy of looking at include (a) Integrated or General Science including Health Education; (b) Mathematics; (c) History (Grenadian and Caribbean); (d) Agriculture Education and (e) Language Arts.

*Pupils at work, St Mary's Junior School*

*Learning can be fun*

3. Full passage cannot be effectively achieved unless teachers and schools are subjected to a set of common assessment and measurement procedures. In this regard a system of continuous assessment becomes indispensable.
   - Each school should be asked to keep a cumulative record card of every student. There should be two sets of cards – one for students currently in school, one for students who have left.
   - In addition to terminal exams and end-of-year exams, students in primary schools should have small quarterly exams during each term and graded accordingly, for example: it should be made clear that the students' end of year mark would be out of 300 as shown below. This will ensure considerable consistency of application and study.

| Time period | 1 | 2 | 3 | Term | 1 | 2 | 3 | Term | 1 | 2 | 3 | End of year | |
|---|---|---|---|---|---|---|---|---|---|---|---|---|---|
| Score | 10 | 10 | 10 | 30 | 10 | 10 | 10 | 30 | 10 | 10 | 10 | 150 | 300 |
| Total | | 60 | | | | 60 | | | | 180 | | | 300 |

The same principle can be applied to secondary schools. Each small quarterly exam would be based on work done in that quarter only; while the term exam would examine the entire term's work and the annual exam the work done for the year. The results of each exam should be entered in the students' card by the teacher for each class. At the end of the year he or she will calculate the raw score as a percentage of points accumulated in all exams out of a possible total of 300 points.

4. The relative importance of the Common Entrance exam will some day have to be examined; but in the medium term it will have to be retained as the system has not been fully developed yet to make it redundant. In fact it is the pace of development of the education system that will determine the length of time the Common Entrance is retained.
5. In the meantime all placements to secondary grammar or comprehensive schools should be based on Common Entrance.
6. At around age 14 those students who have failed to gain a Common Entrance place should proceed to Secondary Skills Training Centres, Agricultural Training Centres, Handicraft Institutes, or Domestic Arts Institutes.
7. After three years of secondary education students should write a national exam to determine their level of achievement at the end of

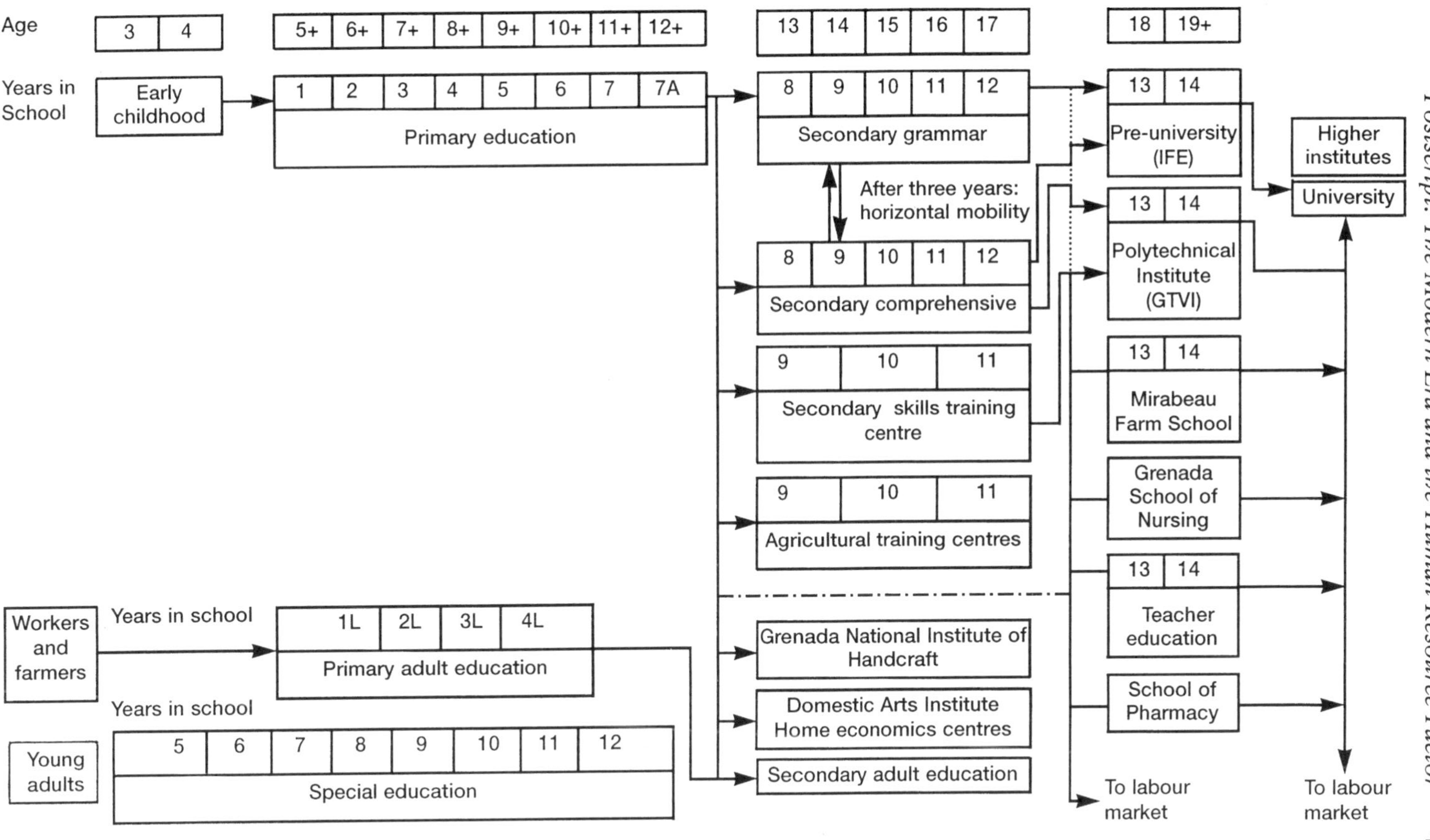


*Structure of the education system to ensure full passage – present and prospective*

the first cycle and to be certificated. At this point cases of mismatch between type of school and interest can be reconciled. If a student interest is in technical education but he is in a secondary grammar school, provision can be made for horizontal mobility.

8. After completing secondary education (five years) students could move on for two years' post-secondary education and training. Those with an academic bent can enter IFE, a post-secondary institution and pursue Advanced Level studies (pre-university) or be trained in one of many vocational areas at the middle-management level, for example:
   - Statistics to operate as a statistician
   - Business Studies
   - Accountancy
   - Laboratory Technology etc.

   Those who wish to make teaching a career can enter a pre-service teacher education programme – primary or secondary. Those who have completed technical secondary and would like additional training to the technician level could go to TVI, the Technical Vocational Institute. This means that TVI would by then have been upgraded to a full tertiary level institution. Those who choose to pursue a career in Agricultural Education can proceed to the Mirabeau Farm School.

### *Improvement in quality*

The fourth goal is the improvement in quality of education. This will require:

- improvement in teacher training, both in quantity and quality – pre-service, in-service, in-college – for all levels in the school system;
- curriculum reform and development, and the reform of educational content;
- reform of examinations;
- improvement of school supervision;
- giving each child as sound as possible a foundation in Maths, Science, Language Arts and History;
- establishing school and community libraries.

### *Advanced learning*

The fifth goal is to develop a creditable institution of advanced learning, to produce academics, professionals and technicians, and at the same time ensure in conjunction with the UWI the proper co-ordination and management of tertiary-level education.

## *Flexibility*

Sixthly, there should be flexibility in education. This ensures that the opportunity is provided for each pupil to develop optimally his personality by a wise individual approach from the didactic quarter. Guidance has to be provided both to the slow learner and to the gifted student. This also necessitates diversified curricula and alternatives in the organization of school work. The system should possess the capacity to cater for the varying abilities and interests of students. Although the comprehensiveness of the curriculum will assist in this regard, there will be need for built-in mechanisms to facilitate the slow learner and the gifted student equally. This can be approached through mixed ability grouping and remedial teaching.

## *Educational and employment pre-orientation*

Finally, the opportunity should be provided to enable a student to discern his or her talents and affinities at a relatively early stage and try them out in properly organized work-oriented activities. This refers to the relationship between education and productive work. The approach should be one which aims at integrating work with study, theory with practice, and education with production, and ultimately preparing students for the workplace. This holds tremendous promise for developing the work ethic and dismantling prejudices associated with certain types of work.

# Appendices

## Appendix 1 Composition of the Executive and Legislature 1900–51

**Composition of the Executive and Legislative Councils 1900–24**

| | *Executive* | *Legislative* |
|---|---|---|
| 1903 | Sir Robert Llewlyn (1800) | Patrick Fletcher McLeod (1890) |
| | Edward Drayton (1888) | John Stuart Martin (1901) |
| | Daniel Thomas Tudor (1903) | Douglas Alexander (1886) |
| | Norman Lockhart (1903) | Francis Gurney (1889) |
| | Charles Macaulay Browne (1885) | Domingo Sebastian de Freitas (1895) |
| | W.S. Commissiong (1896) | N.J. Paterson (1856) |
| | | George Seaton Browne (1901) |
| | | William Graham Lang |
| 1914 | Frederick H. Watkins | Governor Edward Hatton |
| | Nicholas Paterson | John Stuart Martin |
| | Herbert Ferguson | G.W. Paterson |
| | Domingo S. de Freitas | Joseph Terrence de la Mothe |
| | W.S. Commissiong | Domingo S. de Freitas |
| | Acting Governor | N.J. Paterson |
| | W.D. Young (July–Dec) | Peter Johnson Dean |
| | | Richard Geo. deGale |
| | | W.G. Lang |
| | | N. Julian Paterson |
| | | Frederick Watkins |
| | | Herbert Ferguson |
| | | Tyrell M. Commissiong |
| 1920 | Sir B. Haddon-Smith | Governor Edward Daniel La Borde |
| | N. Paterson | John S. Martin |
| | H. Ferguson | G.W. Paterson |
| | Edward La Borde | J.T. La Mothe |
| | D.S. de Freitas | D.S. de Freitas |
| | J.T. La Mothe | N.J. Paterson |
| | John Barclay | W. James Lawrence |
| | | Ruggles Low Ferguson |
| | | W.G. Lang |

| | *Executive* | *Legislative* | |
|---|---|---|---|
| | | John Barclay | |
| | | Frederick Ramsey Harford | |
| | | Herbert Ferguson | |
| | | Tyrell M. Commissiong | |
| 1922 | Sir B. Haddon-Smith | Governor G.E.P. Gentle | |
| | N. Paterson | Fitz Henry Copland | |
| | H. Ferguson | G.W. Paterson | |
| | Malcolm Martin | J.T. La Mothe | |
| | D.S. de Freitas | D.S. de Freitas | |
| | J.T. La Mothe | Reginald C. St Julian Pitt | |
| | Henry W. Sharpe | Alan Wesley Lewis | |
| | | Henry Sharpe | |
| | | Malcolm E.H. Martin | |
| | | (one vacancy) | |
| | | F.R. Harford | |
| | | Herbert Ferguson | |
| | | Tyrrel M. Commissiong | |
| 1925 | | *Official* | |
| | Governor F.S. James | Governor Sir F.S. James | |
| | Herbert Ferguson | Herbert Ferguson | |
| | N.J. Paterson | N.J. Paterson | |
| | Domingo S. de Freitas | | |
| | Malcolm E.H. Martin | *Ex-Officio* | *Elected Unofficial* |
| | | H.E.S. Richards | T.A. Marryshaw |
| | | Daniel I. Kerr | D.A. McIntyre |
| | | G.E.P. Gentle | C.F.P. Renwick |
| | | Herbert A. Baker | C.H. Lucas |
| | | C.L. Wilson | F.H. Copland |
| | | *Nominated Unofficial* | |
| | | John Barclay | |
| | | A.W. Lewis | |
| | | D.S. de Freitas | |
| 1927 | | *Official* | |
| | Seton James | Governor Sir F.S. James | |
| | Herbert Ferguson | Herbert Ferguson | |
| | N.J. Paterson | N.J. Paterson | |
| | H.E. Smith-Richards | | |
| | C.F.P. Renwick | | |
| | | *Ex-Officio* | *Elected Unofficial* |
| | | H.E.S. Richards | T.A. Marryshaw |
| | | E.E. Turner | D.A. McIntyre |
| | | (Chief of Police) | C.F.P. Renwick |
| | | G.E.P. Gentle | C.H. Lucas |

| | *Executive* | *Legislative* | |
|---|---|---|---|
| | | Hugh H. Pilgrim<br>C.L. Wilson | F.H. Copland |
| | | *Nominated Unofficial*<br>P.S. Noel<br>A.W. Lewis<br>R.C. St Julian Pitt | |
| 1931 | <br>Hilary Rudolph Blood<br>Henry W. Steele<br>N.J. Paterson<br>H.E. Smith-Richards<br>C.F.P. Renwick | *Official*<br>Governor Sir T.A.V. Best<br>Hilary Rudolph Blood<br>I. Beauburn<br>James Jarret | *Elected Unofficial*<br>T.A. Marryshow<br>George G. Edwards<br>J.F. Flemming<br>W.E. Julien<br>F.B. Paterson |
| | | *Ex-Officio*<br>H.E.S. Richards<br>Kenneth T. Rae<br>G.E.P. Gentle<br>Bertie H. Carter | |
| | | *Nominated Unofficial*<br>J.T. de La Mothe<br>F.T.T. Alexander<br>John E. Munro | |

**Composition of the Legislature: 1944–51**

| | *Official* | *Nominated* | *Elected* |
|---|---|---|---|
| 1944 | E.F. Twinney (Governor)<br>P.C. Lewis<br>(Attorney General)<br>E.G. Knight<br>(Acting Colonial Treasurer) | A. Williamson<br>S.H. Smith<br>C.A.O. Phillips<br>A.O. Payne | J.F. Fleming<br>J. Wilson (proprietor)<br>T.A. Marryshow<br>F.B. Paterson<br>J.B. Renwick<br>(planter & solicitor)<br>F.C. de Gale (planter)<br>T.E. Noble Smith<br>(merchant & planter) |
| 1947 | Terrence Commissiong<br>P.C. Lewis<br>E.G. Knight<br>(Acting Colonial Treasurer) | C.A.O. Phillips<br>R.O. Williams<br>Cpt. E. Hughes | J.F. Fleming<br>J. Wilson<br>T.A. Marryshow<br>F.B. Paterson<br>J.B. Renwick<br>F.C. de Gale<br>T.E. Noble Smith |

**Composition of the Legislature: 1944–51**

| | *Official* | *Nominated* | *Elected* |
|---|---|---|---|
| 1951 | *Administrator*<br>C.F. Henville<br>C.H. Adams<br>(Colonial Treasurer) | J.B. Renwick<br>D.L. Ferguson<br>W.E. Julien | C. St B. Sylvester<br>(teacher)<br>E.M. Gairy<br>(trade unionist)<br>T.A. Marryshow<br>A.A. McKie (printer)<br>T.J. Gibbs (proprietor)<br>R.C.P. Moore (proprietor)<br>R.A.K. Douglas<br>(proprietor, St Andrews<br>North)<br>F.C. Noel (Planter,<br>St Andrews South) |

# Appendix 2 Persons Imprisoned by Fedon and Eventually Executed

| | | |
|---|---|---|
| Ninian Home | Francis Douglas Carruthers | John Wise |
| Alexander Campbell | Williams Gilchrist | John Reid |
| John Hay* | Christopher McCarthy | William James |
| James Farquhar | Gilbert J. Kerr | Thomas Brae |
| Patrick Fothringham | Richard Davis | Neil Campbell |
| | | Bannister |
| George Rose | Jenkin Rice | William Ker* |
| George Walker | Joseph Shea | James Butler |
| Samuel Ought | Duncan McDougall | Edward Johnson |
| William Muir | Mathew Atkinson | Benjamin Johnston |
| Robert Webster | William Hawkes | William Kennard |
| Michael McCarthy | Joseph Barlow | Hugh McCoull |
| Patrick Cummings | James Cuthbert | Joseph Thomas Guy |
| Anthony Kerr | John Morris | James R. Linton |
| Thomas Johnson | Peter Thompson | Joseph Mercer |
| Phillip Lefelly | John Thompson | Edward Mathers |
| John Livingstone | William Bell | Richard Todd |
| John Jackson | Francis McMahon* | |

* Lives spared

Sources: *Minutes of Legislative Council, 1795–98*; Devas, *History of Grenada*, pp. 199– 201

# Appendix 3 General Election Results: 1951–76

GULP – Grenada United Labour Party
IND – Independent
GNP – Grenada National Party
PDM – People's Democratic Movement
GFLP – Grenada's Federated Labour Party
PPM – People's Progressive Movement

**General Election 1951**

| *Date* | *Constituency* | *Candidate* | *Votes* | *Party* |
|---|---|---|---|---|
| 10 October 1951 | Town of St George | T.A. Marryshow | 1,118 | Action Con. |
| | | Alban Radix | 871 | GULP |
| | Parish of St George | E.M. Gairy | 3,940 | GULP |
| | | E.A. Mitchell | 778 | IND |
| | St John's and St Mark's | H.A. McKie | 2,119 | GULP |
| | | C.G. Ferguson | 595 | IND |
| | | G.A. Glean | 164 | IND |
| | St Andrew's North | Ruthven A.K. Douglas | 1,428 | IND |
| | | Ralph O. Williams | 465 | GULP |
| | | Claude W. Morrison | 95 | IND |
| | St Andrew's South | Franklyn C. Noel | 1,729 | IND |
| | | David Sylvester | 638 | GULP |
| | | T.E. Noble Smith | 242 | IND |
| | St Patrick's | R.C.P. Moore | 1,908 | GULP |
| | | W. Eric Copland | 741 | IND |
| | St David's | J. Joseph Gibbs | 1,693 | GULP |
| | | Daniel Radix | 345 | IND |
| | | Leonard Sargeant | 133 | IND |
| | | L.C.J. Thomas | 12 | IND |
| | Carriacou | Cyril St. Bernard Sylvester | 1,147 | GULP |
| | | F.B. Paterson | 1,040 | IND |

Total electorate: 34,133 Total unspoiled votes: 21,203

| | | | |
|---|---|---|---|
| % of electorate: | GULP | 37.4 | (12,781 votes) |
| | IND | 24.6 | (8,240 votes) |
| % of votes cast: | GULP | 60.2 | |
| | IND | 38.9 | |

Source: Grenada, *Council Papers of 1952*

**General Election 1954**

| Date | Constituency | Candidate | Votes | Party |
|---|---|---|---|---|
| 21 September 1954 | Town of St George | T.A. Marryshow | 988 | IND |
| | | F.J. Archibald | 165 | IND |
| | | George V. Franco | 282 | IND |
| | | Jimmy J. Lewis | 521 | GULP |
| | Parish of St George | E.M. Gairy | 2,675 | GULP |
| | | John M. Knight | 454 | IND |
| | | Dorset M. Paterson | 246 | IND |
| | St John's and St Mark's | L.C.J. Thomas | 1,869 | GULP |
| | | Richard M. Benjamin | 158 | IND |
| | | Gladford J. Boyke | 181 | IND |
| | | Clarence G. Ferguson | 1,262 | IND |
| | | Hawthorne A. McKie | 138 | IND |
| | St Andrew's North | R.A. Keens Douglas | 1,726 | GULP |
| | | Claude W. Morrison | 339 | IND |
| | St Andrew's South | F.C. Noel | 1,310 | IND |
| | | Allan L. Williams | 1,363 | GULP |
| | | Cecil A. Lowe | 386 | IND |
| | | Sydney W. Rennie | 48 | IND |
| | | Leonard Sargeant | 238 | IND |
| | St Patrick's | R.C.P. Moore | 884 | IND |
| | | W. Eric Copland | 991 | IND |
| | | R.O. Williams | 1,138 | GULP |
| | St David's | T. Joseph Gibbs | 1,055 | GULP |
| | | Daniel Radix | 532 | IND |
| | | I.I. Duncan | 416 | IND |
| | | Cyril Hypolite | 358 | IND |
| | | Altinus Whiteman | 134 | IND |
| | Carriacou | F.B. Paterson | 1,296 | IND |
| | | Walter P. McIntosh | 176 | IND |
| | | H.A. Blaize | 517 | IND |
| | | E.L. Sylvester | 590 | IND |

Total Electorate: 36,846 — Total unspoiled votes: 22,476

| | | | |
|---|---|---|---|
| % of electorate: | GULP | 28.1 | (10,347 votes) |
| | IND | 32.8 | (12,089 votes) |
| % of votes cast: | GULP | 46.0 | |
| | IND | 54.0 | |

Source: Grenada, *Council Paper No. 3 of 1955*

**General Election 1957**

| Date | Constituency | Candidate | Votes | Party |
|---|---|---|---|---|
| 24 September 1957 | Town of St George | T.A. Marryshow | 741 | IND |
| | | E.A. Mitchell | 708 | GNP |
| | | L.L. Hee | 522 | GULP |
| | Parish of St George | E.M. Gairy | 2,998 | GULP |
| | | L.A. Purcell | 950 | PDM |
| | | M.A. Bullen | 945 | GNP |
| | St Mark's and St John's | L.C.J. Thomas | 1,340 | PDM |
| | | Herbert McClean | 1,250 | GULP |
| | | Gloria St Bernard | 256 | GNP |
| | | A.J. Felix | 216 | GFLP |
| | St Andrew's North | R.A. Keens Douglas | 1,404 | IND |
| | | R. Forrester | 1,100 | GULP |
| | | Robert Fitz Abraham | 55 | PDM |
| | St Andrew's South | F.C. Noel | 1,912 | PDM |
| | | R.C.P. Moore | 1,352 | GULP |
| | | F.J. Felix | 216 | GFLP |
| | St Patrick's | Hilda E. Mascoll | 458 | IND |
| | | W.E. Copland | 1,653 | GNP |
| | | R.O. Williams | 1,454 | GULP |
| | St David's | T.J. Gibbs | 983 | GULP |
| | | Daniel W. Radix | 972 | GNP |
| | | R. Clyne | 605 | PDM |
| | Carriacou | F.B. Paterson | 920 | IND |
| | | H.A. Blaize | 1,422 | GNP |

Total electorate: 37,738 Total unspoiled votes: 24,551

| | | | |
|---|---|---|---|
| % of electorate: | GULP | 26.4 | (9,955 votes) |
| | GNP | 15.9 | (6,012 votes) |
| | PDM | 12.8 | (4,851 votes) |
| | GFLP | 0.7 | (246 votes) |
| | IND | 9.6 | (3,618 votes) |
| % of votes cast: | GULP | 40.2 | |
| | GNP | 24.3 | |
| | PDM | 19.6 | |
| | GFLP | 1.00 | |
| | IND | 14.6 | |

Source: Grenada, *Council Paper No. 4 of 1958*

**General Election 1961**

| *Date* | *Constituency* | *Candidate* | *Votes* | *Party* |
|---|---|---|---|---|
| 27 March 1961 | Town of St George | E.A. Mitchell | 874 | GNP |
| | | Derek Knight | 396 | PPM |
| | | R.C.P. Moore | 688 | GULP |
| | St George's South | Joshua Thorne | 1,359 | GULP |
| | | Hugh Robertson | 363 | GNP |
| | | George Otway | 186 | PPM |
| | St George's North | Cyril Cambridge | 125 | GNP |
| | | L.A. Purcell | 1,145 | PPM |
| | | George Clyne | 1,517 | GULP |
| | St John's | H. Preudhomme | 1,007 | GULP |
| | | J. DeCoteau | 359 | GNP |
| | | Beaumont Campbell | 316 | PPM |
| | St Mark's | A.O. Forsythe | 725 | GULP |
| | | Walter Duncan | 319 | GNP |
| | St Andrew's North | A. Ken Williams | 1,421 | GULP |
| | | T.E. Noble Smith | 193 | GNP |
| | | R.K. Douglas | 733 | IND |
| | St Andrew's South | David Sylvester | 1,507 | GULP |
| | | F.C. Noel | 857 | GNP |
| | | M.Z. Mark | 506 | PPM |
| | | Lionel Alexis | 180 | IND |
| | | General Noel | 47 | IND |
| | St Patrick's | W.E. Copland | 1,228 | GNP |
| | | R.O. Williams | 1,508 | GULP |
| | St David's | C.B. Gairy | 1,506 | GULP |
| | | L.C.J. Thomas | 822 | PPM |
| | | D.W. Radix | 15 | GNP |
| | Carriacou | H.A. Blaize | 1,493 | GNP |
| | | Charles Cayenne | 368 | GULP |

Total electorate: 31,766 — Total unspoiled votes: 21,107

| | | | |
|---|---|---|---|
| % of electorate: | GULP | 36.5 | (11,665 votes) |
| | GNP | 18.3 | (5,823 votes) |
| | PPM | 10.6 | (3,371 votes) |
| | IND | 3.0 | (960 votes) |
| % of votes cast: | GULP | 54.9 | |
| | GNP | 27.5 | |
| | PPM | 15.9 | |
| | IND | 4.5 | |

Source: Grenada, *Council Paper No. 13 of 1961*

**General Election 1962**

| Date | Constituency | Candidate | Votes | Party |
|---|---|---|---|---|
| 12 September 1962 | Town of St George | E.A. Mitchell | 1,500 | GNP |
| | | M.Z. Mark | 621 | GULP |
| | St George's South | E.M. Gairy | 1,269 | GULP |
| | | A.M. Cruickshank | 1,015 | GNP |
| | St George's North | L.A. Purcell | 1,566 | GNP |
| | | E. James | 1,431 | GULP |
| | St John's | McDonald Welsh | 983 | GNP |
| | | H.J. Preudhomme | 942 | GULP |
| | | C.G. Ferguson | 61 | IND |
| | St Mark's | A.O. Forsythe | 622 | GULP |
| | | W.L. Duncan | 480 | GNP |
| | St Andrew's North | A.L. Williams | 1,315 | GULP |
| | | L.C.J. Thomas | 1,234 | GNP |
| | St Andrew's South | D. Sylvester | 1,076 | GULP |
| | | Ralph Bhola | 1,610 | GNP |
| | St Patrick's | W.E. Copland | 1,795 | GULP |
| | | R.J. Moses | 1,092 | GNP |
| | St David's | C.B. Gairy | 1,337 | GULP |
| | | C. Hypolite | 1,158 | GNP |
| | Carriacou | H.A. Blaize | | GNP |

Total electorate: 31,766 — Total unspoiled votes: 21,107

| | | | |
|---|---|---|---|
| % of electorate: | GULP | 32.8 | (10,428 votes) |
| | GNP | 33.4 | (10,638 votes) |
| % of votes cast: | GULP | 49.4 | |
| | GNP | 50.4 | |

Source: Grenada, *Council Paper No. 3 of 1962*

**General Election 1967**

| *Date* | *Constituency* | *Candidate* | *Votes* | *Party* |
|---|---|---|---|---|
| 25 August 1967 | Town of St George | H.R. Scipio | 1,311 | GNP |
| | | G.E.D. Clyne | 934 | GULP |
| | St George's South | E.M. Gairy | 2,196 | GULP |
| | | A.M. Cruickshank | 1,309 | GNP |
| | St George's North | L.A. Purcell | 1,724 | GNP |
| | | G.F. Hosten | 2,142 | GULP |
| | St John's | M.D. Welch | 920 | GNP |
| | | H.A. Preudhomme | 1,529 | GULP |
| | St Mark's | A.O. Forsythe | 918 | GULP |
| | | S.U. Frederick | 478 | GNP |
| | St Andrew's North | A.L. Williams | 2,124 | GULP |
| | | Ben Jones | 1,020 | GNP |
| | St Andrew's South | D. Sylvester | 2,038 | GULP |
| | | Ralph Bhola | 1,771 | GNP |
| | St Patrick's | W.R.L. Friday | 1,824 | GNP |
| | | J.M. Prosper | 1,689 | GULP |
| | St David's | C. Gairy | 2,026 | GULP |
| | | D. Radix | 1,031 | GNP |
| | Carriacou | H.A. Blaize | 1,807 | GNP |
| | | M.J. Sylvester | 231 | GULP |

| | | | |
|---|---|---|---|
| Total electorate: 38,880 | | | Total unspoiled votes: 29,017 |
| % of electorate: | GULP | 40.7 | (15,827 votes) |
| | GNP | 33.9 | (13,190 votes) |
| % of votes cast: | GULP | 54.5 | |
| | GNP | 45.5 | |

Source: Grenada, *Report of the General Elections for 1967*

**General Election 1972**

| Date | Constituency | Candidate | Votes | Party |
|---|---|---|---|---|
| February 1972 | Town of St George | H.R. Scipio | 1,208 | GNP |
| | | J.M. Morris | 1,229 | GULP |
| | St George's North-east | F. O'Neile | 1,292 | GNP |
| | | F. Dolland | 1,504 | GULP |
| | St George's North-west | K. Mitchell | 558 | GNP |
| | | G. Hosten | 1,340 | GULP |
| | St George's South-east | S.H. Strachan | 638 | GNP |
| | | E.M. Gairy | 1,548 | GULP |
| | St George's South-west | G. Renwick | 768 | GNP |
| | | A. Williams | 1,328 | GULP |
| | St John's | J. Branch | 1,170 | GNP |
| | | H. Preudhomme | 1,777 | GULP |
| | St Mark's | R. Japal | 615 | GNP |
| | | A. Forsythe | 1,037 | GULP |
| | St Andrew's North-east | V. Simon | 564 | GNP |
| | | W. Nedd | 1,461 | GULP |
| | St Andrew's North-west | Ben Jones | 500 | GNP |
| | | N. Benjamin | 1,166 | GULP |
| | St Andrew's South-east | R.M. Bhola | 595 | GNP |
| | | H. Alexis | 1,102 | GULP |
| | St Andrew's South-west | H. Ogilvie | 1,333 | GNP |
| | | D. Sylvester | 1,572 | GULP |
| | St Patrick's West | W. Friday | 1,185 | GNP |
| | | W. White | 1,184 | GULP |
| | St Patrick's East | W. Nyack | 766 | GNP |
| | | O.W.T. Raeburn | 965 | GULP |
| | St David's | C.B. Gairy | 2,404 | GULP |
| | | U. Whiteman | 1,262 | GNP |
| | Carriacou | H.A. Blaize | 1,632 | GNP |
| | | M. Caesar | 538 | GULP |

Total electorate: 41,529 — Total unspoiled votes: 34,241

| | | | |
|---|---|---|---|
| % of electorate: | GULP | 48.5 | (20,155 votes) |
| | GNP | 33.9 | (14,086 votes) |
| % of votes cast: | GULP | 58.9 | |
| | GNP | 41.1 | |

Source: Grenada, *Report of the Legislative Council Elections for 1972*

**General Election 1976**

| *Date* | *Constituency* | *Candidate* | *Votes* | *Party* |
|---|---|---|---|---|
| 7 November 1976 | Town of St George | B. Coard | 1,683 | P. Alliance |
| | | R. St. John | 1,316 | GULP |
| | St George North-west | B. Sylvester | 803 | P. Alliance |
| | | G. Hosten | 1,399 | GULP |
| | St George North-east | U. Whiteman | 1,858 | P. Alliance |
| | | F. Dolland | 1,463 | GULP |
| | St George South-east | S.H. Strachan | 1,103 | P. Alliance |
| | | E.M. Gairy | 1,989 | GULP |
| | St George South-west | M. Bishop | 1,319 | P. Alliance |
| | | N. DeSouza | 1,211 | GULP |
| | St John's | L. Noel | 1,650 | P. Alliance |
| | | H. Preudhomme | 1,096 | GULP |
| | St Mark's | R. Japal | 861 | P. Alliance |
| | | A.C. Forsythe | 1,097 | GULP |
| | St Andrew's North-east | V. Simon | 975 | P. Alliance |
| | | C. Thomas | 1,410 | GULP |
| | St Andrew's North-west | R. Rush | 821 | P. Alliance |
| | | I. Belmar | 1,330 | GULP |
| | St Andrew's South-east | S. Ambrose | 785 | P. Alliance |
| | | H. Alexis | 1,290 | GULP |
| | St Andrew's South-west | N. Bain | 1,771 | P. Alliance |
| | | L. St Louis | 1,516 | GULP |
| | St Patrick's East | W. Nyack | 942 | P. Alliance |
| | | O.W.T. Raeburn | 1,005 | GULP |
| | St David's | K. Radix | 2,007 | P. Alliance |
| | | C.B. Gairy | 2,271 | GULP |
| | Carriacou | H.A. Blaize | 1,542 | P. Alliance |
| | | C. Cayenne | 469 | GULP |

Total electorate: 63,153 — Total unspoiled votes: 40,777

| | | | |
|---|---|---|---|
| % of electorate: | GULP | 33.4 | (21,108 votes) |
| | People's Alliance | 31.4 | (19,669 votes) |
| % of votes cast: | GULP | 51.8 | |
| | PA | 48.2 | |

Source: Grenada, *Report of the Legislative Council Elections for 1976, 1977*

# Appendix 4 Elected Candidates 1837–76

**Elected candidates 1837**

| *Names* | *Office, if any* | *No. of representatives* |
|---|---|---|
| **Town of St George's** | | 4 |
| Alexander Baille | Casual Receiver | |
| James Smith | – | |
| Alexander Horne | Casual Receiver | |
| Ambrose Hayling | Assistant Justice | |
| **St George's & St John's** | | 7 |
| Louis LaGrenada | – | |
| James Glassen | – | |
| William Snagg | Solicitor General | |
| Robert McBurnie | – | |
| Alexander Lamb | – | |
| Richard Gibbs | – | |
| Benjamin Ventour | – | |
| **St Patrick's & St Mark's** | | 6 |
| George Paterson | – | |
| Henry F. Fairclough | – | |
| Henry Waddilove | – | |
| James B. Gaff | Public Treasurer | |
| William Stewart | – | |
| Robert Newbold | – | |
| **St Andrew's & St David's** | | 6 |
| Lewis Hoyes | Speaker of the Assembly | |
| W.H. Whiteman | – | |
| Robert Stromach | – | |
| John Wells | Assistant Justice and Coroner for St David's | |
| George Frazer | – | |
| Henry Berkley | – | |
| **Carriacou** | | 3 |
| Adam Reid | – | |
| Samuel Polson | – | |
| Alexander Fraser | – | |

Source: *Blue Book*, 1837

**Elected candidates 1843 and 1850**

| *1843* | *1850* |
|---|---|
| **Town of St George's** | |
| Alexander Baille | Alexander Baille |
| Alexander Horne | Alexander Horne |
| Robert Gentle | Robert Gentle |
| Richard Walker | Richard Walker |
| **Parishes of St George's & St John's** | |
| Robert Stromach – Speaker | Richard Gibbs – Speaker |
| Benjamin Ventour | John Aird |
| John Aird | William Grant |
| Richard Gibbs | John Fergusson |
| Henry Ross | J.B. DeBellotte |
| William Grant | George Mitchell |
| Jonas Browne | |
| **Parishes of St Patrick's & St Mark's** | |
| John Browne | Robert Jones |
| Henry Waddilove | Charles Alexander |
| George Weston | Adam Reid |
| John Paterson | George Weston |
| William McEwen | George Walker |
| Robert Keith | Robert Keith |
| **Parishes of St Andrew's & St David's** | |
| Alexander Bain | Alexander Browne |
| John Wells | Hugh Henwood |
| George Fraser | Henry Garraway |
| W. Whiteman | John Cameron |
| Hugh Henwood | Samuel Cockburn |
| Francis Jammeth | John Munroe |
| **Carriacou** | |
| Adam Reid | James Browne |
| Alexander Fraser | DeBellot Ramsey |
| James Nibbs Browne | Peter Belfon |

Source: Grenada *Blue Books*, 1843–50

**Elected Candidates: 1856–76**

| *1856* | *1862* | *1869* | *1876* |
|---|---|---|---|
| **Town of St George's** | | | |
| Henry Garraway | Henry Garraway | Paul Orgais | William Simmons |
| David Davidson | Felix Preudhomme | Henry Otway | |
| William Simmons | William Simmons | Felix Preudhomme | |
| Charles Wells | Charles Wells | Charles Simmons | |
| **Parishes of St George's & St John's** | | | |
| Alexander Horne | David Webster | W.A. Sherrif | **St George's Parish** |
| Alexander Turnbull | Charles Simmons | L.B. Otway | W.S. Commissiong |
| Ewen Cameron | W.J. Sinclair | W.J. Sinclair | |
| John Donell | H.B. Beckwith | G. Gun-Munroe | |
| James N. Browne | J.M. Gay | George Palmer | **St John's Parish** |
| Clarke Christy | John Walcott | William Simmons | John McPhail |
| John Aird | John Aird | John Aird | |
| **Parishes of St Patrick's & St Mark's** | | | |
| David Gibbs | William Loran | H.B. Beckwith | **St Mark's Parish** |
| Hall Alexander | John Munro | William Shears | Charles Simmons |
| George Merrywater | Jonathan Date | Henry Langdon | |
| William McEwen | A.J. Rouget | John Langdon | |
| David McAlpin | W.E. Killikelly | John Munro | **St Patrick's Parish** |
| Charles Alexander | J.M. Stervington | James McIntyre | George Munro |
| **Parishes of St Andrew's & St David's** | | | |
| William Wells | William Wells | Thomas Begg | **St Andrew's Parish** |
| Alexander Bain | W.J. Whiteman | J.B.S. Bedeau | William Shears |
| Hugh Henwood | William Date | Felix Renwick | **St David's Parish** |
| Henry Berkley | John Langdon | Francis Bain | William Wells |
| William J. Whiteman | Francis Bain | W.J. Whiteman | |
| **Carriacou** | | | |
| James Mill | James Mill | John R. Desbat | Keith Fulharton |
| Lucius Dill | William Steele | C. Julien Wells | |
| Samuel Cockburn | George Humphrey | W.S. Commissiong | |

Source: Grenada, *Blue Books*, 1850–76

# Appendix 5 Return Showing Provisions on Estates for Well-Being of Indian Immigrants 1867

| *Plantation* | *Proprietor/ attorney* | *Hospital arrangements* | *Buildings* |
|---|---|---|---|
| Balthazar | Salvo Caesar/ Salvo Caesar | Good hospital, doctor, nurse, all employed | Need repairs to floor and lime washing |
| Grand Bras | Thomas Hankey/ William Shears | Hospital, arrangements for doctor; a nurse employed; adequate medicants | Dwellings good |
| Dunfermline and Simon | Thomas Hankey/ Thomas Chichester | Good hospital, doctor, nurse | Barracks, good cottages and floors |
| Carriere and Conference | Jonathan Date/ William Date | Good building on Conference, doctor, nurse regularly employed | Dwellings on Carriere, good water; need repairs |
| Paradise | A. Paul & Co./ William Shears | Hospital, doctor | Buildings good but need white-washing |
| Bolougne | Theophilus Law/ William Shears | Small hospital, insufficient | Dwellings pretty good |
| Pearls | Theophilus Law/ William Shears | Good hospital, doctor, sick nurse | Dwellings good |
| Mount Horne | Henry Berkley/ J.R. Walcott | Hospital (small), doctor, nurse | Dwellings good |
| Tuileries | Charles Sutherland & Co/ W.J. Whiteman | Hospital incomplete, doctor, nurse | Dwellings good |
| Hope | Thompson Hankey & Co./ Thomas Chichester | Small hospital | Dwellings good |
| Telescope | Colonial Company /Charles Simmons | Hospital, doctor, nurse | Dwellings good |
| Mirabeau and St Cyr | Hugh Henwood, James Langdon/ J.R. Walcott | Small hospital | Dwellings good; some require flooring |
| Belmont and Mt Rose | Heirs of Houston, John Campbell/ William Date | Hospital at Belmont Estate used for both | Dwellings good |
| River Antoine | Thomas Hankey & Co./ Thomas Chichester | Hospital, doctor, nurse | Barracks good, but need lime washing |

| Plantation | Proprietor/ attorney | Hospital arrangements | Buildings |
|---|---|---|---|
| La Taste | Thomas Hankey & Co./ Thomas Chichester | Small hospital, doctor | Dwellings good |
| Plains and Mt Fendue | John Shand/ Thomas Chichester | Good hospital | Dwellings good |
| Snell Hall, Samaritan, La Fortune, Mount William | | Good hospital for four estates | Houses need lime washing |
| River Sallee | Hall Alexander/ Hall Alexander | Hospital, doctor | Dwellings insufficient |
| Mont Reuil | Heirs of C. Alexander/ Hall Alexander | | |
| Mt Rich | M. McInnis/ W. McEwen | Small hospital | Dwellings good but need lime washing |
| Marli and Union | Heirs of Paterson | Hospital, doctor | Houses good |
| Mt Rodney | William McEwen/ William McEwen | Hospital, doctor | Houses good |
| Mt Craven | Henry Langdon | Hospital, doctor | Houses good |
| Mt Alexander | A.C. Smith | Hospital, doctor | Houses good |
| Calivigny | Thompson Hankey | Hospital, doctor | Houses good |
| Clarks Court | Thomas O'Neale/ Thomas Crawford | Hospital, doctor | Coolie barracks |
| Grenville-Vale | Richard Neckles/ Richard Neckles | Arrangements made with the Colony Hospital | Coolie cottages in good order |
| Requin | Thompson Hankey/Kent | Doctor, nurse | Cottages in good condition |
| Corinth and Bailles Bacolet | G.A. Whiteman/ G.A. Whiteman | Hospital on Corinth for use of both | Cottages in good condition |
| Westerhall | Felix Whiteman/ A. Preudhomme | Hospital here but the proprietor has arranged to send his sick coolies in the Colony Hospital | Dwellings in good order |
| Black Bay | J.R. Walcott/ G. Walcott | Hospital, a medical man | Coolie houses good |
| Gouyave | Captain Duncan/ J.A. Duncan | Hospital, a medical man | Coolie houses good |

# Appendix 6 Occupation of the Population 1871 and 1881

| *Occupation* | *1871* | *1881* | *Increase* | *Decrease* |
|---|---|---|---|---|
| Government officers | 83 | 36 | – | 47 |
| Police | – | 56 | 56 | – |
| Clergy | 16 | 14 | – | 2 |
| Law | 3 | 3 | – | – |
| Physic | 9 | 8 | – | 1 |
| Merchants & Shopkeepers | 141 | 195 | 54 | – |
| Clerks | 108 | 223 | 115 | – |
| School teachers | 64 | 90 | 26 | – |
| Scholars | – | 9,141 | 9,141 | – |
| Tradesmen & Artificers | 1,818 | 2,297 | 479 | – |
| Engineers, Architects & Builders | 13 | 23 | 10 | – |
| Mariners & Fishermen | 548 | 472 | – | 76 |
| Porters & Jobbers | 45 | 61 | 16 | – |
| Washerwomen & Launderesses | 633 | 879 | 246 | – |
| Milliners & Seamstresses | 2,197 | 2,667 | 470 | – |
| Domestics | 969 | 1,665 | 696 | – |
| Agricultural labourers | 8,658 | 12,483 | 3,825 | – |
| Other Labourers | 7,168 | 1,032 | – | 6,136 |
| Planters & Proprietors | 74 | 505 | 431 | – |
| Managers & Overseers | 250 | 241 | – | 9 |
| Variously employed | 1,030 | 869 | – | 161 |
| Unemployed | 2,064 | 2,868 | 804 | – |
| Wives not otherwise employed | – | 408 | 408 | – |
| Children (not Scholars) | 11,265 | 5,721 | – | 5,544 |
| Inmates of hospitals and other institutions | – | 205 | 205 | – |
| Criminals in confinement | – | 45 | 45 | – |
| Blind, deaf, dumb, etc. | 528 | 196 | – | 332 |
| Total | 37,684 | 42,403 | 4,719 | – |

Source: Grenada, *Census* of 1881

# Appendix 7 Comparative Study of the Number of Valid Votes Received by Political Parties in the General Elections 1984, 1990 and 1995

| Constituency | 1984 | | | | | | 1990 | | | | |
|---|---|---|---|---|---|---|---|---|---|---|---|
| | Valid votes | CDLP | GFLP | GULP | MBPM | NNP | Valid votes | GOD | GULP | MBPM | NDC |
| Town of Saint George | 2,677 | 25 | – | 756 | 151 | 1,745 | 2,301 | 6 | 555 | 42 | 771 |
| Saint George North east | 3,386 | 31 | – | 818 | 99 | 2,438 | 3,357 | – | 607 | 34 | 1,952 |
| Saint George North west | 2,386 | – | – | 956 | 60 | 1,370 | 2,387 | – | 604 | 38 | 323 |
| Saint George South | 3,239 | – | – | 1,173 | 153 | 1,905 | 3,113 | – | 1,088 | – | 1,278 |
| Saint George South east | 2,536 | – | – | 642 | 220 | 1,674 | 2,387 | – | 585 | 43 | 1,214 |
| Saint David | 4,723 | – | – | 1,756 | 111 | 2,856 | 4,493 | – | 1,507 | 51 | 1,748 |
| Saint Andrew South east | 2,143 | 18 | 10 | 997 | 24 | 1,094 | 2,139 | – | 802 | – | 446 |
| Saint Andrew South west | 3,400 | – | – | 1,206 | 185 | 1,964 | 2,960 | – | 690 | 63 | 424 |
| Saint Andrew North east | 2,416 | – | – | 1,276 | – | 1,140 | 2,332 | – | 819 | 28 | 573 |
| Saint Andrew North west | 2,304 | 18 | – | 1,004 | – | 1,282 | 2,272 | – | 716 | 63 | 629 |
| Saint Patrick East | 1,800 | 12 | – | 787 | 66 | 935 | 1,799 | – | 607 | 34 | 510 |
| Saint Patrick West | 2,516 | – | – | 905 | 173 | 1,438 | 2,515 | – | 674 | 140 | 909 |
| Saint Mark | 1,819 | – | – | 750 | 139 | 930 | 1,861 | – | 488 | 130 | 436 |
| Saint John | 3,699 | – | – | 1,576 | 512 | 1,611 | 3,550 | – | 1,227 | 239 | 878 |
| Carriacou and Petite Martinique | 1,979 | – | – | 119 | 146 | 1663 | 2005 | – | 136 | 33 | 1,346 |
| Total | 41,023 | 104 | 10 | 1,4721 | 2,039 | 2,4045 | 3,9471 | 6 | 11,105 | 938 | 13,637 |

Source: Report on the 1995 General Elections, Grenada, 1996

# Appendix 8 Battle Order, 6 July 1779 and 29 April 1781

### Line of Battle on 6 July 1779

| | Ships | Guns | Commanders | |
|---|---|---|---|---|
| | | Van Division | | |
| 1 | *Suffolk* | 74 | Rear Adm.<br>Captain | Rowley<br>Christian |
| 2 | *Boyne* | 70 | | Sawyer |
| 3 | *Royal Oak* | 74 | | Fitzherbert |
| 4 | *Prince of Wales* | 74 | Vice Adm.<br>Captain | Barrington<br>Hill |
| 5 | *Magnificent* | 74 | | Elphinston |
| 6 | *Trident* | 64 | | Molloy |
| 7 | *Medway* | 60 | | W. Affleck |

# Appendix 7 (Continued)

| | 1990 Cont'd | | 1995 | | | | | | | |
|---|---|---|---|---|---|---|---|---|---|---|
| | NNP | TNP | Valid votes | GOD | GULP | MBPM | NDC | NNP | TNP | URP |
| Town of Saint George | 350 | 566 | 2,401 | – | 640 | 54 | 748 | 791 | 165 | 3 |
| Saint George North east | 553 | 207 | 3,704 | 9 | 757 | 56 | 1,887 | 917 | – | – |
| Saint George North west | 1,348 | 74 | 2,659 | – | 504 | – | 292 | 1,850 | – | 13 |
| Saint George South | 454 | 293 | 3,741 | – | 1,195 | 58 | 1,084 | 1,349 | 48 | 7 |
| Saint George South east | 253 | 292 | 2,684 | – | 630 | 48 | 1,196 | 774 | 36 | – |
| Saint David | 639 | 548 | 5,070 | – | 1,641 | 68 | 1,746 | 1,503 | 96 | 16 |
| Saint Andrew South east | 246 | 645 | 2,336 | – | 830 | – | 574 | 676 | 256 | – |
| Saint Andrew South west | 153 | 1,430 | 3,063 | – | 935 | 56 | 697 | 712 | 663 | – |
| Saint Andrew North east | 414 | 498 | 2,582 | 2 | 804 | 40 | 643 | 828 | 258 | 7 |
| Saint Andrew North west | 134 | 730 | 2,611 | – | 755 | 36 | 659 | 782 | 379 | – |
| Saint Patrick East | 361 | 287 | 2,037 | – | 645 | 25 | 604 | 686 | 74 | 3 |
| Saint Patrick West | 385 | 407 | 2,716 | – | 699 | – | 1,063 | 798 | 156 | – |
| Saint Mark | 564 | 243 | 1,876 | 5 | 432 | 54 | 479 | 621 | 235 | – |
| Saint John | 1,027 | 179 | 3,865 | – | 1,032 | 160 | 935 | 1,720 | – | 18 |
| Carriacou and Petite Martinique | 35 | 455 | 2,263 | – | 109 | 39 | 765 | 147 | 460 | – |
| Total | 6,916 | 6,854 | 43,719 | 16 | 11,608 | 694 | 13,372 | 14,154 | 2,826 | 67 |

(1984) 104 Votes went to Independents (3) (1990) 15 Votes went to Independents (2)
(1995) 892 Votes went to Independents (3)

# Appendix 8 (Continued)

| | | Centre Division | | |
|---|---|---|---|---|
| 8 | *Fame* | 74 | | Boutchart |
| 9 | *Nonsuch* | 64 | | Griffith |
| 10 | *Sultan* | 74 | | Gardner |
| 11 | *Princess Royal* | 90 | Vice Adm.<br>Captain | Byron<br>Blair |
| 12 | *Albion* | 74 | | Bowyer |
| 13 | *Stirling Castle* | 64 | | Carkett |
| 14 | *Elizabeth* | 74 | | Truscott |
| | | *Rear Division* | | |
| 15 | *Yarmouth* | 64 | | Bateman |
| 16 | *Lion* | 64 | Hon. Wm. | Cornwallis |
| 17 | *Vigilant* | 64 | Sir Digby | Dent |
| 18 | *Conqueror* | 74 | Rear Adm.<br>Captain | Parker<br>Harmood |

**Line of Battle on 29 April 1781**

| | Ships | Guns | Commanders |
|---|---|---|---|
| | | | *Red Division* |
| 1 | *Alfred* | 74 | Captain Bayne |
| 2 | *Belliqueux* | 64 | ——— Brine |
| 3 | *Prince William* | 64 | ——— Douglas |
| 4 | *Alcide* | 74 | ——— Thompson |
| 5 | *Invincible* | 74 | ——— Bickerton |
| 6 | *Monarch* | 74 | ——— Reynolds |
| 7 | *Barfleur* | 90 | Rear Adm. Sir Samuel Hood, Bart. Commander in Chief<br>Captain Knight |
| 8 | *Terrible* | 74 | Ferguson |
| 9 | *Princessa* | 70 | Sir Thomas Rich, Bart. |
| | | | *Blue Division* |
| 10 | *Ajax* | 74 | Captain Symonds |
| 11 | *Resolution* | 74 | Lord Robert Manners |
| 12 | *Montague* | 74 | Captain Houlton |
| 13 | *Gibraltar* | 80 | Francis Sam. Drake, Rear Adm. of the Blue<br>Captain Knatchbull |
| 14 | *Centaur* | 74 | ——— Nott |
| 15 | *Russel* | 74 | ——— Sutherland |
| 16 | *Torbay* | 74 | ——— Gedoin |
| 17 | *Intrepid* | 64 | ——— Molloy |
| 18 | *Shrewsbury* | 74 | ——— Robinson |

# Appendix 9

**Sources of Revenue and Expenditure Re-Immigration 1855–95**

| | Revenue | | | | | | | Expenditure |
|---|---|---|---|---|---|---|---|---|
| Year | Rum duty | Duty on exports | Interest r'cd | Miscellaneous planters' contribution | Loan | Legislature vote | Total revenue | Total expenditure |
| | £ | £ | £ | £ | £ | £ | £ | £ |
| 1855 | | | | | | | 892 | 24 |
| 1856 | | | | | | | 1,165 | 95 |
| 1857 | | | | | | | 1,450 | 3,464 |
| 1858 | | | | | 7,000 | | 3,001 | 1,384 |
| 1859 | 943 | 2,272 | 62.7s | 1,233.10s | | | 4,511 | 4,171 |
| 1860 | 1,048 | 2,179 | 56.18s | 1,006 | | 1,500 | 5,791 | 1,511 |
| 1861 | 1,046 | 1,922 | 639 | | | | 3,607 | 959 |
| 1862 | 1,092 | 1,654 | | 3,798 | 5,000 | | 11,544 | 19,024 |
| 1863 | 1,250 | 2,225 | | 2,471 | | | 5,996 | 5,056 |
| 1864 | 1,047 | 1,065 | | 1,452 | | | 3,545 | 1,167 |
| 1865 | 1,127 | 525 | 152 | 1,834 | | | 3,639 | 1,312 |
| 1866 | 1,642 | 574 | 243 | 1,215 | | | 3,674 | 4,508 |
| 1867 | 1,670 | 654 | 284 | 1,007 | | | | |
| | | | | 136 } | | | | |
| 1868 | 1,799 | 585 | 257 | 889 } | | | 3,751 | 4,881 |
| | | | | 1,073 } | 1,000 | | 5,602 | 5,099 |
| 1869 | 1,269 | 598 | 204 | 809.10s | | | 2,881 | 3,592 |
| 1870 | 1,166 | 528 | 192 | 377 | | | 2,213 | 1,429 |
| 1871 | 1,247 | 545 | 199 | 348 | | | 2,339 | 6,213 |
| 1872 | 1,285 | 1,709 | 80 | 421 | 1,800 | | 5,296 | 6,302 |
| 1873 | 1,333 | 1,863 | 61 | 467 | | | 3,724 | 2,923 |
| 1874 | 1,147 | 1,706 | 1 | 826 | | | 3,680 | 4,999 |
| 1875 | 727 | 26 | | 64 | | | 817 | 874 |
| 1876 | 963 | | 15 | 13 | | | 991 | 859 |
| 1877 | 1,138 | 643 | 9 | 400 | | | 2,190 | 2,154 |
| 1878 | 1,186 | 2,012 | 15 | 5,552 | 10,800 | | (8,965) | 7,772 |
| 1879 | 1,399 | 2,378 | 16 | 1,131 | | | 4,924 | 6,081 |
| 1880 | 1,600 | 2,617 | 327 | 639 | | | 5,184 | 3,445 |
| 1881 | 1,151 | 2,518 | | 2,460 | | | 6,131 | 4,747 |
| 1882 | 1,616 | 2,037 | 91 | 1,206 | | | 4,949 | 7,391 |
| 1883 | 984 | 2,590 | 141 | 2,829 | | | 6,546 | 4,558 |
| 1884 | 1,202 | 2,836 | 113 | 335 | | | 4,488 | 2,905 |
| 1885 | 1,047 | | 111 | 333 | | | 1,494 | 5,193 |
| 1886 | 895 | | 141 | 368 | | | 1,407 | 1,903 |
| 1887 | | | 252 | | | | 828 | |
| 1888 | | | | | | | | 4,331 |
| 1889 | | | 171 | | | | 4,598 | 2,904 |
| 1890 | | | | | | | 96 | 55 |
| 1891 | | | | | | | | 137 |
| 1892 | | | | | | | | 61 |
| 1893 | | | | | | | | 78 |
| 1894 | | | | | | | 710 | 879 |
| 1895 | | | | | | | | 1,668 |

Source: Grenada, *Blue Books*, 1885–95

# *Bibliography*

## Documents and Manuscripts


A letter to the Right Honourable Earl of Hillsborough on present situation of affairs in Grenada, London, J. Wilkie, 1769.

**Grenada:**

Raymond Devas, *A Short History of The New Scheme For Primary Education*, 1930.

Abstract of Statistics. 1978.

Address of Sir Arthur Grimble at the Opening of Grand Roy School and Farm, 1947.

'Agricultural Development', Council Paper No. 2 of 1945.

Amendment of Constitution, Council Paper No. 6 of 1931.

Annual Administrative Reports, 1890–96.

An Act to encourage the Introduction of Labourers from the USA, in Inter-Colonial Despatches 11 May 1852.

Commissions, 1784.

Laws of Grenada, 1763–1836.

Minutes of the Legislative Council, 1793–95.

Home Correspondence, 1814–29.

Letter Books: 1763–1895. Selected Volumes: 1763–71, 1771–99, 1815–95.

Blue Books: 1829–34, 1835–39, 1840–78, 1900–40.

*Free Press & Public Gazette,* Vols 1–11, 13, 1826–50.

Miscellaneous Correspondence, 1834–41.

Outgoing Despatches, 1850–55.

Censuses: 1844, 1851, 1881, 1891, 1921.

'Report upon the appearance and progress of Cholera in Grenada', Keate to Colebroke, October 1854.

Report of stipendiary magistrates for the first half of 1850, September 1850.

Reports of the stipendiary magistrates for 1852, June 1852.

Reports of the Society for the Education of the Poor, 1824–1850 (selected reports).

Council Paper No. 12 of 1932, 'Report on the Education Department for 1931'.

Outgoing Despatches, 1862.

Debates of the Legislative Council, 1930–56.

Minutes of the Legislative Council, 1891–1914.

*Commissions* 1856–68; 1875–97.

*Government Gazette*, 1888–1920.

*Free Press and Public Gazette*, 1827–45: selected volumes.

Council Paper No. 1 of 1954.

Papers connected with an enquiry into the state of the Colony Hospital of Grenada (1850).

Governor to Secretary of State, *Dr. Nicholls' Mission to the Windward Islands* (1891).

Great Britain, *Parliamentary Papers*, Vol. XXX.
*St George's Chronicle & Grenada Gazette*, 1852–1902: selected volumes.
Indian Mortality for the Half-Year Ended 30 June 1867.
General Report on the Sanitary Conditions of Indian Immigrants (1867).
Council Paper No. 8 of 1938, 'Commission of Enquiry into the Economic Conditions of Wage Earners in Grenada', 1938.
Report of the Peasant Proprietary Commission, 1907.
Report of the West India Royal Commission, 1939.
Report of the Inquiry into the Nutmeg Industry of Grenada, 1951.
The *West Indian*, 1933–60: selected volumes.
Reports of the Agricultural Department, 1931–49: selected years. (All contained in annual Council Papers for the period.)
Council Papers:
No. 1, 1931, 'Cocoa Research Scheme' (January 1931).
No. 4, 1931, 'Co-operative Societies' (January 1931).
No. 13, 1931, 'Economic Cocoa Survey' (June 1931).
No. 18, 1931, 'Tenants Compensation Ordinance' (June 1931).
No. 19, 1931, 'Cotton Cultivation Carriacou' (October 1931).
No. 1, 1932, 'The Nutmeg Industry' (February 1932).
No. 7, 1932, 'Loans to Smallholders' (June 1932).
No. 11, 1932, 'Ginnery and Oil Extracting Plant' (October 1932).
No. 16, 1933, 'Poor Relief Commission' (October 1933).
No. 7, 1933, 'Proposals of the Education Commission Relating to Grenada – Marriot/Mayhew Report' (May 1933).
No. 15, 1934, 'Closer Union Commission' (October 1934).
No. 13, 1934, 'Land Settlements' (October 1934).
No. 14, 1934, 'Children and Young Persons' (October 1934).
No. 2, 1934, 'Statement of S.O.S. on Closer Union' (March 1934).
No. 18, 1938, 'Report on Land Settlement in Grenada and Carriacou for 1938' (November 1939).
No. 2, 1940, 'West Indian Royal Commission – Proposals for a ten-year programme of improvements' (June 1940).
No. 5, 1940, 'Report on Land Settlement in Grenada and Carriacou for 1939' (June 1940).
No. 1, 1945, 'Constitutional Reform' (February 1945 – this includes a minority report by T.A. Marryshow).
No. 3, 1945, 'Tuberculosis survey' (February 1945).
No. 4, 1945, 'Scheme for the Improvement of the Cocoa Industry of Grenada'.
No. 6, 1945, 'Constitutional Reform' (April 1945).
No. 14, 1945, 'Report by the Director of Agriculture on Land Settlements in Grenada' (October 1945).
No. 13, 1945, 'The Grenada Sugar Factory Company by C.Y. Shepherd' (October 1945).
No. 12, 1945, 'Federation of the West Indies' (July 1945).
No. 12, 1947, 'Resolutions of the St Kitts Conference on Closer Union of the Leeward and Windward Islands' (August 1947).
No. 10, 1949, 'Report of the Select Committee appointed by the Legislative Council in connection with the Bill to amend the Nutmeg Industry Ordinance of 1946'. (August 1949).
No. 1, 1950, 'Report on the Survey of Land Settlements in Grenada' (February 1950).

No. 9, 1950, 'Report on Yaws and VD Control Programe' (June 1950).
No. 4, 1951, 'Report on Inquiry into the Nutmeg Industry of Grenada, 1951' (May 1951).
No. 6, 1951, 'Report of the Select Committee Appointed to Examine the Sedition Ordinance of 1951'.
No. 12, 1951 'Financial Report 1950' (August 1951).
No. 4, 1951, 'Financial Report 1951' (October 1952).
No. 7, 1953, 'Report of Committee on Workmen's Compensation Ordinance' (October 1953).
No. 10, 1954, 'Report of Select Committee on Land Settlements' (June 1954).
No. 5, 1962, 'Report of the Commission of Inquiry into the control of public expenditure in Grenada during 1961 and subsequently' (October 1962).
No. 6, 1962, 'Reply of E.M. Gairy, Chief Minister and Minister of Finance to the Report of the Commission of Inquiry into the control of public expenditure in Grenada during 1961 and subsequently' (October 1962).
No. 3, 1963, 'Report on the Legislative Council General Elections of 1962' (February 1963).
No. 12, 1953, 'Metayer System in Carriacou' (1935).

The Primary education Ordinance, 1931.

'Stipendiary Magistrates' Reports 1850–1954', in Inter-Colonial Despatches (1850–54).

'State of Liberated Africans in Grenada', in Inter-Colonial Despatches (12 May 1852).

'List of estates employing East Indians', in Inter-Colonial Despatches (February 1867).

'Shervington to Walker on the Treatment of East Indians', in Inter-Colonial Despatches (9 September 1867).

Inter-Colonial Despatches – Lieutenant-Governor Keate to Governor Colebroke (1854–56).

Inter-Colonial Despatches: Lieutenant-Governor Kortright to Governor Huicks (1857).

Inter-Colonial Despatches 1867, 1870–84, 1895–99.

Report of the Agricultural Department (1958).

Grenada Disturbances 1951 (special government compilation).

Annual Reports of the Labour Department. (1939–69; most of these are contained in Council Papers of the period.)

Report on the Department of Education in 1906 (1907).

The Secondary Education Ordinance of 1915 (1915).

Annual Reports of the Department of Education (1898–1924).

Annual Reports of the Inspector of Schools (1931–1950; contained in Council Papers for the period).

*A Review of the Historical Development of Education in Grenada* (1923).

The 1924 Constitutional Order in Council (1924).

Grenada Constitutional Order in Council (1959).

(1965–66) Government Publication 1968.

Associated States Constitution (1967).

Legislative Council Elections Reports (1951–76).

New Jewel Movement, *Manifesto for Power to the People* (1973).

Report of the Duffus Commission of Enquiry into the Breakdown of Law and Order and Police Brutality in Grenada (1975).

Newspaper (Amendment) Act 1975 – 'An Act to Amend the Newspaper Ordinance' (1975).

Grenada Cooperative Nutmeg Association Financial Statements (1970–80).
Grenada Cocoa Industry Board Financial Statements (1974–79).
*Grenada 1961–62*, London HMSO (1964).
*Grenada 1963–64*, London HMSO (1965).
Grenadan Government of, Economic Survey and Development Plan 1960–64.
*The New Jewel*, Vol. 1, 36, February 1973; also other selected volumes.
Proclamation of the Comte de Durat (1779).
*Relation de la Prise de la Grenade* (1779).
Report of the West Indian Royal Commission (1884).

## Articles

Auchinleck, 'Peasant Agriculture in Grenada', in 'Agricultural Conference of 1912', *West Indian Bulletin*, Vol. XIII (1912).

Bullbrook, J.A., 'Aboriginal remains of Trinidad and the West Indies', *Caribbean Quarterly*, Vol. 1, No. 1 (April–June 1949).

——— 'Aboriginal Remains of Trinidad', *Caribbean Quarterly*, Vol. 1, No. 2 (July–September 1949).

Fletcher, L., 'The decline of Friendly Societies in Grenada', *Caribbean Studies*, Vol. XII, No. 2.

Green, W.A., 'James Stephen and British West Indian Policy', *Caribbean Studies*, Vol. 13 No. 4.

Harewood, Jack, 'Population growth in Grenada in the 20th century', *Social & Economic Studies*, Vol. 15, No. 2 (1960).

——— 'Employment in Grenada in 1960', *Social & Economic Studies*, Vol. 15, No. 3 (1960).

Lobdell, Richard, 'Patterns of investment and sources of credit in the BWI sugar industry', *Journal of Caribbean History*.

Marshall, W.K., 'Notes on peasant development in the West Indies since 1938', *Social & Economic Studies*, Vol. XVII (September 1968).

Moore, Richard B., 'Carib cannibalism: A study in anthropological stereotyping', *Caribbean Studies* Vol. 13, No. 3 (October 1973).

Pitman, Frank W., 'The settlement and financing of the BWI plantations in the 18th century' in *Essays in Colonial History*, New York, Books for the Libraries Press Inc. (1966).

Roberts, G.W. & J. Bryne, 'Summary statistics on indenture and associated migration', *Research Papers*, No. 4 (1967).

Sheridan, Richard, 'The West Indian sugar crisis & British slave emancipation, 1830–33', *Journal of Economic History*, Vol. XXI, No. 4 (December 1961).

Smith, M.G., 'The transformation of land rights by transmission in Carriacou', *Social & Economic Studies*, Vol. 5, No. 2 (December 1961).

Smith, R.T., 'Social Stratification', in *Caribbean Integration* by S. Lewis & T.G. Matthews, Rio Piedras, University of Puerto Rico (1967).

Steele, Beverly, 'East Indian indenture and the work of the Presbyterian Church among the Indians in Grenada', *Caribbean Quarterly*, Vol. 22, No. 1 (March 1976).

Valenta, Jiri and Virginia, 'Leninism in Grenada', in *Soviet Cuban Strategy in the Third World After Grenada*, a conference report, August 1984.

## Selected Books

*A Short History of Grenada*, San Fernando Unique Services, 1974.
Augier, F.R. & S. Gordon, *Sources of WI History*, London, Longman.
Augier, R. *et al., The Making of the West Indies*, London, Longman, 1960.
Bishop, Maurice. *Selected Speeches 1979–81* Havana, Casa de las Americas, 1982.
Brizan, George, *The Grenadian Peasantry and the Social Revolution 1930–51*, UWI, ISER, 1979.
Bullen, Ripley P., *Archaeology of Grenada*, Gainesville, University of Florida, 1964.
Burn, W.L., *Emancipation and Apprenticeship*, NY, Johnson's Reprint Corporation, 1970.
Burrow, John, *The Earl of Macartney*, London, 1807.
Columbus, Christopher, *Journal of Christopher Columbus* (trans. Cecil Jane), New York, 1960.
Cumpston, I.M., *Indians Overseas in the British Territories*, London, Dawsons of Pall Mall, 1969.
Curtin, Phillip D., *The Atlantic Slave Trade*, Madison, University of Wisconsin Press, 1969.
Devas, Raymond, *The History of the Island of Grenada*, St George's, 1964.
Devas, Raymond, *Conception Island*, London, Sands & Co., 1932.
Deerr, N., *History of Sugar*, Vols. I & II, London, Clapham & Hall Ltd, 1950.
Du Tetre, R.P. Jean-Baptiste, *Histoire Générale des Iles de l'Amerique*, Paris, 1722.
——— *Voyages aux Iles de l'Amerique* 1693–1705, Paris, 1931.
Edwards, Bryan, *History Civil & Commercial of the BWI*, Cheapside, T. Miller Publishers, 1815.
Emmanuel, Patrick, *Crown Colony Politics in Grenada 1917–1915*, Barbados, ISER, 1978.
Fletcher, David, *The Development of a Policy Towards Land Reform in Grenada,* 1970–71.
Garcia, A., *History of the West Indies*, London, George G. Harrap & Co. Ltd, 1965.
Gill, W.E., *Illustrated Views & History of Delightful Grenada*, Grenada, 1958.
Gordon, S., *A Century of West Indian Education*, London, Longman, 1963.
Goveia, E.V., *The West Indian Slave Laws of the 18th Century*, Aylesbury, Ginn & Co, 1970.
*Grenada Handbook*, Barbados, Advocate Co. Ltd (1946). Colonial Report Grenada 1948–53; annual.
*Grenada Documents: An overview and selection*, Washington DC, Dept of State and Dept of Defence, September 1984.
Groome, J.R., *A Natural History of the Island of Grenada*, 1961.
Henry, Zin, *Labour Relations and Industrial Conflict in the Commonwealth Caribbean,* P.O.S. Columbus Publishers, 1972.
Hitchins, Fred H., *The Colonial Land & Emigration Commission*, Philadelphia, University of Pennsylvania Press, 1931.
*Independence For Grenada – Myth or Reality,* Trinidad, IER, 1974.
Knapland, Paul, *James Stephen and the British Colonial System*, Madison University of Wisconsin Press, 1953.
Lawrence, K.O., *Immigration into the West Indies*, Aylesbury, Ginn & Co. Ltd, 1971.
Lewis, W.A., *The Evolution of the Peasantry in the BWI*, CO Pamphlet, 1936.
*L'Histoire de L'Isle de Grenade en Amerique*, anonymous manuscripts presented by Jacques Petitjean Rojet, Monteral, Montreal University Press, 1975.

Mannix, Daniel P., *Black Cargoes*, NY, The Viking Press, 1962.
*Martin's British Colonies*, London, W.H. Allen & Co., 1839.
Matheison, W.L., *British Slavery and Its Abolition* 1823–38, NY, Octagon Books, 1967.
*Memoirs of Père Labat 1693–1705*, London, Constable & Co. Ltd, 1931.
Menendez y Pelayo, Marcelino, *Historiadores de Indias*: Ch. 10 'Apologetica Historia de las Indias' by Bartolome de las Casas, Madrid, 1909.
*Narrative of the Revolt & Insurrection of the French Inhabitants in the Island of Grenada*, by an eyewitness, Edinburgh, Vernor & Hood, 1795.
Oviedo y Valdez, Gonzalvo Fernandez de, *Historia General y Natural de Las Indias*, Madrid, 1851–55.
Parry, J.H., *The Establishment of European Hegemony*, NY, Harper & Row, 1959.
Pitman, Frank W., *The Development of the West Indies to 1763*, New York, Frank Cass & Co. Ltd, 1967.
Popino, *Brazil*, Oxford, Oxford University Press, 1968.
Ragatz, Lowell J., *Statistics for the Study of the British Caribbean Economic History* London, Bryan Edwards Press, 1929.
Ragatz, Lowell J., *The Rise and Fall of the Planter Class*, NY, Octagon Books Inc. 1963.
Raynall, Guillamme T.F., *Philosophical & Political History of the Settlements and Trade of the Europeans in the East and West Indies*, Edinburgh, Vol. III, 1804.
Rouse, Irvin, *Handbook of South American Indians*, Washington, Bureau of American Ethnology, 1948.
Sauer, Carl Otwin, *The Early Spanish Main*, Berkeley, University of California Press, 1969.
Sewell, George, *Ordeal of Free Labour*, London, Frank Cass & Co. Ltd, 1968.
Sheridan, Richard, *Sugar and Slavery*, Baltimore, Johns Hopkins University Press, 1974.
Sherlock, P.M., *A Short History of the West Indies*, London, Macmillan, 1965.
Spackman, Ann, *Constitutional History of the West Indies*, Puerto Rico, Caribbean University Press, 1975.
Steward, Julien, *Nature and Peoples of South America*, Toronto, McGraw Hill, 1959.
UNCTAD, Marketing and Distribution System for Cocoa (1975).
UNCTAD, Marketing and Distribution System for Banana (1975, 1978).
UNCTAD/GATT, *Spices*, Geneva (1977).
UNCTAD/GATT, *Cocoa Products*, Geneva (1975).
Weller, Judith Ann, *The East Indian Indenture In Trinidad*, University of Puerto Rico, Institute of Caribbean Studies, 1968.
Wells, Septimus, *Historical Description Sketch of Grenada*, Kingston, Jamaica, 1890.
Williams, Eric, *Capitalism and Slavery*, London, Andre Deutsch, 1964.
——— *From Columbus to Castro*, London, Andre Deutsch, 1970.
——— *Documents of West Indian History 1492–1655*, Trinidad, PNM Publishing Co. Ltd, 1963.
Winsor, Justin, *Christopher Colombus*, NY, 1896.
Wood, Donald, *Trinidad in Transition*, Oxford, Oxford University Press, 1868.

# *Index*

Numbers in *italics* refer to Tables; Figures are marked 'Fig.' and illustrations are indicated in **bold** type.